Understanding the British

Understanding the British Empire draws on a lifetime's research and reflection on the history of the British empire by one of the senior figures in the field. Essays cover six key themes: the geopolitical and economic dynamics of empire, religion and ethics, imperial bureaucracy, the contribution of political leaders, the significance of sexuality, and the shaping of imperial historiography. A major new introductory chapter draws together the wider framework of Dr Hyam's studies and several new chapters focus on lesser known figures. Other chapters are revised versions of earlier papers, reflecting some of the debates and controversies raised by the author's work, including the issue of sexual exploitation, the European intrusion into Africa, including the African response to missionaries, trusteeship, and Winston Churchill's imperial attitudes. Combining traditional archival research with newer forms of cultural exploration, this is an unusually wide-ranging approach to key aspects of empire.

RONALD HYAM is Emeritus Reader in British Imperial History at the University of Cambridge, and Fellow and former President of Magdalene College. He is the author of several books on the British empire, including most recently *Britain's Declining Empire: the Road to Decolonisation 1918–1968* (2006) and, with Peter Henshaw, *The Lion and the Springbok: Britain and South Africa since the Boer War* (2003).

Understanding the British Empire

Ronald Hyam

CAMBRIDGE
UNIVERSITY PRESS

CAMBRIDGE
UNIVERSITY PRESS

University Printing House, Cambridge CB2 8BS, United Kingdom

Published in the United States of America by Cambridge University Press, New York

Cambridge University Press is part of the University of Cambridge.

It furthers the University's mission by disseminating knowledge in the pursuit of education, learning and research at the highest international levels of excellence.

www.cambridge.org
Information on this title: www.cambridge.org/9780521132909

© Ronald Hyam 2010

First published 2010
3rd printing 2012

A catalogue record for this publication is available from the British Library

ISBN 978-0-521-11522-3 Hardback
ISBN 978-0-521-13290-9 Paperback

To the Master, Fellows, and Scholars of the College of
St Mary Magdalene in gratitude for a fifty-year association

Contents

Plates

Figures

Maps

Tables

Preface

It is fifty years since my engagement with the British empire and world history began, and so this volume is something of a celebration; it is also my swansong.

Whatever else historians may claim to do, they are likely to be students of human nature. Indeed, for Hume, the chief value of history is discovery of the principles of human nature: 'Human Nature is the only science of man.'[1] Two aspects of this have long fascinated me: how people arrive at decisions, and how they manage sexuality. As fields of intellectual inquiry, these are not quite so disparate as they might seem, at least not if we view them as the twin axes around which much of active life revolves. Both can be observed playing out on the imperial stage at their most complex and contentious. Understanding the British empire needs – among other things, of course – engagement with the realities of government decision-making as it related to overseas territories, and scrutiny of sexualities expressed in the context of other communities and other traditions.

These two aspects of empire underpin many of the six themes which form the backbone of this set of essays: geopolitical and economic dynamics, religion, bureaucracy, individual agency, sexuality, and historiography. Each of these contributes, I believe, to a better appreciation of the nature of the imperial system. The book cannot, however, be a comprehensive guide to the understanding of the British empire, which would be a presumptuous undertaking indeed, now that historical approaches to it are so riven with methodological diversity. It is not an advice manual, more of an academic confection. Nor – with one exception (chapter 4) – does it engage much with other historians' theories. Not that I have anything against the intussusception of new ideas or fresh approaches. But theories and methodological fashions come and go. When the excitement about post-colonial studies has died down, it should be possible to re-examine the enduring and elemental bedrock laid down by 'old' imperial history. As Jonathan Clark writes: 'A new pattern is beginning to emerge which will soon demand a reconsideration of the nature of imperialism and identity . . . ideas, policy and religion will take the place of post-modernism's weakness for symbol and ceremony, and allow us to answer the harder historical questions of when and why.' This, he suggests, can only come about when we free ourselves from the preoccupation with history's 'present-day function'.[2]

To this it might be added that history also needs to be freed from the pitfalls of any abstract theorising which is not grounded in a basic understanding of the way the world works, human beings behave, and governments think. So let us immerse ourselves in the study of the tendencies of human nature, the operation of governments, the motives of rulers, the predicaments of the governed, the reasonings of politicians, and the techniques of bureaucrats. Let us contemplate the diversity of interests and the complexities of policies, as well as the mechanisms of change, the circuits of continuity, the wiring of interaction and response. Let us register the significance of what people thought *at the time*; and let us relish the explanatory power of taking broad and protean perspectives.

One of the themes in this book deals with imperial historians. I suggest that we should know something of their background and assumptions. Perhaps, therefore, I may be allowed to explain where I am 'coming from'. Why is it, as a survivor from the late imperial age, that I do not feel myself to be a child of empire – still less to be 'saturated with imperialism', which post-colonial historians claim should have been the case?

My upbringing was, I think, fairly typical of the 'popular culture' which 'popular imperialism' is said to have sustained. I come from a family of lower-middle class shop-keepers.[3] I can be classified as an archetypal post-war 'scholarship boy', attending a small suburban grammar school, from 1947 to 1954, where there was nothing imperial to be seen or heard. (We did once consider a topic from Kipling in our lively and popular debating society, but it was only whether we preferred 'flannelled fools to muddied oafs'.) The colonies did not surface in the history syllabus after 1776. I doubt if any of us could have named an 'empire' figure, apart from Don Bradman, the Australian cricketer knighted in 1949, and Gandhi, famous for his skeletal appearance (one especially gaunt and bony boy was nicknamed 'Gandhi'). If you had asked us about the Empire, we would have assumed you meant the Chiswick Empire, a music hall two miles down the road. Henty and Haggard passed me by – I read about Sherlock Holmes and Biggles. If I was 'saturated' in anything it was monarchy not empire. I was taken to Ludgate Hill to see the victory procession to St Paul's Cathedral in 1945; and I stood on the Embankment (with 30,000 other schoolchildren, chosen by ballot) for the coronation procession in 1953; on both occasions the whole point was to see the king or queen, and there was little to help us make sense of all those colourful marching contingents; they were essentially *royal* not *imperial* occasions.[4] In its wisdom, Middlesex County Council commemorated the coronation by presenting each of its grammar school boys with a handsomely bound copy of Hardy's *Tess of the d'Urbervilles* – not exactly overflowing with imperial resonances, though Brazil is mentioned.

Apart from the coronation, the great events of my schooldays were the end of the war, the London Olympic Games of 1948 (no colonial athlete caught the imagination like Emil Zatopek of Czechoslovakia or Fanny Blankers-Koen of Holland), the Festival of Britain in 1951, and the much-lamented death of King George VI in the following year. The Festival of Britain, by the way, was purely a celebration of domestic achievements, the organisers displaying an invincible (and surely realistic) determination to ignore the empire. Apart from a neighbour who grumbled occasionally about the Labour government's groundnuts scheme, such exposure as I had to the empire came solely from the newsreels which formed an integral part of every cinema performance – brief but grim presentations of upheavals like the Malayan emergency and Mau Mau in Kenya, faraway countries of which we knew nothing, except that 'our brave soldiers and people' were there, exposed to danger. Between 1950 and 1956 I saw 133 films – a demotic sampling, some old, some new, but barely a handful with imperial settings, and these easily outnumbered by Westerns.[5]

National Service with the Royal Air Force, from 1954 to 1956, provided no enlightenment about British imperial responsibilities, not even why we might be posted to hot-spots like Cyprus or Aden, fortunately not my fate. It was only when I was taught as an undergraduate by 'Robbie' Robinson that I became interested in, or even properly aware of, the empire. This was in my finals year, 1959.

For most of my working life I have been essentially an 'archival' historian, with the bulk of my research taking place on government files in the old Public Record Office, now The National Archives at Kew. I spent twelve years with the prestigious British Documents on the End of Empire Project after it was launched in 1987. However, since I also had students to teach and to stimulate, my intellectual horizons moved beyond official files and embraced wider themes, especially the cultural aspects of empire. By the 1970s I was becoming convinced that sexuality ought to be an accepted subject of academic inquiry. I had always lectured as much as I could on the problems of race, and my 'turn to sexuality' seemed to be a good way of thinking about 'otherness' and the unexpected outcomes of interaction between Europeans and indigenous peoples.[6]

In accordance, then, with what has been for me a varied pattern of historical activity, several of these essays examine metropolitan motivation and decision-making, for example by the post-war Labour government, and the outlook of famous men, such as Churchill and Smuts. Not all of the chapters are about 'high politics', however. Some of the central ones focus upon people hardly known to history at all. These include an eighteenth-century preacher (Dr Peter Peckard), a twentieth-century Indian Army officer (Captain Kenneth Searight), a middle-ranking Colonial Office official (John Bennett), and a lowly, lecherous member of the Colonial Service in Kenya (Hubert Silberrad). The case-studies of individuals are used to illuminate larger problems, from the abolition of the slave trade to the 'official mind' and the 'end of empire', as well as masculinity and sexual promiscuity. In a similar spirit, the historiographical chapters deal with research students as well as Robinson and Gallagher and other leading historians. Some chapters consider how economic interests fit into the larger scheme of things, how the interlocking of global and local situations shaped the partition of Africa, and how engagement with 'other' peoples not only affected missionary enterprise, but also influenced the doctrines of trusteeship, and even perceptions of the male body.

This is not a conventional volume of 'collected essays'. It is not even a representative selection of my papers. Several of what I might regard as my 'core' publications are omitted, either because they have not stood the test of time well (or at least have served their purpose, such as 1960s or 1970s review articles), or because they have already been absorbed into book form.[7] Half of the eighteen essays are newly written or heavily revised. The result, I hope, manages to span a diverse group of subjects, combining traditional documentary history with at least some of the newer types of cultural exploration, within the covers of a single-authored book, in an integrated way not perhaps often attempted.

All the drafts of the new and revised essays have been read by a number of friends and colleagues, and I have been happy to draw on their good sense and unrivalled knowledge. The long introduction – a reflective commentary attempting to pull the collection together – has benefited from the scrutiny of two of my most loyal associates, Roger Louis (with whom I edited BDEEP documents on decolonisation) and Ged Martin (my former pupil, and later collaborator on a previous book of essays about the empire).[8] Roger also commented on the last two chapters about imperial historians, while both he and Ged made helpful suggestions about my account of John Bennett. Tim Harper, Peter Hennessy, Ashley Jackson, and Tom Licence kindly gave me their reactions to other sections. But above all, I am hugely indebted to another of my distinguished former students, Piers Brendon. The shaping of this entire project owes an enormous amount to his guidance, criticism, and enthusiasm, and to his generosity in providing congenial lunches. Piers has read every word, and suggested many improvements, though I'm afraid he will disapprove of my unwillingness to purge every last concession to contemporary jargon. Finally, once again I acknowledge gratefully the support of Andrew Brown and Michael Watson at Cambridge University Press – to say nothing of their exceptionally helpful expert anonymous readers.

RH
Magdalene College

Notes

1. David Hume, *A treatise of human nature* (1739, 1888 edn), book I, pt IV, section vii (p. 273).
2. Jonathan Clarke, review of T. Claydon, *Europe and the making of England, 1660–1760*, in *Times Literary Supplement*, no. 5489 (13 June 2008), p. 7.
3. In other words, that class of people which Sir John Seeley, first among imperial historians, described as sunk in 'dead-level, insipid, barren, abject, shop-keeping life', and to whom university education should be brought with missionary zeal: J.R. Seeley, *A Midland university: an address* (Birmingham, 1887), p. 16.
4. The coronation was a public holiday and took up all day for many people. I got up at 5.15 a.m., to catch the train to Waterloo, and later watched television replays at my great-uncle's until 11 p.m. (incidentally the first time I had seen TV) – my diary entry for the day ends, 'So I was thoroughly soaked in the Coronation.'
5. Since the evidence for all this comes from my teenage diaries, unpublished, the best I can offer by way of verification is the two-volume memoir of the 1940s and 1950s by my contemporary Tony Betts, who lived a few hundred yards away from me and went to the same schools (though we were not friends): *Wassa matter mate, somebody 'itchyer? A suburban childhood* (Brighton, 2001), and *The key of the door: rhythm and romance in a postwar London adolescence* (Wimborne, 2006). By its absence he does, I think, confirm my assertion that the empire had no meaning for lower-middle class suburban families like ours. (See more on this, p. 16 below.)
6. It is even possible that, if I am remembered at all, it will be as a 'pioneering and contentious' historian of sex: see Stephen Howe's description of my *Empire and sexuality: the British experience* (1990, 1991, 1998) in Sarah Stockwell, ed., *The British empire: themes and perspectives* (2008), ch. 7, 'Empire and ideology', p. 174, n. 37. It simply is not true that it took Edward Said to 'reorient studies of empire towards cultural encounters, loosening the vice-like grip of Robinson and Gallagher (and their students) over the

study of the imperial past' (Tony Ballantyne, writing in the same volume, p. 178). The development of the cultural dimension owes more to James (Jan) Morris than it does to Said: *Pax Britannica: the climax of an empire* (1968) was an inspiring landmark for many of us, published ten years before Said's *Orientalism*, which itself appeared two years after my *Britain's imperial century* (1st edn, 1976), with its emphasis on many cultural themes, such as sport and social life, masculinity and medical praxis, missions, freemasonry, and scouting, as well as sex and race relations.

7. In particular, the articles on Anglo-South African relations are now embedded in my joint book with Peter Henshaw, *The lion and the springbok: Britain and South Africa since the Boer War* (Cambridge, 2003).

8. *Reappraisals in British imperial history* (1975).

Acknowledgements

The author is obliged to the following journals and publications for the reproduction of essays which first appeared in their pages:

Journal of Imperial and Commonwealth History (chapters 1, 8, 13, 15, and 17)
Historical Journal (chapter 10)
Oxford history of the British empire (chapter 7)
Round Table: the Commonwealth Journal of International Affairs (chapter 12)
Erotic Review (chapter 14).

All quotations from Crown copyright material in The National Archives appear by permission of the Controller of HM Stationery Office. The co-operation of the archivists and special collections librarians of the Cambridge University Library, the Churchill Archives Centre, of Christ's College, and St John's College Cambridge is also gratefully acknowledged. As for Magdalene College Archives, since I am the archivist my thanks are formally directed to the Master and Fellows for permission to quote from them. My best thanks are due to Aude Valluy-Fitzsimons for help with the illustrations. The photograph of John Bennett appears courtesy of St Hilda's College Oxford; the photograph of E.A. Benians by permission of the Master and Fellows, St John's College Cambridge.

Abbreviations

ANC	African National Congress
BDEEP	British Documents on the End of Empire Project
CAB	Cabinet Office records
CBE	Commander of (the Order of) the British Empire
CHBE	*Cambridge history of the British empire*
CIE	Companion of (the Order of) the Indian Empire
CMG	Commander of (the Order of) St Michael and St George
CMS	Church Missionary Society
CO	Colonial Office
COS	Chiefs of Staff
CRO	Commonwealth Relations Office
CUP	Cambridge University Press
DFC	Distinguished Flying Cross
DLitt	Doctor of Letters (higher degree)
DNB	*Dictionary of national biography*
DO	Dominions Office/CRO records
FBA	Fellow of the British Academy
FCO	Foreign and Commonwealth Office
FO	Foreign Office
HMG	His/Her Majesty's Government
HMSO	His/Her Majesty's Stationery Office
IBEA	Imperial British East Africa (Company)
JICH	*Journal of Imperial and Commonwealth History*
LMS	London Missionary Society
LSE	London School of Economics
OBE	Officer of (the Order of) the British Empire
ODNB	*Oxford dictionary of national biography* (2004)
OHBE	*Oxford history of the British empire* (1998–9)
OUP	Oxford University Press
PD	Hansard's *Parliamentary Debates*
P&O	Peninsular & Orient (Steamship Company)
PM	Prime Minister

PREM   Prime Minister's Office records
PRO   Public Record Office (The National Archives)
TRHS   *Transactions of the Royal Historical Society*
UN(O)   United Nations (Organisation)
USPG   United Society for the Propagation of the Gospel

Introduction: perspectives, policies, and people

At the beginning of the fifth century, St Augustine, bishop of Hippo, contemplated from his North African home the still-vast domains of the Roman empire. He debated the question of whether it was fitting for good men to rejoice at the expansion of empires over less civilised peoples. He concluded that extending rulership over subjugated nations might seem to bad men felicity, but good men could accept it as a necessity. Many generations since have asked the same question as Augustine, when they encountered empires of all kinds, from theocracies to thalassocracies. Some have been called beneficent, designated with the honorific 'Pax'. Some have been called evil. All of them have excited controversy and continue to do so. The British empire is no exception. None, however, rivalled it for complexity and geographical spread. Those who ran it firmly believed in its fundamental Augustinian necessity. Their sense of duty perhaps blinded them to an inherent infelicity.[1]

To understand this complicated and ambivalent British enterprise is a challenge, but a rewarding one. Writing about British overseas experience has been opened up fruitfully in several directions in the past fifty years. Fresh perspectives have come from the concept of 'informal empire', and from different disciplines, such as global and comparative history,[2] from anthropology and 'history-from-below', and from various manifestations of cultural history, such as sport, masculinity, and women's history. 'Wider still and wider, shall thy bounds be set' may be an undesirable motto for an empire, but it is a good one for imperial history.

All empires occupy simultaneously two different kinds of space: the world stage – alongside and sometimes in geopolitical competition with other empires – and alien localities over which some degree of rulership is established. They may also occupy a third arena, the historical imagination, as the Roman empire did for the British. Globally, wars were fought between imperial powers: Britain against France and Spain in the eighteenth century, through to Britain against Germany in East Africa, and against Japan in South-East Asia in the twentieth. International competition helped to drive forward imperial boundaries on the North-West

Frontier of India and in the partitions of Africa and the Pacific. For these reasons, a global context for the empire is called for. At the same time, dynamic situations in the localities need to be examined, as European 'bridgeheads' in overseas territories were enlarged. Once begun, the process of interaction between European and non-Western societies never stopped. The empire cannot therefore be properly understood without moving beyond the metropolis and into the periphery.

Within the arena of the historical imagination, Rome was the obvious comparison for the classically educated British ruling elite to make. Many administrators had visited the Eternal City and read Gibbon on *Decline and fall*. Commentators like James Bryce, Lord Cromer, and the Colonial Office senior official Sir Charles Lucas, explored comparisons between the Roman and the British empires. 'In spite of the obvious dangers', wrote Lord Cromer, 'and making allowances for differences, the history of Imperial Rome can never cease to be of more than academic interest to the statesmen and politicians of Imperial England.' Rome, he added, 'bequeathed to us much that is of inestimable value, both in the way of precept and example', such as the preference for allowing diversity over imposed uniformity.[3] However, perhaps the most influential writer on the Roman theme was Robert Baden-Powell. 'B-P' originally conceived of the Scout movement as a means of preserving the British empire against the fate of the Roman empire. The same causes of decay were, he believed, at work: 'the decline of good citizenship . . . the growth of luxury and idleness'. British boys must not be disgraced like the young Romans of old who lost the empire of their forefathers by neglecting their 'bodily strength', becoming 'wishy-washy slackers without any go or patriotism in them'.[4]

When it came to the contemporary context, the United States of America was the overshadowing reality. The Americans were the first breakaway colonials, and ever thereafter, right through to the emergence of the USA as the sole superpower, what the Americans did challenged, fascinated, and dogged the British. In the nineteenth century it was a continuing necessity to contain or accommodate to the rival expansion emerging across the Atlantic. In the twentieth century it was a question of staying on the right side of an ever-more ascendant America – 'a state twenty-five times as large, five times as wealthy, three times as prosperous, twice as ambitious' as Britain.[5] Preserving the most cordial relations with 'our kinsmen', said Joseph Chamberlain in 1897, was 'almost a religion'.[6] But how to tell if the so-called 'special relationship' was genuinely reciprocal? And how serious was the long-term threat of the 'Americanisation of the world'? One answer was provided by the comforting illusion that the USA was still in some sense within the British orbit, fusing its immigrants 'into an English mould'. 'Greater Britain', declared Sir Charles Dilke in 1868, included 'our Magna Graecia of the United States', which could offer the 'English race the moral dictatorship of the globe'.[7] Cecil Rhodes as a young man hoped for the recovery of the USA as an integral part of the British empire, and made it his ambition to roll the Anglo-Saxon race into one empire. (This is why his scheme for Rhodes Scholars reserved scholarships for Americans.) In similar vein, Kipling urged the Americans in 1898 to 'take up the white man's burden'; while, after 1945, there were officials who hoped to 'educate the Americans' for the role of propping up the British empire 'in the interests of American security' (see p. 276 below). If the 'special relationship' failed to fulfil the more euphoric expectations, it remains the case that alignment with the USA has been, for good or ill, the most remarkable British geopolitical achievement of the twentieth century.

Sir John Seeley (Regius professor of modern history at Cambridge, 1869 to 1895), described the loss of the American colonies as an event 'pregnant with infinite consequences'. It had left behind permanent doubts, misgivings, and despair. But mutual influence and close contact remained, and 'the whole future of the planet depends on it'.[8] Certainly there were enduring lessons to be learned. The evolution of colonial responsible self-government was a long-term constitutional effect of the American Revolution. Above all there was a visceral determination never again to go through the psychological nightmare of fighting 'kith and kin'. Between the 1920s and the 1960s this had major implications for dealing with recalcitrant settler groups in Kenya and Rhodesia, who could not be brought into line by force, whether gunboats, or what Harold Wilson called 'a thunderbolt'. Nevertheless, historians still broadly accept that there is a legitimate division into 'first' and 'second' empires at around 1781, despite reservations about continuities of motive and method. There clearly was a fundamentally different 'feel' to an integrated transatlantic empire with thirteen American colonies and one without them. Accordingly, few modern histories deal with both the 'first' and 'second' empires together. The emphasis here is on the latter.

Perhaps surprisingly, until very recently British observers seldom developed comparisons between the American empire after 1898 and their own. The Philippines were simply too far away to attract any interest in Britain. Even Attlee in 1945 did not know exactly where they were, and mispronounced 'Filipino'.[9] What was true of British ignorance of the American empire was little different elsewhere. British administrators were not really interested in how other empires were run, and certainly did not think there might be useful guidance in making comparisons. (Kenneth Robinson, developing an expertise in the Colonial Office,

1936 to 1948, on the French colonial empire, seems to be the exception which proves the rule.) Before the 1940s there was little English historical writing about the Spanish and Portuguese empires. What the Dutch did in Indonesia was essentially out of view until the Second World War. The German empire was short-lived and had a bad reputation after the suppression of the Maji-Maji and Herero revolts. Tanganyika, however, had been Germany's 'jewel in the crown'. Before 1914, in railway development, mapping, the promotion of sisal, rubber, and cotton growing, and in agricultural research, the Germans in Tanganyika were far ahead of the British in Kenya.[10] The Belgians seemed tainted by association after King Leopold's 'red rubber' scandal in the Congo, which British investigators did so much to publicise. The Russian empire was a specialist interest for nervous Indian experts like Lord Curzon, although 'the Great Game' came before a wider public in Kipling's great novel *Kim* (1901).

Only the French and British in the New Hebrides Condominium and in Africa as imperial near neighbours had much awareness of each other. There were differences of approach. M. Sarraut addressed the African Society in 1933, suggesting that the British had an 'excess of scepticism', whereas the French had 'an excess of faith' about the possibility of improving the lives of Africans. 'You build day by day on what already exists. We dream of new and rectilinear architecture. You listen especially to the prudent but rather cold counsel of experience. We warm our action to the flame of apostleship.'[11] In other words, the French took a more constructionalist approach. The French policy of 'assimilation' included the fiction by which colonies were regarded as parts of France. Chiefs became more obviously agents of the central government in a way they were not under the British system of 'Indirect Rule'. The French *mission civilisatrice* meant there was no teaching in the vernacular as in British colonies. But while the French made it possible for privileged individuals to 'evolve' into culturally recognised black Frenchmen, few succeeded and this was not the goal for most *indigènes*.[12] After the Second World War there was a brief attempt by officials of the two countries to co-operate on a number of development policies for Africa, but the experiment was not a success.

As far as the indigenous peoples were concerned, the main difference between the European rulers was felt in terms of which foreign language they had to speak. French policy may have produced a more uniform nationalist elite than the British, but this did not give them much advantage in achieving independence. Decolonisation occurred in both empires at roughly the same time.

The methodological attempt to move beyond preoccupation with elites and colonial administrators and government files is especially associated with Indian 'subaltern studies' led by Ranajit Guha. The first of these appeared in 1982. The term is derived from Antonio Gramsci, and paradoxically it takes its name from the designation for junior army *officers*. 'Subaltern studies' aims to describe the history of ordinary folk in indigenous society, and to study them not as excluded categories or passive victims, but as 'the subject in their own history'.[13] But 'history-from-below', even in 1982, was nothing new, and if one looks for a foundational text it is probably E.P. Thompson's *Making of the English working class* (1963), which famously sought to rescue ordinary men and women from 'the enormous condescension of posterity'.[14] However, five years even before that, there was a landmark publication in the empire field: George Shepperson and Thomas Price's book about the Chilembwe uprising in Malawi, *Independent African*. Shepperson was also alive to its international links, with his studies of black American influences on African nationalism.[15] Imperial historians interested in Africa were now beginning to try to recover an African voice and agency. R.E. Robinson's essays on 'non-European foundations' and 'indigenous reactions' firmly shifted the emphasis to the study of European rule as it interacted with local societies, which retained a surprising ability to influence the terms of engagement. For Robinson, 'the possibilities of imperial dominion were calculated in terms of indigenous collaboration and resistance'. Older Eurocentric theories were founded on 'a grand illusion': 'Any new theory must recognise that imperialism was as much a function of its victims' collaboration or non-collaboration – of their indigenous politics – as it was of European expansion.'[16]

The concept of 'the Other' has been one of the more unavoidable historical *tropes* to establish itself in recent years. 'Othering', at its simplest, is the attempt to understand the actions and thought-worlds of communities perceived as culturally alien, often by comparing them with a supposed 'norm'. In a sense this is what anthropologists have always done. But there is a twist. As now understood, 'the Other' stands in apposition to Self. 'Othering' has tended to develop into a 'process by which a group of people establishing a sense of their own identity creates a hostile image of a second group which embodies all the characteristics and features the first group most dislikes and fears'.[17] This is not unlike what psychoanalysts call 'projection', and it certainly has pathological implications, since this kind of self-evaluation leads to gratuitous denigration of others. The 'othering' of indigenous peoples, within the framework of colonial relationships, became in the nineteenth century an inherent function of empire-building. It lies at the root of much of the racial prejudice associated with empires. It hardly needs to be said that inability to see the

Other as human is a recipe for disaster. Or that states trying to impose their will on cultures of which they are ignorant can be dangerous.

Inaccurate Western stereotypes spoke of 'inscrutable orientals' and 'naked savages' as fanatics and fatalists, as vicious and libidinous. It was not simply a one-way process. For their part, Africans and Asians might see a threatening 'otherness' in Europeans. Until well into the twentieth century, Chinese peasant mothers would shield their babies from the foreigner's unlucky gaze, particularly that of the British 'red [hair] devils'. For many societies, the whites might be irreligious (infidel and unclean), vulgar, and materialistic barbarians, and their priests might be feared as cannibals or vampires (see p. 203 at n. 24). One of the early chaplains in India, Frederick Swartz, was berated by an Indian in Tanjore: 'Christian religion! Devil religion! Christian much drink, much do wrong, much beat, much abuse others'; and when Swartz warned a trainee dancing-girl that no bad person went to heaven, she retorted, 'Alas, sir, in that case hardly any European will ever enter it.'[18]

Towards the end of the eighteenth century there was a serious attempt by Warren Hastings as governor-general in India, and those British scholars he encouraged, to understand Indian culture. Sir Charles Wilkins translated one-third of the *Mahabharata*, the longest epic poem in the world, starting with the famous *Bhagavad Gita* in 1785. This was the first major translation of Hindu Sanskrit into a European language. Wilkins thus opened up the path to modern Indology. In Calcutta in 1784 Sir William Jones, jurist and philologist, founded the Asiatick Society of Bengal to encourage enquiry into the history, arts, sciences, and literature of Asia. Two years later he disconcertingly proposed that Greek and Latin may have descended from Sanskrit, which he eulogised as 'more perfect than the Greek, more copious than the Latin'. In 1789 he published a translation of *Shakuntala*, a play by the Indian dramatist Kalidasa, derived from the *Mahabharata*. Jones was a polymath with a pathbreaking output on many aspects of Indian civilisation. What he achieved shows that 'the production of colonial knowledge could involve Western enquirer and Eastern informant in a dialogue characterised by reciprocity, pluralism and equality'.[19] In Germany the Romantic enthusiasm for the culture of the East was if anything even more pronounced; nevertheless, this group of Britishers brought 'unexpected gifts of knowledge and sensibility . . . from the periphery in the eighteenth century'.[20]

For all foreigners, China was unquestionably alien. To the Victorians it was a chaotic, baffling, and annoying society with an unyielding ethnocentricism. It had not always been seen like that. The pundits of the European Enlightenment idealised China in the eighteenth century as a model stable polity governed by reason, a Pax Sinica. Voltaire's *Essai sur les moeurs* (begun in 1740) actually started off with China, and in an admiring way. He praised Confucianism for its rationalistic ethics and freedom from priestly mystifications. But the assessment of China radically changed from the 1790s, as contact became closer (and realities emerged), and as Europe itself, and Britain especially, entered a period of unprecedented change. What had once been admired as stability was now derided as stagnation.[21] Two entirely different worlds began to confront one another: one dedicated to openness, innovation, and free exchange of goods; the other closed, introspective, cursing change and interchange, rejecting novelty – and both of them, proud and ethnocentric. For the Chinese what was codified could not be changed. Rituals established long ago, and once and for all, were the very foundation of civilisation. Alteration meant tampering with the written characters of the language, which was an assault on reality itself. What might displease the ancestors was interdicted, for ancestor-worship sanctified an unassailable paternal perfection. The tenets of Confucianism legitimised both imperial rule at Peking (Beijing) and family patriarchy in the village. It was not that China was inert, but it was mired in inertia, both personal and institutional. And so the Ch'ing (Qing) government rebuffed British embassies seeking freedom of trade, in 1792–4 (led by Lord Macartney), and again in 1816 (led by Lord Amherst), and in 1834 (led by Lord Napier). In the loftily dismissive words of the edict of Emperor Ch'ienlung (Qianlong), 'The Celestial Empire . . . does not value rare and precious things or ingenious articles, nor do we have the slightest need of your country's manufactures.' The residence of a Western representative at court was not allowed by protocol, and would be of 'no advantage to your country'. It required two wars to open China to British trade, in 1839–42 and 1856–60. Only from the 1860s did a change of Chinese attitudes slowly unfold.[22]

Despite frustration with the Chinese, a handful of Britishers made great efforts to understand them. None was more remarkable than Isabella Bishop, who, after a visit to Canton in 1878–9, in the mid-1890s made an astonishing journey to Korea and Chinese Manchuria, immediately followed by an exuberant plunge into the Yangtse Valley, through Szechwan (Sichuan) to the Tibetan border, travelling alone by horse, sedan-chair, and boat across eight thousand miles, an epic 'long march' hardly equalled by Mao Tse-tung himself in 1934–5. For all the faults and mysteriousness of the Chinese, she believed 'their tenacity, resourcefulness . . . and respect for law and literature place [them] in the van of Asian nations'.[23] Another who understood the potential of China was Sir Robert Hart, who ran the Customs from 1868 to 1907: 'If China will only do the right thing, she will be in a century the most powerful empire on earth – the least aggressive – the most tolerant – and the greatest patron of learning' (1900).[24] Towering above all Sinologists is the enigmatic figure of Joseph Needham, CH, FRS, FBA, initiating author of the hyper-massive *Science and civilization in China*, first conceived in the 1940s when he was a cultural attaché in China. Needham was a biochemist of repute, who began learning Chinese in about 1937. He came to think of himself as above all 'an honorary Taoist', but without relinquishing his commitments to Morris-dancing, high-church Anglicanism (he was a lay reader), and a Marxism which welcomed the Chinese communist revolution. As a vocal critic of 'Western imperialism and cultural arrogance', he advocated a dialogue of civilisations.[25]

Needham was of course highly exceptional in his wide-ranging intelligence and sympathies. Outsiders are usually best qualified to understand societies *relatively* like their own and to penetrate their myths and realities. Consider, for example, the astonishing insight which three Frenchmen attained into the working of democracies in other countries: Alexis de Tocqueville for America (1835), André Siegfried for New Zealand (1914), and Elie Halévy for England (1912–32). It was, however, an Englishman, J.E.C. Bodley (in his book *France*, 1907), who saw the French better than they could see themselves. Or consider how much American historians have contributed to British imperial and naval history (L.H. Gipson, A.J. Marder, and others), not least in our own day, the Texas-based historian (via Harvard, Oxford, and Yale) Wm. Roger Louis. But the more unlike our own societies other countries are, the harder it is to fathom them. Even European offshoot societies within the so-called 'British world' can seem obtuse. Looking for similarities can help. South Africa's Afrikaner apartheid regime, for example, showed parallels with ancient Sparta holding down the helots, or Prussia confronting the Slavs, or Israel the Palestinian Arabs; all four are examples of communities feeling themselves to be superior to, but threatened by, a numerically larger, alien population, an Other. In each case the dominant minority developed authoritarian, intransigent, and militaristic attitudes and strategies. It is, however, much harder for Westerners to enter into the mentalities of pre-literate peoples, or those, like the Chinese, whose structures of thought are sophisticated but radically different. Nevertheless, we have to get beyond the intellectual barriers and the simplistic clichés ('the Confucian ethic', 'fanatical Islam', 'unchanging Africa'). Like Needham we have to recognise that Western philosophies and systems are not the only valid way of summing up the whole of human experience and wisdom. As the great literary theorist and Sinophil I.A. Richards came to realise in China in the early 1930s:

This is how we all think – to us the Western world is still the World; but an impartial observer would perhaps say that such provincialism is dangerous. And we are not yet so happy in the West that we can be sure that we are not suffering from its effects . . . For with the increasing pressure of world contacts we do pitiably need to understand on a scale we have never envisaged before.[26]

Accordingly, we cannot be content to look in upon other cultures from the outside, but must draw upon imaginative and empathetic resources to understand them from within, looking outward.[27]

What does it mean, for instance, to study Africa 'from within', looking outward? The historian tries to comprehend the implications of living in small-scale, pre-literate, polygynous, and perhaps 'stateless' communities (where horizontal age-mate structures hold things together, rather than any vertical hierarchies). These may be societies with sophisticated notions of honour and family duty (expressed in kinship obligations, and in subtle distinctions between 'mother's brother' and 'father's brother', instead of a crude blanket term like 'uncle'). Traditional African marriage was a contract between kin-groups rather than between romantically involved individuals, and pastoral peoples thought in terms of 'wives and other cattle'.[28] Incalculable importance has been attached to the possession of cattle for social, ritual, political, and aesthetic reasons. Cattle are a measure of status, a means of mediation with ancestor spirits, and a necessity for ratifying marriage. Amongst many African peoples, too, land has been traditionally viewed as a commodity to be enjoyed in common, which, no more than the air we breathe, could be regarded as unilaterally alienable private property. Dead ancestors had rights in it, and although chiefs might convey rights of *use* and obligations of responsibility to individuals, this was still miles away from Western ideas of property rights. Only with such considerations in mind can we register the full significance for Africans of the alienation of land to Europeans, or the 1890s rinderpest epidemics. In the twentieth century, too, this 'thought-world' explains their alarm about land-apportionment and rehabilitation schemes, or veterinary embargoes or government destocking programmes. Furthermore, most African societies were not 'static'. The readiness with which they could adopt innovation was striking. To give just one example: guns sometimes became new symbols of masculinity so completely for Africans that European attempts to disarm them were greatly resented, as was the case for the Basotho, or the Yao of Nyasaland, who protested 'we are now as children'.

Important as it is to see them 'from within', the history of other societies can also be illuminated by instructive parallels with European ones. In terms of purely military innovation and growing megalomania, Shaka Zulu between 1818 and 1828 can bear comparison with Alexander the

Great in the fourth century BC. The preoccupations of African leaders or Chinese scholar-officials in the nineteenth century were similar to those of their sixteenth- and seventeenth-century European counterparts, and in some respects to those of their contemporary counterparts too. The gradual resolution of tensions between centre and periphery, as consolidating and unitary state-building processes advanced (or receded), the reduction (or growth) of regional autonomies and provincial resistance, all formed part and parcel of the history of every major country in the world, of Mughal India and Maoist China as well as medieval France and modern Germany. What Julius Caesar did for the Roman Republic, what Henry II did for the Angevin empire, what the early Tudors did for England, was to rescue states from overmighty subjects, lack of governance and bureaucratic breakdown, local warlords, and internecine conflicts within ruling elites. They then reconstituted popular allegiance and administrative machinery. Understanding this makes it easier to measure the achievement of Moshoeshoe in re-creating and holding together nineteenth-century Lesotho, or Mao Tse-tung in the 1930s and 1940s imposing some sort of central control (however nasty) on the amorphous chaos of China. In these circumstances government becomes of necessity a personal *tour de force*.[29]

Moreover, the ways in which more impersonal bureaucracies emerge are not totally dissimilar in Tudor England and in late eighteenth-century Asante in the Gold Coast.[30] Techniques of warding off external attack show similarities throughout the world. Sparta in sixth-century Greece avoided fighting in much the same way as Dahomey in nineteenth-century West Africa, both achieving immunity from attack for long periods through manipulating a range of propaganda weapons which cumulatively created an impression of terrifying invincibility. While Sparta manipulated the Delphic Oracle, Dahomey contrived to frighten off Europeans by deliberately exaggerating the extent of its 'cannibalism'. The Maori, however, rather foolishly let it be known that European flesh was not sweet enough for their taste.[31] Conspicuous largesse and hospitality as the test of rank and the most admired virtue among leading squires and nobles in sixteenth- and early seventeenth-century Britain are reflected exactly in the attributes expected of the chief in African societies.[32] Many pages of Thompson's *Making of the English working class* deal with the kind of millenarian expectations which have been so widespread in African history. In particular his treatment of Joanna Southcott of Devonshire (*c.*1800) forms an ideal prelude to studying the upheavals caused by African prophetesses, from Nongqawuse in Xhosaland in 1856–7 to Alice Lenshina a hundred years later in Zambia.[33] In short, whilst being ever alert to complex difference, we should also be wary of European 'exceptionalism'. There are common experiences and transformational similarities across the world, and we can use them for two-way illumination.[34]

We have thus far taken a wide-angled lens to pan around some of the contextualities of the empire, the global setting in which it moved and had its being, and some of the ways in which Britons perceived the Asian and African peoples with whom they had contact. The focus can now narrow down, and we can begin to examine policies, and the people who made and implemented them. We can also ask what the British thought of their imperial enterprise, beginning with the political elite.

The letters, memoirs, and biographies of nineteenth- and twentieth-century politicians reveal one thing quite clearly. Their overriding interest was in domestic politics, in the personalities of their leaders, in the prospects for Liberalism, or Toryism, or the Labour Party, or social democracy, amid the shifting currents of electoral change. Foreign policy, generally understood as relations with European powers and the USA, issues of war and peace and cold war, also loomed large for many of them. 'Imperial policy' was mainly subsumed under foreign policy. Occasionally there would be an imperial crisis and an explosion of concern – the Indian Mutiny-Rebellion (1857), the Governor Eyre controversy in Jamaica (1865), the Irish Home Rule debate (1885–6), the South African Anglo-Boer War (1899–1902), the Government of India Act (1935), the Suez fiasco (1956), the Falklands War (1982) – but otherwise the empire receded into the background. Among front-rank politicians, only Joseph Chamberlain (secretary of state for the colonies, 1895–1903, and thereafter a campaigner for tariff reform) showed any sustained interest in imperial affairs, but even he never visited India and he seldom spoke about it. Gladstone – to take an important example, as four times prime minister – never visited Ireland nor travelled further afield than the Ionian Isles. He was singularly ill-informed about British imperial, military, and naval responsibilities and interests. India seems hardly ever to have entered his thoughts, and only once did it arouse his enthusiasm, when the possibility of arranging Cook's tours there was mooted. Gladstone resented the intrusion of the Egyptian question into the Eurocentric world of his government, because it was an issue which 'does not turn upon clear principles of politics, and about which the country understands almost nothing and cares, for the most part, very little'.[35] Most other prime ministers, too, only bothered about the empire when they had to. Historians have to go to the next layer down of the governing elite to find men with a deep interest in imperial problems: to the 8th Earl of Elgin, Sir Charles Dilke, Lord Cromer, Lord Curzon, and L.S. Amery.

As for the less committed members of the elite, few were actively opposed to empire. 'The empire on which the sun never sets' and 'Ubi virtus, ibi Victoria' were just two of the triumphalist slogans which were happily bandied about. When formal opinions were expressed about the empire by Victorians and Edwardians, what strikes us today is the smugness and hyperbole. But as well as this, there was also pungent criticism, from Richard Cobden in the 1840s onwards.[36] By the late nineteenth century, Liberal Party leaders were echoing Sir Charles Dilke in denouncing 'bastard imperialism'. Campbell-Bannerman attacked 'the vulgar and bastard imperialism of . . . provocation and aggression . . . of grabbing everything even if we have no use for it ourselves' – and he spectacularly lashed out against 'methods of barbarism' in the conduct of the South African War. Winston Churchill, keen to assert his Liberal credentials, in 1904 contrasted an honourable imperialism 'which unites us to our colonies' with a 'bastard imperialism', the 'cheap and flashy doctrine ground out by the Conservative Party machine'.[37] The Liberals, however, did not repudiate empire, so long as it could be represented as a system uncorrupting at home and contributing to world peace and improvement. Lord Rosebery (prime minister, 1894–5) admitted that the empire had often used the sword and could not exist without it, but 'it does not live by the sword'.[38] Similarly, imperial righteousness was stressed by Lord Lugard, famous proconsul, laying the foundation stone of the University of Hong Kong in 1910, when he put the empire firmly on the side of the angels:

It will pass away, as other empires have passed away before it, but I believe that history will record of it that it was founded on something higher than territorial conquest or national aggrandisement – that it was founded on the respect and affection of all the races which compose it, and that its effect has been to bring them increased prosperity and higher standards of life.[39]

Lugard had earlier charged about Africa like a ruthless knight-errant, believing all his actions were justified because he was – he thought – humanely trying to bring benefits to the backward, who had endured 'the appalling waste of life and misery in Africa before we came'. He was mightily indignant when the Colonial Office under the Liberals tried to rein him in, criticising his violent methods: 'Am I less an English gentleman because I am here?' The proconsuls of Lugard's generation, like Sir Frank Swettenham in Malaya and Sir Hesketh Bell in Uganda, all felt that what they were doing was important, 'lighting the dark places', supervising 'great works, roads, railways, telegraphs, wharfs', and model plantations, directing African and Asian progress through a 'wise and benevolent guardianship'.[40]

To have improved the lot of subject peoples was indeed held to be the main justification of empire. Those on the receiving end were not necessarily impressed. Jawaharlal Nehru comprehensively punctured all such justifications which the British could muster in defence of the empire. The Pax Britannica was not enough: 'We can have the perfect peace of the grave and the absolute safety of a cage or of prison. Or peace may be the sodden despair of men unable to better themselves.' Peace imposed by an alien conqueror 'has hardly the restful and soothing qualities of the real article'. As to the benefits of science and technology, the railways, the telegraphs, and the rest of it, these were hardly altruistic tests of 'the goodness or beneficence of British rule'. Was it, Nehru asked, being needlessly cantankerous and perverse to suggest that 'some such technical progress would have come to us anyhow in this industrial age, and even without British rule'? Trusteeship was not enough either. He found himself 'singularly irritated' by the British 'calm assurance of always being in the right and having borne a great burden worthily'; moreover, 'in spite of their amusing assumption of being the trustees and guardians of the Indian masses, they know little about them and even less about the new aggressive *bourgeoisie*'.[41]

Apart from radical critics like Wilfrid Blunt and J.A. Hobson,[42] few Britons working in imperial administration would have endorsed Nehru's critique, though they would have seen what he meant. The most thoughtful of the servants of empire often felt ambivalent about it. This was never better expressed than by the writer Leonard Woolf. He was in the Ceylon Civil Service, 'an extraordinary, hierarchical and complicated engine', from 1904 to 1911. He enjoyed the position, 'the flattery of being the great man and the father of his people'. But as time went on, 'I became more and more ambivalent, politically schizophrenic, an anti-imperialist who enjoyed the fleshpots of imperialism, loved the subject peoples and their way of life, and knew from the inside how evil the system was beneath the surface for ordinary men and women.' In his unease, trying to balance benevolence and ruthlessness, he exaggerated his 'imperialist, stern Sahib attitude to compensate for or soothe a kind of social conscience which began to condemn and dislike the whole system'. He liked the people without idealising them, 'as a good district officer should', unsentimentally working hard to try to 'increase their prosperity, diminish the poverty and disease, start irrigation works, open schools'. But, and in a distinctly Gibbonian final analysis, for Woolf there was an absurdity in a people of one civilisation trying to impose its rule upon an entirely different one.[43]

District officers can bear important witness. Many of them in their memoirs recognised that things had been far from perfect, but, however critical they were prepared to be, almost all of them felt that the record was positive, better than that of the other European empires, and that if Britain had given up, those others would step in, to the detriment of the people concerned. Three unpublished assessments have recently come to light and may be quoted here. They deal with Kenya, Aden, and Palestine. The first is by 'Dick' Cashmore, who felt that in Kenya there had been many mistakes, with injustices as well as good intentions. He feared future generations would 'judge us more harshly for failing in our trust; because we did not prepare our successors adequately for the perils of independence, and left too soon'. Alternatively they would 'curse us for not going sooner, or for even coming at all'. In the second memoir, Reginald Hickling, the high commissioner's legal adviser in Aden, suggested that the 'historian of colonialism' in the Arabian peninsula 'will see our whole exercise, from 1799 to 1968, as one of selfish power-politics, overtaken in its decline by a casual interest in self-government. If he is something of a philosopher, he will also conclude that a nation cannot successfully govern a people it dislikes.'[44] Hickling was unconsciously echoing Thomas Munro, an early administrator in India, who said, 'We can never be qualified to govern men against whom we are prejudiced.'[45]

Thirdly, and pithily, Sir Ronald Storrs, governor of Jerusalem under the Palestine Mandate, believed the British had brought material benefits but not made people more contented: 'Thou hast multiplied the harvest but not increased the joy, is my epitaph for the British empire.'[46]

It is, perhaps, as good an epitaph as the British empire can hope to get. It is not easy to make a definitive judgment. 'Balance-sheets of empire', whether it was worthwhile, a good thing or a bad thing, have a long future in front of them. Subjective judgments are bound to prevail. Evidence can as easily be found for useful benefits and altruistic efforts as for brutality and exploitation and sheer indifference. All these ambiguities have to be taken seriously into account.[47] Like most things in life, 'the empire' was neither black nor white, but a mixture, a not altogether hopeless shade of grey perhaps.

This said, and having considered something of the views of the governing elite, we can now proceed to ascertain what the empire may have meant to ordinary members of the British public. A great deal of recent writing about 'colonialism' stresses the significance of 'identity', and the extent to which the idea of 'Britishness' itself might be in some sense a product of imperial experience. I take a sceptical view of two post-colonial assertions: (1) that a preoccupation with 'identity' (including sexual identity: see p.42 below) has always been as prominent as it is now, and (2) that empire, 'imperialism', was somehow thoroughly embedded in British life and thought.

For those who actually served overseas it could be an absorbing, even a romantic business. They might see themselves at the end of a long line of devoted administrators,

the final executive blood vessel in the network of arteries that stretched out, long, efficient and complex, from the distant heart of empire: the true *ultima ratio regum*. The ghosts of dead colleagues rise up: in the Club at Mandalay, saddling their horses in Peshawar, haranguing the tribes in the Khalahari . . . The powers and privileges, the discomforts and the eccentricities . . . and the fun.[48]

But for ordinary people at home? The first point to make is that however much they may have been surrounded by evidence of empire, they were unlikely to interrogate it, or connect it all up. Shopping at 'Home & Colonial' grocery stores, reading the *Daily Mail* ('For King and Empire'), seeing maps with big splodges of red, or encountering their first West Indian immigrant, seem unlikely to have made them more imperially aware or more patriotic than children playing with their favourite golliwog, or with toys stamped 'Empire Made' (a euphemism for Hong Kong and a byword for shoddiness), or contemplating their first post-war bananas. Being asked to celebrate the empire, wrote the author of 'Land of Hope and Glory', no less, 'leaves me cold. I think that most people have quite enough to do without thinking about their neighbour.' How, he wondered, 'can little minds think about the colonies & India, & the world at large . . . a great dim abstraction' – and all that it means?[49] Neville Chamberlain in the 1930s thought that 'the people of this country' might have a deep underlying sentiment for the empire, 'but it is remote from their ordinary thoughts'. Most people, wrote Noel Annan (b. 1916), 'had always been bored with the Empire', and this fixed a great gulf between them and the ruling class who found employment in imperial administration.[50]

However, the post-colonial historians, purveyors of the so-called 'new imperial history', insist that Britain and the British people were 'steeped', 'saturated', 'suffused', 'permeated', even 'imbricated in imperialism' (really? – imbricated means 'overlapping like roof-tiles or fish-scales'). Empire is said to have played an integral part in metropolitan values, thoughts, ideas, and practices. Now, there are two ways of reacting to this. One is to dismiss it as an intellectually lazy assumption – that so large an enterprise '*must have*' loomed large in contemporary consciousness. The other is to suggest that it all seems like an attempt to make twenty-first-century British people feel uncomfortable about present problems and guilty about 'their' imperial past. This is because they are represented as implicated – whether consciously or unconsciously is said to be immaterial – in the 'evils of imperialism'. Thus they become tainted by its supposedly inherent racism, complicit through their consumption of foodstuffs imported from the empire ('product imperialism'), and – it is assumed – their support of missionary endeavours, their reading of books and watching of films with imperial settings. Even becoming a 'nation of tea-drinkers . . . with the highest sugar consumption in the world' can be made to look suspect.[51]

The empire is seen by these post-modernist historians as 'inexorably shaping' – 'constituting', in their favourite jargon – a sense of 'Britishness', with imperialism as culturally a 'core ideology'. And if this cannot be readily demonstrated, the empire is said, through its 'taken-for-grantedness', to be influential in small but significant everyday ways, and despite being 'almost unseen'. The empire is reckoned to be 'part of everyday life for Britons' between the late eighteenth century and the beginning of decolonisation, even though it might be a largely unconscious 'background assumption', 'a consensual understanding'. According to Catherine Hall, really clever theorists can interpret what was not explicitly stated; but historians who cannot see this should be excoriated for their 'fall into the darkness of empiricism'.[52] The empirical historian's response to this kind of argument is likely to be concern at such a cavalier dismissal of the need for evidence, followed by an attempt to suggest that fundamental assumptions – for example, that food, health, sex, and the weather play a big part in life – are usually made very explicit indeed, and are made so by constant discussion. The insistence on unconscious assumptions about the empire has a worrying whiff of pseudo-Freudianism about it, and, even more alarmingly, echoes of the portentous fantasies of Professor Cramb's *Origins and destiny of imperial Britain* (1900).[53] Post-colonialists at their most extreme have even tried to argue that Victorian novels which do *not* refer to the empire only prove how crucial it was.[54] All this is now a minefield of difficult and contested interpretation about the impact of the empire, the extent of imperial awareness, and whether or not there was a distinctively 'imperialist ideology' and culture.[55] It is a minefield which will take years to clear. Perhaps agreement might at least eventually be reached on a conclusion that whatever the extent of 'popular imperialism' in the formation of a British identity, by the 1940s it was in terminal decline.[56] This may well have been an effect of war, and the cold war which soon succeeded it. A generation (like mine), brought up dodging bombs of various kinds (high-explosive, incendiary, V1 flying-bombs, and V2 rockets, all coming uncomfortably close), and then being confronted with threats of nuclear annihilation, had vastly more worrying issues to concern it than whether or not Britain had, or could retain, an overseas empire, and what sort of impact it was having.

These are complex questions of theory and interpretation. The main aim of the essays in this book is simpler: to explore how the British empire functioned, and to examine the determinants of imperial management. The chapters are organised into six themes or sections. The first two deal with the dynamics of the enterprise, the interlocking of strategic, economic, religious, and ethical concerns through two centuries from 1763. With the aid of a comparative global context, 'geopolitics' is established as an explanatory motif. The third theme is about the civil service (an aspect of the 'official mind'), and the way decisions were arrived at; it concentrates upon the first half of the twentieth century. The next chapters look at individual agency, the role of major figures, with Churchill and Smuts as the examples. The fifth theme explores problems of sexuality, how it is connected to perceptions of 'otherness', and how it had an inherent potential for exploitativeness. Finally, suggestions are made about understanding the practitioners of imperial history themselves, within the shaping of a historiographical framework.

The remainder of this Introduction therefore serves to provide a reflective background and explication for each of these six themes. Accordingly, it is organised into sections with the following headings: I Dynamics: geopolitics and a structural framework; II Religion and an ethical empire?; III Bureaucracy and policy: government decision-making; IV Great men: the individual and responsibility; V Sexuality: putting sex into perspective; VI Imperial historians: historiography or ancestor worship?

I Dynamics: geopolitics and a structural framework

'A vast imperial nodality has been accumulated in London during the centuries characterised by oceanic mobility.' So wrote Sir Halford Mackinder in 1907. His geopolitical hypothesis demonstrated the economic advantages of being geographically 'the central, rather than the terminal, land of the world', an archipelago offshore to the great Eurasian landmass or 'world island' (if Africa was included in the 'inner global crescent').[57] This gave Britain easy access to the 'world's unified ocean', facilitated its expansionist enterprise, and secured its immunity from effective containment or attack by continental rivals. (See Figure 1.) Certainly the British empire developed as a result of a particular combination of favourable world circumstances. The geopolitical preconditions for the empire were: first, a strategic balance in Europe, with no single power dominant; secondly, freedom of movement through the Mediterranean (the route to India) and around the world's oceans – sea-power itself being dependent on the absence of the need to keep

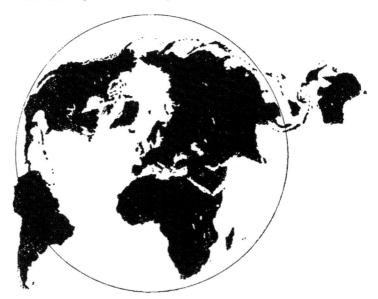

Figure 1 Mackinder's sketch-map showing Britain as 'the central land of the world' – and the importance of the Mediterranean. *Source*: *Britain and the British seas*, p. 4.

a large standing army; and thirdly, a relatively quiescent Islam and East Asia. Once these favourable external factors were eroded, and the whole international context for operating the British empire was compromised, then the days of imperial Britain were numbered.

But what do we mean when we speak of 'the British empire'? It was not monolithic. There was a global network of interests on which, to be sure, the sun never set. But there was no uniformity in its structure, nor was the nature of this 'empire' unchanging over time.

The most fundamental question to ask about it is exactly what the British empire was; whether, even, there was in any real sense an empire at all, about which generalisations can be made.[58] It is one thing to assert that the British 'ruled' much of India and Africa, quite another to argue that they controlled what happened there. For, in certain crucial respects, 'empire' was a myth, an illusion based upon a gigantic confidence trick perpetrated by the 'rulers'. Mostly this illusory system was accepted by the 'ruled', but in different ways: some were duped, some deferred, and some collaborated. Authority over non-European peoples, however deferential they might sometimes appear, was distinctly fragile. The cohesiveness of settler colonies – Canada, South Africa, and the rest of the

'British world' (or Greater Britain as it used to be called) – was weaker than it seemed, even before they became self-governing 'Dominions'.

Seeley thought the term 'possession' for the white colonies in the 1880s inappropriate, and only a little less so for India: we must, he wrote, 'dismiss from our minds the idea that India is in any practical sense of the word a possession of England'.[59] He was right. The Olympian magnificence of the empire, so often celebrated, is not a sustainable historical concept. It was in world terms influential, certainly, but not in the strict sense hegemonic. The empire was not a unified multilateral association at all, but rather a series of bilateral relationships with a lot of weaker units, 'a chaotic conglomerate' in John Darwin's striking description.[60] Quite late in the day, the one triumphantly unifying factor was cable construction (see Map 1); 'the nerves of the empire', by the 1890s, girdled the world with 121,000 miles of telegraph wires. The web of submarine cables transformed the conduct of trade and diplomacy, as well as colonial administration.[61] Even so, a late Victorian and Edwardian rightwing project to tighten the constitutional structure through such devices as a federal council and imperial preference failed utterly. A loose-strung 'Commonwealth' was the best that could be achieved.

In these circumstances the British relied on prestige, on conveying an impression of unquestionable omniscience. A Turkish dragoman in Kinglake's *Eothen* (1844) believed that 'wherever the Irish, or the French, or the Indians rebel against the British, whole armies of soldiers and brigades of artillery' were rapidly deployed to 'utterly exterminate the enemies of England from the face of the earth'. Without this convenient semi-delusion – the cultivation of a 'wholesome dread of our power', as one Victorian governor put it – the empire could hardly have functioned at all.[62] The reality is that imperial resources of all kinds, money and manpower, even support at home and abroad, were in short supply. India itself was conquered for the British by other Indians – or, in Seeley's brilliant insight, there was 'an internal revolution within Indian society rather than a foreign conquest'.[63] The Delhi uprising during the Indian Mutiny-Rebellion of 1857 was in part put down by paid mercenaries of Sikh, Muslim, Punjabi, and Pathan extraction.[64] South African blacks provided indispensable logistical support during the Anglo-Boer War. Mau Mau was brought under control by African vigilante 'home guards', askaris or policemen. The exercise of imperial power depended on organising these mechanisms of indigenous collaboration – and on bluff and racial arrogance. Two stories, one by George Orwell ('Shooting an elephant'), the other by Hans Christian Andersen ('The emperor's new clothes'),[65] tell us much that is vital to know about the nature of imperial rule. Orwell, an Old Etonian serving

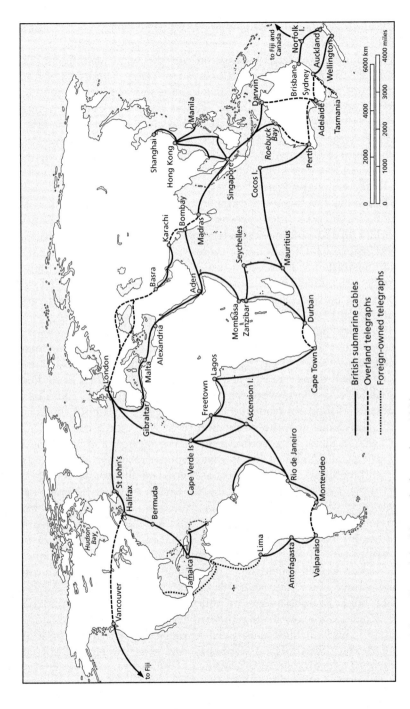

Map 1 Imperial cables and telegraphs, c.1920.

with the Imperial Police in Burma, describes a 'public order' episode, in which the hollowness of the white man's dominion was revealed to him, through the feeling that he was no more than 'an absurd puppet pushed to and fro' by 'natives' who expected a sahib to act like a sahib.[66] In Andersen's tale, it was left to a small boy to point out the awful naked truth about the emperor's supposedly magnificent apparel. Nationalist reactions, from uprisings to full-blown demands for independence, were almost inevitable when people woke up to the essentially fraudulent nature of imperial rule, to a sense that they had been duped.[67] They had succumbed not only to hierarchical plausibility, but also perhaps to their own 'dependency' complex,[68] and slowness to realise that a white man's skull under his vainglorious pith-helmet (sola topee) was as thin as anyone else's. When the scales were lifted from the eyes of subject peoples, then the administrators of empire ran out of local political collaborators, and their future was bleak. Mechanisms which had been devised to consolidate British rule – everything from sport to the English language – were appropriated by the nationalists to challenge it. The devices of the British were made to serve the desires of the colonised. In this way, English education, said the Indian nationalist leader B.G. Tilak, became 'the milk of the tigress'.[69]

Whatever the empire was, then, it was not structurally an impressive monolithic organisation closely governed from London. It was not a steel frame – more a cat's-cradle. Its name was DIVERSITY. It was not an entity driven by some mythical juggernaut called 'imperialism'. It meant different things to different people. The empire was a loose aggregation of diffuse elements, often uncertain, inherently complex, endlessly uneven in its impact.

Whether a territory was conquered or not, was kept quiet or not, depended crucially on geopolitics, on its size, measured geographically and demographically. Despite coastal enclaves, there could never have been a British empire in China, simply because of its remoteness, vastness, turbulence, and amorphous character, 'a vast repository of incalculable forces' (J.A. Hobson). Attempting even limited military action against China on the coast was 'like flogging a jelly-fish' (Winston Churchill).[70] In 1851, China's population was at its nineteenth-century peak, 430 million; Britain's was just 16 million. For the British, it was comparatively easy to control small territories like landlocked Swaziland (no bigger than Wales, population 2 million), small islands like Ceylon (about half the size of England and a population not much greater than London's), and neat peninsulas like Malaya (about the same size as England but with a population of only 5 million). It was a task of a totally different order of magnitude to attempt the government of India, the size of fifty Ceylons, a population of 294 million (by 1900), with 179 main languages and 544 dialects, myriad castes, and the home of an ancient and highly persistent civilisation. To be sure, the establishment of the British Raj was one of the most astounding facts in world history – 'prodigies to which the world has seen nothing similar. Reason is confounded. We interrogate the past in vain' (Macaulay, 1833).[71] But it was almost bound to end in tears.

It could be a great mistake to challenge the British, who then mustered all their limited resources to defeat and punish such temerity. They preferred sensible unresisting peoples who asked for protection or accepted the flag, like the Fijians, the Baganda, the Bangwato, the Swazi, and the Bulozi of Barotseland – even if the Basotho were a little too insistent (Moshoeshoe: 'My country is your blanket, O Queen, and my people the lice on it'). Vexatious resisters could expect no mercy. The diplomatically submissive were allowed to retain their traditional chiefs, but there was declared to be 'no place' for ancient monarchy in conquered states. Such deposition happened slowly in India, with the Mughal dynasty finally being abolished in 1858, when Bahadur Shah Zafar II was exiled; but it was more sharply catastrophic for the Sinhalese and the Burmese, for the Zulu and the Ndebele.

In order to get an effective handle on the imperial structure, a working typology of the dependencies is required. The scheme offered by Anthony Low more than forty years ago remains helpful.[72] He distinguishes between authority 'superseded', 'incorporated,' and 'created'. Mughal India and Southern Rhodesia were in the first category. The princely states of India, the Persian Gulf sheikdoms, Buganda, Muslim Northern Nigeria, Malaya, Zanzibar, and Barotseland were examples of the second, allowing pre-existing authorities to continue, but incorporated into slightly differing patterns of collaboration and dominance. 'Stateless' societies, without a single head (acephalous), such as those in northern Ghana, eastern Nigeria, southern Sudan, and Kenya, formed a third category, where authority was artificially imposed, the British seeking out various types of people thought suitable to be created 'chiefs', within an Indirect Rule system. Thus imperial authority gathered the threads of traditional legitimacy, where this existed, or forged collaborative alliances, or 'invented tradition' – or used force to establish a Pax Britannica which might evoke gratitude, and thus reconcile to alien rule. In Low's scheme there can be stages in the establishment of domination: from external sway (where the British might be welcomed as arbiters in internal African disputes, as by the Ankole in Uganda, or by the Tonga wanting protection from Ngoni raiding), to a stage of *ad hoc* influence, and then on to regular interference. But the exercise of power need not be uniform within a dominated state. It might be 'dictatorial' over land policy, 'predominant' over law, but only 'ascendant' when it came to regulating marriage customs. Similarly, acceptance of British power might be whole-hearted, willing, acquiescent, grudging, or resented.

'Informal empire' is a further structural variant, in situations where influence was considerable but the flag was never formally run up. The obvious examples were in Latin America, China, and the Middle East. But there were many differences in the way it operated in Buenos Aires, Shanghai, and Cairo.

The opening chapter provides an analytical overview of two centuries, and proposes an interpretative model for resolving some of the polarities in the debate about 'strategy' and 'economics' (chapter 1). The next two chapters develop the argument, by probing again at a canonical problem, the partition of Africa, and the variables in the British approach (chapter 2); this is followed by comparing the nineteenth-century British empire with other empires, in a global context (chapter 3). The last chapter in Part I suggests that isolating economic factors and building them into a large theory can be misleading, because such a method is unable either to accommodate 'geopolitics' adequately, or to convey enough of the multi-form structural complexity of the empire (chapter 4).

II Religion and an ethical empire?

It is a commonplace to observe that in our secularised and sceptical modern age, when children are no longer brought up in fear of hell-fire, it is difficult to appreciate the dominance of a religious outlook in life and thought during Victorian times. But it is essential. In 1876 the *Spectator* commented that 'the chief distinction of this generation has been the revival of religious earnestness'. If confirmation is needed, we need look no further than to the ubiquitous legacy of Victorian church-building and restoration, one of the quintessential characteristics of the period. The following remarkable figures for the rapid multiplication of places of worship are probably underestimates: 1,727 new Anglican churches in England and Wales built between 1840 and 1876, with 7,144 old ones or cathedrals renovated or extended, at a cost of £25.5 million; the Methodists had more than 11,000 chapels by 1851, and by the end of the century the Roman Catholics had 1,536 places of worship, the Baptists 6,313, and the Congregationalists 4,579. Victorian society, especially in mid-Victorian times, is said to have been a religious society 'in a deeper and more complete sense than any country in the West since the Reformation'.[73] It was essentially a Protestant faith, committed to good works, complacent, and virulently anti-Catholic. (Remarkably, the imperial historian Sir John Seeley, imbued with convictions about the regenerative power of religion, and England's destiny as a Christian State, forwarding the intentions of Providence, 'did not hesitate to assert even in the bland and cool pages of the *English Historical Review* that the Papacy was the "burning heart of all human discord"'.)[74] The Protestant world-view made it possible for the British to see themselves as a chosen people, with God once more visible in history. Britain was the new Israel. The anti-slavery movement and its related philo-Semitism and concern for indigenous rights, drew on a deep-rooted religious preoccupation with sin and redemption.[75] For most politicians and pundits, politics continued to have a religious dimension.

The entire British expansionist enterprise overseas was infused with and energised by a profound sense of moral and religious purpose. Palmerston's objective was 'the regeneration of rotten empires', the promotion of Britain's standing as 'the head of moral, social and political civilisation'. Charles Kingsley, novelist and cleric, regarded 'the spinning-jenny and the railroad, Cunard's liners and the electric telegraph', the achievements of doctors and political economists, sanitary reformers and engineers, 'as signs that we are, on some points at least, in harmony with the universe . . . the Ordering and Creating God' – a God who had entrusted Protestant England (freed from the 'saints and virgins, relics and miracles' of Catholicism) with the 'glorious work . . . to replenish the earth and subdue it'. Livingstone likewise spoke of the British as 'co-operators with God' in the 'renovation of the world', through 'Christianity and commerce'.[76] Even those with no such programme tended to speak in a religious language about the empire. For J.A. Froude the empire was 'our spiritual salvation'.[77] Lord Rosebery declared the empire to be 'the greatest secular agency for good that the world has seen'. He seems genuinely to have believed this, writing privately:

How marvellous it all is! Built not by saints and angels, but the work of men's hands; cemented with men's honest blood and with a world of tears, welded by the best brains of the centuries past; not without the taint and reproach incidental to all human work, but constructed on the whole with pure and splendid purpose. Human and yet not wholly human, for the most heedless and the most cynical must see in it the finger of the Divine.[78]

As early as 1826 the London Missionary Society had dedicated itself to 'the moral revolution of the world'. Thereafter, 'the evangelisation of the whole world in our generation' inspired many a missionary. Parallel to the missionary invasion of the globe was the consolidation of the Anglican Communion, which arose in consequence of the American

Revolution, the first bishops being consecrated to 'foreign' sees in Philadelphia and New York in 1787. This marked the emergence of the Church of England from an insularity to which it was condemned by the Reformation. By the time of the great Pan-Anglican Congress in London in 1908, 250 bishops from every overseas diocese were able to attend. (The Roman Catholics had 166 bishops in the British empire.) Church leaders expected the Church 'to strengthen the moral force of the Empire', to claim it for God (rather than vulgarly claim God for the empire).[79] As late as 1960 it could be asserted in a government survey that 'the Churches provide some of the strongest personal links that exist within the Commonwealth'.[80]

The disregard in the inter-war period and beyond of 'the expansion of Christianity' by imperial historians is surprising.[81] After all, clergy and missionaries had an extraordinary impact on almost every country in the world outside Islamic regions, and often a disruptive impact. Quasi- or pseudo-Christian elements were embedded in the greatest upheaval known to the nineteenth-century world, the Taiping Rebellion in China; violent protest against Christian intervention was integral to the Boxer uprising. The hold which Christianity now has on America and Africa is among the salient facts of the modern world.

So how did these religious forces affect the British empire?[82] The mental framework of the empire shifted dramatically over time, and with it perceived priorities and motivations. In an important sense 'imperial history' is but a sub-set of a larger species, the world history of race relations and human rights. If we use this perspective, there is one 'paradigm shift' above all others which stands out, and it arises directly out of a religious motivation: the attempt to maintain an ethical imperial policy – and its failure.

The most fundamental belief of late eighteenth-century thinkers was in humanity as a homogeneous whole, with a common origin (the biblical Adam – the theory of monogenesis). Differences were explained by environment and not by an immutable heredity, so there could be optimism about the potential of the backward. There was respect for religions other than Christianity (as having elements in common), and for non-European and especially oriental civilisations, since their material levels were all similar in the pre-industrial age.[83]

These characteristic late eighteenth-century attitudes provide one of the main contexts for the abolitionist movements, successful first against the slave trade (1807), and then against the institution of slavery itself within most of the British empire (1833), and perhaps its greatest achievements. They also underpinned the establishment of an ethical humanitarian policy in the 1830s, a policy associated with Lord Glenelg as secretary of state (1835 to 1839) and James Stephen as permanent under-secretary at the Colonial Office (1836 to 1847). Their challenging interventionism has attracted less attention than it deserves.

Lord Glenelg was educated in a broadly evangelical atmosphere (see below page 168).[84] He was responsible as president of the East India Company Board of Control for the renewal of the company's charter in 1833. In a major speech, almost as noble as Macaulay's more famous one, Glenelg declared that British rule in India should be conducted on 'the great and just principle' that 'considerations of wealth, of commerce, of revenue should be as nothing compared with the paramount obligation' to consider the interests of Indians and promote 'the welfare and prosperity of that great empire which Providence had placed in our hands'. He believed that Britons and Indians could be united in friendship.[85] As secretary of state for the colonies he applied similar principles. His most famous – or notorious – decision was to disallow Sir Benjamin D'Urban's annexation of the Ciskei in Eastern Cape, which had been named 'Queen Adelaide Province'. The region was thickly populated with the Xhosa people, but greedy Europeans wanted to dispossess them. Here was a highly significant moment. For the first time, British government had to decide whether or not to rule an African people. Glenelg – so often unfairly accused of indecisiveness – decided unequivocally against this, and tried to secure Xhosa independence. With advice from James Stephen and the missionary Dr John Philip, Glenelg's 150-page despatch, dated 26 December 1835, is probably the greatest state paper ever issued from the Colonial Office. An impassioned and scathing refutation of D'Urban's report, it rehearsed past history and laid down future guidelines.

'It would be difficult', wrote Glenelg, 'for me to describe the pain' with which he had read D'Urban's description of the Xhosa as 'irreclaimable savages'. Remarkably, Glenelg could see that responsibility for the disputes lay not with the 'Caffres' but with the Europeans, who had 'unavoidably converted them into a nation of depradators'. The despatch spoke the language of victimising and harassment: 'a long series of aggressions . . . victims . . . unjustly despoiled of their country . . . injustice . . . disastrous results'. The British claim to sovereignty was rejected since it rested 'on no solid foundation of international law or justice'. We are, D'Urban was reminded, 'a humane and Christian people', so they should try 'a systematic and persevering adherence to justice, conciliation, forbearance, and the honest arts by which civilisation may be advanced, and Christianity diffused amongst them'. Such a system must be 'immediately established and rigidly enforced'. In his conclusion Glenelg suggested that relations generally between Christian

Plate 1 Charles Grant, Lord Glenelg.

Europeans and heathen Africans were marked by events on which 'every humane mind dwells with such settled aversion and shame': 'of all the chapters in the history of mankind, this is perhaps the most degrading'. South Africa must not be added to the 'history of the regions which have seen their aboriginal inhabitants disappear under the withering influence of European neighbourhood, thus bringing down on ourselves the reproaches of mankind and the weight of national guilt'. Respect for 'the inalienable rights of nations to their lands' was 'the only policy which it becomes this country to observe'. He was caustic a little later about the unprincipled motives of Dutch-descended trek-Boers and the 'uncontrolled self-indulgence' of the Great Trek.[86]

Glenelg also opposed the incursion of settlers into New Zealand and wanted at least some 'interposition by the British government' for the protection of the Maori. He resisted unscrupulous measures which affected Maori lands. In Australia he upheld strongly the rights of the Aborigines, which he insisted must be fully acknowledged and protected, since their lives must be considered 'as equally valuable and entitled to the same protection as those of any European settlers'. He reprimanded the governor of Swan River Colony for threatening the vengeful general destruction of the local Aborigines. Those Europeans who claimed to have shot them in self-defence must be brought to trial. In 1838 he set up a five-man Protectorate of Aborigines at Port Philip; 'Protectors of Aborigines' followed in each Australian colony. In similar fashion, Glenelg kept a watchful eye on the interests of the American Indians in

Canada, and the predicament of ex-slaves in Jamaica after emancipation in 1834. And he refused to allow Mauritius and Guiana to indenture Indian labourers as a substitute for African slaves.

Meanwhile a parliamentary select committee was sitting to consider the general policy towards 'aborigines' in British settlements. The (Fowell) Buxton Report of 1837, taking its inspiration from the humanitarians' 1835 victory in Xhosaland (giving 'life itself, and liberty, and lands and tenements to a whole nation'), insisted that 'the oppression of the natives of barbarous countries is a practice which pleads no claim to indulgence'. Any constitutional changes in government should ensure that the Colonial Office retained powers to decide all questions concerning native interests. Revenue should be set aside for the education and religious instruction of indigenous peoples. The report, it has been said, 'supplied the definitive humanitarian missionary-informed analysis of the evils of settler colonialism', the most developed expression of an anti-settler model of a Christian humanitarian empire. This was based on Glenelg's principle of 'the inalienable rights of nations to their lands' as the only proper policy for Britain.[87] Fowell Buxton, for his part, was also closely involved in a series of measures designed to tackle the persistence of slaving in West Africa.[88]

Glenelg's tenure of the Colonial Office thus marks the high watermark of humanitarian influence upon government, a serious but ultimately unsuccessful attempt to promote an ethical imperial policy based upon indigenous rights. Within a dozen years his Aborigines' Protectorates had been abolished or neutered; Aboriginal land-title was legally denied (and not recognised again in Australia until 1992); the Transkei had been annexed with the approval of Earl Grey;[89] the settlers were firmly in control of New Zealand and not held back by the equivocal Treaty of Waitangi (1840); and Indian indentured labour was spreading across the globe. Buxton had lost his parliamentary seat, and his 1841 Niger expedition to set up a model farm was a disaster. There was widespread disappointment about the results of slave emancipation in the West Indies.[90] Everywhere the settlers were gaining ground, and this was fatal to the humanitarian project. As concessions to white-dominated self-government multiplied, the metropolitan government was left with very little practical influence. The humanitarians were increasingly marginalised. Prominent Victorian commentators like Carlyle, Dickens, and Matthew Arnold ridiculed the whole humanitarian philosophy. In his own day, Glenelg was mocked and condemned for foolishness.[91] The truth is, however, that the humanitarians had more moral seriousness, honesty, and breadth of vision than many of those who came after them. The history of the British empire would have been signally different if their 'eighteenth-century' ethical principles had prevailed over the cultural insensitivities and racial arrogance of the Victorians.

The original motives of the Protestant missionary movement, evident in the planning of the Church Missionary Society in the 1790s, were nothing if not broad-minded and well-intentioned. Christianity was seen as a way of making reparation for the slave trade, and in India, as offering a compensation for territorial conquest: 'We have annihilated the political importance of the natives, stripped them of their power, and laid them prostrate, without giving them anything in return.' The British had '70 million fellow-men who are now our fellow subjects, pagan or Mahomedan, and it is a reproach so far to have done so little for them'; the best gift the Indians could be given was the Christian religion.[92] The first missionary in New Zealand admired the Maori as a 'noble and kindly race', who needed only the introduction of 'the arts of civilisation and the knowledge of the Christian religion to make them a great nation'.[93] The evangelicals of the Clapham Sect and the Cambridge practitioners of 'universal benevolence' had an enlightened and thoughtful view of all their 'fellow-men', but the next generation was much narrower and more aggressive in outlook. Evangelicalism was gradually transformed into a volatile, pessimistic, bigoted, extreme fundamentalist, Calvinist, anti-Catholic, anti-rationalist creed.[94] It saw Satan, the Prince of Darkness, everywhere, not least in Papist 'antichristianity' and the 'Mahometan delusion'. In consequence, by the 1850s in Delhi the English had acquired a reputation as 'the people who overthrow all religions'.[95]

Along with the dark certainties of evangelical doctrines came the iron laws of utilitarianism, and the arrogance produced by intoxicating industrialisation and technological advance. Respect for non-European achievements was severely eroded, as profound differentials in material standards emerged. But for the time being the optimistic assumption that mankind was a homogeneous whole lingered on in some quarters. Lord Palmerston – to take an important example – as late as 1856 said that since Indians and Chinese were 'human beings like ourselves' they were amenable to 'the same general principles as regulated the conduct of all mankind'.[96] The Indian Mutiny-Rebellion in the following year destroyed the last vestiges of this enlightened optimism, especially coming as it did against a background of mounting evidence for a recalcitrant reaction against Western ideas and demands. The conjuction of revolts around the globe amounted to 'a decade of crisis, 1855 to 1865'. At the same time, scientists began to lay stress on heredity rather than environment, and pseudo-Darwinian theories of 'survival of the fittest' gained in popularity.[97]

The decline of the environmentalist view of civilisation, and the increasing importance attached to race, were fatal ingredients in – to use modern jargon – the construction of later nineteenth-century discourse. Experience on the ground dictated much of this, perhaps particularly the failure of the missionaries to make many converts, leading to what has been called 'the closing of the missionary mind'. It has also been suggested that ever more rigid class distinctions and snobbish aspirations, 'aspirations to gentility', tended to emphasise distance between people of different race and colour.[98] This hardening of attitudes was only reinforced by a new breed of ethnocentric anthropologists.

In India, when the Sikhs were conquered and subjugated in 1849, the British had defeated the last of their military rivals. They felt they had nothing to learn from India and much to teach. British officers became increasingly distant, rude, and dismissive. Gone were the days of the 'white Mughals', who joined their men in talking, hunting, dancing, or playing chess, and cohabiting with their sisters. Sitaram Pandey, a sepoy who wrote his memoirs after 1857, measured the change exactly:

I have lived to see great changes in the sahibs' attitudes towards us. I know that many officers nowadays only speak to their men when obliged to do so, and they show that the business is irksome and try to get rid of the sepoys as quickly as possible. One sahib told us he never knew what to say to us. The sahib always knew what to say, and how to say it, when I was a young soldier.[99]

The humanitarian project was wrecked by soldiers, settlers, and sceptics. Although moralising and missionary voices were never quite silenced in the nineteenth century, they had lost their power to influence government decisions. The mournful truth was contained in Lord Salisbury's lapidary dismissal of moralistic objections: 'If our ancestors had cared for the rights of other people, the British empire would not have been made' (1878). The collapse of the early human rights movements between the 1840s and 1860s represents the biggest single change of mentality within the time-frame of the history of the empire since the American Revolution. 'Universal benevolence' gave way to 'the omnipresence of racial differences'. Thereafter there would be disagreements about expansion and how the empire should be run. But there would be no more seismic changes of direction.[100]

In theory 'an ethical empire' should have been possible. But in practice this would have meant the denial of basic facts. The British empire would not have been the British empire without the migrations overseas, the great diaspora, the 'white deluge', of English, Scots, and Irish: perhaps 21.5 million emigrants, between 1815 and 1914.[101] These inhabitants of Greater Britain, or 'neo-Britains', had interests which were bound to clash with the rights of indigenous peoples, particularly over land. Perhaps it was hard to believe, when there was a conflict of interest, that black should prevail over white in the interests of multi-racial harmony. Was there not a moral commitment to an alternative vision, the beauty of a *civitas dei*, the loyal white 'commonwealth' of kith and kin? And it was George Orwell who diagnosed another inescapable fact: an empire has to hold its troublesome subjects down, and 'In order to rule over barbarians, you have got to become a barbarian yourself.'[102]

The British empire could not legitimately claim to have been 'an ethical empire', since the British employed, at various points in time, slavery, Indian and Chinese indentured labour, African and Malayan forced labour; since they trafficked in opium, guns, and liquor, seized native lands, mounted punitive expeditions, obstructed missionaries, exploited native women, conscripted colonial manpower to fight in European wars; and since they indulged in legal violations and intimidation, and implemented counter-terrorist measures with shocking brutality. But if it was not an ethical *empire*, it was not an empire without an ethical *policy*. Humanitarian and trusteeship doctrines staged something of a revival in Whitehall after 1905,[103] so much so that some historians speak of 'a deep sense of ethical responsibility that remains one of the distinguishing characteristics of the colonial age'.[104] Almost all officials in the Colonial Office believed in their role as trustees, and saw themselves as inheriting a noble tradition. One of its leading lights, Sir Andrew Cohen, wrote:

The spirit of the anti-slavery movement is in fact enshrined in the evangelical tradition of Britain – a tradition which has found expression in a deep and practical concern for the welfare of have-nots overseas, a tradition kept alive by reformers, colonial administrators, and liberal societies.[105]

There were publicists, notably Margery Perham, and MPs, including Fenner Brockway and Barbara Castle, who called on government to maintain a strict ethical stance, sometimes mounting a withering critique of policy. Officials and ministers had the harder task, however, as they faced head-on the unresolved ambiguities and limitations of trusteeship.

To discover the effects of moral influence on imperial decisions is far from simple. It is perhaps an unfashionable line of enquiry today, even though the decisions themselves are often criticised. We worry that high-flown protestations of morality are mere rhetorical humbug, that politicians too readily cover mundane motive with an ethical veneer. But as R.E. Robinson insisted, 'Until the role of moral force in the imperial process is more sharply defined, it is not easy to be sure of the role of high velocity guns or surplus capital.' His own conclusion was that

'Ethics were most influential when allied to expediency; expediency was most practicable when approved by ethics.'[106]

The two chapters in Part II address religious themes in imperial history. The first examines the place of doctrinal and humanitarian considerations in the anti-slavery movement, which in turn provided antecedents for the experiment in 'ethical empire' in the 1830s (chapter 5). The second is a foray into mission history, but from the less-usually-explored angle of the African reception of Christianity, by turning the historical gaze upon Europeans, with a 'view from below'. And then the three essays in Part III all explore, in part at least, the attempts to implement trusteeship (chapters 7, 8, and 9). The example of one leading official, John Bennett, shows how difficult it was to reconcile the desire for ethical policies with the demands of government for practical compromise (chapter 9).

III Bureaucracy and policy: government decision-making

There was an almost comic ignorance of imperial geography in the eighteenth century. Newcastle as prime minister at the start of the Seven Years War in 1756 had no idea where the fortress of Annapolis (Royal) was, though it was crucial to the defence of Nova Scotia against the French. At the time of peacemaking, he said he *thought* the king had confused the Ganges and the Mississippi, but admitted to his own ignorance of 'exactly the state and limits of those countries'. The *Annual Register* of 1758 described the Niger as having its source in East Africa. The editor of a government newspaper quoted as a serious argument for keeping Florida the hoax proposition that it would supply peat for the fires of 'our cold, frozen West Indian islands'. Towards the end of peacemaking the Board of Trade could not supply any systematic statistics (or any statistics at all?) on the size of the African trade, which was widely accepted as being the foundation for the whole North Atlantic 'triangle' of trade.[107]

The information deficit lingered on. The old machinery of government remained almost useless for many decades yet. Between 1801 and 1854 the colonies and the War Office were linked together under a single secretary of state. Only in mid-Victorian times was a civil service properly established, on the triune principles of merit, neutrality, and anonymity. Gradually it became accepted that for these principles to work, political masters must carry responsibility. As late as 1833 James Stephen had to beg Lord Grey not to let his name be associated with the Emancipation Act, because his unpopularity would prejudice the measure.[108] But also in 1833 the principle of entry by examination was established in Indian administration, with Macaulay saying he hoped it would enable them to 'fill the magistracies of our Eastern Empire with men who will do honour to their country, with men who may represent the best part of the English nation' (that is, men with an Oxbridge education). However, it was only from 1853 that the principle of *competitive* examination for the Indian Civil Service and the Home Civil Service (which included the Colonial Office) replaced that of merely attaining a certain pass level, a change recommended in the Northcote–Trevelyan Report. Macaulay believed this would infallibly raise the standard of administrative excellence.[109] Great faith was placed in this principle, the cornerstone of recruitment to the Civil Service. Graham Wallas wrote that 'The creation of this Service was the one great political invention in nineteenth-century England.'[110]

Selection by competitive examination certainly enabled the Colonial Office by the beginning of the twentieth century to obtain officials of the highest calibre. Joseph Chamberlain as secretary of state (1895–1903) had shaken the department up. Before that it had been a backwater. (One senior official did all his work at home; less fortunate juniors arrived at noon and left at 5.30 p.m., having meanwhile taken time off for lunch and games of fives and darts; the medical missionary Mary Kingsley described colonial policy in the early 1890s as 'a coma, accompanied by fits'.[111]) From about 1900 the contribution the bureaucracy could make to the running of the empire steadily improved, at its best providing continuity, stability, and expert advice, in partnership with politicians. What has been called 'the official mind of imperialism' relied on accumulated assumptions, well-tried techniques, and 'the cold rules for national safety' handed down from one generation to another.[112]

It is dangerously easy for historians to criticise the politicians and governments of a former era. It is not simply that we know the outcome and they could not, and that hindsight may operate unfairly, applying changed criteria, but that an understanding of how politicians and governments operate may be hazy. There are, however, a few things it is well to bear in mind. First, it should be recognised that at all times, whether in office or out of it, politicians have to use the words they judge appropriate to persuading their hearers, whether colleagues, opponents, constituents, foreign allies, or interviewers. Rhetoric is one of the tools of the political trade. We need not assume that every appeal to popular sentiment represents intellectual conviction, or that politicians always said in public what they thought in private. This is why policy-formation has to be studied archivally. Secondly, it cannot be stated too emphatically that 'politics is the art of the possible'. Bismarck's famous aphorism goes right to the heart of the nature of government. Decisions cannot always be about what is objectively 'best', but have to reflect what is acceptable, affordable, implementable. The 8th Earl of Elgin as governor-general in Canada lamented how rare it was to have a simple choice 'between a clearly right and a clearly wrong course' (1849).[113] Lord Cromer in Egypt a generation later noted that sometimes it was necessary to make 'a choice of evils or act on imperfect evidence'; the result was that 'the conduct of public affairs . . . is at best a very rough and unscientific process'.[114] Attlee, the master-pragmatist among British prime ministers – who testily told Ernest Bevin he was himself 'not defeatist but realist' about India – adopted as his motto 'accept the inevitable pleasantly'.[115] Thirdly, the pressures towards continuity of policy through changes of government are considerable. In 1881 Gladstone wrote (in typically prolix fashion), 'We were certainly not returned to Parliament to carry forward the Foreign Policy of the last Government . . . Nevertheless, sensible of the expediency of maintaining as far as may be a continuity in Foreign Policy we sought for a ground of action which might be common to both political parties.' It follows that little reliance should be placed on what is said in Opposition. Here is Gladstone again, an honourable man, who said 'statements made in Opposition are not to be taken too literally when in office', and who explained to an unamused Queen Victoria that he would not have said the things he did in the Midlothian campaign if he had been in office, 'which is more constricting'.[116] Office forces a change in perspective, and gives access to information not available outside it. Striking changes in direction can result.

In addition to pressures towards continuity, with treaties and contractual obligations to be observed, there are manifestos to remember, political alliances, voting patterns, and parliamentary majorities to calculate, and authoritative advice to ponder, to say nothing of the interdepartmental rivalries and media reactions – all of which have to be taken into account. In other words, government is about taking almost impossibly wide perspectives, and it is an extremely difficult business. Historians should respect that fact, at least when they are assessing intelligent men of goodwill and sound mind. There is a memorable unpublished letter from Lord Cromer to John Morley, written after reading his *Life of Gladstone*:

More than forty years experience behind the scenes of political life has led me to be a very indulgent critic on the faults of political men. I have come to the commonplace but very true conclusion, stated by Taine in the preface to his great work – namely, that the government of human beings is a very difficult task, and that in dealing with them it is far easier to go wrong than to go right.[117]

So then: if all forms of government are difficult to get right, how much the more is this true of government of an empire, especially one so structurally diverse as Britannia's. Seeley wrote of India: 'we cannot delude ourselves here as we do in questions of franchise or taxation, so as to fancy that commonsense or common morality will suffice to lead us to a true opinion'; in ruling distant dependencies, 'the national interest [is] hard to discern and hard to protect'.[118]

Politicians may struggle to take decisions. To have 'a right judgment in all things' is indeed something to be prayed for. It is always easier to make a diagnosis than to suggest a workable remedy. The civil servants are there to help, and it is the essence of modern British government that experienced advice should be available. In a general sense it is indispensable. But it can be ignored, and officials do not necessarily agree, leaving a secretary of state or cabinet free to choose between conflicting advice and options. And there is another problem. Historians often criticise policy-makers for not devising long-term policies. But for politicians and officials alike, the pressure of everyday business is, in the main, such as to preclude taking the longer view. Members of the Liberal government of 1905 to 1908 pondered this. The worst of cabinet government, remarked John Morley (secretary of state for India), was that ministers lived for the day and were content to leave their successors to fend for themselves; a minister who presumed for a few minutes to draw attention to a possible day after tomorrow was dismissed as a bore, and of the worst kind, an irrelevant bore. Moreover, as Lord Elgin (the secretary of state for the colonies) put it, there was a real danger 'in looking too far ahead and not observing the rocks that may be under the bows'.[119] In the 1940s, an official anxious to develop forward planning for the empire was told this was a foreign and un-English thing to do (see below, chapter 9, pp. 284–5).

There is little place in governmental decision-making for acting upon doctrinaire principles or the fiercer dictates of morality. We have seen how hard it was to have an ethical colonial policy, but at least in that sphere inter-state power adjustments were not automatically involved, except in Anglo-Russian relations on the North-West Frontier of India. (See map 3.1.) However, international relations are inescapably and always about power and prestige. An 'ethical foreign policy' invariably fails. Force and power exist: that is the reality, whether politicians, or any of us, like it or not. You do not have to be in favour of physical force to recognise its operation in the real world.[120] To quote Gladstone once more: 'however deplorable wars may be, they are among the necessities of our condition'.[121] And for Bismarck, the true morality in politics was not the application of an ethical code, but 'freedom from prejudice', the 'habit of deciding, independently of any feelings of antipathy to, or preference for, foreign states and their rulers'. A surrender to 'sympathies and antipathies' could not be reconciled with the duty of governing: anyone who acted in this way, Bismarck declared, 'ceases to be a politician and acts according to his personal caprice'.[122] Churchill was equally explicit in rejecting the error of confusing morals and politics. In 1936, as war approached, he said:

If the circumstances were reversed we would equally be pro-German and anti-French. It is a law of public policy which we are following, and not a mere expedient, dictated by accidental circumstances, or likes or dislikes, or any other sentiment, so we should not be accused of being pro-French or anti-German.

The safety of the state must be defended by force if necessary, for in Churchill's view it was not on the terms of Christian ethics that 'ministers assume their responsibility for guiding states'.[123] (Of course not all politicians have comparably realistic insights.[124])

If there is little scope for the application of panaceas, pacifism, or the more challenging Christian precepts, is there a greater role for history? A knowledge of what has happened before can be valuable, and the civil service should be able to provide it. Seeley said politicians should read history to guard against the false analogies of those who do not.[125] Politicians have always been attracted by analogies, and, like preachers in their sermons, tend to rely on them, if only because they seem attractive rhetorical devices. But, lacking historical knowledge, politicians can have an unhappy knack of seizing upon the wrong analogy. The classic case of this – the apotheosis of an embarrassing tendency – was Sir Anthony Eden's use of analogy during the Suez Crisis of 1956. Eden later unrepentantly described the theme of his memoirs as 'the lessons of the thirties and their application to the fifties'. (He conceded that this might have been more easily displayed if he had written volume one first – but of course priority had to be given to his Suez apologia.)[126] Eden seemed to forget that much had changed in the meantime – despite the efforts of officials to remind him. The correct analogue for Colonel Abdul Nasser in the 1950s was not Adolf Hitler or Mussolini in the 1930s, but the Egyptian army officer Urabi Pasha in the 1880s. Even so, false analogies alone do not a disaster make. What was fatal was the devious way Eden, a sick man, bypassed the normal processes of government decision-making, refusing all advice except from one or two people who only encouraged him in his tragically mistaken and atavistic attempt to play power-politics without American support. The Cabinet itself was kept at the fringes of operational planning for Suez.[127]

Normally, in the final analysis, the British Cabinet is at the apex of decision-making machinery. It is in the nature of collective decisions that most things considered are controversial, capable of being looked at in different ways. This indeed is why they had to come to Cabinet for resolution. In any case on really important issues, opinion around a table will tend to divide participants almost evenly for and against. People have to allow their own commonsense opinions (for thus they will see them) to be set aside by the pressure of a group dynamic, and the convention of cabinet government is that ministers accept the consequences of 'collective responsibility'. The result can only be 'an approximation of ideas', a compromise.[128] The minutes of British Cabinet meetings are full of statements to the effect that 'on the one hand it was argued', but also 'as against this' or 'on the other hand it was felt'. The ministerial conclusions arrived at are then formulated in the official phrase, 'the balance of advantage' lay with one particular line of action rather than any alternative.

The art of good decision-making often resides in no more than identifying the simplest solution. Historians of high politics are apt to make rather a lot of assertions which rationalise decisions taken. This proceeding is methodologically more problematic than sometimes realised. Do we read into them aims which were not there? When was a decision taken, why at one time rather than another? Why did it involve a choice between some options and not others? Do historians over-complicate the way decisions are arrived at? What about intuition and snap judgments? Is a decision always the best route forward?[129] 'Sometimes', wrote Churchill, 'there are great advantages in letting things slide for a while,' or adopting what he used to call 'a patient sulky pig' posture.[130]

The three chapters in Part III all draw on government records. The first is an operational sketch of the imperial bureaucracy in the twentieth century, paying special attention to one of the Colonial Office's main concerns, the implementation of trusteeship (chapter 7). The second intensively deploys archival material to discuss African policy under the Labour government of 1945 to 1951 (chapter 8). The third puts under the microscope the career of a little-known official, who nevertheless, under a left-wing administration, played a big part in the early post-war stages of what became the dismantling of the empire (chapter 9).

IV Great men: the individual and responsibility

The relationship between 'statesmen' (not now a term in favour) and events and their causes remains a contentious issue for historians. For some it is not leaders who determine outcomes so much as the societies and systems in which they operate, their history or their lack of history. A great deal has been written analysing impersonal structural forces, conditioning contexts, long-term trends, and so forth. Some writers insist that a nation's actions, especially in war and diplomacy, are determined as much or more by the moves of other states than by their own objectives and actions. Plenty of historians are, however, persuaded that individuals can have a profound influence, that different decisions at specific moments in time can effect turning points, even change the course of history.

Whatever the truth of the matter, there is certainly a need for caution in assessing the responsibility of individuals for events. Imperial historians are aware that there has been much propagandist and historiographical emphasis on hero-figures, almost a relentless search for heroes of 'our empire story'. Some are popular figures, others admired only by academics. The list includes Captain Cook, Admiral Nelson and General Gordon, Cobden and Lord Durham, Disraeli and Churchill, Livingstone and Gandhi, Rhodes, Smuts, and Mountbatten. Several of these men made large, even boastful claims for their own influence and importance.

Churchill appears to be an example of an individual who can survive the historian's scrutiny of his reputation and self-promotion. In any case, it is plain that any study of the British empire in the twentieth century cannot escape the ubiquitous presence of Winston Churchill. He was a central actor in its fortunes, decline and fall no less: first as a soldier in late Victorian years, on the North-West Frontier of India, and in the Sudan, and as a war correspondent during the South African War; then as a politician – under-secretary of state for the colonies (1905–8), first lord of the Admiralty (1911–15), minister for munitions (1917), secretary of state for war and air (1919–21), and for the colonies (1921–2), chancellor of the Exchequer (1924–9), from 1929 to 1935 a leading opponent of Indian constitutional reform, first lord of the Admiralty (again, 1939–40), and finally prime minister in war and peace, 1940–5, and 1951–5. In addition, Churchill is popularly regarded as Britain's 'best' prime minister, even as 'the greatest Englishman', a virtual canonisation. Be that as it may, Churchill had a remarkable intelligence, flair, and talent, an exceptionally long and varied political career (though he thought of himself primarily as someone who had 'always earned my living by my pen and my tongue'[131]). Above all he 'continues to glow', and has an almost unique and continuing capacity to fascinate.[132] Strangely, though, among the bewildering array of monographs on every conceivable aspect of the great man, a comprehensive study of 'Churchill and the empire' is almost the last gap to be filled.[133] Piers Brendon's brief overview has remained unpublished.[134]

The conclusion I draw from my own studies of Churchill and the colonial empire is that Churchill saw it in the wider perspective of concerns about Britain's international standing or prestige, and the need for domestic and imperial policies capable of supporting it. I agree with the view that Churchill was 'never really an empire man'. By contrast, Piers Brendon argues that 'the empire was the grand theme informing his world-view', believing it to be 'integral to the greatness – one might say the racial superiority – of Britain and (to a lesser extent) because it meant that his own career was acted out on a suitably grand stage'. This is not necessarily incompatible with my argument that Churchill appreciated the empire more for its rhetorical value than anything else. However, Brendon makes two suggestions which usefully modify the picture I paint. One is that Churchill's enthusiasm for empire was subject to inconsistencies, ambivalences, and fluctuations. The author of *The River War* (in the Sudan) (1899) is a more racially sensitive man than the Indian army soldier in *The story of the Malakand Field-Force* (1898). Churchill became more liberal about imperial policy, even high-minded, after he moved into the Liberal Party in 1904 and rapidly into responsible ministerial office. For a while he was even able to satisfy Wilfrid Blunt, the 'anti-imperialist' critic of empire, as 'sound on the native question in India and in general about the enslavement of the coloured races by the white races' – until, that is, his preoccupations at the Admiralty returned him to a more 'militaristic groove'.[135] Churchill's attitude hardened even further in the 1920s (back now in the Conservative Party). This was crystallised by his persistently 'Victorian', and indeed extreme right-wing, approach to Indian constitutional advance, and by his commitment to Zionism in Palestine. Wartime leadership and colonial contributions to the war effort stamped themselves into his eloquence ('If the British Empire and its Commonwealth last for a thousand years, men will say, "this was their finest hour".'). Although unhappy about independence for India in 1947, thereafter he reluctantly realised that imperial attitudes were obsolescent.

The other main modification to my picture which Brendon demonstrates is that, however moderate and pragmatic Churchill's involvement with African and broad colonial issues may have been, it was, before 1947, very different with India and the Indians. Churchill seems to have retained an almost lifelong dislike of Indians, and a considerable contempt for them. It is therefore with India that we see the most important illustration of Leo Amery's opinion that 'the key to Winston is to understand that he is a mid-Victorian'. Amery observed that India could raise in Churchill 'a wholly uncontrollable "grand passion" on the whole subject of the humiliation of being kicked out of India by the beastliest people in the world next to the Germans'.[136]

Investigating Churchill needs to be balanced against analysis of a colonial politician, and Smuts suggests himself. For forty years of his life, Jan Smuts was identified in Britain as the representative figure of the Union of South Africa. The intertwining of his career with the empire and Commonwealth was more or less contemporaneous with Churchill's, and almost equally long, and it has many echoes. They were friends. Smuts invented the term 'British Commonwealth of Nations' which became in its day the accepted designation. Professor Mansergh chose him as one of his three 'Men of Commonwealth' accorded special treatment in *The Commonwealth experience*.[137] Understanding Smuts will certainly lead us to some central features of the South African state, notably that it was inherently expansionist, though unsuccessful in a formal geopolitical sense. It is a career which shows up sharply the nature of the relationship between charismatic individual leaders and the society from which they spring, and which they may or may not genuinely represent.

Smuts, with his historical and philosophical turn of mind, always had a sense of how difficult it was for leaders to 'make a difference'. He was sometimes depressed by a feeling of powerlessness in the face of the world's problems. Nevertheless, leaders had 'to labour on with our little palliatives and keep the show going with some appearance of human decency'. Since the effectiveness of political action could only be limited, his instinct was to 'let the situation develop', before having to decide between awkward alternatives. From the election of 1929 onwards the harder-line Afrikaners in the National Party began to make this characteristic into an accusation, and to represent it as a threat. Smuts, they said, stood for *niksdoen*, drifting ('letting things develop'). This in combination with his northward expansionist policies – the electors were told by his opponents – meant letting white civilisation drift on to the rocks, until South Africa drowned in a black sea. These accusations and threats proved fatal to Smuts in the election of 1948. He had been aware of the danger, and it is one reason why he seemed so slow to deal with 'the native question'. He claimed that he would do 'whatever is politically possible . . . But I dare not do anything which will outpace public opinion too much.'[138]

With Smuts, people felt themselves to be in the presence of greatness. Smuts himself thought that 'great men have an air, a form about them which stamps them apart from their fellows'. But he was appalled by Hitler, 'small, beastly and brutish'. How was it, he wondered, that 'so small and commonplace a person can wield such influence for evil'?

For Smuts, greatness could be identified in humane and magnanimous spirits like President Kruger, Campbell-Bannerman, Churchill, and Emily Hobhouse.[139]

Of course, not all persons of great influence have to be 'great men'. To return our analysis to the management of the empire, if we look at the role of the 'men on the spot', the commanders and governors, the viceroys and proconsuls, it seems incontestable that masterful individuals could play a definite part in determining policy, provided they had the support of their political bosses, and even, sometimes, if they did not. It would be a gross distortion of the high commissioner's role in South Africa to reduce causation of the Anglo-Boer War simply to its being 'Milner's War'. But Milner was without doubt instrumental in escalating the crisis. In decolonisation, too, there are examples of proconsuls who had a big impact. Lord Mountbatten in India, Sir Charles Arden-Clarke in the Gold Coast, and Sir Richard Turnbull in Tanganyika were not the strategic architects deciding upon independence as the goal, but they exercised major influence on its timing, in each case speeding up the timetable. Any theory of 'imperialism' ought to be able to accommodate the role of individuals, and I have attempted to do this in chapter 1, where I suggest that the proconsul stood in a pivotal position between metropolitan decision-making and local pressures.

Is it possible from the (relatively limited) arena of the empire to suggest any generalisation about the individual's responsibility for events in history? Although Churchill's history of the Second World War revolves around the overriding theme that history is determined by men at the top,[140] when his colleagues tried to credit him with having inspired the British people to victory, Churchill corrected them. It had fallen to him to express the will of the nation, what was in the hearts of the British people, but 'It was a nation and a race dwelling all round the globe that had the lion's heart. I had the luck to be called upon to give the roar. I also hope that I sometimes suggested to the lion the right places to use his claws.'[141] This seems to point us in the right direction. It is indeed probable that the most profound truths about the influence of 'great men' on events were articulated by Bismarck. A statesman, he said, cannot create the stream of time – he can only try to navigate it. Or again: 'A statesmen cannot create anything himself; he must wait and listen until he hears the steps of God sounding through events and then leap up and grasp the hem of his garment.'[142]

The chapter on Smuts in his South African context (chapter 12) seems to demonstrate limits on the ability of even the most impressive and intelligent leaders to determine the direction of events in their own societies. The two snapshots of Churchill, concentrating on his earlier periods in office, 1905–11 (chapter 10) and 1921–2 (chapter 11), aim to elucidate the formation of his views on empire, and put them in the perspective of his concerns as a whole.

V Sexuality: putting sex into perspective

Sex is an area which demonstrates powerfully the cultural distance between European and other societies. To an extraordinary extent, promiscuity, prostitution, and sodomy were depicted as central characteristics of the Asian Other; and it was this which could be invoked to represent Asians as inferior and unfit for self-rule.[143] Cultural differences of perception about sex are profound, whether located in past time or contemporary experience. There can also be angry disagreements within cultures as to what is acceptable, and changes can occur from generation to generation, as morality is recalibrated. For example, the Victorian taboo against juvenile masturbation has been slowly removed – perhaps there was no need to worry that it would bring about the fall of the empire once the empire had gone. But fundamentally it is clear that today's understanding of sexuality in Western societies is rooted in gender, in dividing people into clumsy categories of heterosexual and homosexual.[144] Such a sexual schema identifies and emphasises sexual orientation (being something) as against focusing on actual experience and roles adopted (doing something – which can blur the categories). This dichotomy of 'being' would be unintelligible in most other times and most other places. And indeed 'homosexuality' is comparatively recent even as a Western classification – the term was invented in the 1860s and only reached England in the 1890s. The idea of invented categories in the late nineteenth century is often associated with Foucault. It is now unpopular with many in the gay community (who prefer to see their sexuality as inborn, rather than socially constructed, and with a much older pedigree). On the other hand, most human societies do seem to have got along well enough without such labels and concepts. Some have regarded sex between males as normal and noble. Moreover, fixing a sexually dimorphic identity not only ignores the possible plurality of sexualities, but would also appear to have pushed 'homosexuals' into the position of an Other (leading to homophobia). As an alternative, it has been argued that perhaps the world's most widespread way of dividing sexual preference, since the Greeks and the Romans, has been between active and passive. Under such a code, 'the normal active male' would have partners of both sexes; if there were any 'homosexuals' in the Western sense (in the main, men exclusively attracted to males) in other cultures, at other times, and in other places, it is unlikely they would have known themselves to be such, nor would they have been recognised in this way.[145]

Put simplistically, much of the rest of the world has traditionally had attitudes towards sex which were open and uncomplicated, and accordingly were regarded by the West as libertarian, to put it mildly. The Eurocentric imposition on the rest of the world of its own local code – with Judaeo-Christian prohibitions about sex – has had a profound impact on other traditions. Sometimes this has been positive in terms of human rights, especially for women. Sometimes, however, Western sexual chauvinism has led to entire indigenous male-to-male systems being wiped out, amounting in China and Japan, in the opinion of some historians, to 'a cultural vandalism' of the first order. Of course a degree of agency must be allowed to non-Western peoples for their moral choices in the modern world, and they have had a degree of autonomy in reinterpreting European notions of sexual identity and sexual politics. But there is no doubt what has caused the choices to be made.[146]

Nowhere were divergent interpretations of sexuality more obvious than between the West and China. Westerners found two aspects of the Chinese tradition particularly hard to come to terms with. One was footbinding. The other was sodomy, endemic and openly indulged. Footbinding of girls was a painful deforming process, in which a child's toes (except the big toe) were bent underneath and fused, forming a soft contoured arch and a protuberant big toe. Adult feet required daily bandaging. Footbinding has been described as an amazing piece of 'physio-psycho-sociological engineering', and it spread to all ranks of Chinese society. The preferred length of a woman's foot was three to four inches. The 'lotus foot' could be reckoned more alluring than facial beauty, and it was a primary focus of sexual attention. The tiny foot, thus rendered highly sensitive by the compacting together of nerve-endings, could be sucked: 'pedo-fellatio' we might call it, and there were other podo-erotic delights too, such as phallic manipulation. The Chinese believed that footbinding increased female erogenous response by fifty per cent, especially by improving vaginal tautness.[147]

British visitors, from Lord Macartney's entourage in the 1790s to Sidney and Beatrice Webb in 1911, might become aware of prevalent sodomy. John Barrow in the 1790s noticed that many high officials at the emperor's court were constantly attended by handsome pipe-bearers in their early teens; by their gestures, the officials 'left us in no doubt what use they made of them'. The Webbs dismissed the Chinese as 'essentially an unclean race', physically and mentally rotten, 'a horrid race', devastated by drugs and 'abnormal sexual indulgence'.[148] In between Macartney and the Webbs, the German writer G. Schegel in 1866 drew an alarming picture of Fujian, where 'unnatural vice had reached its peak' during the recent Opium War: 'English and French troops found entire institutions where boys of eleven or twelve years old were trained for male prostitution.'[149] 'The chosen people of debauchery' was how Sir Richard Burton described the Chinese, and he knew a lot about such things. But even he was rather shocked by the extraordinary range of their erotic artifices and artefacts.[150] No other people indeed has ever produced so many elaborate sex manuals ('pillow-books'), erotic ornaments, or dildoes. The Chinese were obsessed by dildoes – dildoes of every size and shape, dildoes of wood, of ivory, of china. Prostitution was well established, not least through a quasi-servile domestic *au pair* arrangement (*mui tsai*). Brothel-owners were usually members of secret societies, and the atmosphere in their establishments could be cruel and unpleasant. In leading brothel-towns like Tientsin, brothels existed in five different grades, with a complicated system of taxation. According to a Western observer in 1860, there were thirty-five Tientsin male brothels, housing eight hundred boys. Sex between males was said to be especially characteristic of China north of the Yellow River, where some towns were notorious for their lascivious actors, barbers, and bath-house attendants; indeed, any man from Tientsin was automatically assumed to practise anal intercourse. Generally speaking, Chinese men expected to pursue a variety of sexual outlets, rather like the ancient Greeks and Romans.[151] With all-male scholar-official elites and training schools, and commoner sworn-brotherhoods in innumerable secret societies, 'this was a culture where we could expect homosocial bonding to reach the state of a very high art'.[152] Moreover, the theatrical profession was synonymous with male sex and boy prostitution. Boy actors were trained in their dual arts from the age of eight or nine, sleeping naked in well-heated dormitories. There are graphic representations of this kind of scenario in the film directed by Chen Kaige, *Farewell my concubine* (1993). Boy-love had a widespread presence among all classes and in all regions, with a considerable presence in Peking (Beijing) and other major cities. Sodomitically orientated, the sexual training of young boys was geared to effeminisation, anal dilation, and acrobatic flexibility, and it was enforced with sadistic punishments, such as caning on the soles of the feet. Some boys were also subjected to footbinding.[153] The resulting situation, if it did not repel European men, completely fascinated them. Many sought out Chinese boy-brothels, in sufficient numbers, at any rate, for it to be the subject of official annual warnings to the populace by the superintendent of trade at Canton: do not indulge the Western barbarians with all our best favours. However, for almost all Westerners, different attitudes towards 'homosexuality' formed a fundamental barrier, for, as an imperial Chinese compilation of the 1750s had noted, with puzzlement, of European sexuality: 'Their custom is to esteem women, and they think lightly of males.'[154]

Awareness of different cultural traditions in the understanding of sex is one essential perspective. There are two more to be considered. One is how to determine the place of sexual activity within the framework of an individual's life as a whole. The other involves a moral perspective: how to assess the extent to which Europeans overseas seeking out sexual opportunities were being exploitative.

What, then, did sexual relationships, whether with European or non-European partners, with boys and men as well as women, actually mean to those who had them?[155] Conceptually, we may employ the theory that the sexual activities we study were essentially *parergal*: that is to say, they were recreational side-lines, subordinate interests, subsidiary to the main business of life, sometimes divergent from the principal characteristics of a public persona. To conceptualise them in this way is not, however, to argue that these relationships were unimportant (or trivial for those on the receiving end). These sexual activities may have had no specific direct impact on an individual's public performance, but this does not mean that the historian can ignore them. Their indirect significance could be subtly fundamental. The careless sensuality of promiscuous relationships – which can often strike us as frivolous, adolescent, or reckless – could be the hidden side of responsibility and maturity, the obverse of achievement, perhaps even of fame, won through self-discipline. In the total structure of personality, the *parergon*, as a concealed sexual hobby, can be a major component, perhaps even energising or stabilising the whole. Especially in a war-zone, or in an unfamiliar environment, in times of hardship, readjustment, and loneliness – and this is after all what life on the imperial frontier invariably involved – it is not at all certain that men could function properly as agents of empire without an effective parergon life, and all the memories, fantasies, and expectations that could go with it. In this sense, the sexual aspects of personality do matter. And it does make a difference that overseas service of the empire, whether as trader, soldier, or administrator, could sometimes, and especially in the Victorian era, provide easy opportunities for finding sexual outlets. Whether these activities have automatically to be described as exploitation is hard to say. Our (Western) impulse may be to condemn them outright. But sometimes they manifestly fitted in to local cultural norms, and it is perhaps worth reminding ourselves how little actual evidence exists about individual non-European feelings. We make assumptions, but we simply do not know enough about what these sexual encounters meant to the recipients. Sometimes pride might be taken in them; there might in some circumstances even have been a certain prestige in having a foreign lover with a lighter skin. But this could be the case whether the encounter was within a specifically imperial framework or not.

The question of sexual exploitation of non-Europeans is obviously an important one. Power is the issue here: and whether sexual activity within the colonial relationship has a heightened reprehensibility. Feminists insist that all sex between white men and black women was contaminated by the unequal power relationship within colonialism itself. This is partly because they envisage all sex between men and women as an exertion of male power, thinly disguised rape in many cases. This seems unduly cynical. The truth is, surely, that the vast majority of men have no such selfish agenda. They just want pleasurable sex. But what, it may be asked, about sex in a colonial setting? Victorious soldiers the world over and at all times have, notoriously, raped the women of defeated peoples. But within the settled structures of imperial administration it was quite different. After all, what sanctions, let alone support, could a district officer call upon to coerce women if, as certainly happened, they said 'no' to his advances? Once imperial regimes were put on a proper and regular footing, the British government officially set its face against concubinage and all types of 'immoral behaviour' with subject peoples. The French, by contrast, had a more relaxed attitude. And the historian of *métissage* and miscegenation (race-mixing) in French West Africa warns about interpreting inter-racial sex 'simply in terms of French strength and African powerlessness'; he urges us to recognise that *métissage* might be 'mutually beneficial to French and Africans alike'.[156] In practice, British authorities also often took a fairly indulgent view of the predicament of unmarried, lonely young officers serving overseas, who found restraint difficult, or who were, in the words of one official, 'cursed with an unruly member'.[157] 'Immoral conduct with native women' was not, after all, a criminal offence.[158]

Although I am prepared to use the term 'sexual exploitation', this by no means implies that I think it is a straightforward issue. I try to be non-judgmental in my accounts of sexual desire which found expression within service of the empire. (This perhaps raises problems of its own: see note, p. 417 below).[159] The two case-studies printed in Part V present the evidence, and readers will decide for themselves how far they involve truly exploitative behaviour. Hubert Silberrad was a compulsive womaniser in the Kenya colonial service in Edwardian times (chapter 15). His contemporary, Captain Ken Searight, was a boy-loving soldier in the Indian army (chapter 16). These case-studies have been selected not only to represent the range of sexual options which might be encountered overseas, but also because of the attention their stories attracted when I first laid them before the reading public. Searight is now a seriously discussed figure,[160] while the Silberrad episode, and the Crewe Circular to which it largely gave rise, is now widely recognised as important.[161] The preceding chapters on sexuality are very different in scale. 'Empire and sexuality' is a synoptic survey covering almost the whole world (chapter 13). This is followed by a chapter which throws the spotlight on to one specific image, looking at the Other through perceptions of the penis, and it engages with the myth of the 'black super-penis'; it also considers the meaning of 'identity' with respect to eighteenth-century European captives (chapter 14).

VI Imperial historians: historiography or ancestor worship?

In order properly to appreciate the histories of empire we read, how much do we need to know about the imperial historians who wrote them? Historiography – the history of history, of changing interpretations – sounds rather grand, but is it academic self-indulgence?[162]

Historians should not avoid giving opinions and making judgments. Without them we risk killing off the subject. So perhaps it helps to know where the opinions are coming from. That is one thing. But presuppositions and commitments may induce less obvious underlying forms of bias, imputing our values to people of the past. Nowadays everyone is well aware of the dangers of this, and personal bias is no longer as common as once it was. Historians today try to be objective. In some fields this is harder than others. Although the 'heavy weight of pietistic flapdoodle that once passed for ecclesiastical history' has long since disappeared,[163] it remains the case that when we are reading about the Reformation, it is useful to bear in mind that Knowles, Scarisbrick, and Duffy are Roman Catholics, and Dickens, Collinson, and MacCulloch are not. In imperial history there is no such obvious difference or potential predisposition to a particular interpretation. There is merely a broad distinction to be made, perhaps, between those who think the empire was a good thing, and those who do not, or who are at least ambivalent about it. Nor is there any clear national divide: not all Indians denounce the Raj and not all Brits praise it. Unlike ecclesiastical historians who differ by denomination and confession, those who have written about the empire seem to differ mainly according to the generation to which they belong. Since the Second World War, and now that the era of historians as devotees of the Commonwealth and advisers to government has passed away, eulogising the empire is out of fashion academically.[164] We are all of us Young Turks these days – or we are if we hope to be taken seriously. This does not mean we can disregard our ancestors. We ought as historians to know where we stand today in relation to the evolution of our subject. There are two foundational texts to consider briefly.

Sir John Seeley has a good claim to be regarded as the founder of imperial history. His famous book, *The expansion of England* (1883), has attracted differing assessments. For John Morley it was 'one of the cardinal books of the time', while G.M. Trevelyan dismissed it as 'merely a clever and timely essay', however important.[165] The book originated as a double set of lectures, covering in the first group the eighteenth century generally, and then British India. The approach Seeley adopted fused two of his prior interests, international relations and the art of politics. He aimed, at one level, to throw light on current problems, the questions of whether the British could reconcile being 'despotic in Asia and democratic in Australia', and whether Greater Britain could be expected to prosper or to fall (p. 156). Seeley was not neutral about this. If Britain thought in terms of being 'simply a European state', it could, he warned, lead to eclipse by the United States and Russia with their superior territorial strength. Britain might, however, join them among the first rank of nations by bringing about some sort of federal union of imperial territories.

Seeley's view of history as a subject for academic study – barely as yet emerging in Cambridge in the 1880s – was that everything depends on 'turning narrative into problems' (p. 202), breaking 'the fetters of narrative' with its 'artless, chronological method' (p. 166). He was interested in 'large considerations', studying broad effects: 'his method was, as it were, astronomical' (J.R. Tanner). One of his principal interpretative insights was that 'The expansion in the New World and in Asia is the formula which sums up for England the history of the eighteenth century' (pp. 10 and 18). The influence of the New World had been underestimated. In fact it was a transforming experience, and 'the expansion of England is historically far more important than all domestic questions and movements' (p. 167). The 'English Exodus', overseas settler migration, was the greatest event of the eighteenth and nineteenth centuries (p. 17). The British had conquered and peopled half the world in 'a fit of absence of mind', by which he meant with indifference and without letting it 'affect our imaginations or in any degree to change our ways of thinking' (p. 10). The acquisition of India may have been blind and accidental (p. 307), but its governance was the most momentous responsibility assumed 'by any nation since the world began' (pp. 205–7). Nor was it clear what could replace the Raj. Yet Britain remained a distinct organism, 'complete in herself', and the empire 'could easily be peeled off' (p. 296). These things needed to be said. They remain stimulating propositions.[166]

Hobson's *Imperialism: a study*, published in 1902, was not altogether dissimilar in character, though its emphasis is on economic explanations. The tone is more critical and politically driven, easier to dismiss as a tract for the times. Whereas for Seeley the important issues were the 'mutual influence' of states (p. 176) and the 'religious question' (such as its importance in nationality, p. 137), for Hobson 'the imperialism of England is essentially though not exclusively an economic thing'. The under-consumptionist 'economic taproot of imperialism' (p. 105) was to be found in the manipulations of financiers, capitalists, and 'the great controllers of industry' (pp. 85, 97). Hobson was a social theorist rather than a historian, and there are elements of conspiracy theory here and not too much hard historical evidence. Hobson had written a previous book attacking the South African War.[167] Contrary to what is often thought, in *Imperialism* his fire was directed not so much to what was happening in South Africa as to China. He regarded the uncontrolled instinct for taking land ('kilometritis' or 'milo-mania') as at its most rampant and irrational in the struggle for Chinese concessions. The conduct of European powers there was 'the clearest revelation of the nature of imperialism', and it was dangerous, since so little could be predicted about the Chinese reaction. As for Africa, there was more resounding denunciation: 'The Pax Britannica, always an impudent falsehood, has become a grotesque monster of hypocrisy', with almost incessant fighting (p. 126). Such bold strictures against the irrational nature of contemporary 'imperialism' aligned the book with Liberal Party thinking, as a plea for a return to sane values, although there was plenty to make it of continuing appeal to Marxists.[168]

After the striking aphorisms and 'large considerations' suggested by Seeley and Hobson, with their emphasis on the international or economic dimensions of empire, imperial history as a subject of study in the early twentieth century became imprisoned in constitutionalism. Purely constitutional history, using published selections of documents, was the dominant mode of a university education in history. It took a long time to release imperial history from these narrow confines, and it was economic historians who led the way in the 1930s. The most influential of these was the Australian Keith Hancock, writing within an apparently limited commission to review contemporary affairs in the British Commonwealth. The spacious horizons, historical depth, illuminating concepts, and literary style that Hancock developed for his *Survey of British Commonwealth affairs* were an inspiration.[169] The return of ex-servicemen students after the war reinforced his message: that it was time to learn more about the British colonies. The war thus provides a striking demonstration of how the experiences which life throws up can cause a reorientation of the historian's focus. The modern framework of imperial study began to emerge.

What happened next has been authoritatively called 'the historiographical revolution of the early 1960s'. 'We live today', writes Roger Louis, 'in the shadow of the reshaping of imperial history by Robinson and Gallagher and others in the 1950s and 1960s.'[170] Briefly stated, what 'R. and G.' did was to produce, in a seminal article (1953) and a major monograph (1961), a definitive shift in the way imperial history is written, 'neither sentimental nor celebratory', embracing parts of the 'informal empire' never under the flag, emphasising continuities of motive and method, and the functionality of 'collaborative bargains' with local elites,[171] and generally adopting fresh angles of vision.[172] The result was a soaring interest in a revitalised subject, freed from its constitutional shackles, and spilling over into the development of regional histories, or 'area studies' as they became known. For a relatively short period of productive excitement it seemed that the history of empires and non-European countries was destined quickly to move into the central position in historical study. But then two developments caused a stalling of progress in this direction. The first was 'the end of empire', decolonisation, entry into the European Community, and the rediscovery of Britain as a part of Europe. The second was a vigorous (and unexpected) 'comeback' staged by traditional British and European history, fuelled in part by rediscovering the salience of the history of religion for understanding the past. As a by-product of the disorientation which resulted from these two developments, there was eventually a search for a 'new imperial history'. It would be based on forms of cultural history, employing the scepticism, the techniques, and the jargon of post-modern literary criticism. The 'new imperial history' (alternatively known as 'post-colonial studies' or 'critical imperial studies') does not show much respect for anything that has gone before it, or for the old masters of the craft. This needs to be challenged.

Nelson Mandela was brought up to believe that 'to neglect one's ancestors would bring ill-fortune and failure in life'. To him it seemed a perfectly natural belief.[173] And why not? The original statutes of my college, dated 1555, laid down that at the beginning and the conclusion of every term all the students should be called together to listen to a reading of the forty-fourth chapter of the book Ecclesiasticus.[174] It would remind them of their spiritual and intellectual debts to 'our fathers that begat us . . . giving counsel by their understanding . . . their knowledge of learning'. The reading honoured the heroes of the Old Testament, Noah and Abraham and the prophets, and others 'such as found out musical tunes, and recited verses in writing', all those richly furnished

Introduction: perspectives, policies, and people

with ability – but also those righteous men who had lived peaceable lives and left no memorial.

I pay my own tribute as a Cambridge historian, not uncritically, to our forerunners, in the two chapters in Part VI. The first brings to the surface the often forgotten contributions of research students. The topics they chose to work on – or had chosen for them – are excellent indicators of changing historical fashion, of what is of primary interest to those at the so-called cutting edge. It names some neglected ancestors and finds for many people a place within a pattern. Perhaps it is even a genuine contribution to historiography (chapter 17). The second chapter, the final one in the collection, turns to the professorial level, and may seem closer to ancestor worship. It includes personal reminiscences of some of the giants of our profession whom I was fortunate enough to know and to be influenced by (chapter 18). It is right that we should remember 'our fathers that begat us', recalling just how much they understood in their own day about the empire, and how they helped us to try to realise the moral philosopher's vision of becoming our own cosmography, and 'carry within us the wonders we seek without us: there is all Africa and her prodigies in us'.[175]

Notes

1 St Augustine, *The City of God* (AD 413–26), quoted by Sir Alfred Lyall: see John, Viscount Morley, *Recollections*, vol. II (1917), p. 346.

2 D.K. Fieldhouse, *Economics and empire, 1830–1914* (1973) was a notable pioneering survey not restricted to Britain. Anthony Low has written with unique perception on the arc of territories from East Africa to the Philippines, for example *The egalitarian moment: Asia and Africa, 1950–1980* (Cambridge, 1996), and most recently *Fabrication of empire: the British and the Uganda kingdoms, 1890–1902* (Cambridge, 2009). John Darwin's *After Tamerlane: the global history of empire* (2007), spanning six centuries and all the empires of Eurasia, is on such an ambitious scale that it has left us all slightly reeling (see the round-table discussion in *British Scholar*, vol. 1 (2008), pp. 110–25). Sir John Elliott's *Empires of the Atlantic world* (2007), a comparative study of Britain and Spain in the Americas, has been highly acclaimed. Stephen Howe's admirable *Empire: a very short introduction* (Oxford, 2002) makes the point that 'a great deal of the world's history is the history of empires. Indeed, it could be said that *all* history is imperial – or colonial – history' (p. 1).

Regrettably, however, the accumulation of knowledge has killed off comparative study at the undergraduate level. My generation was encouraged to learn by writing essays which built up comparisons: between French and Russian expansion, between the acquisition of the Dutch East Indies and British India, between colonial settlement in Australia and South Africa; we considered why Japan's 'response to the West' was more successful than China's, why the French Canadians were more easily reconciled to the British flag than South African Boers. All this is now considered too difficult a weekly assignment for students, and also too superficial, as specialist literatures have developed.

3 Earl of Cromer, *Political and literary essays, 1908–1913*, vol. I (1913), no. 21, p. 340, 'Rome and municipal government', repr. from *Spectator*, 19 July 1913; and *Ancient and modern imperialism* (1910). See also James Bryce, *The ancient Roman empire and the British empire in India; and the diffusion of Roman and English law: two historical studies* (Oxford, 1914); C.P. Lucas, *Greater Rome and Greater Britain* (Oxford, 1912). The influence of Rome is carefully brought out by Piers Brendon, *The decline and fall of the British empire, 1781–1997* (2007), pp. xv–xviii and *passim*.

4 R.S.S. Baden-Powell, *Scouting for boys: a handbook for instruction in good citizenship* (1908, reissued 2004, 2005), pp. 309–15. See also W.S. Adams, *Edwardian portraits* (1957), pp. 99–146.

5 B.L. McKercher, *The second Baldwin government and the United States, 1924–1929* (Cambridge, 1984), p. 174, FO memo, by R. Craigie (12 November 1928).

6 J. Chamberlain, *Foreign and colonial speeches* (1897), p. 232 (30 January 1897).

7 C.W. Dilke, *Greater Britain: a record of travel in English-speaking countries* (1868, 8th edn 1885), p. viii.

8 J.R. Seeley, *The expansion of England* (1883, 2nd edn repr. 1909), pp. 16, 85, 162, 173. (There is a modern edn by J. Gross, Chicago, 1971.)

9 Beth Day, *The Philippines: shattered showcase of democracy in Asia* (New York, 1974), p. 56. The British may not have known much about the Philippines, but the Filipinos have a theory about the British empire: Ramon Mitra, Speaker of the Philippines House of Representatives, in 1988 told Western diplomats that the British empire fell because England had outlawed cockfighting (*Daily Telegraph*, 31 October 1988, p. 23). Cock-fighting was made illegal in 1849. For the emergence of Anglo-American comparisons, see A.G. Hopkins, 'Comparing British and American empires: review article', *Journal of Global History*, vol. 2 (2007), pp. 395–404.

10 H. Brode, *British and German East Africa: their economic and commercial relations* (1911); J. Iliffe, *A modern history of Tanganyika* (Cambridge, 1979), pp. 164–201.

11 Quoted by Lucy Mair, *Native policies in Africa* (1936), p. 189.

12 M.D. Lewis, 'One hundred million Frenchmen: "assimilation" theory in French colonial policy', *Comparative Studies in Society and History*, vol. 4 (1962), pp. 129–53; M. Crowder, 'Indirect rule, French and British style', *Africa*, vol. 34 (1964), pp. 197–205.

13 Tapan Raychaudhuri, 'India, 1858 to the 1930s', *OHBE*, vol. V, *Historiography*, p. 224.

14 E.P. Thompson, *The making of the English working class* (1963), p. 13.

15 G. Shepperson and T. Price, *Independent African: John Chilembwe and the origins, setting and significance of the Nyasaland rising of 1915* (Edinburgh,

1958); G. Shepperson, 'Notes on Negro American influences on the emergence of African nationalism', *Journal of African History*, vol. 1 (1960), pp. 299–312.

16 R.E. Robinson, 'Non-European foundations of European imperialism: sketch for a theory of collaboration', in R. Owen and R. Sutcliffe, eds., *Studies in the theory of imperialism* (1972), pp. 117–42; 'European imperialism and indigenous reactions in British West Africa, 1880–1914', in H.L. Wesseling, ed., *Expansion and reaction* (Leiden, 1978), pp. 141–63.

17 John Tosh, *The pursuit of history* (1984, 2006), p. 244. For further exploration: M.J. Daunton and R. Halpern, eds., *Empire and Others: British encounters with indigenous peoples, 1600–1800* (1999), esp. P.D. Morgan, 'Encounters between British and "indigenous" peoples', ch. 4, pp. 42–78. The concept of 'othering' can be extended beyond European attitudes: see C. Talbot, 'Inscribing the Other, inscribing the Self: Hindu–Muslim identities in pre-colonial India', *Comparative Studies in Society and History*, vol. 37 (1995), pp. 692–722.

18 T.G.P. Spear, *The nabobs: a study of the social life of the English in 18th-century India* (Oxford, 1932), pp. 59–60. Not all Asian assessments of European religion were so negative. The charismatic Sinhalese reformer Anagarika Dharmapala wrote: 'Europe is progressive. Her religion is kept in the background . . . [used] for one day in the week, and for six days her people are following the dictates of modern science. Sanitation, aesthetic arts, electricity, etc., are what made the Europeans and American people great. Asia is full of opium-eaters, ganja-smokers, degenerating sensualists, superstitious and religious fanatics – Gods and priests keep the people in ignorance.' (See R.F. Gombrich, *Theravada Buddhism* (1988), p. 193.) It sounds as if Dharmapala had thoroughly assimilated an 'orientalist' critique.

19 Michael J. Franklin, 'Jones, Sir William, 1746–1794', *ODNB*, vol. XXX, pp. 665–74, a most important reassessment.

20 Richard Drayton, 'Knowledge and empire', in *OHBE*, vol. III, *The eighteenth century*, p. 243. In Germany, Schegel declared, 'The primary source . . . of the whole of human culture is unquestionably to be found in the traditions of the East': R. Taylor, 'The East and German Romanticism', in R. Iyer, ed., *The glass curtain between Asia and Europe: a symposium* (Oxford, 1965), p. 200.

21 E.G. Pulleyblank, *Chinese history and world history* (inaugural lecture, Cambridge, 1955); P.J. Marshall and G. Williams, *The great map of mankind: British perceptions of the world in the age of Enlightenment* (1982), esp. pp. 149–76.

22 J.L. Cranmer-Byng, ed., *An embassy to China: Lord Macartney's journal, 1793–1794* (1962); Alain Peyrefitte, *The collision of two civilisations: the British expeditions to China in 1792–1794* (1989, tr. J. Rothschild, New York, 1992) is more wide-ranging than the sub-title suggests.

23 Dorothy Middleton, 'Bishop (née Bird), Isabella Lucy', in *ODNB*, vol. XV, pp. 870–1. Isabella Bishop, *The Yangtze Valley: an account of journeys in China, chiefly in the province of Sze Chuan and among the Man-tze of the Somo territory* (1899), esp. pp. 1–13, 531–35; Isabella Bird (Mrs Bishop),

The Golden Chersonese and the way hither (1883; 1967 edn, Kuala Lumpur, with intro. by Wang Gungwu).

24 J.K. Fairbank, K.F. Bruner, and E.M. Matheson, eds., *The I.G. in Peking: letters of Robert Hart, 1868–1907* (2 vols., Harvard, 1975), vol. II, pp. 1192 (1899) and 1226 (1900).

25 Gregory Blue, 'Needham, (N.) J.T.M.', *ODNB*, vol. XL, pp. 328–33; Simon Winchester, *Bomb, book & compass: Joseph Needham and the great secrets of China* (2008); C.N.L. Brooke, in *A history of the University of Cambridge*, vol. IV, *1870–1990* (Cambridge, 1993), pp. 400–4. For Asian scholarship more generally, see Robert Irwin, *For lust of knowing: the Orientalists and their enemies* (2006, 2007).

26 I.A. Richards, *Mencius on the mind: experiments in multiple definition* (1932, repr. as vol. V, *I.A. Richards, Selected works, 1919–1938*, ed. John Constable, 2001), pp. 9, 89–90. Edward Said, *Orientalism* (1978, 1991), p. 254, quotes this passage approvingly as the 'genuine type of pluralism', showing a 'true understanding'. Certainly Richards's most remarkable but seriously under-rated work brilliantly analyses the problems of translating the psychological thought of Meng Tzu (372–289 BC). Richards's world-view and pioneering zest for 'comparative studies' ('we live in an age which offers unparalleled opportunities for intellectual adventure', p. 122) put him at least a generation ahead of most historians.

27 O. Lattimore, *From China looking outward* (Leeds, 1964); M. Vaughan, 'Africa and the birth of the modern world', *TRHS*, vol. 16 (2006), pp. 143–62.

28 They were connected through *lobola*, 'bridewealth', wherein marriage was ratified between kin, sealed and insured by exchange of cattle: see Adam Kuper, *Wives for cattle* (1982). The best introduction to African history is John Iliffe, *Africans: the history of a continent* (Cambridge, 1995, 2nd edn 2007); see also his *Honour in African history* (Cambridge, 2005) for the reconstruction of a mentality that scholars had ignored. For an exemplary analysis of Xhosa history 'from within', see Richard Price, *Making empire: colonial encounters and the creation of imperial rule in nineteenth-century Africa* (Cambridge, 2008).

29 L.M. Thompson, *Survival in two worlds: Moshoeshoe of Lesotho, 1786–1870* (1975). The most accessible introduction to Mao Tse-tung is now Jonathan Fenby, *The Penguin history of modern China: the fall and rise of a great power, 1830–2008* (2008), pt 4, pp. 351–527 ('The rule of Mao', particularly good on the building of the state).

30 Max Weber, *The theory of social and economic organisation* (tr. A.M. Henderson and T. Parsons, Glencoe, IL, 1947), pp. 3, 324–407; Ivor Wilks, 'Aspects of bureaucratisation in Ashanti', *Journal of African History*, vol. 7 (1966), pp. 215–32.

31 J. Lombard in *West African kingdoms in the nineteenth century*, ed. D. Forde and P.M. Kaberry (1967), pp. 71–90, and chapter by I.A. Akinjogbin in *A thousand years of West African history*, ed. J.F.A. Ajayi and I. Espie (Ibadan, 1965), pp. 309–26. Richard Burton, *A mission to Gelele, king of Dahomey* (1864) specifically called Dahomeans a 'breed of black Spartans' (vol. I, p. 85). For the Maori finding European flesh too salt, see J.R. Elder, ed., *Letters and journals of Samuel Marsden, 1765–1838* (Dunedin, 1932), p. 214.

32 Compare L. Stone, *The crisis of the aristocracy, 1558–1641* (1965) and R.H. Tawney, *Business and politics under James I: Lionel Cranfield* (1958), pp. 141–2, with I. Schapera, *Government and politics in tribal society* (1956, 1963), pp. 40–93.

33 Compare E.P. Thompson, *The making of the English working class* (1963), esp. pp. 382ff., with J.B. Peires, *The dead will rise: Nongqawuse and the great Xhosa cattle-killing movement of 1856–1857* (Pietermaritzburg, 1989), A.D. Roberts, 'The Lumpa Church of Alice Lenshina', in R. Rotberg and A. Mazrui, eds., *Protest and power in Black Africa* (1970), pp. 513–71, and R.I. Rotberg, 'The Lenshina movement in Northern Rhodesia', *Rhodes–Livingstone [Institute] Journal*, no. 29 (1961), pp. 63–77. Alice Lenshina was born in 1919 or 1920 and the cult developed from 1955.

34 This is a powerful theme in C.A. Bayly, *The birth of the modern world, 1780–1914: global connections and comparisons* (2004).

35 Agatha Ramm, ed., *The political correspondence of Mr Gladstone and Lord Granville, 1876–1886* (Oxford, 1952; new edn, H.C.G. Matthew, ed., *The Gladstone–Granville correspondence*, Cambridge, 1998), vol. I, p. 326; [A. Godley], *Reminiscences of Lord Kilbracken* (1931), p. 135; R.T. Shannon, *Gladstone and the Bulgarian agitation, 1876* (1963), p. 8.

36 A significant point was established by Miles Taylor – that much of nineteenth-century radical criticism of the empire focused, not on concern with the effects on other peoples, but on its adverse and destabilising effect on politics and society in Britain itself: see his valuable article, 'Imperium et libertas? Rethinking the radical critique of imperialism during the nineteenth century', *JICH*, vol. 19 (1991), pp. 1–23. There are two important complementary books: Bernard Porter, *Critics of empire: British radicals and the imperial challenge* (1968, reissued 2008), and Stephen Howe, *Anticolonialism in British politics: the Left and the end of empire, 1918–1964* (Oxford, 1993).

37 S. Gwynn and G.M. Tuckwell, *The life of the Rt Hon. Sir Charles Dilke* (1918), vol. I, p. 68; Sir Henry Campbell-Bannerman, *Speeches, 1899–1908, reprinted from 'The Times'* (1908), 'A declaration of Liberal policy', speech to the National Liberal Federation (8 March 1899); W.S. Churchill, speech on the Finance Bill, *PD, Commons*, vol. 134, c. 1488 (16 May 1904).

38 Marquis of Crewe, *Lord Rosebery* (1931), vol. II, p. 598; A.S. Thompson, 'The language of imperialism and the meaning of empire: imperial discourse in British politics, 1895–1914', *Journal of British Studies*, vol. 36 (1997), pp. 147–77.

39 Chan Lau Kit-ching and Peter Cunich, eds., *An impossible dream: Hong Kong University from foundation to re-establishment, 1910–1950* (Oxford and Hong Kong, 2002), pp. 4–5; Margery Perham, *Lugard*, vol. II, *The years of authority, 1898–1945* (1960), p. 349.

40 Perham, *Lugard*, vol. II, pp. 188, 200, letters to his wife Flora (7 October 1904, 7 April 1906); F.A. Swettenham, *British Malaya: an account of the origin and progress of British influence* (revised edn, 1948); H. Bell, *Glimpses of a governor's life* [n.d., 1940s], esp. pp. 121–2.

41 Jawaharlal Nehru, *Autobiography* (1936, 1938), esp. pp. 428–9.

42 W. Blunt, *My diaries: Part Two, 1900–1914* (1920); J.A. Hobson, *Imperialism: a study* (1902). See p. 49.

43 Leonard Woolf, *Growing: an autobiography of the years 1904 to 1911* (1961), pp. 157–9, 180, 193. For a recent assessment, see P. Wilson, 'Leonard Woolf: still not out of the jungle?', *Round Table*, vol. 97, no. 394 (2008), pp. 147–60.

44 Brendon, *Decline and fall of the British empire*, pp. 507, 568.

45 G.D. Pearce, *British attitudes towards India, 1784–1858* (Oxford, 1961), p. 134. Nicholas Mansergh, believing that mutual incomprehension was a basic cause of difficulty in and about Ireland, also quoted Munro's dictum: *The Irish question, 1840–1922: a commentary* (new edn, 1965), p. 295.

46 Brendon, *Decline and fall*, p. 466.

47 See the marvellously subtle discussion of 'imperialism and settler colonialism' in Kenya by John Lonsdale, 'Britannia's Mau Mau: controversies and complications', in W.R. Louis, ed., *Penultimate adventures with Britannia: personalities, politics and culture in Britain* (Austin, TX, 2007), ch. 19, pp. 259–72. Another recent study, which steers a balanced course between narratives of celebration and indictment, is Martin J. Wiener, *An empire on trial: race, murder, and justice under British rule, 1870–1935* (Cambridge, 2009), esp. pp. 230–3.

48 A.J.M. Craig (HM Political Agent, Trucial States, 1961–4), despatch, 'Impressions of a Dubai post' (27 September 1964), in S.R. Ashton and W.R. Louis, eds., *East of Suez and the Commonwealth, 1964–1971* (BDEEP, 2004), pt I, pp. 395–7 (document no. 116).

49 A.C. Benson, diary (24 May 1917), Magdalene College Archives, F/ACB/165, ff.36–7. He would later joke about 'the cheap jingoism' of 'Land of Hope and Glory': *Magdalene College Magazine*, no. 48 (March 1925), p. 139.

50 Neville Chamberlain to Edward Grigg, 30 September 1931, quoted in John Darwin, *The empire project: the rise and fall of the Brtitish world-system, 1830–1970* (Cambridge, 2009), p. 449; Noel Annan, *Our age: portrait of a generation* (1990), p. 32.

51 Shula Marks, 'History, the nation, and empire: sniping from the periphery', *History Workshop Journal*, no. 29 (1990), pp. 111–19. Of course tea and sugar are obviously evidence of the country's 'imperial experiences', but how many tea-drinkers actually realised this? Might not people be affected by empire without knowing anything about it? – a point well made by Troy Bickham: 'When a woman in Edinburgh drank a cup of tea, or a family in Bath sat down to a meal of Indian curry, did they consider the cultures they might be mimicking, or how these products reached Britain?' ('Eating the empire: intersections of food, cookery and imperialism in eighteenth-century Britain', *Past and Present*, no. 198 (2008), pp. 71–109 – an article which suggests awareness of 'empire-related foods' may have been most widespread at the time of their introduction, round about 1760). See also Woodruff D. Smith, 'Complications of the commonplace: tea, sugar and imperialism', *Journal of Interdisciplinary History*, vol. 23 (1992), pp. 259–78, on the eighteenth-century growth in consumption, as part of the patriotic 'formation of respectability'.

52 See particularly Catherine Hall, 'Culture and identity in imperial Britain',

in S.E. Stockwell, ed., *The British empire: themes and perspectives* (2008), pp. 199–217; together with Catherine Hall and Sonya Rose, eds., *At home with the empire: metropolitan culture and the imperial world* (2006), and Hall, *Civilising subjects: metropole and colony in the English imagination, 1830–1867* (Cambridge and Chicago, IL, 2002).

53 J.A. Cramb, *Reflections on the origins and destiny of imperial Britain* (1900), seven lectures, 315 pages. Cramb defined imperialism as 'patriotism transformed by a light from the aspirations of universal humanity', and imperial Britain as based upon 'the ideal of national and *constituted* freedom [which] takes *complete possession* of the English people', emerging in the nineteenth century 'from the sphere of the *Unconscious* to the Conscious . . . *insensibly* but surely' (pp. 15–16), 'its *intangible* and even mystic character' (p. 215) emerging from 'the *dark Unconscious* . . . not unlike an empire of mist uprising under the wands of magic-working architects' (p. 74) (emphasis added). Its ideal was 'to bring to the peoples of the earth beneath her sway the larger freedom and the higher justice' (p. 160), moving towards 'an ever higher conception of man's relations towards the Divine, towards other men, and towards the State' (p. 127). With 'the will of God behind her' (p. 303), England could claim to be 'the earth's central shrine and this race the vanguard of humanity' (p. 262), the very representative of humanity itself (p. 308). Cramb traced the identity of imperial Britain from the Roman occupation, the Viking and Norse invasions, through Simon de Montfort and Henry V, to John Milton and especially Oliver Cromwell – in the 'Unconscious' period, which seemed 'to foreshadow the Empire of the World' (p. 123). The South African War exemplified imperialism's ideal of 'heroic suffering'. It was not a war for gold and diamonds, but 'the mandate of destiny to our race in the future' (p. 35), and 'never since on Sinai God spoke in thunder has mandate more imperative been issued to any race' (p. 5); it was a conflict between 'the moribund principle of Nationality – in the Transvaal an oppressive, an artificial nationality – and the vital principle of the future', a British conquest 'less for herself than for humanity' (pp. 139–40). Unsurprisingly, Cramb did not believe 'national independence' was any sort of remedy for Ireland (pp. 111–12).

Cramb was a lecturer in modern history at Glasgow before becoming professor of modern history at Queen's College, London from 1893 until his death in 1913; he was a contributor to the *DNB* (*Who Was Who*, vol. I, *1897–1916*).

54 Bruce Robbins, 'Colonial discourse: a paradigm and its discontents', *Victorian Studies*, vol. 35 (1992), pp. 209–14, poses pertinent questions about the adequacy of these approaches. See also R. Price, 'One big thing: Britain, its empire, and their imperial culture', *Journal of British Studies*, vol. 45 (2006), pp. 602–27.

55 I align myself with Bernard Porter in this debate. In *The absent-minded imperialists: empire, society and culture in Britain* (2004) he examined hundreds of magazines, memoirs, and school textbooks to establish a lightness of impact. More recently he has updated his views in 'An imperial nation? Recent works on the British empire at home', *Round Table*, vol. 96, no. 389 (2007),

pp. 225–32, and patiently re-examined the whole issue in 'Further thoughts on imperial absent-mindedness', *JICH*, vol. 36 (2008), pp. 101–17, where he makes the point that the context should extend beyond the empire, and bring in cosmopolitan and American influences. Stephen Howe, 'Empire and ideology', in S. Stockwell, ed., *The British empire*, pp. 157–76, provides a subtle and helpful discussion; still worth reading is P.J. Marshall, 'Imperial Britain', in Marshall, ed., *The Cambridge illustrated history of the British empire* (Cambridge, 1996), pp. 318–37.

56 Andrew S. Thompson, *The empire strikes back? The impact of imperialism on Britain from the mid-nineteenth century* (2005), p. 204, drawing on material in R. Weight, *Patriots: national identity in Britain, 1940–2000* (Basingstoke, 2002), pp. 63–6, 286–93. Similarly, Martin Pugh suggests that the inter-war period 'marked the start of a gradual *disengagement* from Empire by the British people': the imperial spectacles of the 1920s 'coincided with the ebbing of the naive Victorian enthusiasm for Empire and the growth of a more critical and sophisticated attitude', the 1924 Wembley exhibition marking 'the decline of the phenomenon not its climax' (*'We danced all night': a social history of Britain between the wars* (2008), ch. 19, esp. pp. 400–5).

57 Halford J. Mackinder, *Britain and the British seas* (Oxford, 1907), esp. ch. 20, 'Imperial Britain', pp. 341–52; Mackinder worried about the potential dominance of Russia from the Eurasian heartland – see his famous article, 'The geographical pivot of history', *Geographical Journal*, vol. 23 (1904), pp. 421–44. Of today's historians of the British empire, none has a better grasp of its geopolitical underpinnings (and reverses) than John Darwin, *The empire project: the rise and fall of the British world-system*.

58 See Ged Martin's famous article, 'Was there a British empire?', *Historical Journal*, vol. 15 (1972), pp. 562–9; also our joint book, *Reappraisals in British imperial history* (1975), 'Introduction: personal and impersonal forces and the continuity of British imperial history', pp. 1–20.

59 Seeley, *Expansion of England*, pp. 209–13.

60 John Darwin, 'Britain's empires', in Stockwell, ed., *The British empire*, p. 3.

61 George Peel, 'The nerves of empire', pp. 249–87, in C.S. Goldman, ed., *The empire and the century* (1905), a volume which has only seven maps, six of them about the cable network.

62 A.W. Kinglake, *Eothen, or traces of travel brought home from the East* (1844; 1903, 1931 edn by H. Spender), p. 8: William Denison, *Varieties of vice-regal life* (2 vols., 1870), vol. II, p. 155 (1862).

63 Seeley, *Expansion of England*, p. 237, quoted approvingly by C.A. Bayly, 'The second British empire', in *OHBE*, vol. V, *Historiography*, p. 57.

64 William Dalrymple, *The last Mughal: the fall of a dynasty, Delhi 1857* (2006, 2007), p. 338n.

65 H.C. Andersen, *Eventyr, fortalte for Børn*, vol. I, no. 3, 'Keiserens nye Klaeder' (Copenhagen, 1837).

66 George Orwell, *The collected essays, journalism and letters*, vol. I, *1920–1940* (1968), pp. 235–42.

67 The great French novelist, Henri de Montherlant, wrote: 'There is a study to be made of naivety, which seems never to have been undertaken. It is

one of the main cogs in the machinery of the world; in fact it is what makes everything run smoothly. What would the world be without dupes?' At the time of the making of the Nazi–Soviet Pact, Stalin observed to Ribbentrop: if weak England dominated the world, it was only because 'stupid nations allowed themselves to be bluffed' – 'It was ridiculous, for example, that a few hundred Englishmen should dominate India' (quoted by Piers Brendon, *The dark valley: a panorama of the 1930s* (2000), p. 682).

68 O. Mannoni, *Prospero and Caliban: the psychology of colonisation* (tr. P. Howesland, 1956). For commentary, G. Jahoda, *White man: a study of attitudes of Africans to Europeans in Ghana before independence* (Oxford, 1961).

69 Anil Seal, 'The emergence of Indian nationalism' (PhD thesis, University of Cambridge, 1962), p. 145, but not quoted in *The emergence of Indian nationalism* (Cambridge, 1968), ch. 3, 'The rewards of education', pp. 114–30.

70 J.A. Hobson, *Imperialism: a study* (1902), pp. 224, 313–24; for Churchill's remark in 1927, see W.R. Louis, *British strategy in the Far East, 1919–1939* (Oxford, 1971), p. 133. Basic facts reflect the huge scale of China. The most-spoken language in the world as late as 1953 was not English, but Northern Mandarin (Northern Dialects), spoken by 387 million people (Jacques Gernet, *A history of Chinese civilisation*, tr. J.K. Foster, Cambridge, 1982, pp. 7–13). Dragon-boat racing rivals football as the world's most popular sport, with about 50 million *participants* by 2006, and of course it is older by millennia (see www.wikipedia.org/wiki/Dragon_boat_racing: my thanks to Andrew Ward for this reference). Other statistics are also highly indicative: the death toll in the Taiping Rebellion was anything from 20 million to 30 million, and in the rebel heartlands the population did not recover to its previous level for a century. In the 'global great drought' of 1876 to 1879, China suffered worse than anywhere else, certainly more than India: between 13 million and 20 million died in China, 5.5 million in India (Mike Davis, *Late Victorian holocausts: El Niño famines and the making of the Third World* (New York and London, 2001), pp. 64–9). When in 1895 Li Hung-chang (Li Hongzhang), provincial governor-general of Chihli (Zhili, centred on Peking (Beijing)), discussed with Japan's Prince Ito Hirobumi the relative progress of their countries, Li explained that China lagged behind mainly because it had eighteen semi-autonomous provinces, with 'too many strong and sectional interests' (S.-Y. Teng and J.K. Fairbank, eds., *China's response to the West: a documentary survey, 1839–1923* (Harvard, 1954; New York, 1963), p. 126 (document no. 35).

71 *PD, Commons* (Hansard 3rd series), vol. XIX, c. 516 (10 July 1833), 2nd reading of the East India Company's Charter, repr. in G.M. Young, ed., *Speeches by Lord Macaulay* (1935), p. 129.

72 D.A. Low, 'Lion rampant', *Journal of Commonwealth Political Studies*, vol. 2 (1963–4), pp. 235–50; this brilliant formulation was reprinted in *Lion rampant: essays in the study of British imperialism* (1973), pp. 8–38 ('Empire and authority'). However, Low himself would probably now want to urge the greater refinement of his analytical procedure in *Fabrication of empire: the British and the Uganda kingdoms*, which unfortunately appeared too late for me to absorb. For a lucid explanation of the nuances of the terms 'crown

colonies' and 'informal empire', turn to Darwin's essay in Stockwell, ed., *The British empire*, pp. 1–20.

73 Owen Chadwick, *The Victorian Church, Part II* (1970), pp. 238–43; G. Kitson Clark, *The making of Victorian England* (1962), pp. 167–205; Shannon, *Gladstone and the Bulgarian agitation, 1876*, pp. 28–9. For a powerful statement of the importance of the 're-invention of religion' as a historical theme, see Bayly, *The birth of the modern world*, pp. 363–4.

74 Quoted by R.T. Shannon, 'John Robert Seeley and the idea of a National Church: a study in churchmanship, historiography and politics', in R. Robson, ed., *Ideas and institutions of Victorian Britain: essays in honour of George Kitson Clark* (1967), pp. 236–67. Seeley's principal publications prior to *The expansion of England* were *Ecce Homo* (ostensibly a life of Jesus, but really about the place of religion in contemporary society, and its moral organisation), and *The life and times of Stein, or Germany and Prussia in the Napoleonic age* (3 vols., Cambridge, 1878), Stein being, according to Seeley, the architect of a 'moral conception of the state': see Sheldon Rothblatt, *The revolution of the dons: Cambridge and society in Victorian England* (Cambridge, 1981), pp. 155–80 ('Ecce Homo').

75 Abigail Green, 'The British empire and the Jews: an imperialism of human rights?', *Past and Present*, no. 199 (2008), pp. 175–205; Linda Colley, *Britons: forging the nation, 1707–1837* (New Haven, 1992).

76 Charles Kingsley, *Yeast: a problem* (1851; Eversley edn 1881, 1902), ch. 5, p. 97 (letter from the hero Lancelot Smith to his Roman Catholic cousin); I. Schapera, ed., *Livingstone's African journal, 1853–1856* (1963), vol. II, p. 244; W.E. Houghton, *The Victorian frame of mind, 1830–1870* (1957), pp. 43–4.

77 Michael Bentley, *Modernizing England's past: English historiography in the age of modernity* (Cambridge, 2005), pp. 70–81 ('Empire'). See n. 53 above for Prof. J.A. Cramb. For Prof. V.T. Harlow, pp. 511–12 below.

78 Eric Stokes, *The political ideas of English imperialism*, inaugural lecture, University College of Rhodesia and Nyasaland (Oxford, 1960), p. 18.

79 The Bishop of Stepney, 'The empire and the Church', in Goldman, ed., *The empire and the century*, pp. 166–73.

80 The National Archives, PREM 11/4640, CRO confidential print, 'The British legacy: the "intangible" links of the Commonwealth association', para. 74.

81 In the two thousand pages of the the two 'general' volumes of the *Cambridge history of the British empire*, covering the periods 1783 to 1870 and 1870 to 1919, there is no separate chapter on missions, only passing references in vol. II, and ten pages in vol. III: Norman Etherington estimates that 'missionaries receive about fifty pages in the entire *Cambridge history of the British empire*' ('Missions and empire', in *OHBE*, vol. V, *Historiography*, p. 306, n. 8). One of the first 'imperial' historians to signal a change was Anthony Low in his lively pioneering essay, 'Empire and Christianity', in *Lion rampant*, pp. 113–47, especially the section 'Breakthrough in Africa'.

82 The central study is now Andrew Porter's award-winning *Religion versus empire? British Protestant missionaries and overseas expansion, 1700–1914* (Manchester, 2004).

83 Marshall and Williams, *The great map of mankind*, pp. 113–15; M. Hunt, 'Racism, imperialism and the traveller's gaze in 18th-century England', *Journal of British Studies*, vol. 32 (1993), pp. 333–57; A.J. Barker, *The African link: British attitudes to the Negro in the era of the Atlantic slave trade, 1550–1807* (1978).

84 Ged Martin, 'Grant, Charles, Lord Glenelg', *ODNB* (2004), vol. XXIII, pp. 293–6, and 'Two cheers for Lord Glenelg', *JICH*, vol. 7 (1979), pp. 213–27; R. Hyam (hereafter RH), *Magdalene, anti-slavery, and the early human rights movement from the 1780s to the 1830s* (Magdalene College Occasional Paper, no. 35, 2007). G.R. Mellor, *British imperial trusteeship, 1783–1850* (1951) remains the closest analysis of Glenelg's policies.

85 *PD, Commons*, vol. XIX, cc. 547–50 (10 July 1833).

86 J.S. Bell and W.P. Morrell, eds., *Select documents on British colonial policy, 1830–1860* (Oxford, 1928), pp. 463–77 (extracts); J.S. Galbraith, *Reluctant empire: British policy on the South African frontier, 1834–1854* (Berkeley, CA, 1963), pp. 19–21, 116–32; W.M. Macmillan, *Bantu, Boer and Briton: the making of the South African native problem* (Oxford, revd edn 1963), pp. 145–59; Price, *Making empire*, pp. 1–15.

87 Alan Lester, 'British settler discourse and the circuits of empire', *History Workshop Journal*, no. 54 (2002), pp. 25–48, and Alan Lester, 'Humanitarians and white settlers in the 19th century', in Norman Etherington, ed., *Missions and empire* (*OHBE* Companion Series, 2005), pp. 64–6; Andrew Porter, 'Trusteeship, anti-slavery and humanitarianism', *OHBE*, vol. III, *The nineteenth century*, ch. 10, pp. 198–221.

88 J.A. Gallagher, 'Fowell Buxton and the new African policy, 1838–1842', *Cambridge Historical Journal*, vol. 10 (1950), pp. 36–58. Buxton called West Africa 'a universal slaughterhouse'.

89 The result on the South African frontier, according to W.M. Macmillan, was terrible and systematic havoc by military means: 'The one thing never tried was honest civil government which recognised the Xhosa as subjects with a secure place in their own land' – as Glenelg had in fact urged (*Bantu, Boer and Briton*, p. 293).

90 The abolition of the slave trade and the slave emancipation itself actually made race relations worse: 'the law refusing to recognise a difference, the social line was drawn the harder' (J.A. Froude, *The English in the West Indies* (1888), p. 106).

91 Glenelg received a bad press from those who interpreted his principled rulings on behalf of indigenous peoples as confused and obstinate attempts to block the proper expansion of the empire. Glenelg was an early riser, and once fell asleep at a Cabinet dinner. Thereafter he was invariably portrayed by cartoonists and in editorials in *The Times* as narcoleptic. *The Times* pursued a veritable vendetta against him, calling him 'His Somnolency', this 'drowsy Lord', this 'piece of official still-life', and once apologised to him for disturbing him at the beginning of the shooting season by demanding his resignation. Other wags said that the Canadian uprisings of 1837 must have cost him 'many a sleepless day', and, after he left office in 1839, it was being asked 'who is to have Glenelg's night-cap?' Glenelg consoled

himself against such uncivilised behaviour by learning German in order to read Goethe in the original.

92 William Farish, *A sermon preached before the Church Missionary Society on May 5, 1818* (1818); J. Sargent, *The life of the Revd Thomas Thomason* (1833), p. 115.

93 Elder, ed., *Letters and journals of Samuel Marsden, 1765–1838*, p. 79 (1814), p. 364 (1823).

94 D.N. Hempton, 'Evangelicalism and eschatology', *Journal of Ecclesiastical History*, vol. 31 (1980), pp. 179–94; Rowan Strong, *Anglicanism and the British empire, c.1700–1850* (Oxford, 2007), ch. 1.

95 Dalrymple, *The last Mughal*, p. 220.

96 Robert Gavin, 'Palmerston's policy towards the east and west coasts of Africa' (PhD thesis, University of Cambridge, 1959), p. 12, quoting *PD, Commons*, vol. 60, c. 2225 (1858).

97 RH, *Britain's imperial century*, pp. 145–54, 'A decade of crisis for the grand design, 1855–1865', and pp. 155–66, 'The hardening of racial attitudes'.

98 Price, *Making empire*, ch. 6, 'The closing of the missionary mind', pp. 127–53. D.A. Lorimer, *Colour, class and the Victorians: English attitudes to the Negro in the mid-nineteenth century* (1978) – this book plays down unduly the role of imperial experience, partly because the author subscribes to the outdated idea of the 1860s as 'the climax of anti-imperialism'.

99 Dalrymple, *The last Mughal*, p. 137.

100 Andrew Roberts, *Salisbury: Victorian Titan* (1999), pp. 169, 185. Price, *Making empire*: 'The displacement of evangelical humanitarian discourse from its controlling place in British politics was a profoundly important event' (p. 128).

101 'The white deluge' is C.A. Bayly's description, see *The birth of the modern world, 1780–1914*, pp. 439–40. For a persuasive argument that the white dominions were a crucial element within the empire, see Darwin, *The empire project*: along with India 'the great auxiliary engines of British world power', the most reliable component, as their mobilisation in two world wars suggests (pp. 11–16).

102 Orwell, *The collected essays, journalism and letters*, vol. I, p. 235. The British were not of course alone in reacting to revolt with draconian measures and the death penalty: for a comparison, consider China. In the suppression of the Taiping Rebellion, Yeh Ming-ch'en (Yeh Mingchen) claimed to have decapitated 100,000 rebels, action described by Sir John Bowring, governor of Hong Kong, as the worst example in history of 'such holocausts of human sacrifice'. Perhaps one million people were executed in Kwangtung. As a Ch'ing official said, 'who would have expected that the atrocities of the imperial army would be so much worse than the rebels themselves?' (L.B. Bowring, ed., *Autobiographical recollections of Sir John Bowring, with a brief memoir* (1877), p. 223; Jonathan Spence, *The search for modern China* (New York, 1990), p. 186; F. Wakeman, Jr, *Strangers at the gate: social disorder in South China, 1839–1861* (Berkeley, CA, 1966) p. 150).

103 H. Samuel, *Liberalism: an attempt to state the principles and proposals of contemporary Liberalism in England* (1902), p. 335: Samuel urged trying to reclaim 'the same cosmopolitan and humanitarian spirit' of Clarkson and

Wilberforce, by way of Gladstone. But the centenary of the abolition of the slave trade was barely noticed in 1907, and in the same year Wilberforce's house in Battersea Rise was demolished; a suggestion that it might become a memorial was received by the public with total indifference. (See Boyd Hilton, 'St John's most historical moment? The abolition of the slave trade', *The Eagle*, The Magazine of St John's College, Cambridge, 2007, pp. 65–7). Yet only two years before, there was tremendous enthusiasm throughout the land to mark the centenary of the battle of Trafalgar and pay tribute to Nelson; a commemorative volume about the empire, sumptuously bound, was published to mark this naval-imperial centenary, *The empire and the century: a series of essays on imperial problems and possibilities by various writers* (1905). By 1933 the shift was apparent, though, and decent attention was focused on the centenary of the abolition of slavery.

104 W.R. Louis, 'Introduction', *OHBE*, vol. IV, *Twentieth century*, ch. 1, p. 20.

105 Andrew Cohen, *British policy in changing Africa* (1959), pp. 7–8. Another one-time CO official, Kenneth Robinson, explored this theme in *The dilemmas of trusteeship: aspects of British colonial policy between the wars*, Reid lectures, Acadia (Oxford, 1965). His conclusion was that though trusteeship did not always prevail, 'in some areas it significantly affected the outcome' (p. 75).

106 R.E. Robinson, 'The moral disarmament of African empire, 1919–1947', *JICH*, vol. 8, no. 1 (1979), repr. in N. Hillmer and P. Wigley, eds., *The first British Commonwealth: essays in honour of Nicholas Mansergh* (1980), pp. 84–104. This is an extremely thoughtful paper, based on his PhD thesis (Cambridge, 1950).

107 RH and Martin, *Reappraisals in British imperial history*, ch. 2, 'Imperial interests and the Peace of Paris (1763)', pp. 36–7; Brendan Simms, *Three victories and a defeat: the rise and fall of the first British empire, 1714–1783* (2007), p. 495.

108 G. Kitson Clark, '"Statesmen in disguise": reflections on the history of the neutrality of the Civil Service', *Historical Journal*, vol. 2 (1959), pp. 20–38.

109 *PD, Commons*, vol. XIX, cc. 525–6 (10 July 1833); G.O. Trevelyan, *The life and letters of Lord Macaulay*, vol. II (1932 edn), p. 275 (23 June 1853).

110 G. Wallis, *Human nature in politics* (1908, 4th edn 1948), p. 249; John Roach, *Public examinations in England, 1850–1900* (Cambridge, 1971), pp. 3–4.

111 Mary Kingsley, *West African studies* (1899, 1900), p. 310.

112 R.E. Robinson and J.A. Gallagher, *Africa and the Victorians: the official mind of imperialism* (1961, 1981), pp. 21, 463. Edward Ingram, *The British empire as a world power* (2001), traces a 'geopolitical template', dating from the late eighteenth century, which guided British policy-makers.

113 T. Walrond, ed., *Letters and journals of James, Eighth Earl of Elgin* (1872), pp. 96–7.

114 Cromer, *Political and literary essays, 1908–1913*, vol. I, p. 93. Cromer complained that although he had served British governments all his life, he never knew a minister who had a steady policy (quoted in Darwin, *The empire project*, p. 91).

115 RH, *Britain's declining empire*, pp. 96, 116. Compare Edmund Burke, 'not

the least of the arts of diplomacy is to grant graciously what one no longer has the power to withhold' – almost the guiding injunction for British decolonisation.

116 Ramm, ed., *The political correspondence of Mr Gladstone and Lord Granville, 1876–1886*, p. 181 (memo, 23 September 1880); S. Gwynn and G.M. Tuckwell, *The life of the Rt Hon. Sir Charles W. Dilke* (1918), vol. I, p. 320 (Dilke's diary, 20 May 1880).

117 The National Archives: Cromer Papers, FO 633/8/3, no. 4, 11 April 1901. Hippolyte Taine wrote *Les origines de la France contemporaine* in the last eighteen years of his life, from 1875.

118 Seeley, *Expansion of England*, pp. 193, 203.

119 Quotations from RH, *Elgin and Churchill at the Colonial Office*, pp. 542–3.

120 H. Butterfield, *Man on his past* (1955), p. 126.

121 James Joll, ed., *Britain and Europe* (1950, 1961), p. 189, Gladstone's speech at Edinburgh, 17 March 1880.

122 Geoffrey Barraclough, 'History, morals and politics', Stevenson Inaugural Lecture, 8 October 1957, *International Affairs*, vol. 34 (1958), pp. 13–14; A.J.P. Taylor, *Bismarck: the man and statesman* (1955), p. 87.

123 W.S. Churchill, *The Second World War*, vol. I, *The gathering storm, 1919–1939* (1948), minutes, pp. 162–3 (1936), 251. See also vol. III, *The Grand Alliance* (1950): 'We must not let our vision be darkened by hatred or obscured by sentiment' – hence he would speak of Nazis rather than Germans (p. 638, 5 January 1941).

124 On 'political morality', there are the exaggerated but indicative words of Sir Humphrey Appleby: 'You can't put the nation's interests at risk just because of some silly sentimentality about justice. If we took moral positions on individual injustices and cruelties we'd never have been able to hand Hong Kong over to the Chinese, or put Mugabe in power in Zimbabwe. Morality was what fouled up the Foreign Office's plans for a quiet handover of the Falklands to Argentina' (Jonathan Lynn and Antony Jay, eds., *Yes, prime minister: the diaries of the Rt Hon. James Hacker*, vol. I (1986), p. 214).

125 Seeley, *Expansion of England*, p. 345.

126 A. Eden, *The memoirs of Sir Anthony Eden*, vol. II, *Full circle* (1960).

127 Tom Little, *Egypt* (1958), pp. 210–12; John Marlowe, *Anglo-Egyptian relations, 1800–1953* (1954), p. 403, which shows that the correct analogy was already available. For Eden's failure to consult, see S. Kelly and A. Gorst, eds., *Whitehall and the Suez Crisis* (2000).

128 Ramm, *Political correspondence of Mr Gladstone and Lord Granville*, p. xv.

129 Ged Martin, *Past futures: the impossible necessity of history* (Toronto, 2004, based on the Joanne Goodman Lectures, 1996), ch. 4, 'The moment of decision'.

130 Martin Gilbert, *Winston S. Churchill*, vol. VIII, *Never despair, 1945–1965* (1988), p. 15, PM's minute 14 May 1945, facing the chaos of defeated Germany. For the 'sulky pig', see RH, *Britain's declining empire*, p. 224 (1953, on Egypt).

131 W.S. Churchill, *Unwritten alliance: speeches, 1953–1959* (ed. Randolph Churchill, 1961), p. 202.

132 David Reynolds, *In command of history: Churchill fighting and writing the*

Second World War (2004, 2005), p. 527; Ashley Jackson, 'Churchill: warrior and writer', *Round Table*, vol. 96, no. 389 (2007), pp. 193–9.

133 Richard Toye, *Churchill's empire: the world that made him and the world he made* (2010), a comprehensive and illuminating study, rigorous but fair minded in its assessment.

134 Piers Brendon's typescript, 'Churchill and empire', was a lecture given at the Imperial War Museum in 2002 (18 pages), and is summarised in his *Decline and fall of the British empire*, pp. 205–6. R.A. Callahan's *Churchill: retreat from empire* (Delaware, 1984) is essentially about the Second World War. Kirk Emmert's obscure and idiosyncratic monograph, *Winston S. Churchill on empire* (Claremont Institute, Durham, NC, 1989), has a limited purpose, exploring his writings about 'civilising and democratic empire'. Ian S. Wood, *Churchill* (2000) gives a good short account of 'Churchill and the British empire': ch. 9, pp. 156–75.

135 Blunt, *My diaries: Part Two, 1900–1914*, p. 287 (21 October 1909), p. 350 (18 January 1911), p. 417 (21 October 1912).

136 Wm. Roger Louis, *'In the name of God, go!': Leo Amery and the British empire in the age of Churchill* (1992), p. 20. See also pp. 329, 337 below.

137 P.N.S. Mansergh, *The Commonwealth experience* (1969, 1982), 'General J.C. Smuts: he was defeated', pp. 370–8. His other Commonwealth 'heroes' were Mackenzie King and Nehru.

138 W.K. Hancock, *Smuts*, vol. II, *The fields of force, 1919–1950* (Cambridge, 1968), pp. 19, 85–6, 218, 488, 500, 517. Churchill also believed there was 'wisdom in reserving one's decisions as long as possible and until all the facts and forces that will be potent at the moment are revealed' (*The Second World War*, vol. VI, *Triumph and tragedy* (1954), minute 4 January 1945, p. 306).

139 Hancock, *Smuts*, vol. II, p. 325. Smuts arranged for the ashes of Emily Hobhouse to be brought to South Africa for burial, 'like a princess', at the foot of the Women's Memorial (1912–13) near Bloemfontein (pp. 169–70). Hobhouse had gone out from England during the South African War, and befriended women in the concentration camps. Her meeting with Campbell-Bannerman influenced the latter's 'methods of barbarism' speech: see *ODNB*, vol. XXVII, pp. 405–7.

140 Reynolds, *In command of history*, p. 486.

141 Churchill, *Unwritten alliance: speeches*, pp. 202–3.

142 Taylor, *Bismarck: the man and statesman*, p. 115. Herbert Butterfield believed that individuals should try to take control of 'the processes of history': 'The role of the individual in history', *History*, vol. 40 (1955), pp. 1–17.

143 Philippa Levine, 'Sexuality, gender and empire', in Levine, ed., *Gender and empire* (*OHBE* Companion Series, 2004), p. 151, and *Prostitution, race and politics: policing venereal disease in the British empire* (2003), pp. 177, 322–5.

144 But see Barry Reay's recent plea for permeable categorisation, for historians to resist present-day sexual assumptions, which insist on taxonomies and construct simplistic teleological accounts of a shift from 'doing to being': 'Writing the modern histories of homosexual England: historiographical review', *Historical Journal*, vol. 52 (2009), pp. 213–33.

145 For a carefully presented perspective from a cultural anthropologist, see

Gilbert Herdt, *Same sex, different cultures: explaining gay and lesbian lives* (Boulder, CO and Oxford, 1997). For the active/passive 'Roman' theory, see H.N. Parker, 'The teratogenic code', in J.P. Hallet and M.B. Skinner, eds., *Roman sexualities* (Princeton, NJ, 1997), esp. pp. 47–9. Professor William Empson noted that assuming a 'homosexual' was a distinct character, 'incapable of pleasure with women', was 'a very recent delusion': 'I was astonished to have a bit of linguistics talked at me by a distinguished Chinese pansy my wife and I met at a Peking dance-hall; he said that in Chinese there were many words for a male invert like himself but no word meaning men who enjoyed them, because it was presumed that any man did, as he claimed to have proved; but the English word implied only that special men did, and he could go right on with anecdotes about it wasn't only special men' (to G. Wilson Knight, 3 February 1957, in J. Haffenden, ed., *Selected letters of William Empson* (Oxford, 2006), p. 264).

146 Bret Hinsch, *Passions of the cut sleeve: the male homosexual tradition in China* (Berkeley, CA, 1990), pp. 159–69. Hinsch deplores the 'pathetic end' to male-to-male sex, the change from a tradition of prominent openness, toleration, and classical literary expression, to a Western-derived interdiction and terrified obscurity, with that tradition now not only dead but forgotten by the Chinese. See more generally, Richard Phillips, 'Histories of sexuality and imperialism: what's the use?', *History Workshop Journal*, no. 63 (2007), pp. 136–53, and *Sex, politics and empire: a postcolonial geography* (Manchester, 2006).

147 H.S. Levy, *Chinese foot-binding: the history of a curious erotic custom* (New York, 1966); J.K. Fairbank, *The great Chinese revolution, 1800–1985* (New York, 1986), pp. 68–73.

148 Peyrefitte, *The collision of two civilisations*, p. 228; J.M. Winter, 'The Webbs and the non-white world: a case of socialist racialism', *Journal of Contemporary History*, vol. 9 (1974), pp. 181–97.

149 Quoted by Rudi C. Bleys, *The geography of perversion: male-to-male sexual behaviour outside the West, and the ethnographic imagination, 1750–1918* (1996), p. 175.

150 Sir Richard F. Burton, ed., *A plain and literal translation of the Arabian Nights . . . The book of the thousand nights and a night* (1885–6), 'Terminal essay', p. 238.

151 R. Gullik, *Sexual life in ancient China* (Leiden, 1961); M. Beurdeley *et al.*, *The clouds and the rain: the art of love in China* (Fribourg, 1969), pp. 159–68; V.W. Ng, 'Ideology and sexuality: rape laws in Qing China', *Journal of Asian Studies*, vol. 46 (1987), pp. 57–70. See also pp. 379, 390 below.

152 Susan Mann, 'The male bond in Chinese history and culture', p. 1606, and Norman Kutcher, 'The fifth relationship: dangerous friendships in the Confucian context', p. 1624, both in *American Historical Review*, vol. 105, no. 5, special issue on 'Gender and manhood in Chinese history' (2000).

153 Hinsch, *Passions of the cut sleeve*, pp. 152–4. 'Cut sleeve' is a reference to an emperor who cut off his sleeve rather than disturb a sleeping catamite. See also Dominique Fernandez, *A hidden love: art and homosexuality* (2001, Munich and New York, 2002), pp. 158–67.

154 Wakeman, *Strangers at the gate*, p. 50; Teng and Fairbank, *China's response to the West*, p. 20.
155 The argument here follows that in RH, *Empire and sexuality*, pp. 210–11.
156 Owen C. White, *Children of the empire: miscegenation and colonial society in French West Africa, 1895–1960* (Oxford, 1999), pp. 7–9.
157 The Administrator of Southern Rhodesia, describing Thomas Raikes in 1903, quoted in RH, *Empire and sexuality*, p. 172.
158 This certainly was Churchill's view: see especially the judgment he made in a CO minute, 12 April 1922 (case of Lieut. H.W. Andrews), Churchill Archives Centre, Chartwell Papers 17/26; Martin Gilbert, ed., *Winston S. Churchill*, vol. IV, *Companion Pt 3: Documents, April 1921 to November 1922* (1977), p. 1860.
159 Ged Martin, *Past futures*, pp. 181–3.
160 Searight is mentioned by well-known writers such as Niall Ferguson and Graham Robb, and he gets a chapter in Richard Aldrich's major study, *Colonialism and homosexuality*: see detailed references below, p. 461, n. 11.
161 In Jeremy Paxman's *The English: a portait of a people* (1998), pp. 66–9, he appears under 'True-born Englishmen and other lies'; I am grateful to Guy Walker for this reference. Helen Callaway discusses Silberrad in her substantial essay on 'The cultural construction of gender, sexuality and race', in T. Ranger and O. Vaughan, eds., *Legitimacy and the state in 20th-century Africa: essays in honour of A.H.M. Kirk-Greene* (1993, 2001).
162 For some highly germane reflections on imperial historiography, see A.G. Hopkins, 'Development and the Utopian ideal', *OHBE*, vol. V, *Historiography*, pp. 635–52.
163 G.M. Trevelyan, 'Bias in history', presidential address to the Historical Association, 1947, in *An autobiography and other essays* (1949), p. 73.
164 Stephen Howe, writing in 2001, says that when he was studying at Oxford twenty years ago, 'most of the senior figures in the field had spent their youth either as servants of Empire, or, in Tapan Raychaudhuri's case, as activists against it. Today few even of the most senior active scholars have that kind of connection': 'The slow death and strange rebirth of imperial history', review article on *OHBE*, vol. V, in *JICH*, vol. 29 (2001), p. 133.
165 Morley, *Recollections*, vol. II, p. 79; Trevelyan, *Autobiography*, p. 17. J.R. Tanner, a leading historian of the sixteenth and seventeenth centuries, as an undergraduate had heard Seeley's lectures, which he described (in a eulogistic obituary) as almost 'transcendently inspiring': 'John Robert Seeley', *English Historical Review*, vol. 10 (1895), pp. 507–14. For a helpful modern assessment, see P. Burroughs, 'John Robert Seeley and British imperial history', *JICH*, vol. 1 (1973), pp. 191–211.
166 Seeley's view of the relative importance of empire as against European involvement is challenged by Simms, *Three victories and a defeat*, p. 1.
167 J.A. Hobson, *The war in South Africa: its causes and effects* (1900). This was a book marred by anti-Semitism.
168 D.K. Fieldhouse, 'Imperialism: an historiographical revision', *Economic History Review*, vol. 14 (1961), pp. 187–209.

169 W.K. Hancock, *Survey of British Commonwealth affairs*, vol. I, *Problems of nationality, 1918–1936* (1937), and vol. II, *Problems of economic policy, 1918–1939* (in two parts, 1942).

170 W.R. Louis, 'Introduction' to *OHBE*, vol. V, *Historiography*, pp. 1–41: this essay is essential reading. See also Bentley, *Modernizing England's past*, pp. 89–91.

171 J.A. Gallagher and R.E. Robinson, 'The imperialism of free trade', *Economic History Review*, vol. 6 (1953), pp. 1–15; Robinson and Gallagher, *Africa and the Victorians: the official mind of imperialism* (1961, 1981). More than thirty years of commentary has now accumulated, from W.R. Louis, ed., *Imperialism: the Robinson and Gallagher controversy* (New York, 1976), to John Darwin, 'John Andrew Gallagher, 1919–1980', *Proceedings of the British Academy*, vol. 150 (2007), pp. 57–75, a particularly acute assessment.

172 What Dane Kennedy calls 'an exceptionally handy and heterogeneous tool-kit of ideas they handed out about the dynamics of imperial expansion': 'The boundaries of Oxford's empire', review article on *OHBE*, in *International History Review*, vol. 23 (2001), pp. 604–22, at p. 611.

173 Nelson Mandela, *Long walk to freedom: the autobiography of Nelson Mandela* (1994, 2001), p. 13.

174 Peter Cunich, ed., *Foundation statutes of Magdalene College Cambridge (1555/1565)* (privately printed, Cambridge, 1995), p. 75.

175 Sir Thomas Browne, *Religio Medici* (c.1635), pt I, section 15.

Part I

Dynamics: geopolitics and economics

1   The primacy of geopolitics: the dynamics of British imperial policy, 1763–1963

[Reprinted from the *Festschrift* for Professor Roger Louis, *The statecraft of British imperialism: essays in honour of Wm. Roger Louis* (ed. R.D. King and R. Kilson, 1999), appearing first in the *Journal of Imperial and Commonwealth History*, vol. 27 (1999). The formulation of my ideas on this subject particularly benefited from discussions with Professor Sir Christopher Bayly and Dr T.N. Harper. As yet, the most systematic attempt to apply the 'interaction' model suggested here has been Peter Henshaw's account of the origins of the South Africa War: 'Breakdown: into war, 1895–1899', in our joint book *The lion and the springbok: Britain and South Africa since the Boer War* (Cambridge, 2003), pp. 37–56.]

When in the early 1960s Roger Louis began writing on the history of the British empire, the dominant historiographical fashion was to invoke economic interpretations, even to subscribe to economic determinism. Hobson, Lenin, and the 'export of surplus capital' threw a long and intimidating shadow over the subject.[1] *Capitalism and slavery* by Eric Williams was a key text,[2] 'Economic factors in the history of the empire' by Richard Pares an essential article.[3] Vincent Harlow's monumental *The founding of the Second British Empire, 1763–1793* argued that a preference for 'trade rather than dominion' was the general characteristic from the late eighteenth century.[4] Keith Hancock's great work, the *Survey of British Commonwealth affairs*, was built around the organising concept of moving frontiers of migration, money, and markets.[5] Symptomatically, the most seminal of all essays in the field, Gallagher and Robinson's 'The imperialism of free trade', appeared in the *Economic History Review*.[6] Moreover, neo-Marxists were about to launch a massive takeover of South African history.

Roger Louis's initial studies were concerned with the partition of Central Africa.[7] These immediately led him into a world of officials and statesmen with perceptions and preoccupations of an apparently quite different kind. He focused upon Sir Percy Anderson of the Foreign Office, a practitioner of Francophobia and *realpolitik*, who saw the scramble for Africa 'mainly as a problem of maintaining British power and prestige'. With A.J.P. Taylor as his research supervisor, Roger Louis thus quickly became convinced that British imperial policy only made sense within the context of international relations. The empire for him is above all about power politics and international prestige, strategy and inter-state perceptions, the Anglo-American relationship, diplomacy and defence.[8] He continued to find its most revealing records in the Foreign Office political archives. In some ways he maintained a strong American tradition exemplified in such classic works as William Langer's *The diplomacy of imperialism*[9] and A.J. Marder's studies of British sea-power.[10] At all events he provided for a generation a necessary corrective and effective challenge to the prevailing fashions of British writing about the empire.

Why had post-war British historians become so dangerously addicted to an assumption that 'economic imperialism' would explain more or less everything? They admitted such obvious political exceptions as Anglo-Russian rivalry in Central Asia, in pursuit of the 'Great Game'. They were prepared to concede that Bismarck's bid for colonies might be a move either in his European policy (*Primat der Aussenpolitik*) or in his domestic policy (*Primat der Innenpolitik*). They acknowledged the central role of army officers in driving forward the frontiers of the French and Russian empires. They had no difficulty in accepting that 'prestige' might have considerable explanatory power for French expansion. But as far as the British empire was concerned they insisted – perhaps arrogantly – that this was an altogether more complex phenomenon, demanding (supposedly) more sophisticated explanations, which an economic interpretation might yield. Certainly they operated against a background in which economic historians were gaining a powerful grip over all branches of history after the Second World War. A suspicious and sceptical generation was perhaps bound to look to material self-interest and entrepreneurial conspiracy for explanations in history. Concurrently, too, any alternative approach to empire through 'geopolitics' – more or less invented by a British historical geographer, Sir Halford Mackinder, in the years before the First World War – had been discredited by its association with Nazi and Fascist expansionist programmes in the 1930s, in which 'geographical imperatives were used to legitimize imperialism'.[11]

I

If we are now to assert or reassert the primacy of geopolitics in governmental decision-making about the empire, the underlying assumption will be that there is a fundamental flaw in all theories of economic determinism. This flaw is that they are not grounded in any real under-standing of how governments think. Decisions are taken not by trends or abstract phenomena, but by individuals in very small inner groups, such as a Cabinet sub-committee. Governments – elders, oligarchs, politicians, fighting services chiefs, and their various advisers – are by definition elites. All elites have their own particular 'cosmologies', ways of looking at the world and interpreting their responsibilities within a bureaucratic tradition. In Britain the relevant training of most govern-ment ministers for ruling the empire has always been minimal. They can mostly be made to grasp the basic principles of survival-politics but not the technicalities of economics. The British elite, drawn in part from the aristocracy for a long period of time, and mostly with an Oxbridge educa-tion overwhelmingly classical (or more recently historical) in its empha-sis, was frequently disdainful of business interests. It served a form of government heavily committed to laissez-faire, which before 1945 at the earliest, had no machinery to hand for formulating national economic policy. In any case, government is mostly about response to immedi-ate problems, in the face of which ministers must concentrate on the essentials. Apart from holding office, these are primarily concerned with protecting the 'national interest', which is most obviously interpreted to mean the security of the state against attack. Thus government seems to them to be about 'high politics', especially relations with other states, also pursuing their own national interests. The dynamics of this rarefied world are frequently driven by prestige. This will be a central concept for the argument of this chapter. What is prestige? Harold Nicolson defined it as 'power based on reputation', an amalgam of the two, something which has to be acquired by power but can only be retained by reputa-tion; prestige is thus more durable than power alone. According to Dean Acheson, 'prestige is the shadow cast by power'.[12] The estimate formed by rival states of another's power may be crucial, and so all governments worry about prestige.

British governments in the two centuries since the middle of the eighteenth century have tended to be temperamentally detached from non-governmental representations and from special interest groups of whatever kind, resistant to attempts to put pressure on them to advance individual enterprises which cannot be equated with 'the national interest'. Ministers might accept a vague duty generally to 'promote trade' but would almost never allow themselves to be dictated to by particular lobbies.[13] It has, however, all too often been argued that governments acted on behalf of interest groups, such as sugar-planters, merchants, businessmen, mining magnates, or 'gentlemanly capitalists', simply because government decisions happened to coincide with what commercial or industrial leaders wanted. This emphatically does not mean, however, that they were genuinely influential, still less instrumental, in bringing those decisions about. It is no longer possible to maintain that William Pitt, the Earl of Chatham, during the Seven Years War was a 'spokesman of City interests', or that Lord Palmerston as foreign secretary a hundred years later was acting primarily in the interests of merchants. Marie Peters has shown Chatham's priorities to have been firmly rooted in the political aspects of winning the war against the French: if he aimed at 'the total extirpation of French commerce from the seas', this was not primarily for economic reasons as such.[14]

Similarly, Palmerston's famous statement about its being 'the business of the government to open and secure roads for the merchant' has to be returned to its context. The reference was to Afghanistan and Turkestan, where Palmerston was pushing trade as a means of increasing British political influence against Russian penetration. As Ingram puts it, for Palmerston trade was an extension of diplomacy by other means, the cheapest method of injecting stability and security into the region.[15] Governmental priorities were clearly articulated in discussions in 1852 over opening up Japan, when the foreign secretary, Lord Granville, declared that ministers did not accept the view that 'all considerations of a higher nature . . . be sacrificed to the pushing of our manufactures by any means into every possible corner of the globe'.[16] The government can also be shown to have ignored trading interests even when traditional mercantile activities were directly concerned or adversely affected by a change of policy, as in Tunis in 1878 or Persia in 1907. (Britain gave way to France in Tunisia and in Persia influence was to be shared with Russia.) Public opinion was to be treated with suspicion at best, contempt at worst. Even when government appears to have been responding to popular pressure to act in a particular way, only a little research will usually expose the error. Thus in the case of the retention of Uganda in 1894, we now know that Rosebery's Cabinet, far from responding to missionary demands, had itself asked missionaries to whip up a campaign in its favour, in support of a decision already taken on strategic grounds (to protect the headwaters of the Nile).[17] Similarly, it can now be agreed that in South Africa the neo-Marxists were wrong. The truth is that Milner and Chamberlain manipulated the mining magnates and not vice versa, and that they used public opinion to further their own ends, rather than being dictated to by it.[18]

It is not in dispute that the British empire took its origin in trade, or that in the eighteenth century colonies were valued for trade. But it was a politically 'mercantilist' trade in colonial raw materials, especially those strategic naval supplies which would make possible self-sufficiency in time of war. In order to extract such materials from the periphery (or overseas world) it might be necessary to plant settlers or impose order on indigenous chaos by establishing formal rule. But then two imperatives followed ineluctably. What you held you had to defend against rivals. And what you defended you began to value for its own sake, irrespective of the original intention. The first point was well put by Mackinder in 1907:

It is only when a state desires to secure or is driven to avert a monopoly of trade in any region, that the imperial motive becomes effective . . . When order breaks down, or foreign interference is threatened in a land in which large British interests are at stake, Britain has often been compelled to add to her possessions by assuming authority among an alien and distant population.[19]

The second point was understood by Henry Dundas (as secretary of state) as early as 1790, when he defined 'the great objective' of the British in the East as 'to preserve the empire . . . in comparison of which even trade is a subordinate or collateral consideration'.[20] Thus strategic imperatives, taking more territory to maintain imperial prestige or pre-empt the challenges of the foreigner, began to operate almost from the beginning of formal rule. Effective defence meant thinking strategically. The very nature of strategic planning created a snowballing process of expansion: to be safe in the valley the overlooking hill must be controlled, to be secure on the hill the next valley must be taken, and so on. As Prime Minister Lord Salisbury observed, 'the constant study of maps is apt to disturb men's reasoning powers', and he more than once complained that his naval and military advisers would have liked to 'annex the moon in order to prevent its being appropriated by the planet Mars'.[21] Strategic geopolitics indeed had a distinct tendency to take on a life of its own. This happened spectacularly in the process of reinsuring the British presence in India, internally by gradually incorporating more Indian states until brought up sharp by the Mutiny-Rebellion of 1857, and externally until control of the Indian Ocean rim, from Cape Town to Rangoon, together with the Middle East routes to India, was virtually complete by 1922.

Considerations of strategic security were a particularly strong concern for Britain in the eighteenth century, confronting France as a hated and formidable rival imperial power. The two states were locked into an antagonism which was historical and total, a 'Second Hundred Years' War'. This was not just about trade competition but a duel between two different ways of life, not least that of a Protestant nation against a Catholic one, and ultimately a monarchical against a republican one as well. This rivalry coloured everything which happened in British expansion before 1815, and it left a potent residue for the remainder of the nineteenth century.[22] Expansion was seen in the context of 'competing empires'; the pre-emption of rivals was an important motive for acquiring territory.

These strategic preoccupations were scarcely modified by the promotion of economic opportunity. At the end of the eighteenth century political nervousness made the British government more pessimistic than optimistic about overseas territories, more concerned with a defensive strategic survival than with a positive expansionist blueprint, except spasmodically. In any case, ignorance about economic possibilities was so deep-rooted that no master-plan for any imperial project could be effectively implemented. Geopolitical priorities alone can explain why strategically important Canada and Florida were retained in the peace treaty of 1763 – to round off imperial control of the continent against the French – while the captured rich sugar-island of Guadeloupe was handed back.

Concern for trade was no more developed twenty years later. Shelburne's dictum, 'we prefer trade to dominion', propounded bravely in respect of North America, where the dominion had been lost in 1783, was ripped out of context by Harlow and elevated by him into the 'enunciation of the general principle on which the Second Empire was being established'. He argued that there was a diversion of interest and enterprise from the Western world to the potentialities of Asia, a 'swing to the East'. For Harlow and those historians who followed him, all acquisitions were seen as parts of an economic design to open up world markets. In point of fact, however, the retention of Cape Town in 1806 was determined solely to make the route to India secure against the French.[23] The founding of Australia might well have been related to a plan to make convicts produce vital naval stores (timber and flax for shipbuilding), but this was much less important than the need to find somewhere to dump convicts after the loss of the American colonies, all other possibilities having been eliminated. But another strand was the pre-emption of a possible French move to establish themselves in Australia.[24] Harlow's thesis is further unsustainable in that the North Atlantic world remained the principal centre of imperial concern and trade, despite the acquisition of India. Four-fifths of British investment in 1798 remained in the West Indies alone; the West Indies remained vital to British naval strength and to sustaining the war effort against Revolutionary France.[25]

In the Asian sector itself, it is no more clear that trade for its own sake was driving everything forward. At least in part, Sir Stamford Raffles envisaged Singapore (which he founded in 1819) as 'a fulcrum whence we may extend our influence politically'. Commercially valuable Indonesian territories were handed back in the Anglo-Dutch Treaty of 1824. The main outlines of the empire as it had emerged by that date essentially constituted a system of strategic bases in support of an Indian Raj.

The long-term problem of a large-scale territorial empire, which grew ever larger in the nineteenth century, was to keep the whole imperial structure safe and manageable without too much expense to the metropolis. By the end of the century the most favoured device was to promote the regional federation of provinces. After the successful establishment of the Canadian Confederation in 1867, the 'federal panacea' almost became an imperial obsession. Carnarvon tried to make it work in South Africa in the 1870s, where local economic concerns about control of African labour coincided with his grandiose strategies, but were opposed by Boers and Africans. Federations are quintessentially geopolitical constructions. To say that they were adopted for economic reasons is not saying very much. There are always economic arguments in favour of federations. Whether they are worth creating, or holding together, depends on political criteria, notably security against external threat. Canada's Confederation was fundamentally a means of preventing its absorption in an American empire, a counterpoise to the alarming expansion of the United States. As Lord Elgin (governor-general, 1847–54) realised, 'Let the Yankees get possession of British North America with the prestige of superior generalship – and who can say how soon they may dispute with you the Empire of India and of the Seas?'[26] Canadian shipbuilding timber, the Halifax naval base, and a sizeable merchant marine were strategic assets which the United States had to be denied. In some ways the new Canada represented a revamped imperial defence posture on the North American continent. As for Australia's coming together, a crucial motive concerned its geographical vulnerability to the 'yellow peril' and desire to consolidate a 'white Australia' on the basis of tougher immigration restrictions against Asians. Unless this purpose is given due weight, historians (such as Norris) are reduced to the tame explanation that Australian federation was no more than a 'businessman's merger'.[27] South African Union also had its economic rationale and racially motivated components, though the British government was more concerned with strengthening the region strategically against an anticipated German attack in the expected general war.

During the 1930s, the federal panacea was canvassed in connection with the problems of India and Palestine. It was actively resurgent if not actually triumphant after the Second World War. These proliferating post-war federations were predicated upon the supposed political desirability and superior defensive capability of larger units.[28] The Central African Federation, the most problematic and artificial of them all, was essentially a geopolitical construct to contain the threat of South African expansion, reinforcing the Zambesi as the northern frontier of Afrikanerdom, with its repugnant doctrine of apartheid.[29] In Malaysia, federation was undertaken to improve the defence posture in South-East Asia and 'absorb' Chinese communism in Singapore.

II

At the 'high politics' level of imperial decision-making, strategic and geopolitical calculations were dominant. International rivalries and anxieties about prestige were central to the machinations of bureaucratic cosmologists. However, this is not to contend that in the totality of historical explanation economic considerations have no place. They do. But they operated at a different, and secondary, level from governments preoccupied with their global perspectives. At this 'private sector' level, the interests of individuals or pressure groups were decidedly limited, parochial, and selfish: investors, traders, and businessmen seeking profit, concessionaires and adventurers seeking fame and aggrandisement, army officers playing out the strategic games of 'military fiscalism',[30] missionaries seeking converts. The significance of such interests to historical explanation is that they created the situations which might force metropolitan statesmen to make decisions or which they could utilise for their own policies. Once interest groups were established overseas – whether settler communities, mining magnates, or army garrisons – they tended to demand government help in consolidating and protecting their interests. It was hard for them to make effective direct contact with ministers. Often their demands for running up the flag and imposing formal territorial rule were ignored or rebuffed. For example, the British government refused pressing offers to take over Sarawak (1860) and Katanga (1874, 1890), and offers of protectorates in Uruguay and Basutoland. At one time the annexation of Fiji was refused (1872), while Lord Derby snubbed the Australians by initially refusing to confirm Queensland's annexation of New Guinea (1883). Those cases which did result in formal imperial rule, however, did so because of convergence between private interests at the local level overseas and the dictates of geopolitics as perceived by rulers at the centre. This convergence was often mediated by a proconsul or 'man on the spot' who had a good relationship with his political bosses in London. If he did not have such a sympathetic relationship, his initiative might be repudiated, as Lord Glenelg repudiated Sir Benjamin D'Urban's annexation of Queen Adelaide Province in South Africa in 1834–5. (See above, pp. 26–7.)

Exertions of the imperial factor or the imposition of territorial rule have to be explained at two levels, the one making final politically determined decisions within a European framework of reference, and the other contributing to the creation of preparatory conditions in a non-European context, frequently requiring, but certainly not always obtaining, governmental control. Where local indigenous regimes were unable to maintain an adequate system of law and order for the successful operation of European economic or other activities, the government might step in. But it did so chiefly because it believed these chaotic conditions could lead to international conflicts or humanitarian abuses (as, for example, in New Zealand) which it was its function to avert or contain. Territory was thus acquired, or colonial wars broke out, when the two levels of interest interlocked. Individuals overseas could create the circumstances which made an acquisition possible or even probable, but they could never ensure or determine it.[31]

Existing models for a 'theory of imperialism' usually involve an interacting centre and periphery. The dynamic forces at the centre may include strategic as well as economic pressures. European states are regarded as being sucked into an overseas territory through troubles on an unstable frontier. Essentially a 'crisis in the periphery' would lead to territorial takeover, an enlargement of 'bridgeheads'. The dynamic interaction took place in a spatial location, the turbulent frontier.[32] This theory may be expressed diagrammatically (Figure 1.1, p. 80).

My alternative model proposes that we should, so to speak, raise this periphery-oriented model from the horizontal to the vertical, and give more weight to the metropolitan dimension. We should envisage two different *levels* of activity (rather than two different *spheres*), two sets of interests interacting along the axis of a chain of command. Thus we generate a model in which metropolitan policies (at one level) were being handed down from the elite group at the centre or political apex, and (at another level) local pressures – set in motion by concessionaires, colonial adventurers, missionaries, settlers, revenue-seeking army officers, etc. – were being transmitted upwards from the base-line of the geographical periphery. Neither the metropolitan nor the local level of action was in itself unilaterally decisive. What clinched matters was an effective interaction between the inner and outer pinions of imperial political power. This interaction was mediated by or funnelled through an individual. In this model a key role thus exists for the 'man on the spot' – the proconsuls, the ambassadors, the high commissioners, the governors, the viceroys, the commanders-in-chief. For it is they who could determine

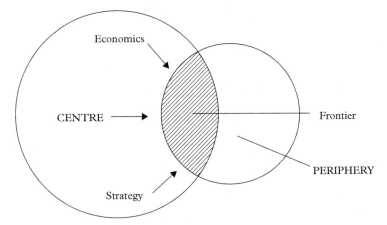

Figure 1.1 The 'turbulent frontier' model.

the extent to which imperial policies worked out at the centre, or local pressures erupting overseas, would be implemented or endorsed. They stood at the intermediate point of interlock in a chain of responsibility between decisions handed down and self-seeking initiatives mediated to the centre. It was General Sir William Butler who once illuminatingly defined the high commissioner in South Africa as 'a kind of pointsman on the railway of thought between two stations'. John Benyon, building upon my theory as first adumbrated in 1976, has glossed this by describing the high commissioner as an imperial agent who 'worked as a half-way relay station that could charge up, or scale down the impulses transmitted in either direction'. In an equally helpful alternative metaphor, Benyon speaks of an 'intermediate proconsulate', which, 'like a connecting-rod, joined the metropolis to periphery at the political level, within the reciprocating engine of empire'.[33]

This model may be expressed diagrammatically for an individual case-study as in Figure 1.2. The principal advantage of this 'two-levels' approach is that, unlike the rather one-dimensional and impersonal 'horizontal' model of interaction between the forces of centre and periphery (with the point of interaction located in a place, the unstable frontier), the 'vertical' model is much more precise in assigning economic and geopolitical-strategic motives. Instead of saying 'both may be present', the two-levels model allocates economic motives primarily to the periphery-level, and political or strategic considerations primarily to the elite-level. The other advantage is that it also accommodates properly the role of masterful individuals, both decision-makers in the metropolis and proconsuls 'on the spot'. Instead of reducing everything in an overly

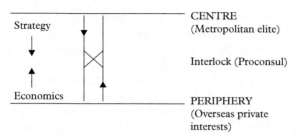

Figure 1.2 The 'interaction' model: for a case-study.

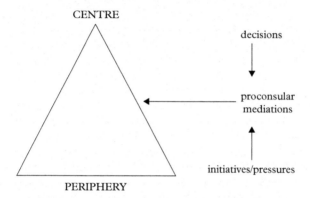

Figure 1.3 The 'interaction' model: for a general theory.

theoretical way to impersonal forces ('imperialism'), it unequivocally incorporates into the historical process the policies and decisions of particular men, whose actions can sometimes only be understood by reference to their personal ambition or psychological drives. In this way the model forces analysis to go beyond mere considerations of 'peripheral crisis' or 'turbulent frontier'. Accordingly, it has much greater explanatory power when applied to the German case of expansion, in which Bismarck had such a central role. His policies need no longer seem obscure or exceptional. Finally, the model does not require any monocausal emphasis on either metropolitan or peripheral dynamics, but allows for both. If it gives primacy to the former, it certainly does not make it exclusive. The integrated, comprehensive nature of the model (in its globally accumulated form) can be represented as in Figure 1.3.

Let us now test the validity of this model by juxtaposing in rapid succession an analysis of the two most important episodes in the British imperial process: territorial acquisition in India from the late eighteenth century and territorial acquisition in Africa in the late nineteenth.

After the French defeat in 1763 there was a continuing British fear that France would use a European war to re-establish an empire in India. Not until 1815 did France finally accept that there was no longer any possibility of a French Indian empire. The existence of the Napoleonic Wars was a critical precondition for the major phase of British territorial expansion in India, providing Richard Wellesley (governor-general 1798–1805) with the excuse as well as the opportunity. In Ingram's conceptualisation, France was his 'necessary enemy'.[34] As Bayly reminds us, this was an empire 'forged in the context of war . . . and the ideological challenge of Republican France'.[35] Castlereagh was right: 'It has not been a matter of choice but of necessity that our existence in India should pass from that of traders to that of sovereigns. If we had not, the French would long since have taken the lead in India to our exclusion' (1804).[36] Tipu Sultan of Mysore was in diplomatic contact with the French between 1797 and 1799, and so Wellesley argued for the reduction of Tipu's power and resources before he could avail himself of the advantages of formal alliance. Otherwise Mysore would be 'a perpetual source of solicitude, expense, and hazard'. In accordance with Wellesley's plan, Tipu's power was smashed, and collectors of revenue were sent in.

Further north, the most powerful leader of the Mahratta Confederacy was Sindhia, who controlled the fugitive Mughal emperor and held sway over a large area of Hindustan, which Wellesley feared might afford facilities to the French, whose man on the spot was Perron. Wellesley's declared aim was to destroy the 'French state on the banks of the Jumna'. He urged that Sindhia's domains presented to vindictive Napoleon 'an instrument of destruction adapted to wound the heart of the British empire in India'. However, he also claimed that the international war against France would have induced him to attack Perron 'even independently of his contest with Sindhia'. In this sense, territorial expansion in India was his contribution to the general war effort.[37] Next, Oudh had to be tackled, because of its strategic importance as a buffer to protect the Bengal territories from Zaman Shah in Afghanistan. Though an economic dimension existed – exports in raw cotton, saltpetre, opium, and indigo were being rapidly developed – this was not (as P.J. Marshall has shown) influential upon Wellesley, whose concern was about its supposed 'misrule' and consequent strategic weakness.[38] On the west coast, Wellesley's political decisions suited the Bombay merchants very well, but this does not mean he was genuinely concerned with their trade in raw cotton and pepper for Canton. In fact the Bombay merchants, led by Miguel de Souza, seized their chance to persuade Wellesley to keep commercially valuable pieces of territory in the Treaty of Bassein (1802) by dressing up their supposed strategic significance. It was difficult for them to transport indigenous products out of Gujarat and the Malabar coast because of the confused political conditions and Mahratta interference. The hugely increased demand for China tea after 1784 made Indian raw cotton and pepper, and ultimately opium, important as a payment. All these emerging interests enabled Wellesley to mobilise support in overcoming London's reluctance to agree to territorial extension.[39] This was paid for by raising Indian revenue. As Wellesley recognised early on, the establishment of a territorial revenue was 'that necessary foundation of European power in India'.[40] Wellesley was thus successful in pushing conquest much further forward than Dundas and his other London bosses would otherwise have been prepared to tolerate.

Once the Indian empire existed, the imperatives for its defence were subject to continual escalation. Almost all further extensions had a strategic objective. Despite some interest in teak, Burma began to be added from the mid-1820s mainly to protect the eastern flank of India.[41] The last big acquisitions in India proper in the 1840s demonstrated the same pattern. In Sind and Punjab, economic expectations and commercial opportunities were in the background. The idea of pushing British goods into populous regions was important in creating the conditions for conquest and gaining support for it in Britain. But strategic requirements were the central cause of imperial advance: the need to stabilise turbulent frontiers was especially significant in the case of Punjab, which bordered on Afghanistan. In part the acquisition of Sind was an act of pre-emptive expansion against the French. Prestige entered in, because the British had been defeated in Afghanistan and needed a victory in order to halt the erosion of imperial confidence. Personal factors also played a part, with ambitious Lord Ellenborough as governor-general supporting General Sir Charles Napier, himself determined to redeem an otherwise lack-lustre career. Napier exaggerated the strategic importance of the Indus Valley.[42]

Turning now to the partition of Africa: whether or not this was triggered off by an Egyptian crisis, the British occupation of 1882 has always been a test-case of imperial controversy. Did Britain move in to protect the bondholders or the route to India? The question of Gladstone's investments is not highly relevant, granted his relative sympathy for Egyptian protonationalists, together with his positively Palmerstonian geopolitical understanding that 'for India the Suez Canal is the connecting link between herself and the centre of power – the centre of the moral, social, and political power of the world'. The Canal, he said, was 'the great question of British interest'.[43] A broad spectrum of British interests existed in Egypt, but ministers were primarily concerned with the strategic security of the Canal, in the context of the local situation developing chaotically from the 1870s, when excessive rates of interest led to Egyptian bankruptcy. The bondholders provided the context, but they did not determine the form of government action, which as Schölch first convincingly demonstrated, was the result of manipulation by its 'men on the spot', notably Sir Edward Malet, the consul-general (who exaggerated the dangers), and Admiral Sir Beauchamp Seymour (who exceeded his instructions).[44] Prestige mattered too. Failure to act after the riots in Cairo, Sir Charles Dilke believed, 'would destroy not only the prestige of this country, but also of Europe in the East'. Chaos in Egypt, unless brought under control, might also have led to a renewed French attempt to obtain a permanent footing.[45]

In general, the partition of sub-Saharan Africa was the response of European 'high politics' to fears of a widespread, ever-increasing, and fundamental destabilisation of Africa. Externally, Leopold of the Belgians and Bismarck broke the international 'gentleman's agreement' to avoid territorial seizures. Internally, partition meant the imposition of control on the dangerously chaotic scenario brought about by the activities of gun-runners, slave-traders, ivory-hunters, greedy concessionaires, aggressive explorers, treaty-extorters, importunate missionaries, and Islamic fundamentalists. It was, as so often, the frontiers of fear which were being edged forward, especially the fear that local confrontations between frontiersmen could spark off a war between European powers.[46] Bismarck rebuked the explorer Wolf in 1888: 'Your map of Africa is very fine, but my map of Africa lies in Europe. Here lies Russia, and here . . . lies France, and we are in the middle. That is my map of Africa.'[47] Locating African disputes within the parameters of European politics was a conception which British statesmen shared. Diplomatic bargaining determined the finalisation of cartographical claims. All the participants were worried that their interests would be squeezed out in a situation of ruthless economic competition. Pre-emption was the name of the game. As Sir Percy Anderson encapsulated it: 'Protectorates are unwelcome burdens, but . . . are the inevitable outcome' of international competition.[48]

The partition took place in an extraordinarily fevered atmosphere of geopolitical excitement and apprehension. The profile of geographers, explorers, and engineers was suddenly raised.[49] Engineers made striking pronouncements about the technical feasibility of railways (Trans-Sahara, Cape to Cairo, Berlin to Baghdad, Paris to New York); they pontificated about the ease with which dams could be constructed to regulate the Nile waters, or even flood the Sahara. The spreading network of submarine cables added yet another potent strategic imperative. This was especially true of the main cable east from Cape Town, which reached Mauritius in 1879, making the retention of the east coast of southern Africa more significant than ever. The Germans had to be kept away from it. 'In the main,' concluded Robinson and Gallagher, 'British Africa was a gigantic footnote to the Indian empire.'[50]

The security of the Cape route to India also explains why Britain went to war with the Boers of the Transvaal and Orange Free State, another prominent case where the supposed primacy of economic interests has been strongly canvassed. Yet it is easy to be mesmerised by gold. The truth is that some sort of war might well have broken out in 1899 even if gold had never been discovered in the Transvaal in 1886. The historic long-term causes driving the two sides apart pre-dated the discovery of gold. The incompatibility of outlooks, of local requirements, and basic political aims had been apparent at least since the provocative British annexation of the Transvaal in 1877. No war, however, is inevitable, but the South African War could not be averted because of the way in which the 'man on the spot', High Commissioner Milner, was determined to 'work up to a crisis', being anxious to prevent the snapping of 'the weakest link in the imperial chain' of global communications. He was supported by Secretary of State Chamberlain, worried about prestige.[51] Imperial federation was an ultimate goal. There were fears of German intervention. Control of the hinterland provided the focus for a regional geopolitical conflict. But the existence of economic interests at the local level – the archaic Transvaal as a 'source of unrest, disturbance, and danger' to the needs of mining magnates and hopes of *Uitlanders* – remain a necessary part of the overall explanation, even if the geopolitical concerns of strategy and prestige represent a primary level of causation.[52]

The 'two-levels' model thus appears to make good sense of interpreting the dynamics of British expansion over a long period of time. Any convincing model, however, must also hold good for other expanding states too. That it does so for the empires of the continental states, France,[53] Germany,[54] Russia,[55] and Italy,[56] should be readily apparent, and there is no space for demonstration here. (See below, chapter 3.) The alignment of American expansion, as analysed by Phillip Darby and Roger Louis, also seems to present no particular difficulty.[57] More problematic, at least at first sight, is the case of Japan. Actually, the study of Japanese expansion has long been bedevilled by the attempt to harmonise it with the prevailing European theory of 'economic imperialism'. This has proved difficult.[58] For one thing, Japan had an actual capital shortage when its expansion began in the late nineteenth century. Myers and Peattie, however, in 1984, put forward the argument that the Japanese empire was designed to create a strategic ringfence in surrounding territories which were regarded as ineptly governed: a process which ultimately snowballed into over-extension and disaster. Japan fought its first wars against China and Russia essentially because of strategic worries about Korea, which according to General Meckel, Prussian adviser to the Meiji army, was a 'dagger thrust at the heart of Japan', potentially fatal in Russian hands. Myers and Peattie concluded: 'No colonial empire of modern times was as clearly shaped by strategic considerations . . . in large part undertaken to guarantee the nation's strategic frontiers against Western advance.' Thus economic considerations provided a context, and economic advantages – such as control of the oil of Indonesia – were sought as an adjunct to strategic requirements. Only Japanese aggression had created the need for new raw materials and for bolstering prestige against the Americans. Japanese expansion thus clearly confirms the theory of the primacy of geopolitics and the utility of the 'two-levels' paradigm.[59]

III

Halford Mackinder first unveiled his famous thesis that the 'heartland' of Eurasia constituted a geographical pivot, a 'world island' if Africa was included, in 1904. Control of this land mass could lead to the creation of 'a world empire'. The sub-text was a geopolitical warning that sea-power alone might not be sufficient to save the British empire.[60] One of the members of Mackinder's audience at this lecture in 1904 was L.S. Amery, who became under-secretary of state for the colonies in 1919 and secretary of state from 1924 to 1929; he was also secretary of state for India, from 1940 to 1945. As Roger Louis has made plain, Amery has a fair claim to be 'the architect of the British geo-political system that endured until the crack-up at Suez in 1956'.[61] This system was still mainly designed to uphold the Indian empire. In 1917 Amery envisaged the removal of the Germans from East Africa and from possible influence in the Middle East as giving a strategical security 'which will enable that Southern British World which runs from Cape Town through Cairo, Baghdad, and Calcutta to Sydney and Wellington to go about its peaceful business without constant fear of German aggression'.[62] The keystone of this geopolitical arch would be in Palestine, with British influence established on the ruins of a defeated Ottoman empire and linked with the patronage of Zionism. If Germany emerged from the war able to dominate the Middle East, it would 'threaten our whole position in Egypt, India, and the Eastern Seas'. If left in Tanganyika and installed in Palestine, Germany might try to link up the two with a railway from Hamburg to Lake Nyasa, 'the greatest of all dangers which can confront the British empire in the future'. (Mackinder himself was arguing that Germany had gained command of Tanganyika and Kiaochow in order to mobilise African and Chinese manpower, and would make them the termini of projected overland railway routes on the 'world island' land mass.) Although Amery became a committed Zionist, excited by the potentialities which Jewish energy, released in a National Home, might bring to the regeneration of the Middle East, he admitted in his memoirs that the origin of his interest was strategic. Doubting whether Britain could control Egypt much longer, he believed a plan to hold the area to the east of the Canal would provide 'a central pivot of support for our whole Middle Eastern policy as well as assuring the effective control of our sea and air communications with the East'.[63]

The Palestine Mandate thus commended itself to the British government for essentially geopolitical reasons. To a large extent it was a pre-emptive measure against a possible German initiative to become the patron of Zionism, which was after all an Austrian idea. Foreign Secretary Lord Curzon argued – in language strongly reminiscent of Wellesley – that a teutonised Turkey, in possession of Syria and Palestine, 'would be an extreme and perpetual menace to the Empire'. The Balfour Declaration of 1917 was also an attempt to rally Jewish support for the faltering allied war effort.[64] The importance of Palestine to the empire developed in the 1920s, as it became not only the protective buffer of the Canal Zone, but the indispensable geopolitical link in the Iraq route to India and the outlet for oil, at Haifa. Sitting on the land bridge between Eurasia and Africa (or, as Mackinder saw it, at the 'physical and historical centre of the world'), it became known as the 'Clapham Junction of the British empire'. By 1939, however, it had become clear that Arab friendship was more valuable to Britain than Jewish, not least because of the ever-increasing importance of oil. By 1948 the Palestine Mandate was given up, basically on the ground that to antagonise the Arabs further would throw them into the arms of the Russians, and it was vital to forestall this. And the military experts had ceased to regard Palestine as a 'strategic reserve'.[65]

The geopolitical problems of an over-extended empire explain all the policies of the 1920s and 1930s, from the Singapore Base to appeasement. If the former became a symbol of unrealistic defence commitments, the latter was a strategic necessity, since the empire could not realistically fight three enemies (Germany, Italy, and Japan) or in the Mediterranean and Far East simultaneously.[66] Extraordinary plans were made for a further paper repartition of Africa, in order to give German ambitions some satisfaction. This represented the apotheosis of diplomatic bargaining with respect to the map of that continent.[67] It was also in this period that the Chiefs of Staff acquired enormous power over overseas policy, which persisted well into the 1950s.

As Britain moved into the post-war era, the gradual dismantling of the empire became the dominant theme. The central hinge of governmental debate about decolonisation was whether British prestige would be best served by holding on or getting out. Timing was the critical factor, and increasingly calculations about the feasibility of the continuation of imperial rule were made within the framework of the cold war. Long-term international friendships came to be seen as much more important than transient local control. In 1946 the viceroy of India, Wavell, concluded that 'on the whole Great Britain should not lose, but on the contrary, may gain in prestige and even in power, by handing over to Indians'. Most importantly, the Chiefs of Staff agreed. Even Amery had argued that 'in surrendering control from here we should not be sacrificing anything that mattered'. The Labour government's greatest anxiety in the whole process of transferring power in India was that it should not be done in a way which could be criticised as 'scuttle'.[68] Independence for India in 1947 was obviously a major turning point for the British empire, even if its geopolitical significance was insufficiently understood at the time. In Field Marshal Lord Alanbrooke's assessment:

With the loss of India and Burma, the keystone of the arch of our Commonwealth Defence was lost, and our Imperial Defence crashed. Without the central strategic reserve of Indian troops ready to operate either east or west, we were left impotent and even the smallest of nations were at liberty to twist the lion's tail . . . but few realized what the strategic loss would amount to.[69]

Attlee as prime minister tried hard to initiate the strategic reassessment which was required in the Middle East and North Africa, but was thwarted by the inertia of the traditional nostrums and by the intensification of Russian expansion.[70] But with India independent, it could be argued that many of the British political elite fundamentally lost interest in empire. This holds true for Churchill as well as Attlee, for Macmillan and Duncan Sandys as well as Enoch Powell.[71] From 1947, the gradual end of empire was not seriously contested at the highest level of government. Not so much a failure of will, just a fit of absence of mind.

With the onset of the cold war, Mackinder's warnings and predictions came into their own. In a major state-paper of 1948, the foreign secretary, Ernest Bevin, used the conceptual language of Mackinder: 'Physical control of the Eurasian landmass and eventual control of the whole World Island is what the Politburo is aiming at – no less a thing than that . . .'[72] This had profound consequences for the continuation of unwanted European rule. In Attlee's famous phrase, 'an attempt to maintain the old colonialism would, I'm sure, have immensely aided communism'.[73] The whole process of decolonisation is best interpreted within the geopolitical context of the cold war. The long-term aim with respect to future relations with Afro-Asian countries was to ensure their alignment with the West, thus containing communism within Mackinder's 'heartland'.[74] According to Macmillan, writing privately in 1962, the ideological struggle against communism 'really dominates everything'. Consequently, the new multi-racial Commonwealth must be made to work, because its worldwide dispersion made it a useful weapon in the global contest, 'while the Communist/Free World division really holds the front of the stage'.[75] Macmillan's view reflected that of the senior civil servants who compiled the 'Future Policy Study' in 1959–60, which emphasised the 'overriding importance of countering the threat from the communist world'; this would be the first, the ultimate objective of British policy in the 1960s.[76] Iain Macleod (secretary of state for the colonies, 1959–61) also based his policy in East Africa on the belief that 'the overriding consideration' was to make sure that its territories did not become sympathetic to the Sino-Soviet cause.[77] In general, he believed, it would be better to grant too much and too soon than too little and too late. This policy was not without its risks: reluctance to move forward with independence might turn African opinion towards the Soviet Union, but going too fast might equally well plunge large areas of Africa into chaos, ripe for communist exploitation. Sir Andrew Cohen, the Colonial Office expert, was worried by 1961 that 'killing communism' seemed to have become the chief objective of African policy, rather than the desirability of preparing stable and viable regimes for independence.[78]

In this way political considerations were paramount in decolonisation. Economic considerations were in the nature of *nihil obstat*. Just as economic interests had once facilitated the acquisition of territory, so now they operated in reverse. Territories could be given up when nothing essential seemed likely to be irretrievably lost by transfers of political power – a conclusion reached for India by the 1940s and Africa by the 1960s.[79] Business firms exercised no influence on decolonisation, as is clear from studies made of such widely differing territories as Malaya, Egypt, Rhodesia, and the Congo.[80] The mainspring came from the international context. To 'Joe' Saville Garner, a civil servant who was well placed to know (as permanent under-secretary of the Commonwealth Relations Office), the reason why the pace of independence was speeded up was primarily because 'other people's empires were crumbling all around': Germany, Italy, Holland, and Japan had all ceased to be imperial powers after the war, and from 1958 to 1960 there were major advances to self-rule in French West Africa and the Belgian Congo.[81] From the end of 1960 there was pressure from the United Nations (Resolution 1514) to promote the early independence of all colonial territories. Macleod warned the Cabinet in January 1961: 'we must recognize that pressures from the United Nations, now that Belgium and France are dropping out as colonial powers, will increasingly concentrate on us'.[82] Britain had no wish to be pilloried as an international pariah. It was widely understood in any case that colonial territories could not be insulated from developments in neighbouring countries: if not a 'domino theory' of decolonisation, at least a recognition of the salience of 'chain reactions'. Insulating ring fences were impossible, as the governor of Nigeria, Sir John Macpherson, reluctantly realised in 1952; they had had to give Nigeria a constitution 'in advance of its true capacity', because of what was happening in the Gold Coast, the Sudan, and Libya.[83] Similarly, just as the Gold Coast became the pacemaker in the first phase of decolonisation, in West Africa, so Tanganyika became the pioneer in the next and crucial phase, in East Africa. As its governor, Sir Richard Turnbull, recognised, 'it could not be expected that Tanganyika would remain immune from the trend of events' in the neighbouring Congo, Ruanda-Urundi, and Nyasaland.[84] Charismatic proconsuls painting frightening scenarios had a vital role to play in converting reluctant ministers to nationalist political advancement in Africa.

Britain did not want to be found in the last colonial ditch with the Portuguese, the 'wily, oily Portuguese' as Churchill once called them. Britain did not take the initiative in the decolonisation of Africa, any more than Britain had spearheaded the partition. Great power rivalry led Britain into the nineteenth-century scramble for Africa, and great power rivalry – in the shape of the cold war and a competition for international respectability and support – induced the twentieth-century scramble to get out of Africa. Britain's policy was essentially reactive, that is to say, it was one of following other powers into empire-building in Africa (in order not to be excluded), and into decolonisation (so as not to be ostracised).

Geopolitical considerations were decisive in withdrawal from empire, and they remained so until the end of the cold war. It may or may not be possible to make sense of the Falklands War of 1982, a war which never should have taken place, between two countries that had long been friends. But the familiar dictates of prestige and strategy may be tellingly invoked. From the end of the 1970s the Soviet Union was establishing close relations with Argentina, and this made a vital difference. The strategic importance of the Falklands grew with the mobility of nuclear submarines capable of entering the Atlantic through Drake's Passage (south of Cape Horn) from the Pacific. The Russians might thus max-imise the unity of what Mackinder had called 'the world's ocean', and there were almost no other islands from which submarine movements in the area could be monitored. Thus the cold war expansion of Soviet naval power gave a new geostrategic significance to the Falklands and its dependencies. These, ironically, had seemed to the Foreign Office in 1952 to be the one overseas commitment which might possibly be offloaded.[85]

The end of the cold war had many ramifications, unfreezing all manner of constraints from Ulster to Hong Kong. The 'new' South Africa was a principal beneficiary, since fears of communism could no longer underpin apartheid. At least potentially, a solution to the problem of Northern Ireland could be put on the agenda: there was profound significance in the phrase of the Downing Street Declaration of 1993 that the British government no longer had any strategic interest in the retention of Ulster within the United Kingdom. The removal of strategic constraints elsewhere in the empire has frequently led to rapid impe-rial withdrawals. However, strategic re-evaluations of themselves do not automatically solve everything. It has been a major premise of this chapter that effective action has to arise out of a conjunction of local and metropolitan interests, and such conjunction in Northern Ireland was particularly hard to achieve.

Metropolitan decision-making equally does not operate in a global vacuum. Empires compete. A broad geopolitical basis to imperial policy-making is thus unavoidable. Rulers of empires have to study maps. It is not difficult to construct plausible geopolitical rationales and strategic arguments. They can be made to justify almost any policy. By their arcane nature they have often become dangerously overvalued by the governing elite. They are specialist judgments which are difficult to remove and, notoriously, the planners are always fighting the last war over again. As Roger Louis has so pertinently observed: 'strategic cal-culations with emotional origins can become absolute. When they carry over into a different era, they can become irrational.'[86] This is an insight which no historian of empire can afford to neglect.

Notes

1 J.A. Hobson, *Imperialism: a study* (1902). A historiography which began with R. Koebner, 'The concept of economic imperialism', *Economic History Review*, vol. 2 (1949), pp. 1–29, culminated in P.J. Cain and A.G. Hopkins, *British imperialism, 1688–1990*, 2 vols. (1993). But as Theodore Hoppen has sagely observed, the findings of economic history 'have not proved as con-clusive as its practitioners might once have hoped', and it is not at all easy 'to

discern "economic motives" in the specific *details* of government action': *The mid-Victorian generation, 1846–1886* (Oxford, 1998), pp. 5, 156.

2 E. Williams, *Capitalism and slavery* (New York, 1944).

3 R. Pares, 'Economic factors in the history of the empire', *Economic History Review*, vol. 7 (1937), pp. 119–44.

4 V.T. Harlow, *The founding of the Second British Empire, 1763–1793*, 2 vols. (1952, 1964).

5 W.K. Hancock, *Survey of British Commonwealth affairs*, especially vol. II, *Problems of economic policy, 1919–1939* (Oxford, 1940).

6 J. Gallagher and R.E. Robinson, 'The imperialism of free trade', *Economic History Review*, vol. 6 (1953), pp. 1–14.

7 Wm. Roger Louis, 'Sir Percy Anderson's grand African strategy, 1883–1896', *English Historical Review*, vol. 81 (1966), pp. 292–314; *Ruanda-Urundi, 1884–1919* (Oxford, 1963).

8 Wm. Roger Louis, *Imperialism at bay, 1941–1945: the United States and the decolonization of the British empire* (Oxford, 1977), ch. I; *British strategy in the Far East, 1919–1939* (Oxford, 1971).

9 W.L. Langer, *The diplomacy of imperialism* (New York, 1935, 1950); *European alliances and alignments, 1871–1890*, 2nd edn (New York, 1950), chs. 8, 9.

10 A.J. Marder, *The anatomy of sea power: British naval policy, 1880–1905* (New York, 1940).

11 M. Bell, R. Butlin, and M. Heffernan, eds., *Geography and imperialism, 1820–1940* (Manchester, 1995); Geoffrey Parker, *Western geopolitical thought in the twentieth century* (1985).

12 Harold Nicolson, *The meaning of prestige* (Rede Lecture, Cambridge, 1937); Dean Acheson, *Present at the creation: my years in the State Department* (1969), p. 405; see also J. Ferris, '"The Greatest Power on Earth": Great Britain in the 1920s', *International History Review*, vol. 13 (1991), pp. 726–50.

13 Two books have helped me greatly in developing this argument: E. Ingram, *The beginning of the Great Game in Asia, 1828–1834* (Oxford, 1979), and Phillip Darby, *Three faces of imperialism: British and American approaches to Asia and Africa, 1870–1970* (New Haven, 1987).

14 M. Peters, 'Myth of William Pitt, Earl of Chatham, great imperialist', I, 'Pitt and imperial expansion, 1738–1763', *JICH*, vol. 21 (1993), pp. 31–74.

15 Ingram, *Beginning of the Great Game*, pp. 10–12, 27; C.K. Webster, *Foreign policy of Lord Palmerston, 1830–1841* (1951), vol. II, p. 751.

16 Quoted in W.G. Beasley, *Great Britain and the opening of Japan, 1834–1858* (1951), p. 74.

17 R. Oliver, 'Some factors in the British occupation of East Africa, 1884–1894', *Uganda Journal*, vol. 15 (1951), pp. 49–64; G. Martel, 'Cabinet politics and African partition: Uganda debate reconsidered', *JICH*, vol. 13 (1984), pp. 5–24; J. Darwin, 'Imperialism and the Victorians: the dynamics of territorial expansion', *English Historical Review* (1997), vol. 112, pp. 634–40.

18 N.G. Garson, 'British imperialism and the coming of the Anglo-Boer War', *South African Journal of Economics*, vol. 30 (1962), pp. 140–53; A.N. Porter, *The origins of the South African War: Joseph Chamberlain and the diplomacy of imperialism, 1895–1899* (Manchester, 1980).

19 H.J. Mackinder, *Britain and the British seas* (Oxford, 1907), p. 344.
20 N. Tarling, *Anglo-Dutch rivalry in the Malay world, 1780–1824* (Queensland, 1962), p. 27.
21 Quoted in RH, 'The partition of Africa', *Historical Journal*, vol. 7 (1964), p. 161.
22 H.M. Scott, 'The Second "Hundred Years' War", 1689–1815', *Historical Journal*, vol. 35 (1992), pp. 443–69; C.I. Hamilton, *Anglo-French naval rivalry, 1840–1870* (Oxford, 1993).
23 RH, 'British imperial expansion in the late eighteenth century', *Historical Journal*, vol. 10 (1967), pp. 113–24; 'Imperial interests and the Peace of Paris (1763)', in *Reappraisals in British imperial history* (with Ged Martin, 1975); L.C.F. Turner, 'The Cape of Good Hope and Anglo-French conflict, 1797–1806', *Historical Studies, Australia and New Zealand*, vol. 9 (1961), pp. 368–78.
24 A.M. Roe, 'Australia's place in the "Swing to the East", 1788–1810', *Historical Studies, Australia and New Zealand*, vol. 8 (1957–9), pp. 202–13; A. Frost, *Convicts and empire: a naval question* (Melbourne, 1980); Ged Martin, ed., *The founding of Australia: the argument about Australia's origins* (Sydney, 1978).
25 M. Duffy, *Soldiers, sugar, and seapower: the British expeditions to the West Indies and the war against Revolutionary France* (Chapel Hill, NC, 1987), pp. 21, 385.
26 A.G. Doughty, ed., *The Elgin–Grey Papers, 1846–1852* (Ottawa, 1937), vol. I, p. 166; Ged Martin, *Britain and the origins of Canadian Confederation, 1837–1867* (1995).
27 R. Norris, *The emergent Commonwealth: Australian federation, expectations, and fulfilment, 1889–1910* (Melbourne, 1975).
28 R.L. Watts, *New federations: experiments in the Commonwealth* (Oxford, 1966); see also Louis, *Imperialism at bay*.
29 RH, 'Containing Afrikanerdom: the geopolitical origins of the Central African Federation, 1948–1953', in RH and Peter Henshaw, *The lion and the springbok: Britain and South Africa since the Boer War* (Cambridge, 2003), ch. 9.
30 C.A. Bayly, 'The first age of global imperialism, *c.*1760–1830', in P. Burroughs and A.J. Stockwell, eds., *Managing the business of empire: essays in honour of David Fieldhouse* (1998), repr. from *JCIH*, vol. 26 (1998), pp. 28–47.
31 RH, *Britain's imperial century, 1815–1914: a study of empire and expansion* (2nd edn, 1993; 3rd edn, 2002), pp. 285–90; see also 1st edn (1976), pp. 373–5.
32 J.S. Galbraith, 'The "turbulent frontier" as a factor in British expansion', *Comparative Studies in Society and History*, vol. 2 (1959/60), pp. 150–67.
33 J. Benyon, *Proconsul and paramountcy in South Africa: the High Commission, British supremacy, and the sub-continent, 1806–1910* (Natal, 1980), especially pp. 3–4, 333, 341–2. See also H.L. Wesseling's observation: 'neither the local nor the metropolitan factor alone was decisive – their interaction was' (in S. Förster, W.J. Mommsen, and R.E. Robinson, eds., *Bismarck, Europe,*

and Africa: the Berlin Conference, 1884–1885 (Oxford, 1988), p. 534). The idea of making the diagrams came from G. Arrighi, *Geometria dell' imperialismo* (Milan, 1977), translated by P. Camiller as *The geometry of imperialism: the limits of Hobson's paradigm* (1978).

34 E. Ingram, ed., *Two views of British India: the private correspondence of Mr Dundas and Lord Wellesley, 1798–1801* (Bath, 1970), and *Commitment to empire: prophesies of the Great Game in Asia, 1797–1800* (Oxford, 1981).

35 C.A. Bayly, *Imperial meridian: the British empire and the world, 1780–1830* (1989), and *Indian society and the making of the British empire* (Cambridge, 1988), ch. 3.

36 S.J. Owen, ed., *A selection from the despatches of the Marquess of Wellesley* (Oxford, 1877), pp. 264–5.

37 S.P. Sen, *The French in India, 1763–1816* (Calcutta, 1958); R.A. Huttenback, 'The French threat to India, 1799–1809', *English Historical Review*, vol. 76 (1961), pp. 580–9; G.S. Misra, *British foreign policy and Indian affairs, 1783–1815* (1963).

38 P.J. Marshall, 'Economic and political expansion: the case of Oudh', *Modern Asian Studies*, vol. 9 (1975), pp. 465–82; M.E. Yapp, *Strategies of British India: Britain, Iran, and Afghanistan, 1798–1850* (Oxford, 1980).

39 P. Nightingale, *Trade and empire in western India, 1784–1806* (Cambridge, 1970).

40 Owen, *Despatches of the Marquess of Wellesley*, p. 34, minute 12 August 1798.

41 D. Peers, *Between Mars and Mammon: colonial armies and the garrison state in India, 1819–1835* (1995).

42 R.A. Huttenback, *British imperial experience* (New York, 1966), ch. 7, 'British acquisition of lower Indus Valley', repr. from *Journal of Indian History*, vol. 36 (1958).

43 D.A. Farnie, *East and west of Suez: the Suez Canal in history, 1854–1956* (Oxford, 1969), p. 316.

44 A. Schölch, 'The "men on the spot" and the English occupation of Egypt in 1882', *Historical Journal*, vol. 19 (1976), pp. 773–85.

45 J.S. Galbraith and A.L. Al-Sayyid Marsot, 'The British occupation of Egypt: another view', *International Journal of Middle East Studies*, vol. 9 (1978), pp. 471–88.

46 The best accounts of the partition are R.E. Robinson and J. Gallagher, *Africa and the Victorians: the official mind of imperialism* (1961, 1981), and G.N. Sanderson, 'The European partition of Africa: coincidence or conjuncture', *JCIH*, vol. 3 (1974), repr. in E.F. Penrose, ed., *European imperialism and the partition of Africa* (1975), pp. 1–54.

47 W.O. Aydelotte, *Bismarck and British colonial policy: the problem of South-West Africa, 1883–1885* (Philadelphia, 1937), p. 21.

48 C.W. Newbury, *The Western Slave Coast and its rulers* (Oxford, 1961), pp. 120–1.

49 D.V. McKay, 'Colonialism in the French Geographical Movement, 1871–1881', *Geographical Review*, vol. 33 (1943), pp. 214–30; J.M. MacKenzie, 'The provincial geographical societies in Britain, 1884–1914', in Bell *et al.*,

eds., *Geography and imperialism*; J.D. Hargreaves, *Prelude to the partition of West Africa* (1963).

50 R.E. Robinson and J. Gallagher, 'The partition of Africa', in F.H. Hinsley, ed., *New Cambridge modern history*, vol. XI (Cambridge, 1962), p. 616.

51 Milner to Sir G. Parkin, 28 April 1897, in C. Headlam, ed., *The Milner Papers: South Africa, 1897–1905* (1931), vol. I, p. 42; J.L. Garvin, *The life of Joseph Chamberlain*, vol. III, *1895–1900* (1934), pp. 458–9; J.S. Marais, *The fall of Kruger's Republic* (Oxford, 1961).

52 Three essential contributions are Iain R. Smith, *The origins of the South African War, 1899–1902* (1996), A.N. Porter, 'The South African War (1899–1902) reconsidered', *Journal of African History*, vol. 31 (1990), pp. 43–57, and Peter Henshaw's chapter in *The lion and the springbok*, pp. 37–56 ('Breakdown: into war, 1895–1899').

53 D.K. Fieldhouse, *Economics and empire, 1830–1914* (1973, 1984); A.N. Porter, *European imperialism, 1860–1914* (1994); A.S. Kanya-Forstner, *The conquest of the Western Sudan: a study in French military imperialism* (Cambridge, 1969); R. Aldrich, *French presence in the South Pacific, 1842–1940* (1990); H. Brunschwig, *Mythes et réalités de l'impérialisme colonial française, 1871–1914* (Paris, 1960; English translation, 1966).

54 P.M. Kennedy, *The rise of Anglo-German antagonism, 1860–1914* (1980); H.U. Wehler, 'Bismarck's imperialism, 1862–1890', *Past and Present*, no. 48 (1970), pp. 119–55; H.A. Turner, 'Bismarck's imperialist venture: anti-British in origin?', in P. Gifford and W.R. Louis, eds., *Britain and Germany in Africa: imperial rivalry and colonial rule* (New Haven, CT, 1967), pp. 47–82.

55 D. Gillard, *The struggle for Asia, 1828–1914: a study in British and Russian imperialism* (1977); D. Mackenzie, 'Russian expansion in Central Asia: St Petersburg versus the Turkestan generals', *Canadian Slavic Studies*, vol. 3 (1969), pp. 286–311; R.A. Pierce, *Russian Central Asia, 1867–1917* (Berkeley, CA, 1960); D. Geyer, *Russian imperialism 1860–1914* (translation 1987).

56 D. Atkinson, 'Geopolitics, cartography, and geographical knowledge: envisioning Africa from Fascist Italy', in Bell *et al.*, eds., *Geography and imperialism*; D. Mack Smith, *Mussolini's Roman empire* (1976).

57 Darby, *Three faces of imperialism*, part 3; W.R. Louis and R.E. Robinson, 'The imperialism of decolonization', *JICH*, vol. 22 (1994), pp. 462–511.

58 W.G. Beasley, *Japanese imperialism, 1894–1945* (Oxford, 1987).

59 R.H. Myers and M.R. Peattie, eds., *The Japanese colonial empire, 1895–1945* (Princeton, NJ, 1984); M.R. Peattie, 'The Japanese empire, 1895–1945', in P. Duus, ed., *Cambridge history of Japan* (Cambridge, 1988), vol. VI, pp. 217–70.

60 H.J. Mackinder, 'The geographical pivot of history', *Geographical Journal*, vol. 23 (1904), pp. 421–44; *Democratic ideals and reality: a study in the politics of reconstruction* (1919). For commentary, see C. Kruszewski, 'The pivot of history', *Foreign Affairs*, vol. 32 (1954), pp. 388–401; B.W. Blouet, *Halford Mackinder: a biography* (College Station, TX, 1987); P.M. Kennedy, *Rise and fall of British naval mastery* (1976), ch. 7, 'Mahan versus Mackinder'.

61 W.R. Louis, *In the name of God go! Leo Amery and the British empire in the*

age of Churchill (New York, 1992), pp. 54, 68–9, 77, 86–7; L.S. Amery, *My political life* (1953), vol. I, *England before the storm, 1896–1914*, pp. 228–9.

62 M. Howard, *The continental commitment: the dilemmas of British defence policy in the era of the two World Wars* (1972), pp. 65–72.

63 Amery, *My political life*, vol. II, *War and peace, 1914–1929*, p. 115.

64 I. Friedman, *The Palestine question: British–Jewish–Arab relations, 1914–1918* (1973); W.R. Louis, *Great Britain and Germany's lost colonies, 1914–1919* (Oxford, 1967).

65 W.R. Louis, *The British empire in the Middle East, 1945–1951: Arab nationalism, the United States, and post-war imperialism* (Oxford, 1984); 'British imperialism and the end of the Palestine Mandate', in W.R. Louis and R.W. Stookey, eds., *The end of the Palestine Mandate* (Austin, TX, 1986), pp. 1–31.

66 Louis, *British strategy in the Far East*; W.D. McIntyre, *Rise and fall of Singapore Naval Base, 1919–1942* (1979); N.H. Gibbs, *Grand strategy*, vol. I, *Rearmament policy*, in *History of the Second World War, UK Military Series* (HMSO, 1976); L.R. Pratt, *East of Malta, west of Suez: Britain's Mediterranean crisis, 1936–1939* (Cambridge, 1975).

67 W.R. Louis, 'Appeasement and the colonies, 1936–1938', *Révue Belge de Philologie et Histoire*, vol. 49 (1971), pp. 1175–91.

68 N. Mansergh *et al.*, eds., *Transfer of power in India*, vol. V (HMSO, 1974), p. 620, and vol. VIII (1979), p. 51.

69 Viscount Alanbrooke, *Triumph in the West, 1943–46* (1959), p. 533.

70 Louis, *British empire in the Middle East*, pp. 107–9; RH, ed., *The Labour government and the end of empire, 1945–1951*, pt III, in *British Documents on the End of Empire Project* (HMSO, 1992), pp. 207–29.

71 Philip Murphy, *Party politics and decolonization: the Conservative Party and British colonial policy in tropical Africa, 1951–1964* (Oxford, 1995), pp. 30–1, 227.

72 RH, ed., *Labour government and the end of empire*, pt II, pp. 329 (CAB 129/25, CP(48)72, 3 March 1948).

73 C.R. Attlee, *As it happened* (1954), p. 190.

74 For further development of this argument see RH, 'Winds of change: the empire and Commonwealth', in W. Kaiser and G. Staerck, eds., *In search of a role: British foreign policy, 1955–1964* (1999), pp. 190–208.

75 Macmillan to Menzies, 8 February 1962, Prime Minister's Office, PREM 11/3644, T 51–62.

76 Cabinet memorandum, 24 February 1960, CAB 129/100, C(60)35.

77 Macleod, minute to Macmillan, 6 January 1961, PREM 11/4083, M 15/16.

78 Discussion in Foreign Office, 16 May 1961, FO 371/154740, no. 59.

79 B.R. Tomlinson, *Political economy of the Raj, 1914–1947: the economics of decolonization in India* (1979).

80 R.L. Tignor, 'Decolonization and business: the case of Egypt', *Journal of Modern History*, vol. 59 (1987), pp. 479–505; N.J. White, 'Government and business divided: Malaya, 1945–1957', *JICH*, vol. 22 (1994), pp. 251–74; Murphy, *Party politics and decolonization*, pp. 26, 118; Alan James, *Britain and the Congo Crisis, 1960–1963* (1996), p. 31.

81 J.S. Garner, *The Commonwealth Office, 1925–1968* (1978), p. 344.
82 Memorandum by Macleod, 3 January 1961, CAB 134/1560, CPC(61)1.
83 Sir J. Macpherson to Sir T. Lloyd, 18 January 1952, CO 554/298, no. 13.
84 Letter from Turnbull to Gorell Barnes, 12 May 1959, CO 822/1449, no. 229.
85 Y. Lacoste, 'The sea and key geopolitical changes: the Falklands', in P. Girot and E. Kofman, eds., *International geopolitical analysis: a selection from 'Hérodote'* (1987), pp. 46–58.
86 Louis, *Imperialism at bay*, p. 569.

2 The partition of Africa: geopolitical and internal perspectives

[Most historians have a fondness for their first published work, though few would be able to eclipse Sir Geoffrey Elton, who astonished readers of his collected essays (1974) on Tudor political history by kicking off with a paper on 'The terminal date of Caesar's Gallic proconsulate' (reprinted from *Journal of Roman Studies*, vol. 36, 1946).

My first publication was a review article entitled 'The partition of Africa' (*Historical Journal*, vol. 7, 1964), a subject which I have revisited more than once. Instead of reprinting this, what follows is a chapter from *Britain's imperial century* (2nd edn 1991, 3rd edn 2001), which develops more fully some of the major themes tentatively put forward in the original essay. It has been lightly revised.]

You may roughly divide the nations of the world as the living and the dying . . . In these [dying] states, disorganisation and decay are advancing almost as fast as concentration and increasing power are advancing in the living nations that stand beside them . . . the weak states are becoming weaker and the strong states are becoming stronger . . . For one reason or another – from the necessities of politics or under the pretence of philanthropy, the living nations will gradually encroach on the territory of the dying, and the seeds and causes of conflict among civilised nations will speedily appear . . . These things may introduce causes of fatal difference between the great nations whose mighty armies stand opposed threatening each other.[1]

No historian has ever succeeded in improving on this description, made by Lord Salisbury, of the atmosphere in which the partition of Africa took place. As an analysis of its causes, it directs attention unerringly to the geopolitical disequilibrium of power which made the acquisition of territory possible in Africa; it is rooted in the European considerations which conditioned ministerial thinking; it warns us not to pay too much attention to the rhetoric of philanthropy.

One of the first events to focus public attention on Africa was Samuel Baker's expedition to the Sudan, 1869 to 1873. In 1876 King Leopold of the Belgians began his Congo enterprise. France made forward moves in Senegal in 1879. In 1881 France occupied Tunisia, and in 1882 Britain occupied Egypt. In April 1884 Bismarck annexed

Angra Pequena (German South-West Africa), German East Africa, the Cameroons, and Togoland. Britain declared a Somaliland protectorate. In December 1884 the Berlin Conference apportioned the Congo and Lower Niger regions. In 1885 Britain declared protectorates over Bechuanaland and the Oil Rivers (Nigeria), and a year later chartered George Goldie's Niger Company. In 1889 the British South Africa Company was chartered to secure Rhodesia. In 1890, by the Anglo-German 'Heligoland' Treaty, British interests in Uganda, Zanzibar, Pemba Island, Witu, and Nyasaland were secured. In 1894 Rosebery's Cabinet declared a protectorate of Uganda, and in 1895 took over the Kenya area as well from the Imperial British East Africa Company. In 1896 Asante was likewise declared a British protectorate. In 1898 the Sudan was reconquered and an Anglo-Egyptian condominium set up over it in the following year. Two large Nigerian protectorates were organised in 1899.

I

Explanations of the partition are legion. There is no agreement among historians as to when it began, or who began it. The view taken here is that it was not Britain who initiated it, but that when other countries (France and Germany in particular) decided to embark on territorial acquisition, it was impossible for Britain to stand aside if it wished to protect its interests. The opportunity – as well as the necessity – for taking territory arose out of the widespread breakdown or stagnation of indigenous political and economic systems. It is easy to condemn extension of Western rule as sheer acquisitiveness. But the brutal alternative would have been rule by irresponsible European adventurers, armed with all the resources of their civilisation to work their selfish will as they wished, without any superior control at all.

Africa in the last thirty years of the nineteenth century was a notable example of what Sir Edward Grey described as an area 'in a position of minimum stability', or, as a modern political scientist might describe it, of 'power vacuum'. The collapse of the Turkish empire in North Africa was accompanied by a variety of movements further south. Some African authorities were seriously weakened, but there were also some expanding African powers on the upgrade, notably the Ethiopians, the Baganda, the Lozi, and the Ndebele. In Buganda, for example, sixty raids by land and water are recorded for the twenty-seven years of Mutesa's reign down to 1884. And in the next four years, Buganda was in almost continuous war with Nyoro. Africa was a much-disturbed continent. Islam was widely reviving and pursuing its own expansionist policy.

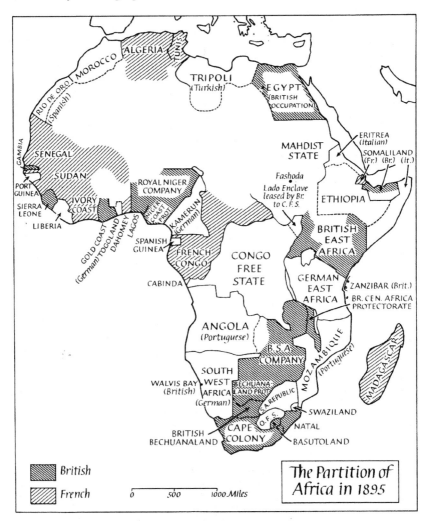

Map 2.1 The partition of Africa in 1895.

If the partition had been delayed even thirty years, most of Africa to the north of the Zambesi might have passed into the world of Islam. Sir Richard Burton predicted a Muslim conquest of the continent. Rivalries in Africa were not simply between Europeans. In one sense the partition of Africa was a device to contain or counteract the expansion of militant Islam, which the British as well as the French feared greatly. Partition could be described as a struggle for control of north, west, and central

Africa between Christian European and Muslim Arab-Africans. By 1880 politicians in Paris and London had begun to talk of a dangerous pan-Islamic conspiracy, a fanatical Muslim resurgence, giving the slave trade a new lease of life. The most famous events in the Islamic revival were Urabi's rising in Egypt, the revolt of the Mahdi in the Sudan, and the persecution of Christian missionaries and their followers in Buganda in 1884–6. It was thought that the Mahdist *jihad* was precursor of a general and formidable offensive movement through the Islamic world. There was certainly a later parallel in Somaliland, where the so-called Mad Mullah was in rebellion (1899–1904 and 1908–20). As far as the West African situation is concerned, Kanya-Forstner has shown how fear of Muslim resistance and determination to crush it had dominated French military thinking for almost half a century by 1890.[2] Britain's Lugard was vitally interested in controlling and limiting Islam. This fear of Islam provided one reason for keeping Uganda. Uganda was important to British interests throughout north and south-central Africa as a Christian state – for it seemed definitely to have thrown in its lot with Christianity as the new 'established' religion. Buganda was one of the few states to experience a 'Christian revolution', and already had more than thirty martyrs by 1886. It was therefore not likely to originate any fanatical Muslim movement, but instead could form a barrier against the spread of any such movement as might arise, and perhaps be a means of spreading Christianity to the surrounding areas. Likewise Nyasaland, in the opinion of officials in the Foreign Office, could not be abandoned, because the Arabs would make it their stronghold and the consequences would be disastrous. Retention of these two states seemed to produce the desired result. In 1905 Sir Charles Eliot, sometime governor of Kenya, wrote of Uganda: 'In view of the power which Islam has shown of spreading among African races, and the damage done on the Upper Nile by the Khalifa and the Dervishes, the existence of this Christian state must be regarded as a great guarantee for the preservation of peace.'[3]

Africa had one widely occurring asset of international significance: ivory. Competition for ivory was the cause not only of ecological degradation but of political instability. By the 1820s ivory had entered a phase of unprecedented popularity in Europe for an extraordinary range of industrial products and decorative arts. Its principal uses were as billiard balls, knife handles, and piano keys. Only the finest quality would do for billiard balls. One tusk would yield no more than three top-grade billiard balls – and a single manufacturer was reputed to keep 30,000 balls in stock. In fact so refined was the marketing of billiard balls that by the end of the nineteenth century they sold in Britain in twelve different grades. As for cutlery, Rodgers of Sheffield consumed about twenty tons

Table 2.1. *British imports of ivory, 1827–1900 (cwt)*

1827	3,000 ⎱	into London only: the total British figure
1850	8,000 ⎰	would be higher
1890	14,349	
1895	10,911	
1900	9,889	

of ivory a year. But there were all manner of lesser uses, from crucifixes to dildoes, chess sets and cribbage pegs, doorhandles and napkin rings, sealing punches, and umbrella handles. Ivory was also used as an inlay to furniture and gun butts. Even the chips and the dust could be used in polishes and the preparation of Indian ink; there was even a food called ivory jelly. Peak imports were reached by 1890. (See Table 2.1.)[4]

London was the principal centre for the distribution of ivory in Europe for most of the nineteenth century, until Belgium became a competitor, as the outlet of King Leopold's Congo venture. But there was also a Muslim and Asian demand for African ivory. (Indian elephants have poor tusks, and only one per cent of Sri Lankan elephants even have tusks.) The Asian market pre-dated – and outlived – European demand. Probably in the nineteenth century, in fact, *most* African ivory went to India, the Middle East, China, and Japan, with Zanzibar and Egypt dividing the export approximately evenly between them. In Asia the particular uses were to make bangles for Hindu and Muslim weddings and Chinese and Japanese name-stamps. By 1870 Africa, and especially East Africa, supplied 85 per cent of the world's total ivory consumption.

Wild rubber grew in central Africa, and from the 1870s world demand created a sensational boom, until the world rubber market collapsed after 1914. Rubber was second only to ivory in bringing central Africa into the world economy, and it supplied one-third of the world's demand. These hunting and gathering activities tended to be very destructive. But there were other ecological problems as well. Simultaneously throughout southern Africa the cattle trade was also expanding rapidly. The Boer pastoral economy moved north, its herds increasing all the time. By 1886 the Boers were interested in crossing the Limpopo in a new Great Trek. The movement of armed bands of Boers in the wake of the droughts of the 1870s caused turmoil in many African societies. The whole of southern and central Africa suffers periodic droughts, with the droughts spanning a number of consecutive years. This dismal ecological fact had been a main cause of institutionalised cattle-raiding and enslavement among African states. Inevitably the resultant famines were followed by locusts, smallpox, typhoid, and rinderpest. The movement of white men was responsible for further ecological degradation. Waggon-trains along the fringes of the Khalahari desert destroyed the grassland, while wheel ruts caused erosion. But even this was preferable to what was to follow with the coming of the railways. Their wood-burning locomotives caused deforestation along the lines of rail, at least until coal replaced wood in the twentieth century. But then again, coalmines (like all other mines) consumed huge quantities of timber.[5]

II

The breakdown of control in Africa made it difficult to obtain economic advantages from the continent. Chamberlain defended the expedition against King Prempe of Asante in 1895 as necessary, because since the mid-1870s the Gold Coast area, which was:

certainly rich in natural resources – has been devastated, destroyed, and ruined by inter-tribal disputes, and especially by the evil government of the authorities of Ashanti . . . I think the duty of this country in regard to all these savage countries over which we are called upon to exercise some sort of dominion is to establish, at the earliest possible date, *Pax Britannica*, and force these people to keep the peace amongst themselves . . . The people are not a bad people. The natives are, on the whole, perfectly willing to work . . . but in such cases as that we are considering, the government is so atrociously bad that they are not allowed to do so. No man is safe in the enjoyment of his own property, and as long as that is the case, no one has any inducement to work.[6]

Warfare between Africans imposed severe handicaps on European trading. For example, early in 1879 many roads in Sierra Leone were closed by internal wars, and the number of caravans visiting Freetown dropped by 80 per cent. Rivalries among African rulers were complicated by European traders who sought to draw business to their own establishments, and to avoid customs duties; they, in turn, drew in the governments. The condition of Africa was potentially dangerous. The local claims which were being staked out became increasingly entangled and confused. British politicians were worried lest the Africans, being divided among themselves and indulging frequently in petty wars, should tend to support one of the adjacent or overlapping incipient European spheres of influence (often emerging out of economic pressures, but sometimes as a result of missionary activity) against the other; and that the Africans, by fighting one another partly on the basis of allegiance to rival European interests, might lead Europeans on the spot to fight each other as well, and so ultimately perhaps embroil the European powers themselves in war. This was the constant fear at the back of the mind of governments. It was nourished by the large number of small incidents occurring between Europeans, and by risings and disturbances against Europeans, at the end of the nineteenth century, as well as by the classic example of missionary entanglement with local politics in Buganda. Salisbury's analysis quoted above provides the vital clue to the British motive in the partition. To prevent European conflict was a major reason for the partition. Only by imposing a strict control on the chaotic power vacuum could European powers feel safe from future disaster. Despite acute – but in fact peaceful – rivalry, European powers generally acted in political co-operation. There is support for this thesis in a book by a distinguished Victorian historian, W.E.H. Lecky, *Democracy and liberty* (1899):

Experience has already shown how easily these vague and ill-defined boundaries may become a new cause of European quarrels, and how often, in remote African jungles or forests, negroes armed with European guns may inflict defeats on European soldiers which will become the cause of costly and difficult wars.[7]

At first the widespread absence of formal European governmental control enabled European adventurers and concession-hunters to pursue their rivalries without much restraint. Lugard and others pointed out the dire results of leaving vast areas of Africa in a state of indefinite and dangerous suspense, with firearms flooding in, with traditional rule violated, and no new system of control to take its place.

The unrestricted arms trade was one of the most serious problems. As European weapons improved in the 1860s and 1870s, especially with the introduction of repeating rifles, so vast quantities of obsolete guns were thrown on to the African market. The volume of this arms traffic must have been immense. In addition, by 1907 Birmingham may have made 20 million guns for the African market. It has been estimated for the German and British areas of East Africa *alone* that between 1885 and 1902 something like a million firearms and more than 4 million pounds (weight) of gunpowder entered the region. Even by 1880 firearms seem to have been more than one-third of the total imports of Zanzibar. Estimates have been made which suggest that the Lozi of Barotseland had about 2,300 guns by 1875, the king of the Nyoro 2,000 by 1888, the kabaka of Buganda somewhere between 6,000 and 9,000 by 1890. Menelik of Ethiopia had about 100,000 guns with which to defeat the Italians at Aduwa in 1896. By 1896 the Shona and Ndebele probably had 10,000 guns of considerable variety. In 1904 the Herero were said to have 5,000 modern breech-loaders. The Pedi had 4,000 guns by 1860, and held Boer commandos at bay until 1876, while the Zulu had at least 8,000 by 1879. Guns penetrated some South African societies deeply. The Venda traded guns to the Shona, teaching them how to manufacture ammunition and to repair the weapons. In Basutoland a virtual mania to possess them developed; attempted disarmament was a dominant issue in the Sotho rebellion in 1880. In the last nine months of 1873 more than 18,000 guns were imported into Griqualand West. The diamond- and gold-fields were major points of distribution. They in turn were largely supplied from Lourenço Marques – 15,000 guns were sold from there to Africans in the interior between January and October 1875; by 1879, 20,000 percussion guns, 300 breech-loading rifles, and 10,000 barrels of gunpowder were sold there annually, the Zulu and Shangaan being major buyers. This caused much anxiety in Natal and the Transvaal, and it was one of the main incentives to the confederation schemes of the 1870s. Firearms were sold in mining camps in order to attract labour.

A Colonial Office memorandum prepared by A.A. Pearson in 1879 indicated this official anxiety about arms in South Africa, recording wide agreement that the traffic could only be stopped by co-operation between all European governments from Walvis Bay to the mouth of the Zambesi. With extraordinary accuracy Pearson prophesied that unless they could prevent the Ndebele getting arms, their eagerness to obtain them was such that 'we may in twenty years time, or less, find ourselves engaged in another equally serious Zulu war'. Kimberley as colonial secretary was working for an agreement between the British, the French, the Portuguese, and Liberia to prohibit the introduction of arms and ammunition in West Africa, in order to diminish the constant petty wars and disturbances. But there were always two difficulties in such proposals. The first was simply that of obtaining agreement between the parties. The second was that it was a matter of legitimate debate whether or not such a prohibition, if achieved, was really wise. It could always be argued that guns were useful for hunting and crop protection, that they shortened wars and therefore the numbers of deaths, and that Africans should be allowed, or at least not prevented from having, arms with which to protect themselves and their lands. Otherwise it could come about that pro-British chiefs, such as Khama of the Bangwato, were under-provided with arms, whereas the 'unfriendly' Lobengula might obtain large quantities of them from the Boers. By the end of the 1880s, however, opinion had swung towards the necessity of control. An old gas-pipe type of gun might plausibly be said to be less bloody than the assegai, but breech-loaders, and even more superior weapons available at nominal prices, were giving fresh life to the gun-runners of South Africa. By 1889 a blockade was in force to prevent the importation of arms and gunpowder from Somaliland to Pemba Island. The General Act of the Brussels Conference in 1890 arranged for agreed steps to be taken to

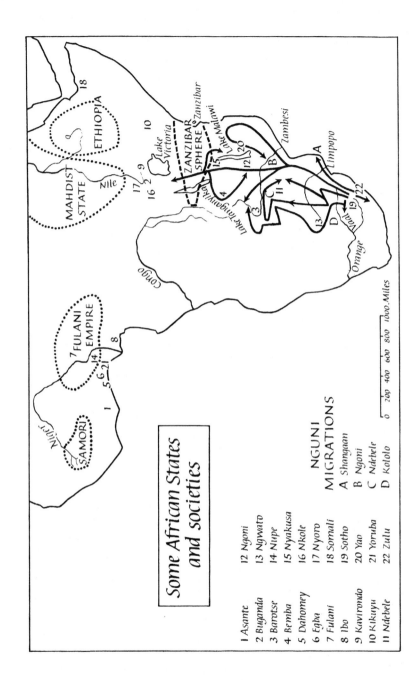

Some African States and societies

1 Asante	12 Ngoni
2 Buganda	13 Ngwato
3 Barotse	14 Nupe
4 Bemba	15 Nyakusa
5 Dahomey	16 Nkole
6 Egba	17 Nyoro
7 Fulani	18 Somali
8 Ibo	19 Sotho
9 Kavirondo	20 Yao
10 Kikuyu	21 Yoruba
11 Ndebele	22 Zulu

NGUNI MIGRATIONS

A Shangaan
B Ngoni
C Ndebele
D Kololo

Map 2.2 Some African states and societies.

diminish inland wars between Africans, by means of arbitration and by
the prohibition of the import of the firearms between 20°N and 22°S,
that is to say, in all tropical Africa as far south as the Limpopo.[8]

A close look at Africa in the last thirty years of the nineteenth century
suggests that Europeans were indulging not only in gun-running but in
concession-hunting on a big scale. There was widespread and intensi-
fying rivalry between localised European economic interests. In fact,
the most conspicuous and characteristic feature of the scramble on the
spot was concession-hunting, as it had been in Egypt and as it was to
be in China. The Congo was an outstanding example, though there
it followed Leopold's annexation rather than preceded it. Europeans
committed atrocities in the Congo at an early stage: thirty-two Africans
were tortured and executed for alleged incendiarism in 1879 – which
shows how fragile was the basis of law and order on the Zaïre River. In
Swaziland the tangle of overlapping concessions was so serious as eventually to compel compulsory expropriation and land apportionment by
a British government. King Mbandzeni conceded in land alone more
than the total area of his kingdom, and sold all his private revenues to
John Harrington in 1889 for £12,000 a year. He even conceded the right
to concede concessions – the culmination of concessions for mining,
minting, tanning, for collecting customs and importing machinery, for
oil and tobacco, for the right to establish everything from glassworks
to pawnbrokers', from soda-water factories to orphanages, the right to
hold auctions and sweepstakes, to take photographs and set up billiard
tables and law courts. John Thorburn obtained a concession to build a
hotel for the concession-hunters. Not unnaturally Swazi folklore came to
speak of the 'documents that killed us'.[9] In such circumstances British
officials were inclined to think that it would be better for the Swazi and
other peoples to be taken over even by a formal Transvaal administration
than by a set of wild or seedy adventurers. In backing Rhodes, Hercules
Robinson (as high commissioner) argued that he could 'check the inroad
of adventurers', since the rush of concessionaires to Matabeleland had
'produced a condition of affairs dangerous to the peace of that country'.
The first concession from Lobengula was the grant of mining rights to
Sir John Swinburne in 1869 in the Tati area to the extreme south-west
of Matabeleland. Rhodes secured his own foothold by the concession
negotiated by C.D. Rudd in 1888, by which Lobengula granted away
his mining rights in return for a thousand Martini-Henry rifles and
100,000 rounds of ammunition. This covered a wider area than the
Tati concession, but unlike it, did not involve sovereign rights. The
charter of the British South Africa Company could not in fact have
been granted if there had not been concessions obtained from African

Plate 2.1 Swazi deputation in London, 1923. Left to right: Benjamin Nxumalo, Mandanda Mtetwa, Amos Zwane, King Sobhuza II, Loshini Hlope, Suduka Dhlamini, Sol Plaatje, and Pixley Seme (the two legal advisers from the ANC). Sobhuza was installed as Ngwenyama on the last day of 1921, and immediately began planning a deputation to present Swazi grievances in London. A petition by 'the King and Council of Swaziland' was submitted to the high commissioner, 30 May 1922. It laid claim to Swazi independence, and challenged the validity of the land apportionment proclamation (1907), which had recognised two-thirds of Mbandzeni's overlapping concessions, but converted leaseholds into copyholds, depriving the Swazi of formerly reserved rights of occupation, grazing, and tillage (CO 417/681, no. 30892). The deputation left South Africa in mid-December and returned in February 1923. A test-case on the lands dispute and an appeal in 1924 failed. *Source*: the store at Malkerns, Swaziland (1970).

chiefs. The charter gave permission to certain British subjects to exercise any rights that African chiefs had conceded or might concede. Because Matabeleland and Mashonaland were reputedly rich in gold, speculators rushed in: German, Portuguese, Transvaalers and Cape Colonists bartered gin and rifles with Lobengula for mineral rights. Lobengula was seriously alarmed by the influx of concession-seekers by 1888.

Petty adventurers without political aspirations helped to upset the balance and produced friction on many frontiers – men like Carl Weise, a German-Jewish elephant hunter who became a political power in

Ngoniland in Zambia. In Nyasaland, taking advantage of African trust-fulness, ingenuousness, and inexperience, individuals and companies obtained ownership of land on which large numbers of Africans lived and tilled the soil. John Buchanan, a coffee planter, bought 3,065 acres in the future city of Blantyre for a gun, thirty-two yards of calico, two red caps, and several other tiny items. Sir Harry Johnston had to make a report in 1892 after a survey of land claims. He noted that some claim-ants had obtained thirty, forty, or fifty square miles of territory with exclusive rights of mining and road-making. He sorted this out, but left the Africans in control of no more than two-fifths of the total land area of Nyasaland. It has been concluded on the basis of a study of Ruanda-Urundi that by 1890 the scramble for East Africa threatened to become uncontrollable. Concession claims became increasingly entangled, and any solution might rapidly have become impossible. The explorer H.M. Stanley in particular may have aggravated the situation. Britain used Stanley's treaties for all they were worth, and perhaps much more than they were worth. Regardless of economic value, competition for scraps of territory increased. Ruanda-Urundi was the object of much European bickering down to the 1910 Kivu-Mfumbiro Conference.

Sometimes local administrations were in private hands. It was this fact which generated intense Anglo-German friction in East Africa after 1887. Lord Granville as foreign secretary in 1885 explained to the German government how 'unnecessary complications' must unavoid-ably result from imposing no check over the action of individuals, and even officials, in such distant places. Sir William Vernon Harcourt in the same year complained that British agents were getting Britain into difficulties in every quarter of the globe. Lord Salisbury plainly feared the growing chaos in Africa. He worried about British officials with pro-consular pretensions, but he was even more apprehensive of European adventurers, doubting the possibility of effectively restraining them: 'It is impossible to prevent the danger of collisions, which might be mur-derous and bloody.' In South Africa for this reason he was anxious to obtain agreement with Portugal, whose agents were especially active in seeking concessions. Anarchy was undoubtedly endemic in many areas of southern Africa.[10]

In West Africa French and British firms behaved more aggressively towards one another after 1875, when France deliberately tried to break into the richer and British-dominated markets, especially on the Niger and Oil Rivers between 1880 and 1883. There were fears too that de Brazza would move north and seize the Ibo palm-oil producing lands of the hinterland. More European traders had been brought in by the steamship, while African merchants had also begun to compete. The increasingly difficult economic situation of the 1870s led to strains, misunderstandings, and conflicts between all the participants. There was a sharp drop in prices for palm oil in the mid-1880s. In this crisis a trade war was fought out in Lagos among Europeans, and with African traders and producers, in an attempt to pass on as much of their losses as possible. As Professor Hopkins has established, of twelve European firms in Lagos in 1880, only five remained in 1892, and two of these were present in name only. Merchants pressed for political action to resolve economic conflicts. This was not a simple question of the government being 'manipulated' by traders. It made its own decisions in the light of what it assessed were the national interests of British commerce, and it made them from a fundamental belief in the hopelessness of achieving improvement by relying any more on African agency. Hence the establishment of the Oil Rivers Protectorate of 1885 and the chartering of the Royal Niger Company in 1886.[11]

Colin Newbury has drawn attention to the intense commercial rivalry on the west coast in the 1870s and 1880s. Local disputes arising from differential customs zones, sometimes operating in a protective manner (against German or French spirits in British areas, and against British cloth and arms in French and German areas), created, he believes, a situation only to be remedied by the 'rationalisation' of partition: the impulse to extend European rule over the interior came mainly from local traders, supported by commercial and shipping interests in Europe.[12] Both Britain and France wanted to extend the area of their customs collection, either to raise more revenue or to assert sovereignty or title, and every sign of an advance by one power was usually counterbalanced by a move from its rival. For example, Gouldsbury's expedition up the Gambia River (1881), prompted by Rowe's desire for a counter-demonstration against French policy, had the effect of accelerating the French penetration of Fouta Djallon. Salisbury suggested to the French ambassador, Waddington, that the cause of many territorial disputes in West Africa might be removed by an agreement to assimilate French and British tariffs along the coast. The French were very aware that Salisbury's main preoccupation was the effect of a conflict between French protectionist policy and British commercial interests. This fear of potential foreign tariffs was deep-rooted. With so many eager competitors in the field, *The Times* felt, Britain could not afford to neglect any country likely to yield new opportunities for commercial enterprise. Ministers and officials might not have gone so far as this, but even Lord Derby as colonial secretary drew a distinction between keeping what was threatened and wanting new acquisitions. As the Francophobe head of the African department of the Foreign Office (1883–96), Sir Percy Anderson,[13] put it in 1883, British trade in West Africa must not be placed at the mercy of French officials, partly because this would increase France's political and military power: 'Protectorates are unwelcome burdens, but in this case, it is . . . a question between British protectorates, which would be unwelcome, and French protectorates, which would be fatal. Protectorates, of one sort or another, are the inevitable outcome of the situation.'[14]

III

That the established on-the-spot British interest in West Africa was basically a trading interest is unlikely to be contested. More controversial is the nature of British interest in East Africa. Analysis of Clement Hill's Foreign Office memoranda reveals a strong economic interest here too, though Gladstone complained that Hill's attitude savoured of 'annexationism'. Since the slave trade had been checked, commerce had made great strides. Hill contended that the region was rich in minerals, that cereals could be grown and cattle raised with success. He pointed to an excellent climate in the mountain ranges of Kilimanjaro and Kenya. He posed the question whether, in view of French trading rivalry on the west coast, it might not be better to exploit the commercial possibilities of the east coast instead. Consul Holmwood also urged the commercial possibilities. Colonists might grow rice, coffee, sugar, wheat, and fruit, and supplement a trade tapping ivory, wax, iron, and hides. The imports of Zanzibar increased from £500,000 in 1875 to £850,000 in 1884, and exports from £600,000 to £1,000,000 in the same period. The hinterland might fall to the sultan of Zanzibar; 'the healthiest, and perhaps, the most valuable portion of East Africa' was around Kilimanjaro. Outside pressure came from men, many of them powerful, such as Lord Aberdare, Mackinnon, Baron Rothschild, Jacob Bright (brother of John), who regarded East Africa as a new Australia as well as a new India, and a place of potential for Manchester goods. Lugard argued that Uganda, as an El Dorado, should 'be secured at all costs' (1891). The Germans also saw it as an El Dorado, and although the British gained a large field for enterprise they had to sacrifice Kilimanjaro.

There were of course other considerations, essentially geopolitical in nature. As Clement Hill defined them these were the importance of the Cape route to India, and the existing trading connection between India and the east coast, especially at Zanzibar; the intrusion of a foreign power could damage both. There was also the fact of a Muslim population on the coast with a connection with co-religionists in Sudan, the Red Sea area, and the Persian Gulf, which, 'if not close, is none the less real'. He emphasised the desirability of Britain exercising 'a preponderating influence' over these Islamic and Indian elements.[15] But there was also the commercial potentiality, though this was not pressed by Zanzibar merchants. East Africa had been made much more accessible after the opening of the Suez Canal in 1869. British desire for cloves, tea, coffee, and ivory was strong.

Nevertheless, strategy was what mattered in the East African acquisitions, and especially in Uganda. The east coast was strategically significant, as Foreign Secretary Granville minuted in 1884: 'Its annexation by France or Germany, and the seizure of a port would be ruinous to British . . . influence on the East Coast. The proceedings of the French in Madagascar make it all the more necessary to guard . . . our sea route to India.'[16] By which he meant the Cape route. What gave this consideration enhanced force was the laying of the cable linking Cape Town and Zanzibar, Seychelles, and Mauritius. This reached Zanzibar in 1879 and Mauritius by the early 1890s. It was intended to be Britain's first line of communication with India and the fleet in eastern waters in time of war. In view of the strength of France in the area – annexing Madagascar in 1893 – it was expected that many ships would be required for the protection of the route. Zanzibar, as the turning point for the cable across the Indian Ocean, had to be held at all costs (Map 1, p. 20). It was almost equally as important to secure Mombasa – the only decent port (apart from Portuguese Lourenço Marques) north of Durban – for the use of the ships required to protect and repair the cable. No one expected that the Suez Canal could remain operational in wartime, if only because of prohibitive insurance premiums on ships and cargoes. So it became 'an object of supreme importance that we should retain complete command of the only alternative and only feasible route in case of war' (Lugard).[17] Even in peacetime the Cape route continued to carry 37 per cent of the total value of British trade with the East.

When Lord Rosebery as prime minister made the decision to keep Uganda, the strategic argument for controlling the Nile headwaters was kept in view, and the Uganda railway (the purpose of which was troop movement) was built on the same gauge as Egyptian railways, in case a link were ever to be made. The strategic case could be presented by reference to two other considerations. Uganda was 'the paradise of slave-dealers', and if they were given back their 'happy hunting-ground', Britain would be 'guilty of a grave and perhaps criminal dereliction of duty'. Moreover, withdrawal would also involve the massacre of Christians, with an effect on the public mind comparable to that produced by the fall of Khartoum in 1885. Acting for the Imperial British East Africa Company, Lugard had entered Buganda in 1890, and two years later, in alliance with the Protestants, defeated the kabaka Mwanga and the Roman Catholics. This dominant and victorious Protestant Christian elite secured its own position by alliance with Britain – an alliance valuable to both, especially against their mutual enemy, the Baganda Muslims. Uganda was retained in 1894 with British public opinion clearly pronouncing in favour on account of the Christian stake there, although it seems clear that public support was inspired by the government, who asked their mission societies to whip up a campaign.[18]

'British prestige' was a significant motive in the partition of Africa, as it had been in the occupation of Egypt. Sir Percy Anderson, *éminence grise* of the British part in the partition, saw the scramble mainly as a problem of maintaining British power and prestige in an increasingly hostile world, though to this end he seems to have thought that Manchester should be stirred to look after its interests. He favoured counter-moves against every French and German advance. Professor Sanderson's monumental investigation of activities on the Upper Nile leads convincingly to the conclusion that at the turn of the year 1898–9 considerations of national prestige and territorial possession were more decisive than any supposed imperial defence strategy on the headwaters of the Nile. The condominium of the Sudan went far beyond anything required by the latter consideration, but was necessary because the British public wanted a tangible reward for its exertions and regarded Gordon and Kitchener as heroes to be honoured. Moreover, it would seem that, ultimately, the quarrel between Britain and France which culminated in 1898 at Fashoda was not about the security of Egypt and the Nile, but about the relative geopolitical status of the two powers. Fashoda has to be seen in the context of the British plan to assert control over the whole of the Sudan. 'The national or acquisitional feeling has been aroused,' lamented Salisbury in 1897.[19]

Perhaps the clearest example of running up the flag purely from an unalloyed desire to keep the foreigner out comes from South Africa. The fear of Germany in this region was very strong. The Victorians had been unnerved by German seizure of the Cameroons. 'Predatory proceedings', Derby called them. It was suspected that Bismarck would then try for St Lucia Bay, which might lead him formally into the Transvaal if appealed to as protector. In the Colonial Office it was feared that 'a hostile cordon drawn round the Cape from Angra Pequena to Zululand would effectually cripple us'. One official, returning from the Berlin Conference, gained the impression that the Germans were almost certain to annex any place on the coast of southern Africa which was left open for them. British difficulties would, it was thought, then increase tenfold, because Germany might try to use its position to interfere between the British government and the Boers. A German presence was regarded as 'a dangerous complication' which would increase the difficulty of dealing with Africans and Afrikaners. German traders would almost certainly try to prevent British control of arms supply to both. Britain became interested in Bechuanaland only after Germany had annexed South-West

Africa. Annexation of British Bechuanaland then became of urgent importance as the territorial wedge between the German hinterland and the Transvaal.[20] The same fear of a junction between Germany and the Transvaal led to the annexation of St Lucia Bay and the hitherto unoccupied coastal region between the Cape and Natal. Gladstone saw that apprehension of German rivalry was a factor in the South African aspect of the partition. He said on 9 December 1884: 'It seems that wherever there is a dark corner in South African politics there is a German spectre to be the tenant of it.' Accordingly, Gladstone thought that Derby was quite right in wishing to have 'a continuous line of coast in South Africa'.[21]

All European powers were anxious that Africa should not threaten international peace. In the last resort all agreed that their friendship was more important than their African interests. It was one of the aims of the Berlin Conference of 1884/5 to limit the effect of future African disputes on international relations in Europe and to reduce the danger of friction which lay in general ignorance of Central Africa. According to Sir Edward Malet, who attended it, Britain's aim was to help prevent 'the anarchy and lawlessness which must have resulted from the influx of traders of all nations into countries under no recognised form of government'. There was quite a strong move, supported by Britain, to neutralise the whole African continent.[22] It was generally understood at the time that the African activities of different powers had to be adjusted within the context of their European relationships and their mutual concern about Africa. Somaliland was declared a British protectorate in 1884 in order to contain the anarchy consequent upon the dissolution of the indigenous government, and to prevent the danger of foreign encroachment on the line of communication to India; it was also a major source of food supply for the Aden garrison. But in 1896 the administration of Somaliland was transferred from the Government of India (acting through Aden) to the Foreign Office. Although Aden was geographically a convenient centre from which to administer the Somali coast, the viceroy of India could not know enough of the political considerations which would decide the action to be taken there as in other parts of Africa, 'because they are inseparably bound up in European politics'.[23]

IV

It would be wrong, however, to end on this note. Partition, and the related 'pacification' of African territories, was something above all which affected indigenous peoples. Their experience of it was far from uniform, and cannot be properly examined here. One regional example will have to stand for all.

Geographically, it mattered profoundly where you were. A graphic illustration is provided by Central Africa in the 1890s, where two very similar polities had widely differing fates.[24] The Bulozi and Ndebele states, Barotseland in today's Zambia and Matabeleland in Zimbabwe, are strictly comparable in the sense that they were both more or less centralised kingdoms, ethnically similar, neither worn down by prior European influences, and both under the sway of the British South Africa Company. The Lozi were farmers and fishermen, inhabiting a great floodplain stretching along the Zambesi for about 120 miles. This was a notoriously unhealthy place for the white man, with a significant malaria threat. It was, in European terms, remote, isolated, an inaccessible backwater, of little economic value. Moreover, no one expected to find gold in a marshy floodplain. By contrast, the Ndebele were a warlike people who built military raiding into an economic system, alienating their neighbours. So they could expect no allies when they found themselves standing smack in the front line of a major European settler thrust on the ground, backed by the rich and powerful Cecil Rhodes. The Ndebele occupied a region of geopolitical significance to the British, of expected mineral wealth (the settler pioneers were searching for a 'second Rand'), and of known pastoral potential. By 1897 the railway was at Bulawayo, thus depriving the Ndebele of protective inaccessibility. The upshot of these differences was that Barotseland survived as a compact entity, with a continuing monarchy, and a direct, privileged relationship with the British Crown. The Ndebele state, after first going to war with the British and then rebelling (*chimurenga*), was dismantled. Social cohesion was smashed, the monarchy abolished, and much of the land and cattle confiscated. This led to Southern Rhodesia's Africans being much more closely administered than Africans in any other British territory. The imposing Ndebele leader Lobengula reflected sadly that he felt like a fly caught by a calculating chameleon (the British); but the diplomatic skills of Lozi's Lewanika were rewarded by an invitation to the coronation of Edward VII, where everybody said he looked just like 'a dusky Disraeli'.[25]

Notes

1 *The Times*, 5 May 1898.
2 A.S. Kanya-Forstner, *The conquest of the western Sudan: a study of French military imperialism* (1969), p. 195; Earl of Cromer, *Political and literary essays* (1913), vol. I, p. 101.
3 C.S. Goldman, ed., *The empire and the century* (1905), p. 865.
4 *Encyclopaedia Britannica* (11th edn, 1910), vol. XV, 'Ivory', p. 93.
5 R.S.S. Baden-Powell, *The downfall of Prempeh* (1896), pp. 18–19.
6 J.D. Hargreaves, *Prelude to the partition of Africa* (1963), pp. 240–4.

7 W.E.H. Lecky, *Democracy and liberty* (1899), vol. I, p. 309.
8 CO 879/31, no. 381, correspondence about trade in arms and liquor, 1881–9 (1890); CO 879/16, no. 200, memo, 21 July 1879, 'The South African arms question'.
9 H. Kuper, *An African aristocracy: rank among the Swazi* (1961), pp. 19–31.
10 L.M. Thompson, in M. Wilson and L.M. Thompson, eds., *Oxford history of South Africa*, vol. II, *1870–1966* (1971), p. 250.
11 A.G. Hopkins, *An economic history of West Africa* (1973), pp. 124–66, and 'Economic imperialism in West Africa: Lagos, 1880–1892', *Economic History Review*, vol. 21 (1968), pp. 581–606.
12 C.W. Newbury, *The Western Slave Coast and its rulers* (Oxford, 1961), pp. 100–20, and 'Victorians, republicans and the partition of Africa', *Journal of African History*, vol. 2 (1962), p. 500.
13 W.R. Louis, 'Sir Percy Anderson's grand African strategy, 1883–1896', *English Historical Review*, vol. 81 (1966), p. 303.
14 Newbury, *Western Slave Coast*, pp. 120–1.
15 M.E. Chamberlain, 'Clement Hill's memoranda and the British interest in East Africa', *English Historical Review*, vol. 87 (1972), pp. 533–47.
16 A. Ramm, ed., *Political correspondence of Mr Gladstone and Lord Granville, 1876–1886* (Cambridge, 1962), vol. II, p. 304; R.E. Robinson and J.A. Gallagher, *Africa and the Victorians* (1961, 1981), p. 190.
17 [F.D. Lugard], 'Imperial interests in East Africa', *Blackwood's Edinburgh Magazine*, vol. 155 (1894), pp. 860–1.
18 R. Oliver, 'Some factors in the British occupation of East Africa, 1884–1894', *Uganda Journal*, vol. 15 (1951), pp. 49–64.
19 G.N. Sanderson, *England, Europe and the Upper Nile, 1882–1899* (Edinburgh, 1965), pp. 381–403.
20 D.M. Schreuder, *Gladstone and Kruger: the Liberal government and colonial 'Home Rule', 1880–1885* (1969), pp. 370–1.
21 Ramm, *Political correspondence of Mr Gladstone and Lord Granville*, vol. II, p. 304.
22 R.J. Gavin and J.A. Betley, eds., *The scramble for Africa: documents on the Berlin West Africa Conference* (1973), pp. 116–19.
23 *PD, Lords*, 5th series, vol. 5, cc. 557–8 (6 April 1910); Elgin Viceroy Papers, F 84/14, f. 79, Elgin to secretary of state for India, 9 January 1896.
24 E. Stokes and R. Brown, eds., *The Zambesian past: studies in Central African history* (Manchester, 1966), esp. chapters by the editors, pp. 63–93, 261–301; C. Youé, 'The politics of collaboration in Bulozi, 1840–1914', *JICH*, vol. 13 (1985), pp. 139–50; M. Gluckman, 'The Lozi of Barotseland', in E. Colson and M. Gluckman, eds., *Seven tribes of Central Africa* (Manchester, 1959), pp. 1–87.
25 Philip Mason, *Birth of a plural society: the conquest and settlement of Rhodesia* (Oxford, 1958), p. 105.

3   The empire in a comparative global context, 1815–1914

[Reprinted from the third edition of *Britain's imperial century*, for which it was specially written in 2002. Not all libraries will have this edition, and comparative perspectives are increasingly fashionable, so the reprinting seems justified.]

Historians have often supposed that the British empire was an unusual case in the history of European expansion and that the expansionist motivation of other states was quite different. But what if it could be shown that in fact these differences have been greatly exaggerated?[1]

I

At first sight, the Russian empire, land-based, with a contiguous metropolis and periphery, might appear to have little in common with the British.[2] The Russian sense of geopolitical vulnerability and strategic insecurity on the open and agriculturally marginal north Eurasian plain has been deep-rooted, and appears to persist even after the collapse of the communist regime.[3] However, the ways in which this worked out in territorial acquisition will be familiar to students of British expansion. In Central Asia from the 1860s the driving force was the search for stable frontiers and sound administration in areas of local political power vacuum and nomadic Muslim raiding. Support might be mobilised by reference to commercial opportunity, particularly the development of the cotton supply, but essentially it was the frontiers of strategic manipulation which were being advanced. Army generals were the directing force. The architect of the conquest of Tashkent (1865), a key event in control of the region, was General M.G. Cherniaev. His new administrative machine put much power in the hands of the army, and the governor-general was always an army officer. The government in St Petersburg found it hard to control its agents in these remote frontier regions. Army officers tended to make life-long careers in Central Asia, and they formed a close-knit group in the war ministry.[4] Strategic arguments snowballed: every little campaign generated the necessity for another. The common perception was that 'it gave idle Russian generals something to do'.[5] All in all, between 1830 and 1880 Russia advanced 1,200 miles south towards India, and a further 600 miles towards Herat between 1880 and 1884 – causing much anxiety to the Government of India (see Map 3.1).

In the Far East, the Russian 'urge to the sea' through Manchuria was important, and railways the principal instrument. Herein lay the roots of the Russo-Japanese War of 1904–5. By the end of the nineteenth century, a central figure was Count Sergei Witte, the man who saw the Trans-Siberian Railway through to Vladivostok. As minister of finance from 1892 to 1903, he had effective charge of the empire. His aim was to strengthen Russia in an age of geopolitical rivalry, believing that only through economic strength could states become 'fully able to assert their political power'.[6]

Lord Curzon singled out lower Russian emphasis on Christian mission as the principal difference between British and Russian expansion.[7] In Central Asia, where 90 per cent of the inhabitants were Muslim, that is unsurprising, and Britain was equally wary in Northern Nigeria. Yet in general the Russians by the end of the eighteenth century had 'a thoroughly European ideology of cultural superiority and civilising mission in Asia' (Lieven), and, where populations were non-Muslim and animist, Russian Orthodox missionaries were active. In Alaska from 1794, the missionaries left behind 12,000 indigenous Christians in 1867, still perhaps the most enduring monument of Russian rule there. Orthodox missionaries also entered Japan in 1858, with Monk Nikolai doing sterling work for fifty years in that most religiously eclectic of countries, becoming Orthodox bishop of Japan in 1880. The Trans-Siberian Railway had a lavishly fitted-out 'church' car.[8]

Russian expansion exhibits little support for a theory of 'the economic taproot'. The consolidation of Siberia and the movement into Central Asia pre-dated the need to find new sources of raw cotton from the mid-1860s and the huge increase in cotton outflow came only after 1908. Here as elsewhere, economic interests formed a backdrop to nineteenth-century expansion rather than supplying its motive force.

French expansion showed marked similarities with Russian expansion, especially in the tendency to concentrate effort geographically at any one time, in the weak grip of higher political direction from the centre, and in the prominent role of army officers. In France the army was more professional and more influential in society than it was in Britain. A cadre of eight hundred officers formed an elite of marines, bonded by freemasonry not only to each other but also to civilian administrators: three-quarters of French governors-general in West Africa in the twentieth

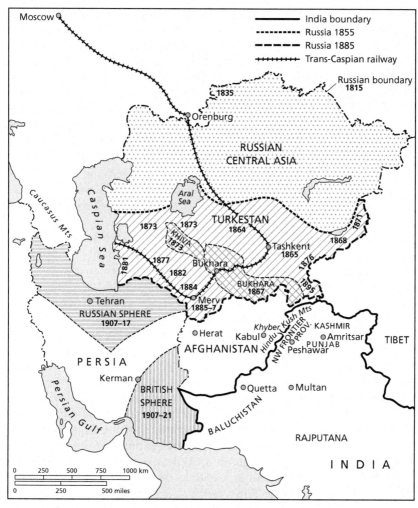

Map 3.1 Russian expansion in Central Asia, 1863–87: the 'Great Game'. Lord Curzon described Turkestan, Afghanistan, Transcaspia, and Persia as 'pieces on a chessboard upon which is being played out a game for the dominion of the world'. The danger posed by Russian expansion to the security of India was not acute so long as mountains and deserts and buffer states kept the two empires separated. But by 1884 Russian frontiers were coterminous with Persia and Afghanistan, and the distance from the most advanced outposts of British India had been almost halved in twenty years.

century were freemasons, a much higher percentage than among British governors.

Henri Brunschwig advanced the thesis that French expansion was 'essentially political', always 'une politique de prestige', an affirmation to the world of 'la présence, la grandeur, le rayonnement de la France'. Unlike the British, the French 'did not need' world commerce, and the expansionist activities of merchants were sporadic and ephemeral. Most French exported capital went to Russia. R.E. Robinson appeared to endorse this comparison with Britain: a French obsession with prestige made French expansion almost 'unnatural, even superfluous', 'very different' from the supposedly more materialistic aims of the British.[9] These views, however, seem to underestimate the importance of prestige for the British, at the same time as overestimating their commercial motivation.

Although the invasion of Algiers in 1830 could be said to have an obvious geopolitical imperative behind it – Algiers is no further from Marseilles than is le Havre – and although there may have been some hope of economic gain, the motives were opportunistic. Reasons of internal political expediency suggested an attempt to bolster a tottering regime by a spectacular foreign adventure. Long-term plans were notably absent and less than half the settlers (perhaps 40 per cent) were French. The occupation of the coastal region, however, produced a Muslim reaction based in the interior, and a prolonged and bloodthirsty conquest had to be embarked upon. Unlike British India, Algeria did not 'conquer itself'. Even when, by the late 1860s, the French army had established its mastery in Algeria, it was still impossible to secure the artificial boundaries of the colony. There were 2,365 violations of the Algerian border from Tunisia in the ten years before the annexation of Tunisia in 1881. The French main aim, though, in 1881 was to pre-empt the planting of an Italian colony, and to consolidate their naval command of the Mediterranean. (By 1869 Tunis was bankrupt and thus vulnerable to European takeover.)[10] As international competition intensified, France became ever more obsessed with its world-ranking. Jules Ferry (president of the council) declared in 1885: 'Our country must place itself in a position to do what all the others are doing', or be 'reduced to third or fourth class'.[11] By the 1890s something like a 'grand design', such as the British had had since the 1830s, was beginning to emerge. But for most of the nineteenth century, with an empire of almost insignificant proportions after 1815, what mattered to Frenchmen was not imperial expansion as such, but the promotion of the French language (the vital symbol of the *mission civilisatrice*), and, above all, rivalry with Britain, or rather, an attempt to assuage a political pride and prestige so completely wounded by British successes overseas. From the 1830s ministers and officials in the foreign ministry recurred to the idea of 'a French India' in Africa: 'Africa must be for us what India is for England.' From the 1850s they began to wonder whether Indo-China might also serve as a replacement for 'our miserable remnants of Indian colonies'. Only by opening up Indo-China, said the explorer Francis Garnier in 1873, could France recover the empire of which Dupleix had dreamed in mid-eighteenth-century India.[12]

If France could not match the overwhelming economic pre-eminence of industrialised Britain, a supposed cultural superiority could be aggressively promoted instead, projecting France as a more enlightened and intelligent ruler of non-Europeans. Perhaps it was true. Whereas Napoleon before the Great Pyramid made an oration to his soldiers about how 'forty centuries of history look down upon you', the British lugged a theodolite up it and established a triangulation point. In 1882, victorious from Tel-el Kebir, British squaddies carelessly swarmed over the Sphinx. Napoleon is certainly credited with initiating the cultural component of French imperial rule, and, by his understanding of its potential power, with beginning the spread of European science to the Third World. He went to Egypt in 1798 with more than a hundred and fifty *savants* – scientists, technicians, and artists – to record and collect the information required to rule Egypt on an informed basis. No previous European expedition to any part of the world had ever been accompanied by such a prestigious official effort to discover the history and material resources of an overseas land (Captain Cook's voyages were privately funded). The result was the splendid twenty-four-volume *Description de l'Egypte* (1809–29) in 'elephant folio' format, still one of the outstanding monuments of European scholarship – even Edward Said recognises it as a 'great collective monument of erudition'.[13] Again, forty years later, Louis Philippe's government established a commission to undertake a 'scientific exploration' of Algeria: thirty-nine volumes were published (1844–67): zoological, biological, geographical, economic, sociological; there was even a pioneering study of prostitution. In Hanoi in 1898 France set up the Ecole Française d'Extrême Orient, which also produced notable scholarship.

Missions had long been the principal preoccupation of Frenchmen in Indo-China and gave some substance to the claims of *mission civilisatrice*. Catholic missions had slowly rebuilt themselves from the 1820s, and the missionary strand became every bit as important in French expansion as it was in British, even though some of it was directed against Protestants. The difference was that the French government did not leave indigenous education to local voluntary or missionary enterprise, but opened government schools. There were five hundred of them in the Levant by 1914 and 5 per cent of the French budget was dedicated to their support. French rather than English thus became the 'international' language of most of the Middle East until well into the twentieth century.

One other characteristic of French expansion deserves emphasis. This was the French love of euphoric geopolitical gestures, often with rivalry with Britain in mind. They wanted to join Paris and New York by an intercontinental railway, linking Alaska and Siberia (by an extension to the Trans-Siberian) with a fifty-mile tunnel under the sea, through the Bering Strait. De Lobel took up this thirty-year-old project in 1900, but Russia finally refused permission in 1907. It may yet be built.[14] Also planned was a France-to-China route via a Panama Canal (begun by de Lesseps, 1881, but interrupted in 1888), the Marquesas and Tahiti (acquired in 1842, and midway to South-East Asia in the Pacific), and back via Réunion in the Indian Ocean. In Africa, Captain E. Roudaire, an engineering officer, planned in the late 1870s to create an inland Saharan sea with a canal from the Gulf of Gabes (Tunisia), while Donald MacKenzie offered an alternative project from Cape Juby (south Morocco). Flooding the Sahara would be one way of dealing with a recalcitrant and expanding Islam in the interior. The other was by the construction of strategic railways. Proposals included linking Algeria and Niger, Algeria and Senegal, Senegal and Niger, Algeria and Djibouti (French Somaliland, on the Red Sea), Algeria and Lake Chad, Lake Chad and Johannesburg (the French riposte to Rhodes's 'Cape-to-Cairo' dream). A Trans-Saharan railway received support from a parliamentary commission in 1879 and a vote of 400 million francs was supported by Charles de Freycinet, the prime minister and a former engineer.[15] But less than 200 miles of it has ever been built. In 1899–1900 a grandiose tripartite geopolitical rendezvous was planned at Lake Chad (the moves to occupy which have been described by one historian as the 'peak of the [French] colonial orgasm'[16]). This was to be a symbolic demonstration of how Chad could be the pivot of a unified all-embracing African empire, with expeditions converging from Algeria, the west, and the south, but it ended in acutely embarrassing disaster. On the line of march from Senegal, after much rampaging and village-burning, a senior officer sent to restore order was murdered by another officer and two more officers were killed by their men. The advance from the south was by way of Brazzaville, the Congo, and Ubangui–Chari rivers. This route had also been taken by a remarkable expedition under Captain J.B. Marchand, making for the Nile, where he was supposed to meet a group from Djibouti (who got fed up with waiting) and search for a dam site. He became embroiled with the British at Fashoda (Kodok) in 1898. French army engineers such as P.L. Monteil agreed with the British 'experts' Sir Samuel Baker and Sir Colin Moncrieff that with the right location it would be 'an easy operation' to regulate the Nile waters.[17] A fantasy world of hydropolitics.

II

Like all other European leaders, Bismarck would have preferred to stick to informal empire ('I want no colonies', 1871), but this became impossible for Germany through the new wave of international competitiveness and destabilisation in the periphery.[18] For Bismarck, as for all other participants in the 'partition of the world', it was the frontiers of fear that drove him forward. Bismarck of course made a famous geopolitical pronouncement, rebuking E. Wolf, the explorer: 'My map of Africa lies in Europe. Here lies Russia, and here . . . lies France, and we are in the middle. That is my map of Africa' (December 1888).[19] Accepting as part of a government's duty some protection of the commercial interests of its nationals, the acquisition of colonies seemed above all a question of preemption. Bismarck, like all other European leaders, and probably more than most, can be shown to have used and manipulated overseas interests to his own advantage as a politician concerned with other, political issues, including protection of his own power-base. To do this he could work upon the local conditions created by German businessmen, such as the Bremen trader Adolf Lüderitz, or adventurers like Carl Peters. Almost all Bismarck's acquisitions were made between April 1884 (the protectorate over Angra Pequena at Lüderitz Bay in South-West Africa) and April 1885 (the protectorate over north-east New Guinea).

All of them were pressing hard up against, though not actually directly overlapping, existing British interests. Togo impinged on the Gold Coast, Cameroon on the Niger delta, while the most provocative was Tanganyika (February 1885) opposite Zanzibar, but carefully avoiding the port of Mombasa. Domestic political anxieties as well as diplomatic concerns seem to have pointed to a controlled, limited, tactical quarrel with Britain. Bismarck at all costs wanted peace and order in Africa on a European basis and did not care much who provided it. Indeed, his anger with Britain over South-West Africa stemmed from his realisation that he could not rely on Britain to protect German interests there without formal German rule.[20] He alleged that British consuls, missionaries, and traders in the Cameroons had incited the Africans to rebel against Germans. In 1876 German agents had urged him to annex the Transvaal. Bismarck was also worried about the increasing aggressiveness of France in Africa and its tariff policies. By summoning the

Berlin Conference, he clearly signalled his concern that Africa must not become the cause of major political disputes between European nations and his determination that its dangerous destabilisation must be brought under international control. Bismarck's speech to the closing session of the Berlin Conference (26 February 1885) put the point well:

The special conditions in which you have opened up wide tracts of territory to commercial enterprise have required special guarantees for the preservation of peace and public order. The evils of war would assume a specially fatal character if the natives were led to take sides in disputes between the civilised powers. After careful consideration of the dangers which might attend such contingencies, in the interests of commerce and civilisation you have sought to devise means to withdraw a large part of the African continent from the oscillations of general politics, and to confine the rivalry of nations therein to the peaceful pursuits of trade and industry.[21]

In order to make the withdrawal from the 'oscillations of general politics' as comprehensive and valid as possible, ten days after inviting the obvious powers (Britain, Belgium, the Netherlands, Portugal, Spain, and the United States, with Germany and France as co-hosts), on 18 October 1884 he issued a second batch of invitations to those with, in most cases, little or no existing direct interest in Africa: Austria, Russia, Italy, Denmark, Sweden, Norway, and finally Turkey – fourteen participants in all, at a conference lasting three months. Unfortunately, whatever the statesman-like restraint Bismarck imposed, his successors were unable to resist the temptations of a more aggressive German drive towards world power, 'a place in the sun'.

The Dutch in the nineteenth century did not indulge in territorial extension, as the main lineaments of their empire were already in place. However, from 1880 they were forced to make good their Indonesian holdings in a closer assertion of their authority, both because of internal instability and Islamic challenge, and because of external pressures. The Aceh War in north Sumatra lasted from 1873 to 1903 and cost 100,000 lives. Dutch policy was marked by defensive pre-emption: 'Fear of American intervention and later of England, Germany and Japan forced the Dutch government to plant the flag and have it respected in areas which they would rather have left alone . . . In short the only reason for Dutch imperialism was the imperialism of others.' Wesseling thinks this feature, this attitude of 'reaction rather than action', 'almost exclusively a function of international politics', may be unique. But that is probably because he accepts a more economic motivation as the norm, and I question that. However, the way Wesseling articulates Dutch activity is congruent with my 'two-levels' model, since he points to the different *levels* represented by private interests and local officials on the spot, the mediating governor-general in Batavia and the colonial ministry at The Hague. Positive actions could be initiated but also be stopped or misfire at any level, and in general 'slackened with every step to a higher level'.[22]

'The Italians are exceedingly tiresome', complained Lord Salisbury in 1889, 'with their misplaced and suicidal African ambitions.'[23] The volatile and reckless Italian leader, Francesco Crispi, believed 'colonies are a necessity of modern life. We cannot remain inactive and allow other powers to occupy all the unexplored parts of the world.' Italian acquisitions – Tripoli, parts of Somalia, Libya, and Eritrea – arose from elitist conceptions of the prestige requirements of a newly unified state and were not economically driven. Defeat in Ethiopia (1896) marked the ruin of an imperial venture 'based almost entirely on a romantically grandiose vision of Italy's place in the world . . . a well-nigh mystical conception of national grandeur' (Sanderson). Things were scarcely much different a generation later when Mussolini tried again.[24]

The historiography of the Portuguese empire is dominated by two diametrically opposed interpretations: Hammond's 'non-economic' version and Clarence-Smith's attempt to align it with 'economic imperialism'. Hammond's interpretation remains persuasive. The insight of Eça de Querioz in 1903 seems to catch an authentic essence: 'Precisely what preoccupies us, what gratifies us, what consoles us, is to contemplate *just the number* of our possessions; to point here and there on the map with the finger; to intone proudly "we have eight, we have nine; we are a colonial power, we are a nation of seafarers".'[25] In a word, prestige was what mattered to the Portuguese.

As for the 'Belgian' empire, although the interpretative options narrow sharply, prestige was certainly present and there is demonstration of the fact that initiatives might indeed arise 'at every level' – in this case at the very top. The establishment of the Congo Free State confronts us with the actions of a single individual, acting on his personal initiative without support from any business interests (it was not yet known that the Congo would yield huge profits from wild rubber). King Leopold opportunistically, obstinately, and voraciously pursued for Belgium new sources of plunder and prestige. From the early 1860s he was impressed with the revenue the Dutch drew from Indonesia and hoped to find an equivalent, looking first to Sarawak, Formosa, or the Philippines. Acquisition of the Congo as a personal fief did not satisfy him. Not content with portentous plans to link (in the French manner) the Atlantic and the Red Sea (a domain stretching from Leopoldville to Eritrea), he was also avidly on the lookout for leases and concessions in the Canary Islands, Uganda, Ethiopia, Macao, and China. Despite the attempt of Stengers to defend him against 'insane megalomania', it is hard not to agree with the king's cousin, Queen Victoria, who feared in 1896 that Leopold 'must have wished goodbye to his reason'. Quixotic, rabid fantasies he may have had, but Leopold's grab at 'ce magnifique gâteau africain' from 1877 was a trigger to the partition. And this bizarre case is an important reminder of the sometimes crucial role of metropolitan individuals.[26]

III

If 'surplus energy' and a sense of superiority are the taproots of the expansionist spirit,[27] the Americans had plenty of both. The United States was inherently expansionist. By the end of the nineteenth century, 'the regeneration of the world' was for some becoming part of the American dream, to which it might give a new sense of purpose. Senator A.J. Beveridge hailed the takeover of the Philippines from 1898 as part of 'the mission of our race, trustee under God, for the civilisation of the world'. This was the moment when an American informal Pacific empire of commerce and Christianity became a formal responsibility and many Americans regarded it indeed as an enlightened 'extension of civilisation' not as territorial expansion.

It is easy enough to see how the geopolitical imperative might lead the United States into its southward thrust, conceiving the Caribbean as an American lake, eliminating an unstable and oppressive Spanish rule in Cuba in order to provide a strong naval station and to secure the route to the projected Panama Canal; easy, too, to see that the Alaska purchase (1867) would be welcomed; or how the Hawaiian islands might be regarded as a 'natural' part of the American outer defence network, with internal stability a necessity for the naval base at Pearl Harbor. But why the Philippines? The attack was launched in 1898 in the wake of a successful Filipino revolt against Spanish rule. President McKinley probably saw it as the logical result of the emergence of the United States to world-power status. There had been a vague sense of Russia, Japan, and China as 'bordering' the United States and of the Pacific as potentially a theatre of American enterprise. The Aleutian island chain thrust out from Alaska a big-brotherly arm, a prong into the north Pacific. American missionaries were established in Honolulu from 1820 and in China from 1830. By the 1890s Americans were worried about destabilisation in China and anxious not to miss their part in concession-hunting.

Clearly, America's leaders profoundly believed the international stakes in Asia were high. Manila was almost ideally placed to give the United States 'a base at the door of all the East', a base of its own, instead of having to use British facilities, and from which American 'influence and trade' and the Protestant religion could be more effectively diffused in China. This trans-Pacific thrust, however, does seem to have had some strategic planning behind it. The islands of Wake (uninhabited) and Guam (Spanish) were acquired, nicely spaced on the shipping lane from San Francisco to Manila via Honolulu in the Hawaiian islands, which were finally annexed in 1898. There was an element of pre-emption in the Philippines. The Germans were seen as the principal rivals in the Pacific and they were actually holding aggressive naval manoeuvres in Manila Bay. There was potential interest from Britain (which had captured Manila in 1762 but returned it to Spain), and Japan, if Spanish rule should collapse. In fact the British, fearing a German colony, informally urged the United States to retain the Philippines. Despite the rhetoric of 'overproduction', there appear to have been no genuine economic motives for this acquisition. The Philippines had little economic value. American exports went overwhelmingly to Europe. Less than 5 per cent of exports left from America's Pacific ports, mostly grain bound for Europe via Cape Horn. The Protestant religious and missionary establishments were, however, keen supporters of keeping the Philippines, apparently unaware that 90 per cent of the population were Catholics.[28]

Ideally the United States wanted no more than bases at Manila and Cavite, but as so often in the history of territorial acquisition, this could only be made good by control of the hinterland and the eventual annexation of the entire 7,107-island archipelago. Uncle Sam was far from avuncular in the Philippines. Perhaps it was hardly to be expected that soldiers who had, in many cases, spent an entire lifetime bashing the American Indians would show much respect for the Filipinos, who were perceived as an uncivilised, treacherous enemy who armed young children and mutilated captives. According to one American solider, 'We all wanted to kill "niggers". This shooting human beings is a "hot game", and beats rabbit-shooting all to pieces . . . We killed them like rabbits; hundreds, yes thousands of them. Everyone was crazy.' Women and children were not spared.[29] Even in the racially motivated violence of their methods of conquest, it seems, the Americans conformed to the pattern and model of European expansion.

Japan had a geopolitical advantage in its remoteness from western Europe, which fended off a premature interest by Britain, at any rate. It exhibits a rare example of an 'indigenised colonial state'. Japan's self-managed modernisation was highly eclectic. The founding fathers of the Meiji government determined in their charter oath of 1868 that 'knowledge shall be sought throughout the world'. Prince Ito Hirobumi, who became prime minister, and was chiefly responsible between 1868 and 1909 for the creation of the administrative system, went to England as early as 1863, and he met Bismarck several times. The government by 1875 employed 520 foreign advisers, perhaps half of them British, and many of those engineers. Key slogans proclaimed the policy: 'Japanese spirit, Western method', 'Eastern ethics and Western techniques'. The best models were deliberately selected (with some switches): the British for navy, railways, industry, and seismology; the German for police, army, local government, the constitution, and medicine; the French for the civil and criminal codes; the American for agriculture and university education; the Italian for silk management. And then, determined to assert an equality with the Western powers, Meiji Japan embarked within a generation on expansion: to Taiwan (Formosa) in 1895, to Sakhalin (from Russia) in 1905, to the Kwantung peninsula (Liaotung, from China) in 1905, and to Korea in 1910.[30]

The study of Japanese expansion was for long bedevilled by the attempt to harmonise it with the prevailing European theory of 'economic imperialism'. This proved difficult.[31] For one thing, Japan had an actual capital shortage when its expansion began. Silk was the engine of Japan's industrial revolution and by the end of the nineteenth century the country produced one-third of the world's raw silk.[32] This did not of itself require expansion. There was very little Japanese commitment to empire-building as such. Their preference was always for informal control. There was, however, a strong sense of being an expansionist society, of wanting to emulate the classic British model of 1815 to 1858. The Japanese may well have wished informally to influence the future of the Pacific rim and spread the Japanese way of life, but they did not want to rule it. The largest group of overseas Japanese settlers was in Hawaii – 20,000 of them by the 1890s – but Hawaii became an American and not a Japanese colony. The reasons for empire must be sought elsewhere. Myers and Peattie in 1984 put forward the geopolitical argument that the Japanese empire was designed to create a strategic ring fence in surrounding territories which were regarded as ineptly governed: a standard kind of diagnosis, initiating a process which ultimately snowballed into over-extension and disaster. Japan fought its first wars against China and Russia essentially because of geopolitical worries about Korea, potentially fatal in Russian hands.[33]

IV

Inevitably the attempt to sketch briefly the salient characteristics of nine other empires will be open to charges of selectivity in the use of evidence. However, I am attempting to draw out possible points of comparison with the British empire, to see whether other empires had more in common

with it than is usually supposed. Several themes-in-common do seem
to emerge. (1) Expanding states have an initial preference for informal
empire. This is hardly surprising: no state wants to saddle itself with the
burdens of formal rule if another will do the work for it; informal control
is thus seen as the cheapest, most sophisticated way to exert influence.
(2) Informal control tends to break down in unstable frontier zones, and
indigenous regimes on the periphery often fail to provide the minimum
standards of law and order sufficient for European purposes. Hinterlands
have to be secured. (3) Much of the periphery was dominated by Islam,
and engagement with Islam was a common preoccupation for many
European empires: not just the British and French in Africa and India,
but the Russians in Central Asia, the British in the Malay world, the
Italians in Libya, the Americans in the southern Philippines – although
none of these could match the fearful scale of involvement by the Dutch
against the Muslim Acehnese in Indonesia.[34] To say that all shared a fear
of Islam is perhaps pitching it too high: on the whole what is striking is
European confidence that Islam could be controlled and contained. (4)
If European expansion was in a sense always in competition with Islam,
inter-state competitiveness within the Western international system
is clearly also an overarching theme. Almost all states take territory
reactively, that is to say because a rival has already done so. There is a
geopolitical preoccupation with world-ranking and status: 'the frontiers
of fear' are driven forward, and strategic concerns take on a dynamic of
their own. (5) All European leaders were worried that existing interests
would be squeezed out in any aggressively competitive situation. Thus
pre-emption was frequently a dominant immediate motive for acquiring
territory. (I have used the term pre-emption simply to mean forestalling
foreign rivals in places where maintenance or consolidation of existing
interests was perceived as desirable, and not in the German sense of
Torschlusspanik, 'the pegging out of claims for the future' just for the sake
of it, though this did sometimes happen in the heightened competitiveness of the late nineteenth century.) (6) Most expanding states seem
to have 'less' of an economic motivation than Britain, but this should
alert us to the likelihood that historians have overestimated the role of
economic interests in the British case. Examining other empires seems
to confirm that while many political leaders thought collateral economic
gain was possible, businessmen were usually noisy but essentially secondary influences in decisions to take territory. (7) The reasons for territorial
acquisition are almost always complex and multi-faceted. Frequently
they have a cultural dimension, at least at the local level. Expanding
states produce people keen to spread their way of life and will often
have missionary elements seeking religious converts among indigenous

communities. (8) Crucially and fundamentally, obsession with prestige assumed a primary significance for all expanding states, since concern for prestige 'is the essence of being a great power' (Hinsley).[35] So pervasive is the determining influence of prestige on governments that it can also be shown to be intimately related to geopolitical assessments, and thus a root cause of the wars which they fight.

Notes

1 The best starting points for comparisons between European empires since 1815 are A.N. Porter, *European imperialism, 1860–1914* (1994) and D.K. Fieldhouse, *Economics and empire, 1830–1914* (1973, 1984).
2 D. Lieven, *Empire: the Russian empire and its rivals* (2000), esp. 'Comparisons between the British and Russian empires', pp. 120–7.
3 G. Hosking, *Russia and Russians: a history* (2001), pp. 15, 611.
4 D. Mackenzie, 'Russian expansion in Central Asia: St Petersburg versus the Turkestan generals', *Canadian Slavic Studies*, vol. 3 (1969), pp. 286–311; P. Morris, 'The Russians in Central Asia, 1870–1887', *Slavonic and East European Review*, vol. 53 (1975), pp. 521–38; D. Gillard, *The struggle for Asia, 1828–1914: a study in British and Russian imperialism* (1977); D. Geyer, *Russian imperialism, 1860–1914* (Göttingen, 1977; English translation, 1987).
5 E. Allworth, ed., *Central Asia: a century of Russian rule* (New York, 1967), ch. 1, p. 58.
6 T.H. von Laue, *Sergei Witte and the industrialisation of Russia* (Columbia, 1963).
7 G.N. Curzon, *Russia in Central Asia in 1889 and the Anglo-Russian question* (1889), pp. 382–414.
8 R.A. Pierce, *Russian Central Asia, 1867–1917* (Berkeley, CA, 1960); J.R. Gibson, *Imperial Russia in frontier America: the changing geography of the supply of Russian America, 1784–1867* (New York, 1976).
9 H. Brunschwig, *Mythes et réalités de l'impérialisme colonial française, 1871–1914* (Paris, 1960; English translation, 1966, with an introduction by R.E. Robinson, repr. from *Journal of African History*, vol. 2 (1961), pp. 158–9).
10 A.S. Kanya-Forstner, *The conquest of the western Sudan: a study in French military imperialism* (1969), reviewed by B.O. Oloruntimehin, 'Theories of "official mind" and "military imperialism" as related to the French conquest of the western Sudan', *Journal of the Historical Society of Nigeria*, vol. 5 (1970), pp. 419–34; C.M. Andrew and A.S. Kanya-Forstner, *France overseas: the Great War and the climax of French imperial expansion* (1981), esp. pp. 9–42, and 'Centre and periphery in the making of the second French empire, 1815–1920', *JICH*, vol. 16 (1988), pp. 9–34, repr. in A. Porter and R. Holland, eds., *Theory and practice in the history of European expansion overseas: essays in honour of Ronald Robinson* (1988); C.W. Newbury and A.S. Kanya-Forstner, 'French policy and the Scramble', *Journal of African History*, vol. 10 (1969), pp. 253–76; R. Aldrich, *French presence in the South Pacific, 1842–1940* (1990).

11 Quoted by J. Stengers in P.J.M. McEwan, ed., *Nineteenth-century Africa* (1968), p. 283 (repr. from *Journal of African History*, vol. 3 (1962), pp. 469–91). T.F. Power, *Jules Ferry* (New York, 1944) remains a safe guide.

12 J.F. Cady, *The roots of French imperialism in eastern Asia* (Cornell, 1954), pp. 100, 282. For another view, see J. Marseille, *Empire colonial et capitalisme française* (Paris, 1984).

13 E. Said, *Orientalism* (1978), pp. 42, 84–7.

14 A sceptical British explorer travelled the route in 1901: see Harry de Windt, *From Paris to New York by land* (1903). In 1995 it was reported that plans were still being made by the Interhemispheric Bering Strait Tunnel and Railroad Group, under the chairmanship of a Czech-American, with the hope of bringing about 'the greatest engineering project the world has ever seen' (*Sunday Telegraph*, 3 September 1995, p. 15).

15 J.D. Hargreaves, *West Africa partitioned*, vol. I, *Loaded pause, 1885–1889* (1974), p. 16; D.R. Headrick, *The tools of empire: technology and European imperialism in the nineteenth century* (1981), pp. 200–1.

16 S.H. Roberts, *History of French colonial policy, 1870–1925* (1929), pp. 341–3.

17 J.D. Hargreaves, *West Africa partitioned*, vol. II, *The elephants and the grass* (1985), pp. 235–7.

18 P.M. Kennedy, *The rise of Anglo-German antagonism, 1860–1914* (1980); H.-U. Wehler, 'Bismarck's imperialism, 1862–1890', *Past and Present*, no. 48 (1970), pp. 119–55; E. Feuchtwanger, *Imperial Germany, 1850–1918* (2001), pp. 90–1; F. Stern, *Gold and iron: Bismarck, Bleichröder and the building of the German empire* (New York, 1977).

19 W.O. Aydelotte, *Bismarck and British colonial policy: the problem of South-West Africa, 1883–1885* (Philadelphia, 1937), p. 21.

20 H.A. Turner, 'Bismarck's imperialist venture: anti-British in origin?', in P. Gifford and W.R. Louis, eds., *Britain and Germany in Africa: imperial rivalry and colonial rule* (New Haven, CT, 1967), pp. 47–82.

21 W.H. Dawson, *The German empire, 1867–1914*, vol. II (1919), pp. 198–9; see also W.J. Mommsen, in S. Förster, W.J. Mommsen, and R. Robinson, eds., *Bismarck, Europe and Africa: the Berlin Conference, 1884–85 and the onset of partition* (1988), p. 166.

22 H.L. Wesseling, 'The giant that was a dwarf: or, the strange history of Dutch imperialism', *JICH*, vol. 16 (1988), pp. 58–70, repr. in Porter and Holland, eds., *Theory and practice . . . essays in honour of Ronald Robinson*; for an alternative view, applying the 'Cain and Hopkins' theory, see M. Kuitenbrouwer, *The Netherlands and the rise of modern imperialism: colonies and foreign policy, 1870–1902* (1985, English translation 1991), esp. pp. 349–69 on comparisons with Britain, Portugal, and Belgium.

23 G. Cecil, *The life of Robert, Marquis of Salisbury*, vol. IV (1932), p. 326; W.L. Langer, *The diplomacy of imperialism, 1890–1902* (New York, 2nd edn, 1951), p. 272.

24 G.N. Sanderson, *England, Europe and the Upper Nile, 1882–1899* (1965), pp. 383–4; J.-L. Miège, *L'impérialisme colonial italien de 1870 à nos jours* (Paris, 1968); R.A. Webster, *Industrial imperialism in Italy, 1908–1915* (Berkeley, CA, 1975); D. Mack Smith, *Mussolini's Roman empire* (1976), pp. 32–44.

Most work on Italian expansion concentrates on the Fascist era, including E. Serra and C. Seton-Watson, eds., *Italia e Inghilterra nel' età dell' imperialismo* (Milan, 1990; proceedings of a conference at Catania, 1987).

25 R.J. Hammond, 'Imperialism: sidelights on a stereotype', *Journal of Economic History*, vol. 21 (1961), p. 583, and *Portugal and Africa, 1815–1910: a study in uneconomic imperialism* (Stanford, CA, 1966); G. Clarence-Smith, *The third Portuguese empire, 1825–1975: a study in economic imperialism* (1985).

26 J. Stengers, 'King Leopold's imperialism', in R. Owen and R. Sutcliffe, eds., *Studies in the theory of imperialism* (1972), pp. 248–75.

27 The driving force of empire-building can be regarded as the overspill of a restless people with a theory of regeneration: as the explorer Sir Samuel Baker put it (1855), there was 'an innate spirit of action' which was 'the mainspring of the power of England'. See the discussion of 'surplus energy' in RH, *Britain's imperial century* (3rd edn, 2002, p. 280).

28 R. van Alstyne, *The American empire: its historical pattern and evolution* (Historical Association pamphlet, 1960), and *The rising American empire* (1960), esp. 'The lure of East Asia', pp. 170–94; J.A. Field, Jr, 'American imperialism: "the worst chapter in almost any book"', *American Historical Review*, vol. 83 (1978), pp. 644–83; H. Wayne Morgan, *Road to empire: the war with Spain and overseas expansion* (New York, 1965); J.C. Thomson, P.W. Stanley, and J.G. Perry, *Sentimental imperialism: the American experience in East Asia* (New York, 1981), pp. 93–120.

29 S.C. Miller, *'Benevolent assimilation': the American conquest of the Philippines, 1899–1903* (New Haven, CT, 1982), p. 188.

30 M.B. Jansen, ed., *Cambridge history of Japan*, vol. V, *The nineteenth century* (1989).

31 For example, W.G. Beasley, *Japanese imperialism, 1894–1945* (1987).

32 S. Sugiyama, *Japan's industrialisation in the world economy, 1859–1897* (1988), p. 78.

33 R.H. Myers and M.R. Peattie, eds., *The Japanese colonial empire, 1895–1945* (Princeton, 1984); A. Iriye, 'Japan's drive to great power status', in *Cambridge history of Japan*, vol. V, ch. 12; M.R. Peattie, 'The Japanese empire, 1895–1945' in P. Duus, ed., *Cambridge history of Japan*, vol. VI (1988), pp. 217–70.

34 E. Tagliacozzo, 'Kettle on a slow boil: Batavia's threat-perceptions in the Indies' outer islands, 1870–1910', *Journal of South-East Asian Studies*, vol. 31 (2000), pp. 70–100.

35 F.H. Hinsley, *Power and the pursuit of peace: theory and practice in the history of relations between states* (1963), p. 170. See also the conclusion of P.J. Marshall: from the mid-eighteenth century British expansion was fuelled by 'international rivalry, fear of others, above all of France, and increasingly about ambition and regard for Britain's status as a great power. That heady mixture was to spread the British across the globe for a long time to come.' ('Britain and the world in the eighteenth century', *Transactions of the Royal Historical Society*, 6th series, vol. 8 (1998), pp. 1–18. See also P.J. Marshall, *The making and unmaking of empires: Britain, India, and America, c.1750–1783* (Oxford, 2005).)

4   The myth of 'gentlemanly capitalism'

[Not previously published, this chapter does not seek rigorously to review a debate which has become controversial and even heated; rather it tries to show that economic history cannot be treated separately from political and diplomatic history if a comprehensive picture is the aim. This conclusion could perhaps be an enduring legacy of the debate, even when interest refocuses elsewhere. (New directions are strikingly suggested by Professor Hopkins himself, into globalisation and empires as transnational organisations with supranational connections: A.G. Hopkins, 'Back to the future: from national history to imperial history', *Past and Present*, no. 164 (1999), pp. 198–243.)]

The City of London was at the centre of a commercial empire, remarkable in its global reach. Britain was the world's banker, and its mercantile marine and overseas investments were among its most significant 'imperial' attributes. This remarkable economic system is the subject of a comprehensive study by P.J. Cain and A.G. Hopkins. Now in its second edition, *British imperialism, 1688–2000* is an impressively learned book of 739 pages, developed from an influential pair of articles in the *Economic History Review*, entitled 'Gentlemanly capitalism and British overseas expansion', published in 1986 and 1987.[1] In *British imperialism*, the authors propose a large-scale simplification and hold a strong interpretative line through a long period of time (although 1688 to 1850 is dealt with in a forty-page 'prospective'). They attempt to redefine the whole of the imperial process of expansion, and even the nature of British society itself. Unsurprisingly, their work has attracted a lot of comment and criticism,[2] to which they have generally responded with their usual courtesy and ready appreciation of the contributions of other historians.[3]

The essential Cain and Hopkins proposition is the 'importance of metropolitan interests in shaping Britain's presence abroad' (p. 13). Their overriding aim is the laudable one of making systematic connections between British imperial history and the history of the British economy and state-building, by reintegrating the two (p. 542). The 'causes of British imperialism' (p. 24) are located within 'impulses emanating from

the centre' (p. 645). They have focused on 'the domestic roots of imperialism' because this approach 'seems to us to have greater explanatory
power than one pitched at the level of international relations and removed
from the interests which shape national policy' (p. 685). (The word
'removed' here is surprising, since inter-state concerns about prestige
are normally held to determine 'the national interest', as its very essence,
and not something 'removed' from it.) Thus Cain and Hopkins propose
a reversion to the old narrow idea of the primacy of economic interests
as the basis of Britain's global expansion. There is, however, a new twist:
'gentlemanly capitalists' of the City of London and south-east England
are substituted, in the key role, for the bourgeois industrial capitalists of
the older accounts.

I

In *British imperialism*, the engine of expansion is driven by home coun-
ties investors and City financiers, as opposed to northern manufacturing
tycoons, of whom they were suspicious (p. 31).[4] The 'expansionist forces
of investment, commerce and migration' were promoted by 'the gentlemanly capitalist class' (p. 449), superintending the service-economy of
banking, insurance, and communications (p. 37). 'Gentlemanliness' is
defined as the snobbish, amateur, Christian, upper-middle class character of the English public school Establishment elite; they had capitalist
assumptions and a willingness to make money and calculate profit (pp.
34, 37, 84), but paradoxically this was allied to a contempt for 'mere
money-making' (p. 120). A crucial connection – the authors argue – was
the link between the economic power of this gentlemanly elite and the
political authority of government in its decision-making, a link inherent
in the 'high social status' of those in financial and commercial services.
Government officials 'moved in the same circles and shared the same
values' as City businessmen – 'an essential likemindedness', the authors
call it (pp. 400–2). The leading politicians were 'invariably gentlemen',
and they protected and promoted 'income-streams which fed gentlemanly interests', giving much less weight to industrial interests in the
formulation of policy (p. 647). Both the political and economic members
of the elite had shared priorities and a common view of the world and
how it should be ordered.

Thus far, it might be thought, Cain and Hopkins have presented their
thesis clearly, but the argument becomes much less tangible in the latest
version, when they suggest almost metaphysical conclusions: 'in our
account, capitalism is actually absorbed by the elites and adapted to suit
their needs' (p. 33); 'the imperial mission was the export version of the

gentlemanly order' (p. 47); 'imperialism was an integral part of the con-figuration of British society' (p. 56) – and this when 'imperialism' itself is defined as 'an incursion, or an attempted incursion, into the sovereignty of another state' (p. 54).

Although it may be paradoxical to explain *British* imperialism by an essentially *English* characteristic, there is of course nothing particularly controversial about describing the political elite as 'gentlemanly'. The pervasive grip of genteel middle-class values on English society is not in doubt, with all that we now understand about the Victorian aspirations to respectability and godly manliness. The trouble starts when 'capital-ism' is claimed to be one of its central values. What is problematic is the attempt to isolate, and then to magnify, from the totality of gentlemanly elements the narrowly financial and fiscal concerns of the elite, and then to suggest that these were able to exert a powerful influence on the whole direction of the British economy and government policy, even in India and elsewhere (p. 542).

So where might this thesis be said to be vulnerable? To start with a notorious quotation from Lord Salisbury: as the South African War approached, the prime minister lamented the fact that Milner had led the British government into having to make 'a considerable military effort – and all for people whom we despise'.[5] This contemptuous and dismissive dissociation from Johannesburg mining magnates is a vivid example of a more general unease in the relations between politicians and businessmen. Years later, the Labour minister Richard Crossman pronounced the government's distance from the world of the City 'ter-rifying'. Contrary to the Cain and Hopkins picture, there was in truth a deep mutual mistrust, a serious disparity of outlook: as one empire historian puts it, 'status, merit, honour and success were judged very differently in these two worlds'.[6] The 'gentlemanly class' may or may not have formed 'the backbone of the Colonial Office' (p. 121) (its most obvious characteristic in the first half of the twentieth century was surely its scholarly donnishness). But it is another matter entirely to position its civil servants as in effect sympathetic agents of City financiers, or indeed of any other interest group. More plausibly, they can be described as austere and objective guardians of national reputation, of trusteeship for those peoples administered from the CO – even if this was of limited effectiveness – and disdainful of vested interests of all kinds. There is here exactly the same kind of historiographical problem as that which confronted the now largely discredited neo-Marxist interpretations of the relationship between government and mining capitalists on the Witwatersrand before and after the South African War.

The problem for proponents of neo-Marxism or gentlemanly capitalism is the same. How do you prove – especially when you work from theory and secondary accounts rather than government documents – that the magnates, or businessmen, exercised a *determining* influence over political decision-making? The fact is that in South Africa such a link has not been proved, and the archival evidence is that the government manipulated the mining magnates, and not the other way round.[7] Similarly, those studying Malaya have rejected the idea of capitalist manipulation, and stressed the handicaps imposed by Colonial Office opposition.[8] More generally, having concerns in common, perhaps a convergence of interests – businessmen giving support to government, or even being consulted – none of this *proves* them to be exercising a decisive influence on government. Sometimes government did defend private economic initiatives overseas. But not often and never automatically. Where decisions suited economic interests, and government appeared to back commercial objectives, this was seldom for commercial reasons. It was much more likely to be applying geopolitical-strategic, international-prestige diplomatic calculations. Plainly, in some cases interests diverged.

If the authors are right that Whitehall attitudes were sympathetic to settlers in East Africa, and were 'broadly the same' (p. 581), then they have to explain why there was continual tension between them, and why, in the long run, settler aspirations failed. In China, it is claimed, British planners valued stability simply for the security of 'public sector loans'; too much is made in their account of China of the influence on government policy of Jardine, Matheson & Co. and the Hongkong and Shanghai Bank (HSBC) (pp. 605, 612). The authors assume that the Foreign Office and the HSBC were 'manned by the same sort of people' (pp. 379–80), a view which the haughty mandarins of the FO would have dismissed with scorn.[9] The actual disconnection between the FO and business leaders would be most strikingly illustrated by Sir William Fraser (1888–1970). This dour ungentlemanly Glaswegian oil industrialist, chairman of the Anglo-Iranian Oil Company – in which the government had a 51 per cent stake – never won the confidence of ministers or civil servants; his suitability for such an important post was questioned, and during the crisis of 1951 he was heavily criticised by diplomats. For his part, Fraser 'had a fire-eating contempt for civil servants'.[10] In short, the final admission of Cain and Hopkins that more work is needed on 'the connection joining financial interests to political authority' (p. 659) can only be welcomed.[11]

The analysis of the characteristics and influence of the 'gentlemanly capitalist class' (p. 449) will seem to some readers rather too tentative. But there is an even more fundamental problem involved in the attempt to explain the reality of something called 'British imperialism', and to do so along monocausal lines. One can only admire the courage of scholars who try to develop a thesis about 'imperialism', after the magisterial dismissal of its 'muddle-headed historians' by Sir Keith Hancock, more than half a century ago: 'It is a pseudo-concept which sets out to make everything clear and ends by making everything muddled; it is a word for the illiterates of social science, the callow and the shallow who attempt to solve problems without mastering a technique.'[12] The essential trouble with this 'pseudo-concept' is, as Ged Martin has demonstrated more than once, that it is 'a reified term that can all too easily take on a life of its own', which in its analytical looseness, can all too readily become 'an autonomous monster': 'Imperialism comes to life, becomes a historical player in its own right, a self-propelled bulldozer that roams the world creating level playing-fields for capitalism. Real people and even other processes, such as industrialisation, are reduced to the status of "agents".'[13] Moreover, those who persist with this 'pseudo-concept' are unable to agree upon a definition of 'imperialism'. Each makes his or her own theory ('it means what I say it means'). They may admit that it is complex, as well as ideologically loaded. But if complex, then it is absolutely not reducible to a single set of motives, in the Cain and Hopkins manner,[14] and, if emotive, then surely it is suspect as a working category.

Historians of empire have worked hard since the 1950s to elucidate the relative balance of a subtle and comprehensive range of variables in order to describe empires and expansionist motivations – not just economic explanations, but strategic, geopolitical, and prestige considerations, and religious, missionary, ethical, cultural, even sexual influences. They have understood that imperial activities cannot be comprehended by a restriction to 'metropolitan impulses', but have raised awareness of what was happening overseas, on 'the periphery', where turbulent frontier situations and indigenous reactions might draw European powers further from their bridgeheads into territorial control. Major contributions along these lines have been made, for example, by R.E. Robinson, acknowledged by Cain and Hopkins as a master of the field (p. 5, n. 18).[15] But by refocusing on the primacy of metropolitan initiatives and economic motives, Cain and Hopkins are aware that they may be committing themselves to a retrograde exercise.[16]

The inevitable result of confining discussion to the economic elements is a sheaf of lopsided interpretations, oversimplifications with insufficient context. Here are some examples. The purpose of taking (strategic) naval bases is said to have been simply 'to police the new economic order' (p. 650). Policy towards the Ottoman empire is depicted as prompted by financial interests, especially after its bankruptcy in 1875 (pp. 342–51)

– yet Christopher Platt established long ago that 'in no sense could it be said government intervened as part of a general policy of promoting British finance overseas'.[17] In the chapter on the partition of Africa, only ten pages are devoted to the tropical areas. These contain predictable generalisations: the 'City's needs were very much to the fore' (pp. 400–2), and, 'in general Britain enlarged her sphere of influence in areas where the value of existing trade indicated that expansion could be self-supporting' – but is that true for Somaliland, or Kenya, or Nyasaland? Britain's active South African policy in the 1890s 'owed little to strategic considerations' – but Cain and Hopkins ignore regional geopolitical concerns, and give the impression that the only strategic aim was the security of the Simon's Town naval base (pp. 324–6). The occupation of Egypt in 1882 is explained as 'a direct result of the Khedive's external indebtedness' (p. 652) – an interpretation sidelining such salient considerations as the 'routes to India'. The Anglo-Japanese alliance in 1902 emerges as if it were concluded merely to help 'the Treasury to control naval expenditure at a critical time by making Japan Britain's watchdog in the Far East' (p. 373) – rather than meeting Foreign Office concerns about Russian expansion. Chamberlain's failure with tariff reform after 1903 is much more complicated than is implied by their bald statement that he failed to unite industry behind him (pp. 194–7). The Union of South Africa was set up in 1909–10 for reasons other than just 'a preoccupation with finance', or hopes of realising its economic potential (p. 653): see below, p. 345. Afrikaner politicians of the 1930s would be amazed to see themselves described as having become 'servants of foreign business' (p. 511). As for Indian policy in the 1930s, because the authors assume gentlemanly representation of the national interest 'gave first place to financial considerations', they tell us that in cotton tariff reductions, 'Lancashire took second place to London'. This, they say, was because 'preserving textile exports was less important than defending sterling' (p. 563) – but what about political and ethical reasons for such a policy? Cain and Hopkins further suggest that Britain's constitutional policy for India was about seeking alliances which promoted fiscal and monetary objectives, and that radical political advance in India in the 1930s was constrained by the fear that an independent government would renege on its financial obligations (p. 543) – not in fact an argument advanced by Winston Churchill in his comprehensive die-hard attempt to hold up constitutional advance in the subcontinent.

Discussion of the issues of decolonisation after 1945 shows the same predictable emphasis on finance. In the case of Ghana, the authors write as follows: the nationalist leader Nkrumah 'agreed to respect the rules governing the sterling area in 1956, and he led his country to independence in the following year' (p. 638) – a seriously misleading *non sequitur*. The 'importance of financial priorities' in decolonisation is a hypothesis which finds little support outside their own work and that of their students (see their footnote 58 on p. 11). The authors are right to the extent that declining economic importance did remove obstacles to decolonisation in India and elsewhere (pp. 561, 620, 630).[18] But this negative factor needs relating to more positive ones, especially the international and geopolitical contexts of the cold war. Furthermore, domestic political and social constraints were also significant. The tenacious attempt of Wilson's Labour government after 1964 to avoid devaluation had everything to do with sterling as guarantor of living standards and symbol of British greatness, and very little to do with defending City interests.[19] Generally, and unfortunately, the statements in *British imperialism*, not necessarily untrue in themselves, tend to be advanced as if they alone were the key to understanding. Is this really the case?

II

The book is said to be based on 'research', but this turns out to be intensive reading of secondary materials, books, and articles by others. The authors' knowledge of this literature is second to none, and can only evoke awe. But of unpublished business records and diaries, official letters and despatches – archival documentation, or research as properly understood – there is little sign. The entire character of the project places much emphasis on theorisers at the expense of actual historical agents, with surprisingly meagre information about individual 'gentlemanly capitalists'. Marx and Marxist-Leninism score twenty-six references in the index. Marx, Schumpeter, Weber, Veblen, and Hobson are regularly referred to, while several of the expected historical actors, big players like Warren Hastings and Sir George Grey, are never mentioned. Others, such as Lord Curzon, appear only tangentially. Some are brought in solely to buttress the thesis, regardless of how reductionist this is. For example, many interesting things might be said about Sir Harry Johnston, influential and hyperactive in Africa, but there is just a single sentence, dealing with his unimportant youthful report on the economic prospects for an agricultural settlement in East Africa. This they admit was 'lyrical, almost chimerical' (p. 334). Or, for an earlier period, what about Sir Stamford Raffles? He was the founder of Singapore (*partly* for its economic prospects), a significant and complex participant in the development of Indonesia and South-East Asia before and after 1815. Driven by geopolitical plans and hatred of the Dutch, Raffles was a 'Renaissance man' with multifarious interests, including the founding of

London Zoo. He simply cannot be pinned down by an economic label such as 'gentlemanly capitalist'. Cain and Hopkins solve the problem neatly – by not dealing with him at all.[20]

Their defence for this approach is that they 'are concerned less with anatomising the biographical entrails of a Dilke or a Rhodes than with explaining why Dilke-like and Rhodes-like figures arose in the first place' – as if there were anybody 'like' these unique men in any case. Rather than analysing 'individual actions in terms of motivation', they are trying to understand 'trends and events and causes' – but not everyone will agree that the two can be profitably separated (p. 59).

William Pitt, the Earl of Chatham – surely an obvious figure for discussion in the context of possible links between City and government – is not even in the index, though he is mentioned once in passing (p. 89). Perhaps his absence is owing to the fact that it was shown a few years ago that Chatham was not the spokesman for the City in the way once supposed.[21] Still, the issue remains worth consideration, especially since without him, there appears to be no eighteenth-century minister of the Crown plausibly involved in such links. Moving on to the Victorians, Palmerston has just two paragraphs, equivalent to one page of text (pp. 99–100). He is claimed as representing aptly 'a particular brand of gentlemanly capitalism' (mixing economic liberty with paternalist interventionism). Commendably, the authors have a better understanding of Palmerston's extra-European policies than many of his biographers. But it is less helpful when they quote out of context the phrase about 'opening and securing roads for merchants', making it into a general economic aim, when it was in fact part of his diplomatic strategy for Afghanistan (see above, p. 74). Gladstone and Chamberlain alone among the politicians receive any extended coverage: Gladstone, who was not (as they admit) a foreign policy or empire man (p. 186), and Chamberlain, who was definitely not a gentleman. They rightly lay considerable emphasis on Gladstone's financial policies and determination to maintain Britain's economic supremacy (p. 187). But what is the convincing evidence for saying he was 'an *enthusiastic* subscriber' (my emphasis) to Egyptian stocks, and that this influenced his judgment in the crisis of 1882 (pp. 188–9)?[22] As for Chamberlain, Asquith thought he had the manners of a cad and the tongue of a bargee, and Salisbury even described him as 'the Cockney' – but he earns his place negatively, for his 'direct assault on gentlemanly culture' through the tariff reform campaign (pp. 194–7).

In general, there is a real difficulty, of which the authors are well aware, of deciding who is a genuine 'gentlemanly capitalist'.[23] Cain and Hopkins concede that one important financial group, joint-stock bankers or managers, were not gentlemen (p. 125). They recognise that many of the leading City figures were Jewish or cosmopolitan (Germans and Greeks as well as Scots), but extend to them the benefit of the 'gentlemanly' doubt (p. 123) – which is dubious, because Jews laboured under civil disabilities until 1858 and were kept out of Oxbridge colleges, the essential training ground for the Victorian gentleman. Candidates for inclusion in the elite, within the definition of 'gentlemanly capitalists', tend to be multiplied until it almost seems that none can be allowed to escape, such as those accorded 'honorary membership' ('gentlemen' for this purpose, rather like Queen Victoria being an honorary man as required).

There are several examples of this in the chapter on 'Britain and the partition of Africa, 1882–1902' (ch. 11, pp. 303–39), where Sir William Mackinnon, Sir Donald Currie, and Sir Alfred Jones are all blithely included among those 'most successful entrepreneurs who descended on Africa [bringing] the gentlemanly code with them'.[24] Yet Alfred Jones (who founded Elder Dempster Line at Liverpool in 1879, dominated West African shipping, and brought bananas to Britain), began his working life as a cabin-boy and remained essentially a provincial Liverpool merchant. Currie (founder of the Castle Line in 1862, which became Union-Castle) was a Scotsman, the son of a barber, hated by London-based officials and by businessmen everywhere for his willingness to strike mutually advantageous bargains with German capitalists. There was nothing very gentlemanly about Currie, and he seemed untouched by imperial sentiment. Mackinnon (founder of the British India Steam Navigation Co. in 1856, and chairman of the Imperial British East Africa Company, 1888–95), with his Indo-Scottish interests, developed overseas regional networks without reference to any British metropolitan financial-cum-service elite. Mackinnon's family raised capital in Calcutta, the Netherlands, and Indonesia. He had no access to Treasury mandarins, and Rosebery allowed him no influence on the political future of Uganda. Mackinnon has been described by one acute historian (with no axe to grind) as 'quite free from capitalist ambitions', encouraging support for the IBEA Company from missionaries and military men rather than the big capitalists.[25] As to the prime movers on the spot in the partition, they seem equally ambiguous. Sir George Goldie may have been an entrepreneur, but he was of Manx origins, commissioned in the Royal Engineers, and defiantly his own man. A convinced atheist, he lived for three years in isolation in the Egyptian Sudan with an Arab woman, before more publicly offending Victorian sexual morality by eloping to Paris with the family governess. Settling down somewhat, he set up a Nigerian administration through the Royal Niger Company. From this vantage-point, Goldie looked to the conversion of the North

African belt from the Niger to the Nile (the 'Sudan') into 'an African India', to be a source of military manpower rather than a field of commercial development. Its races were 'at once capable of fighting and amenable to discipline', and could usefully reduce a dependence on Indian troops in the tropics, undesirable on several grounds.[26] Lugard, the most famous of Britain's colonial governors, was a seriously confused young man from an army and clerical family, an ex-soldier with fantasies of becoming an elephant hunter. As high commissioner for Northern Nigeria he was determined to control, or in some spheres to prohibit, business enterprise, attaching primary importance to the interests of the Africans.[27] Cecil Rhodes in southern Africa was a country vicar's wayward son, regarded by many as a vulgar, bad-tempered upstart. His crony, the diamond magnate Barney Barnato, had the reputation of being a 'dreadful little Whitechapel Jewish Cockney'. None of these men was a conventional 'gentlemanly capitalist'. At the same time, the bankers in the City showed no propensity to invest in the newly acquired African territories.[28]

It is no more persuasive to characterise as 'associates' of the gentlemanly-capitalist entrepreneurs such people as the representatives of the Church Missionary Society, supposedly 'drawn from established gentry families and from the professional classes of southern England' (p. 308). In fact, most missionaries were of lowly social background and often ill-educated. Many of the earliest were from Yorkshire farming stock and were craftsmen. The most important of all, Samuel Marsden, second chaplain to the penal colony in New South Wales (where he was known as 'the flogging parson') and 'the Apostle of New Zealand' (1814), was a rough-and-ready Yorkshire blacksmith, with a late-applied veneer of Cambridge education. By the 1820s he had recruited as missionaries a fruit-grower, a ropemaker, a flax-dresser, a shoesmith, four carpenters, and a schoolteacher.[29] The great Livingstone himself was born in a one-room Glasgow tenement, son of a self-employed tea-dealer, and he worked in a mill from the age of ten.[30] The Welsh, the Scots, and women were always prominent, and several British missionary societies fell back on German recruits. Nearly all missionaries in any case, and especially the ubiquitous Evangelicals, felt almost no affinity with the ideals of the ruling classes, let alone settlers or businessmen.[31]

And again, the systematisation of the values of the gentlemanly elite into a powerful independent force has been overdrawn. After all, even the Rothschilds were able only to provide finance for policies already decided by politicians; they 'never shaped important policy'.[32] The authors exaggerate the coherence, the insulation from industry, and the self-containedness of this elite. Like most interest groups, they were far from monolithic in their concerns and representations, holding conflicting views of what was and was not appropriate. This significantly reduced any effectiveness they might have had, as it does for all loose interest groups. Historians used to think the West India sugar lobby in the eighteenth century exercised a powerful political influence, but this was not so, because the planters were in fact split into at least three sub-interest groups.[33] Martin Daunton likewise convincingly showed – well before the final working out of the Cain and Hopkins thesis – that 'The City was fluid and divided in terms of its economic and social structure,' and, for example, split at least four ways on the Edwardian issue of free trade versus tariff reform.[34] As for the politicians, the undoubted gentlemen of the Liberal Party from the 1890s articulated a strong critique of what they disparagingly called 'stock-jobbing imperialism'. This was described by Sir William Harcourt as 'squalid and sordid' (1896), while according to John Morley, Rhodes was surrounded by those 'with whom imperialism is, and can't be anything else, but a name for [stock-jobbing] operations of that ignoble kind' (1897).[35]

Following on from this objection, the thesis has met with criticism from historians about the way it involves downgrading the contributions made to an expanding Britain by regions of the UK other than south-east England, like Merseyside and the 'Celtic fringe'. There was a large financial and mercantile class in northern industrial districts, and Manchester merchants were able at least to talk to government.[36] West and central Scotland was the base for one of the UK's biggest concentrations of heavy industry and commercial enterprise, cemented by Scottish clannishness and freemasonry (an alternative manifestation of 'linked values'?). Only about a fifth of the British mercantile marine was registered in London. Several of the leading British steamship companies operated out of Glasgow, including the Mackinnon group, which was second to none. Glasgow benefited from its northern location, since the northerly sea-route to America (the Clyde to Virginia, say) usually took a little more than two weeks *less* in each direction than the transatlantic journey from more southerly embarcation points. Glasgow was the principal port for Canada. The leading business-firm in Upper (British) Canada by the mid-1850s was the import-export merchant house of Peter and Isaac Buchanan, brothers from a Scottish farming family, operating out of Glasgow, with annual sales of $2 million. The entire Canadian business world to this day retains a strong Scottish tinge and character, and the south-east of England is just not in the frame.[37]

The authors admit that not everything can be explained in economic terms. They recognise, for instance, that trusteeship policies cannot be reduced to economic motives (p. 571). They concede that geopolitical considerations 'have their place in the story' (p. 645), but only, it seems, within the context of 'the importance of financial priorities in the formulation of international policy' (p. 11) – which is a pretty big retracting qualification to their concession. Moreover, what is lacking is any systematic attempt to measure the exact relative dynamic balance of geopolitical, economic, or ethical considerations in imperial policy. Several revealing test-cases will suggest themselves to readers, including such standard 'topics' as the partition of Africa (see chapter 2) and the South African War. The case I have chosen here is one neglected in recent historiography, though it figured prominently for an earlier generation of empire historians. This is the making of the Peace of Paris in 1762–3, especially the 'Canada versus Guadeloupe' controversy.[38]

The Seven Years War was the most successful war Britain ever fought. The spoils piled up magnificently. From France, Britain conquered Canada, slaving-ports in West Africa, trading-stations in India, and virtually all the French West Indian islands except St Domingue, but including the prizes of Guadeloupe and Martinique. From Spain, Britain captured Havana in Cuba (Spain's most important colonial possession) and Manila in the Philippines. The British government accepted the eighteenth-century international convention that victors should not retain all their conquests, but should seek a stable future balance of power. The British prime minister, Lord Bute, who was determined to pursue a permanent peace, had to decide which conquests to keep and which to let go. Within the grand strategy, keeping Canada was the priority. Britain yielded the main French West Indian islands in order to consolidate all the American territory on the left bank (to the east) of the Mississippi. Florida was taken from Spain in return for handing back Havana. Although there was a lively pamphlet controversy about 'Canada versus Guadeloupe', with arguments that Guadeloupe was economically much more valuable than Canada, the government ignored the public dispute. Bute accepted the principal war aim, defined by William Pitt in 1761 as 'the entire safety' of North America, and especially 'the secure possession of that most valuable conquest of Canada'. Canada was seen within a Eurocentric context of rivalry with another European power. Attempts have been made to suggest that the government was intelligently seeking to open up economic opportunities in eastern Louisiana and Canada ('as a great potential market for British producers').[39] However, there can be no doubt that the peace terms were constructed simplistically and solely in order to realise the essential war aims, by providing a strategic security for the American colonies. Canada pre-eminently fulfilled this geopolitical requirement, although it was also no disadvantage to be able to claim that retention would protect the interests of the fisheries and the fur trade. Expanding territorial holdings westward to the banks of the Mississippi provided an incontrovertible boundary, and removed the French from dangerous contact with the Amerindians; but this decision flew in the face of the fact that the Mississippi Valley was an economic unit which could not rationally be divided. The acquisition of Florida was expected to remove the threat of a French-inspired Spanish incursion from the south. France had tried to save Florida for Spain by offering Britain a million square miles of Louisiana lands to the west of the river, a striking offer rejected on geopolitical grounds. In short, there was no searching out of economic opportunity in the peace terms, and the great sugar-producing island of Guadeloupe was therefore returned to France.

Nor did the government in 1762–3 pay any significant attention to the interests of the big commercial companies, and this despite the fact that their loans had been a vital part of the government's ability to finance the war effort. (Up to 70 per cent of the cost of the Seven Years War was met by loans, mainly from merchants.) The government did consult the East India Company about the Indian peace terms, but chose to find its claims excessive and unsatisfactory, preferring to stick to a reversion to the *status quo ante*, generous to France. The company was told it must either accept these basic terms or be left out of the negotiation, and the directors were then given an official draft to accept or amend in one day.[40] Nonetheless, the East India Company was accorded better treatment than the Hudson's Bay Company, which seemed to be largely forgotten even within the salient Canadian context, until March 1763, *after* the conclusion of the final treaty, when it was asked for a statement of the limits of its claims in Labrador. As the company's historian observes, it was not able to sway discussions at the highest political level.[41] The Board of Trade had little grasp of British overseas trading interests, and could not furnish any useful information about the West African trade; when Bute was petitioned by Liverpool merchants trading to Africa in October 1762, he expressed surprise at the size of their operations, but said it was too late to do anything to assist them.

III

British imperialism stands at the end of a long line of investigation into 'economic imperialism', perhaps the apotheosis of this strand of historiography. But whereas their predecessors were content to write of 'the economic *elements*' in the Pax Britannica, or 'economic *factors*' in the history of the empire,[42] and accepted that '*economic* imperialism' was a sub-set of a larger species, Cain and Hopkins have been much more audacious.

British imperialism continues to attract attention (and qualification),[43] particularly among economic historians, who might be sceptical but take it seriously as a basis for discussion.[44] Imperial historians have, on the whole (with the notable exception of Bernard Porter[45]), been much less impressed and respectful. Some agree with the lethal dismissal by Peter Burroughs, that those who accept Cain and Hopkins could 'comfortably assemble in a telephone kiosk'.[46] If the book had been modestly and more accurately entitled 'An economic history of the British empire',[47] it would of course have generated much less interest, but it would also have been much less open to attack as 'an invitingly large target'.[48] For the stumbling block is precisely its claim fundamentally to explain the dynamics of 'British imperialism', when the limit of what it effectively does is to advance a theory summarising the recent historiography of its economic aspects. That is of course valid and worthwhile – especially on some of the twentieth-century issues – and it is done with an enviable command of the specialist literature. But we should not mistake its wider value for understanding the empire.[49] There is an intriguing theory, but much of the actual history has been left out. The words of one of the greatest of all economic historians ought perhaps to apply: 'If it is the theoretician's job to remove from his argument the considerations which do not happen to be "strictly" economic, it is the historian's function to bring them together again.'[50]

Notes

1 P.J. Cain and A.G. Hopkins, 'The political economy of British overseas expansion, 1750–1914', *Economic History Review*, vol. 33 (1980), pp. 463–90, and 'Gentlemanly capitalism and British overseas expansion', Part I, 'The old colonial system, 1688–1850' and Part II, 'New imperialism, 1850–1945', *Economic History Review*, vol. 39, (1986), pp. 501–25, and vol. 40 (1987), pp. 1–26. For an incisive evaluation of their work within the historiography of imperial economic history, see A.R. Dilley, 'The economics of empire', in Sarah Stockwell, ed., *The British empire: themes and perspectives* (2008), pp. 101–29.

2 Among the most sustained critiques are: D.K. Fieldhouse, 'Gentlemen, capitalists and the British empire', *JICH*, vol. 22 (1994), pp. 531–41; Geoffrey Ingham, 'British capitalism: empire, merchants and decline', *Social History*, vol. 20 (1995), pp. 339–48; while M.J. Daunton, 'Home and colonial', *Twentieth Century British History*, vol. 6 (1995), pp. 344–58, develops a powerful critique from the perspective of British economic development and state formation. Further comment may be found in H.V. Bowen and T.J. Barron, 'The British empire, I and II', review article in *History*, vol. 79 (1994), pp. 263–8; and in Edward Ingram, *The British empire as a world power* (2001), which is highly critical, especially for 'inadequate attention to the Middle East' (pp. 11, 49–52, 242–3).

3 'Foreword: the continuing debate', pp. 1–19 of the second edition. The one exception is their reaction to criticism by Andrew Porter (pp. 5–6, nn. 18, 19, see also p. 55, n. 89), criticism which is not nearly as hostile as they seem to think: A.N. Porter, '"Gentlemanly capitalism" and empire, the British experience since 1750?', *JICH*, vol. 18 (1990), pp. 265–95, and 'Birmingham, Westminster and the City of London: visions of empire compared', *Journal of Historical Geography*, vol. 21 (1995), pp. 83–7, which compares the first edition (two volumes) of *British imperialism, 1688–1990* (1993) with my *Britain's imperial century* (2nd edn, 1993).

4 The downgrading of industry historically in itself implies a dubious revision. Although it follows some (once) fashionable questioning of the 'reality' of the Industrial Revolution and the importance of industry in British economic development, the Industrial Revolution remains 'real' as a motive force in overseas expansion because its revolutionary nature (increases in textile exports) depended on *anticipated, overseas,* demand, notably for cotton clothing in tropical climes; this is why cotton was the leading sector. Therefore: 'The British case is the classic prototype of an industrial revolution based on overseas trade' (W.A. Cole and P. Deane, in *Cambridge economic history of Europe,* vol. VI, *The industrial revolutions and after,* ed. H.J. Habakkuk and M. Postan (1965), p. 5.). See also J.R. Ward, 'The Industrial Revolution and British imperialism, 1750–1850', *Economic History Review,* vol. 47 (1994), pp. 44–65.

5 E. Drus, 'Select documents from the Chamberlain Papers concerning Anglo-Transvaal relations, 1896–1899', *Bulletin of the Institute for Historical Research,* vol. 27 (1954), p. 189, Salisbury to Lord Lansdowne, 30 August 1899.

6 John Darwin, *The empire project: the rise and fall of the British world-system, 1830–1970* (2009), p. 89; R.H.S. Crossman, *The diaries of a Cabinet minister,* vol. II, *1966–1968* (1976), p. 603 (14 December 1967).

7 A.N. Porter, *Origins of the South African War: Joseph Chamberlain and the diplomacy of imperialism, 1895–1899* (Manchester, 1980), for the role of public opinion and the manipulation of it; see also P.J. Henshaw, 'Breakdown: into war, 1895–1899', in RH and Henshaw, *The lion and the springbok: Britain and South Africa since the Boer War* (Cambridge, 2003), ch. 2, pp. 37–56.

8 Keith Sinclair, 'Hobson and Lenin in Johore: Colonial Office policy towards British concessionaires and investors, 1878–1907', *Modern Asian Studies,* vol. 1 (1967), pp. 335–52; V. Ponko, Jr, 'The Colonial Office and British business before World War I: a case-study', *Business History Review,* vol. 43 (1969), pp. 39–58.

9 It was suggested to Hopkins back in 1972 that he might be exaggerating the influence of Lagos merchants on the West Africa policy of the Foreign Office and Colonial Office: J.F.A. Ajayi and R.A. Austen, 'Hopkins on economic imperialism in West Africa', *Economic History Review,* vol. 25 (1972), pp. 303–6, commenting on A.G. Hopkins, 'Economic imperialism in West Africa: Lagos, 1880–1892', *Economic History Review,* vol. 21 (1968), pp. 581–606; see also Hopkins, 'The economic basis of imperialism', in *An economic history of West Africa* (1973), ch. 4, pp. 124–66.

10 J.H. Bamberg, 'Fraser, William Milligan', *ODNB,* vol. XX, pp. 884–6; W.R.

Louis, *The British empire in the Middle East, 1945–1951* (Oxford, 1984), pp. 643–6. Similarly, of an equally influential businessman, Sir Ronald Prain, chairman of the Rhodesia Select Trust, 1950–72 (a copper-mining baron who held innumerable chairmanships and directorships in the metallurgical industry), it can be said 'his outlook and behaviour sit uncomfortably with the homogeneity of interests between business and state which is central to the "gentlemanly capitalist" model'; born in Chile, son of a mine manager, Prain never went to a university. See L.J. Butler, 'Business and decolonisation: Sir Ronald Prain, the mining industry and the Central African Federation', *JICH*, vol. 35 (2007), p. 477, and *Copper empire: mining and the colonial state in Northern Rhodesia, c. 1930–1964* (Basingstoke, 2007).

11 There seems no reason to revise the authoritative conclusions of one of the world's most eminent economic historians, David S. Landes, that there was no unity between government and economic interests, and in such linkage as there might seem to be, business or economic pressure was invariably in the service of diplomacy: 'Economic imperialism', *Journal of Economic History*, vol. 21 (1961), special issue on *Colonialism and colonisation in World History*, p. 508.

12 W.K. Hancock, *The wealth of colonies* (The Marshall Lectures, Cambridge, 1950), pp. 8, 17.

13 Ged Martin, *Past futures: the impossible necessity of history* (Toronto, 2004), pp. 60–4.

14 Cain and Hopkins declare that Denmark was 'just as much within the orbit of British overseas economic influence as were the smaller newly-settled countries' (p. 231). Why then was Denmark not recognised as part of Britain's formal or informal empire? Cain and Hopkins cannot say. The answer must be that finance-capital interests *alone* are not sufficient to explain outcomes: other factors have to be present as well.

15 R.E. Robinson, 'The non-European foundations of European imperialism: a sketch for a theory of collaboration', in R. Owen and B. Sutcliffe, eds., *Studies in the theory of imperialism* (1972), pp. 117–42, and the related paper on 'European imperialism and indigenous reactions in British West Africa, 1880–1914', in H.L. Wesseling, ed., *Expansion and reaction* (Leiden, 1978), pp. 141–63.

16 *British imperialism* is not merely metrocentric and Eurocentric, it is *Anglocentric*. An overarching theory about a modern empire, if it is to persuade, should surely be valid (or at least reasonably congruent) for the analysis of other contemporaneous empires. (In case this seems an unreasonable demand, perhaps I may be allowed to point out that I have tried to test my own 'geopolitical' interpretation of British expansion against other empires: see RH, *Britain's imperial century* (3rd edn, 2002), pp. 317–31, 'Global context: the empire in comparative perspective', repr. above, chapter 3.) Aware that such a criticism will be made, Cain and Hopkins mention the issue, arguing that 'the evidence currently available is insufficiently detailed to allow generalisations to be made with confidence' about other European powers (p. 659). Presumably what this means is that there is insufficient evidence to support their *own* hypothesis. After all, D.K. Fieldhouse dealt with France and

Germany as well as Britain in his great work *Economics and empire, 1830–1914* (1973, 1984), to say nothing of *The colonial empires: a comparative survey, from the 18th century* (2nd edn, 1982, 1987). More recently, equally broad in scope, there is Jonathan Hart, *Empires and colonies* (2008), and Robin A. Butlin, *Geographies of empire: European empires and colonies, c.1880–1960* (Cambridge, 2009), with a pertinent criticism of 'gentlemanly capitalism' at pp. 27–8.

17 D.C.M. Platt, *Finance, trade, and politics in British foreign policy, 1815–1914* (Oxford, 1963), pp. 204–18. According to Platt, the 'overriding considerations in forming Ottoman policy were strategic, political and humanitarian'; he quotes Lord Salisbury as saying that all he could offer Turkish bondholders was 'a tender but perfectly platonic expression of sympathy' (1887). Similarly, McLean's work on Persia shows how economic tools were used to confirm Britain's political presence: Lord George Hamilton told Curzon that the main object of the loan 'is political rather than financial' (D. McLean, *Britain and her buffer-state: the collapse of the Persian empire, 1890–1914* (1979, p. 49). Cain and Hopkins themselves quote Edward Grey admitting that financial assistance was given in order 'to obtain leverage over the Persian government': see their section on 'Persia: financial diplomacy – with limited finance', pp. 351–7.

18 The main discussion of decolonisation is in ch. 26, 'The City, the Sterling Area and decolonisation', pp. 635–40, which is more about sterling than decolonisation. The equation of City and empire may be weakened by their admission that decolonisation did not lead to the fall of the City (p. 658). But in any case, any number of regional studies have agreed in their conclusion that economic interests had almost no direct influence on 'transfer of power' policies, or, as John Darwin puts it magisterially in his essay on decolonisation, there was 'an Olympian disregard of official policy for commercial interests in the formation of its political and constitutional programme': *OHBE*, vol. V, *Historiography* (ed. R.W. Winks, 1999), p. 555. Sarah Stockwell confirms that from the late 1950s 'geopolitical considerations emerge as more significant [than economic interests] in determining Britain's handling of colonial nationalism': 'Trade, empire and the fiscal context of imperial business during decolonisation', *Economic History Review*, vol. 57 (2004), pp. 142–4. See further, 'Ends of empire', in Stockwell, ed., *The British empire: themes and perspectives* (2008), pp. 269–93.

19 J. Tomlinson, 'The decline of the empire and the economic "decline" of Britain', *Twentieth Century British History*, vol. 14 (2003), pp. 206–8. Tomlinson points out that 'the same kind of criticisms made about Cain and Hopkins's treatment of the pre-1939 period have relevance to the post-war decades', and that making economic considerations the defining issue in decolonisation is 'implausible'.

20 For Sir George Grey, see the splendid article by James Belich, *ODNB*, vol. XXIII, pp. 839–45. For Harry Johnston, see R. Oliver, *ODNB*, vol. XXX, pp. 366–8; for Raffles, see C.M. Turnbull, *ODNB*, vol. XLV, pp. 788–93.

21 M. Peters, 'The myth of William Pitt, Earl of Chatham, great imperialist', Part I, 'Pitt and imperial expansion, 1738–1763', *JICH*, vol. 21 (1993), pp.

31–74, which in particular stresses his geopolitical concerns and casts doubt on the earlier interpretations of J.H. Plumb in *Chatham* (1953) and Kate Hotblack, *Chatham's colonial policy: fiscal and economic implications* (1917), esp. pp. 12–26.

22 Even Cain and Hopkins admit no more than that it was 'likely' Gladstone would see the 'creditors' point of view with some clarity'. The subtle and definitive discussion of this issue is by H.C.G. Matthew, which certainly does not allow the 'enthusiastic investor' claim; Gladstone was a 'bondholder at *second hand*'; his holding was 'substantial' (this was not unusual), but he was unaware of a damaging link (H.C.G. Matthew, ed., *The Gladstone diaries*, vol. X, *January 1881–June 1883* (Oxford, 1990), pp. lxxi–lxxiii.

23 One notices the circularity of the scholarly mechanisms by which the validation of hypotheses tends to take place. For example, D.E. Torrance, a young historian, wanting to assimilate his portrait of Lord Selborne to the exciting Cain and Hopkins thesis, the 'new debate on imperialism', portrays Selborne as a 'gentlemanly capitalist' (unconvincingly, in my view), and then Torrance in turn is gratefully seized upon by Cain and Hopkins as lending further support to their hypothesis (p. 10): D.E. Torrance, *The strange death of the Liberal empire: Lord Selborne in South Africa* (Liverpool, 1996), which is hard to square with the more persuasive characterisation by D. George Boyce in the aptly entitled *The crisis of British power: the imperial and naval papers of the Second Earl of Selborne, 1895–1910* (1990).

24 My material here closely follows Porter, 'Birmingham, Westminster and the City of London', p. 85. See also A.N. Porter, *Victorian shipping, business, and imperial policy: Donald Currie, the Castle Line and southern Africa* (Woodbridge, Suffolk, and New York, 1986).

25 R. Koebner, 'The concept of economic imperialism', *Economic History Review*, vol. 2 (1949), pp. 1–29, a particularly full and well-argued investigation of the problem, and still worth serious attention. The important large-scale monograph by J. Forbes Munro, *Maritime enterprise and empire: Sir William Mackinnon and his business network, 1823–1893* (Woodbridge, Suffolk, 2003) discusses Cain and Hopkins at pp. 8–9 and 505–11, and poses the question of whether those around Mackinnon ever did escape 'from the values of small burgh and urban Scotland'. Forbes Munro's study supersedes J.S. Galbraith, *Mackinnon and East Africa, 1878–1895: a study in the 'new imperialism'* (Cambridge, 1972), which came to conclusions similar to Koebner's.

26 George Goldie, 'Introduction', to S. Vandeleur, *Campaigning on the Upper Nile and Niger* (1898), repr. in D. Wellesley, *Sir George Goldie* (1934), pp. 165–81.

27 M. Perham, *Lugard*, vol. II, *The years of authority, 1898–1945* (Oxford, 1960), p. 171; see also a most illuminating re-assessment by A.H.M. Kirk-Greene, 'Lugard, Frederick J.D.', *ODNB*, vol. XXXIV, pp. 927–32.

28 J.E. Flint, review of *British imperialism*, in *International History Review*, vol. 16 (1994), pp. 787–90.

29 J.R. Elder, ed., *The letters and journals of Samuel Marsden, 1765–1838* (Dunedin, 1932), p. 445n.; Elisabeth Elbourne, 'Religion in the British empire', in Stockwell, ed., *The British empire*, p. 139.

30 A.D. Roberts, 'Livingstone, David', *ODNB*, vol. XXXIV, pp. 73–82: an important re-evaluation.

31 Andrew Porter, *Religion versus empire? British Protestant missionaries and overseas expansion, 1700–1914* (2004).

32 R. Davison, *The English Rothschilds* (1983); R.V. Turrell, '"Finance . . . the governor of the imperial engine": Hobson and the case of Rothschild and Rhodes', *Journal of Southern African Studies*, vol. 13 (1987), pp. 417–32, which distinguishes between the 'governor' mechanism and the *motive force*, a difference too often obscured, and points out the difficulty of empirical proofs: for all the evidence of financial influence there is equal evidence that 'politicians distanced themselves from the City'.

33 Richard Pares, *War and trade in the West Indies, 1739–1763* (1936).

34 Martin Daunton, 'Gentlemanly capitalism and British industry, 1820–1914', *Past and Present*, no. 122 (1989), pp. 119–58, esp. pp. 148–9.

35 Koebner, 'The concept of economic imperialism', pp. 16–19.

36 Martin Daunton, 'Home and colonial', review article, *Twentieth Century British History*, vol. 6 (1995), pp. 344–58; A. Redford, *Manchester merchants and foreign trade*, vol. I, *1794–1858* (Manchester, 1934).

37 D. McCalla, *The Upper Canada trade, 1834–1872: a study of the Buchanans' business* (Toronto, 1979). Additionally, Ged Martin has shown how Canadian politicians – presumably part of Cain and Hopkins's 'gentlemanly diaspora' (p. 56) – in the first seven years of Confederation after 1867 failed to conform to expectation, and 'showed themselves to be very ungentlemanly capitalists indeed': *Past futures*, pp. 63–4. Martin also showed how Cain and Hopkins have misunderstood Britain's capital contribution to sustaining an independent British North America, in part because they adumbrate a 'St Lawrence seaway' acting as a conduit for late nineteenth-century British trade to Midwest America – a seaway which was in fact opened only in 1959: Ged Martin, *Britain and the origins of Canadian Confederation* (1995), p. 307, n. 31.

38 Brendan Simms, *Three victories and a defeat: the rise and fall of the first British empire, 1714–1783* (2007), pp. 475–500. For older discussions, see Pares, *War and trade in the West Indies*, pp. 216–22; L.B. Namier, *England in the age of the American Revolution*, vol. I, *Newcastle and Bute, 1760–1763* (1930, 2nd edn 1961), pp. 317–27. Harlow recognised the Peace of Paris as an almost ideal example for the study of the interplay of various imperial concerns: *The historian and British colonial history: an inaugural lecture, 1950* (Oxford, 1951), p. 16. See RH, 'British imperial expansion in the late eighteenth century', *Historical Journal*, vol. 10 (1967), pp. 113–24, and 'Imperial interests and the Peace of Paris (1763)', in *Reapprasials in British imperial history* (1975), pp. 21–43.

39 V.T. Harlow, *The founding of the second British empire, 1763–1793*, vol. I, *Discovery and revolution* (1952), pp. 162–6.

40 Lucy Sutherland, *The East India Company in 18th-century politics* (1952), pp. 94–7, and 'The East India Company and the Peace of Paris', *English Historical Review*, vol. 57 (1947), pp. 179–90. The lack of concern for commercial interests is reinforced in Simms, *Three victories and a defeat*, ch. 17,

although one may not entirely accept his overall 'Eurocentric' reinterpretation of imperial policy.

41 E.E. Rich, *The history of the Hudson's Bay Company, 1670–1870*, vol. I, *1670–1763* (1958), pp. 656–60.

42 Richard Pares, 'Economic factors in the history of the empire', *Economic History Review*, 1st series, vol. 7 (1937), pp. 119–44; A.H. Imlah, *Economic elements in the Pax Britannica: studies in British foreign trade in the nineteenth century* (Cambridge, MA, 1958); D.C.M. Platt, 'Economic factors in British imperial policy during the "New imperialism"', *Past and Present*, no. 39 (1968), pp. 123–38.

43 R.E. Dumett, ed., *Gentlemanly capitalism and British imperialism: the new debate on empire* (1999).

44 For example, Daunton's powerful analyses, 'Gentlemanly capitalism and British industry', in *Past and Present*, and 'Home and colonial', in *Twentieth Century British History* (notes 34 and 36 above).

45 Bernard Porter, *The lion's share: a short history of British imperialism, 1850–1995* (3rd edn, 1996), pp. xiv–xvii, 151–2.

46 Peter Burroughs, review of M. Kitchen, *British empire and Commonwealth: a short history*, in *JICH*, vol. 25 (1997), pp. 344–5. R.E. Robinson's appraisal of their work was perhaps more muted than Cain and Hopkins suggest (p. 5, n. 18) – he said merely that it was 'an original view of a major movement in British imperial history' (*JICH*, vol. 27, 1999, p. 11).

47 On the lines of Hopkins's *An economic history of West Africa*, which remains a much-admired and useful book, likely to out-live *British imperialism*.

48 Fieldhouse, 'Gentlemen, capitalists and the British empire'.

49 After the initial euphoria, the tide is now beginning to turn: see, for example, a former pupil of Cain and Hopkins, Anthony Webster, 'The strategies and limits of gentlemanly capitalism: the London East India agency houses, provincial commercial interests, and the evolution of British economic policy in South and South East Asia, 1800–1850', *Economic History Review*, vol. 59 (2006), pp. 743–64, which strongly challenges the supposed separation between the City and the provincial mercantile and industrial interests. This is an issue to which Daunton had first drawn attention in *Past and Present* (note 34 above) – Daunton showed that ties between industrialists on the one hand, and the financial and commercial middle class on the other, could be strong: even Nathan Rothschild first came to England to finance trade in cotton goods in Manchester.

50 M.M. Postan, *Fact and relevance: essays on historical method* (Cambridge, 1971), p. 121.

Part II
Ethics and religion

5   Peter Peckard, 'universal benevolence', and the abolition of the slave trade

[Newly written for this volume, this chapter is based upon parts of two pamphlets published as Magdalene College Occasional Papers (nos. 16 and 35): *Peter Peckard: liberal churchman and anti-slave trade campaigner* (with J.D. Walsh, 1998), and *Magdalene, anti-slavery, and the early human rights movement, from the 1780s to the 1830s* (2007).]

The Atlantic slave trade, it is now believed, despatched 11,863,000 Africans to America and the West Indies. Estimates tend to get revised upwards, so we can safely say 'about 12 million, and maybe more'. Fewer actually arrived in the New World, of course, the death toll on the notorious fifty-one-day 'middle passage' across the Atlantic being on average about 15 per cent. During the eighteenth century, Britain became the major contributor to the traffic, shipping a total of about 30,000 slaves every year in the hundred years before abolition in 1807.[1]

This was social engineering on a huge scale, and of a particularly cruel kind. Even after the horrors of the Holocaust and the anguish of apartheid, the African slave trade remains one of the most appalling chapters in the history of humanity's inhumanity. Not just European inhumanity, it has to be said – but Arab and African inhumanity and complicity too. So why did it last for so long, more or less unchallenged? The economic realities of producing sugar, rice, tobacco, and cotton on tropical plantations in sparsely populated regions were held to make imported African labour indispensable. It was not illegal, and African indigenous slavery was well established. There was a legitimising if shaky so-called 'biblical defence' of slavery, which argued that Noah had cursed the sons of Ham into servitude, and Africans were their remote descendants.

Acquiescence was compounded by the fact that Europeans themselves might be enslaved by Muslims, perhaps 20,000 of them – which is why 'Rule, Britannia!' (1740) proclaims 'Britons never will be slaves'.[2] But above all the Atlantic slave trade persisted simply because of inertia, ignorance, unthinking indifference, and a sense of its being an unalterable necessity, part of the natural order of things.

All that was to change from the 1780s. Quakers, Enlightenment thinkers, revolutionary ideologues, and even some poets had made their protests, but they had little impact. It was essentially the Cambridge and Anglican campaigners who really forced the abolition issue into take-off. They were working against the grain, and it was a tremendous counter-cultural achievement.

It was not that the slave trade was suddenly becoming less profitable than it had been. So why did people turn against it? There is a lively and continuing controversy.[3] W.E.H. Lecky, in his *History of European morals* (1869), described the crusade against slavery as 'among the three or four perfectly virtuous acts recorded in the history of nations'. Subsequent generations have treated this judgment with considerable scepticism. Most famously, there was Eric Williams with his contrary thesis in *Capitalism and slavery* (1944), which argued that abolition came about as a result of obsolescence and disillusionment, and that changing economic conditions actually required it. 'The humanitarians', he wrote, 'could never have succeeded in a hundred years when every important capitalist interest was on the side of the colonial system.' Yet the fact is that the development of a climate of opinion objecting to the slave trade on moral grounds was unprecedented. The aim in this chapter is to examine the contribution of one individual, an Anglican clergyman, so as to understand the religious or 'humanitarian' case better. An intense public reaction was created against the slave trade. This had a crucial – if not all-sufficient – part to play in demolishing the long-standing near-universal acceptance of it. Not 'all-sufficient', because no responsible government could have abolished it manifestly *against* the national economic interest. Nevertheless, for campaigners to have successfully reversed such deeply entrenched public and governmental perceptions was remarkable – something which Edmund Burke as late as 1780 had considered a hopeless task ('a very chimerical object').[4] The year 1807 probably marked the heyday of the profitability of the Atlantic slave trade, with perhaps four-fifths of British overseas investment tied up in the West Indies. Some historians have argued that the slave trade was a nationally important and dynamic system 'aborted in its prime'.[5]

I

Peter Peckard (1717–97) was appointed Master of Magdalene College Cambridge in 1781 and remained there until his death. He was vice-chancellor of the University of Cambridge in the years 1784 and 1785. Unusually for an abolitionist, he was neither a Quaker nor an Evangelical, but a latitudinarian (broad-church) Anglican divine, who believed in a religion of 'universal benevolence', 'earnest, but rational'.[6] In fact he was

regarded by Evangelicals as a dangerous heretic, since he had shed the
doctrines of the Trinity and original sin. If 'as a theologian he travelled
light', he was also an eighteenth-century 'pluralist on a generous scale',
rector of two parishes in Huntingdonshire, and holding prebendal stalls
at Lincoln and Southwell. Towards the end of his life he was also dean
of Peterborough, though that was near his base in Fletton vicarage. He
was by then the most serious and abstemious of men, with wide scholarly
interests, a fine library, an exquisite cursive handwriting; distinguished-
looking too, after his red hair had turned grey. But Peter Peckard had
a reprobate past behind him. After losing an arm in boyhood, through
messing about with a gun with a companion, he became a wild undergraduate at Corpus Christi College Oxford. Notorious for foul-mouthed
rowdiness in the quad, and drunkenness even in chapel, he was much
talked about for having had a woman in his rooms at night. For most of
his life he was a convivial army chaplain in the Grenadier Guards. The
early rebelliousness seems to have been transmuted into a progressive
radicalism. He needed a cause, and it was anti-slavery which came to
dominate his last years. This was something which fitted perfectly into
his framework of patriotic reformism, as set out in a brief anonymous
statement about himself in 1788. He professed to be 'a sincere and
zealous friend to the Rights of Man, to the Civil Constitution, and real
Honour of his Country, and to the Christian Religion; particularly to
that divine precept of doing every possible kindness to all our fellow crea-
tures . . . [with] a General Good-will, and . . . Universal Benevolence'.[7]
'Universal benevolence' was his preferred gloss on Christian 'charity',
and he interpreted it to include the promotion of civil and religious rights
and liberties, equality and freedom for all.

In most historical accounts of the abolition of the slave trade, Peckard
is given one standard sentence: that he set the prize essay won by
Thomas Clarkson in 1785.[8] He deserves more. One reason why he is
under-recognised is that his letters and papers – in contrast to those of
Clarkson and Wilberforce – have disappeared, other than his five published sermons referring to the slave trade.[9]

We do not know exactly when Peckard began preaching against
the slave trade, but it may have been in the chapel of his college as
Master. His first published reference to it was in a university sermon
in November 1783, preached at a service in celebration of the anniversary of deliverance from the Gunpowder Plot. Peckard touched on
the 'horror and enormity' of the slave trade, which made 'the Natural
Liberty of Man an article of public Commerce . . . A crime founded on
a dreadful pre-eminence in wickedness', worse than murder. This must
'sometime draw down upon us the heaviest judgment of Almighty God;

Plate 5.1 The Revd Dr Peter Peckard.

who . . . cannot suffer such deliberate, such monstrous iniquity to pass long unpunished', since he made 'of One Blood all the Sons of Men, and gave to All equally a natural Right to Liberty'.[10]

This preliminary salvo was followed up quickly. Early in 1784, already aged sixty-six, finding his strength declining and believing he was not long for this world, he decided upon one 'last public act' on behalf of a cause which had long been close to his heart. He was due to preach the university sermon on 30 January, the Feast of King Charles the Martyr. It sounds an improbable occasion on which to launch an attack on the slave trade, but a sermon on 'Piety and benevolence' provided a genuine opportunity for reflection on issues of civil rights and good government. Taking as his text 'Honour all men, love the brotherhood, fear God, honour the king', Peckard asked what it meant to 'honour all men'. It was, he suggested, a solemn Christian duty. It also involved recognising our common humanity, 'the natural equality of the human race'. There was a God-given, natural, 'inherent right to liberty'; yet, by participation in the slave trade, and gripped by 'an imperious spirit of unjust domination', the British people were, by selling them, depriving Africans of their liberty: 'With conscious deliberation, and unexampled tyranny, we doom them to daily misery, and drive them by inexpressible cruelty to unceasing torments, and an untimely death.' This, he declared, was a barbarous iniquity, an avaricious crime, a national disgrace, 'a Sin against the light of Nature, and the accumulated evidence of divine Revelation', and thus doubly rebellious against God.[11]

It is recorded that Peckard spoke nervously – as well he might, in view of his daringly subversive words. Equally shocking, he abandoned the formulaic set prayers in order to pray 'for our brethren in the West Indies', so outrageously ill-used.[12]

One of the young graduates in the congregation on that astonishing occasion was Thomas Clarkson of St John's. When, a few months later, by now vice-chancellor, Peckard set a Latin prize-essay competition for senior BAs on the subject *Anne liceat invitos in servitutem dare?* ('Is it right to make slaves of others against their will?'), Clarkson remembered Peckard's sermon and realised that the appropriate theme for him to write about would be, not, as would come naturally to a classics scholar, slavery in the ancient world, but the Atlantic slave trade. He duly won the prize in 1785 after considerable research, and in so doing discovered his life's vocation. Clarkson founded the Anti-Slave Trade Committee in London in 1787 and then recruited another Old Johnian, William Wilberforce, to lead the parliamentary campaign. Meanwhile he set about translating his Latin essay into English, a task he found difficult: graduates in those days had much less experience of formal writing in English than in Latin. Published as *An essay on the slavery and commerce of the human species, particularly the African* (1786; revised and enlarged edition, 1788), it was dedicated to the vice-chancellor and heads of house in Cambridge, 'but particularly the Revd Dr Peckard'. Clarkson always acknowledged Peckard as the man who had inspired him; among 'the activists' of the campaign, he wrote, 'the first of these was Dr Peckard' (*History of the abolition of the slave trade*, quoting a portion of Peckard's 1784 sermon). In his 'hydrographical' chart, representing the abolition movement over time as a river with tributaries, Clarkson placed Peckard at the head of the 'activist' stream, with himself second, relegating Wilberforce way down stream in ninth place.[13] (This was Clarkson getting his own back in a squabble for primacy, in which class tensions were reflected, for the posh Wilberforces looked down on Clarkson.[14])

As an aged scholarly don, in what he called his 'sequestered situation'

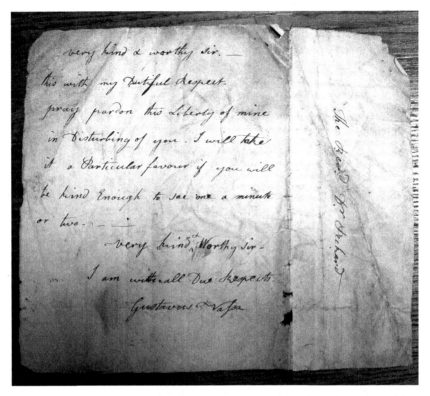

Plate 5.2 Letter from Olaudah Equiano to Dr Peckard, undated but probably 1788, requesting an interview. *Source:* Magdalene College Archives, Ferrar Papers, F/FP/2273.

in unworldly Magdalene, now with 'a very contracted' sphere of action, and mildly surprised still to be alive, Peckard would have been content quietly to encourage the young men in his charge in right ways of thinking, while keeping out of the limelight himself. He was proud that Clarkson had become in some sense his instrument: 'thus, through him, I look upon myself as in some small degree a Promoter of the glorious attempt to set the Slave at Liberty'.[15] He was also pleased to become the friend and patron of Olaudah Equiano (Gustavus Vassa), the freed slave (he bought his freedom in 1766), who with Peckard's help, emerged as the leading black abolitionist from 1789.[16]

At Equiano's request, they had met in 1787 or 1788. Peckard's interest was aroused by the fact that Equiano had worked as a slave in the plantations of Virginia (which was in Peckard's mind, for reasons discussed below). Peckard's letters of introduction and commendation helped

Equiano to turn his autobiography into a best-seller, *The interesting narrative of the life of Olaudah Equiano or Gustavus Vassa, the African* (1789). Later editions, and there were many, printed Peckard's endorsement, written to the chairman of the Committee for the Abolition of the Slave Trade (from Magdalene, 26 May 1790): 'I take the liberty, as being joined with you in the same laudable endeavours to support the cause of humanity in the abolition of the Slave Trade, to recommend to your protection the bearer of this notice, Gustavus Vassa, an African; and beg the favour of your assistance to him in the sale of this book.' Peckard's lead in endorsing the work meant that other prominent persons were also prepared to lend their names to it, including Clarkson. *The interesting narrative* has of course been rediscovered as the classic foundational text in the modern genre of black writing.[17]

But there is more. It is possible that through Peckard, Equiano met and in 1792 married Susannah Cullen of Soham in Cambridgeshire. There were two children. Susannah died three years later, probably giving birth to the second, Joanna. The first daughter, Anna, died on 21 July 1797 as an orphan, midway between the death of her father (31 March 1797) and that of Peckard (8 December 1797). An intriguingly large, elegant, and prominent memorial to the four-year-old was placed at Chesterton Church, just a mile away from Cambridge. But who paid for it? Could it have been Peckard, more or less on his deathbed? – with the verse supplied by his wife, Martha Peckard, a minor poet? She is, at any rate, known to have composed elegies for tombstones in Fletton Churchyard, including one for a parish clerk.[18]

In the later 1780s, Peckard noticed that ridiculous arguments about African racial inferiority were gaining renewed currency, and, anticipating Clarkson's further writings, published anonymously – which he thought might be more effective – a hundred-page pamphlet, *Am I not a Man? and a Brother?* (1788). This had the epigraph 'Nihil HUMANI a me alienum' (a slight adaptation from Terence).[19] The arguments for abolition were rehearsed. Africans might be slaves in their own country, 'but does this give us Title to enslave them?' (p. 84). If Britain surrendered profit, at least the British would also clear themselves of guilt (p. 91). More interestingly he then examined – from writings about Africa – such things as African capacity for music, poetry, medicine, and moral exhortation. In music, he pointed out, Africans had instruments, could sing with 'a delicate and most enchanting harmony', and had 'a turn and power for composition'. Phillis Wheatley ('Phyllis Whateley') he cited as an exemplar of poetry. Ignatius Sancho he praised as a writer infused with 'Universal Benevolence'.[20] As for medical skills, it was a slave in Carolina who discovered the specific remedy for the bite of the rattlesnake (p. 18). All in all, he considered, it

*Juſtice and Mercy recommended, parti-
cularly with reference to the* SLAVE
TRADE.

A

S E R M O N

PREACHED BEFORE THE

UNIVERSITY OF CAMBRIDGE,

By P. PECKARD, D.D.

MASTER OF MAGDALEN COLLEGE.

CAMBRIDGE,

Printed by J. ARCHDEACON Printer to the UNIVERSITY;

For J. & J. MERRILL, in Cambridge; T. CADELL, in the
Strand; B. WHITE & Son, in Fleet-ſtreet; T. PAYNE
& Son, at the Mews Gate; T. EVANS, in Paternoſter-
Row; and G. & T. WILKIE, in St. Paul's Church
Yard, London.

MDCCLXXXVIII.

AM I NOT A MAN?

AND A BROTHER?

WITH ALL HUMILITY

ADDRESSED TO THE

BRITISH LEGISLATURE.

Nihil HUMANI a me alienum.

CAMBRIDGE,

Printed by J. ARCHDEACON Printer to the UNIVERSITY;

And ſold by J. & J. MERRILL, Cambridge; T. PAYNE
& Son, London; and J. & J. FLETCHER, Oxford.

MDCCLXXXVIII.

Plate 5.3 Title-pages, from Peckard's 1788 sermon (above) and his 1788 pamphlet (below). (The University Library copy was deposited by Magdalene College.) Reproduced by kind permission of the Syndics of Cambridge University Library.

could be 'fairly proved' that 'Negroes are *Men*', that they had sensitive capacities comparable with Europeans, 'that they are capable of an idea of *Civil Government*, of *Moral Distinctions* of *Religion*, of a *God*, and a *Future State of Existence*' (p. 94). The analysis was brought to a conclusion by the argument that '*greater national advantages* would really arise from a different mode of commerce with Africa, by taking in exchange for our commodities, instead of Natives, the Salt Petre, Ivory, Gums, Medicinal Drugs, Silver, Gold and many other very valuable articles, of which the Continent of Africa is a Source absolutely inexhaustible' (p. 92). The phrase 'Am I not a man and a brother?' became the campaign slogan, displayed on the seal of the Anti-Slavery Society. Peckard may well have invented it; he certainly helped to launch it; and Josiah Wedgwood ('Vasemaker General to the Universe') popularised it, supervising Hackman's production of a cameo, the slave kneeling in chains, which was endlessly reproduced on mass-produced campaign buttons, chinaware, and medallions, decorating brooches, bracelets, and snuff-boxes.

It troubled Peckard that no one seemed to come forward to maintain the campaign in Cambridge, and he seized upon the anniversary of the Revolution of 1688 to suggest that this should be celebrated, 'not in noisy riot and drunkenness, not in disorder and tumult, but by extending the blessings we enjoy to those who are deprived of them; by breaking every yoke, and setting the poor captives free'. In February 1788 he returned to the pulpit of Great St Mary's to denounce once again 'that abominable violation of the laws of God and the Common Rights of Man'. Compared with the 'convulsive horrors' of the slave trade, he thundered, the ravages of war were but innocent pastimes: 'The Annals of the whole world cannot produce its equal in perfidy, injustice and cruelty: being radically, absolutely, and essentially Evil, loaded with all possible malignity.' For 'unexampled barbarity' no one in human history stood equal to 'the British Man-Merchant' in his dreadful depravity, habitually dealing in violence, rape, and murder.[21]

This fierce and fearless sermon was a personal triumph for the seventy-year-old Master. The *Cambridge Chronicle* published poems saluting him. One contained the lines:

> See Peckard rise, whose moving accent draws
> Entranc'd Attention, and mute applause!
> Hail, reverend sire, whose light our mist removes.

Another ode, rather touchingly, was by a Magdalene undergraduate:

> Reviving Pity hails the new-born day,
> And Peckard's precepts must confirm her sway.[22]

The sermon was designed to coincide with the Cambridge University Senate's Anti-Slave Trade Petition to Parliament, for which the dons voted on 26 January 1788. The petition was organised by the Revd Professor William Farish, Fellow of Magdalene, and the wording strongly suggests the hand of Peckard:

the Petitioners hope, that the Legislature will take this Subject into its most serious Consideration, and adopt such Measures as shall appear most effectual for abolishing a Commerce supported only by Violence and Rapine, and which, by encouraging Treachery, by exciting War, as well as by forcing into Slavery Multitudes of the Inhabitants, desolates a most extensive and fertile Country: Commercial Interest can never justify a Crime, nor atone for the Guilt incurred by an Action which Reason and Revelation forbid: But the Petitioners are far from apprehending, that the Abolition of this Traffick will be attended with Consequences detrimental to the state, inasmuch as a firm Belief in the Providence of a Benevolent Creator assures them, that no System, founded on the Oppression of one Part of Mankind, can be beneficial to another.

Parliament was urged to stop supporting a traffic 'replete with Misery and Oppression', violating 'every Principle of Humanity and Justice, as well as of the precepts of the Christian Religion', so that 'this continued Outrage against Humanity be no longer the Disgrace of our National character, and the Reproach of our Christian Profession – thus shall Peace be restored to that afflicted and desolated Country, and a friendly Commercial Intercourse enable us to introduce into it the Comforts of social Life, and the advantages of true Religion'.[23]

Peckard continued to preach against the slave trade, and it seems plain that his series of university sermons – four in all – must rank as the most galvanic heard in Great St Mary's since the Reformation. The later sermons bluntly and uncompromisingly rejected all arguments old and new which were advanced in defence of what he now called the 'infernal traffic in human blood'. He dismissed with confidence the claim that there was biblical authority for slavery: this was merely 'to twist and torture' the holy scriptures, for the Bible might record slavery as a historical fact but it conferred no approbation. He dismissed with contempt the protest that abolition would upset property rights: 'Be it so. They who hazard their property knowingly for the commission of Evil, deserve at least to lose it.' He dismissed with conviction the argument that Africans were constitutionally inferior: 'God made of one blood all the sons of men,' and Africans had all the same excellencies and imperfections as themselves. As to the question of commercial gain, he claimed there was misrepresentation of the facts, for 'it had been fairly proved that it may be more effectively obtained by honest means'.[24]

In his final sermon on the slave trade, in Peterborough Cathedral (which John Walsh calls 'a magnificently sulphurous Jeremiad'), he reaffirmed his commitment to the slaves: 'My feeble voice and fervent prayer shall always be exerted on their part, so long as God shall be pleas'd to give me power to utter a syllable.' The slave trade was, in a word, 'Execrable!' – but 'what words can be equal to the description of our guilt? We must form a new language for the purpose.' Finally, the sermon ended on a note of high drama, with his cry that 'God will no more hide his face from us, when our hands are no longer DEFILED WITH BLOOD.'[25]

II

Peckard's abolitionist and Africanist views seem to us so right – especially in comparison with those of a generation later, after the post-Indian Mutiny-Rebellion deterioration of racial sympathies – that it is hard to realise they are more than two hundred years old and belong to another era entirely. How on earth did it come about that Peckard developed such a challengingly radical position? Why was it Peckard and not some other Cambridge cleric who broke the mould of theological ambivalence and ethical obfuscation – and thus wrote himself into a central if, alas, not always properly recognised position in the history of human rights?

Essentially Peckard's vision arose out of his own special brand of religion, his concept of 'universal benevolence' as the essence of an accessible Christianity, his personal commitment to justice and humanity. (It was a triumph for latitudinarianism, and a decisive disproof of the view that 'Broad Church is no church at all'.) As early as 1753 he had preached about the 'indefensibleness of anti-semitism', a full hundred years and more before the removal of Jewish civil disabilities in Britain.[26] He had an intense and passionate conviction that personal freedom was the very essence of 'civil and religious liberty'. The natural rights of man were God-given, and therefore men could not 'in any respect approach so near to divinity of character as by conferring happiness on men'. But there was a more chilling line of reasoning as well. He believed in the reality of divine judgment *in this world*. Individuals might be judged at the Last Day, but states and societies risked judgment and punishment here and now. It was this conviction that gave a sharp, apocalyptic cutting edge to his sombre later sermons on the slave trade: 'It is an evil utterly inconsistent with our religion.' Jesus expressed affection for the whole human race, proclaiming a gospel for all mankind irrespective of 'accidental circumstances of Climate, of Form, or of Complexion . . . a gospel of peace and liberty'. So the slave trade, 'an abominable commerce, defeats the gracious purposes of God, crucifying his Son again'.

Thus Britain was, by defeats during the early years of war against France, being judged and punished for the appalling crime of the slave trade, and if it were not soon abolished, the British trading empire would suffer the eclipse of ancient Tyre.[27]

Peckard was familiar with the writings of Granville Sharp, and we know that they were in touch with each other.[28] Many of Sharp's pamphlets were nicely bound in his library. It is also of interest that he clearly treasured his copy of Charles Wilkins's pioneering translation of the Hindu Sanskrit classic, the *Bhagavad Gita* (1785), writing his name in it with a flourish. And he was deeply influenced by James Ramsay's *Essay on the treatment and conversion of African slaves in the British sugar colonies* (298 pp., 1784), which had an epigraph from the Acts of the Apostles, 'God hath made of one Blood all Nations of the Earth', which Peckard was fond of quoting. Ramsay had a chapter on the 'natural capacity of African slaves indicated', which Peckard drew upon for his own demonstrations of African potential. There was also a chapter devoted to a 'plan for conversion'. Peckard would have found plenty of information about Africa, especially its products and trade, in volumes 36 and 37 of the *Universal History* (1760), which was also on his library shelves.

His religion and his reading, his commitment to 'universal benevolence', thus made Peckard a passionate abolitionist. But there are, I want to suggest, two further possible lines of explanation.

The first concerns the influence of his wife, Martha Ferrar, and his scholarly investigations into the history of her virtuous family. By marriage into the Ferrar family, Peckard inherited its voluminous papers and came to write the biography of Nicholas Ferrar, director of the Virginia Company of America in the early 1620s, and later founder of the Little Gidding religious community in Huntingdonshire. The Ferrar brothers, Nicholas and John, had strongly opposed the use of slaves in Virginia, had favoured the religious conversion of American Indians, and proposed schemes of comprehensive American education, irrespective of class or colour, with a plan for a multi-racial university for Virginia and a school for Bermuda. These were ideals which profoundly influenced Peckard, as, over a long period of years, he slowly completed his life of Nicholas Ferrar, finally published in 1790.[29]

The other influential source of inspiration was the Evangelical Fellows of Magdalene, led by the President, Samuel Hey, his brother Richard Hey, Henry Jowett, and Professor William Farish, a scientist who astonished the world by declaring that steam-trains could safely travel at thirty miles per hour and that sixty miles an hour might one day be achieved. Farish was a close friend of Henry Venn and Charles Simeon. As we have seen, he undertook zealous work on the university petitions against the slave trade, and he was 'also among the earliest and most anxious advocates for the abolition of slavery'. Furthermore, these men were right at the heart of the emerging Protestant missionary movement from the mid-1780s. And it was thus to Magdalene that Wilberforce and John Newton looked as the recruiting ground for pioneer missionaries to send to India and the Antipodes. Indeed, the college must have been brimming with excitement in the second half of Peckard's mastership, as one godly undergraduate after another was pulled from his studies and packed off for immediate sailing to preach the gospel in Bengal or New South Wales, or in one case the West Indies.[30]

It was, however, painfully clear to all those involved in planning the emergent Church Missionary Society (1799) – including Wilberforce, who regarded the campaign for the admission of missionaries to India as a 'cause analogous to the abolition of the Slave Trade'[31] – that any credible British missionary endeavour would depend on prior repudiation of the slave trade. Otherwise, as Professor Farish declared, preaching the gospel to Africans would be nothing better than 'hypocrisy and insult'.[32] Peckard himself, in *Am I not a Man? and a Brother?*, advocated a missionary movement, since the Society for the Propagation of the Gospel had not bothered with conversion of Africans ('presumably on the groundless prejudice that Negroes are not men'). But continuation of the slave trade 'must always be an insuperable bar against their conversion', because all they see in Christianity is 'action of Oppression, and Rapine, Cruelty and Murder'. On the other hand, and anticipating Livingstone, a civil commerce and friendly mutual exchange would open the way for moral and religious instruction. Peckard took up this theme in his 1790 sermon. Christianity was a gospel of goodwill, but

What a contradiction to these gracious intentions is the whole of our conduct respecting the innocent and unoffending nations of Africa! if we consider the treatment they receive from us; first in being torn from their country and their friends by the violence of hard hearted ruffians, then doomed to chains and excruciating misery, and if they survive these calamities, in being sold for Slaves to merciless masters, not less cruel than the ruffians who forced them from their native land. Is this our Gospel of Peace and Liberty? Is this our proclamation of the acceptable year of the Lord? If such be the conduct of Christians, the unconverted world must hear the name of Christ with horror.[33]

And so the study of seventeenth-century Virginia Company policies, and conversations with the godly Fellows of Magdalene about the future of Protestant missions, together helped to persuade Peckard that the slave trade must be ended.

Peckard's influence did not stop at his contribution to anti-slavery. Among his college star pupils in the 1790s were evangelical men who had a defining impact on aspects of British imperial policy in the 1830s. Samuel Marsden, 'the Apostle of New Zealand', inaugurated the mission there in 1814. In his preaching he often drew on Peckard's sermons. He was a great admirer of the Maori as a 'noble race', and in April 1830 he conducted the first inter-racial marriage between a European and an (unconverted) Maori bride. Marsden may thus be regarded as the founding father of New Zealand as a multi-cultural nation.[34] Charles Grant, Lord Glenelg, became Irish chief secretary, supporting Catholic emancipation; after this he was president of the East India Company Board of Control, and secretary of state for the colonies, 1835 to 1839, promoting 'universal benevolence', and in distinctively Peckardian language. (See Introduction, pp. 26–7). His brother Robert Grant, author of the noble hymn 'O worship the king, all glorious above', was governor of Bombay presidency from 1834 until his death in 1838, bringing Aden into the empire as part of a large geostrategic scheme for India. His views on Indian policy set him at odds with Macaulay in some ways, because Robert encouraged education in the vernacular as well as English. His Indian plans were cut short by his early death, so he is perhaps better remembered for his efforts to remove the civil disabilities of British Jews, a cause which had also been one of Peckard's concerns. He was a member of the Philo-Judaean Society founded in 1826. As MP for Finsbury for two years he initiated two bills for Jewish emancipation, which passed through the House of Commons in 1833 and 1834, but were rejected by the Lords, who continued to hold up this reform until 1858. Grant's argument was that religious opinions should not operate against civil rights: to inflict political disabilities on account of sectarian differences was persecution, so a Christian parliament should behave towards the Jews like the Good Samaritan, and settle 'this great question . . . on the basis of charity and . . . goodwill to men'.[35] The echoes of Peckard are very clear: 'universal benevolence' in action. Robert and Charles Grant and Samuel Marsden all carried the Peckardian principles forward into the early human rights movement and the humanitarian attempt to follow an ethical imperial policy.

III

This final section will elaborate upon the earlier assertion that the humanitarian campaign had a crucial but not all-sufficient part to play in abolition – it aims to put religious arguments in context, and to assess the balance of motivation between moral and material interests, humanitarian concern, and commercial calculation. The 'economic' theory of abolition, crudely stated, maintains that shifts in capitalist engagement were what mattered. However, Sir George Stephen, reflecting on anti-slavery and particularly the emancipation movement which he had done so much to mastermind in the five years or so before 1833, contended that support had been 'created by adherence to the text that to uphold slavery was a crime before God'.[36] In this he was echoing Peckard, and it seems likely that appeal to the religious conscience and a sense of guilt and sin was a vital factor in spearheading the campaigns, persuading where other arguments could not.

Nevertheless, it was also the case that it could not *by itself* have brought about abolition. This was recognised early on by the Committee of the Society for Abolition, which produced a report (dated 15 January 1788 and signed by its chairman, Granville Sharp), stating that the committee was 'not insensible of the natural influence which interest has in biassing the judgments of men', even on matters involving the 'plainest dictates of religion and morality'. It was therefore essential that they should persuade merchants and traders, and government itself, that a 'legitimate commerce' would be more profitable.[37] Ministers were hard-headed pragmatic men, even if at the same time godly believers. The efficacy of pure humanitarian argument with them may be doubted. A government which in 1806 held Demarara (Guyana), contemplated getting hold of Cuba, and shot its way up the River Plate to Buenos Aires, was certainly not a government unmindful of economic considerations and prospects, or concerned only with ethical behaviour in international relations.[38]

Thoughtful 'mercantilist' theorisers of British trading interests had long 'disliked the slave trade and wished it could be ended', but it seemed that 'the necessity, the absolute necessity, then, of carrying it on, must, since there is no other, be its excuse'.[39] Prime Minister Lord North in 1783 had dismissed representations by a delegation of Quakers, complimenting them on their humanity, but saying that abolition was impossible because the slave trade was necessary to almost every trade in Europe.[40]

It was, however, becoming clearer by the 1790s, and largely as a result of Clarkson's researches, that the slave trade was speculative and inherently risky, 'abounding in imponderables', in Jack Gallagher's memorable phrase.[41] Few people had realised, until Clarkson told them, that higher percentages of the European crew died on the 'middle passage' than of the slaves: perhaps 20 per cent as against 15 per cent. Hazards ranged from piracy and shipwreck to rats and rebellions. Rats urinated on the biscuits, chewed up the sails, and even nibbled at people when they were asleep. John Newton, as a slave-trade captain, recorded in his diary: 'At work all spare times mending the sails, yet cannot repair them so fast as the rats destroy' (15 May 1751).[42] Profits on capital investment for successful slave traders averaged about 8 per cent, but with marked fluctuations, and with a high proportion of failures and bankruptcies. It was far from certain that individual voyages would make a profit. Overall, it is now calculated that the slave trade represented less than 1 per cent of total domestic investment in about 1790.[43] Moreover, there was increasing instability in the West Indies, and in consequence the possibility of a serious financial crash.

As Boyd Hilton has pointed out, governments of the day 'were inclined to define economic well-being not in terms of growth, but in terms of stability, and that was a test which the British slave trade, for political and economic reasons, failed'.[44] Professional and mercantile men who really knew about the West Indies were turning against the slave trade: men like John Newton, James Stephen (who had been a lawyer in St Kitts), and Zachary Macaulay (formerly a plantation manager in Jamaica). Liverpool merchants, led by the abolitionist James Cropper, were already diversifying and adapting themselves to the hope of making decent alternative profits out of palm oil, soap-making, and cotton goods, and could thus persuade themselves that the moral imperatives were not incompatible with commercial profit – as indeed Peckard had argued. New market opportunities were opening up on a global scale.[45] In this situation of expansionist activity and buoyant expectation, the government could be satisfied that abolition would *not* mean economic disaster – 'econocide' in Seymour Drescher's terminology.

The limits of the efficacy of public pressure in its wider sense have to be recognised. In fact, in his historical account, Clarkson did no more than mention in passing 'the enthusiasm of the nation', confining his analysis to what he thought really mattered, the ideas of the elite circles based in London.[46] The new strength that public pressure had acquired by the 1830s had not by 1807 been established. The limits, too, of humanitarian influence on government policy-making must also be reckoned with. It must surely be the case that by 1792 the intellectual argument had been won, but it was fifteen years before abolition finally triumphed over the economic and political obstacles, notably those thrown up by the French Revolution. The cynic would go further and say that 'humane' actions by the state seldom come about through the diffusion of humanitarian ideas. The repeal of numerous capital offences, for example, was enacted because of the logistical impossibility of hanging so many felons.[47] Humanitarian abolitionists of the next generation were unable to prevent the emergence of what was recognised in the 1840s as 'a new system of slavery', the development of Indian indentured labour from the 1830s as a substitute for slavery; nor were they able to stop cheap sugar imports after 1846 from foreign slave-grown sources.

On the other hand, the reality of the moral conscience in a religious age, and respectful attention to religious arguments, such as those so powerfully articulated by Peter Peckard, cannot be ruled out of the explanation of abolition. Lord Grenville reflected the concerns of most of his ministerial colleagues when he spoke of taking Cabinet responsibility for the administration of the slave trade in newly acquired Trinidad in 1806 as 'a dreadful responsibility to those who feel upon it as I do, and believe that the responsibility of public men in public stations is not confined to impeachments in *this* world'.[48] Far from being altruistic, then, the motivation of abolitionists was strongly influenced by the sense that their own moral redemption, even their eternal salvation, seemed to be at stake. Abolition might be regarded as a kind of 'spiritual insurance policy'.[49]

The old polarities of the debate[50] can perhaps be collapsed by emphasising the facilitating link between the moral and the material explanation: the test of viability. It is estimated that 15,000 slaves had died of starvation directly attributable to cutting off supplies during the American War of Independence – something engendering a heightened sense of the vulnerability of the whole system, and threatening to turn the Caribbean islands into a contingent liability.[51] Then came the slave revolt in France's premier colony, St Domingue, in 1791, leading after much upheaval and bloodshed to the establishment of the world's first black ex-colonial independent state, Haiti, in 1804. The death toll was massive, perhaps half a million. The British watched in horror, particularly as an intervention force in 1793–4 was brought to its knees by the brilliant rebel leader Toussaint l'Ouverture and by yellow fever – the most costly and demoralising colonial campaign the British had ever fought until then.[52] Henry Dundas, for many years a powerful minister in all that related to overseas policy in the 1790s, expressly turned against the slave trade because of fear that risings similar to St Domingue's might occur in the British West Indies. And it was not long before they did: in Grenada and St Vincent in 1794–5, in Barbados in 1816, in Demarara (Guyana) in 1823, and, above all, in Jamaica in 1831, the latter being the immediate trigger for slave emancipation in 1833.[53]

So perhaps the collapse of faith in the slave trade was in large measure the result of fears about its continuing feasibility, and alarm that it would become more trouble than it was worth, as British and international opinion turned against it, and as slaves mounted rebellions in protest. Just as would be the case in the twentieth century with the fall of the British empire as a whole, economic shifts removed obstacles to change but were not in themselves determinant. And just as with the implementation of decolonisation – in the context of international criticism and increasing alarm at nationalist protests if they turned violent – so the historiographical polarities between competing interpretations of abolition can be resolved by flagging up the salience of pragmatic tests about the relative costs of holding on as against giving up. Abolition was driven both by religious concerns and by economic re-evaluations, but also by anxious expediency.

Notes

1 For the statistics on the slave trade, see P. Curtin, *The Atlantic slave trade: a census* (Madison, 1969); P.E. Lovejoy, 'The impact of the Atlantic slave trade on Africa: a review of the literature', *Journal of African History*, vol. 30 (1989), pp. 365–94; J.D. Fage, 'African societies and the Atlantic slave trade', *Past and Present*, no. 125 (1989), pp. 97–115; John Iliffe, *Africans: the history of a continent* (Cambridge, 1995), p. 131; David Richardson, 'The British empire and the Atlantic slave trade, 1660–1907', in *OHBE*, vol. II, *The eighteenth century* (ed. P. Marshall, Oxford, 1998), p. 46.
2 For the Europeans enslaved in the seventeenth and eighteenth centuries, see Linda Colley, *Captives: Britain, empire and the world, 1600–1850* (2002), p. 44.
3 For the general background of the debate, see D. Brion Davis, *Inhuman bondage: the rise and fall of slavery in the New World* (2006); R. Anstey, *The Atlantic slave trade and British abolition, 1760–1810* (1975), 'A reinterpretation of the abolition of the British slave trade, 1806–1807', *English Historical Review*, vol. 87 (1972), pp. 304–32, and 'Capitalism and slavery: a critique', *Economic History Review*, vol. 21 (1968), pp. 307–20; R. Anstey and P.E.H. Hair, eds., *Liverpool, the African slave trade, and abolition: essays to illustrate the current knowledge and research* (Historical Society of Lancashire and Cheshire, 1976); D. Eltis and J. Walvin, eds., *Abolition of the Atlantic slave trade: origins and effects in Europe, Africa and the Americas* (Madison, WI, 1981); S. Drescher, *Econocide: British slavery in the era of abolition* (Pittsburgh, 1977). The classic, opposing, accounts remain worth reading: R. Coupland, *British anti-slavery movement* (1933; 2nd edn, 1964, ed. J.D. Fage), and Eric Williams, *Capitalism and slavery* (Chapel Hill, NC, 1944; New York, 1961); but see also C.J. Robinson, 'Capitalism, slavery and bourgeois historiography', *History Workshop Journal*, no. 23 (1987), pp. 122–40, and Barbara L. Solow and Stanley L. Engerman, eds., *British capitalism and Caribbean slavery: the legacy of Eric Williams* (Cambridge, 1987).
4 Coupland, *The British anti-slavery movement*, pp. 64–9.
5 Drescher, *Econocide: British slavery in the era of abolition* is the leading example.
6 J.D. Walsh, 'Peckard, Peter', in *ODNB*, vol. XLIII, pp. 374–5, and *Peter Peckard: liberal churchman* (Magdalene College Occasional Papers, no. 16, Cambridge, 1998).
7 *Am I not a Man? and a Brother?* (1788), preface, p. i.
8 The 'standard sentence' is all that appears even in the 924-page book by

Hugh Thomas, *The slave trade: the history of the Atlantic slave trade , 1440–1870* (1997), p. 491. The first step towards a more official national recognition of Peckard as a leading abolitionist was in the Westminster Abbey 'Service to Commemorate the Bicententary of the Abolition of the Slave Trade Act, 27 March 2007', when a specially commissioned piece of music, set to words by Olaudah Equiano, was performed in memory of Peckard.

 9 Magdalene College Archives, 'Catalogue of the books left at Magdalen [*sic*] College by Mrs Peckard', 26 January 1798, p. 2, described as 'Octavo: A bundle of papers respecting Slave Trade', and annotated 'missing' – but as there is no date to the annotation it is impossible to tell whether the item was actually received, or subsequently lost. Another reason for the lack of recognition given to Peckard may be the fact that by the time of abolition he had been dead for nine years. Thus the commemorative volume of *Poems on the abolition of the slave trade* by James Montgomery, James Grahame, and E. Benger (R. Bowyer, London, 1809, with engravings by R. Smirke) celebrates the work of Granville Sharp, Clarkson, and Wilberforce alone, and even erroneously states that Sharp 'was the first to encourage Mr Clarkson in his adventurous career' (preface); Ramsay is also mentioned honourably. Clarkson's essay is referred to, but not Peckard as having set it. My thanks to Denis Murphy for showing me a copy of this rare volume. For further reflections on this theme, see my article 'Peter Peckard and the abolition of the slave trade', *Magdalene College Magazine*, no. 51 (2006–7), pp. 92–5.

10 Peter Peckard, *The nature and extent of civil and religious liberty: a sermon preached before the University of Cambridge, November the 5th, 1783* (J. Archdeacon, Cambridge, 1783), 37pp.

11 Peter Peckard, *Piety, benevolence, and loyalty recommended: a sermon preached before the University of Cambridge, January the 30th, 1784, published at the request of the Vice-Chancellor and the Heads of Colleges* (Cambridge, 1784), 18pp.

12 Henry Gunning, *Reminiscences of the University, Town and County of Cambridge from the year 1780* (2 vols., 1852; 2nd edn 1855), vol. I, pp. 112–13: Peckard's 'enthusiasm in favour of abolition was unbounded', and he preached 'warmly against it'.

13 Thomas Clarkson, *The history of the rise, progress and accomplishment of the abolition of the African slave trade by the British Parliament* (2 vols., 1808), esp. pp. 203–5. For the best short account of Clarkson, see Hugh Brogan, *ODNB*, vol. XI, pp. 937–40.

14 A. Tyrell, 'A house divided against itself: the British abolitionists revisited', *Journal of Caribbean History*, vol. 22 (1988), pp. 42–67. Clarkson and Wilberforce had almost nothing in common, not just socially, but in politics and religion too. Clarkson followed Peckard in subscribing to a humanitarian *this*-worldly Christianity, whereas Wilberforce followed the Evangelical missionary *other*-worldly emphasis on sin and salvation: see Boyd Hilton, 'St John's most historical moment?: the abolition of the slave trade', *The Eagle* (2007), pp. 63–79.

15 Peckard, 'Introduction' ('To the Rt Revd Beilby, Lord Bishop of London'), *Justice and mercy recommended, particularly with reference to the slave trade: a*

sermon preached before the University of Cambridge (Cambridge, 1788), pp. vii–ix.

16 James Walvin, in *ODNB*, vol. XVIII, pp. 481–2. Gustavus Vasa was king of Sweden, 1523–60; but adding another 's' in 'Vassa' implied a slave. The *Cambridge Chronicle* published a letter from Equiano thanking the 'gentlemen of the University and the inhabitants of the town' for their kindness and civility (1 August 1789).

17 In modern editions: *The interesting narrative and other writings* (ed. V. Carretta, 1995), and P. Edwards, ed., *Equiano's 'Travels'* (1988); J. Walvin, *An African life: the life and times of Olaudah Equiano, 1745–1797* (1998).

18 Joyce Fullard, 'Peckard, Martha', in *ODNB*, vol. XLIII, pp. 373–4. The verse at Chesterton Church:

> Should simple village rhymes attract thine eye,
> Stranger, as thoughtfully thou passest by,
> Know that there lies beside this humble stone
> A child of colour haply not thine own.
> Her father born of Afric's sun-burnt race,
> Torn from his native field, ah foul disgrace:
> Through various toils, at length to Britain came
> Espoused, so Heaven ordain'd, an English dame,
> And follow'd Christ; their hope two infants dear.
> But one, a hapless orphan, slumbers here.
> To bury her the village children came.
> And dropp'd choice flowers, and lisp'd her early fame;
> And some that lov'd her most, as if unblest,
> Bedew'd with tears the white wreath on their breast;
> But she is gone and dwells in that abode,
> Where some of every clime shall joy in God.

19 *Am I not a Man? and a Brother?: with all humility addressed to the British legislature* (Cambridge, 1788). Attributed to Peckard in S. Halkett and J. Laing, *Dictionary of anonymous and pseudonymous literature* (new edn, ed. J. Kennedy, W.A. Smith, and A.F. Johnson, Edinburgh, 1928), vol. I, p. 62 (but wrongly dated to 1778).

20 *ODNB*: 'Wheatley, Phillis', by J.C. Shields, vol. LVIII, pp. 420–2; 'Sancho, Ignatius', by Vincent Carretta, vol. XLVIII, pp. 835–7; Ignatius Sancho, *Letters of the late Ignatius Sancho, an African* (1782). Phillis Wheatley was born in the Gambia region, becoming a domestic slave in Boston, Massachusetts; a learned and sophisticated poet who visited London in 1773; she has 'a secure place as one of early America's best poets'. Sancho (*c.*1729–80), author, critic, composer, born on the 'middle passage', but brought up as an orphan in England; painted by Thomas Gainsborough, and 'the first African to get an obituary in the British press'.

21 Peckard, *Justice and mercy recommended; particularly with reference to the slave trade.*

22 *Cambridge Chronicle*, 1 March 1788.

23 *Cambridge Chronicle*, 2 February 1788; Charles Henry Cooper, *Annals of Cambridge*, vol. IV (1852), p. 426.

24 Peter Peckard, *The neglect of a known duty a sin: a sermon preached before the University of Cambridge on Sunday, Jan. 31, 1790* (Cambridge, 1790).

25 *National crimes the cause of national punishments: a discourse delivered in the Cathedral Church of Peterborough, on the fast-day, Feb. 25th 1795* (Peterborough and London, 5th edn), vi + 28pp.

26 Peter Peckard, *The popular clamour against the Jews indefensible: a sermon preached at Huntingdon, October the 28th, 1753* (Cambridge, 1753). This was preached at the time of the Naturalisation Bill for British Jews. See Abigail Green, 'The British empire and the Jews: an imperialism of human rights?' *Past and Present*, no. 199 (2008), pp. 75–105.

27 Peckard, *National crimes*; Walsh, *Peter Peckard: liberal churchman*, p. 14.

28 Jane Webster, 'The *Zong* in the context of the 18th-century slave trade', *Journal of Legal History*, vol. 28 (2007), p. 295. It seems likely that it was Sharp who encouraged Olaudah Equiano to meet Peckard.

29 Peter Peckard, *Memoirs of the life of Nicholas Ferrar* (Cambridge, 1790), 316 pp.

30 P. Cunich, D. Hoyle, E. Duffy, and R. Hyam, *A history of Magdalene College Cambridge, 1428–1988* (Cambridge, 1994), pp. 185–93.

31 J. Wolffe, 'Wilberforce, William', *ODNB*, vol. LVIII, p. 885.

32 William Farish, *A sermon preached before the Church Missionary Society . . . on May 5, 1818* (London, 1818), 33 pp. Obituary in *Christian Observer* (1837), pp. 611–13, 674–7. See also Richard Hey, *Some principles of civilisation, with detached thoughts on the promotion of Christianity in British India* (Cambridge, 1815), 135pp.; Charles Grant, *A poem on the restoration of learning in the East* (Claudius Buchanan Prize Essay, 1805), 29pp., in rhyming couplets (Cambridge, 1805).

33 Peckard, *The neglect of a known duty a sin*.

34 A.T. Yarwood, *Samuel Marsden: the great survivor* (Melbourne, 1977).

35 *PD*, *Commons*, vol. XII, cc. 205–22 (17 April 1833), 2nd Reading, Jewish Disabilities Bill, and vol. XIX, c. 1081 (23 July 1833), 3rd Reading; Green, 'The British empire and the Jews: an imperialism of human rights?', pp. 175–205, esp. 189; Robert Gavin, *Aden under British rule* (1975), pp. 28–33.

36 George Stephen, *Anti-slavery recollections, in a series of lectures addressed to Mrs Beecher Stowe at her request* (2nd edn, 1971, ed. Howard Temperley). The Agency Committee of the Anti-Slavery Society insisted that anti-slavery was 'a question essentially of a religious character' and slavery a sin (H. Temperley, *British anti-slavery, 1833–1870* (1972), p. 14).

37 Printed at the back of Peckard, *Justice and mercy recommended*, pp. 45–8.

38 V.T. Harlow, *The founding of the second British empire, 1763–1793* (2 vols., 1952, 1964).

39 Malachi Postlethwayt, *Britain's commercial interest explained and improved*, vol. II (1757), pp. 217–21; John Hippisley, 1764, quoted in F.W. Pitman, *The development of the British West Indies, 1700–1763* (New Haven, CT, 1917), p. 63: Hippisley believed 'the impossibility of doing without slaves in the West Indies will always prevent this traffic being dropped'.

40 Coupland, *The British anti-slavery movement*, p. 64.

41 J.A. Gallagher, 'Economic relations in Africa', ch. 24, in *New Cambridge modern history*, vol. VII, *1713–1763* (ed. J.O. Lindsay, 1957), p. 573; Anstey

and Hair, *Liverpool, the African slave trade, and abolition*; B.B. Parkinson, F.E. Hyde, and S. Marriner, 'The nature and profitability of the Liverpool slave trade', *Economic History Review*, vol. 5 (1953), pp. 368–77; R.E. Sheridan, 'The commercial and financial organisation of the British slave trade', *Economic History Review*, vol. 11 (1958), pp. 249–63; K.G. Davies, *The Royal African Company* (1957), esp. pp. 292–349.

42 B. Martin and M. Spurrell, eds., *The journal of a slave trader (John Newton), 1750–1754*, p. 52, 'Thoughts upon the African slave trade' (1788), p. 101.

43 Richardson in *OHBE*, vol. II, p. 461.

44 A.J. Boyd Hilton, review of Drescher, *Econocide* (which he finds not very plausible) in *English Historical Review*, vol. 94 (1979), pp. 135–7, and *A mad, bad and dangerous people? England, 1783–1846* (Oxford 2006), pp. 184–8, 'Slavery and the national mission: the politics of virtue', where he concludes that 'emancipation was analogous to conversion'.

45 David Eltis, *Economic growth and the ending of the transatlantic slave trade* (New York, 1987), and in James Walvin, ed., *Slavery and British society, 1776–1846* (1981); R.B. Sheridan, *Sugar and slavery: an economic history of the British West Indies, 1623–1775* (Barbados, 1974), p. 483.

46 S. Drescher possibly overstates the importance of 'public opinion' in his two articles: 'People and Parliament: the rhetoric of the slave trade', *Journal of Interdisciplinary History*, vol. 20 (1990), pp. 561–80, and 'Whose abolition? Popular pressure and the ending of the British slave trade', *Past and Present*, no. 143 (1994), pp. 136–66; he argues that popular pressure was used to break the stalemate of 1805 and it was the revelation of 'humanitarian priorities within public opinion that first dislodged the economic rationale from its hegemonic political position in the parliamentary discourse about slavery'. But is this the same as *proving* its effectiveness?

47 V.A.C. Gatrell, *The hanging tree: execution and the English people, 1770–1868* (Oxford, 1994).

48 Grenville to Viscount Sidmouth, 1 June 1806, quoted in G.R. Mellor, *British imperial trusteeship, 1783–1850* (1951), p. 420; see also further quotations, pp. 31–80, and in Hilton, *A mad, bad and dangerous people*, pp. 187–8.

49 Temperley, *British anti-slavery*, pp. 43–6; Hilton, 'The abolition of the slave trade,' *The Eagle*, p. 78.

50 It should, however, not be forgotten that Eric Williams was reacting against what he saw as the misleading and gross exaggerations of the 'humanitarian' historians: his study deliberately subordinated humanitarianism in order to redress the balance, but 'to disregard it completely, however, would be to commit a grave historical error and to ignore one of the greatest propaganda movements of all time. The humanitarians were the spearhead of the onslaught which destroyed the West Indian system' (*Capitalism and slavery*, p. 173).

51 K.M. Dallas, 'The first settlements in Australia considered in relation to sea-power in world politics', in Ged Martin, ed., *The founding of Australia: the argument about Australia's origins* (Sydney, 1978), pp. 39–49; S.H.H. Carrington, 'The American Revolution and the British West Indies' economy', *Journal of Interdisciplinary History*, vol. 17, no. 4 (1987), pp. 823–50, special issue on

Caribbean slavery and British capitalism, repr. in Solow and Engerman, *British capitalism and Caribbean slavery*.

52 Glyndwr Williams, *The expansion of Europe in the eighteenth century* (1966), pp. 243–4; C.L.R. James, *The Black Jacobins* (1938). The cost was estimated at £4.5 million, and the toll in manpower, including slave battalions, as 20,000 'British' dead, deserted, or incapacitated.

53 David Geggus, 'British opinion and the emergence of Haiti, 1791–1805', in Walvin, ed., *Slavery and British society*, p. 126; W.A. Green, *British slave emancipation: sugar colonies and the great experiment, 1830–1865* (1976). Peckard was aware of the unfolding tragedy in St Domingue, printing as a postcript to the 1790 sermon a report that planters had assassinated M. Ferrand, one of the Seneschal Judges, and paraded his head on a pole, for maintaining and publishing the Declaration of the Rights of Man, and speaking in favour of the liberty of the slaves (p. 33).

6 The view from below: the African response to missionaries

[In 1969 I spent five weeks with the two Mirfield Fathers of the Community of the Resurrection at the USPG Mission at Usutu in Swaziland. I was impressed with the extraordinary range of activities required of them. Part of the Diocese of Zululand and Swaziland, they had to be fluent in Zulu. They ran not only a parish church but a large and important boys' secondary school, together with outlying primary schools, for which they acted as governors and inspectors and occasionally as teachers. They had to be not merely pastors, but farm proprietors; they had to make medical diagnoses, employing and supervising nurses for peripatetic clinics; they acted as amateur architects and building suppliers for any new mission churches in the bush. They trained indigenous auxiliary clergy, led a scout troop, and generally dispensed advice of all kinds. I gained a fascinating insight into cultural interaction. Shortly afterwards I wrote as follows: 'When a British missionary abandons his Volkswagen or Datsun, strips naked, balances his ordinary clothing, his priestly vestments and communion plate upon his head, and takes horrible risks by wading across a bilharzia-riddled river in flood, and returns to carry across his Swazi acolyte who cannot swim and is not tall enough to wade – all in order to celebrate the Eucharist in Zulu with a few Africans in a hut in a remote kraal – is not a meaningful interaction taking place which deserves at least some decent and sympathetic acknowledgement in the historical record?'[1] This chapter is written in that spirit and arises from that experience. African history has made immense strides in the past fifty years, but what I seldom seem to hear are ordinary *African voices*, so I hope they can be heard here.]

One of the strangest features, perhaps, of European influence upon Africa was the extent to which Africans exchanged their traditional religions for an alien world religion, Christianity. By 1970 Africa could be seen as the site of vigorous expansion and innovation in Christianity. As the twentieth century opened, the British deployed some 10,000 missionaries overseas, and well over fifty different mission societies were operating in Africa. In 1900 there were about 9 million African Christians, out of a total population of 100 million. By 1990 the figure had moved towards 200 million, out of 450 million. Christianity became particularly strong not only in southern Africa, Mozambique, and Angola, but also in the Congo, Southern Nigeria, Ghana, and Uganda. An African in the countryside during the imperial era was much more likely to see a missionary than a district officer. Mission stations were highly visible, villages with a church, a school, and a clutch of houses; they might have attached a farm, a clinic, a printing press. Missionaries were highly mobile, moving out on foot or on horseback, by ox-cart, canoe, or bicycle, and eventually by motor-car. Only in the Muslim north was there little or no missionary effort.[2]

For Africans, any missionary encounter was but part of a much larger process. A basic problem for Africans coping with the European intrusion was facing an 'enlargement of scale'. The widening of horizons and possibilities involved 'thinking bigger', co-operating among themselves over larger areas, seeing Africa as a whole, and so forth. The twentieth century is sometimes described as the period in which Africans moved from self-sufficient, microcosmic societies, to wider macrocosmic entities in unavoidable relationships extending beyond the narrow traditional limits of their own small communities. Africans were incorporated into global economic systems created by others. Economic restructuring led to the introduction of cash-cropping and the spread of labour migration. New material ambitions and objectives developed – to own guns, clothes, and bicycles, or to obtain a Western education. There were new impositions such as the white man's hut-taxes and poll-taxes to pay for. Africans were also incorporated into a world disease-pattern. Above all, perhaps, there was the enlargement of religious options, the prospect of incorporation into one of the world religions. As the old gods seemed to fail in a succession of crises, military, sociological, and personal, so alternatives might be worth considering. It was this aspect of 'enlargement of scale' which could most help adjustment to other challenges. The universalism of Christianity might seem attractive when tribally based horizons had weakened.

In traditional Africa, religion was more than just religion. It was an all-pervasive reality which served to interpret society and give wholeness to communal life: 'The village world and the Spirit world were not two distinct separate realms; there was a continuous communication between the two . . . a totality, a comprehensive whole.'[3] Sharp distinctions were not made between natural/supernatural, body/spirit, or living/dead. African religions had two main functions. One was to control and explain evil and misfortune. Evil was that which destroyed life, fertility, prosperity; the eradication of evil was necessary and believed to be possible. The other function was to integrate communities through ritual – religion as 'an all-purpose social glue'. 'Religions' were thus cosmologies rather than theologies, about ways of looking at the world, performing actions rather than holding dogmas. There were perhaps five main 'types'. Theistic religions maintained a belief – though often a vague one – in a supreme being, a creator-god, among other gods. This was quite a widespread belief, though God went under various names, *Olusun* (Yoruba), *Mulungu* (East Africa), *Katonda* (Baganda), *Ngai* (Kikuyu), *uThixo* (adopted by the Xhosa). Secondly, there were ancestor cults, which indeed honoured ancestors, but they were talked to rather than worshipped; the dead were very much alive and active. Animism is the third type, a term which covers belief in spirits inhabiting objects such as sacred trees, rivers, rocks, caves, waterfalls, so that these things and places were also 'alive'. Territorial cults were religions which divinised human beings and erected shrines to them, sometimes with monarchical associations; they were especially characteristic of the area now covered by Zimbabwe, Zambia, and Malawi. Finally, there were witchcraft eradication cults. The witchdoctor was the good guy, 'a sacred specialist' who aimed to counter evil forces believed to be physically inhabiting unfortunate human agents, thus causing hurtful events. Oracles and magic were two different ways of combating witchcraft.[4]

These 'types' were often held in combination, with one form usually dominant. African spirituality was nothing if not eclectic. Under the impact of Christianity, animism and ancestor cults tended to die out fairly rapidly, but witchcraft eradication cults persisted. Indeed, as witchcraft panics persisted, they were even extended to apply not merely to wives, as so often formerly, but to colleagues and job-competitors.[5] Among the theistic cults, Jesus was often an added spirit in the traditional pantheon.

I

A principal theme in African history for much of the nineteenth and early twentieth centuries is to be found in demographic change. There were large-scale population movements, in the redistribution of people, as refugees or for new forms of work, and in urbanisation. African encounters with missionaries often developed out of this mobility. How Africans might respond to Christianity was largely determined by their experience of uprooting, whether as voluntary migrants or involuntary refugees – whether, out of military crisis and conflict, they were victors or losers. The Yoruba Wars were a major cause of disruption in West Africa. In south-east Africa, the term *mfecane* loosely describes the Nguni dispersion believed to have arisen out of military conquests and state-formation spreading from the storm-centre of Zululand in the 1820s.

This instability resulted in refugee movements radiating as far north as Lake Malawi (see Map 2.2). One group of refugees from Xhosaland, remnants of a broken society who had lost all their cattle, took the name Mfengu ('beggars for food') and adopted Western ways more readily than those who stayed put. Mostly under Wesleyan Methodist influence, the Mfengu are a classic case of refugees accepting the Christian faith corporately and not just as individuals. They did so as an expression of social revolt and reconstitution, and they came to be regarded as a model Nguni Christian community.[6] Further resettlements and refugee movements occurred as a result of the disastrous and suicidal Xhosa cattle-killing of 1856–7 instigated by Nongqawuse, a female prophet, and her associate Nonkosi, a nine-year-old girl. The crisis produced thousands of converts, mainly brought in by other Xhosa. Traumatised survivors came to the mission stations as desperate, homeless, starving beggars. This could also be the pattern elsewhere. Battered groups who emerged from violent upheavals might be prepared to look for security and new futures with the missions.

This process of conversion was not confined to southern Africa. In East Africa, too, the 'refugee factor' operated as a result of the spread of the Arab slave trade. Africans fearing enslavement, an omnipresent threat, sought the protection of the missions. These promised help, refuge, access to learning, and a better life. East African ex-slaves, both liberated and runaways, might become the nucleus of a Christian community, just as they had done at an earlier time in West Africa.

After the radiating impulses of the *mfecane* had eventually settled, the next demographic phenomenon, from the later nineteenth century, involved European-induced labour migration. Tens of thousands of young men moved into the white man's farms, mines, and towns. Migration, usually but not always seasonal, was essentially a sporadic activity, 'peasants raiding the cash economy for goods'.[7] Some migrants wanted guns, and actually called themselves 'rifle-seekers'. Generally, the more usual cover-story was that they were 'away, clothing their wives'. Huge distances were traversed, especially to the mines. It is a thousand miles from northern Malawi to the Rhodesian copper-belt, two thousand miles to the southernmost gold mines in South Africa. Journeys were often on foot. Mortality was heavy.

By the mid-twentieth century, several African societies regularly found themselves without 50 per cent of their menfolk, a percentage which was even higher in Mozambique, the principal source of labour recruitment for the mines of Witwatersrand. Through migrancy a man might acquire a gospel book or a New Testament. Returning home, armed with a rifle and a Bible, he might be regarded as having mastered the secrets of the white man's world – the firearm and the written word. In Basutoland, there was a young man called Nguana Ngombe, who in the late 1880s joined François Coillard at the Paris Evangelical Mission as a servant-boy. He began to act as a translator, and eventually sought baptism. He provides a rare insight into what happened to him and other young men like him. It was not, he explained, that he 'wanted to be a white man', but 'God is not the God of the Whites only':

When I took service with the missionary, a gun was the object of all my desires. When I had got it I thought myself the happiest man in the world. A gun! *My* gun! . . . I used to get up in the night to make sure that I really possessed it. I was always admiring it. But now I know the Lord Jesus, it is he who has taken possession of all my thoughts and all my love and I almost forget that I have a gun.[8]

A similar perceived connection between desirable new objects was made by Sebato, a Bagandan refugee, who in 1890 asked CMS missionaries for a book – the New Testament would do – and a gun, as he had lost both.[9]

African mobility and new aspirations paved the way for the missions. One of the major insights of the leading authorities, Bengt Sundkler, Richard Gray, Andrew Porter, and Norman Etherington, is that it was 'largely Africans who evangelised other Africans'. Missionaries on arrival in a village often found a group who had the rudiments of the revelation, 'a "conventicle" of faithful', young men who had returned from travels, already influencing others with a new message.[10] Sundkler said he was sometimes tempted – 'perhaps irresponsibly' – to propose a law: 'The first missionary arriving in a certain African village, there to proclaim for the first time the name of Christ – was never the first.' Partial contact and rumour had done essential preparatory work. This African initiative centred on young men who were essentially rebels, young men who challenged the elders and consciously sought change. Sundkler emphasised that in nineteenth-century Africa, it was 'a young man's Church'. (In the twentieth century it was to become more of 'a women's church'.[11]) As the Jesuits had found in seventeenth-century China, missionary technology was more appealing than their doctrine. Africans could be highly selective too. For these reasons, Sundkler saw the role of the missionary as catalytic rather than dominant.

In the early 1990s, however, a theory was developed on the basis of an examination of what happened among the Tswana. It proposed that Christianity in Africa was something imposed by powerful missionaries, who were, ultimately, 'cultural imperialists', transforming African culture in conformity with their own 'hegemonic world-view', privileged implementers of the 'colonising project'. Its authors were theoretical anthropologists, who were not really reacting against an orthodoxy (for which mission history was largely if inadvertently responsible), but articulating it with a fresh panache derived from emerging 'post-colonialism' and the speculations of Edward Said.[12] But historical ethnographers like Isaac Schapera, and historians of Tswana missions such as Anthony Dachs, had always quietly understood the reality to be more complex. Moreover, way back in 1972, R.E. Robinson had drawn attention to Dachs's proposition about the way Tswana elites had exploited missionaries to their own ends, neutralised potentially disruptive effects, and largely frustrated European objectives. As Robinson realised, in Bechuanaland in the mid-nineteenth century, a missionary was 'irrigation expert, chief of defence staff, gunsmith, commercial and diplomatic agent in dealings with the outside world'. The missionary may have thought he was playing a European role, but the role he actually played was assigned and determined by the Tswana. Robinson used this missionary example as an essential part of his theory about the nature of empire as a whole, the way it rested on collaborative 'non-European foundations'.[13] Post-colonial theory, however, bypassed this evidence of missionaries being manipulated. In the rush to denounce 'imperialism', it was strangely deaf to African 'agency'.

It was largely left to Andrew Porter to bring historians back again to the essential weakness of missionary enterprise, its disjunction from 'imperialism'. Porter emphasised the realities of 'agency' and 'appropriation', the successful African 'indigenisation' of Christianity.[14] Missionaries and Africans, he writes, were involved, whether consciously or not, in 'a constant process of mutual engagement'. He concludes: 'The continued presence and success of missionaries almost anywhere depended on their value and usefulness, the willingness of local leaders and their people to co-operate with them and the possibility of Christianity being construed in a manner answering to local circumstances.' African societies possessed considerable power 'to deflect or selectively absorb western influences'. Porter suggested two particular spheres where missionary activities had ambiguous consequences: biblical translation and school education. Helping with translation presented Africans with opportunities for rendering the gospel within traditional concepts and language: in other words, indigenisation. There was significant 'give and take' between missionaries and their collaborators in translation.[15]

It could indeed be suggested that a turning point significant for the whole future of Christianity and biblical scholarship was reached when William Ngidi, a former waggon-driver, and from 1856 a catechist assisting the bishop of Natal in translating the Bible into Zulu, asked questions about the Flood: 'Is all that true? Do you really believe that all this happened thus?' Could Noah's Ark with those relatively limited measurements really have contained so many animals? Bishop John Colenso was much-loved by the Zulu. They called him 'Sobantu' ('our father', who 'abandoned whiteness and became a true human/black'). He was a gifted Cambridge-educated mathematician, so he made calculations on the Ark and other issues. As a result, he 'felt compelled to take a totally different view from what I once did'. He started to tell questioners that the Bible could not be literally true. When he published 'proof' of this in *The Pentateuch and the Book of Joshua critically examined* (vol. I, 1862) there was a sensational reaction, a firestorm, among British readers and church leaders. From an African's astute questioning, however, has come much of modern Anglican understanding of the Bible as a text like any other, requiring careful interpretation.[16]

Missionaries were unable to prevent their madrassa-style education (which was not really meant to do much more than enable their charges to read the Bible) from being exploited for non-religious ends. The cultural impact of their schools was determined by what Africans wanted to take from them. At first the whole concept of education seemed unattractive: sitting in the heat listening to a white-skinned foreign tutor going on about the Word of God was thought to be a waste of time and essentially frivolous. But as European rule spread, it was realised that this education would provide entry into the white man's world. Christianity was one of the few sectors of European culture to which the capable and energetic African found entry unbarred. What had not been foreseen by the missionaries was that the 'brotherhood of man' and 'equality before Christ' were ideas capable of being interpreted in special senses in conditions of profound social and emotional upheaval. Singing hymns about the prisoner leaping to lose his chains, belted out unthinkingly in English public schools, could have different implications in a conquered colony. (In much the same way, Nehru's reading of G.M. Trevelyan's *Garibaldi* trilogy was more political and inspirational than a British schoolboy's.)[17]

Almost all the early nationalist leaders were mission-educated. These included the founders of the (South) African National Congress, Sol Plaatje and John Dube, and independence politicians such as Kenyatta and Banda (Church of Scotland), Nkrumah, Nyerere, and Mugabe (Roman Catholic), Awolowo and Azikiwe (Wesleyan and Baptist), Seretse Khama (LMS), and Mandela (Methodist). At primary school, Kwame Nkrumah came under the influence of a German priest, Fr George Fischer, who did much to help him: 'He was almost my guardian during my early school-days, and so relieved my parents of most of the responsibility with regard to my primary education.' Young Nkrumah took his religion seriously, frequently serving at mass, but as he grew older, 'the strict discipline of Roman Catholicism stifled me'. He became 'a non-denominational Christian and a Marxist socialist'. Nkrumah studied theology in the USA and preached in the Black Church. Perhaps only a mission-educated nationalist could launch the slogan 'Seek ye first the political kingdom and all things shall be added unto you.' Mandela went to a Methodist school at Qunu at the age of seven, proudly wearing trousers for the first time, instead of a pinned blanket. On his first day, Miss Mdingane gave him an English name (as missionaries did not approve of African ones), so Rolihlahla became Nelson – the teacher did not explain why she chose this name. 'The education I received', Mandela recalled, 'was a British education, in which British ideas, British culture and British institutions were automatically assumed to be superior. There was no such thing as African culture.' Mandela's education continued at the mission school at Mqhekezweni in Thembuland, where he felt the powerful presence of the Revd Matyolo. This Methodist missionary preached sermons of the 'fire and brimstone variety, seasoned with a bit of African animism'; God was omnipotent and vengeful and would not permit a bad deed to go unpunished. Mandela attended church every Sunday: 'I saw that virtually all of the achievements of Africans seemed to have come about through the missionary work of the Church. The mission schools trained the clerks, the interpreters and the policemen, who at that time represented the height of African aspirations.' As for Kenyatta, though he was not yet known as such (the name was later given him because of his shiny belt, *kinyatta*), he was one of the first boarding pupils at the Church of Scotland mission at Thogoto near Nairobi. He was baptised as 'Johnstone' in 1914, and became prominent among the mission-educated intelligentsia, or *athomi* ('the readers') as they were known locally. Banda, with the new name 'Hastings', attended the Livingstonia Mission, but as a migrant worker on the Rand he joined the black American-led African Methodist Episcopal Church there, which sponsored him to study in the USA, though he later returned to the Church of Scotland and became an elder. Meanwhile in Tanganyika, Nyerere, a pupil at Tabora Boys Secondary School, was baptised as a Catholic aged twenty; formerly known as Kambarage, he took the name Julius. He remained in the faith. In Rhodesia, Robert Gabriel Mugabe emerged from the Jesuit Kutama mission school, where he was befriended by Fr Jerome O'Hea, a member of the Anglo-Irish gentry. Mugabe later returned there to teach, and he was also a teacher in several other mission schools.[18]

The essential paradox about the missionary impact is this. It was both destructive and reintegrative. In this way it differed from other European

Plate 6.1 Traditional Swazi 'reed dance'. The Mhlanga is typical of the dances that missionaries objected to – an annual gathering, more or less compulsory, of all young Swazi virgins, at Lobamba, the queen mother's cattle kraal, where they repair the wind-breaks with reeds. Wearing only bead-skirts, one of the girls will be chosen at the final dance to be an additional wife for the king. The tradition continues to this day.

influences which acted in a solely disintegrating fashion. Missionaries wilfully interfered with and interdicted a whole range of traditional practices without understanding their purpose in preserving social cohesion. They attacked polygamy and bridewealth cattle exchange (*lobola*, which strengthened kinship relations), initiation and circumcision ceremonies (which marked a disciplined entry into adulthood), dancing and drumming (which promoted a comforting sense of community well-being). A Scottish missionary in Zambesia in the early 1860s argued that the whole of mankind could be divided into those who built square houses, who were civilised, and those who built round ones (*rondavels*), who were not. Some missionaries insisted on a man building a house before marriage. When they pointed to 'advances in civilisation', they often simply meant that European clothing was becoming common.[19] This might in itself become a visible sign of divisions in a community resulting from Christianity. In South Africa there was a widespread distinction between 'red' Africans (wearing red ochre decoration on their blanket) and trousered 'school' people, who lived apart.

Most Africans expected a religion to provide answers to the immediate troubles and ultimate mysteries of life. Their greatest need so often was for a remedy against witchcraft. Unable to take this seriously, Christianity was made to appear irrelevant. Africans found it hard to understand Christian doctrines, such as the incarnation and atonement. 'The Word is great, but it has gone in at one ear and out at the other,' confessed a Xhosa man. The Xhosa had problems with the idea of death as completely separate from life (the ancestors were 'alive', after all), and therefore with the concept of the soul as a purely 'spiritual body'. So, was the soul of a good man in heaven the same as the soul he had on earth? Missionaries were defeated by such sophisticated and difficult questions, and sometimes resorted to rebukes about being frivolous. To which a dignified Xhosa response came in 1826: 'I have too much wisdom to ask idle questions, but being ignorant, I wish to learn.'[20]

Many Africans were puzzled by the idea of an after-life: the Yoruba said, 'We know nothing of the other world and therefore we do perfectly right to confine our concern to this one.' A yet more serious objection was expressed by the Yoruba: 'Our fathers gave us *orisas* [idols] and we must honour them.' In 1890 a CMS missionary was confronted by an angry old Yoruba man who burst into his church crying that if his son as well as his nephew became a Christian there would be no one after his death to keep up the spirit worship inherited from his ancestors, indispensable to the well-being of his family.[21]

But at the same time as it caused social disruption and cut people off from their roots and supports, Christianity also provided new and powerful forms of religious consolation. It gave new confidence and self-understanding to individuals, liberating them from a sometimes almost overpoweringly fear-filled environment. An indigenous church provided a new focus of loyalty and interest apart from the locality, for it was a trans-tribal bond. It could be empowering to women, especially in the twentieth century. It could become a way of 'getting on' in the modern world. Some vigorous peoples, suffering much pressure on land resource, such as the Ibo of eastern Nigeria, found it attractive.[22] Missionaries became valuable intermediaries with new alien administrations, explaining their enigmatic demands, interceding against excessive ones, giving advice about the assessment and payment of taxes. Above all, they provided schools. The British government did not significantly move into the provision of education until the 1920s, and for decades after that, mission schools remained a major instrument of African education. Schools encouraged a positive encounter with modernisation.[23]

II

Nothing better illustrates the essential ambiguities of mission Christianity than the ambivalent response to it of African rulers. Almost everywhere missionaries began by aiming at top-down conversions, the winning over of the chief who could bring his people with him – a strategy which seldom worked. There was a handful of individual converts, Khama III of the Bangwato, King Kama of the Gqunukwebe, Faku of the Pedi, Sechele of the Bakwena. Strong resistance came from leaders of patriarchal and heroic cultures like the Xhosa, the Zulu, the Swazi, and the Ndebele. But rulers sometimes invited missionaries to court (the royal cattle kraal), because a 'tame missionary' could bring prestige. Generally, though, there was deep suspicion of an alien supernatural power.[24] The demands of the Christian religion were recognised as little short of awe-inspiring, as well as potentially subversive. The state council of Asante in the Gold Cost declared of the New Testament, 'It is the Word of God; it had better remain unopened.'[25] Sekgoma I (father of Khama III) used a striking analogy: 'When I think of entering the Word of God, I can compare it to nothing except going to the plain and meeting single-handed all the forces of the Matabele.'[26] Many rulers saw quite as clearly as Roman emperors in the earliest centuries of Christianity (or the Tokugawa Ieyasu who expelled the Jesuits from Japan in 1614, or the Chinese emperor who proscribed them in 1724) that this was a politically dangerous religion. Zulu chiefs in the 1870s complained that if a Zulu did anything wrong, or planned to run away with a girl without *lobola*, he went to a mission station and said he wanted to become a Christian: 'The missionaries desire to set up another power in the land and as Zululand has only one king that cannot be allowed.' Dingane (Shaka Zulu's heir) was prepared to use Francis Owen of the CMS as his secretary from 1837, but that was as far as it went. In the 1860s, Sekhukhune, king of the Pedi, said missionaries acted as 'his eyes'. He liked the idea of a sabbath and he kept it – but he also kept his wives. This selective response was far from untypical. And so were his doubts: 'You missionaries are lions. You have stolen my people and want to make yourself kings' – and then Sekhukhune accused them of causing drought.[27]

A closer look at some of the outstanding African rulers of the nineteenth century will reveal the ambiguities more sharply. King Moshoeshoe (*morena a moholo*, c.1786–1870) welcomed the Paris Evangelical Mission into Basutoland from 1833. At first he looked upon Eugène Casalis and Samuel Rolland as friends, and they rapidly became respected counsellors. Between 1839 and 1843 Moshoeshoe made many changes. He scrapped royal funeral parades of a thousand cattle, abolished circumcision rites in his family, divorced some of his 'additional' wives after his senior wife was baptised, and repudiated the killing of witches. The missionaries made some two thousand converts. But after a brief 'golden age', there was a reaction.[28] A considerable section of the BaSotho threatened the king with deposition if he persisted in encouraging Christian innovations.[29] Moshoeshoe – who was never prepared to have only one wife – decided it would in any case be better not to run the risk that his people would not follow him into conversion, or that he would lose his influence with them altogether. And so from 1848 under pressure he reversed the reforms, reinstated circumcision schools, and increased the number of his wives – some estimates say up to 200. Nearing death, however, he was about to be baptised, but died first.[30]

Mzilikazi, the greatly feared Ndebele warlord, first met Robert Moffat (Livingstone's father-in-law) in 1829. Moffat became a father-figure to Mzilikazi, and was indulged by him in all sorts of ways, after Moffat had cured the chief of a debilitating illness, diagnosing it as dropsy. However, despite this remarkable friendship, it took many years to obtain permission to open mission stations in Matabeleland, and Mzilikazi remained dubious and impatient about their activities.[31]

One of Mzilikazi's antagonists, Khama III (c.1835–1923), was much more amenable. Khama the Great was king of the Bangwato, the largest of the eight Tswana 'tribes' of Bechuanaland. His mentor was John Mackenzie of the LMS. Khama was baptised in 1862. During the 1870s he abolished rain-making, circumcision rites, infanticide, bridewealth, nocturnal dances, polygyny, and the levirate; he introduced the sabbath, and from 1879 he prohibited alcohol. But nothing was done to jeopardise his authority or that of the Bangwato nation. According to Schapera, 'all the new Church services were essentially tribal rites'; Schapera also pointed out that although missionaries welcomed the reforms as complying with their insistence on Christian requirements, there could be good indigenous reasons for making changes. Circumcision, for example, was abolished by several nineteenth-century rulers, not actually in response to Christian demands, but because of frequent fighting and military insecurity – initiation schools took too many boys and young men out of action for prolonged periods.[32] Although the Tswana case remains controversial, there seems no reason to doubt that Khama kept strict control of missionaries; the consolidation and expansion of the Bangwato kingdom with its new state religion 'clearly hinged on their successful appropriation and control of Christianity'. The Bangwato Church was made to serve the purpose of the Bangwato monarchy in its control of the kingdom.[33] Or, in the crisp formulation of Elisabeth Elbourne, 'missionaries were relatively marginal, but Christianity was nonetheless enormously important'.[34]

Lewanika, the astute ruler of the Bulozi kingdom (from 1878 to 1916), had a tame missionary in François Coillard of the Paris Evangelical Mission. Coillard had real influence on him in some ways, more perhaps than any other Protestant missionary in the nineteenth century anywhere in Africa, and for almost twenty years. But Lewanika was cautious. He often attended church services, hoping to hear his favourite hymn, a Lozi rendering of 'What a friend we have in Jesus'. But in an irritated outburst in 1892 he declared:

What have I to do with the Gospel and their God? . . . Had we not got gods before their arrival? What *I* want is . . . especially missionaries who build big workshops and teach us all the trades of the white men: carpenters, blacksmiths, armourers, masons and so on. That's what I want . . . we laugh at all the rest.[35]

Lewanika certainly made good use of the missionaries, who helped him develop a canal network. This was to prove very important in coping with ecological crisis and threatened mass starvation in Barotseland in the 1890s. His experience in dealing with missionaries in the 1880s stood him in good stead when faced with the European political challenge. He obtained technical, diplomatic, and secretarial aid, but what he seems to have valued above all was 'the reinforcement of Lozi self-confidence in the face of white encroachment'.[36]

Among ordinary Africans, two questions were frequently asked when a missionary first appeared. One was 'what useful things does he bring?' The other was 'can he make rain?' They looked for ecological not theological expertise, and for material benefits. Even into the twentieth century, especially among drought-ridden peoples like the Tswana, 'the real measure of a missionary's usefulness was: could he bring rain?' Since missionaries opposed traditional rain-makers, it was a reasonable expectation, and success would prove they enjoyed the favour of God. The substitution of a day of fasting and prayer did sometimes bring results. But more reliable were irrigation practices, 'the missionary's water-furrow', and indeed the plough. Missionaries were, however, often accused of causing drought. When Sechele of the Bakwena was baptised by Livingstone (his one and only convert), an old man complained to Livingstone, 'you might have delayed till we got rain'. A rain-doctor of the Bakwena rebuked him for saying God should be prayed to in his name alone and not by means of medicines: God 'made black men first, and he did not love us, as he did the white men. He made you beautiful, and he gave you clothing, and guns . . . [but] God has given us one little thing, which you know nothing of . . . the knowledge of certain medicines by which we can make rain.' They did not dispute the things the whites possessed, though ignorant of them, and 'you ought not to despise our little knowledge, which you are ignorant of' – for the idea of 'waiting patiently on God' for rain was silly: 'whoever thought of making trial of starvation?'[37]

Nothing endeared missionaries to Africans more than the ability to make agricultural improvements. As Samuel Marsden had understood in New Zealand, 'a nation can do nothing without iron', and he ensured the Maori were given a plentiful supply of the best axes, hoes, and spades.[38] The missionaries in Africa used a similar strategy. A delighted Nguni chief praised the introduction of the plough by the Wesleyan Methodists: 'This thing that the Whites have brought into the country is as good as ten wives.'[39] From the beginning missionaries had realised the value of being able to dispense goods. From 1799 in the Cape, the LMS missionaries carried 'Bibles in one hand, beads in the other', in order to attract attention and make rewards and payments. They soon learned, as any slave-trader could have told them, that taste and fashion in Africa were fastidious and fickle; beads must be of the right colour, size, shape, and translucency. And from this arose a demand for blankets and other forms of clothing, for tools, guns, and ploughs, in exchange for feathers, skins, and ivory. Some missionaries took to full-time trading, notably at Kuruman in Bechuanaland. In this way missionaries helped to create a dependency on the white man's goods.[40]

Christianity had other attractions. Africans were profoundly interested in acquiring some form of invulnerability in conflict with warring neighbours. There was a growing belief in southern Africa that a community with its own missionary could not be defeated in battle. Livingstone noted that the Bakhatla asked for a missionary: 'It is merely a desire for the protection and temporal benefit which missionaries are everywhere supposed to bring.'[41] The Tonga wanted missionaries in order to get help against Ngoni raids.[42] Another attraction was the idea of a day of rest: the sabbath was a natural aid to conversion.[43] Yet another could be the 'new way of death'. Indeed, this was sometimes the supreme attraction. Africans had not speculated much about life after death, and heaven sounded good. In Uganda, Roman Catholic prayers to and for the dead, and the baptism or blessing of the dying to assure them of heaven, 'living for ever with Mary', 'had a great appeal to the converts'.[44] But then, there was hell, too.

Perhaps no idea was more popular, though, than the mission station as a refuge and hiding place: 'I have found a haven, a place of constant hiding.'[45] Most early Christians were refugees, slaves, children, marginalised adults (especially women), even princes who could not succeed to the throne. Christianity was an especial opportunity for suppressed or aspiring teenagers, for whom, Professor Iliffe has written, 'Christianity was a generational revolt much as communism was in twentieth century Asia.'[46] In 1912 every member of the first Anglican Church Council in western Kenya was still at mission school (though some were older than teenagers). Missions attracted depressed social groupings and outcasts (though less so than in India with its 'rice Christians'): twins, mothers of twins, disabled people, epileptics, lepers, pregnant girls, girls escaping circumcision, barren women, women accused of witchcraft.[47] However, it is important not to overemphasise this. Not all early converts were from marginal groups. In fact they came from a wide social spectrum.[48] Nevertheless, there was a strong element of self-emancipation and protection-seeking by those who were young, poor, or female.

Syncretism was sometimes a weapon in the mission armoury. Important decisions about 'rites controversies' were not as prominent as they had been for Jesuits in China and Japan, since most missionaries in Africa did not favour syncretist techniques. An extraordinary exception was Bishop Vincent Lucas in Tanganyika (1926–44), with his famous Masasi experiment. In total, Bishop Lucas put seven hundred boys aged thirteen to sixteen through a Christian *jando* (or circumcision school), combining it with confirmation – cutting off foreskins as a prelude to first communion. He did it with some relish, declaring it to be 'a wonderful opportunity' for a priest to get 'into real personal touch with his boys'. Most European observers regarded the Masasi experiment with scorn and disgust ('it's nothing but an orgy' – or, in today's terminology, nothing but an organised system of child abuse). However, this form of syncretism was popular with the African communities of the diocese, and had in fact been initiated several years earlier by African clergy and teachers.[49]

III

Conversion sometimes resulted from gratitude for services given or insights provided. One estimate suggests that at least a third of converts in Bantu South Africa were won by missionary doctors and hospitals.[50] But is there a more theoretical way of understanding the phenomenology of conversion? The best-known attempt is that of Robin Horton in 1971.[51] Horton suggested an interpretation of 'traditional religion' as being flexible and open, a religion which sought to provide 'explanation, prediction, and control' of events. 'Traditional religion', he argued, operated at two levels: at a microcosmic level of lesser spirits for the control of everyday events, and at a macrocosmic level of a supreme being for bigger things – but ideas about this God were not highly developed because he was regarded as more distant and not so influential as the lesser spirits. As horizons widened, an African might become more interested in the macrocosmic layer of his 'traditional religion', without missionary intervention. Conversion depended upon 'enlargement of scale' brought by European presence generally, 'the modern situation'. Operating in a vacuum, Horton suggested, would have brought little missionary success.

It is certainly true that missionaries often sought to develop the embryonic concept of 'supreme being'. They would try to establish his local name, and then represent their God as the 'true' manifestation of this high god. Certainly, too, there is widespread acceptance of Horton's placing of a great deal of initiative on the African side, and regarding missionaries as catalysts rather than dominants. Horton knew about eastern Nigeria, but his thesis lacks historical specificity, and 'is probably inherently unprovable using normal procedures of investigation and verification'.[52] It is an abstract theory, and it makes almost no reference to the demographical background of conversion which seems so important. There are questions too about this rather simplified concept of 'traditional religion'. Was the 'high god' always sufficiently immanent, or valued, as to be something which could be built upon? Was the Christian God even regarded as a convincing or admirable alternative? The evidence from New Zealand in the 1820s is instructive. The Maori told Samuel Marsden that your God and our God could not be the same, otherwise you would have sweet potatoes and we would have cattle: 'were he our God as well as yours he could not have acted so partially'. Nor would he have made 'such a mistake as to make us of different colour'. More than this: missionaries introduced new diseases, with fatal effect: 'Your God is cruel and we do not want to know him.'[53] These concerns would surely have resonated with many Africans.

The Xhosa frequently asked awkward questions about the nature of God. Did he have many cattle as a mark of his greatness? Why did he not use his power to solve the problem of sin by cutting it off at source and destroying Satan? Missionaries in Xhosaland were repeatedly asked why if Christianity was meant for all people, it was 'detained for so long amongst the white people?' In the 1860s, an evangelist called Tiyo Soga challenged fellow countrymen to explain why they did not accept Christianity. A senior Xhosa chief argued that their ancestors should have known of it, if it was so important, and would not have withheld it from them. Soga replied that they hadn't had hoes, spades, and blankets in the old days either.[54]

IV

African objections to the missionary enterprise can be further explored. The three obstacles which loomed largest were polygamy, Islam, and independency. Africans' engagement with each of these will explain much about their response to missionaries.

Differing understandings of sexual moralities have always been and still remain potent sources of division between Christians and non-Christians, and nowadays between liberal Western churches and conservative African ones. The example set by European communities in Africa was not always appealing. Bishop Frank Weston in the early twentieth century worried about their corrupting influence in Zanzibar: 'more and more immoral – Piccadilly, Sodom and public bar!' This bad example he thought quite as threatening to mission work as the omnipresent expansion of Islam and the practices of witchcraft.[55] The behaviour of missionaries and priests was also sometimes scandalous.[56] Celibate Catholic priests and nuns were certainly not above suspicion in African eyes. Celibacy was incomprehensible, the mark of a boy, and few Africans believed anyone could stick to it. Victorian missionary discomfort about African sexuality often focused on circumcision. As 'a badge of manhood' it was extremely difficult to discourage.[57] But it was the rejection of polygamy which was the most fundamental bone of contention. Opposition to it became the essential dogma of nineteenth-century Christianity in Africa: at best it was repellent, at worst the devil's own institution.[58] To polygynists, the incendiary missionary demand to repudiate a second wife would put them in a state of illegality among their own people and would require dowry fines; it involved an inhumane act towards both discarded wives and their children. Traditional society had no place for unattached women who were neither immature nor senile. Inevitably it was always the least attractive women who were put away and the least likely to be remarried. As Livingstone observed, those who knew a bit about the gospel 'hate it cordially because of monogamy'. Indeed, Christianity often became known as the 'religion of one wife only'. Livingstone himself, with a real sympathy for African culture, was prepared to be more relaxed about polygamy than most, but the inflexibility of all missions on this issue was constantly reaffirmed.[59]

Polygyny was practised and admired in almost every African society.[60] Traditionally, it has been calculated that about 35 per cent of men had more than one wife. Of those who were pluralists the average number of wives was about 2.5 each. To understand the system, it has to be remembered that African marriage was aimed not at personal happiness on a basis of love or friendship between the sexes, but at the production of children within a framework of kinship alliance. An Mfengu elder told the 1883 commission on law and custom, 'it is all this thing called love. We do not understand it at all. This thing called love has been introduced' – and everything had gone wrong.[61] Multiple wives were reckoned important for several reasons. They would minimise the stigma, indeed the calamity, of childlessness; they conferred personal prestige, status, and the chance of high office; they compensated for the taboo on sexual intercourse with a breastfeeding wife (in societies where this was often prolonged until infants were two or three years old); they were important for getting work done in the fields, for food supply, and for meeting the obligations of hospitality. The Kikuyu have a proverb: 'One wife is a passport to death.' From the female point of view polygyny had advantages as well. It freed women from constant pregnancies, from a man's insistent sexual expectations, from loneliness, where convention did not expect companionship between husband and wife (they seldom ate together); and it ensured that widows and children were cared for in extended families. It also meant there was among polygynists little or no call for prostitutes. Thus, as far as family life was concerned, Christian reorientation and insistence on monogamy could have devastating consequences.[62] Men complained that they lost control of their women and missions turned their daughters into whores.[63] Even among urban, modernised, and committed African Christians, only a minority ever actually wanted to be married in a Christian ceremony. For example, in early twentieth-century Lagos, on average only some fifty Christian unions a year occurred in a Christian population of about 100,000; perhaps only two-fifths of the Lagosian elite made Christian marriage work. Or again, in eastern Uganda, only about one in eight Christian Africans ever married in a church.[64] Polygamy was a major factor in the establishment of breakaway and independent churches. Missionaries were often devious over the issue, turning a blind eye when it suited them, but then employing it as a way of asserting their authority or blocking African leadership.[65] The issue remains unresolved and controversial. In 1998, the new archbishop of Cape Town, the Most Revd Njongonkulu Ndungane, became the highest-ranking prelate yet to launch a campaign to persuade the Church to embrace polygamy. 'It has', he claimed, 'long been recognised in the Anglican Communion that polygamy in parts of Africa genuinely has features of both faithfulness and righteousness.'[66]

Second only to polygamy as a problem was competition with Islam. In a way, everything the Europeans did in Africa was part of a struggle with Islam for control.[67] Edward Steere, bishop of Zanzibar from 1875, was keenly aware of this: 'It is a race with Islam which shall have the tribes [of the interior].'[68] Islam of course had the advantage along the northern part of the east coast of having been first in the field. Like Christianity, it needed calamities and mobility to flourish, but it was prepared to be more adaptable than Christianity, and, despite its emphasis on the individual, to Africans it seemed to require less disruption of traditional practices. Most importantly, it permitted polygamy. It more readily validated the militarism of honour cultures. It required circumcision, male and female, but that was not a problem for circumcising African societies like the Yao, who transformed it into an Islamic purification rite. Islam's rules and injunctions were clear and precise, its worship simple. It was highly audible, with the muezzin's cry, and highly visible, with men praying in the open and in public. It was quite easy to set up a mosque using existing huts and local materials, as opposed to purpose-built churches, which had to provide pews and import brass eagles and lecterns from Birmingham.[69] The agents of Islam – its missionaries – were often African chiefs, confident and well organised, or wandering mallams, with much closer links to the laity than the Christian missionaries. Islam, like traditional religions, but unlike Christianity, was much concerned with the explanation of events. Its expansion proved, as one bishop put it, that Christianity was 'not the natural sublimation of African animism'; or, in modern scholarly parlance, Islamic ideas had a more workable 'significant equivalence', recognisable to the 'African mentality'.[70] Its death rites and food taboos were readily adopted. The Muslim paradise was confidently promised to believers.

Islam was not, however, automatically preferred to Christianity where there was direct competition, as in Uganda. Mutesa, kabaka of the Baganda, waveringly weighed up the counter-claims of Allah and Messiah, Friday and Sunday, and thought that the Bible might be better than the Qur'an because it was older.[71] Some scholars have suggested that perhaps the real key as to whether Islam or Christianity gained the converts was the answer to the question 'who had been the

Plate 6.2 USPG mission church under construction at Mankaiana, western Swaziland, 1969. The first Anglican church in Swaziland was built of brick in 1881 and would not have looked out of place in a British town; it was subsequently abandoned. Out-station churches were later built in a more vernacular style, with thatched roof and cow-dung floor.

slave-traders?' For this reason, Islam made no progress in the southern Sudan.[72] Conversely, Islam sometimes had the advantage of promoting a different faith from that of the dominant white rulers.[73] Ironically, the expansion of Islam was actually promoted by the extension of European control. The Pax Britannica and transport improvements enabled Islam to be spread more easily. Islam also gained an elevated status in African eyes because of the number of Muslims who served the colonial state as soldiers, policemen, and officials. In these ways acceptance of Muslims by the colonial state encouraged a more general respect for Islam.[74]

A third problem for the missions was the rejection of orthodox Christianity, the attractions of the independent church movement, or even more radical offshoots associated with eschatological millennialism. These breakaway movements (African Initiated Churches) arose from (1) dissatisfaction with what privileged missionaries offered, (2) an attempt to reassert African cultural identity, and (3) acute resentment at the blocking of indigenous promotion and leadership in mainstream churches. From the perspective of this last point, a disastrous moment occurred in the history of African Christianity when Bishop Samuel Ajayi Crowther was forced to resign in Nigeria in 1890. Crowther was the first black bishop (of West Africa); and James Johnson, another African bishop, superintendent of interior missions, was also dismissed. After these retrogressive steps by the CMS, part of a bitter reaction against the earlier strategy of promoting an indigenous ministry, there was no full diocesan African Anglican bishop again until 1953.[75] Of the fifteen ordained Africans who worked on the Niger between 1880 and 1890, twelve were either disconnected or recommended for disconnection. From the 1890s, throughout West Africa, 'Africans found themselves victims of a new hardening of attitude, an uninformed intolerance, a pushing and grasping for absolute authority'. In Nigeria, 'three great schisms' within the churches took place: Baptist in 1888, Anglican in 1891, and Methodist in 1917.[76] In South Africa, a Wesleyan minister, Nehemiah Tile, left the Methodist Church when missionaries criticised his political views. He founded the Thembu Church in 1884, in opposition to European control, and with the positive desire to adapt the Christian message to the needs of Thembu society. A similarly motivated secession from the LMS took place in Bechuanaland in 1885. An ex-Wesleyan, Isaiah Shembe, founded the Nazareth Baptist Church near Durban in 1911, defending polygyny and Zulu patriarchal values. In South Africa there were about thirty independent churches by 1913. Numbers grew to more than 800 in 1948, 2,000 in 1960, 3,000 by 1970, and up to an estimated 10,000 by the year 2000. The roll-call extended all the way from the 'Al Zion Elected Church' to the 'Zulu Ethiopian Church', and included the 'International Four Square Church', the 'Fire Baptised Holiness Church of God', the 'African Castor Oil Dead Church', and the 'King George Win the War Church'.[77]

Independency involved two comparable but unrelated strands. Not only are independent churches in one sense inheritors of an entire history of schism in the Christian Church (especially the highly visible disjunction of Protestant and Catholic churches) – 'as it were, the arithmetical progression of sectarian divisions in the West'[78] – but also they reflect the inherent tendency to split off from a father's kraal, and the fissiparousness of 'tribal' society. The leaders of independent churches, brought up in cultures with a strong sense of honour,[79] rejected the autocratic paternalism of missionaries, and sought greater respect and improved status in new centres of power. Their followers were in search of something perhaps more fundamental still, a genuinely local, intimate, autonomous community, a space which gave them personal significance and made them feel at home. Hence the stress on the ritual recovery of traditional practices.

In Nyasaland during the First World War, John Chilembwe, a charismatic African Baptist minister, protested that the fruits of Christian civilisation, promised by missionaries, were being denied. He had a vision of a national African church and was prepared to fight for it, leading to his rebellion in 1915 with tragic consequences.[80] In Kenya in the 1920s, the attack by the Church of Scotland Mission and the Africa Inland Mission on the practice of clitoridectomy was regarded as an attempt to bring about the disintegration of the Kikuyu social order; it led to the founding of the African Independent Pentecostal Church and to the politically significant Kikuyu Independent Schools Association.[81] In Uganda, Reuben Spartas founded the African Orthodox Church in 1929 for 'men who wish to be free in their own house, not always being thought of as boys'.[82] Throughout the independent churches there was dissatisfaction with a Western religion which denied polygamy and gave too little healing in church services, which did not provide enough of Horton's 'explanation, prediction, and control' of events. Africans wanted a more prophetic vision, a more vigorously developed, and preferably mystical, ministry of healing. At the more extreme end were the Zionist churches. These expressed faith through healing and purification rites, drawing heavily upon, and aiming to protect, traditional witchcraft eradication cults.[83] Women became especially prominent, in some places accounting for perhaps two-thirds of independent church membership.

Africans strikingly and enthusiastically took up eschatalogical Christian millenarianism, a feature of the Bible which missionaries were no longer keen upon, though it had featured among the original motivations of the Protestant missionary movement from the 1790s. It lost some of its power for missionaries when the predicted millennium failed to arrive in 1866. Christian millenarianism envisages the 'glorious thousand years of the saints', Christ's thousand-year rule on earth (pre-millennialism), or the culmination of Christ's Second Advent (post-millennialism, or millennialism proper).[84] Either way, Africans were inspired by the expectation that Christ would punish wicked rulers and raise up the blacks to be the preferred ones in glory everlasting. One of the most powerful millenarian movements was Kimbanguism in the Lower Congo. Simon Kimbangu was a former member of the Baptist Mission, active in the 1920s. He himself was reluctant to cut all ties with missionaries: 'We are like wives to our Whites . . . if we leave them they will be sorely afflicted.' But such was his growing prophetic reputation, and such the enthusiasm generated by the miracles ascribed to him, that men and women flocked to Kimbangu as a messiah, deserting the Roman Catholic missions. People said, 'We have found the God of the Blacks.' Intoxicated by success, Kimbanguism moved further and further from its European roots. It developed into the 'greatest mass Christian movement in West Africa', the biggest independent church in all Africa. This was despite the ambiguity of Simon Kimbangu's own beliefs. He died in 1951, but after his death the movement grew exponentially.[85]

V

It should perhaps not be too surprising that some observers consider mainstream missionary enterprise to have been largely a failure, especially in the nineteenth century.[86] There were, in a lapidary phrase, 'not all that many converts' – at least not won by Europeans, as opposed to the work of local African agents.[87] Large-scale adherence only came with independency. The often heroic educational and medical efforts of missionaries are not recalled today with much gratitude. While many Africans simply rejected the mission call, others embraced Christianity only superficially or partially. Archdeacon Watts in Swaziland in the early twentieth century wondered how far Africans 'regard the sacraments as simply "white man's medicine" of a stronger kind than can be produced by their own witchdoctors'.[88] Sundkler mentions a Zionist prophet, a graduate, who told him that a woman in his church was barren because she had a snake in her stomach which ate the foetus;[89] many years later I myself was assured by a Swazi ordinand that his stomach pains were caused by a snake, and he would be visiting a traditional healer. (It should perhaps be explained that this 'snake' is not quite like the usual reptile, but it has a head and can crawl about and bite, thus causing indigestion and stomach ache; in the male it is sometimes believed to be the source of semen, and in the female, the snake must accept the semen for conception to take place.)[90]

The apparently impressive statistics for African Christianity thus conceal a good deal of syncretism, reinterpretation, and unorthodoxy. Africans – though not unique in this – have always taken what they wanted of the Christian message, and they do so still. They believe what they want to believe. But then again, given the sceptical questioning of Bishop Colenso by William Ngidi some 150 years ago, it is ironic that many African bishops today are amongst the world's most vocal and hard-line upholders of the literal truth of the Bible and the moral teaching of the Old Testament. It is not clear yet whether present disputes will lead to a split in the Anglican Communion. But whether they do or not, explanations will be needed. It will be more important than ever to understand the history of the complex African response to Christian missions.

Notes

1 'Are we any nearer an African history of South Africa?', review article on *The Oxford history of South Africa*, vol. II, *1870–1966*, in *Historical Journal*, vol. 16 (1973), pp. 616–26, criticising (among other things) its neglect of the history of religion.

2 Richard Gray, 'Christianity and religious change in Africa', *African Affairs*, vol. 77 (1978), pp. 89–100, and *Black Christians and white missionaries* (New Haven, CT,1990); Norman Etherington, 'Missions and empire', in *OHBE*, vol. V, *Historiography* (Oxford, 1999), pp. 303–14; Etherington, 'Introduction', pp. 1–18, and Andrew Porter, 'An overview, 1700–1914', ch. 3, pp. 40–63, in Etherington, ed., *Missions and empire*, OHBE Companion Series (2005); Elisabeth Elbourne, 'Religion in the British empire', in S.E. Stockwell, ed., *The British empire: themes and perspectives* (2008), pp. 131–56.

3 Bengt Sundkler and Christopher Steed, *A history of the Church in Africa* (*Studia Missionalia Upsaliensia*, vol. 74; Cambridge, 2000), p. 91. No other study carries quite the authority, let alone the comprehensiveness, of this one. Sunkler (1909–95) was a Swedish bishop, and professor of church history at the University of Uppsala, who had been a missionary in Zululand, and became the first Lutheran bishop of Bukoba in north-west Tanzania. Steed was his research assistant, teaching African history at Uppsala.

4 Key books by anthropologists include E.E. Evans-Pritchard, *Witchcraft, oracles, and magic among the Azande* (Oxford, 1937), and *Nuer religion* (Oxford, 1956), esp. pp. 311–22; G. Parrinder, *West African religion: a study of the beliefs and practices of Akan, Ewe, Yoruba and Ibo* (2nd edn, 1961); and, from a sympathetic missionary perspective, J.V. Taylor, *The primal vision: Christian presence amid African religions* (1963); and Adrian Hastings, *The Church in Africa, 1450–1950* (Oxford, 1995).

5 Peter Geschiere, 'Witchcraft and the state': Cameroon and South Africa, ambiguities of "reality" and "superstition"', *Past and Present*, supplement no. 3 (ed. S.A. Smith and A. Knight, 2008), pp. 313–35.

6 Sundkler and Steed, *A history of the Church in Africa*, pp. 352–4; J.D. Omer-Cooper, *The Zulu aftermath: a nineteenth-century revolution in Bantu Africa* (1966), pp. 164–5.

7 G. Hunter, *The new societies of tropical Africa* (1962), p. 194.

8 Sundkler and Steed, *A history of the Church in Africa*, pp. 392–3, 461–2.

9 Ibid., p. 579. For African gun-culture, see pp. 104–5, above.

10 Sundkler and Steed, *A history of the Church in Africa*, p. 402; Gray, *Black Christians and white missionaries*, p. 80; Etherington, *Missions and empire*, pp. 7–8; Andrew N. Porter, *Religion versus empire? British Protestant missionaries and overseas expansion, 1700–1914* (Manchester, 2004), esp. pp. 320–3. For further development of the 'hidden history' of this theme, see Peggy Brock, 'New Christians as evangelists', in Etherington, ed., *Missions and empire*, ch. 7, pp. 132–52.

11 Sundkler and Steed, *A history of the Church in Africa*, pp. 83–4, 333, 1039.

12 Jean and John Camaroff, *Of revelation and revolution*, vol. I, *Christianity,*

colonialism and consciousness in South Africa (Chicago, IL, 1991). For commentaries, see C.C. Crais and L. De Kock, 'For and against the Camaroffs', *South African Historical Journal*, no. 31 (1994), pp. 273–309, and Elisabeth Elbourne, 'Word made flesh: Christianity, modernity and cultural colonialism', *American Historical Review*, vol. 108 (2003), pp. 435–59.

13 Adam Kuper, 'Schapera, Isaac', *ODNB, 2001–2004* (ed. L. Goldman, 2009), p. 974; Anthony J. Dachs, 'Missionary imperialism in Bechuanaland, 1813–1896' (PhD thesis, University of Cambridge, 1968): 'the missionary's policy is determined not so much by what his home society or his conscience suggest it ought to be, as by the roles in tribal society that its native leaders chose to allocate to him' (p. 352). R.E. Robinson, 'Non-European foundations of European imperialism: sketch for a theory of collaboration', in R. Owen and R. Sutcliffe, eds., *Studies in the theory of imperialism* (1972), pp. 117–42.

14 A.N. Porter, 'Religion, missionary enthusiasm and empire', *OHBE*, vol. III, *The 19th century* (1999), pp. 222–46; 'Religion and empire: British expansion in the long nineteenth century', *JICH*, vol. 20 (1992), pp. 370–90; '"Cultural imperialism" and Protestant missionary enterprise, 1780–1914', *JICH*, vol. 25 (1997), pp. 367–91; and *Religion versus empire?*, ch. 12, 'Conclusion: the "anti-imperialism" of Protestant missions', pp. 316–30. See also the commentary in Rowan Strong, *Anglicanism and the British empire, c.1700–1850* (Oxford, 2007), ch. 1, 'Anglicans and empire: historical interpretations', pp. 10–40.

For the creation by African agency of a Tswana 'Christian textual orthodoxy', see S. Volz, 'Written in our hearts: Tswana Christianity and the "Word of God" in the mid-nineteenth century', *Journal of Religion in Africa*, vol. 38 (2008), special number, *Inventing orthodoxy: African shaping of mission Christianity during the colonial era*, pp. 112–38.

15 Conclusions strongly supported by an important thesis dealing with Buganda: Christian results reflected not so much the religion and ideals presented by Catholic missionaries, as 'characteristics which showed the people's active involvement in the attempt to shape Catholicism and make it their own, able to build on whatever they valued in their culture and to answer their spiritual and material needs, especially their new urge for progress'; it supplemented but did not entirely supplant traditional religion (John M. Waliggo, 'The Catholic Church in the Buddu Province of Buganda, 1879–1925', PhD thesis, University of Cambridge, 1976, p. 337).

16 Sundkler and Steed, *A history of the Church in Africa*, p. 371; Jeff Guy, 'Imperialism and literary criticism: William Ngidi, John Colenso, and Matthew Arnold', *Journal of Southern African Studies*, vol. 23 (1997), pp. 219–40, and *The heretic: a study of the life of John William Colenso, 1814–1883* (Johannesburg, 1983), pp. 90–105; P. Hinchliff, 'Colenso, John William', in *ODNB*, vol. XII, pp. 332–5; Hlonipha Mokoena, '"The queen's bishop": a convert's memoir of John W. Colenso', *Journal of Religion in Africa*, vol. 38 (2008), pp. 312–42. Colenso wanted to Christianise Zulu culture rather than remove individuals from their traditional way of life; he never believed polygamy was incompatible with Christian morality. He was accused of

being converted into heresy by his Zulu congregations. But because of his theological insight and vigorous championship of African rights, his life and work should today be celebrated by the Church more than it is. The popular hymn 'The Church's one foundation' was written contra-Colenso, and its verse about 'by schisms rent assunder' should now be omitted from all decent hymn-books.

17 R.I. Rotberg, *The emergence of Northern Rhodesia: the missionary contribution, 1885–1924* (*St Antony's Papers*, no. 15, African Affairs, no. 2, ed. K. Kirkwood, Oxford, 1963), pp. 101–19; P. Worsley, 'Religion and politics in Central Africa', *Past and Present*, no. 15 (1959), pp. 73–81. For Nehru, see his *Autobiography* (1936, 1938), p. 19.

18 *The autobiography of Kwame Nkrumah* (1957, 1964), pp. 11–12; Nelson Mandela, *Long walk to freedom: the autobiography* (1994, 2001), pp. 15–16, 22–23.

19 H.A.C. Cairns, *Prelude to imperialism: British reactions to Central African society, 1840–1890* (1965), pp. 85, 228.

20 Hildegarde H. Fast, '"In at one ear and out at the other": African response to the Wesleyan message in Xhosaland, 1825–1835', *Journal of Religion in Africa*, vol. 23 (1993), pp. 147–74; Richard Price, *Making empire: colonial encounters and the creation of imperial rule in nineteenth-century Africa* (Cambridge, 2008), ch. 4, pp. 57–92, which confirms for the Xhosa the ingenious fitting of Christianity to indigenous beliefs and requirements.

21 John Iliffe, *Honour in African history* (Cambridge, 2005), p. 79; J.D.Y. Peel, 'For who hath despised the day of small things? Missionary narrative and historical anthropology', *Comparative Studies in Society and History*, vol. 37 (1995), pp. 599–600.

22 Ruth Slade, *King Leopold's Congo: aspects of the development of race relations in the Congo Independent State* (1962), pp. 158–64; J.S. Coleman, *Nigeria: background to nationalism* (Berkeley, CA, 1958), pp. 91–107.

23 Richard Gray, 'Christianity', in *Cambridge history of Africa*, vol. VII, *From 1905 to 1940* (1986), pp. 140–90. Teaching by Africans was not always efficient, however. At Mutwankolo school in Zambia, the Universities Mission to Central Africa in 1915 found the alphabet being taught upside down: see Rotberg, *The emergence of Northern Rhodesia*.

24 Gray, *Black Christians*, p. 59; Iliffe, *Honour in African history*, pp. 149–52. An extreme form of suspicion arose in the copper-belt in the 1930s, when the White Fathers were accused of vampirism: Luise White, 'Vampire priests of Central Africa: African debates about labour and religion in colonial northern Zambia', *Comparative Studies in Society and History*, vol. 35 (1993), pp. 746–72.

25 John Iliffe, *Africans: the history of a continent* (Cambridge 1995, 2007), p. 154 in 1st edn, p. 160 in 2nd edn.

26 Sundkler and Steed, *A history of the Church in Africa*, p. 438.

27 C.P. Groves, *The planting of Christianity in Africa*, vol. I, *To 1840* (1948), p. 267 (Dingane); Sundkler and Steed, *A history of the Church in Africa*, pp. 388–9 (Sekhukhune).

28 Victor F. Ellenberger, *A century of mission work in Basutoland, 1833–1933*

(1932, tr. E.M. Ellenberger, Morija, Lesotho, 1938), esp. pp. 14, 44, 61; L.M. Thompson, *Survival in two worlds: Moshoeshoe of Lesotho, 1786–1870* (Oxford, 1975). Moshoeshoe acquired his name from the sound made by a razor-shearer on cattle (sound the 'o' as 'w').

29 B. Hutchinson, 'Some social consequences of nineteenth-century missionary activity among the southern Bantu', *Africa*, vol. 27 (1957), pp. 160–75.

30 C.C. Saunders, 'Moshoeshoe', in *ODNB*, vol. XXXIX, pp. 465–7.

31 Omer-Cooper, *The Zulu aftermath*, pp. 129–31; Elisabeth Elbourne, 'Moffat, Robert', in *ODNB*, vol. XXXVIII, pp. 495–500.

32 Sundkler and Steed, *A history of the Church in Africa*, pp. 427–40; Isaac Schapera, *Tribal innovators: Tswana chiefs and social change, 1875–1940* (1970), p. 44. Circumcision was abandoned by the Mpondo, the Taung, the Swazi, and the Zulu without missionary prompting: Isaac Schapera, *Government and politics in tribal societies* (1956, 1963), p. 90; Omer-Cooper, *The Zulu aftermath*, p. 27.

33 Porter, *Religion versus empire?*, p. 321. Porter draws here on Paul S. Landau, *The realm of the Word: language, gender and Christianity in a South African kingdom* (1995).

34 Elbourne, 'Religion in the British empire', p. 145.

35 Sundkler and Steed, *A history of the Church in Africa*, pp. 462–5.

36 Gwyn Prins, *The hidden hippopotamus: reappraisals in African history: the early colonial experience in western Zambia* (Cambridge, 1980), pp. 164, 236.

37 Sundkler and Steed, *A history of the Church in Africa*, pp. 355, 463; James Morris, *Heaven's command: an imperial progress* (1973, 1979), p. 321.

38 J.R. Elder, ed., *The letters and journals of Samuel Marsden, 1765–1838* (Dunedin, 1932), pp. 371, 445n.

39 Sundkler and Steed, *A history of the Church in Africa*, pp. 358, 377; J.B. Webster, 'The Bible and the plough', *Journal of the Historical Society of Nigeria*, vol. 2 (1963), pp. 418–34.

40 R.B. Beck, 'Bibles and beads: missionaries as traders in southern Africa in the early 19th century', *Journal of African History*, vol. 30 (1989), pp. 211–25; Dachs, 'Missionary imperialism', p. 82.

41 Isaac Schapera, ed., *Livingstone's missionary correspondence, 1841–1856* (1961), p. 36; Sundkler and Steed, *A history of the Church in Africa*, p. 429.

42 J. van Velsen, 'The missionary factor among the Lakeside Tonga of Nyasaland', *Rhodes–Livingstone Journal*, no. 26 (1959), p. 6.

43 Sundkler and Steed, *A history of the Church in Africa*, p. 463.

44 Ibid., p. 96; Waliggo, 'The Catholic Church in the Buddu Province', ch. 5, 'Tensions of change and continuity'. One of the most popular mass 'intentions' was *muddembuga* ('take your enemy to the court of justice'): p. 251.

45 Sundkler and Steed, *A history of the Church in Africa*, p. 377.

46 Iliffe, *Africans*, pp. 232–3 (2nd edn).

47 Richard Elphick, 'Africans and the Christian campaign in southern Africa', in H. Lamar and L.M. Thompson, eds., *The frontier in history: North America and South Africa compared* (New Haven, CT, 1981), pp. 270–307.

48 Justin Willis, 'The nature of a mission community: the Universities Mission to Central Africa in Bonde', *Past and Present*, no. 140 (1993), pp. 127–54.

49 T.O. Ranger, 'Missionary adaptation of African religious institutions: the Masasi case', in T.O. Ranger and K. Kimambo, eds., *The historical study of African religion: with special reference to East and Central Africa* (1972); W.V. Lucas, 'The educational value of initiatory rites', *International Review of Missions*, vol. 16 (1927), pp. 192–8; Sundkler and Steed, p. 533. These accounts are now modified by Anne Marie Stoner-Eby, 'African clergy, Bishop Lucas and the Christianizing of local initiation rites: revisiting "the Masasi case"', *Journal of Religion in Africa*, vol. 38 (2008), pp. 171–208.

50 B.G.M. Sundkler, *Bantu prophets in South Africa* (2nd edn, Oxford, 1961), pp. 220–1.

51 Robin Horton, 'African conversion', *Africa*, vol. 41 (1971), pp. 101–7. For commentary, see Gray, *Black Christians and white missionaries*, pp. 63–9, and Etherington, 'Missions and empire', p. 310.

52 Etherington, 'Missions and empire', p. 310.

53 Elder, *Letters and journals of Samuel Marsden*, pp. 231, 441.

54 Brock, 'New Christian evangelists', p. 137.

55 Quoted by Porter, *Religion versus empire?*, p. 229. A 'public bar' was regarded as the disreputable part of a pub.

56 For example, see M. Erlack, 'Sexual misconduct and church power in Scottish mission stations in Xhosaland South Africa in the 1840s', *Gender and History*, vol. 15 (2003), pp. 69–84. See also p. 381 below, and, generally, RH, *Empire and sexuality*, pp. 103–6.

57 Price, *Making empire*, pp. 62–5.

58 J.F.A. Ajayi, *Christian missions in Nigeria, 1841–1891: the making of a new elite* (1965), pp. 106–7.

59 Schapera, *Livingstone's missionary correspondence, 1841–1856*, p. 9; Waliggo, 'The Catholic Church in Buddu', p. 252. Colenso's friend William Ngidi was much exercised by insistence on monogamy: surely 'God would not call a man and say "Come thou and be saved, though thyself alone", and cast the others away to be lost?' (Guy, 'Imperialism and literary criticism', p. 225). There is an important reappraisal of David Livingstone by Sir Andrew Roberts, 'Livingstone, David', in *ODNB*, vol. XXXIV, pp. 73–82.

60 V.R. Dorjahn, 'Polygyny', in W.R. Bascom and J. Herskovits, eds., *Continuity and change in African cultures* (Chicago, 1959), pp. 103–8; A.R. Radcliffe-Brown and D. Forde, eds., *African systems of kinship and marriage* (1950); Lucy Mair, *African marriage and social change* (1969).

61 Max Gluckman, *Custom and conflict in Africa* (1956, 1963), p. 78.

62 Isaac Schapera, *Married life of an African tribe* (1940): 'as far as the family is concerned, Christianity was the most directly subversive factor' among the Kgatla of Botswana (p. 249).

63 N. Etherington, 'Education and medicine', in *Missions and empire*, p. 263; Iliffe, *Honour in African history*, pp. 202–3.

64 Adrian Hastings, *Christian marriage in Africa: being a report commissioned by the archbishops of Cape Town, Central Africa, Kenya, Tanzania, and Uganda* (1973), pp. 12–20, 45–60; K. Mann, *Marrying well: marriage, status and social change among the educated elite in colonial Lagos* (Cambridge, 1980), esp. pp. 43–53.

65 J.B. Webster, *The African churches among the Yoruba, 1888–1922* (Oxford, 1964), esp. p. 65, and 'Attitudes and policies of the Yoruba African churches towards polygamy', in C.C. Baëta, ed., *Christianity in tropical Africa: studies presented at a seminar in Ghana, 1965* (1968), pp. 224–46.

66 As reported in the *Sunday Telegraph*, May 1998; see also for the stand on monogamy, Stephen Neill, *A history of Christian missions* (2nd edn, 1986, ed. O. Chadwick), pp. 452–3.

67 This theme is elaborated in RH, *Britain's imperial century* (2nd and 3rd edns): 'In one sense the partition of Africa was a device to contain or counteract the expansion of militant Islam' (p. 216); this idea has been found useful by Porter, *Religion versus empire?*, p. 215. And see p. 100 above.

68 Quoted by Sundkler and Steed, *A history of the Church in Africa*, p. 530.

69 Peter B. Clarke, *West Africa and Islam: a study of religious development from the 8th to the 20th century* (1982), esp. pp. 259–61; J. Spencer Trimingham, *Islam in West Africa* (Oxford, 1959), esp. pp. 24–45; Iliffe, *Honour in African history*, pp. 73–82 on Yorubaland.

70 Bishop Gresford Jones, quoted by Roland Oliver, *The missionary factor in East Africa* (1952), p. 207; E.A. Alpers, 'Towards a history of the expansion of Islam in East Africa', in Ranger and Kimambo, eds., *Historical study of African religion*, pp. 172–201; J. Spencer Trimingham, *Islam in East Africa* (Oxford, 1964), esp. pp. 54–60.

71 Sundkler and Steed, *A history of the Church in Africa*, pp. 567–76.

72 P.E. Lovejoy, *Transformations in slavery* (Cambridge, 1983), p. 280.

73 Francis Robinson, 'The British empire and the Muslim world', *OHBE*, vol. IV, *The twentieth century* (1999), p. 418.

74 Sundkler and Steed, *A history of the Church in Africa*, pp. 648–9.

75 Ajayi, *Christian missions in Nigeria*, pp. 232–72.

76 Webster, *The African churches among the Yoruba, 1888–1922*, p. 65.

77 Sundkler, *Bantu prophets in South Africa*. Castor oil of course was used for purgation, a prominent feature of 'spirit' churches, and a symbol of entry into new life. As to 'King George Win the War', well into the 1970s in Lesotho, two of the most popular designs for blankets remained Second World War Spitfires and victory-V signs. For further analysis of independency, see Robert Edgar, 'New religious movements', in Etherington, *Missions and empire*, ch. 11, pp. 216–37.

78 Sundkler, *Bantu prophets*, p. 296.

79 Iliffe, *Honour in African history*, p. 225.

80 George Shepperson and Thomas Price, *Independent African: John Chilembwe and the origins, setting and significance of the Nyasaland Native Rising of 1915* (Edinburgh, 1958), and 'Nyasaland and the millennium', in S. Thrupp, ed., *Millennial dreams in action: essays in comparative study* (supplement no. 2 to *Comparative Studies in Society and History*, vol. 5, The Hague, 1962), pp. 144–59; Worsley, 'Religion and politics in Central Africa'; R.I. Rotberg, 'Chilembwe's revolt reconsidered', in R.I. Rotberg and A. Mazrui, eds., *Protest and power in Black Africa* (New York, 1970), pp. 337–73.

81 J. Kenyatta, *Facing Mount Kenya* (1938), pp. 130–5; RH, *Empire and sexuality*, pp. 189–97 ('Clitoridectomy in Kenya').

82 F.B. Welbourn, *East African rebels: a study of some independent churches* (1961), p. 81.

83 V. Lantenari, *The religions of the oppressed: a study of modern messianic cults* (tr. L. Sergio, 1963).

84 See 'Chronological index of Scripture History' in John Brown's *Self-interpreting Family Bible* (1st edn, Edinburgh, 1778), for a prediction that the millennium would begin in 1866, or failing that, 150 years later, that is, 2016. For background, see J.F.C. Harrison, *The Second Coming: popular millenarianism, 1780–1850* (1979), and D.N. Hempton, 'Evangelicalism and eschatology', *Journal of Ecclesiastical History*, vol. 31 (1980), pp. 179–94.

85 Efraim Andersson, *Messianic popular movements in the Lower Congo, Studia Ethnographica Upsaliensia*, vol. 14 (1958); Sundkler and Steed, *A history of the Church in Africa*, pp. 780–3.

86 Elphick, 'Africans and the Christian campaign in southern Africa', pp. 285–6.

87 Etherington, 'Education and medicine', p. 261; Waliggo, 'The Catholic Church in Buddu', p. 273: a failure to eliminate traditionalism.

88 C.C. Watts, *Dawn in Swaziland* (1922), p. 105.

89 Sundkler, *Bantu prophets*, p. 237.

90 Helen Kuper, *An African aristocracy: rank among the Swazi* (1961), p. 187 (the Swazi believe the snake produces worms, and turns food into faeces); E.J. and J.D. Krige, *The realm of an African rain-queen: a study of the pattern of Lovedu society* (1943), p. 212.

Part III

Bureaucracy and policy-making

7   Bureaucracy and trusteeship in the colonial empire

[Reprinted from the *Oxford history of the British empire*, vol. IV, *The twentieth century* (ed. J.M. Brown and W.R. Louis, 1999), an essay which drew in part upon material first published in 'The Colonial Office mind, 1900–1914', a contribution to the *Festschrift* for Professor Mansergh, *The first British Commonwealth: essays in honour of Nicholas Mansergh* (ed. N. Hillmer and P. Wigley, 1980), reprinted from the *Journal of Imperial and Commonwealth History*, vol. 8 (1979).]

You might say that a chapter with this title ought to test the hypothesis of 'the official mind of imperialism', the idea that there was a definable directing theory (or 'invisible hand') behind the British empire. This essay does not quite do that, although it does ask some of the main questions relevant to such an enquiry, at least for the first half of the twentieth century. How was the central bureaucracy of the empire organised? What was its role and function, and where did it stand in relation to other agencies? What sort of officials ran it? (They were almost entirely male, though we should not forget the pioneering women, Mary Fisher – see pp. 274–5 below – and Eleanor Emery.) Did they have any sort of agreed outlook? To the extent that 'trusteeship' can be identified as an institutionally defining doctrine, how did this work in practice? How did it change to meet post-war challenges after 1945?[1]

I

Colonial affairs had been dealt with in Whitehall by a secretary of state since 1768, though sometimes in combination with other ministerial portfolios. Towards the end of the eighteenth century the secretaryships of war and colonies were combined and not finally separated until 1854. At this time the Colonial Office operated out of Downing Street, in a seriously dilapidated building, later pulled down and replaced by the Whips' Office. In 1875 the Office was moved to the north-east corner of the prestigious block containing the Home, Foreign, and India Offices. There was a further move to Great Smith Street in 1945. Plans for a grand

Table 7.1. *Colonial Office staff, 1935–64*

Year	Number of staff
1935	372
1939	450
1943	317
1947	1,189
1954	1,661
1964	530

new Colonial Office building in Parliament Square were abandoned in 1954 because of Winston Churchill's objection – on the grounds not that the empire was contracting, but that it would ruin his own grandiose scheme for an enlarged Parliament Square, 'to be laid out as a truly noble setting for the heart of the British Empire'.[2] Before the routine use of the typewriter and telegraph from the 1890s, the Colonial Office was a sleepy, humdrum place. It was also, before the arrival of Joseph Chamberlain (secretary of state, 1895–1903), a political backwater. In 1870 incoming communications totalled a mere 13,500 items. By 1900 this had risen to 42,000 and by 1905 to 50,000 a year. It was one of the smallest departments in Whitehall, with a staff of 113 by 1903. Numbers were to increase, although the Office remained comparatively small (see Table 7.1). Of some 400 in the 1930s only about 70 were administrative grade secretaries.

In response to criticism that the Colonial Office was insensitive to the emerging and developing self-governing communities (Canada, Australia, New Zealand, and South Africa), a separate Dominions Department was established within the Office in 1907. This led eventually to the creation of a separate secretaryship of state for Dominion affairs in 1925, but until 1930 the post was held by the secretary of state for the colonies, L.S. Amery. The two posts remained distinct after 1931 until they were recombined in 1962 in the person of Duncan Sandys. Meanwhile the Dominions Office was renamed the Commonwealth Relations Office in 1947, when it took over residual India Office work after independence. Probably only at this point did the 'Dominions Office' (DO) acquire any real sense of purpose, even though Kashmir was to provide plenty of headaches in Commonwealth relations. A merger took place between the Colonial Office (CO) and the Commonwealth Relations Office (CRO) in 1966. Two years later a final merger with the Foreign Office (FO) established the Foreign and Commonwealth Office (1968). These changes were not uncontested. Cabinet Secretary Norman Brook, as early as 1956, was in favour of a

united 'Department of Commonwealth Affairs', which would get rid of
the word 'Colonial', fast becoming a term of abuse. He thought Australia
and New Zealand were now mature enough not to feel threatened by
this change, and all ought to appreciate the need to dispel criticism of
colonial policy. Neither Office was enthusiastic, but it was increasingly
recognised that there were problems in maintaining the post-1925 structure. By 1958 Alan Lennox-Boyd (secretary of state, 1954–9) believed
'we should be thinking in terms of an ultimate merger' of colonial and
Commonwealth affairs. In 1959 high commissioners were asked for their
views about the suggested amalgamation. All believed Commonwealth
governments would regard being linked with colonial territories unfavourably: it would be a retrograde act which might increase the taint of
'colonialism'. (Only the government of the Central African Federation
welcomed it, as leading to the disappearance of its bogey, the Colonial
Office.) The high commissioners warned that the result would probably
be that the Commonwealth governments would bypass the new office
and deal directly with the Foreign Office. The existence of a separate
office, they argued, was living proof of the importance attached to the
Commonwealth connection, and Commonwealth relations were, after
all, supposed to be 'different in kind' from foreign relations.[3] However,
by the end of 1962 the winding up of the colonial empire had proceeded
to such an extent that the prime minister, Harold Macmillan, was in
favour of amalgamating the two. Meanwhile, the Plowden Committee
had tentatively recommended amalgamation of the Commonwealth
Relations Office and Foreign Office as the two 'diplomatic' departments,
engaged on different work from the Colonial Office's 'administration' of
dependencies. But Macmillan was vehemently opposed to this further
merger: 'No. I think the Plowden Ctee. are on the wrong track *altogether*.
I should *oppose* strongly merg[ing] Commonwealth with FO. *Politically*,
it would be worse for us than the Common Market.'[4] An incoming
Labour government after 1964 thought differently. The establishment
of the Commonwealth Secretariat in 1965 (on Afro-Asian initiative) also
fundamentally changed the situation.

Until 1925, when the separate Dominions Office was created, the
work of the Colonial Office was subdivided essentially along geographical or regional lines, and these country departments were relatively
self-contained. The role of the Office was supervisory. Colonies were
administered not from London, 'the one rank heresy which we all shudder
at', but by their governors on the spot. Governors, however, acted
under a general metropolitan supervision. The feasibility of a governor's proposals would be assessed by the CO, whose officials saw their
task as being 'an essential function of cautious criticism'. They were

Plate 7.1 Secretary of state's room, Colonial Office, early twentieth century.

unperturbed by the argument that they lacked practical experience and firsthand knowledge of particular colonies: 'one can criticize a pudding without being a cook' (Charles Strachey). From the 1930s the colonial empire gradually began to be seen more as a whole, and as a stage upon which more interventionist and generally applicable policies might be evolved, beginning with Colonial Development and Welfare. Attempts at regional co-ordination increased. Administration became more and more complex and technical. Accordingly, the subject departments became more important. There had long been a General Department, dealing with promotions and transfers in the Colonial Service, postal communications and copyright inventions, uniforms and flags; only to a limited extent was it genuinely concerned with general policy. The Personnel Division was created in 1930, and the General Department developed its subject functions which then again subdivided, starting with the Economic Department (trade, colonial products) in 1934, followed by International Relations (dealing with the League of Nations Mandates), Defence, Social Service (labour, education, and health), and Development. By 1950 there were twenty-one subject departments as against eight geographical departments. A parallel development was the increase in specialist advisers. There had been a legal adviser since 1867. The secretary of the advisory committee on Native Education in Tropical Africa became in 1934, in effect, the educational adviser. A chief medical adviser was appointed in 1926, an economic and financial adviser in 1928, a fisheries adviser in 1928, an agricultural adviser in 1929, an animal health adviser in 1930, and a labour adviser in 1938. By 1960 there were thirty scientific and technical advisers, and twenty-three advisory committees. All these changes were reflected from the late 1930s in subject files becoming increasingly the focus of business, until by 1950 there were about three times as many subject files as country files. The country or geographical classes of records between 1925 and 1954 are now represented in the National Archives by about 55,000 surviving files for thirty years, while the subject classes for the period 1939 to 1954 alone are represented by 31,000 files for fifteen years. Co-operation between geographical and subject departments remained close. Ministers, when they took decisions, were usually advised not simply by one of the geographical departments or one of the subject departments but by both working together. And the country departments remained more important politically than the mere statistics suggest.[5]

Was there in the Colonial Office an 'official mind' on empire problems? Although technically only the instrument of the secretary of state, 'as a continuous institution it had in fact a corporate "mind" of its own, built up on its long tradition, the experience and personal characteristics of its staff, and the effectual influence of its constant and intimate contact with the Colonial Service'.[6] By contrast, it would have to be a powerful secretary of state who could impose his own policy on all but a highly selected number of individual issues. The vast majority of files only went to the secretary of state at the discretion of officials. Changes of government were seldom a problem. Political bipartisanship generally prevailed, although apparently fractured from 1964. Before then little adjustment to new parties in power was required. Temperamental differences between ministers of whatever political colour were more important, as garrulous character succeeded taciturn, slave-driver replaced indulgent, intellectual followed near-illiterate, or lazy amateur succeeded dedicated professional. Like all civil servants, Colonial Office officials were expected to be unbiased politically. However, in the broadest terms, the 'mind' of the Colonial Office was humane and progressive, unable to identify with extreme right-wing attitudes to empire. They were proud of the empire, but also sceptical about it. They were happiest and worked most effectively under radical administrations, such as that of the Liberal government of 1905 to 1915 and the Labour government of 1945 to 1951.

It is manifestly the case, however, that there was never a time in the twentieth century when the Colonial Office staff was of a single mind. As in all small communities of intelligent people, there were tensions and strongly argued disagreements which could quickly acquire a personal dimension. The argumentativeness of its officials was remarked on ruefully by a new permanent under-secretary, Sir Francis Hopwood, coming in from the outside in 1907, who found he suffered a great deal and wasted too much time every day 'endeavouring to convince or coerce' the remarkable 'self-confidence in opinion' of those below him. Chamberlain, he believed, had to a certain extent 'fomented contentiousness'. In a later generation there were marked differences of approach between traditional conservatives such as Sir Hilton Poynton and Sir John Martin, and radical Young Turks such as J.S. Bennett. Nevertheless, the atmosphere was clubbish and donnish. It was also rather patronising towards public opinion and pressure groups. Officials were generally impatient of humanitarian and missionary pressure. This was not because they did not care about human rights; on the contrary, they regarded themselves as the true and efficient guardians of 'the moral tradition', to which outside bodies, with imperfect access to full information, could add little. Too often the representations of the latter seemed inaccurate, exaggerated, sentimental, and unrealistic. And where matters of high policy, like strategic considerations or delicate diplomatic relations, were concerned, it was not possible to provide proper and convincing explanations to outsiders.

These officials were a true elite of scholar-official mandarins. They were clever men, richly furnished with ability. Many of them passed high in the open competition for the Home Civil Service, some of them head of their year, among them C.P. Lucas, S. Olivier, W.A. Robinson, and A.B. Keith, the last-named passing in 1901 with more than a thousand marks more than any previous candidate. Keith had an Oxford triple first on top of his previous first-class degree from Edinburgh; he took a law doctorate by thesis in 1907, and became a professor of Sanskrit and comparative philology, as well as an acknowledged authority on the constitutional history of the empire. First-class degrees were common (as they were not in the Colonial Service, dominated by the 'Blues and 2.2s'). Of the later generation, J.S. Bennett had a double starred first in history from Cambridge. Andrew Cohen was within six marks of first place in the 1932 entry, but had sixty marks deducted for 'bad handwriting' (he practised a large, vague script which looked like gothicised Hebrew with all the diacriticals omitted), a penalisation which demoted him to fourth place. Kenneth Robinson left for an academic career which embraced the directorship of the Institute of Commonwealth Studies in London and vice-chancellorship of the University of Hong Kong.

Almost the entire routine of the Colonial Office consisted in the circulation of paper among its officers in strict hierarchical sequence, each person recording his – it was usually his – opinion in minutes. Minuting tended to be more extensive and meticulous than it was in the sparser, less reflective Foreign Office tradition. Minuting is a more time-consuming process than might be thought, as it required good composition combined with mastery of a great deal of documentation. But in this painstaking way the Colonial Office was able to function efficiently as a memory-system of data storage and retrieval, as hard-working officials recorded the reasoning behind decisions and made themselves able to give an expert opinion or draft appropriately worded despatches reasonably quickly, make precedents available, and warn politicians of actions already proved futile.

II

One aspect of bureaucracy which became increasingly central as the twentieth century progressed was inter-departmental relations. In the early days it had not much troubled the Colonial Office what other government departments thought about the empire. The relationships which came to matter were principally those with the Foreign Office, Commonwealth Relations Office, and Treasury. The approach of the Foreign Office was radically different, its main interest being in diplomatic accommodations without the responsibility of actually running any territories. All too often it seemed to think the Colonial Office could well afford to make gestures within the colonial empire in order to make its own general task in the international arena simpler. The Colonial Office often felt it received no help from the Foreign Office permanent officials, and frequently a good deal of hindrance, since they seemed to regard colonial matters as rather a nuisance, especially as they appeared not to be much concerned to stand up for British rights, let alone those of the inhabitants of colonial territories. The Foreign Office thought the Colonial Office too legalistic, and rather resented the fact that British Honduras bedevilled 'normal' relations with Guatemala, or the Falkland Islands with Argentina. Above all, it was annoyed that Cyprus upset relations with Greece. The Foreign Office view tended to be that British policy itself caused discontent in Cyprus because of an unduly high-and-mighty attitude emanating from Government House, Nicosia (but then, the Colonial Office would have agreed with that). They also thought the Colonial Office attitude too ambivalent: was Enosis (union with Greece) a serious problem or not? ('The Colonial Office are supreme wishful thinkers.') There was a major disagreement between the Foreign

Office and Colonial Office about the recognition of the Yemen Republic in 1963, with the Foreign Office much more disposed to be nice to the 'Nasserite' Yemenis, and the Colonial Office evaluating the question from the narrow standpoint of the Aden base. The Foreign Office was contemptuous of the Colonial Office's reluctance to see it move into a more significant role in African policy. They thought the Colonial Office 'Bourbon-minded' in resisting a more planned and inter-departmental approach. In 1949 the Foreign Office suggested there should be a Nile Valley Board (made up of Egypt, Sudan, Ethiopia, Uganda, and the Belgian Congo) to sort out the problem of the Nile waters, foster good relations with Egypt, and generally improve the British reputation at the United Nations. But to Cohen and the Colonial Office this was wholly disadvantageous to East Africa: 'we cannot sacrifice the interests of colonial territories for these purposes'. It was not in Uganda's interest to risk Egyptian and Ethiopian interference. Hilton Poynton agreed: 'This is a characteristic piece of Foreign Office nonsense. I agree that it should be vigorously opposed.'[7]

Differences of approach with the Commonwealth Relations Office are best illustrated with reference to two major surveys conducted at the request of the prime minister in 1957 and 1959, entitled respectively 'Future Constitutional Relations with Colonies' and 'Future Policy Study, 1960–1970'. In response to the former (vulgarly known as Macmillan's 'profit and loss account'[8]), the Commonwealth Relations Office indicated that it would like Britain to divest itself of responsibility for the Solomon Islands and the New Hebrides (a condominium with France), which could be more sensibly administered by Australia and New Zealand. The Colonial Office could not see this working and doubted whether it would be in accordance with 'the wishes of the natives'. Two years later Macmillan himself raised the matter again, after 'some interesting' representations from the Duke of Edinburgh who had just visited the Pacific. Macmillan agreed there was 'much to be said for a rationalization of colonial responsibilities' in the south-west Pacific. Australia spent more on its dependent territories than Britain did per head, and if it were interested in taking over, this could be of advantage to the peoples involved. A transfer 'within the Commonwealth' would involve no loss of prestige. The New Hebrides were of no importance to Britain. If the British held on they would have to spend more on them: 'otherwise the disparity between our standards and those of the Australians and the French will become so marked that the inhabitants may become disaffected'. If the Gilbert and Ellice Islands could be rejoined to Fiji, a 'general co-ordination' of dependencies in the region might be secured.

Such arguments were familiar to the Commonwealth Relations Office, and had been mooted by them before, but for the most part, and certainly since 1952, Australia had seemed reluctant to take on new responsibilities. Macmillan's interest polarised departmental attitudes sharply. The Colonial Office took its stand on 'trusteeship': the people themselves must choose for themselves when they had been brought to a sufficient stage of political and economic advancement. The Commonwealth Relations Office focused on the admittedly poor reputation of European rule in these territories – the 'Pandemonium' of the New Hebrides, and the 'discreditable backwater' of the Solomons – and argued that it was a nonsense for six Western powers to be exercising jurisdiction in the south Pacific. John Chadwick of the Commonwealth Relations Office minuted: 'This has now become an open battle between the Colonial Office paternalists who wish to retain control until they have led their South Seas protégés into the best of all possible worlds, and CRO devolutionists, who believe in the lessons of geo-history and see some chance of lessening the white man's burden . . . It is clear that we and the CO are poles apart.'

A special committee of ministers discussed the issue in July 1959. The principal points made were that Britain could not indefinitely undertake the financial commitment of administering territories of no particular strategic significance, especially where they could be more appropriately administered by other Commonwealth countries; but the peoples might not welcome transfer and the French might not agree. The prime minister then directed the matter to be remitted to the 'Future policy study' group of officials – which in the event could make no clear recommendation because of the continuing irreconcilability of views between the Colonial Office and Commonwealth Relations Office, but they did incline to the Colonial Office basic arguments of 'moral responsibility' and allowing the wishes of the inhabitants to prevail.[9]

The production of this 'Future policy study' paper provided a major occasion for inter-departmental co-ordination, particularly over perceptions of the future of the Commonwealth, the most contentious section as originally drafted by the Commonwealth Relations Office. Both the Colonial Office and the Foreign Office felt the Commonwealth Relations Office exaggerated the importance of the Commonwealth as a factor in British relations with the United States when they argued that Americans listened to the British *because* of the Commonwealth. The Commonwealth Relations Office draft also seemed to contain too much special pleading and too much optimism about the value of economic ties to the United Kingdom for future African states. But much of the imprecision of the Commonwealth Relations Office paper arose from internal disagreements within that office. The Foreign Office view was that the Commonwealth was not a possible source of power (as the United States was and Europe might be) for Britain, but was nevertheless important as an instrument of such limited power as Britain still had. The Colonial Office valued the Commonwealth highly, but to some extent simply because it was a non-American grouping in international affairs. However, these differences of official perception were ironed out, and the final version of the paper on the future of the Commonwealth was accepted by the Colonial Office officials as 'very satisfactory'. They too believed that the Commonwealth was of great significance in the crucial matter of relations between advanced and underdeveloped nations: that it was the only alternative to the growing political and economic deterioration of Britain, as well as a useful instrument of Western influence in the global struggle against communism. Moreover, its very existence provided a good answer to the charge of 'colonialism', and it enabled emerging nations to begin to learn about international relations within 'a sort of family circle'. By 1962, when the Commonwealth had changed from a cohesive and small group of relatively large countries into a large association of mainly small states, the value of the Commonwealth – according to Norman Brook – was that it was a means of attracting Western as opposed to communist allegiance, and might make a valuable contribution to world peace if Britain could reduce racial tension in the world by co-operation within this multiracial organisation. 'Two-tier' concepts of the Commonwealth, with different levels of participation for the old 'white' members and the new Afro-Asian ones, were firmly rejected by the officials.[10]

There were departmental differences, too, about how to treat the United Nations. The Foreign Office and Commonwealth Relations Office felt that the collapse of the United Nations would be disastrous, and Britain must not let discontent with it lead to policies which might damage it. They wanted a more robust attitude to colonial problems when these were debated at the United Nations: the British delegation should be more active and publicise the British case more effectively, instead of thinking more in Colonial Office terms of disdainful silence or walkouts. They thought the Colonial Office attitude – at least as exemplified by Hilton Poynton, obsessed with resisting the United Nations and seeing no real need to work with either it, the United States, or even the Commonwealth – profoundly unsatisfactory and legalistic. Some years of inter-departmental debate (defy or co-operate?) reached a climax in 1962.[11]

After the Foreign Office and Commonwealth Relations Office, the other main department the Colonial Office dealt with was the Treasury

– a relationship in which the Colonial Office is commonly supposed to have been at a disadvantage. Things were not quite as difficult as might be thought. The Treasury had no positive input into colonial policy. It simply reacted to proposals. In the vast majority of cases all it had to do was declare 'no Treasury interest'. What it did do was to provide funding for colonial projects, and its scrutiny then was, quite properly, rigorous. But it certainly was not the case that the Colonial Office pressed for the expenditure of limitless sums of money. Before 1940 its own fundamental principle was that the 'colonies should pay for themselves', usually by taxation. When the Colonial Office entered a serious argument with the Treasury it was because it felt compelled to do so, and on the whole the Treasury respected this and its response was not necessarily unsympathetic. The testimony of a notable deputy under-secretary, Sir Charles Jeffries, throws useful light on this. He described Treasury officials as always courteous and helpful, but naturally 'some were more inclined than others to take a real interest in colonial affairs', which often raised questions 'for which normal "Treasury practice" did not provide clear answers'. Even in the titanic debate over the funding of pensions for the new Overseas Civil Service (HMOCS) between 1955 and 1961, the Treasury officials were, Jeffries found, 'anxious to be as helpful as possible within the limits of what they regarded as the correct approach'. And in the end, 'the Colonial Office substantially achieved all that it had fought for over the years' in the scheme established under the Overseas Service Aid Act (1961).[12]

It has often been argued that the Colonial Office lacked respect in Whitehall, that it suffered from 'political weakness'. Such an interpretation would seem hard to sustain in the light of detailed examination of the evidence. How did this evaluation come about? In part because influential prime ministers, such as Attlee or Macmillan, are supposed to have had a low opinion of the Colonial Office. We must be careful not to rip out of context their occasional acid comments on particular personalities or issues. Attlee did not get on at all well with Arthur Creech Jones (secretary of state, 1946–50), essentially because he could not stand his talkativeness. Macmillan as foreign secretary despaired of the 'Byzantine ways' of the Colonial Office department which handled Cyprus; but his very choice of adjective shows that it was not meant to be a *general* comment on the Colonial Office. Indeed his assessment of it, based on his experience as parliamentary under-secretary in 1942, praised it as a small, tightly knit department, with intelligent, devoted, conscientious officers.[13] No convincing generalisation that the Colonial Office was not highly regarded by ministers can be constructed: rather the reverse, since the ministers usually expressed themselves well satisfied with the service they received. From the perspective of officials, obviously they preferred a boss who effectively fought the Colonial Office corner at the Cabinet. If Creech Jones could not always do so against Foreign Secretary Ernest Bevin, that was not an unusual situation, for not even Attlee himself could automatically prevail against such a heavyweight opponent. The Colonial Office was certainly powerful enough to impose its views and even take advantage of the change of government in 1951 from Labour to Conservative. A declaration of continuity of policy initiated by Andrew Cohen went ahead despite the disinclination of Churchill to endorse it. The civil servants' project (also masterminded by Cohen) for a Central African Federation was pushed forward relentlessly, and their notions of how best to treat Seretse Khama (heir to the Bangwato chieftainship in Bechuanaland) were imposed on new ministers with vigorous determination.[14]

III

It will now be appropriate to examine the doctrines of the Colonial Office, and its principal contributions to policy-making. Its doctrines were famously embodied in the term 'trusteeship', which in the post-war era was elided into 'partnership', 'multi-racialism', and finally 'non-racialism'.[15]

Edmund Burke declared in 1783 with respect to India, 'all political power which is set over men, being wholly artificial, and for so much a derogation from the natural equality of mankind at large, ought to be some way or other exercised ultimately for their benefit . . . such rights . . . are all in the strictest sense a *trust*; and it is in the very essence of every trust to be rendered accountable.' This was the first occasion upon which governmental 'trust' doctrines were applied to dependencies. The idea was refined by Lord Macaulay and J.S. Mill in ways which envisaged self-government as the desirable long-term outcome of the 'trust'. In the government of dependencies, said Mill, unless there was some approach to facilitating a transition to a higher stage of improvement, 'the rulers are guilty of a dereliction of the highest moral trust which can devolve upon a nation'. Macaulay looked forward to the day when India should be independent. These doctrines, especially as reinforced by anti-slavery ideologies and evangelical missionary religion, had some real and positive influence on the conduct of government policy of the empire in the 1830s – the climax of a genuine period of humanitarian doctrines, when a concern for 'aboriginal rights' was manifestly prominent. Such rights were rather more equivocally set forth in the Treaty of Waitangi (1840) with the Maori of New Zealand, and thereafter were harder to assert in the face of proliferating disillusionment in non-European capacities and amenability – a disillusionment which reached its climacteric as a result of the Indian Mutiny-Rebellion of 1857. Later Victorians might still recognise their 'trust' in a paternalistic and protective way, but its positive and progressive elements (as added by Macaulay and Mill) were at a discount. They began to revive only after 1905, but if there were then some 'gains' towards a less negative trusteeship, there were also some notable 'losses' in terms of promoting self-government in white minority hands in South Africa in 1909–10. Only from 1923, after similar gains for white settlers in Southern Rhodesia, were the more positive aspects of the 'trust' gradually consolidated.

Trusteeship in the early years of the century was in constant counterpoint with the parallel policies of increasing deference to the principles of white self-government. This was especially the case with the terms of the South African transfer of power, but also there was a soft-pedalling of imperial protest at the immigration-restriction policies of the Dominions. The desire of Indians to emigrate freely within the empire posed a difficult issue, as white regimes everywhere wished to exclude them. Whose loyalty was government to forfeit: Indian or European? There was a genuine fear in Whitehall that an attempt to stop restriction of immigration would set up a movement of secession from the empire; some Australians, indeed, had already muttered threats about breaking with the empire if thwarted. When the Colonial Office in 1905 (under Alfred Lyttelton) had tried to persuade self-governing colonies to reserve for imperial consideration all bills containing provisions based on race and colour distinctions, there was uproar. Thereafter an uneasy compromise was worked out. The Dominions found means of discrimination based on vague grounds of 'unsuitability' rather than express prohibition of racial categories. The imperial government was obliged to admit the right of self-governing colonies to exclude those it did not wish to receive, but tried to see that the way they did it did not cause needless offence or hardship, or involve Britain in 'diplomatic' difficulties with India or Japan; they would continue to make selective representations against racial discrimination even if they could not veto offensive legislation; but they knew they must not preach, as that would cause friction and so be counterproductive.

Some definite victories for trusteeship were achieved outside the strictly colonial field. It was agreed to stop selling opium to China from 1907. In 1917 Indian indentured labour – which had been such a central feature of the imperial enterprise since the 1830s – was terminated. But this chapter is concerned with colonial policy and the revival of trusteeship from 1905.[16] Under the Liberal government, bureaucratic heavy-handedness came under attack everywhere, from Curzon's India to Milner's Transvaal. Stern rebukes were issued to Captain Ewart Grogan (president of the Colonists' Association of Kenya), who flogged some Kikuyu men outside the Nairobi courthouse in 1907 for having jolted a rickshaw carrying white women. Colonel Montgomery (conservator of Kenya forests) was also taken severely to task for saying 'natives did irretrievable damage to forests, and whilst the natives themselves could always be replaced, with trees it was different, for it cost much money to plant a forest'. A closer watch was kept on forced labour and flogging, although the former was not effectively brought under control until 1921. The Colonial Office would not accept a political argument for pulling administration out of any part of the newly acquired territories in Africa, not even the unproductive hinterland of Somaliland: 'we have undertaken the responsibility before the world of gradually introducing order and settled government . . . and to withdraw our civilizing agents . . . is a renunciation of our mission which is not admissible' (W.D. Ellis). Nor would they co-operate with the Foreign Office in a diplomatic deal with France involving the handing over of the Gambia, asserting the need to have the consent of the inhabitants. In Nigeria they put (Lord) Lugard on a much tighter rein. In Southern Rhodesia they vetoed restrictions on Asian immigration. They refused permission for large-scale European plantations even to respected firms such as W.H. Lever, the soap manufacturer, in West Africa. This foreshadowed the rebuff to Bovril, denied ranching access to Bechuanaland in 1919. African colonies, officials believed, were administered 'first of all and chiefly in the interests of the inhabitants of the Territories; and secondly in accordance with the views of people in this country (and not a small and interested section of them [the merchants] represented in Parliament)' (R.L. Antrobus, assistant under-secretary). The first consideration was 'to do what was best for Africa', and trusteeship came before development. Not that development was entirely neglected. In July 1906 a circular despatch was issued to promote the work of development through the revamped Scientific and Technical Department of the Imperial Institute. At this date, however, 'development' meant measures to combat disease and improve transport rather than a comprehensive infrastructural programme.

Interlocking with trusteeship were policies of Indirect Rule and promoting peasant cultivation. Central to all of this was the report of the Northern Nigeria Lands Committee (1908) and the resulting Land and Native Rights Proclamation of 1910, an important measure which secured non-alienation of African land, leasehold in preference to freehold, and African priority in undisturbed use. Africans were encouraged to initiate commercial development wherever there were no settlers, especially in cotton growing in Southern Nigeria, Uganda, and in the Sudan, where there was a massive scheme at Gezira. Cocoa was also successfully developed by peasant production in the Gold Coast (Ghana). Broadly speaking, the African policy of the Colonial Office before the First World War was anti-settler and pro-African, in favour of 'rule through chiefs' and the development of traditional organisation; it was wary of chartered companies, excessive expenditure, and indentured labour, and opposed to 'punitive expeditions', monopolies, and concession-hunting. As a former governor, Lord Lugard famously summed up this version of trusteeship as a 'Dual Mandate', with Britain as trustee to civilisation for the development of resources, and to the natives for their welfare.[17]

The story of trusteeship between the wars was essentially played out through eight separate pronouncements about the future of East and Central Africa, especially Kenya and the Rhodesias (Zambia and Zimbabwe), which had the most vociferous settler communities. Analysis of these documents cannot be avoided. As Lord Vansittart of the Foreign Office has written, this was a generation which 'paddled in a purée of words and hoped to catch a formula'. These pronouncements reflected the tussle for control between conflicting interests: the officials as trustees, Parliament as watchdog, the settlers, and the Government of India.[18]

Churchill's statement, 1922: Churchill was secretary of state, 1921–2. He declared that there was no intention of preventing Kenya becoming 'a characteristically and distinctively British Colony, looking forward in the full fruition of time to responsible self-government'. This was not actually quite so much of a charter for settler self-government as it appeared, and it was balanced by a call for a common electoral roll to be established. The Indian community would be the principal beneficiary, and the settlers were furious.

The Devonshire Declaration, 1923: the Duke of Devonshire was secretary of state, 1922–4. This declaration reversed Churchill's approach by giving less to Indians and more to Africans: 'His Majesty's Government regard themselves as exercising a trust on behalf of the African population, and they are unable to delegate or share this trust, the object of which may be defined as the protection and advancement of the native races.' There followed words about 'the mission of Great Britain' to work continuously for 'the training and education of the Africans towards a higher intellectual, moral and economic level' than that which they had reached. And finally there was one of the most famous and powerfully worded declarations of imperial policy ever made: 'Primarily Kenya is an African territory, and His Majesty's Government think it necessary definitely to record their considered opinion that the interests of the African natives must be paramount, and that if, and when, those interests and the interests of the immigrant races should conflict, the former should prevail.'

Amery's White Paper, 1927: L.S. Amery was secretary of state, 1924–9. Amery had a more political programme than was common among colonial secretaries. He proposed to do what the Devonshire Declaration had expressly forbidden: to share the trust with the settlers. This was known as the 'dual policy', and it seemed to give as much weight to European settler interests as to trusteeship for Africans. He was also keen to promote closer association between the East African dependencies and also the Central African territories.

The Hilton Young Report, 1929: Sir Edward Hilton Young was a former Liberal junior minister and Chief Whip, now moving to the Conservative side. His committee was hijacked by Sir George Schuster (Colonial Office financial adviser) and J.H. Oldham (secretary to the International Missionary Council), and the majority report (which Hilton Young himself did not sign) rejected the idea of self-government for Kenya on the Southern Rhodesia model. It rejected also a closer union under white domination for the territories of both East and Central Africa, and instead looked to an imperially directed co-ordination of trusteeship policy. This meant: 'the creation . . . of a field for the full development of native life as a first charge on any territory; the government . . . has the duty to devote all available resources to assisting the natives to develop it'. The report was also significant for introducing a new concept, of which much was to be heard in future: 'what the immigrant communities may justly claim is partnership, not control'.

The Passfield 'Memorandum on Native Policy in East Africa', 1930: Lord Passfield, formerly Sidney Webb, was Labour's secretary of state, 1929–31. His paper tried to reconcile previous statements by promoting the fiction that the 'dual policy' of looking to settler interests was 'in no way inconsistent with trusteeship', but the emphasis was primarily on the paramountcy of African interests.

The Passfield Statement on Closer Union, 1930: to the disgust of the Kenya settlers, this revived the Churchillian proposal of a common roll franchise for all races, based on educational attainments. The two Passfield White Papers together were denounced by the settlers as 'black papers'.

The Parliamentary Joint Select Committee Report, 1931: this asserted that the East-Central African question had become 'a test case of imperial statesmanship in harmonizing the separate interests . . . of different races'. It glossed 'paramountcy' as meaning that African majority interests 'should not be subordinated to those of a minority belonging to another race, however important in itself'. The report was not in favour of East African Closer Union, and it affirmed a continuation of the 'dual policy', 'the complementary development of the native and non-native communities'. This was how the Kenya issue was more or less left for the 1930s.

The Bledisloe Commission Report, 1939: Viscount Bledisloe was formerly parliamentary secretary to the Ministry of Agriculture, and governor-general of New Zealand, 1930–5. He was asked in 1935 to investigate whether some form of closer association or co-operation between Northern and Southern Rhodesia was desirable or feasible, 'having due regard to the interests of the inhabitants irrespective of race, and the special responsibilities of the government for African interests'. He took such a long time to report that he acquired the nickname 'Bloody-slow'. The eventual conclusion was that the only argument against amalgamation was the difference in native policies of the two Rhodesias, with Northern Rhodesia following Colonial Office doctrine: 'It is the fear that the balance is not fairly held between the two races in Southern Rhodesia that alone prevents a recommendation being made for immediate amalgamation.' That single obstacle was of course received as decisive in Whitehall. Bledisloe recommended economic co-operation and a political standstill.

The upshot of the battle of words was clearly resolved in favour of trusteeship and against the settler aspirations in Kenya. It was, however, a hollow victory, because it proved impossible to get the resolutions implemented. With the exception of the statements of Amery, and of Churchill to a lesser extent, these pronouncements represent a consistent Colonial Office view. The Devonshire Declaration of 1923 clearly stands out as historically central and significant, however difficult to turn into effective practical results in the short term. It was a courageous statement which, whatever the equivocations, represented the moment from which Kenya would develop into a black state. The retreat from a settler state, however discontinuous, had publicly begun. It was not an entirely new departure, but picked up a thread inherent in British policy for Kenya since the Foreign Office in 1904 had instructed its officers: 'the primary duty of Great Britain in East Africa is the welfare of the native races'.

Why, then, was it so hard to make trusteeship stick in Kenya? The settlers were strong-willed and often intimidating, and they successfully 'captured' governors selected to control them. Governors with impeccable records in defending native rights elsewhere (Girouard in Nigeria, Mitchell in Fiji) soon succumbed to this bluff and intimidation. Only Sir Joseph Byrne (1931–7) is generally reckoned to have achieved anything like resistance to their seductive pressure. Under provocation, intimidation could mean actual threats of rebellion, as in 1922–3 against putting Indians on a common roll franchise. The Devonshire Memorandum itself held that it was out of the question to use force against the settlers, many of whom were ex-soldiers. It would be costly and unedifying; anything like a blockade to cut trade facilities would be damaging to the entire Indian community, and to Uganda; blacks could not be used to suppress whites. These considerations made Passfield's papers more equivocal than they would otherwise have been. In 1942 Sir Arthur Dawe of the Colonial Office wrote: 'The lesson of 1923 is always there . . . it seems unthinkable that any British government would bring military force to bear upon a community of our own blood who have supported the British cause splendidly in this and the last war.' Compromises *tended* to favour the settler interest, and all the while there was a fear of driving them into the arms of South Africa.[19]

Yet in a fundamental sense Whitehall was never wholeheartedly behind the Kenya settlement, even if it acknowledged some obligations. As early as 1908 a junior Colonial Office official had adumbrated a scheme of wholesale repatriation: 'It would probably pay the British taxpayer to repatriate all the whites and forbid their entry except on payment of a heavy poll-tax' (W.D. Ellis).[20] In 1923 Viscount Peel told a settler delegation directly, 'I think the best solution of this trouble is to buy you all out.' In 1928 he said privately that he had never negotiated 'with a more stiff-necked or unreasonable set of people'. Harold Macmillan, as parliamentary under-secretary of state in 1942, concluded that Kenya was 'not a white man's country', and there would be a clash in which the government would be torn between the rights of the settlers and their obligations to the natives. The solution, he believed, was to buy out the whites and give land back to the Africans; there might be land nationalisation into state and collective farms run by such farmer-settlers who were serious and efficient. This would be expensive, 'but it will be less expensive than a civil war'.[21] After 1945, however, when the Labour Party suggested something similar, Cohen was adamant that it was now too late for such drastic measures, and persuaded Creech Jones that the Kenya problem could not be solved by dramatic gestures of this kind. Instead, an appeal was made to the settlers to see the wisdom and decency of a policy of multi-racialism. In the wake of Mau Mau, this bore fruit in the shape of Michael Blundell and his New Kenya Party. The Lyttelton Constitution of 1954 finally ruled out for all time the prospect of self-government for the Kenya Europeans alone. The officials' report, 'Future constitutional development of the colonies' (1957), described Kenya as an 'unstable multi-racial society . . . the task of statesmanship in the next decade is to manipulate European fears, Asian timidity and African impatience to a delicate but changing balance which allows no member of the team to run off the field'. The whole of East Africa was seen in the Colonial Office at this date as 'the testing ground for the possibility of multi-racial or non-racial development'.[22]

The success of the Colonial Office in blocking the amalgamation of the Rhodesias meant that after the war the settlers switched their objective to a federation of the Rhodesias and Nyasaland. This was, perhaps, only a partial victory for trusteeship in Central Africa. Whatever their reservations, officials in the Colonial Office and Commonwealth Relations Office thought there were good arguments for a link-up which would act as a counterpoise to South African expansion and retain some formal elements of imperial control over African affairs.[23]

IV

Although the issues of trusteeship for East and Central Africa between the wars were fought out in the public arena, there was another equally important battle raging mainly behind the scenes. This concerned the High Commission Territories of Basutoland, Bechuanaland, and Swaziland. From 1925 these became the responsibility of the Dominions Office and second only to Ireland as its principal problem. The continual frustration by the Colonial Office and the Dominions Office of aspirations passionately espoused by all South African governments for fifty years was a notable tribute to imperial trusteeship. In the early years at least it was trusteeship maintained in default of any public knowledge of, or interest in, the question, which only emerged after 1933.[24]

The problem was as follows. The schedule to the South Africa Act (1909) provided for a possible transfer of the administration of the three Territories to the Union. Section 151 was purely permissive; transfer was essentially conditional, and no date was specified. Moreover, important pledges were given during the passage of the Act through the British Parliament that Africans would be consulted and their opinion 'most carefully considered'. It was never clearly explained what this meant: 'consultation means consultation'. Equivocation was part of the tactics; another was playing for time. Since South African native policies became progressively tougher, beginning with the Land Act of 1913, there was never any serious hope that the Colonial Office or Dominions Office would be willing to hand over its trusteeship to South Africa. Accordingly, the Colonial Office took issue with Viscount Gladstone, the first governor-general, over his apparent unawareness that 'it is the natives who really count'. Gladstone seemed to contemplate transfer as something to be prepared for rather than staved off. Overtures were received from the South African government, broadly divided into five main sets: 1911–13 (Botha), 1919–23 (Smuts), 1924–7 (Hertzog), 1932–9 (Hertzog again), and 1939 (Smuts). But even after 1948, all prime ministers (Malan, Strijdom, Verwoerd) until 1961 (when South Africa left the Commonwealth) still hoped to secure substantive negotiations. Despite some differences between British politicians, officials to a man consistently opposed any change in the status quo. The most anyone was ever prepared to contemplate was an experimental transfer of Swaziland before 1925. What they achieved was a containment of South Africa within its boundaries of 1909. Whether this could be made permanent was in doubt as late as the mid-1970s. In dealing with the evil of apartheid, containment of its boundaries was the most effective contribution Britain could have made, and by the end of the 1960s British policy had allowed the emergence of three successful independent states (Lesotho, Botswana, and Swaziland). This was trusteeship exercised at the expense of imperial political advantage. Britain risked the hostility of white South Africans whose loyalty hung in the balance. No comparable advantage could be expected from the goodwill of small African communities enmeshed in the southern African geopolitical structure. Britain's resistance to Union demands was played from a position of steadily decreasing strength. Britain could so easily have bought the favour and co-operation of the South African government, which economic and strategic interests required, by relinquishing the High Commission Territories, since these were a drain rather than an asset, in no sense valuable as showpieces of empire – it was feared any development of their resources would only make them more attractive to the Union. They were, therefore, largely left alone as backwaters.

It was precisely in this contradiction – that development seemed incompatible with active trusteeship – that the weakness of the doctrine was revealed, and it is this which explains its transmutation into multiracial 'partnership'. Protection from exploitation was no longer enough. As Secretary of State Oliver Stanley declared in 1943: 'Some of us feel now that the word "trustee" is rather too static in its connotation, and that we should prefer to combine with the status of trustee the position also of partner.' A little earlier, the under-secretary, Macmillan, had declared that the 'governing principle of the Colonial Empire' should be 'the principle of partnership between the various elements composing it'. This exceedingly general proposition soon became refined in East and Central Africa in an idiomatic sense, where it meant partnership between the different sections of the community. Great faith was pinned upon 'a genuine partnership between Europeans and Africans' in producing prosperity and concord. The planners here did not favour in East Africa either an African or a European nationalism as the basis for the future, believing that one group or the other would always feel threatened by it. Partnership was thus a device to promote stability. There was a definite fear that the progressive withdrawal of European influence might cause the whole central area of the continent to fall into great disorder, which would not be in anybody's interest. It was in regard to the Central African Federation established in 1953 that 'partnership' was most ardently invoked: but the invocation was one more likely to be made by politicians than by officials. The civil servants had propounded the theory that the expansionist pressure of a militant National Party in South Africa and its apartheid doctrines had to be counterbalanced by keeping an active loyal 'British' state on its border, in which the relationship between Europeans and Africans would be progressively improved, and the 'share of the Africans in the political and economic life of the territories . . . progressively increased under the policy of partnership'. It was not to be, and the special association of 'partnership' with the Federation discredited it.[25]

Meanwhile, outside the East-Central African area, trusteeship still held sway. It was particularly in evidence in the arguments advanced by the civil servants in 1957 to discourage Macmillan from offloading colonial responsibilities. In presenting their case, they relied on arguments about the need to maintain 'global prestige', but where these manifestly could not apply they fell back on the 'abdication of moral responsibility'. It would be deplorable, discreditable, and dangerous, they said, to allow colonies to degenerate into chaos, as would happen in the Seychelles, the Solomons, and the Gilbert and Ellice Islands. In other cases, such as Mauritius and Fiji, there were delicate racial problems which Britain must accept the responsibility of having created in the first place by the introduction of Indian labourers.[26]

By the end of 1959 the doctrinal emphasis had shifted again to 'non-racialism'. In the officials' paper 'Africa in the next ten years', it was asserted: 'East Africa must be non-racial, where minorities can contribute.'[27] The future of the High Commission Territories was also from about this date considered to be 'non-racial'. When the 'Future policy study' paper was being prepared, C.Y. Carstairs of the Colonial Office thought it was a good opportunity to reaffirm trusteeship doctrines. Something needed to be included in any statement of the aims of government policy which recognised that: 'In terms of practical politics a large section of opinion in this country will never be easy if it feels that our liberty or property depend directly or indirectly on the servitude or property of others; and a policy which gives rise to such feelings will for that reason not in the long run be capable of steady and effective pursuit.' This was not, Carstairs argued, mere sentimentality, and to ignore it was 'inverted sentimentality': public opinion had a right to feel government was doing what it reasonably could to put an end to possible abuses.[28]

V

From the 1950s the context within which trusteeship could still be invoked was entirely different, and the emphasis was much more on its positive aspects. A new and forward policy emerged from about 1940. Lord Hailey urged the application to the empire of the expanded role of the state which had developed in Britain itself during the 1930s Depression. With the full backing of the Colonial Office, Secretary of State Malcolm MacDonald was determined to align trusteeship to a more active development policy in a new Colonial Development and Welfare Act. Gerard Clauson of the Colonial Office described the two motives behind this as 'to avert possible trouble in certain colonies where disturbances are feared if something is not done to improve the lot of the people', and 'to impress the world with our consciousness of our duties as a great Colonial Power'. MacDonald was anxious to make the colonial position in wartime unassailable. It was 'essential to get away from the old principle that Colonies can only have what they themselves can afford to pay for'. Without such action 'we shall deserve to lose the Colonies and it will be only a matter of time before we get what we deserve'. The introduction of 'welfare' as well as 'development' would provide the genuineness of more altruistic purpose. It was not easy to persuade the Treasury about this new dimension. The Colonial Office had to fight to keep the word 'welfare' in the title of the Act. But by 1944 even Treasury officials were persuaded that 'as regards the money we are conscious that we must justify ourselves before the world as a great Colonial power'.[29]

There is no doubt that, as Wm. Roger Louis writes: 'The Second World War witnessed a moral regeneration of British purpose in the colonial world.' With the impetus of MacDonald's achievement behind them, together with better information in the shape of Lord Hailey's *An African survey* (1938) and the stimulus of Lord Moyne's damning report on the West Indies (1939), the Colonial Office officials entered enthusiastically into the task of redefining colonial policy.[30] This in itself marked a dramatic shift. Formerly the initiative was allowed to rest with innovative governors such as Lugard of Nigeria and Cameron of Tanganyika. Now, as Cohen put it, 'we cannot afford to leave this vital matter to the chance of new Lugards and Camerons coming forward

in the future'. The Colonial Office must itself define a centrally determined and generally applicable clear policy. This became 'political
advancement', the key to which was to look upon African administrations as local authorities, 'in broadly the same relationship to central
government as local authorities in this country'; to provide 'a balanced
system of political representation for the traditional and non-traditional
elements of African opinion', a pyramidal chain of representation
leading up to the legislative councils and national self-government. The
Colonial Office recognised that more social services and educational
facilities would have to be provided. They acknowledged that they
had to respond to 'a rapidly increasing political consciousness among
Africans' (Cohen), as well as international opinion reinforcing 'pressures towards the immediate implementation of trusteeship obligations'
(R.E. Robinson).[31] Officials after 1945 saw themselves as engaged on
not only what they called 'a new policy for Africa', but also 'a gigantic experiment', 'a worldwide experiment in nation building' (H.T.
Bourdillon). The central aim of policy as they redefined it was to lead all
but the smaller isolated colonies into self-government as soon as possible
(though that was not expected to be soon), and to consolidate links with
Britain on a permanent basis, so that ex-colonies would remain in the
Commonwealth. 'In this conception of the evolving Commonwealth,'
wrote Bourdillon, 'I see the boldest stroke of political idealism which
the world has yet witnessed, and on by far the grandest scale'; this great
experiment was something 'surpassing in importance any of the much
publicized political experiments indulged in by the Soviet Union or
anybody else'.[32] Poynton declared at the United Nations: 'the present
time is one of unprecedented vigour and imagination' in British colonial policy, 'one cheerful thing in a depressing world'. A carefully considered formulation of policy by the Colonial Office (probably drafted
by Cohen) in 1948 was certainly high-minded: 'The fundamental
objectives in Africa are to foster the emergence of large-scale societies,
integrated for self-government by effective and democratic political and
economic institutions both national and local, inspired by a common
faith in progress and Western values and equipped with efficient techniques of production and betterment.'[33]

From 1945 onwards the Colonial Office was fully aware that a major
task would be to come to terms with African nationalism. They had not
previously thought much about this problem, as British attitudes to colonial nationalism had originally been responses to it in Ireland, India, and
Egypt. Lessons of Asian and Arab nationalism had been learned fast after
1945, and by the 1950s there was a considerable body of accumulated
experience to draw upon. It was clear that Britain's limited economic

resources made it impossible to resist nationalists everywhere, that strategic bases could not effectively be held without local goodwill, and that it was difficult to withhold equal concessions from similar states (especially if neighbours). Experience also suggested the importance not only of recognising what was feasible, but of retaining the initiative. One had to keep one jump ahead of nationalists, make timely and graceful concessions from a position of control, show willingness to modify ideal timetables in response to circumstances, be prepared to go faster rather than slower, avoid giving too little and too late; recognise the fundamental need to decide who the 'moderates' were, then back them, and outmanœuvre the 'extremists'; and generally find ways of turning nationalism to constructive account. In response to what the Colonial Office thought an unimpressive Foreign Office paper on 'The problem of nationalism' (1952), Trafford Smith summed up their view: 'the important ways in which we should deal with nationalism, both inside and outside the Colonial sphere, are those which depend on publicity and propaganda, especially in the United States and the United Nations, and not by thinking in Edwardian terms of the use of military and economic power which we no longer possess'.[34]

As the end of empire approached, Sir Charles Jeffries described the 'Colonial Office mind' as united on the proposition that: 'the colonial episode would only have made sense if it resulted in the new countries and the old country continuing as friends and partners when the ruler–subject relationship should come to an end. They should at least be started off with a democratic system, an efficient judiciary and civil service and impartial police.'[35] The Colonial Office was anxious not to be rushed. A 1959 statement prepared for the secretary of state contained the following assertion on East and Central Africa: 'We are not prepared to betray our trust by leaving off our work before it is properly finished.'[36] This involved trying to ensure there were in place a good honest political system, rights for all, reasonable standards of living, and trained civil servants. William Gorell Barnes defined the task in East Africa at the end of 1960: 'to regulate the pace of political development so that it was fast enough to satisfy the African desire for self-government but not so fast as to jeopardize economic progress or the security situation'.[37] As late as 1960 in West Africa residual trusteeship notions made Colonial Office officials reluctant to contemplate the independence of a tiny state like the Gambia, even in some form of association with another country, Senegal being the most likely candidate (an association which would take it out of the Commonwealth). The Gambia was costing Britain too much in grants-in-aid, Christopher Eastwood wrote; 'But of course mercenary considerations are by no means all. It would be no light matter for the UK to divest itself of a country which had been associated with it for very many years, and like marriage it is not an enterprise to be lightly or inadvisedly embarked on.'[38] Gambia achieved independence on its own in 1964.

In the end, of course, the imperatives of decolonisation, the growing force of the 'wind of change', simply overwhelmed the maintenance of trusteeship. The Colonial Office would have preferred rather more time to prepare states for independence.

Notes

1 Sir Charles Joseph Jeffries, *Whitehall and the Colonial Service: an administrative memoir, 1939–56*, Institute of Commonwealth Studies Paper, no. 15 (1972); Joe Garner, *The Commonwealth Office, 1925–68* (1978); R. B. Pugh, 'The Colonial Office, 1801–1925', in E. A. Benians and others, eds., *Cambridge history of the British empire*, vol. III, *1870–1919* (Cambridge, 1959), pp. 711–68; RH, 'The Colonial Office mind, 1900–14', *JICH*, vol. 8 (1979), pp. 30–55, reprinted in Norman Hillmer and Philip G. Wigley, eds., *The first British Commonwealth: essays in honour of Nicholas Mansergh* (1980); *The Colonial Office List* (HMSO, annually), *passim*.

2 David Goldsworthy, ed., *The Conservative government and the end of empire, 1951–1957* (British Documents on the End of Empire Project (BDEEP), 1994), pt II, pp. 87–9.

3 Goldsworthy, *Conservative government*, pt II, pp. 89–92: D[ominions] O[ffice] 35/7999, no. 18, and C[olonial] O[ffice] 1023/147, no. 161.

4 Minute by Macmillan, December 1962, PREM 11/3816.

5 Anne Thurston, ed., *Records of the Colonial Office, Dominions Office, Commonwealth Relations Office and Commonwealth Office* (BDEEP, 1995), pp. 1–29; see also a major memorandum by C.J. Jeffries, November 1942, 'A plan for the Colonial Office', in S.R. Ashton and S.E. Stockwell, eds., *Imperial policy and colonial practice, 1925–1945* (BDEEP, 1996), pt I, document no. 4.

6 Jeffries, *Whitehall and the Colonial Service*, p. 72.

7 RH, ed., *The Labour government and the end of empire, 1945–1951* (BDEEP, 1992), pt II, pp. 278–82, 459–65, and pt III, p. 83 (for FO attitudes); for the Yemen, see CAB[inet Office] 134/2371, OP(63)2 and 4 (February 1963).

8 A.G. Hopkins, 'Macmillan's audit of empire, 1957', in Peter Clarke and Clive Trebilcock, eds., *Understanding decline: perceptions and realities of British economic performance: essays in honour of Barry Supple* (Cambridge, 1997), ch. 11, pp. 234–60.

9 Minutes by Macmillan, M.213/59, 16 June 1959, and J. Chadwick, 8 October 1959, DO 35/8095; see also CAB 134/1551, CPC(57)27 and CO 1036/781, no. 1.

10 CAB 129/100, C(60)35; minutes by I. Watt, 11 February and 11 June 1958, CO 1032/167; CO 1032/174; officials' report on 'The evolution of the Commonwealth', April 1962, CO 1032/226; F[oreign] O[ffice] 371/135623,

no. 1; FO 371/135624, no. 9; FO 371/143705, no. 51; minute by P.E. Ramsbotham, 22 September 1959, FO 371/143707, no. 72.

11 Sir Hugh Foot to Sir Patrick Dean, 16 March 1962, FO 371/166820, no. 70; see also FO 371/166819, FO 371/166824, and FO 371/172591, nos. 16, 17, 19 (1963).

12 Jeffries, *Whitehall and the Colonial Service*, pp. 27–8; Goldsworthy, *Conservative government*, pt II, pp. 111–38.

13 Harold Macmillan, *The blast of war, 1939–1945* (London, 1967), p. 163; Alistair Horne, *Macmillan, 1894–1956: volume I of the official biography* (1988), vol. I, p. 365.

14 Goldsworthy, *Conservative government*, pt II, pp. 1–2; RH, 'The political consequences of Seretse Khama: Britain, the Bangwato and South Africa, 1948–52', *Historical Journal*, vol. 29 (1986), pp. 921–47, and 'The geopolitical origins of the Central African Federation: Britain, Rhodesia and South Africa, 1948–53', *Historical Journal*, vol. 30 (1987), pp. 145–72, repr. in RH and Peter Henshaw, *The lion and the springbok: Britain and South Africa since the Boer War* (Cambridge, 2003), chs. 8 and 9.

15 Ronald Robinson, 'The moral disarmament of African empire', *JICH*, vol. 8 (1979), pp. 86–104, repr. in Hillmer and Wigley, eds., *The first British Commonwealth*; Kenneth Robinson, *The dilemmas of trusteeship: aspects of British colonial policy between the wars* (Oxford, 1965). For nineteenth-century trusteeship, see Andrew Porter in *OHBE*, vol. III, ch. 10.

16 RH, *Elgin and Churchill at the Colonial Office, 1905–8: the watershed of Empire-Commonwealth* (1968), esp. pp. 468–74.

17 F.D. Lugard, *The dual mandate in British tropical Africa* (1922), pp. 282–94, 391.

18 R. Vansittart, *The mist procession: the autobiography of Lord Vansittart* (1958), p. 484; Robert G. Gregory, *India and East Africa: a history of race relations within the British empire, 1890–1939* (Oxford, 1971); Edna Bradlow, 'The evolution of "trusteeship" in Kenya', *South African Historical Journal*, no. 4 (1972), pp. 64–80; J.G. Kamoche, *Imperial trusteeship and political evolution in Kenya, 1923–63: a study in the official views* (Washington, 1981); R.I. Rotberg, 'The federal movement in East and Central Africa, 1889–1953', *Journal of Commonwealth Political Studies*, vol. 2 (1964), pp. 141–60; Robert M. Maxon, *Struggle for Kenya: the loss and reassertion of imperial initiative, 1912–1923* (1993). For Amery and Kenya, see Wm. Roger Louis, *In the name of God, go! Leo Amery and the British empire in the age of Churchill* (New York, 1992), pp. 94–9; for Churchill and Kenya, see RH, 'Churchill and the empire', in Wm. Roger Louis and Robert Blake, eds., *Churchill* (Oxford, 1993) – see chapter 11 below, pp. 327–8.

19 E.A. Brett, *Colonialism and underdevelopment in East Africa: the politics of economic change, 1919–39* (1973), pp. 171–212; C.P. Youé, 'The threat of settler rebellion and the imperial predicament: the denial of Indian rights in Kenya, 1923', *Canadian Journal of History*, vol. 12 (1978), pp. 347–60; D. Wylie, 'Confrontation over Kenya: Colonial Office and its critics, 1918–40', *Journal of African History*, vol. 18 (1970), pp. 427–47.

20 RH, *Elgin and Churchill at the Colonial Office*, p. 413.

21 Macmillan to G. Gater, 15 August 1942, commenting on A.J. Dawe, 'A federal solution for East Africa' (July 1942), CO 967/57, printed in Ashton and Stockwell, *Imperial policy*, pt I, document nos. 65, 66; Harold Macmillan, *Memoirs*, vol. VI, *1961–63* (1973), p. 289.

22 RH, *Labour government*, pt III, pp. 14–15; CAB 134/1551, CPC(57)27.

23 Martin Chanock, *Unconsummated Union: Britain, Rhodesia and South Africa, 1900–45* (Manchester, 1977); H.I. Wetherell, 'Britain and Rhodesian expansionism: imperial collusion or empirical carelessness?', *Rhodesian History*, vol. 8 (1977), pp. 115–28; R.E. Robinson, 'The "Trust" in British Central African policy, 1889–1939' (PhD thesis, University of Cambridge, 1950).

24 Garner, *Commonwealth Office*, pp. 134–6; RH, *The failure of South African expansion, 1908–48* (1972), and 'The politics of partition in southern Africa, 1908–61', in RH and Ged Martin, *Reappraisals in British imperial history* (1975), pp. 187–200; J.E. Spence, 'British policy towards the High Commission Territories', *Journal of Modern African Studies*, vol. 2 (1964), pp. 221–46.

25 Lord Hailey, *An African survey revised, 1956* (Oxford, 1957), pp. 185–7.

26 CAB 134/1551, CPC(57)27.

27 May 1959, FO 371/137972, no. 27, AF(59)28.

28 CAB 129/100, C(60)35; CO 1032/172, no. 102.

29 Stephen Constantine, *The making of British colonial development policy, 1919–40* (1984); John W. Cell, *Hailey: a study in British imperialism, 1872–1969* (Cambridge, 1992), pp. 136–7; Joanna Lewis, 'The colonial politics of African welfare, 1939–52: a crisis of paternalism' (PhD thesis, University of Cambridge, 1993), pp. 35–7.

30 Wm. Roger Louis, *Imperialism at bay, 1941–45: the United States and the decolonization of the British empire* (Oxford, 1977), pp. 101–3; J.M. Lee and Martin Petter, *The Colonial Office, war, and development policy: organisation and planning of a metropolitan initiative, 1939–45* (Institute of Commonwealth Studies Paper no. 22, 1982); Nicholas J. Westcott, 'Impact of the Second World War on Tanganyika, 1939–49' (PhD thesis, University of Cambridge, 1982), pp. 230–76; Ashton and Stockwell, *Imperial policy*, pt II, document nos. 100, 101.

31 RH, *Labour government*, pt I, pp. 103–9 (memorandum by A.B. Cohen, 3 April 1946), pp. 153–9 (memorandum by R.E. Robinson, n.d., 1947).

32 RH, *Labour government*, pt I, pp. 320–6 (memorandum by H.T. Bourdillon, 10 May 1948), and Introduction, pp. xxix–xxxiv.

33 Speech by A.H. Poynton at United Nations, 3 October 1947, CO 847/36/4, no. 27; paper to Cambridge Summer School, CO 852/1053/1, CSC(48)4.

34 Minute by Trafford Smith, 22 July 1952, CO 936/217.

35 Jeffries, *Whitehall and the Colonial Service*, p. 73.

36 CO 1027/177, no. 11.

37 FO 371/146504, no. 30.

38 C.G Eastwood to E.B. Boothby (FO), 2 December 1960, FO 371/146485, no. 20.

8   Africa and the Labour government, 1945–1951

[This chapter – summarising some intensive research – occupies a central position among my papers, both by intention and in its effect. Written in homage to my principal mentor in imperial history, 'Robbie' Robinson, it played an unexpected but crucial role leading to my appointment with the British Documents on the End of Empire Project, commissioned to edit the large four-part volume on *The Labour government and the end of empire, 1945–1951* (1992). Ironically though, despite being carefully designed to reflect Robinson's main interests and commitments, replete with several of his best-known concepts and aphorisms, and even a private joke ('bananas to Battersea'), the essay failed to appeal to him as much as another of mine written at about the same time, 'The geopolitical origins of the Central African Federation' (for which see *The lion and the springbok*). It is reproduced here with only minor amendments from the original version in *The Journal of Imperial and Commonwealth History*, vol. 16 (1988), special issue, *Theory and practice in the history of European expansion overseas: essays in honour of R.E. Robinson*. The references have been updated, for example to subsequent publication of BDEEP documents.]

No one has done more than Ronald Robinson to penetrate the inwardness of Britain's post-war African policy. He not only pointed to the central role in it of a Colonial Office official, Sir Andrew Cohen, head of the African department, but also tried historically to relate policy-making to a 'general theory of imperialism'. 'Had British planners decided that nationalism was the continuation of imperialism by other and more efficient means?' he asked, and famously answered, 'Perhaps.'[1] After a lifetime's thinking about Africa and applying his CO experience (1947–9) to its history, Robinson believed profoundly that Africa matters. And so did British ministers and civil servants after the Second World War, when a fruitful period of policy-making was embarked upon.

I

Two essential themes dominated the work of the Labour government between 1945 and 1951: economic recovery and Russian expansion. Both problems pointed to an increased interest in the empire in general and in Africa in particular. 'My mind turns more and more', wrote Chancellor of the Exchequer Hugh Dalton in 1947, 'towards a consolidation in Africa.'[2] In October 1949 the minister of defence, A.V. Alexander ('King Albert Victorious'), defined the government's three main policy objectives as: (1) securing 'our people against aggression', (2) sustaining a foreign policy dominated by 'resistance to the onrush of Communist influence', everywhere from Greece to Hong Kong, and (3) achieving 'the most rapid development practicable of our overseas possessions, since without such Colonial development there can be no major improvement in the standard of living of our own people at home'.[3] (An astonishing admission! – where now is Lord Lugard? where Lord Hailey?) As far as Foreign Secretary Ernest Bevin was concerned, from the moment that neo-Palmerstonian took office he saw 'the utmost importance' from political, economic, and defence points of view of developing Africa and making its resources 'available to all'. Stepping up the flow of strategic raw materials out of Africa would help to free Britain from financial dependence on America. Bevin's pet projects were to sell manganese ore from Sierra Leone to the United States, and coal from Wankie to Argentina in return for beef. Always dreaming cosmoplastic dreams, he also talked about a new triangular oceanic trade between eastern Africa, India, and Australia. But more than this, Bevin feared the Russians would sooner or later 'make a major drive against our position in Africa'.[4] In Attlee's world-picture too, Africa presented the same duality of concern: economically it was immoral not to develop its 'great estates', while politically the cold war pointed to the necessity of an increasing reliance on African manpower, as well as coming to terms with African nationalism. On the one hand, he wanted to increase European settlement in under-populated areas of East-Central Africa, but on the other, recognised that in Gold Coast and Nigeria 'an attempt to maintain the old colonialism would, I am sure, have immensely aided Communism'.[5]

Several Labour ministers believed they were called 'to bring the modern state to Africa'. John Strachey – of all people – as minister of food foisted the mechanised groundnuts project on Tanganyika to improve the British margarine ration, arguing that only by such enterprises could African possessions be rapidly developed, and 'become an asset and not a liability as they largely now are'. Even Sir Stafford Cripps wanted to 'force the pace' of African economic development in order to close the dollar gap.[6] At the same time, if Britain was to remain a world power, they realised they had to control rising nationalist tension in Africa because, as James Griffiths (the able latter-day secretary of state for the colonies) put it in 1950, 'we had to face an ideological battle in the world, especially in the Colonies', and the next ten years would be crucial.[7] 'A glance at Asia', Herbert Morrison declared, was enough to show the kind of troubles which 'could break loose' in Africa if they did not adjust their policies to promote political and economic change as a matter of 'two-way teamwork' between the metropolis and Africans.[8] Beyond that, and for Attlee especially, it was a challenge to statesmanship to meet the susceptibilities of Afro-Asian peoples while maintaining and expanding the Commonwealth. The prime minister believed Britain was its 'material and spiritual head', and that it could be a multi-racial international bridge, as well as an effective global barrier against communist aggression. One of Attlee's principal long-term preoccupations was to prevent newly independent states seceding from the Commonwealth, since this would be exploited by Russia as a failure and would automatically diminish British influence throughout the world.[9]

II

The four great axes of Labour's engagement with Africa were political, strategic, economic, and racial. Not in any one of these spheres was a simple, straightforward policy possible.

By 1946 the Colonial Office planners were acutely aware of the need for a clear policy based on the political advancement of Africans. There were perhaps five main reasons for this. First, African political consciousness had been stimulated by the war, and the white man's prestige destroyed as an instrument of government, particularly in the eyes (it was thought) of returning black ex-servicemen. Secondly, to carry out the new social welfare and economic development programmes, a new political instrument was required, namely African participation ('a metropolitan "new deal" in local collaboration'). Thirdly, Colonial Service attitudes had to be reconstructed: morale was bad, the nostrums of Lugard and Cameron were moribund, and officers felt frustrated by newly emerging African criticisms of them. The men on the spot needed a renewed sense of 'mission', a revitalisation and extension of Malcolm MacDonald's constructive vision on the eve of the war. Fourthly, it seemed Britain had to retain a positive initiative in the formulation of African policy, otherwise control would pass to 'settler' regimes (South African, Rhodesian, and Portuguese), to whom it was a matter of life and death. This would imperil British trusteeship policies; indeed, after the adoption of apartheid in South Africa from 1948, an actual policy conflict existed. Finally, and perhaps most important of all, international pressures from the United Nations, American and 'world opinion' were (as the secretary of state for the colonies, Arthur Creech Jones, said) directing 'the play of a fierce searchlight' over Africa.[10] These outside influences were expected to stimulate the demand for self-government. 'Prejudiced, ignorant and hostile' criticism and interference from 'the anti-colonial bloc' (communist and Latin American countries, together with India, and, most vocal adversary of all, the Philippines) would be grounded not in trying to reform imperial systems but in abolishing them entirely and instantly as anachronistic. Officials regarded this as a recipe for widespread post-imperial disintegration, as it took no account of fitness for self-government: 'We are just as concerned to see our colonial peoples achieve self-government, but in conditions in which they really can stand on their own, without the risk of subsequently falling under foreign political or economic domination, or under the control of an undemocratic minority seeking power for its own selfish ends.' Britain aimed at establishing stable, effective and representative political systems. This was a delicate operation in which it must not be dictated to by '58 back-seat drivers without responsibility'.[11]

These reasons, internal and international, 'demanded a new approach to policy in Africa' (Ivor Thomas, parliamentary under-secretary at the Colonial Office). A unified, logical, coherent, and convincing policy was essential.[12] The process of defining it centred on Andrew Cohen ('*alter ego* of Creech Jones'), head of the African department – he of the purple shirt and spikey handwriting, once a Cambridge Apostle, now 'Emperor of Africa'. Cohen insisted that what was wanted was not another set of platitudinous generalisations but an actual programme of practical policies. 'There will be no question of imposing a stereotyped blueprint. All we can do is to indicate the broad objective.' The first fruit of Cohen's initiative (welcomed by Creech Jones) was a notable state paper, the famous 'local government despatch' of February 1947. It enjoined the promotion of efficient local government as a priority, and represented the victory of conciliar principles over the Indirect Rule tradition. This was the work of Cohen, G.B. Cartland, and R.E. Robinson: Cohen called it 'a joint effort' by the three of them.[13] Robinson – he of the DFC and gravel-voice – was Cohen's special acolyte in the temple of African divination. His most significant job was to make the more conservative governors swallow the new directive, using his historical skills to demonstrate its logical development from previous policy. This most intellectual of Blues ever to think about the Blacks saw the aim of democratising local government as providing 'some measure of political education'. He stressed the 'transition from local government through personalities to local government based on institutions'. It was no longer possible, Robinson argued, to preserve African societies against change, and British rulers must attempt to see the future. The economic bases of

African societies left to themselves were in danger of collapse. Imperial indecision would be fatal: 'No policy of letting sleeping dogs lie is likely to succeed when the dogs are already barking.' (He learned early on that canine metaphors went down well in Great Smith Street.) But young Robinson was optimistic. Communism he thought 'outmoded' and unlikely to have any real future in Africa. Moreover, by constructing a political pyramid with a firm base in local government, there was a good chance that British rulers had 'dug out an adequate system of political irrigation channels before the rains of nationalism have burst into full flood upon them'.[14]

A conference of African governors in November 1947 chewed over the implications of the new local government strategy, not always amicably, together with most other aspects of African policy. A remarkable series of papers was prepared in the Colonial Office for this path-breaking conference. Creech Jones praised them as excellent. The crucial constitutional proposals about the stages of political evolution he did not specifically comment on. The strictly limited nature of this programme (as envisaged by Cohen and Sir Sydney Caine, deputy under-secretary) needs to be stressed, in the light of the wilder misinterpretations which have been placed upon it. Even in the most advanced territory, the Gold Coast, Cohen wrote, 'internal self-government is unlikely to be achieved in much less than a generation'; elsewhere 'the process is likely to be considerably slower'. Accordingly, there must be a long-term plan, 'for 20 or 30 years or indeed longer', for ordered development under continuing British responsibility. Readiness for internal self-government (that is, the stage attained by Southern Rhodesian whites in 1923) was still 'a long way off'; 'independence' (that is, control of external affairs, with freedom to secede from the Commonwealth) was not even mentioned.[15] In his paper Caine assumed merely that 'perhaps within a generation many of the principal territories of the Colonial Empire will have attained or be within sight of the goal of full responsibility for *local affairs*' (my emphasis). There would be a 'redistribution of power' and friendly association would have to replace 'benevolent domination', but he did not see this as involving the elimination of British power: it should continue to be possible to control the pace and 'influence the main line of policy and, provided the right new techniques are developed, the extent of that influence may remain very considerable'.[16]

Cohen was well aware of the probability that any constitutional programme would need to be radically rewritten from time to time. The crux of the problem was the risk that the demand for self-government ('stimulated by outside influences') might outpace the process of building up local government from below. Nevertheless, 'the rapid building up of local government through the process of devolution . . . is the most important of all the methods by which we must seek to foster political evolution in Africa'. Only thus could the 'evils of a class of professional politicians' be avoided. The secretary of state agreed: the 'ignorant and gullable [sic] majority' must not be exploited by 'unrepresentative oligarchies'. Creech Jones was particularly interested in getting things started. The demand for a share in government responsibility was, he thought, certain to be made with increasing emphasis, and the demand must be satisfied. 'Time was knocking at the door and the art of government had to be learned.' Britain had thus to permit trial and error to Africans, reduce its spoonfeeding, and encourage a virile political self-reliance, without waiting for the educational qualifications it would like.[17]

The strategy of promoting political advancement on local government foundations was a policy to which Attlee was already totally committed. Indeed he noted the 'regrettable failure' in several colonies to develop municipal institutions as 'a first school of political and administrative training'. Politics could not be learned from a textbook. In his view also there was a most serious danger in assuming the Westminster Parliament to be the appropriate objective. Democracy could be fundamentally threatened by the concentration and centralisation of powers in the Westminster model. 'It would have been wiser in India to have followed the model of the United States constitution . . .' This sort of mistake must not be repeated in Africa. (Has modern Britain ever had so prescient a prime minister?)[18]

So: *political advancement* of Africans – gradual, smooth, and efficiently controlled – was the central purpose of policy. The goal was self-government, but self-government was not something to be hurried on. Demands for it seemed always to arise out of unrest, and invariably created awkward and unwelcome problems. Creech Jones urged the Cabinet to deal with economic and social discontents first, in order to lessen the immediate pressure for constitutional advance, thereby laying firmer foundations for 'liberal and efficient' self-government. Colonies – it was realised – could not be retained against their will, and any attempt to suppress national desires would be a disaster, but there would be no 'scuttling' out of Africa. Azikiwe would not intimidate them. Government must keep the initiative. Ceylon might be the model. Nor would there be any overall blueprint or prepared schedule. The timetable would be left vague. Fitness for political advancement in any individual colony would depend entirely and solely on its own 'social and political viability and capability'. Regional variations in Africa would be fully recognised. Cohen stated quite categorically: 'The conception of dealing with Africa as a whole in political questions is a wrong one.' (The

Colonial Office accordingly scorned the notion of having a 'secretary of state for Africa'.)[19] The ultimate objective of Commonwealth association must be preserved. To this end, the early nineteenth-century theories of Macaulay and Fowell Buxton were dusted down. A Colonial Office paper on 'our main problems and policies' (1950) declared:

We are engaged on a world-wide experiment in nation-building. Our aim is to create independence – independence within the Commonwealth – not to suppress it. No virtue is seen in permanent dependence. A vigorous, adult and willing partner is clearly more to be desired than one dependent, adolescent and unwilling. But there is no intention to abandon responsibilities prematurely. Self-government must be effective and democratic . . .

Above all it must be within a Commonwealth framework, so as to ensure 'an ever-widening circle of democratic nations exerting a powerful stabilising influence in the world'. (Or, as Robinson later put it, 'We thought we were creating a great practical, cultural Commonwealth.') Premature withdrawal of British responsibility would only create a dangerous vacuum, within which nationalism would be usurped and 'perverted by extremists'. On the other hand, the imperial rulers must accustom themselves to the idea that 'the transfer of power is not a sign of weakness or of liquidation of the Empire, but is, in fact, a sign and source of strength'.[20] A Foreign Office paper on 'the problem of nationalism' (1952) concluded that it was possible to draw the constructive forces of nationalism to the British side and minimise the threatened erosion of British world power. It was a 'dynamic on the upsurge' which could not be stopped, but could be directed and encouraged into 'healthy and legitimate' channels. Destructive, extremist, xenophobic nationalism might be a potent instrument of communist incitement, but a 'new and fruitful' relationship established with moderate nationalists through a policy of self-government could be the 'best prospect of resistance to Communism'. 'Greater maturity of thought in nationalist peoples and leaders' (without which any form of co-operation might prove temporary and illusory) might be induced by 'creating a class with a vested interest in co-operation', and involving it in social welfare and economic development projects. (The articulation of a 'collaborative bargains hypothesis' was thus well advanced by the time Labour left office.)[21]

All this theorising was congenial to Cohen. He believed strongly in a continuing firm metropolitan grip on the situation, in being one jump ahead, in controlling and nurturing nationalist movements. This was, he believed, the only possible policy to secure the future stability and viability of territories. The sooner government acted, 'the more influence we were likely to have for a longer period'. In the best reformist traditions of the Colonial Office, he justified their policies as designed to 'strengthen not weaken the British connection'.[22]

In West Africa, the Colonial Office identified three 'political' categories: nationalists (the educated and part-educated), moderates (professional and business groups and the more enlightened chiefs), and rural populations (who were 'not politically-minded'). 'To be successful, policy must satisfy the second class while safeguarding the interests of the third, and going far enough to meet the aspirations of the first to secure some co-operation at any rate from all but the more extreme nationalists.' Accordingly, African representatives should play a major part in working out constitutional reforms. Executive machinery should be remodelled to give representatives a full share in the formulation and execution of policy. Legislatures should be extended and made 'fully representative of all parts of the country and not merely of the urban and more developed areas'.[23]

When in 1948 the Accra riots broke out in the Gold Coast, Creech Jones, canny and alert as ever, doubted the simplistic theory of 'communist incitement' initially presented by the local administrators. In any case he was worried that this 'factor in the disturbances may be used so as to obscure or belittle . . . sincerely felt causes of dissatisfaction quite unconnected with Communism', or desires 'to accelerate constitutional development' – at however ill-considered a pace. Creech Jones believed the underlying causes were partly political and partly economic.[24] For him the Gold Coast held the key to future success in Britain's West African policy, and so he set up a commission of inquiry, and appointed Sir Charles Arden-Clarke, the very model of a modern colonial governor, to take over the administration. The new governor was a bit of a showman as well as a shrewd politician, with the reassuring appearance of a dog-lover advertising a good pipe-tobacco. Arden-Clarke's plan was to build on Moscow's known abandonment of Nkrumah as a useful contact, and to treat him as essentially a moderate, no longer 'our little local Hitler'; they were, he thought, in many ways lucky he had become so amenable. Nkrumah's position must be underwritten. The alternative was an inevitable further challenge to British authority, with increasing encouragement from communist forces outside the country and later perhaps within it. Considerable African participation in the Gold Coast executive was therefore essential. The Cabinet was persuaded by the Coussey Report and Creech Jones's argument that without such progress 'moderate opinion will be alienated and the extremists given an opportunity of gaining further and weightier support and of making serious trouble'. They took a significant step forward, but of course it fell short of full self-government. Ministers refused to say when they would start discussing that.[25] Ideally, Cohen told them, in order to preserve efficient government there should be no further constitutional advance until 1954 or 1955, and it would not be in anyone's interest to have only a short transitional period to responsible government. But Nkrumah was in 1951 asking to take over from the governor the selection of ministers and to be given the title of prime minister.

> It must, of course, be recognised that we may not be able to adhere to an ideal timetable. We may be forced, if we are to keep on good terms with the more responsible political leaders such as Mr Nkrumah and his immediate colleagues and not to force the Gold Coast Government into the hands of extremists, to move more rapidly than ideally we should wish . . . It would be fatal . . . to forfeit the goodwill of Mr Nkrumah and his colleagues by holding back excessively.

The imperatives of the collaborative mechanism had begun ineluctably to operate. Arden-Clarke diagnosed the salient feature of the situation: there was no alternative to Nkrumah's Convention Peoples Party government, and it could only be replaced by a similar one, or one of even more extreme nationalist tendencies. 'We have only one dog in our kennel . . . All we can do is to build it up and feed it vitamins and cod liver oil . . .'[26]

Nigeria was launched almost automatically on a similar course as a result of Gold Coast developments. Cohen in 1948 quickly alerted Governor Sir John Macpherson to their relevance for neighbouring Nigeria. The principles of Nigerian political advancement were approved by the Cabinet in May 1950: greatly increased Nigerian participation in the executive, both at the centre and in the three regions; increased regional autonomy (within the unity of Nigeria, which was not negotiable); larger and more representative regional legislatures with increased powers. The Cabinet was especially concerned to ensure a smooth transfer of administrative responsibility by speeding up Africanisation of the civil service on the lines that had worked well in India.[27] In 1952 Macpherson reflected that Nigeria had obtained a constitution 'in advance of its true capacity', but 'we could not put a ring-fence round Nigeria, and we had to take the initiative, and not wait to be overtaken by events, because of what was happening, and is continuing to happen, in the Gold Coast, the Sudan, Libya, etc. etc.'.[28]

Where had British planners got to in West Africa by 1951? The aim was self-government within the Commonwealth. But this, as Cohen saw it, meant something different for Nigeria and the Gold Coast, 'which can look forward to full responsibility for their own affairs', and for Sierra Leone and Gambia, which were not yet ready for African ministers, and must expect even in the long run to leave defence and foreign affairs to Britain. The Gold Coast was 'very far on towards internal self-government'; Nigeria was only a degree or two behind; but since there was little comparable nationalism in Sierra Leone and Gambia the two of them should be satisfied with a much more limited advance, and remain 'quite content' for 'a considerable time to come'. In all four, the government was trying to provide constitutions based on 'consent and consultation' – under the governor's ultimate authority. Maintaining confidence in British good faith was the essence of it, since this would slow down the pace. Simultaneously local government was being reformed and modernised, and Africanisation was proceeding. The theory Cohen discerned behind all these changes was that full African participation provided 'the best defence against Communism', 'the only chance of friendly co-operation' with Britain, and the 'best chance' of persuading an African country voluntarily to remain in the Commonwealth. There could be no question of being deflected from political advancement and administrative devolution by the protests of France and South Africa.[29]

As far as East Africa was concerned, the final forms of government were 'less evident and less near' than in West Africa, but essentially the goal was the same. They would build up and improve the status and experience of Africans (through participation in local and central government) until disparities with Europeans and Indians were removed politically, economically, and socially. They could then play a full part in a 'system in which all communities would participate on an equal basis' of genuine partnership. The problem of course was that the settlers objected to this, and indeed disapproved of the speed of African advance in West Africa. To force equality of representation upon the settlers would precipitate a major political crisis. Not that Creech Jones was unduly alarmed by such a prospect: 'whatever privilege they may have had in the past cannot be perpetuated much longer'. Many of the African grievances were, he thought, legitimate, but in such a vast area they ought not to demand exclusive rights, and 'a corrective to their irresponsible nationalism should be applied from time to time'.[30] Viscount Addison (the Cabinet's elder statesman, intermittently concerned with Commonwealth relations) argued for the importance of reassuring settlers in order to avoid 'driving them into undesirable alliance with South Africa'. Griffiths, on the other hand, emphasised the necessity of reassuring Africans that ultimate British responsibility would be retained until they had 'narrowed the gap'. Out of these conflicting pressures came a parliamentary statement in December 1950, balancing irreconcilable interests in the well-worn fashion of the declarations of the inter-war years. The goal was 'true partnership' between races, but the immigrant communities had a part to play in the future of Kenya, and were not being asked to agree to 'their eventual eviction'. A certain *stasis* entered East African political advancement as a result. Resolution of the agonising contradictions of Kenya was deferred, with Mau Mau as the consequence.[31]

North Africa was in many ways acting as the pacemaker for African political advancement. By concentrating on the Gold Coast for the 'beginnings of decolonisation' historians have in fact been looking in the wrong place. Independence for Libya (1951) and Sudan (1956) pioneered the way, and arose out of fascinating international constraints. In the case of Libya, officials felt that the 'prospect of early independence is not unreal'; it was an occupied ex-Italian colony and not a British possession, and thus provided the easiest way in which they could meet the obligations of the Atlantic Charter. It was an ideal chance for once to forestall a nationalist protest, 'recognising the inevitable and cashing in on it in good time', instead of waiting to be forced into granting independence 'by local revolt and/or outside pressure'. Britain had some essential strategic requirements, at least in Cyrenaica, especially as a result of uncertainty over its Egyptian tenure, but promoting Libyan independence could be the best way of securing them.[32] Certainly in Sheikh Idris Britain had an 'ideal prefabricated collaborator'. Idris had indicated his willingness to grant bases and generally to allow the British considerable freedom of military action. At any rate the government concluded that the best solution, resolving a complex international tangle, was to back Idris and the Libyan claims for independence under UN auspices.[33]

In Sudan, too, Britain promoted independence. Validated in this case by Indian analogy, it was basically a means of countering the Egyptian claim to sovereignty (Farouk having been proclaimed 'King of the Sudan'). In part it was also a way of pre-empting a UN trust, with its risks of 'letting Russia into Africa'. But if independence would get the Sudan off its Egyptian hook, refusal to sell the Sudanese into Egyptian slavery dashed all Bevin's hopes of negotiating the crucially important new Canal Zone treaty with Egypt. ('I cannot do what I believe to be wrong and retrograde in order to get a quick treaty of alliance.') This was because the Egyptians insisted on linking the two issues. As to the Suez base itself, Labour policy was to shift its defence on to Anglo-Egyptian co-operation and away from British occupation. Realising that effective use of the base was essentially dependent on Egyptian goodwill, and that ideal strategic requirements would have to be sacrificed in order to ensure it, Attlee in 1946 set the tone for treaty renegotiation. In a masterly summing-up in Cabinet he declared that Britain could 'not remain forcibly on the ground':

There was no more justification for this than for our claiming that our neighbours in the Continent of Europe should grant us bases for our defence. Our oil interests in the Middle East were indeed important, but our ability to defend them would only be impaired if we insisted on remaining in Egypt against the will of the Egyptian people and so worsened our relations with the remainder of the Arab world.

The Labour government continued to try to tempt Egypt into some sort of 'equal partnership' in a new Middle East defence scheme, but negotiations remained deadlocked. Attlee was unable to deliver Britain out of its Egyptian bondage.[34] Meanwhile he ruled out the use of force in dealing with the Iranian oil crisis of 1951. This was welcomed by officials as proof that the days were over of 'thinking in Edwardian terms of the use of military and economic power which we no longer possess'. Nationalism, all seemed to be agreed, must be met with diplomacy and publicity, not intervention and force.[35]

III

Strategically Attlee wanted to give up a 'hopeless' attempt to defend the Middle East oil-producing areas, and to work routinely round the Cape to the East and Australasia, instead of relying on an ever-more problematic Mediterranean route. In addition, he had always been anxious not to be drawn into UN trusteeships for 'deficit areas' in North Africa and the Horn. ('Somaliland has always been a dead loss and a nuisance to us.') His earliest and most iconoclastic initiative as prime minister was to demand a strategic reappraisal to take proper account of the atom bomb, the United Nations, and the impending loss of India. He was worried by the costs of continuing Mediterranean commitments he regarded as obsolescent. Nor did he like the idea of supporting the vested interests of a 'congeries of weak, backward and reactionary states' in the Middle East. With impressive 'Little Englander' pragmatism, remorselessly yet reasonably, and with occasional touches of irreverence, he pursued a confrontation with the Chiefs of Staff on these issues through endless committee meetings, and thoroughly rattled them. Attlee was supported by Dalton. This titanic battle lasted almost eighteen months. It ended with a victory for the traditionalist doctrines of the Chiefs of Staff (apparently threatening resignation), backed by Bevin and his formidable Foreign Office team. Their argument was that withdrawal from the Mediterranean route would leave a vacuum, into which Russia (even if not bent on world domination) would move, since 'the bear could not resist pushing its paw into soft places'. This would make a gift to Russia of Middle Eastern oil and manpower, and would dangerously signal to Russia, America, and the Commonwealth Britain's 'abdication as a world power'. Without a first line of defence in North Africa, the Russians would, they argued, rapidly be in the Congo and at the Victoria Falls. They rejected Attlee's concept of a disengagement from a 'neutral zone', putting 'a wide glacis of desert and Arabs between ourselves and the Russians'.[36]

However, despite this fundamental disagreement, there was common ground between Attlee, Bevin, and the Chiefs of Staff about the desirability of a strategic base located in Kenya, which Attlee had seen as part of a more general shifting of military resources into less contentious and exposed regions. They all agreed that more use ought to be made of Africa as a manpower reserve, compensating for the loss of the Indian 'British barrack in the Oriental seas', and as a way of relieving the strain in Egypt. East Africa was expected to be more important in a future war, as a result of greater weapon ranges and the weakening of the British position in the Middle East. It would become a major training camp and storage depot. It would also defend 'our main support-area in South Africa'. Work began in September 1947 on the new base at Mackinnon Road, some sixty miles inland by rail from Mombasa.[37] All this tied in with new doctrines of colonial development. The new base in Kenya, Bevin argued, would 'modernise the whole character of our defence as well as our trade and bring into the British orbit economically and commercially a great area which is by no means fully developed yet'. Communications would need to be improved over a wide area. Bevin was keen to develop Mombasa as a major port, and link it to Lagos by a trans-African highway ('passing through the top of French Equatorial Africa', thus enabling Britain, if necessary, to protect the strategic deposits of the Belgian Congo). This scheme the experts pronounced impossible because of the administrative and maintenance costs of African 'all-weather' roads, to say nothing of the difficulty of co-operating with foreign powers. Bevin also campaigned to improve the outlets for Rhodesian strategic minerals to the sea. Railway links to the south were in consequence thoroughly investigated.[38]

A rail link between Rhodesia and Kenya from Ndola to Korogwe was the most favoured project. This would mean unifying the gauges (which ministers thought a strategically valuable exercise), by converting 3,520 miles of East African railways from one-metre to 3 foot 6 inch – a five-year task. Tanganyikan authorities naively put their costs at £870,000, while Kenya (with more track and rolling stock) estimated their conversion at £16 million. The new 1,125 mile link itself might be built for £11 million. However, even a 3 foot 6 inch railway could not carry oversize loads (such as big tanks) and would have to be backed up by a much-improved road capable of carrying 70 ton weights. (Only a route able to carry heavy equipment would provide any appreciable saving over the shipping routes.) Cohen strongly favoured the 'great advantage of having an all-British railway link from the Cape to Kenya', possibly with a branchline to Kilwa or Mikindani to evacuate groundnuts. (See Map 8.1.) The project lapsed, however, and for three reasons. There were doubts about the enormous costs and its economic profitability. (Creech Jones was decidedly sceptical – haunted, no doubt, by Labouchere's famous diatribe against the Uganda railway: 'What it will carry there's none can define; . . . It clearly is naught but a lunatic line.') Then there was the growing difficulty of being seen to co-operate with South Africa. Above all, the Chiefs of Staff decided they did not wish to develop Kenya as a major operational base: it was too far from the Middle East theatre, it had insufficient industrial backup, and it was impracticable (for racial and political reasons) to import the quantities of white or Indian labour required. The Ndola rail link was accordingly downgraded to being 'strategically desirable but not essential', and at all events not sufficiently important to warrant a contribution from the UK defence vote. 'Cape-to-Cairo' was as far off as ever.[39] (See map 8.1, next page.)

IV

The fate of the railway project was symptomatic of the sheer difficulty of developing Africa. Yet interest in the potential and the protean problems of Africa was sufficiently aroused for nine visits to be made by Colonial Office ministers in these years, four of them by secretaries of state. Field Marshal Montgomery (the Chief of the Imperial General Staff) also decided to make a tour of Africa at the end of 1947. ('It is terribly important to check up on Africa.') He visited French Morocco, Gambia, Gold Coast, Nigeria, Belgian Congo, Union of South Africa, Southern Rhodesia, Kenya, Ethiopia, Sudan, and Egypt. The result was an electric 76-page report, containing many a caustic phrase, though his most derisive strictures were reserved for Ethiopia (its 'pathetic Emperor', 'Gilbertian army', 'Addis in Wonderland', and elite of 'Hollywoodian ostentation'). He thought there were 'immense possibilities' for African development, enabling Britain to 'maintain her standard of living', if not actually to survive, because 'these lands contain everything we need'. However, 'no real progress was being made', and the way was open for communism. Government should 'think big'. There must be 'a grand design for African development as a whole, with a masterplan for each Colony or nation'. Invoking the spirit of Cecil Rhodes, and roundly condemning the settlers, the African ('a complete savage'), and

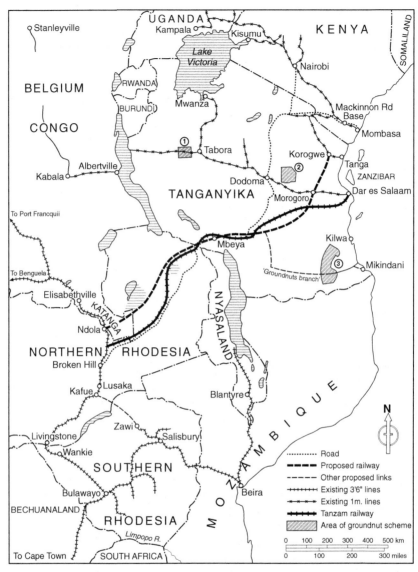

Map 8.1 Proposed Rhodesia–Kenya rail link. The Tanzam Railway as completed in 1975 ran from Dar es Salaam to Kapiri Mposhi. The three main areas of the Groundnuts Scheme are shown as numbered diagonally shaded areas. *Source*: CO 537/1231, no. 102, COS(46)271, report on the development of African communications, 13 December 1946.

the Colonial Service alike, he demanded that those who said it could
not be done should be 'ruthlessly eliminated'. Britain should 'import
brains and "go-getters"'. 'Belly-aching will assume colossal proportions;
it must be stamped on.' Administrative units should be boldly amalga-
mated; federations of Central Africa, East Africa, and West Africa ought
to be established. The High Commission Territories were an anomaly
and should be 'abolished'. Eventually South Africa and Central Africa
should be linked up. There should be much closer co-operation with
other European powers too, and with the Americans.[40]

Despite the staccato tone of the presentation, and an arrogant ama-
teurism masquerading as geopolitical genius, senior ministers took this
report seriously. Bevin called for its 'urgent study'. Attlee was 'much
interested'. With remarkable speed Creech Jones came up with a comprehensive reply, in a fourteen-page memorandum dated 6 January
1948. (It is the central ministerial document on Labour's African policy,
and its preparation must have ruined his Christmas and New Year.)
He agreed that quick and vigorous African development was essential
on strategic, economic, and political grounds to strengthen Britain and
western Europe; it was also needed to secure smooth African progress
in social and political fields, and to augment the world supply of food
and raw materials. British departure from India and the reduction in its
overseas investments generally had still further increased the economic
importance of close links with Africa. But the imposition of a centralised
'grand design' drawn up in and directed from London 'would not be
practical politics' (words which Attlee underlined in his copy). It would
'conflict with our declared policy of devolution in the progress of building up self-government' and ensuring that Africans attained it as 'part of
the western world'. Central direction would not work. It was contrary
to all British policy and historical experience. It would not secure the
co-operation of local peoples, settler or African, without which effective
development could not take place. Developing relationships between
peoples over a period of years could not be dealt with on the analogy of a
military operation. A blueprint could not be operated by orders in a chain
of command, because colonies had powers and responsibilities which
would progressively increase. They should be dealt with by devolution,
which had worked successfully in India, Ceylon, and Sudan. There was
in fact no lack of planning. 'We have a clear and well-understood general
policy for political and economic development in Africa.' All the territories had ten-year development plans. Montgomery had overestimated the
material resources of Africa: 'Africa is not an undiscovered El Dorado.
It is a poor continent which can only be developed at great expense in
money and effort.' Vast areas were barely self-supporting in food, and

could only be made so by a heavy capital expenditure on water, bush clearance, fertilisers, and supervisory manpower. The crucial problem was not lack of brains or vigour, but lack of money and the 'pay your way' philosophy, which was now being rectified. African development might well be vital to the survival of Britain, but if so, it must have a much higher priority in supplies and technicians. The present bottleneck was the lack of capital equipment, especially an acute shortage of steel, and a deficiency of consumer goods to provide incentives.

Politically, too, Creech Jones continued, the right means of countering anti-British movements, the real answer to nationalism, 'does not lie in uniformity of policy, or in federation, or in any other imposed measure', but in 'the maintenance and development of our existing friendly relations with the African peoples'; in giving them 'a real part in the constructive work of government', and in building up responsible native institutions. Communists were *not* exploiting the lack of a uniform native policy; it would in fact be easier to exploit such a policy if it were imposed without regard to local conditions. But there *was* a broad overall uniformity, and regional co-ordination was certainly existing policy. Any link-up of African territories with South Africa was out of the question, and the High Commission Territories could not be handed over.[41]

Notwithstanding this drily devastating critique, the Montgomery Report was a useful weapon in the fight to demand greater attention in Whitehall as a whole for African development needs. Ministers agreed they must urgently have a plan fully co-ordinated and integrated with British domestic economic policy. With some mild breast-beating, they admitted colonial economic development planning to have been defective, because they had not determined on broad lines what proportion of British resources should go overseas, or assessed the relative value of home and colonial projects. For example, there had been no agreed criterion for allocating priorities in agricultural machinery or steel between conflicting British and African demands. All this they would now try to put right. The new chancellor of the Exchequer (Cripps) said the first thing was to inject a spirit of improvisation, and improve the productivity of existing capital equipment, rather than initiating new, large-scale development schemes. The Economic Policy Committee agreed with Creech Jones that, however desirable, a more positive control of the African economic field was not possible, as it would be contrary to the fundamental policy of gradually transferring real power.[42]

Simultaneously with these discussions, Caine submitted a special report on colonial economic development to the prime minister. He too rejected the idea of a single centralised plan: they had to work within the Labour policy of 'political advancement'. He called for more liaison, more international collaboration, the allocation of priorities, and the mobilisation of all available agencies, including private enterprise. All this could be of inestimable value to colonial peoples and to Britain in a few years. They must prepare for the day American aid ran out. 'Prompt action now will mean that we shall by that time be enjoying the first fruits of this new form of colonial investment.' The essential problem was the removal of limitations to development. These were of three kinds: (1) virtually irremovable traditional social barriers (especially land-tenure systems), (2) basic conditions which were remediable in perhaps a generation (soil infertility, scarce labour, and insufficient technicians), and (3) limitations which could in theory be removed at any time by governmental decision (provision of finance, infrastructure, and capital goods). Progress could only be gradual, however. Any revolutionary attack on agrarian problems would only cause serious political trouble. Government must therefore work within the limits set by the tolerable pace of social change. In dealing with soil infertility, too, they must be cautious, since they were not sure of the ecological effect of applying Western methods – they must not create a dustbowl even worse than that in North America. And the provision of government help was bound to be restricted because of Britain's own needs for basic services and capital goods: iron, steel, machines, and cement were all in short supply in Britain itself. A couple of months later Attlee received a report from Hilary Marquand, the paymaster-general, on his seven-week tour of the eastern half of Africa, which reinforced many of these conclusions.[43]

Thus African economic development was faced with multiple obstacles, clearly identified by the spring of 1948 in a cluster of memoranda. Africa was not amenable to the more euphoric hopes of exploiting it in the common good. Shakespeare and Pliny were equally confounded, as well as Strachey and Bevin: it was not filled with 'golden joys' and it was in fact not easy to conjure anything new out of Africa. The stunning recalcitrance of the environment even to mechanised assault was brought home by the groundnuts fiasco. Inadequate transport was perhaps at the heart of the overall problem. There was maddening difficulty in actually transporting essential products out of Africa on an exiguous, congested, war-exhausted rail system; exports of uranium from the Congo, copper from Northern Rhodesia, coal and chrome from Southern Rhodesia, timber from the Gold Coast, and even groundnuts from Tanganyika, were all held up. There were seven different railway gauges in Central Africa, yet the high cost of unifying even two of them surprised everyone. It was all very well for Bevin to demand that 'Africa should be as full as possible of transport', but the difficulties were immense. In this as in other sectors, British and African needs were competing. More generally, with the shortage of clothes and bicycles for export from Britain, African workers could not be given all the incentives they needed. Nutritional problems and debilitating diseases also reduced their efficiency. (The iniquities of the tsetse fly, incidentally, generated more surviving Colonial Office records than any other subject.) Finally, there was the obvious danger that too concerted a policy of demanding African action to meet Britain's domestic needs (a demand already pushed to the limit by the exigencies of the convertibility crisis of 1947) would be endlessly open to the damaging charge of exploitation, as Bevin was among the first to realise. (The Colonial Office thus sought to distance itself from the work of the new Colonial Development Corporation.) For this reason also international collaboration would remain limited: there must be no hint of 'ganging up' to turn Africa into a hinterland of western Europe.[44]

V

Although much thought was given to the ways in which Africa might help to solve Britain's own strategic and economic problems, the empire would not stand or fall on the establishment of a base in Kenya, or poultry farms in Gambia, or the supply of bicycles to Blantyre, or even of peanuts and bananas to Battersea. More fundamental by far was the racial challenge of the stereotypes of Stellenbosch and the precepts of Pretoria.

The advent of the National Party regime in South Africa in 1948, dedicated to apartheid inside its borders and expansion outside them, had worrying implications for the whole of Britain's African policy. Griffiths spoke for all his colleagues when he described apartheid as 'totally repugnant'. South Africa itself, already angry over the perpetual withholding of the High Commission Territories, became alarmed at the Labour government's determination to press ahead with 'arming Africans' (raising troops for the defence of Africa and the Middle East). It was, moreover, outraged by the prospect of the Gold Coast's being turned into 'another Liberia'. Sir Evelyn Baring, the high commissioner, warned that 'to despise or to ignore the strong and expanding force of South African nationalism in 1951 would be as unwise as it was to decry in March 1933 the power of Hitler to do harm'. Ministers took the point: if Afrikaner racial ideas spread northwards of the Union's boundaries the whole of their African policy might be jeopardised. South Africa might even try to seduce the settlers in Kenya and Rhodesia from their British allegiance.[45] On the other hand, South Africa was deeply involved in, and had useful technical resources for dealing with, transport, soil erosion, and disease problems (trypanosomiasis, rinderpest, and locust-plague). Both sides wanted co-operation in these intractable matters, but it was clearly impossible for the British government to agree to extend discussion into the political arena or to be drawn into a local defence pact. Yet they did want South Africa to contribute to a Middle East defence system: this was 'an essential element we could not forgo' (according to P.C. Gordon Walker, Commonwealth relations secretary). In Whitehall there were generally held to be four reasons why the maintenance of good relations was important. First, strategically South Africa was a strong country in a pivotal geopolitical position. It had the basis for heavy industry, together with raw materials important in peace and vital in war (uranium, manganese, diamonds, chrome, and coal); it was the only African country which could in war provide a large body of trained technicians. The Simon's Town naval base was of the 'utmost importance' to Britain; the use of other ports was also required. South Africa would be needed as a transit area, an arsenal, and a troop-reserve for the Middle East. Secondly, economically Britain was 'in dire need of its gold' (Baring), since the stability of the sterling area depended on obtaining a substantial part of its gold output. It was also a valuable export market – indeed it headed the list of Britain's customers in 1947. Thirdly, trusteeship ('the ethical code of the empire') meant protecting the vulnerable High Commission Territories. Departmentally this was seen as the critical reason for staying on the right side of South Africa, especially in the Seretse Khama case.[46] For many ministers, however, the determining factor was the fourth one: to preserve the Commonwealth. A quarrel with a 'founder member' would be highly embarrassing and 'immensely damaging to British world prestige'. A public dispute might 'break up the association overnight'. Philip Noel-Baker (Gordon Walker's predecessor at the Commonwealth Relations Office (CRO)) even invoked some emotional (and inaccurate) 'inherited official historiography' about Campbell-Bannerman and Smuts – 1906 and all that.[47]

Unfortunately South Africa had put itself into the international dock by de facto incorporation in 1949 of the former mandated territory of South-West Africa, for which it was hauled before the International Court. Britain had at first tried to be friendly and helpful over this, but it was becoming harder all the time. How closely could it afford to side with South Africa at the UN over a case which might be thought weak if not bad? Civil servants were undecided. Some thought the British government was the only one which stood any chance of influencing the attitude of South Africa, but would lose what little influence it had if it 'joined the pack howling against them', so driving them out of the Commonwealth 'into an outer darkness of their own'. Others, while not wanting Britain to be 'tarred with the apartheid brush', thought it was hardly worth while imperilling a South African contribution to Middle East defence ('very nearly the biggest strategic interest of the UK') for the sake of making doubly sure British policy would not be confused with South Africa's. Some felt strategic requirements should be the overriding consideration. *Per contra*, many officials argued that unless Britain rejected all visible compromise with the Union's native policy, Britain's own African policy would be endangered. (Sir Thomas Lloyd, permanent under-secretary at the CO, complained of 'numerous and growing embarrassments' flowing from the failure to denounce its reactionary policies.) The South-West Africa dispute was formally analysed as requiring the pursuit of three conflicting objectives. Britain needed to preserve good relations with South Africa, but also 'to keep her reputation as a champion of liberal Western civilisation', avoiding a conflict with Afro-Asian opinion. Above all, it had to defend its rights as a colonial power vis-à-vis the UN, which must not be allowed to establish the right of intervention in non-self-governing territories. If in South-West Africa the UN inserted the thin end of the wedge of a right to dictate policies and decide the future of all African peoples, it would 'bring British authority, peace and good government in Africa tumbling about our ears'.[48]

For the impending Cabinet debate on this difficult controversy, an inter-departmental paper was prepared, signed by Griffiths, Gordon Walker, and Kenneth Younger (minister of state at the Foreign Office). As drafting proceeded, over a period of five months, the recommendation to intervene at the International Court (in order to make British views known) was made stronger. (According to Galsworthy, some aspects of the dispute were 'supremely important' to the Colonial Office.) Griffiths insisted the main issue should be brought out unequivocally: the risk of being misrepresented as supporting South African native policies, as against the threat of the court's making a decision adverse to British colonial interests. Attorney-General Sir Hartley Shawcross favoured intervention, though acknowledging that the arguments were 'very nicely balanced'; they would attract a great deal of opprobrium, but mostly from those 'who already have a pretty poor view of us in colonial matters'. Presenting the issue to the Cabinet, Griffiths declared himself on balance in favour of intervening, but at the same time he wanted it to be made clear that their appearance before the court did not imply support for apartheid. Gordon Walker agreed, on 'strict grounds of British interest'. The Cabinet, however, rejected their recommendation. Most ministers felt that representation at or participation in the court's proceedings would be bound to be misrepresented as implying support for South Africa, and would therefore 'incur political odium'. Indeed, it might actually invite the court to pronounce on the colonial issues of concern to Britain, in a context most unfavourable to its case, which it could argue more convincingly in future if it had not been present.[49]

Following upon this hardening of opinion and unusual rejection of departmental advice, a Cabinet paper was prepared in the CRO to clarify the more general issues of Anglo-South African relations. Again, this was several months in preparation. It was finally presented by Gordon Walker at the end of September 1950. Indian hostility to South Africa was identified as a significant feature in the equation, since Britain was anxious to enlist India's 'great influence in Asia' to help in the solution of various Far Eastern problems. Moreover, 'any suspicion that the United Kingdom sympathised in any way with South Africa's native policies would so deeply disturb African and Indian public opinion in our African Colonies as to constitute a threat to their internal security'. On the other hand, it was important to continue to preserve good relations. The 'four reasons' for this were carefully rehearsed. The conclusion was drawn that Britain ought to show that it appreciated South Africa's difficulties, and not simply condemn and antagonise it. Unnecessary polemics should be avoided, and everything possible done 'to retain South Africa as a member of the Commonwealth, preferably as one owing direct allegiance to the Crown'.[50] Gordon Walker spoke to the paper in the Cabinet, emphasising that strategically South Africa's goodwill was of special importance. Griffiths then examined the other side of the coin, expressing deep concern both about South Africa's expansionist ambitions and about the serious alarm South Africa's policies were arousing throughout black Africa. Aneurin Bevan drew this point out a little more sharply: the time might come when Britain would be forced to consider whether it lost more than it gained by its embarrassing association with South Africa. Other ministers countered this by underlining the strategic importance of securing South Africa's support in any struggle against communism, and the 'great value' of the military support it now seemed likely to promise in the Middle East. (Ernest Bevin still wanted South Africa to 'look after the east coast of Africa'.) The CRO paper was endorsed. At a subsequent discussion in the Defence Committee, Strachey (now a War Office minister) reluctantly accepted that they must look on South Africa as an ally, but Emanuel Shinwell (now minister of defence) remained profoundly unhappy about seeming to give tacit approval to apartheid by any military co-operation. Attlee (who had not yet really turned his mind to southern Africa) summed up correctly if inconclusively: 'it was a matter of great importance'. However, it clearly had been decided that co-operation with South Africa was to remain a prime object of British policy.[51]

But not the only object. Six months later, Gordon Walker produced his own prodigiously thorough and perceptive analysis of the situation, seeking more definitely to balance necessary co-operation by a policy of containing South African expansion. 'This would mean that we do not regard as our sole objective the emancipation and political advancement of the African in all our African colonies.' Of course this would remain a major objective, but 'we must not subordinate all else to it'. A shift towards closer association with Rhodesian settlers had to be faced. There was a real danger that, to avoid domination by Africans (as a supposed consequence of 'political advancement'), white settler communities would throw in their lot with the Union. This was at least as grave a danger as the eruption of African discontent. Containing South African expansion should thus be 'a policy of *equal* weight and importance in our eyes with the political advancement of the Africans in our Central and East African colonies'. If British communities revolted and linked themselves to the Union, the apartheid policies they detested would be established in the heart of Britain's African empire: 'Millions of Africans would be subjected to oppression. Terrible wars might even be fought between a white-ruled Eastern Africa and a black-ruled Western Africa.' They would in the end fatally have 'betrayed our trust to the Africans', who would be 'calamitously worse off'.[52]

This apocalyptic scenario provided the rationale for the Central African Federation. Enthusiastically advised by G.H. Baxter of the CRO and the ubiquitous and utterly pragmatic Cohen, Gordon Walker was the principal ministerial advocate of creating in Central Africa a British bloc to contain Afrikanerdom, provided Africans could be persuaded to accept it.[53] He won Griffiths to his side, but Creech Jones and others remained unconverted to this solution, believing other means could be found for achieving its political and economic purposes without upsetting Africans. Attlee fully understood the case for such a federation in principle, but to him, as always, what mattered was 'tide rather than froth'. Drawing on his Indian experience, he believed the vital thing was the long-term trend of growing African nationalism, which, if given insufficient outlet, might go sour from frustration. The fatal flaw he discerned in the scheme of federation as it ultimately emerged was that it froze the progress of African political advancement by stabilising the whole framework on the Southern Rhodesian model. The federation thus ran counter to the basic premise of Labour's African policy, and he rejected it.[54]

Retiring as high commissioner in 1951 after seven years, Baring summarised the three guidelines which had emerged for Britain's South African policy: (1) counteract the magnetic new South African nationalist expansion in the north; (2) preserve and develop the High Commission Territories; and (3) regularise relations by co-operating as often as possible and always being very careful to avoid sweeping condemnations, which would only 'unite and inflame' all white South Africans behind Malan. There was thus no simple policy for dealing with Afrikanerdom, but a subtle symbiosis of two parallel strategies, co-operation and containment.[55]

VI

In fact there was no simple policy for dealing with any of the problems of Africa. Throughout the continent the Labour government found that the successful adoption of clear new policies was limited by the tension between cold war strategic imperatives and their ideally required rational disengagements or moral stands. Neither politically nor economically were centralised blueprints possible. Inadequate British resources and the stubborn facts of the African environment stopped dead in its tracks any striking advance towards an 'economic new deal'. Politically, in principle Attlee was convinced by Indonesia and Vietnam that 'failure to meet reasonable nationalist aspirations led to an ever-worsening position'. But he did not think Africans were as civilised as Asians, and he foresaw a danger in too rapid a transition.[56] The resultant policy was thus not one of wholesale 'decolonisation' or 'dismantling the empire'. Labour ministers themselves invariably called their policy merely one of 'political advancement'. And this political advancement was not thought practicable as yet in much of Africa. Progress was uneven. The Gold Coast and Nigeria were seen as exceptions. Attlee lectured the Northern Rhodesian African National Congress about there being 'a long way to go' and 'no short cuts to political maturity'. Political advancement in East and Central Africa was held up by the supposedly immature and irresponsible nature of its nationalism, but also by the presence of white settlers.[57] Fear of driving them into the arms of an expansionist South Africa was a major reason why the Labour government did not take up earlier recurrent proposals (most notably those of Harold Macmillan in 1942) for an assault on the privileges of the Kenya settlers.[58] East and Central Africans themselves were not thought ready to be of use as collaborators in the task of containing Afrikanerdom. Every region indeed had leaders who were seen as mere demagogues, bent only on capturing the colonial state and driving the British out as quickly as possible. This was not at all the kind of future the government intended. In the short term, local government would be used 'to call in the masses to keep the balance', and close control would remain meanwhile. The long-term aim was gradual political advancement towards self-governing states which were broadly based, stable, viable, friendly, non-communist, and firmly within the Commonwealth.[59] Labour ministers may well have been involved in a 'controlled colonial revolution',[60] but their emphasis was distinctly on the *control* of the process. This gradualism was essential because they were determined to maintain as far as possible the structure of British global interests in the fight against communism. Paradoxically, however, as Attlee saw so clearly, 'an attempt to maintain the old colonialism would . . . have immensely aided Communism'. Decolonisation was a gigantic footnote to the cold war.[61]

Notes

1 R.E. Robinson, 'Andrew Cohen and the transfer of power in Africa, 1940–1951', in W.H. Morris-Jones and G. Fischer, eds., *Decolonisation and after: the British and French experience* (1980), p. 50.

2 Dalton Papers (LSE), I/35/17, Diary, 24 February 1947; CAB 128/10, CM 75(47)5, 9 September 1947.

3 CAB 129/37(3), CP(49)245, Annex A, 18 October 1949.

4 Bevin Papers, FO 800/435, f. 116, conversation with Portuguese ambassador, 23 October 1948, and 118, minute to prime minister, 6 November 1948; FO 800/444, f. 29, minute to prime minister, 16 September 1947; CAB 21/2278, minute by Attlee, 16 September 1947; Dalton Diary, I/34/13.

5 CAB 21/2277, minute 29 October 1946, and 2280, minute, 23 December 1949; CAB 134/786, CCM(54)1; C.R. Attlee, *As it happened* (1954), p. 189.

6 CO 537/5361, D.R. Rees-Williams (parliamentary under-secretary, CO), report on West African tour, 27 September 1948; CAB 129/16, CP(47)10, memo. 4 January 1947; CO 847/36/2, no. 24, speech by Cripps to African Governors' Conference, 12 November 1947 (AGC.22). RH, ed., *The Labour government and the end of empire, 1945–1951* (BDEEP, 4 pts, 1992, hereafter cited as *BDEEP*), pt I, document no. 66.

7 CO 537/5699, no. 89 A, 16 June 1950.

8 DO 35/4023, no. 62, speech at opening of the African Conference, 23 September 1948. Attlee regarded this occasion as important enough for him to address, but he was prevented by illness (CAB 21/2279, Attlee to Creech Jones, 12 October 1948).

9 Attlee Papers and Gordon Walker Papers (Churchill Archives Centre, Cambridge), ATLE 1/24/1; GNWR 1/7.

10 CO 847/25/7; CO 847/35/6, no. 1 (Cartland memo.) and 7; CO 847/37/1, no. 21.

11 CO 537/4589 (esp. note by colonial secretary, October 1949), and 5708, and 5698; CO 936/56, no. 6; CAB 129/24, CP(48)36; FO 371/107032 (UP.134/1), and 107076 (UP.247/10).

12 CO 847/36/1, minute by I. Thomas, 18 January 1947; PREM 8/922, A(49)1.

13 CO 847/35/6, esp. no. 2, memo. by Cohen, 3 April 1946, and minute, 24 January 1947.

14 CO 847/35/9, no. 3, minute by Cartland, 29 December 1947; CO 847/38/3, memos by R.E. Robinson on some recent trends in native administration policy (March 1947): *BDEEP*, pt I, document no. 49. Robinson described the 'pyramid of councils' as 'essentially an organisation for the political education of the rural Africans, and a scaffolding round which territorial political unity can be built' (CO 847/44/3, memo. on 'The development of British principles of native administration, 1927–47').

15 The distinction between 'responsible' or internal self-government and 'independence' is fundamental. Some historians need to remember what Jim Hacker learned from Sir Humphrey Appleby: 'I *must* be clear on my African terminology, or else I could do irreparable damage' (J. Lynn and A. Jay, *The complete 'Yes, minister': the diaries of a Cabinet minister, by the Rt Hon. James Hacker, MP* (1984), p. 35).

16 *BDEEP*, pt I, document nos. 58–9. CO 847/35/6; CO 847/36/1, no. 9, minutes by Creech Jones, 5 May 1947, and report of the committee on the conference of African governors, 22 May 1947 (? by Cartland), esp. Appendix 2 (AGC.1, 'The general political development of colonial territories', by Caine), and Appendix 3 (AGC.2, 'Constitutional development in Africa', by Cohen). Ivor Thomas wrote that local government would give Africans 'self-government in the matters that really touch them' (minute, 30 May 1947). The most prominent misinterpretation is by D. Williams in *Cambridge history of Africa*, vol. VIII, *From c.1940 to c.1975* (Cambridge, 1984), p. 341, writing about the Gold Coast in 1946 [*sic*]: 'independence – perhaps in 15 years' time. This was a sort of date . . . Creech-Jones [*sic*], or . . . Cohen had in mind.'

17 CO 847/37/5, no. 9, minute 5 of African Governors' Conference, and Cohen to Sir John Hall, 29 October 1947; CO 537/4625, minute by Creech Jones, 1 March 1949.

18 CAB 134/55, CA(48)8, 29 October 1948; CAB 134/56, CA(49)1, 19 January 1949; CO 1015/770, no. 43.

19 CO 537/7098; FO 371/80130.

20 CO 537/5698, no. 69, and 5699, no. 102; *BDEEP*, pt I, document no. 72, pp. 334–5; R.E. Robinson, in A.H.M. Kirk-Greene, ed., *The transfer of power: the colonial administrator in the age of decolonisation: proceedings of a symposium, March 1978* (Oxford, 1979), p. 181.

21 CO 936/217, FO study paper, prepared by Permanent Under-Secretary's Committee, 21 November 1952, and Sir Thomas Lloyd to Sir William Strang, 9 September 1952.

22 CO 537/5921, no. 5; 5929, no. 2; 5698, no. 66; 5699, no. 102.

23 CO 537/5698, no. 69, International Relations department secret paper on 'The Colonial Empire today', May 1950, section III, drafted by S.H. Evans: *BDEEP*, pt I, document no. 72, p. 337.

24 CO 537/3558, no. 122, Creech Jones to Sir G. Creasy, 18 March 1948; CO 96/795, and 796, no. 24 C. See *BDEEP*, pt III, document no. 212.

25 PREM 8/924; CAB 128/16, CM 58(49)3, 13 October 1949; CAB 129/36(2), CP(49)199.

26 CO 537/7181, no. 5, Arden-Clarke to Cohen, 12 May 1951, and minute by Cohen, 11 June 1951. See *BDEEP*, pt III, document no. 226, and R. Rathbone, ed., *Ghana, 1941–1957* (BDEEP, 2 pts, 1992).

27 For Nigeria, see *BDEEP*, pt III, document nos. 222–3 and 227: CO 537/5787, no. 52, and 7166; CAB 128/17, CM 30(50)6, 11 May 1950; CAB 129/43, CP(50)94; PREM 8/1310. See also Martin Lynn, ed., *Nigeria, 1943–1963* (BDEEP, 2 pts, 2001), and '"We cannot let the North down": British policy and Nigeria in the 1950s', in Lynn, ed., *The British empire in the 1950s: retreat or revival?* (2006), pp. 144–63.

28 CO 554/298, no. 13, Macpherson to Lloyd, 18 January 1952.

29 CO 936/198, no. 7, memo. 20 November 1951: *BDEEP*, pt III, document no. 228.

30 CO 967/62, Creech Jones to Sir Philip Mitchell, 17 October 1948; CO 537/5698, no. 69; CO 822/114, no. 2, minute, 20 September 1946; CAB 134/1, A(49)2, 5 July 1949. Creech Jones also told Mitchell he had many doubts about the 'essential rightness of some aspects of our past policy, the basic rightness of our being in Kenya, the conditions and distribution of land in Africa'; British past folly and occasional perversity had brought intractable problems, but equally in Kenya difficulties were 'in no small part due to African suspicion and ignorance, and their own failures in social and political development' (and not only to European settlement), and they ought to be more appreciative of the contribution of Western civilisation, 'which they have almost unwittingly enjoyed'.

31 CO 537/5923; PREM 8/1113, CA(50)2; CAB 128/18, CM 76(50)1; CAB 129/24, CP(48)43; CAB 129/43, CP(50)270. See D.W. Throup, *The economic and social origins of Mau Mau* (1987).

32 CO 537/1468, and 1474, minute by J.S. Bennett, 30 May 1946; CO 537/2081, minute by Cohen, 1 February 1947, and 2087, esp. no. 18, Bennett to Brig. Benoy, 31 March 1947; CAB 129/9, CP(46)165, memo. 18 April 1946.

33 CO 537/2088; PREM 8/1231, DO(48)9, 30 April 1948; PREM 8/1478, COS(49)381.

34 PREM 8/946, and 1388/I (1946), Bevin to Lord Stansgate, 31 August 1946; CAB 128/5, CM 58(46), 7 June 1946; CAB 128/19, CM 23(51)6, 2 April 1951, Cabinet conclusion, *BDEEP*, document no. 33; FO 800/435, f.153, and 457, f.176, minute by Bevin to prime minister, 15 December 1947.

35 CAB 128/20, CM 51(51)2, 12 July 1951, and CM 60(51)6, 27 September 1951; CO 936/217, minute by Trafford Smith, 22 July 1952. See W.R. Louis, *The British empire in the Middle East, 1945–51* (Oxford, 1984).

36 *BDEEP*, document nos. 273–82; CAB 129/1, CP(45)144, memo. on future of Italian colonies, 1 September 1945; CAB 131/1; CAB 131/2; PREM 8/515, memo. 19 February 1946; FO 800/475, and 476. Attlee predicted: 'It may be that we shall have to consider the British Isles as an easterly extension of a strategic area, the centre of which is in the American continent, rather than as a power looking eastwards towards the Mediterranean to India and the East' (memo. 19 February 1946).

37 CAB 131/2–5, *passim*, esp. DO(46)99 (COS, 5 August 1946), and DO(46)40,

memo. by Bevin, 13 March 1946; CO 537/1883, and 2515; FO 800/451, f.144, Montgomery to Bevin, 25 September 1947.

38 CAB 131/2, DO(46)40, memo. by Bevin, 13 March 1946; Dalton Diary, I/34/12–13, 22 March 1946; CO 537/1231, no. 102, COS(46)271; CO 537/1233.

39 CAB 131/2, DO(46)48, COS report, 2 April 1946; CAB 131/4, DO(47)27, memo. by A.V. Alexander, 17 March 1947, and DO(47)9/4, 26 March 1947; CO 537/1230, and 1231, no. 102, COS(46)271; DO 35/2373, JP(48)122, and COS(49)6; FO 371/73042, and 73043; CO 967/58. A tentative alternative was a train-ferry crossing the northern part of Lake Nyasa to an outlet at Mikindani, which would transport Northern Rhodesian minerals to the coast by the quickest route, but not achieve the Cape–Kenya link (PREM 8/923, Marquand Report).

40 *BDEEP*, pt III, document no. 104, DO 35/2380, memo. 19 December 1947; FO 800/435.

41 *BDEEP*, document no. 106, PREM 8/923. P.C. Gordon Walker in the CRO welcomed Creech Jones's paper as 'very sensible' (DO 35/2380, minute, 8 January 1948).

42 CAB 130/31, GEN. 210/1; PREM 8/733, and 923, EPC(48)35/4, 9 November 1948, *BDEEP*, document no. 109.

43 CO 537/3030, 27 February 1948; PREM 8/923, report by H.A. Marquand on visit to Africa, 2 April 1948, and address to press conference, 18 March 1948.

44 FO 800/435, f.3, and 444, f.29; FO 371/73037, and 73038, and 73039; CO 537/3032.

45 CO 537/5896 (Griffiths); DO 35/3140, no. 55; FO 371/76351, and 91171.

46 *BDEEP*, pt IV, document no. 429, memo. by Gordon Walker, 'Relations with the Union of South Africa', 25 September 1950; CO 537/5929; CAB 134/1, A(49)2, CO memo. 5 July 1949; CAB 131/10, DO(51)17/3, 18 June 1951 (Gordon Walker); DO 35/3140; PREM 8/1284, minute by C. Syers, 22 August 1950. See RH, 'The political consequences of Seretse Khama: Britain, the Bangwato and South Africa, 1948–52', *Historical Journal*, vol. 29 (1986), pp. 921–47, repr. in RH and Peter Henshaw, *The lion and the springbok: Britain and South Africa since the Boer War* (Cambridge, 2003), ch. 8.

47 CO 537/4596; DO 35/3811. Noel-Baker told a deputation led by Tom Driberg, MP, 3 March 1949: 'Our policy is not in the slightest degree influenced by economic, financial, or strategic considerations, not at all. It is influenced by this: 40 years ago Campbell-Bannerman made a self-governing unit of the Union, to which our Liberal Parliament then agreed. Since then we have worked with them in the Commonwealth on many matters and many South African statesmen have, in our view, rendered great services to the world: we want to go on doing that, we want to keep that co-operation, we don't want to have an all-out quarrel with another member of the Commonwealth in the creation of whose self-government we still take a considerable national pride.'

48 CO 537/5710, minute by W.I.J. Wallace, 19 September 1950; CO 936/123, minute by W.G. Wilson, 12 March 1952; CO 936/125, no. 162; CO 936/217, Lloyd to Strang, 9 September 1952: *BDEEP*, document no. 428.

49 CO 537/5708, and 5709; FO 371/88560, and 88561, and 88566; CAB 128/17, CM 28(50)3, 4 May 1950; CAB 129/39, CP(50)88. The paper was drafted by Sir E. Beckett, W.G. Wilson, and A.N. Galsworthy, together with suggestions from N. Pritchard, and vetting by Cohen, Lloyd, J. Martin, and Sir K.O. Roberts-Wray (the legal adviser); it was then discussed with ministers H. Shawcross and J. Dugdale.

50 CAB 129/42, CP(50)214, 25 September 1950; DO 35/3839; CO 537/5710, no. 142; FO 371/88566. The paper was drafted by G.E. Crombie of the CRO, but a great deal of consultation went into it (e.g. with R.R. Sedgwick, G.H. Baxter, C. Syers, and J.S. Garner), and it was 'much travelled' between departments too, so that in its final form responsibility for it was spread widely. Griffiths for the CO and Younger for the FO signified their general agreement with it.

51 CAB 128/18, CM 62(50)4, 28 September 1950; FO 800/435, f.153; CAB 131/10, DO(51)17, 18 June 1951; PREM 8/1284: *BDEEP*, pt IV, document no. 429.

52 CAB 129/45, CP(51)109, memo. by Gordon Walker, 16 April 1951, after visit to South Africa, Southern Rhodesia, and High Commission Territories: *BDEEP*, pt IV, document no. 433.

53 See RH and Henshaw, *The lion and the springbok*, ch. 9, 'Containing Afrikanerdom: the geopolitical origins of the Central African Federation, 1948–1953'. For important supplementation, see Philip Murphy, '"Government by blackmail": the origins of the Central African Federation re-considered', in Lynn, ed., *The British empire in the 1950s*, pp. 53–76, and Murphy, ed., *Central Africa, 1945–1965* (BDEEP, 2005, 2 pts); L.J. Butler, 'The Central African Federation and Britain's post-war nuclear programme: re-considering the connection', *JICH*, vol. 36 (2008), pp. 509–25.

54 CO 1015/89, no. 13, BBC talk by Creech Jones, 15 April 1952; CO 1015/144, no. 15, and CO 1015/770, visit of Attlee to Central Africa, August 1952. In this matter Attlee was more far-sighted than Cohen, who had become too personally involved with the federal scheme. Cohen's determination to bring federation into being was not, however, somehow out of line with his West African policy: there is only a paradox if his commitment to 'decolonisation' is exaggerated. His African policy was consistent: in all parts of Africa he wanted to retain the initiative against extremists, and *control* nationalist movements. He opposed withdrawal of the federal proposals on the ground that it would abandon the field to irresponsible 'outright nationalists', which would only give impetus to European extremists. Africans should therefore, as he put it, be brought round to 'a true realisation of their own interests', confronted as they were by the 'Afrikaner menace' (DO 35/3601, no. 104; CO 1015/59, minute, 31 October 1951; CO 1015/64, no. 36 B, to Sir G. Rennie, 16 November 1951).

55 DO 35/3140, no. 55, and FO 371/91171, Baring's 'final review' despatch to secretary of state, CRO, 30 June 1951; see also Gordon Walker Papers, GNWR 1/9, Diary, 2 April 1950.

56 Attlee, *As it happened*, p. 191.

57 CO 1015/770, no. 43. Cohen expressly described Northern Rhodesian

African opinion as 'immature and unorganised politically' (CO 537/7203, no. 7, memo. 18 April 1951).

58 CO 967/57, Sir A. Dawe's memo. on East Africa, July 1942, and 'Mr Macmillan's counter-proposals', 15 August 1942: S.R. Ashton and S.E. Stockwell, eds., *Imperial policy and colonial practice, 1925–1945* (BDEEP, 1996), pt I, document no. 65.

59 CO 847/35, no. 6, minute by Sir F. Pedler, 1 November 1946; CO 537/3561, report on West African tour by Rees-Williams, 27 September 1948.

60 FO 371/107032 (UP134/1), Sir Gladwyn Jebb to foreign secretary, 12 January 1953.

61 But see John Kent, *British imperial strategy and the origins of the cold war, 1944–1949* (Leicester, 1993) for a complementary (rather than a different) interpretation.

Referencing for this chapter has rather remorselessly focused on research sources. But there are good general accounts of the Labour government and the empire, among them P.S. Gupta, 'Imperialism and the Labour government of 1945–1951', in J.M. Winter, ed., *The working class in modern British history: essays in honour of Henry Pelling* (Cambridge, 1983); D.K. Fieldhouse, 'The Labour governments and the Empire-Commonwealth, 1945–1951', in R. Ovendale, ed., *The foreign policy of the British Labour governments, 1945–1951* (Leicester, 1984), pp. 83–118; L.J. Butler, *Britain and empire: adjusting to a post-imperial world* (2002), ch. 3, 'Attlee and post-war re-adjustments, 1945–1951', pp. 63–91; F. Heinlein, *British government policy and decolonisation, 1945–1963: scrutinising the official mind* (2002), pp. 1–86; P. Keleman, 'Modernising colonialism: the British Labour movement and Africa', *JICH*, vol. 34 (2006), pp. 223–44; John Darwin, *The empire project: the rise and fall of the British world-system, 1830–1970* (2009), ch. 12, pp. 527–65.

[Not previously published. Written in 2006.

Although this chapter is a by-product of many years' research at the National Archives, it could not have been written without the help of John Bennett's family: his widow, the late Mrs Mary Bennett, his brother, the late Dr Ralph Bennett, and his nephew, Mr Francis Bennett, to all of whom I am most grateful. I must stress, however, that my views are not necessarily their views.

This chapter is mainly about official policy-formation, but class-based attitudes within the administrative elite emerge as a sub-theme. How significant is this?]

In 1947, as imperial attention swung away from newly independent India to the tropical colonies of Africa and elsewhere, insiders in the Colonial Office would have had no difficulty in identifying the high-flyers who could be expected to be the leading advisers for what proved to be the evolving process of decolonisation. They were Andrew Cohen[1] and John Bennett.[2] But while Cohen is a familiar name to all students of empire – possibly the best-known Colonial Office civil servant since Sir James Stephen in the early nineteenth century – Bennett has dropped out of view for all but a handful of archival researchers who gratefully disinter his incisive minutes.[3] A John Bennett Memorial Lecture on the Middle East is delivered biennially in the University of Cambridge Faculty of Asian and Middle Eastern Studies,[4] but it is safe to assume that most of those attending do not know who John Bennett was. Yet, for more than ten years, up to and including independence for Ghana in 1957, Bennett was at the centre of colonial policy-making, author of a sheaf of remarkable and radical memoranda about trusteeship, decolonisation, Palestine, Mediterranean North Africa, and Cyprus. After that, his career stalled. For the next fifteen years he was confined to the fringes, descending ever deeper into a sense of hopelessness about the future of the remaining colonial territories and his own ability to contribute to the solution of their problems.

The career of John Bennett may illustrate three main themes: (1) how the nature of policy-making in the Colonial Office and the dynamics of decolonisation planning can be deduced from the thoughts of one centrally placed civil servant; (2) how historical intelligence could be deployed to discern policies which would work with the grain of perceived future trends, and therefore how a strategy for ending the empire more quickly might have been articulated;[5] and (3) more tentatively, how although the British educational system could be exploited to create a career genuinely open to the talent of grammar school boys, social mobility might be limited by certain lower-middle class attitudes and attributes which precluded rising institutionally to the very top, given the continuing dominance of public school elitism in 1950s and 1960s Britain.

I

John Sloman Bennett was an Essex man. His family forebears moved from Derbyshire to Havering-atte-Bower (once a tiny Essex village, now part of the London borough of Havering) in the eighteenth century, and then down the hill to Romford in 1894. Three successive generations of the Bennetts were veterinary surgeons, of whom John's father, Ralph, was the last, serving in the First World War in the Army Veterinary Corps. He was second-in-command of a base-hospital at Kantara in the Suez Canal Zone from 1917 to 1919. His services to the cavalry operating in Egypt, Sinai, Palestine, and Syria were sufficiently valued to gain him the freedom of the City of London after the war. Ralph Bennett made the most of his local leave in visits to Cairo and Alexandria, and longer trips to Luxor and Jerusalem, all of which impressed him deeply. Returning home with books on the area and the war campaigns, liberally illustrated with detailed maps, he enthralled his two young sons, Ralph (born 1911) and John (born 1914), with traveller's tales, communicating to them an interest in Near Eastern antiquities, especially ancient Egyptian art, architecture, and religion. He also read the Bible to them, the Book of Samuel being a favourite. As a boy, John absorbed all this with enthusiasm: he could count (up to ten) in Arabic before he could do so in French or any other European language, and even acquired a smattering of hieroglyphics. 'I think the intersection of all this with the Bible was what first made history come alive for me,' he wrote later. 'And without knowing it at the time, I also grew up free from the then prevalent illusion (derived from Renaissance classical education) that the civilised world was confined to Europe and that history began with classical Greece.' Only later did he identify a connection between public school classical education 'and the English habit of mismanaging civilised countries (India, Egypt *et al.* including Palestine and Cyprus), unlike backward black ones which they were not bad at'.[6]

The Bennetts were a lower-middle class family, though with an annual income of £730 their father was financially at the higher, minor-professional, end of the social class. He was also determined to give his clever sons as good a start as possible. The Bennett brothers were educated at the local state grammar school, the Royal Liberty School, Romford. It was not nearly as grand as it sounds, for it was not the school which had royal status but the ground it stood upon, the former 'royal liberty' of Havering-atte-Bower. Nor did it have any sort of tradition. In fact it was just one of a number of brand-new 'county' schools, which had opened in September 1921. The headmaster, S.B. Hartley, was not a Cambridge man, and it is not known why he steered the Bennett brothers to try for scholarships at Magdalene College, Cambridge. Scholarships were awarded at Cambridge by groups of colleges conducting their own examinations, so once application was made to Group II, the choice of a college was automatically narrowed to Trinity, Jesus, Clare, Queens', Trinity Hall, and Magdalene. Both Bennett boys gained open awards to Magdalene, with supplemental state scholarships (that is, in effect, a free university education).[7] John Bennett was in direct competition with a candidate from Mill Hill School, Albert Hibab Hourani, of Lebanese extraction. A history scholarship was awarded to Bennett, but not to Hourani (one year younger), who later gained a scholarship at Magdalen College, Oxford.[8] They were to meet again during the war.

During the 1930s, Magdalene College was in serious danger of becoming mainly a finishing school for Old Etonians, who made up 35 per cent of the intake by 1937. But there was also a traditional group of grammar school boys with scholarships, accounting for a steady 10 per cent of the student body. With a number of Fellows who were leading Nonconformists, there were also connections with the Congregational community, such as members of the Pilkington family of glass manufacturers and the sons of ministers, for example, Kenneth Horne, later well known as a comedian.[9] The problem for talented lower-middle class students in this milieu was whether to assimilate to the public school ethos, or to maintain their grammar school credentials in purity. The two Bennett brothers adopted opposite strategies, and then there was tension between them for the rest of their lives. Ralph worked at his assimilation, smartening himself up, joining the Boat Club, cultivating snobbier friends, and eventually dismaying his parents by becoming known as 'Rafe' instead of Ralph with the 'l' sounded.[10] John, on the other hand, was determined not to conform. Apart from studying history, he

followed his elder brother in one respect only – succumbing to considerable pressure, he took up rowing. He rowed regularly in the bow position
for three years before moving into coaching. As a freshman, he weighed
only 9 stone 3 lb, lighter even than the cox, though by the time of gradu-
ation he had gone up to 10 stone 1 lb.[11] (This slight physique was also
to have a bearing on his future prospects.) One of his rowing partners
was John Field, a South African who joined the Colonial Service in the
same year as John joined the Colonial Office (and became commissioner
of the Cameroons, 1956–61). Another was Robert McDowall, later secretary of the Royal Commission on Historical Monuments (England).
Interestingly, McDowall, in spite of being an Etonian (but presumably unorthodox), became a friend as a fellow-historian. But a more
significant friendship was with Jack Beddoe from Hitchin Grammar
School, who took two firsts in history, entered the Ministry of Health in
1936, and rose to become under-secretary of state in the Department of
Economic Affairs. These three students, together with one or two others,
including his old schoolfriend, Alan Murray, formed their own 'set'.
Bennett was the leader, and coined the name 'Adullamites' for them, the
'discontented', like the followers of David in the Book of Samuel.[12] But
unlike other clever students with a rebellious turn of mind (for example,
the future Lord Listowel, Charles Madge, and J.R. Cumming-Bruce, all
in Magdalene), they were not attracted to communism.[13] Rather, the
Adullamites were cheerful anarchists, mocking their social superiors.
They were members of what Bennett playfully called STRACA, the
Society for Tendentiously Resisting All Constituted Authority. In a satirical story which Bennett wrote for the *College Magazine*, the Magdalene
rebels take part in a proletarian revolution against bourgeois authority. They drive out the vice-chancellor and the Conservative MP (Sir
Kenneth Pickthorn, Tudor historian); they execute college deans, the
proctors, and all the members of the upper-class Pitt Club; they discover
a leader with 'ruthlessly basic principles in the sinister Dr Anarcharsis
Richards'; and thus defeat a counter-revolution of traditional Liberals
and moderates led by historians Professor Sir Ernest Barker and their
tutor Frank Salter, all of whom were deported to the Isle of Ely. It was a
clever and amusing piece, fairly inoffensive.[14]

As to his academic work, John Bennett added a Goldsmith's Exhibition
in June 1934 to his college and state scholarships. He obtained Tripos
results which can only be described as legendary. He was awarded
distinctions ('starred firsts') in both parts of the Historical Tripos. A
distinction in one part is not all that uncommon, but to achieve the
accolade in Part I (1934) and Part II (1935), with their significantly differing coverage, focus, and methodologies, was, in those days at least,

highly exceptional.[15] It put Bennett in the class of such luminaries of the historical profession as future regius professors like Sir John Elliott and Quentin Skinner, the celebrated Marxist historians Eric Hobsbawm and Victor Kiernan, and Robert Latham, who produced the definitive edition of the Pepys Diary. John Bennett was said to be the ablest medievalist examinee in living memory. What had really inspired him was the final-year special subject on 'The First Crusade and the Kingdom of Jerusalem to 1127'. This was run by Miss Helen Pybus; she was not a university lecturer, but a Fellow of Newnham College (director of studies in history, 1927–55). Students had to read original contemporary sources: chronicles, memoirs, and the like in Latin and French, and translations from the Greek and Arabic. Bennett was fascinated by 'the tangled mixture of idealism and material motives on both sides', and the example of relations between Europe and the Levant 'in a previous era of colonisation'. One of the things which remained with him – perhaps because unexpected – 'was the way the Crusaders of the second generation took to wearing eastern dress and so on, and fraternised with Moslems of like social class, and were inclined to be embarrassed by the keen boisterous ways of the new recruits fresh from Europe'. Not unnaturally, the study of the Crusades intensified his schoolboy feeling of involvement with the Middle East.[16]

The natural career for so gifted a scholar would have been a college fellowship. In those days, colleges tended to elect from among their own members, and in Magdalene elder brother Ralph now blocked the way.[17] The college had just taken the decision to appoint Ralph as a medieval history lecturer, to complement the teaching of its modernist, Frank Salter, and John had in fact been taught by his brother. In a small college of limited resources, election of a third teaching Fellow in history was out of the question, while there was only one research fellowship, to which elections were made once in three years, usually at this date to a mathematician. John did become an unregistered research student for a year, but the arrangement with the college was such as to secure his services as a history supervisor in the absence of Ralph Bennett in Munich for a year, rather than to promote John's research. After that year, needing a job, John sat the examination for the Home Civil Service. Passing in fifth in August 1936,[18] he had done well enough to be allowed to choose his government department: 'I chose the Colonial Office from no sense of imperial mission but because it seemed small and friendly and offered the possibility of travel.' (The CO at this time was indeed like a collegiate club.) Three other young men joined at the same time. Quite by chance he was allocated to fill a vacancy in the Middle East department.[19]

II

Nothing could have suited him better than this first assignment, but he had not even known that the Colonial Office covered Palestine. And Palestine was to preoccupy him for the next ten years. 'While colleagues wrestled with the parish-pump affairs of great backwaters in Africa or the Caribbean, Palestine was already a hot seat in the middle of the world stage.' As a result, for a junior, he was soon in unusually close touch with the office mandarins and the secretary of state. Within his first year he was involved secretarially with the royal commission on Palestine chaired by Lord Peel (1937). He accompanied a senior CO official to a meeting of the League of Nations Council in Geneva. He was appointed assistant conference secretary to the London Palestine Conference of 1939, the last pre-war attempt to patch up some kind of settlement, or at least truce, and the first to which representatives from other Middle East countries as well as from both sides of the Palestine conflict itself were invited. In the theatrical atmosphere of St James's Palace, for a whole month he was face-to-face with the main protagonists, from Weizmann to the Saudi Crown Prince, 'not to mention Mr Chamberlain in his frock-coat against a backdrop of Tudor halberds on the wall'. The conference failed to produce any agreement. This, it might be said, was part of his education, but so was the fact that Bennett made personal contacts with Palestinian Arab leaders, almost alone among Whitehall civil servants in doing so in the inter-war years. His sympathies became strongly pro-Arab and anti-Zionist.

Not long after this, he made further Arab contacts as assistant to a Ministry of Information official on a tour of the Middle East in 1940. The work was not, he thought, particularly important, but the journey itself was absorbing, 'though breathless (especially as I had to keep the accounts, in nine currencies)'. They stopped in Istanbul, Ankara, Aleppo, Beirut, Damascus, Jerusalem, Cairo, Baghdad, Tehran, Bushire (Bushehr), and Aden, returning to England (in the middle of the Dunkirk crisis) via Alexandria. Travel was mostly by land (rail or motor-car), but the longer hops were made in old-fashioned, slow, low-flying aircraft, from which Bennett could see his father's maps come to life.[20]

His preparation as a Middle Eastern expert was now nearly complete. His final 'big break' was being drafted to Cairo as assistant to the Australian politician and diplomat Richard Casey, who had been appointed by an admiring Churchill as minister-resident (with a seat in the War Cabinet) in the Middle East. Casey was a very successful trouble-shooter, someone Bennett could look up to. They worked closely together, until Casey was transferred by Churchill to the governorship of Bengal in 1944.[21] Before leaving, Casey let it be known how highly he regarded young Bennett. And it was while in Cairo that Bennett's path once again crossed that of Albert Hourani, who was now Casey's assistant adviser on Arab affairs.[22]

Bennett's Middle Eastern interests and experience, and especially his contacts with the Arabs and Hourani, were to determine his whole subsequent approach to imperial problems. One of his fundamental insights was to identify 'an inherent logical and moral absurdity' in the way Western powers after the First World War had apparently maintained that Arab tribes of the Arabian peninsula were fit for immediate recognition of their independence, whereas the sophisticated townsmen of Beirut and the Mediterranean coast, with their centuries of contact with Europe, required an indefinite period of 'tutelage' by a Western power. It seemed obvious to him, with his studies of the Crusader Kingdoms, that this distinction was based on no principle, but driven by French imperialistic ambitions backed by their claim to 'protect' the Christian minorities in Lebanon. 'It couldn't last and it didn't,' because the whole process was essentially one in which European 'imperialism' artificially tried to peel off a strip of the eastern Mediterranean coast from its natural association with the rest of the Arab world. After the Second World War he feared that another attempt would be made to establish a series of such bridgeheads along the southern Mediterranean coast, including Libya. This would only alienate the Arabs of the interior, when what Britain needed was good relations with 'the Arab world as a whole'.[23]

Returning to the CO, Bennett was assigned to the International Relations department. This, too, was another providential stroke of good fortune, keeping him associated with front-line developments at an eventful time. He always regarded his liaison with the United Nations during its formative days on trusteeship policy as a particular privilege, since the general pattern of relations with the UN was then established, with hard-fought drafting battles. The experience was to leave an indelible mark upon him.[24] (See Plate 9.2.) By 1946 he was an assistant secretary – a very rapid promotion – and head of the International Relations department. He was thoroughly in tune with the ethos of the Labour government, with Attlee, and with Cohen. In 1947 he was transferred to head the Mediterranean department, where he remained until 1952, deeply involved with the Cyprus problem and critical of government policy. In 1953 he was seconded to the Imperial Defence College course, preparatory to taking over the Defence and General department of the CO, 1954 to 1956, where he led the team drafting the constitution for independent Ghana.[25]

In 1955 he got married, rather sensationally, to Mary Fisher, the only child of H.A.L. Fisher, Warden of New College, Oxford, and one of the finest historians of his generation. After working for the BBC during the war, Miss Fisher joined the CO in 1945 as its first female official, and worked for Bennett in the Mediterranean department.[26] It would be misleading to say the courtship was conducted on the minute-sheets of the CO files, but with knowledge of the outcome, all those consecutive minutes beginning 'I agree', and signed 'JSB', seem to have a predictive, even a poignant quality. Miss Fisher was someone who shared John's radical outlook on colonial issues, and whose trenchancy of minuting was a match for his own. In the same year as his marriage he was appointed CMG. It must have seemed that he was, aged forty-one, finally on his way. Paradoxically his career went into free-fall almost at once.

After a brief spell in the West African department 'B' (which excluded the leading colony of Nigeria), he was drafted into the dwindling side-stream of Social Services, mainly concerned with labour relations, trade unions, public health, and the occasional 'colour question'.[27] He had no role in decolonisation strategy during the crucial years of the Macmillan government. By contrast, Leslie Monson significantly raised his profile simply in virtue of his lucky allocation to the East African department. By 1961 JSB was the most senior assistant secretary, but he received no further promotion either then or for the remainder of his service. The years 1963 and 1964 found him working on marketing and investments in the Economic and General department. With CO staff and responsibilities rapidly shrinking from 1965, he took charge of the Atlantic department, and after the merger with the CRO he headed the Gibraltar and South Atlantic department in the Dependent Territories department, with A.N. Galsworthy and J.C. Morgan over him as 'super-intending under-secretaries'. The creation of the FCO made little structural difference to the colonial side, and the Foreign Office's Sir Denis Greenhill became the first permanent secretary in 1969, the post which Bennett thought he ought to have had. He stuck it out until 1971 and then, thoroughly disillusioned, resigned. For the next three years until his formal retirement at the age of sixty, he was in an unestablished post as a part-time adviser in the FCO research department, where he briefly found a niche as something like a historian of the 'official mind'.[28]

I shall return below to the question of why JSB's career stalled so dramatically. The main cause can, however, be stated simply enough here: it was a consequence of the accession of Sir John Martin and Sir Hilton Poynton to the leadership of the Colonial Office in 1956, as joint deputy under-secretaries of state, with Poynton becoming permanent under-secretary (1959–66). Martin was a Zionist and Poynton was old fashioned. If Andrew Cohen had been in charge the outcome might have been different. But no two heads could have been less congenial to JSB than Martin and Poynton. Unfortunately the feeling was mutual, and no two heads could have placed a larger question-mark over his suitability for promotion. He especially seems to have rubbed John Martin up the wrong way. Quite early on, Martin had said to him with an irony which was only half-joking, 'you have introduced a very dangerous element into this department – *thought*'.[29] As for Poynton, JSB had the temerity to criticise him in a minute on the files for all to see. This was in 1947, but its audacious and ruthless sarcasm will certainly not have been forgotten. Poynton's telegrams from the United Nations, JSB complained, created an impression of 'Athanasius contra mundum':

The light of battle was in his eyes [when] he left for New York, and I am sure he is enjoying himself hitting out at all and sundry. My only personal doubt . . . is whether the 1940 spirit is really entirely appropriate to the situation. The parallel is close in some respects: in the last two years it has been largely a matter of waiting for the Americans to swing in behind us, and educating them for the rôle of saving the British empire in the interests of American security. But if the atmosphere which must now be prevailing in the Ad Hoc Committee goes on, in the Assembly afterwards, it is 'open war' – colonial powers versus the rest of the United Nations. Open war is more honest and refreshing than phoney war, yet in the long run I think one is obliged to consider whether the fomenting of international dispute and bad feeling on colonial issues will really operate to the advantage of the colonial peoples themselves. That is quite apart from the question whether the UK, in its present state, can hope to win such a slogging match in the end.[30]

III

It is time to consider JSB's approach to colonial policy in more detail. We have already seen that he was pro-Arab to an exceptional degree. Beyond that, he believed more rigorously than perhaps any other member of the post-war CO that policy must be based on the wishes of indigenous inhabitants, and must be determined by *morality* and *logic*, two words which repeatedly recur in his minutes. He also held fiercely to trusteeship doctrines as updated by the United Nations. Time and again he quoted as an inescapable obligation of colonial rule the UN's formula that the basic objectives of the trusteeship system (as defined in the UN charter) were, *inter alia*, 'to promote the political, economic, social and educational advancement of the inhabitants of trust territories, and their progressive development towards self-government or independence as may be appropriate to the circumstance of each territory and its peoples and the freely expressed wishes of the peoples concerned'.

Palestine was the problem on which he had cut his teeth as an official:

a job he described as 'arduous, fascinating and hopeless'. Precisely what he meant by 'hopeless' was in retirement carefully set down:

The League of Nations mandate bound us to favour Jewish immigration without prejudice to the indigenous inhabitants. Diplomatic double-talk at the best of times; and when Hitler came on the scene, stark contradiction, though nobody was yet allowed to say so. The Mandate might just have been workable in a peaceful world and if Zionism had remained primarily a religious and cultural ideal content to move slowly (and not leading to any sudden major demographic change). But by the mid-1930s, Hitler refugees were transforming it into a political movement in a hurry, backed by much non-Jewish liberal sympathy.[31]

Bennett believed that in essence the refugee problem could not possibly have been solved in Palestine alone, except by military force such as was later imposed by the Israelis. Britain and the USA should have taken in 'a comparable proportion' of refugees themselves. It became inevitable that there would be injustice as the Zionists pressed their claims. As early as 1941, and in the context of illegal immigration, he complained that 'the Jews have done nothing but add to our difficulties by propaganda and deeds since the war began . . . The morally censorious attitude of the US in general to other people's affairs has long attracted attention, but when it is coupled with unscrupulous Zionist "sob-stuff" and misrepresentation, it is very hard to bear.'[32] As far as he was concerned, Zionism had developed into something 'totalitarian, militaristic and National Socialist' in outlook, quite different from Weizmann's intentions.[33] JSB became a formidable, even intemperate, critic of proposals for partition. In a strikingly bold analysis in October 1946 he challenged the CO orthodoxy about this: 'Partition means that, having used our period as mandatory to allow squatters to occupy the premises placed in our trust, we withdraw leaving them in legal possession of the ground-floor flat, and the original residents in a state of considerable congestion upstairs.' Partition, he predicted, would not be final: 'The Jews will only accept it, if at all, as a step towards something further; so far as they are concerned, it will be no more final than Hitler's successive "last territories" claims in Europe.' The case for partition appeared to be based primarily on being the policy most acceptable to Jews. But if – he tartly observed – the basis of policy was to be what Zionism, backed by the sanction of armed force, would accept, then it seemed a waste of time to examine any further what moral commitments there might be 'in any other direction'.[34] However, as Zionist sympathisers, Sir George Gater (permanent under-secretary, 1939–47) and Creech Jones (secretary of state, 1946–50) were not to be moved from their preference for partition.

Palestine was, as Bennett saw it, an acute problem created by European 'imperialism'. It agitated the whole Middle East because it appeared that the Arab majority was deprived of self-government and self-determination in the interests of a European colonial settler minority. This might be a rapidly growing one, but that only made it worse, and thus harder with every passing year 'to create elementary self-governing institutions in the country'. The mandate bequeathed only 'a political vacuum', which the Jews would fill.[35]

Bennett was determined to try to see that the British government did not create a similar problem in North Africa and the Horn by allowing 'power politics' to engineer the return of some of its colonies to Italy and Italian settlers, even in the form of trusteeship. This would be 'a logical and political absurdity', cynically disregarding the interests of the inhabitants, which ought to determine the outcome.[36] He worked closely with Cohen in drafting several Cabinet papers. They argued for the unification of the Somali territories as a way of heading the Italians off, and rectifying 'the mistakes of the nineteenth century' with its arbitrary boundaries. They were to be disappointed over 'Greater Somalia' (until independence was granted, that is), but were more successful in setting Libya on the path to speedy independence, despite what JSB called the defeatist and timid 'negative opportunism of the Foreign Office'.[37] He saw Libya as a practical test-case of British high-minded words about promoting colonial self-government. Britain, he wrote, was under growing international pressure for rapid political advancement to independence, which in 1946 was not really in the realm of practical politics for many African territories, thus obliging planning to move fairly slowly, at the price of increasing criticism. But he believed it was feasible for Libya. Bennett applied his historical lessons from the Middle East. What had happened in Egypt and Iraq after the First World War 'should be sufficient warning of the demerits of excessive caution and of waiting to have statements about independence extracted from us by local revolt and/or outside pressure'. Libya was 'fundamentally an Arab country', and should be treated within the framework of an Arab-friendly Middle Eastern policy. Thus the British government should 'recognise the inevitable' and cash in on it in good time by boldly taking the initiative in promoting Libyan independence.

When Cyprus became part of his remit from the middle of 1947, he immediately began to apply his historical perspectives and principles of 'logic and morality', urging that policy towards it should be seen as part of an overall Middle Eastern strategy. The fundamental weakness of the British position in Cyprus was that it 'did not rest on any moral foundation'. There was 'no real moral basis for administration in the sense in which a moral basis for the state is understood in the democratic countries of the West'. This weakness could only be removed by giving the people of Cyprus a share in making the laws and influencing the actions of the executive. To deny an educated European community self-determination solely on the grounds of Western defence and strategic needs was little different from the Soviet grip on the Baltic states – not an observation that endeared him to his superiors. The right of Cypriots to self-determination he believed ought to have been self-evident, not something they should have to prove; and as a Crown Colony it was after 1948 in a flagrantly exposed position as 'an anachronism without parallel for thousands of miles in any direction'. The complexities of the problem were not being addressed in 'a serious or rigorous way'.[38]

He was sceptical about the strategic argument for the retention of Cyprus, at least as it stood in 1947. The defence of the Middle East in war would, he argued, depend not on the possession of Cyprus, 'but on the degree of friendly relations which we succeed in maintaining with independent Arab states in peace'. Authoritarian imperial rule in Cyprus was a handicap in the cold war. Nor was he as dismissive of Enosis as most of his colleagues. Interestingly, he thought its emotional appeal was a direct result of the authoritarian and repressive British regime, its lofty haughtiness, silly and stuffy provincialism, and officials 'morbidly sensitive to criticism'. Enosis was thus 'inherent in our administration', and it was, he added in an impressive comment, 'no good ignoring and complaining' about 'the deeply embedded general attitude of mind of a whole nation'.[39] He was even prepared to admit that in the long run union with Greece might be the only satisfactory political solution. It would at least be better than the permanent hostility of the Cypriots, and their Greek and Arab neighbours (but this was before the rise of Turkish militancy on the issue).[40] He drew the parallel – inevitable after 1948 – with Palestine. By 1951 this led him to a chilling prediction: 'The Cypriots are not, on past form, the fighters the Palestinian Jews proved to be, but if that should ever change, the parallel would become even more gloomy.'[41] And so it proved to be.

The direction of Cyprus policy increasingly disturbed him. He was appalled – and he was not alone – when the ministerial Commonwealth Affairs Committee in December 1947 rejected a proposed constitution (surprisingly acceptable to Cypriot communists), which would reserve to the imperial government defence, foreign affairs, and protection of minorities. The committee refused all constitutional advance and suggested that Cypriot politicians could be diverted into local municipal government.[42] Bennett's consternation made him seem rather pompous, perhaps: 'I admit to being a little puzzled personally by the strength of the ministerial reaction against any concessions, even mild ones, towards self-government in Cyprus, coming within a few days of the signature of an extremely liberal treaty with Iraq, which lies in the same strategic zone and is quite as important strategically.' In his view, ministers had not behaved with logic any more than with morality. He was convinced that the situation would now deteriorate; and as to local government, that was all very well, but village councils were not a realistic training for a central legislature, and municipal politicians had shown 'no tendency to forget Enosis in their absorption with municipal drainage: very much the contrary'.[43] He continued to regard the decision of December 1947 as a lost opportunity. Another frustration was what he saw as the disastrous governorship of Sir Arthur Wright (1949–54). Again, he was not alone in this, but no one else was so outspoken. He scornfully denounced the 'folly and impracticability' of Wright's policy of hard-line repression. He dismissed Wright's claim that the Cypriot majority would really like and accept a 'strong policy' and all would be well if only he could have the power to lock up a few agitators. This was 'the familiar talk of harassed colonial governors everywhere in the last half-century, not least in Egypt and Palestine'; yet such a line in Palestine in 1937 had seriously increased the scale of the Arab revolt. Was no one learning the lessons? Wright, he urged, should be replaced 'by a governor with the Mountbatten touch', someone who might be able to 'bounce' (Miss Fisher's term) the Cypriots and the government into accepting the 1947 proposed constitution. He kept repeating this: 'In view of Sir A. Wright's inflexible resolve that Cypriots should not be encouraged to think, because all thoughts are dangerous thoughts, I fear I see no hope of progress on this subject until we have a new governor.'[44]

Bennett's views of other colonial problems – so far as I have been able to uncover them – may be dealt with more briefly. Predictably, he was opposed to the proposed integration of Malta into the United Kingdom, not so much on the usual ground of objections to its financial cost and potential for friction, as on that of geopolitical anachronism and logic: 'If after 150 years the Navy has now little further use for Malta, it would seem an odd moment to choose to link the Island permanently with this country by some form of incorporation' (1955).[45] He made an important contribution in 1956, when, during the last stages of decolonisation for the Gold Coast, he held his nerve when all about him (from Secretary of State Lennox-Boyd downwards) were losing theirs. He was satisfied that Arden-Clarke as governor 'can still read the scene correctly', that the differences with Nkrumah were in fact very narrow; there was accordingly no case for delay.[46] He vetoed a last-minute attempt to write human rights into the Ghanaian constitution, because the CO could not within three or four weeks and amid many preoccupations solve a problem 'whose satisfactory solution has evaded the cleverest brains of three continents during the century and a half since the American Revolution'. Rather than botch it they should leave it alone.[47] Always alert to opportunities to speak up for the wishes of indigenous communities, in 1946 when a century of 'white raja' rule was being terminated in Sarawak, he was anxious that the new regime under CO control should conform to UN principles of trusteeship and should initiate a progressive policy.[48]

Furthermore, he supported the desire of the Ewe peoples (split between British and French Togoland and the Gold Coast) for unification. He complained that the French refusal to consider this was 'completely rigid and unrealistic'. He believed that the Ewe question raised fundamental issues of African policy. Africans were at 'a most critical stage of their evolution' and it would be madness to arouse their suspicion and hostility. Britain should side with the wishes of the inhabitants and look to its international reputation, as against friendship and collaboration with France. Not everyone in the CO agreed with him about this.[49] Later he wondered what to do with the Gambia. Some status short of sovereign independence might be considered: perhaps the country would become, in his sardonic phrase, 'a sort of black Gibraltar'.[50] Ever alive to the need to face up to situations before they became acute problems, as early as the summer of 1945 he was drawing attention to the difficulties with Indian immigration and settlement in Kenya and Uganda, and earned Cohen's approval for doing so.[51] On wider issues, he signalled the need for caution over adopting human rights policies generated by the UN's 'rather wild and woolly body' on the subject. A code based too closely on advanced European notions might 'expose our colonial flank', but he saw the attractions of occupying 'the high moral ground' and 'dishing the Soviets'.[52] The politics of aid policy reveals once again his insistence on logically coherent approaches. *Logically*, he wrote, only aid given disinterestedly without strings was effective – but this was increasingly an unpopular view, and one particularly rejected in the Foreign Office.[53] JSB was delighted with Macmillan's 'wind of change' speech, and ensured that copies of it were circulated as widely as possible to government departments and the Colonial Service; it was soon being quoted and invoked in many different contexts.[54]

It was JSB's misfortune to be stuck for most of the years of his prime with the Falklands, and, moreover, the Falklands in a relatively quiescent period. They were so unimportant in British policy in the 1960s that they were quite literally off the map, omitted from the 'diagrammatic map of British interests overseas' prepared by the the FCO research department in 1969.[55] He had little patience with the inhabitants, who were 'European colonial settlers'. Their political sense had atrophied, he thought, and they had let things slip into a 'sorry state' by their apathy and prickly unwillingness to take a responsible and constructive part in managing their own affairs. He waspishly suggested that they would benefit from 'a period of mismanagement' run by their elected representatives, or 'by as many of them as they would bother to elect'. Equally he rejected the validity of Argentina's claims, and believed the Argentinians did not really 'care two-pence about actually administering the Islands, and simply want to paint them [their] colour on the map'.[56] This led him to propose 'leaseback' as a way of resolving the deadlock. In return for ceding sovereignty, Argentina would grant the UK a long lease with the exclusive right of administration. This should give Argentina what it most wanted, a title-deed, and provide Britain with 'a transitional generation during which the practical *status quo* remains but everybody knows that it is coming to an end when the old people are dead'. It sounds plausible, and something similar operated for Hong Kong, but whether it would really have worked is uncertain.[57] The Falklands War in 1982 killed the idea. Bennett's private lament then was, 'If only Attlee had had time to decolonise the Falklands, while nobody would have noticed!'[58] (See Plate 9.2.)

IV

If John Bennett has a claim to some historical significance, it is largely because he presents us with an alternative scenario for the management of decolonisation. If his approach and ideas had been allowed to prevail, the whole process would have moved more briskly. There would certainly have been some advantages for Britain in this – no Falklands War, for example. He saw earlier and more clearly than almost anybody that the dictates of logic and morality, to say nothing of economic reality, meant that the empire had to be comprehensively ended.

His most detailed examination of fundamental general principles was in a memorandum entitled 'International aspects of colonial policy, 1947'. Dated 14 April 1947, it was written in the context of impending Indian independence, the notification to the USA that Britain could no longer fulfil its responsibilities in the Middle East and would refer the Palestine question to the UN, and, economically, the convertibility crisis. His immediate aim was to clarify the line to be taken in the UN discussions of trusteeship and other colonial matters. Its argument – highly significant to his whole philosophy of late colonial rule – may be summarised as follows.[59]

Bennett's starting point was that the UK was 'seriously weakened economically and in manpower', so if the pace of political development was to continue to be set by economic and social development, it was bound to be slow, and this would not be generally acceptable to politically conscious dependent peoples. Britain was no longer effectively in control of this sociological experiment, because of the vulnerable gap between the magnitude of the programme set by the idea of 'colonial development and welfare' and the practical ability, financial resources, and manpower to carry it out. Resources on the major scale required could not be diverted to the colonies for the foreseeable future. The chances of an impoverished empire being able to carry through 'controlled economic and social development of the colonies *within the time which political circumstances will allow* appear to be distinctly questionable' (emphasis in his original). Basic assumptions must therefore be reconsidered. Unless the pace of political advancement was accelerated, 'there is a risk that internal and external pressures may break the "controlled experiment" before it is completed, which would obviously be the worst of all conclusions from the point of view of the colonial peoples themselves'. Britain was vulnerable from two directions: from the 'indigestible colonial intelligentsia', and from the international pressures opposed to the continuance of colonial empires.

This combination of pressures was now more than the UK was in a position to resist indefinitely. Britain was no longer in control of the timetable for political advancement in the colonies. '*Time* has, therefore, become the dominant factor.' Hanging on until pressures were overwhelming would be entirely negative, and British policy had to be brought into line with the realities. The best and most positive way forward would be 'to liquidate as rapidly and satisfactorily as possible those communities which are likely to become untenable, to beat a strategic retreat to shorter and more defensible lines (both territorially and functionally), and as a condition of the manoeuvre to seek to fortify ourselves with the maximum practicable United States support'. The outstanding colonial commitments in those regions exposed to the greatest international pressure, those in the Middle East, North Africa, and South-East Asia, should be wound up as rapidly as possible. Instead, groups of independent states would be created, associated with Western powers by community of interests and treaties. 'By facing the dominant modern political issue, such a policy would offer the best chance, in the long run, of preserving Western friendship and influence in those regions.'

His analysis concluded with some specific recommendations. Britain should support 'an autonomist settlement' for Libya, and run up as quickly as possible the framework of independence for Malaya, bypassing traditional intervening constitutional stages. 'This does not mean an ideally good or stable government (it would probably be neither

– compare India), simply any structure that would just work.' The apparently 'annexationist' arrangements in Sarawak and Borneo should be reversed. Tropical Africa would then become the core of the 'colonial problem' proper, though there could be 'no doubt of the necessity for the continuation of external guidance in some form for a continued period'. Policies for the Pacific islands would be developed in a similar 'but minor key'. His new strategy would impose two broad objectives for Africa:

(a) to devise a means of tapping American resources in order to accelerate the pace of economic and social development, at the price of admitting some degree of United States influence in policy generally;
(b) to accelerate the pace of political development, parallel with (a), by making maximum use of the small minority of educated Africans, at the price of some lowering of standards of administration.

The United States would of course need to be convinced that such involvement was in its own interests. Bennett was not in favour of collaboration with other European powers, seen as less enlightened. Instead, he suggested that regional agencies promoting development should be set up, broadly on the pattern of the Middle East Supply Centre in 1943–4, superintended by resident British regional authorities, perhaps with an advisory body of Africans. Finally, he urged that the proposals before the African Governors' Conference (November 1947) on constitutional progress would need to be rapidly carried out 'and perhaps extended'.

Although JSB was unaware of it, his proposals for immediate disengagement from the Middle East bore an uncanny resemblance to Attlee's radical reappraisal of 1945–6. Since the prime minister was unable to get his views accepted, it is hardly surprising that Bennett's memorandum was also pigeon-holed.[60] The parliamentary under-secretary of state, Ivor Bulwer Thomas, found it 'very stimulating', even if every paragraph 'invited rejoinder', but it was never put before Creech Jones.

V

Bennett's memorandum on colonial policy was by any standard a notable state-paper. But when he followed it up almost immediately with another formidable analysis, this time of the Cyprus problem, he at once ran into criticism. Trafford Smith – not a man to cross – pounced upon him for speculating 'far beyond what is legitimate for us in the Colonial Office' and for trying to plan policy 'on a procrustean bed of logic and coherence', wrong in principle, misconceived and unworkable in practice, 'an analytical "Latin" point of view, the sort of thing French and Jews, but not Anglo-Saxons might do'. (JSB's response was, 'I realised that

I was committing an awfully un-British thing in writing this memo!')[61]
At about this time, Sir George Gater called in Kenneth Robinson – and
probably other colleagues too – and asked for his opinion of Bennett.
Kenneth Robinson replied that Bennett, though undoubtedly brilliant,
seemed to have difficulty in working within the parameters of a professional framework, so that if called upon to write a minute on a specific
issue he was likely to produce a memorandum saying the whole policy
was wrong.[62]

Brian Simpson offers the following judgment: Bennett was 'a person
of the highest intellectual ability [and] something of an iconoclast', who
'consistently comes across as willing to look critically at departmental
dogmas. Perhaps that was why he never rose to the top of the institution.'[63] It is certainly the case that JSB had the obstinacy and scornful
disdain of the man who knew he was right, and that those who patron-
ised him were wrong. He was never afraid to use words like absurd,
ridiculous, and fatuous of policies with which he disagreed. He could
not keep his opinions to himself, such as his disapproval of Sir Hilton
Poynton and Sir John Martin.

An Office Rottweiler had his uses of course. He had the reputation
of being the only civil servant able to stand up to a bully like Duncan
Sandys (secretary of state, 1962–4) and tell him he was wrong.[64] But
essentially JSB was perceived as not a man for accommodation, consensus, or compromise, all necessary attributes, perhaps, for someone to
take the presiding top position. Pragmatic colleagues were disconcerted
by his habit of exposing 'logical and moral absurdities'. He was seen as
unable to take criticism, unable to get on with certain sorts of people,
and too anti-Zionist. He was spoken of as inflexible, accused of lacking
judgment. Too clever by half, he understood perhaps more than was
good for him. And yet I do not think intellectual arrogance and management style alone can explain his failure to reach the top.

'Extremely clever . . . but definitely lower-middle class.'[65] This assessment by his college tutor, Frank Salter, would almost certainly have been
echoed by the mandarins of the Colonial Office. Salter was devastatingly
clear about what he meant. Lower-middle class people like the Bennetts
might be highly intelligent, sometimes even of 'very good stock', but they
lacked a naturally distinguished or impressive presence, were deficient
in *savoir faire*, in instinctive tact and refinement, graceful and polished
manners.[66] JSB in the CO saw no reason to modify his 'lower-middle-
classness' any more than he had in Cambridge, but he spent his career
in an essentially public school world. In 1939, 89 per cent of all entrants
to the administrative civil service came from public schools, a robust
social group with its own rigid and arcane codes of what was done and

Plate 9.1 John Bennett in 1981.

not done, deeply unforgiving of behaviour it disapproved of.[67] Even so, a lower-middle class background need not inevitably have blocked John's promotion, if he had been prepared to follow his brother Ralph's strategy of emollient assimilation, as indeed his chum Jack Beddoe seems successfully to have done (p. 271 above). Ralph had an equally edgy, ingrained dislike of all 'establishments', an intense suspicion of all those who might think themselves better than other folk simply because they had power and influence to deploy; but Ralph had a less abrasive and less egocentric appreciation of how to 'play the system'.[68] The obvious social chip on John's shoulder made it harder to overlook his physical appearance. Thin, blond, foxy, slight of frame and neither tall nor handsome, John Bennett was to the more patrician Hilton Poynton as a Hutu peasant to a Tutsi chief. He simply did not look the part of the archetypal Whitehall mandarin or colonial governor, and crucially, therefore, might be thought unable to command the respect of the Colonial Service.

The merger with the Foreign Office was the final blow to Bennett's chances of promotion. He did not get on with FO types at all.[69] He disliked and distrusted the suave certainties of diplomats, and he contemptuously rejected absolutely their commitment to social hierarchy and a conservatively defined 'national interest', and the priority they gave to good relations with foreign countries. *They* had little time for the interests of non-Europeans and the lofty ideals of trusteeship.[70] *He* was

I am intrigued to hear of the subject of your research, and should be very pleased to help you in any way I can. It is a sobering thought that the outpourings of my official youth are now (I suppose) open to inspection in the PRO! But it was an eventful time, and I had the good fortune to be in on several front-line affairs (including liaison with the U.N. during its formative days on trusteeships etc) which might be of interest to you.

With kind regards

John Bennett

If only Attlee had had time to decolonise the Falklands while nobody would have noticed!

With best wishes

Yours sincerely
John Bennett

Plate 9.2 John Bennett: extracts from two letters to the author. The first was dated 27 January 1982, and the second 20 June 1982, one week after the end of the Falklands War. *Source*: Magdalene College Archives, F/OMP/IV/24.

not much interested in Europe. But he could have been of the greatest value in developing FCO policies for the Middle East during the difficult years of disengagement from Aden and the Persian Gulf, and the 1967 war. Instead his talents were wasted with fretting over a scatter of 'rocks and islands',[71] before taking early retirement.[72]

VI

Certain themes emerge clearly from Bennett's analysis of the problems of post-war imperial rule and the demission of power. He believed fundamentally that the British were trustees and that it was right to enable people to rule themselves if they possibly could. He believed that British policy had to be set in the international context, respect the resolutions of the United Nations, and invoke help from the USA where practicable. He was sceptical of the CO euphoria about superintending a beneficent 'controlled colonial revolution', because of Britain's overstretched resources and shortage of money to commit to development and welfare, and because of the increasing pressure of nationalist aspirations and international criticism. Britain could no longer control the timetable: '*Time* has, therefore, become the dominant factor.' Even if his colleagues did not always share his passion for 'morality and logic', historians are likely to agree that he had a sound appreciation of the underlying realities and dynamics of decolonisation.

John Bennett's upbringing, intelligence, historical studies, and Arab contacts had brought him to see by the spring of 1947 that Britain was doomed as a great power, 'and therefore we must get out quick everywhere'. It was not until after the Accra riots in the Gold Coast a year later that the rest of the CO officials started to realise this too, and not until after Suez in 1956 that the politicians and the country at large also began to see it. Years later, asked by historians how he explained the slowness of the British approach to decolonisation, he replied, 'Because people's minds don't move fast, do they? That's what history is about.' This may seem a somewhat odd observation, but it certainly suggests he thought he had superior powers of discernment. His colleague Aaron Emanuel at the same symposium recalled that 'we didn't occupy our minds . . . with the forthcoming demission of the colonial empire'. If so, then JSB was the exception which proves the rule.[73]

Notes

1 R.E. Robinson, 'Cohen, Andrew B.', in *ODNB*, vol. XII, pp. 418–19, and 'Andrew Cohen and the transfer of power in tropical Africa, 1941–1951', in

W.H. Morris-Jones and G. Fischer, eds., *Decolonisation and after: the British and French experience* (1980), pp. 50–72.

2 *Who was who*, vol. VIII, *1981–1990* (1991), p. 57. The newspapers carried no obituaries at John Bennett's death, apart from a note in *The Independent* (28 August 1990) about his musical interests. This unfortunate omission meant that he had little chance of being included in the *ODNB*.

3 Notably Roger Louis, Brian Simpson, Freddie Madden, Rob Holland, John Kent, and Simon Smith, in works referred to below.

4 *Cambridge University Reporter*, 28 October 1992, p. 172: 'The John Bennett Fund', established by his widow.

5 Ged Martin, *Past futures: the impossible necessity of history* (Toronto, 2004), has some elegant reflections on making sense of the continuum of past, present, and future. Martin's discussion of the accelerated collapse of comfortably envisaged futures (pp. 135–6) seems particularly relevant to Bennett's understanding of decolonisation (see p. 283).

6 John Bennett, 'JSB and the Middle East', unfinished and unpublished memoir-note, drafted in 1986, believed to have been written for an American viol-playing friend, herself half-Jewish and ardently Zionist (Mary Bennett to the author, 9 October 1992); copy in Magdalene College Archives, F/OMP/IV/24 (John Bennett file).

7 Magdalene College Archives, H/FRS/Bennett, J.S. (tutorial file), consulted by kind permission of the Master and Fellows. Unfortunately this file contains no progress reports or references.

8 A. Hourani, 'Thoughts on the writing of the history of the Middle East', the first John Bennett Memorial Lecture, University of Cambridge, 1992 (unpublished). Hourani was able to draw on JSB's 'memoir' – see n. 6 above.

9 P. Cunich, D. Hoyle, E. Duffy, and R. Hyam, *A history of Magdalene College, 1428–1988* (Cambridge, 1994), p. 235. One of the Congregational Fellows was A.S. Ramsey, father of an atheist (the mathematical philosopher Frank Ramsey) and an Anglican archbishop (Michael Ramsey).

10 *Magdalene College Magazine*, no. 46 (2001–2), 'In memoriam, Ralph Bennett, Senior Fellow, formerly President', pp. 12–17; obituaries in *The Times* (9 August 2002) and the *Daily Telegraph* (23 August 2002). RFB did important work on 'Ultra' at Bletchley Park during the Second World War; although his academic field was medieval ecclesiastical history, he will be remembered mainly for his trilogy on military intelligence during that conflict (1979–94).

11 *Magdalene College Magazine*, nos. 70–5, Boat Club reports, 1932–6.

12 'Everyone that was in distress, and everyone that was in debt, and everyone that was discontented' gathered themselves with David as their captain in the cave of Adullam (*First Book of Samuel*, ch. XXII, vv. 1–2; 'cave' was a mistranslation for 'stronghold'). 'Adullamites' was a label often humorously alluded to after it had been famously applied by John Bright to Robert Lowe and his awkward squad of MPs who opposed the reform bills of 1866 and 1867; it was Lowe who complained 'we must educate our masters', though not quite so pithily.

13 T.E.B. Howarth, *Cambridge between two wars* (1978), pp. 224–7. Lord Listowel

became minister of state for colonial affairs, 1948–50, and governor-general of Ghana; Professor Charles Madge was the inventor of 'Mass-Observation'; Sir Roualeyn Cumming-Bruce became a lord justice of appeal.

14 *Magdalene College Magazine*, no. 74 (February 1936), pp. 200–24, 'The first workers' government in Cambridge'. 'Dr Anarcharsis Richards' is I.A. Richards, the famous literary critic; JSB makes punning allusion to his involvement with 'Basic English'. JSB's only other contribution to the *Magazine* was a poem about a nightmare, 'Murder in the examination', satirising Eliot's *Murder in the Cathedral* (no. 75, December 1936), pp. 259–62).

15 *University of Cambridge Historical Register*. For comparison: Ralph Bennett, 2/1 in Pt I, first in Pt II; of JSB's exact contemporaries, R.C. Smail, 2/1 in Pt I, first in Pt II, and (Prof.) J.H. Parry, two firsts but no 'star' – all these three were future lecturers in the Cambridge History Faculty; one year behind him, (Prof. Sir) John Habakkuk and (Prof.) Charles Wilson both had distinctions in Pt II (1936) but not in Pt I.

16 'JSB and the Middle East', typescript, p. l.

17 If John had been the elder brother, then *he* would have become the don, and Ralph might have become a civil servant. John would probably have made at least as good a don as his brother, while Ralph would probably have done better than John in the civil service. In 1938 RFB became an Official Fellow of Magdalene after three probationary years, the first lower-middle class grammar school boy to do so since A.S. Ramsey in 1897.

18 *Magdalene College Magazine*, no. 75 (December 1936), p. 250. For comparison: Cohen passed in fourth, but would have been second, had not sixty marks been deducted for bad handwriting (*OHBE*, vol. IV, *The twentieth century* (1999), p. 259).

19 'JSB and the Middle East', typescript, p. 2.

20 Ibid., p. 3.

21 A.P. Robbins and M. Brodie, 'Casey, Richard', *ODNB*, vol. X, pp. 478–80.

22 R. Owen, 'Hourani, Albert H.', *ODNB*, vol. XXVIII, pp. 289–90. Hourani became a Research Fellow of Magdalen, Oxford, a Fellow of St Antony's, and Director of the Middle East Centre. He converted to Roman Catholicism, and died in 1993. See also J.P. Spagnolo, *Problems of the modern Middle East in historical perspective: essays in honour of Albert Hourani* (Oxford, 1992).

23 The National Archives, Colonial Office records, CO 537/1474, no. 56, JSB to J.A. Marjoribanks (British delegation, Paris), 15 June 1946, printed in British Documents on the End of Empire Project (hereafter BDEEP), *The Labour government and the end of empire, 1945–1951* (ed. RH, 1992), pt III, p. 255 (no. 291). See also W.R. Louis, *The British empire in the Middle East, 1945–1951: Arab nationalism, the United States, and post-war imperialism* (Oxford, 1984), p. 303.

24 JSB to the author, 27 January 1982, reproduced in Plate 9.2; The National Archives, FCO 51/372, minute, 25 October 1974 (I owe this reference, and that in note 35 below, to Professor Wm. Roger Louis). For the way in which British official experience fed into the UN's trusteeship and human rights policies, see Kevin Grant, Philippa Levine, and Frank Trentmann, eds., *Beyond sovereignty: Britain, empire and transnationalism, 1860–1950*

(Basingstoke, 2007), p. 12, and pp. 80–102 (Grant, 'Towards an international human rights regime during the inter-war years').

25 *The Colonial Office List* (annual), listings.

26 *Who's who, 2005*: Bennett, Mary (1913–2005). See also obituaries in *The Times* (4 November 2005), *Independent* (19 November 2005), *Daily Telegraph* (21 November 2005), none of which says anything significant about JSB.

27 His big initiative in the Social Services department was to organise a review of colonial trade union policies and the abuses which seemed to be emerging: RH and W.R. Louis, eds., *The Conservative government and the end of empire, 1957–1964* (BDEEP, 2000), pt II, p. 170 (no. 358), 1959; see also nos. 353, 355, 361 for other subjects.

28 *Colonial Office List*, *CRO List*, and *FCO List*. For his analyses of various constitutional technicalities, see the Research department files in FCO 51/372.

29 Mary Bennett to the author, 2 October 1992. Mrs Bennett also recalled that Sir Andrew Wright came to regard Martin as 'the evil genius of the Colonial Office'. For Martin, see Michael Jackson, *A Scottish life: Sir John Martin, Churchill and empire* (ed. J. Jackson, 1999).

30 CO 537/2058, 13 September 1947. Hugh Foot as Britain's representative at the UN seriously disagreed with Poynton's attitude. For Poynton, see S.R. Ashton, 'Poynton, A. Hilton', *ODNB*, vol. XLV, pp. 191–3; and for Bennett's relations with Martin, note 34 below.

31 'JSB and the Middle East', typescript, p. 2.

32 B. Wasserstein, *Britain and the Jews of Europe, 1939–1945* (Oxford, 1979), p. 50.

33 A.F. Madden, ed. (with John Darwin), *Select documents on the constitutional history of the British empire and Commonwealth*, vol. VII, *The dependent empire, 1900–1948: colonies, protectorates and mandates* (1994), p. 619, n. 2 to no. 195 (August 1942).

34 CO 537/1783, 30 October 1946, printed in BDEEP, *Labour government*, pt I, pp. 26–9 (no. 12). It seems that Martin was angered by this minute, and he refused detailed comment on it. Their antagonism over Palestine went back to 1936–7, when Martin was secretary of the Peel Commission, with Bennett as his junior – Martin made friends with the Jews, Bennett with the Arabs; Martin approved of the recommendation for partition, while JSB did not; Martin's commitment to Zionism was then reinforced by his loyalty to Churchill as his principal private secretary during the war (Jackson, *A Scottish life: Sir John Martin*, pp. 79–101).

35 CO 537/1474, no. 56, to J.A. Marjoribanks, 15 June 1946, printed in BDEEP, *Labour government*, pt III, p. 255 (no. 291); FCO 51/372, minute, 9 October 1974.

36 CO 537/2081, no. 8, JSB, memo, 'Note on the implications of restoring to Italy some or all of the ex-Italian colonies', 11 February 1947; Cohen commented that this was 'brilliant and damning' (minute, 1 March 1947, BDEEP, *Labour government*, pt III, p. 269, no. 296).

37 BDEEP, *Labour government*, pt III, pp. 238–40, Cabinet draft paper, 7 March 1946, and pp. 253–79 (nos. 291–8), June 1946–August 1947; for background, pt I, Introduction, pp. lv–lvii; see also CO 537/1468–1474. For

a lucid and important account, see Louis, *The British empire in the Middle East*, pp. 280–8 ('The death of the Greater Somalia project'), and pp. 300–6 on Libya.

38 BDEEP, *Labour government*, pt III, pp. 105–7 (nos. 241–3); see generally pp. 84–122, and pt I, Introduction, pp. xxxix–xlii.

39 CO 537/2484, minute, 10 November 1947; CO 537/4036, minute, 18 June 1948; CO 537/4979, minute, 11 June 1949.

40 CO 537/2486, no. 4, JSB, memo. 'The future of Cyprus in relation to the withdrawal from Palestine', 14 November 1947, printed in BDEEP, *Labour government*, pt III, pp. 84–90 (no. 235).

41 Minute, 13 December 1949: BDEEP, *Labour government*, pt III, p. 106 (no. 242).

42 The National Archives, CAB 134/54, CA 5(47)3, minutes of Cabinet Commonwealth Affairs Committee, 22 December 1947, and CO reactions: BDEEP, *Labour government*, pt III, pp. 93–100. Attlee disliked the idea of an 'interim' constitution, while Bevin preferred to have no constitution at all, in order to 'hang on' to Cyprus (see CO 537/7463, no. 7, minute by JSB).

43 BDEEP, *Labour government*, pt III, p. 99, minute, 23 January 1948, and p. 122, minute, 1 February 1951.

44 JSB's principal attacks on Wright were in minutes of 24 January 1950, 1 February 1951, and 24 October 1951: for the first two see BDEEP, *Labour government*, pt III, pp. 108–9 (no. 244) and pp. 121–2 (no. 247), and for the last, CO 537/6773. See also R. Holland, *Britain and the revolt in Cyprus, 1954–1959* (Oxford, 1998), pp. 20–2, 66.

45 Simon C. Smith, 'Integration and disintegration: the attempted incorporation of Malta into the United Kingdom in the 1950s', *JICH*, vol. 35 (2007), p. 57 (minute, 10 March 1955), and Smith, ed., *Malta* (BDEEP, 2006), pp. xxxvi–xxxvii, and document nos. 5, 10–14, 35. JSB regarded responsibility for Malta as 'an utterly thankless task', and he thought the Maltese had 'wilfully aggravated' their problems by their Catholic refusal to control the alarming population growth (p. 32).

46 The National Archives, CO 554/808, minutes 14 and 25 September 1956; see also R. Rathbone, ed., *Ghana, 1941–1957* (BDEEP, 1992), pt II, pp. 291–6.

47 A.W.B. Simpson, *Human rights and the end of empire: Britain and the genesis of the European Convention* (Oxford, 2001, 2004), p. 855.

48 CO 537/632, and 1478, minutes, 17 and 18 May 1946.

49 BDEEP, *Labour government*, pt I, pp. 405–9, minutes, 11 and 25 February 1947; see also J. Kent, *The internationalization of colonialism: Britain, France and Black Africa, 1939–1956* (Oxford, 1992), pp. 209, 226, and *British imperial strategy and the origins of the Cold War, 1941–1949* (Leicester, 1993), pp. 132–9.

50 CO 554/801, minute, 15 December 1956.

51 CO 537/1523, minute, 9 July 1945.

52 Simpson, *Human rights and the end of empire*, pp. 340–2, 363, 426–7: CO 936/5, nos. 5 and 6, and CO 936/6, no. 2.

53 BDEEP, *The Conservative government*, pt I, p. 156 (no. 353), minute, 3 September 1964.

54 BDEEP, *The Conservative government*, pt I, Introduction, p. xl.
55 S.R. Ashton and W.R. Louis, eds., *East of Suez and the Commonwealth, 1964–1971* (BDEEP, 2004), pt II, pp. 101–2.
56 Madden and Darwin, eds., *Select documents*, vol. VIII, *The end of empire: dependencies since 1948*, pt I, *West Indies, British Honduras, Hong Kong, Fiji, Gambia, Gibraltar and the Falklands* (2000), pp. 535–6, 541–2, no. 170, minutes, 29 March 1949 and 15 February 1952. JSB thought the job of the governor of the Falklands little better than a mixture of 'old-fashioned squire and chairman of a rural district council' (quoted by Ashton, *East of Suez and the Commonwealth*, pt I, Introduction, p. cxxx, n. 72, from a minute, 25 May 1967).
57 Ashton and Louis, eds., *East of Suez and the Commonwealth*, pt III, p. 143, minute, 13 July 1967; but see the doubts expressed by Ged Martin, *Round Table: Commonwealth Journal of International Affairs*, vol. 95, no. 383 (January 2006), pp. 153–7, in a review of L. Freedman, *The official history of the Falklands Campaign* (2005), a work in which JSB is not mentioned.
58 JSB to the author, 27 January 1982.
59 JSB believed that this major memorandum was perceived as subversive and might well have been destroyed. It certainly took some tracking down, but was eventually found among the CO's United Nations 'secret' files, at CO 537/2057, no. 48, and is printed in BDEEP, *Labour government*, pt III, pp. 409–21 (no. 174); quoted in W.R. Louis and R.E. Robinson, 'The imperialism of decolonisation', *JICH*, vol. 22 (1994), pp. 466–7 – JSB's memo seems to provide stronger support for their 'American' thesis than their paper allows (see especially the quotation on p. 276 above).
60 For the controversy over Attlee's 'Mediterranean strategy', see BDEEP, *Labour government*, pt III, pp. 207–29; see also R.J Aldrich and J. Zametica, 'The rise and decline of a strategic concept: the Middle East, 1945–1951', in R.J. Aldrich, ed., *British intelligence, strategy and the Cold War, 1945–1951* (1992), pp. 236–74.
61 See n. 40 above, and BDEEP, *Labour government*, pt III, p. 84, minutes by JSB, 14 November and 17 December 1947, and pp. 90–1, minute by Trafford Smith, 17 November 1947.
62 Professor Kenneth Robinson in conversation with the author, 28 September 1990.
63 Simpson, *Human rights*, pp. 298, 342.
64 Mary Bennett in conversation with the author, 11 May 1992; Ralph Bennett to the author, 22 August 1990, 12 August 1992.
65 As a cultural concept, 'lower-middle class' is analytically slippery – 'even vaguer than most British social-class terminology' (Brian Harrison, *Seeking a role: the United Kingdom, 1951–1970* (New Oxford History of England, 2009), pp. 206–7). Nevertheless, it can be accepted as 'describing a contemporary reality', especially when seen from above, as here. A social group below the established middle class (and often providing services for it), respectable and traditional but narrow and localised in outlook, any aspirations to betterment were often scornfully observed by its social superiors: see Geoffrey Crossick, ed., *The lower middle class in Britain, 1870–1914*

(1977), pp. 9–60 ('The emergence of the lower middle class'). According to Peter Bailey, the lower middle class is mainly made up of clerks and shopworkers, socially and politically a 'fundamentally unheroic group', but culturally the closest we get to 'ordinary people': 'White collars, gray lives? The lower-middle-class revisited', *Journal of British Studies*, vol. 38 (1999), pp. 273–90. W.D. Rubinstein, 'Education and the social origins of British elites, 1880–1970', *Past and Present*, no. 112 (1986), pp. 163–207, does not give much help on the class issue in the civil service, because insufficiently precise on the 'lower-middle class' as a group (as opposed to what he calls the 'lower end' of the middle class), while 'higher' civil servants are not isolated from civil servants *en masse*. What does emerge, however, is that the situation changed rapidly from *c.*1970, when grammar school products began to rise rapidly.

66 Magdalene College Archives, H/FRS/Bennett, J.S., and Bennett, R.F. (1932–3). Salter was a Gurney-Salter, son of the official shorthand writer to Parliament, and educated at St Paul's School. He was not a historian of any particular distinction, but a valued teaching member of the Cambridge History Faculty. On his retirement as a university lecturer in 1952, at a dinner in his honour, his friend Prof. G.M. Trevelyan said, 'If you want to see a true English Liberal, look at Frank Salter. If you want to see a true English gentleman, look at Frank Salter. And then you will realise the profound historical truth that there is no difference between a true English Liberal and a true English gentleman' (oral tradition).

67 For class issues and values in the Colonial Office and the Colonial Service, see I.F. Nicolson and C.A. Hughes, 'A provenance of proconsuls: British colonial governors, 1900–1960', *JICH*, vol. 4 (1975), pp. 77–102; J.M. Lee, *Colonial development and good government, 1939–1964* (Oxford, 1967), pp. 2, 284–5; and A.H.M. Kirk-Greene, *Britain's imperial administrators, 1858–1966* (2000), esp. pp. 12–22, 290. In a discussion with Professor Mansergh in 1961 about hide-bound 'establishments' and institutional tensions, he told me about a CO permanent under-secretary who refused to acknowledge the secretary of state's 'good morning', adding that he, Mansergh, was 'glad to say the colonial secretary never gave up'. Being Mansergh, he would not reveal names, but the most likely are Sir George Gater (see above, pp. 277, 285), a Wykehamist through and through, and George Hall, the Labour minister from a Welsh elementary school.

68 Compare Ralph Bennett's outburst, 'Masters, professors, bishops: damn them all!', quoted in *Magdalene College Magazine*, no. 46 (2001–2), p. 16 (obituary).

69 Ralph Bennett to the author, 3 August 1990.

70 See, for example, his scathing remarks about R.J.D. Scott Fox (FO Middle East department, 1944–9, and later ambassador to Chile) that Scott Fox made no secret of his contempt for all 'colonial' peoples and 'is the kind of man who would always put the interests of diplomatic convenience first'; Scott Fox, he felt, was 'somewhat shaken' when JSB told him on the telephone that his paper on the ex-Italian colonies was 'incredibly muddled and inaccurate' (CO 537/2087, minute, 18 July 1947). JSB would have loved

James Hacker's aphorism 'The Foreign Office is a hotbed of cold feet', and the idea that the FO believed 'Our job is to get along with other countries. People have said a lot of unpleasant things about the Foreign Office but no one has *ever* accused us of patriotism' (J. Lynn and A. Jay, eds., *'Yes, prime minister': the diaries of James Hacker, MP* (1987), pp. 183, 226).

71 Mary Bennett to the author, 9 October 1992: 'it was all so glum and hopeless and made him so morose'. Gibraltar dogged him: it was in the Mediterranean department when JSB was there, and then transferred to the South Atlantic department when he had charge of that for the last six years of his service. In 1948 Attlee had flown a troublesome kite by asking that the Greek city-state model should be considered for it, amalgamating the city council and the legislature. Miss Fisher (well versed in ancient history) dismissed the idea, and JSB added that there was no useful parallel in the medieval city states, which were 'also sovereign, highly complex and not very good' (CO 91/536/4, minutes, 3 and 6 August 1948).

72 Retirement was to an extent moulded by the fact that Mary Bennett had become principal of St Hilda's College in Oxford (1965–80). He coached the boat for St Hilda's (all women), played the viol and stimulated music in the college, fussed over their cats, and researched into the obscurer bits of sixteenth- and seventeenth-century musicology and recusant history. It sounds rather eccentric, but his commitments were genuine. He developed a passion for English seventeenth-century consort music, and particularly for Gibbons. In 1977 he published an article which successfully established the main outlines of the biography of Richard Mico (c.1590–1661), a neglected composer but highly regarded in his own day. He edited some of his music, wrote the entry for the *(New) Grove Dictionary of Music and Musicians* (2001 edn, vol. XVI, pp. 601–2), published scholarly papers, and generally 'put Mico on the map' (Layton Ring, *The Independent*, 28 August 1990). JSB also published an article on Fr Thomas Whitbread, the most eminent ecclesiastical victim of the so-called Popish Plot, 1679, executed and beatified: 'Who was Fr Thomas Whitbread?', *Recusant History* (Catholic Record Society), vol. 16 (1982), pp. 91–8.

73 Witness Seminar, 'Decolonisation and the Colonial Office', 12 December 1988: see N. Owen, ed., in *Contemporary British History*, vol. 6 (1992), pp. 514–15. See also P. Hennessy, *Never again: Britain, 1945–1951* (1992), pp. 223–4, using the original transcript.

Part IV
Great men

10 Winston Churchill's first years in ministerial office, 1905–1911

[Why Churchill? There is, after all, no shortage of iconic figures in the history of the empire. My interest in him arose, unanticipated, out of my PhD research on the African policy of the Liberal government, 1905–9. On my very first day in the archives, sitting in the Round Room of the old Public Record Office in Chancery Lane, amid the medievalists studying their court rolls, I opened with due solemnity the volumes of the Transvaal correspondence files for December 1905, in their magnificent black-and-red bindings (CO 291/87 and 88). Almost the first interesting things I came across were memoranda and minutes initialled in red ink 'W.S.C.'. I was instantly hooked.

This chapter remixes material published as 'At the Colonial Office', in *Churchill: a profile* (ed. Peter Stansky, New York, 1973), and as a review article ('Winston Churchill before 1914') in the *Historical Journal*, vol. 12 (1969), on Randolph Churchill's official biography, *Winston S. Churchill*, vol. I, *Youth, 1874–1900*, vol. II, *Young statesman, 1901–1914* (1966, 1967). These articles were in turn based upon a lecture to the Historical Association (Cambridge Branch), on 22 January 1965; Churchill died two days later. Detailed comment on the biography is omitted here.]

Pen at the ready, Churchill sat down at his desk (as the Liberal government's parliamentary under-secretary of state) in the Colonial Office for the first time on 14 December 1905, and started to write comments on the files, determined to make his mark.

I

Within a couple of weeks he had completed his first state-paper. Modestly entitled 'A note upon the Transvaal Constitution as established by Letters Patent', it addressed the burning question of the hour, and it was designed to steer his superiors towards a decision in favour of granting responsible self-government.[1] And this is what he wrote:

The vital and fundamental issue is this: who is to govern the Transvaal . . . The question is grave . . . The late government have determined definitely to abandon

299

. . . one practical and defensible position, viz, Crown Colony Government . . .
When one crest line is abandoned it is necessary to retire to the next. Halting at
a 'half-way house' midway in the valley is fatal. What is the next defensible position? I submit that it will not now be possible to deny the Transvaal a representative Assembly with an Executive responsible thereto.

He pointed out that responsible government would be demanded with
'ever increasing vehemence', while the metropolitan government would
already have surrendered all that was necessary to enable the rest to be
extorted:

In the end, which may come quite soon, the Lyttelton Constitution will be recognised as unworkable, and we, or our successors, will be forced to concede full
responsible self-government. The control of events will then have largely passed
from our hands. We may not be able, without the employment of force, to prescribe the electoral basis of the new Constitution, or even to reserve the functions
necessary to the maintenance of public order and the King's authority. What we
might have given with courage and distinction, both at home and in South Africa,
upon our own terms, in the hour of our strength, will be jerked and twisted from
our hands – without grace of any kind – not perhaps without humiliation – at a
time when the government may be greatly weakened, and upon terms in the settlement of which we shall have only a nominal influence.

This was a classic statement of the primary principle in political conduct
for the Victorian and Edwardian ruling elite, the principle of timely
concession to retain an ultimate control. Churchill regarded it as indispensable that Britain should itself prescribe the basis of the responsible
constitution whenever it did come, 'so to shape our policy as to keep the
British party well together, and so to frame the Constitution as to give it
a fair chance of securing the balance of power'.

But Mr Lyttelton's proposals will, if carried out, have the effect, first of dividing
the British party . . . into Responsibles and Progressives, secondly, of putting
the Transvaal Government into a large minority, and thirdly, converting the
Legislative Assembly into a kind of constituent body, which will begin by agitat-
ing the demand for responsible government, and very possibly proceed to dictate
its exact basis. In all this the *beau rôle* is assigned to the Boers, who, in their exertions for responsible government, are admittedly voicing the opinions of men
outside their own party organisation, and appear as the champions of the Colony
as a whole; while the Imperial Government can only fall back to that foundation
of mere force from which we have laboriously endeavoured to raise it.

The paper combines a freshness of presentation with a firm grasp of
purely British interests. Military metaphor, which Churchill frequently
used for major matters, was seldom employed more appositely than in
the opening passage here, or made so integral to the argument. The
ruthless logic, the foresight, the polished phrases, the arresting words

(jerked, twisted, humiliation), the favourite thematic words (courage, grace) – all these features stamp it unmistakably as a memorable piece of Churchilliana. Here is Churchill at his best, expressing the thoughts of older colleagues better than they could themselves. This superlative passage reads like the work of the years when he was an elder statesman, yet it was written when he was a mere under-secretary who had held political office for only three weeks.

After this impressive ministerial debut, which received a great deal of praise, an emboldened Churchill turned his attention in particular to Nigeria. He launched an attack on Lord Lugard's methods in the north: 'Nigeria seems to be a sort of sultry Russia,' British responsibilities were 'serious, indefinite and ever-expanding' – and ought to be diminished, or at least re-examined:

I am inclined to the opinion that we should withdraw from a very large portion of the territories which we now occupy nominally, but really disturb without governing; and that we should concentrate our resources upon the railway and economic development of the more settled and accessible riparian or maritime regions . . . I see no reason why our occupation should be made immediately effective up to the French frontier line; or why these savage tribes should not be allowed to eat each other without restraint, until some much more suitable opportunity than the present shall arise for 'pacifying' them. At present we are simply drifting along upon the current of military enterprise and administrative ambition.[2]

Lugard played into his hands when on 31 December 1905 the Munshi, the only large and important grouping which had never been 'pacified', burned down the Niger Company's station at Abinsi, and the River Benué was closed to navigation. Lugard proposed reprisals and a punitive expedition. Churchill was perturbed:

We are about to be committed to operations of indefinite character and considerable extent without any substantial information . . .

Of course, if the peace and order of the Colony depends on a vigorous offensive we must support him with all our hearts. But the chronic bloodshed which stains the West African seasons is odious and disquieting. Moreover the whole enterprise is liable to be misrepresented by persons unacquainted with Imperial terminology as the murdering of natives and stealing of their lands. HMG seems to have only a nominal control over these grave matters, and yet has to bear the direct responsibility. I do not think we ought to enter upon these expeditions lightly or as a matter of course.[3]

These vigorous and scathing minutes are the kind of thing ministers often tend to write on taking office, hoping iconoclasm will get them noticed, a practice which tends to diminish with experience. The secretary of state, Lord Elgin, put things into perspective: of course they must be consulted and given full information, but 'we engaged in the game of grab in the African continent and we cannot escape the consequences, of which this is one'. But he agreed it would be better to make punitive measures less aggressive.

Policies for South Africa and for Nigeria were prominent issues, and Churchill contributed cogently to the discussion. A few months later, however, and he was penning something rather different. It is the third piece of his writing I want to analyse.

After a usurpation of twenty years' duration, Sekgoma had been removed from the Batawana chieftainship in Ngamiland, Bechuanaland. His suspension from office was in accordance with the wishes of the great majority of the people, among whom he had the reputation of being a bad character, whom they wished to replace by the legitimate chief Mathibi, who was now twenty-four. As Sekgoma was not taking his deprivation quietly, he was put into detention. The high commissioner, Lord Selborne, thought that he should be deported to avoid a general disturbance. Only Churchill saw fit to question this recommendation, and he did so fiercely:

We cannot imprison him or deport him without flat violation of every solid principle of British justice. As at present advised I could not undertake even to attempt a defence of the lawless deportation of an innocent man upon an informal *lettre de cachet*. If we are going to embark on this sort of law-breaking and autocratic action, where are we going to stop? What kind of injustice is there that would not be covered by precedents of this kind? If we are going to take men who have committed no crime, and had no trial, and condemn them to life-long imprisonment and exile in the name of 'State policy' why stop there? Why not poison Sekgoma by some painless drug? No argument, that will justify his deportation to the Seychelles, will not also sustain his removal to a more sultry clime. If we are to employ medieval processes, at least let us show medieval courage and thoroughness. Think of the expense that would be saved. A dose of laudanum, costing at the outside five shillings, is all that is required. There would be no cost of maintenance, no charges for transportation, no legal difficulties, no need to apply to the Portuguese, no fear of the habeas corpus. Without the smallest worry or expense the peace of the Protectorate would be secured, and a 'dangerous character' obnoxious to the Government, removed.

If however, as I apprehend, Secretary of State would be averse to this procedure, the next best thing is to obey the law, and to act with ordinary morality, however inconvenient.

The secretary of state was very cross. He did not think it necessary to carry the argument so far as a five-shilling dose of laudanum – so Elgin's rejoinder begins. He did not mince his words. 'This man is a savage – and is said to be contemplating proceedings in defiance of all law to disturb the peace.' As he saw it, the measures that had only narrowly

Plate 10.1 'An Elgin Marble'. 'Bas-relief in the manner of the Parthenon Frieze (commonly called the Elgin Marbles). Design attributed to Mr W-nst-n Ch-rch-ll.' *Punch* cartoon by Bernard Partridge, 25 April 1906. Was Churchill taking over the Colonial Office from Lord Elgin?

averted fighting had resulted inevitably in Sekgoma's detention. Elgin ended on a militant note; he, at any rate, was ready to take his share of the responsibility for the preservation of peace. This responsibility was, of course, to a Liberal, the primary function of African government.[4]

This minute on Sekgoma reflects many of Churchill's characteristics. It is audacious in the extreme. Indeed, it is doubtful whether there could be found anywhere in the history of British government a more audacious minute than this by a mere under-secretary of state. Moreover it reduces the argument to absurdity. On the other hand, it shows an awareness of the necessity of safeguarding the fundamental principles of British life. It is a splendidly written piece of prose. It could scarcely have been more carefully prepared if it had been a draft for a major public speech, as in fact so many of Churchill's minutes were. It has the characteristic and favourite words: 'solid', 'courage', 'sultry'. And it has the typical flash of impish humour – hell, the more sultry clime. Yet all this effort and brilliance had gone into an ephemeral issue of no intrinsic importance, at least at that date, concerning an insignificant and unpopular usurping chief; into an issue that was properly decided on the spot.

No other minister, let alone an official, would have questioned whether Sekgoma ought even to be in detention, or have seized upon the case in order to squeeze out of it issues of major principle. It is a teasing minute. The humour and the irony call its seriousness into question. It is, in this sense, irresponsible. Nobody ever contrived to get so much fun out of official business as Churchill.

It was decided to detain Sekgoma for such period as would enable the young Mathibi to establish his position completely. Elgin thought that Sekgoma could be more easily managed in a detention compound in the protectorate; setting him free would certainly result in the 'calamity of a breach of the peace'. He accepted Churchill's representations so far as to tell Selborne that Sekgoma's present detention was an act of state for which no actual legal authority existed, and so a special proclamation was issued, indemnifying the officers who had detained him. Elgin also agreed to veto deportation, as too troublesome, and objectionable in principle. Churchill, finally, succeeded in adding to the despatch the observation that Sekgoma had not been formally condemned and that his power to disturb the peace might prove transitory.

II

Churchill at the Colonial Office presents a curious combination of magisterial statesman and mischievous schoolboy. The Pitt in him jostled with the Puck in him. He was just as capable of producing a rash and unrealistic suggestion as he was of producing a reasonable and acute one.[5] Indeed, they could even be yoked together. To state that Southern Rhodesia 'with its British population may ultimately be the weight which swings the balance in South Africa decisively on the side of the British Crown' showed geopolitical insight. But to suggest that such an outcome could be forwarded by government investment in support of General Booth's scheme of Salvation Army colonisation was surely a case of romantic rhetoric overcoming common-sense. Colonial Office officials had rejected the scheme with scorn, but Churchill hit back:

General Booth is the most practical idealist the world can show today. He can exert forces not at the command of ordinary commercial agencies. The difficulties of the wilderness, its loneliness and inaccessibility are not perhaps to be surmounted without the aid of some super-economic influence. I should be very sorry to see this plan shrivel into a polite official reply.[6]

In deference to Churchill, politely positive enquiries were in fact made. But could anything be more different than Churchill's first memorandum on the Transvaal, and this minute on the Rhodesian scheme? In the case of Booth, Churchill's talents were lavished ineffectually upon magnifying out of all proportion the importance of a very vague and eccentric proposal. In the case of the Transvaal constitution, his gifts were exercised on a matter of acknowledged high policy, with considerable effect. And yet he seemed to treat the two issues as equally deserving of attention, at least in the sense of devoting equally brilliant rhetoric to them. His eagerness to support Booth's scheme suggests that he was not always very good at distinguishing between what was practical politics and what was not.

His romantic support of Booth, or of Sekgoma, also suggests that he had not mastered the art of coming to terms with the mundane, repetitive routines of day-to-day human life. He was hardly the man for the humdrum round of ministerial duties. Churchill exaggerated the importance of everything he touched. Every speck on the horizon, he assumed, would turn out to be a Cunarder, not a cockleshell. As a result of historical instincts and histrionic tendencies, he treated too many issues indiscriminately as matters of fundamental concern or historic significance. If important issues did not exist he would invent them. Not even the work of one government department could satisfy his voracious appetite for involvement. He was as fruitful in producing ideas for other departments as he was for the one to which he had been allocated. He was congenitally incapable of relaxing, even on holiday abroad. His power of concentration amounted almost to obsession.

As under-secretary of state at the Colonial Office he was able to make a definite contribution to the work of the department. Not all his ideas were equally valuable, and his recommendations had always to pass the acid test of Elgin's canny common-sense and varied experience. Occasionally he seemed to see the right course of action more quickly and more clearly than others. On the parliamentary side of his duties, he was extraordinarily good at anticipating and representing the House of Commons view, even if he sometimes cleverly enlisted it upon his own side to fight a private battle. Overall, three aspects of his achievement may be selected as standing out.

First, there is his gift for writing arresting minutes and for expounding government policy effectively in Parliament. His preoccupation with phrase-making left behind it a host of attractive aphorisms enlivening the ponderous archives of government. Some of the most trenchant and forceful writing of his life was done in these early minutes and memoranda. His skill and eloquence in the presentation and defence of ministerial policy in the House of Commons brought his talents in this direction before a much wider audience.

Secondly, despite his subordinate position, Churchill was able, by the sheer power of his mind and his imagination, and by the force and persistence of his rhetoric, to take a real part in the formulation of policy. He played his part in the Transvaal settlement, the major work of the Liberal government in the Edwardian empire. He provided much of the written analysis and argument upon which the Cabinet decisions were based and justified. He was himself the originator of specific points of policy, such as the establishment of the Land Settlement Board. His official biographer is, however, wrong to claim that he was 'the prime mover behind the new Transvaal constitution'.[7]

Thirdly, he had a generous and sensitive, if highly paternalistic, sympathy for subject peoples, and a determination to see that justice was done to humble individuals throughout the empire. He had this sympathy to a degree that was rather rare among British administrators, and even politicians, at this time. Human juices must be injected into Olympian mandarins. By vigilant reading of routine official files he frequently uncovered what he thought were 'flat' or 'shocking' violations of the elementary principles of law and justice. He insisted that the principles of justice, and the safeguards of judicial procedure, should be 'rigidly, punctiliously and pedantically' followed.

He insisted, too, on questioning the Colonial Office assumption that officials were always in the right when complaints were made against government by Africans or, as was more probable, by Asians. He campaigned for an earnest effort to understand the feelings of subject peoples in being ruled by alien administrators, 'to try to measure the weight of the burden they bear'. The business of a public officer, he maintained, was to serve the people he ruled. The officer must not forget that he was as much their servant, however imposing his title, as any manufacturer or tradesman was the servant of his customers. It was a salutary but unpopular reminder. Churchill supported Hofmeyr's[8] suggestion that British civil servants in South Africa should learn Dutch, for if the people 'like to talk to him in Volapük, he must learn Volapük. If they have a weakness for Sanskrit [*sic*], it must become his study. By humouring them, and understanding them, he will be able very often to make their wishes and their welfare coincide.' At the same time he was also a watchful

Plate 10.2 Minutes by Churchill and Lord Elgin on a draft reply to a parliamentary question relating to the South African Constabulary in the Transvaal, June 1907 (CO 291/121, no.19519). Although broadly in agreement on the main outlines of policy, Elgin and Churchill had several minor disagreements. Elgin, whose minute appears in the right-hand margin, has drawn a line through the most important part of Churchill's suggested reply dealing with the reduction of the Constabulary. Churchill signs himself 'WSC' and Elgin as 'E'.

Copy

While the Imperial troops in South Africa are maintained at their present strength, it is obvious that no large volunteer force equipped with artillery equipped as the hon. member suggest with artillery is needed for the maintenance of peace & order; or Real notice of the withdrawal of the Imperial troops will be given and & it is not proposed that any such force should be organised.

In regard to the second part of the question of the hon. member, I must refer him to the answer given by me to the hon. memb. for Preston on June 3. & in regard to the last part of the question — I am not yet able to say that namely that I understand that reductions will be made in the Constabulary; but I should expect that they would be substantial reductions are certainly to be expected I think & & hoped.

ber. 5. 6

I do not think it could be fair to the hon. gent. to forestall the opinion which they may come to with regard to Constabulary &c—

the Transvaal Govt. have not so far as I am aware, as yet given any intimation of the reduction of the Constabulary champion of the interests of the Colonial Service, more narrowly considered. He defeated the threat to make marriage a disqualification for candidates proposing to enter the civil service in Ceylon.[9]

In a sense, it could be argued that Churchill's interest in the empire was never more than circumstantial and tangential. L.S. Amery once observed that Churchill's patriotism had always been for England, rather than the empire or Commonwealth.[10] There is a good deal of truth in this. It could hardly be claimed that Churchill's Colonial Office days left an indelible mark on all his future political development. His interest in the empire never absorbed him entirely at the Colonial Office, and it may indeed have been very nearly exhausted by it. At any rate, he had already begun to devote much thought to domestic problems. When he reflected upon the 'fine homogeneous' majority conferred by the electoral victory of 1906 he dwelt chiefly upon its significance for domestic legislation: 'I do not suppose we are likely to attain the millennium; but a few Big Acts by way of instalment ought certainly to be put on the Statute Book.'[11]

A speech at Glasgow on 11 October 1906 marks his emergence as a social reformer. Starting from the proposition that 'the whole tendency of civilisation' was towards the 'multiplication of the collective functions of society', he wished to see 'the State embark on various novel and adventurous experiments', increasingly assuming the position of 'the reserve employer of labour'. He much regretted that they had not got the railways in state hands. He looked forward to the 'universal establishment of minimum standards of life and labour'. The state must mitigate the consequences of failure in the struggle for existence and 'spread a net over the abyss'.[12]

These thoughts were always at the back of his mind while he was at the Colonial Office. In this post, Churchill was much more influenced by the Webbs and Lloyd George, and their schemes for domestic change, than he was by any of the theorists of empire.

In October and November 1909 Churchill spoke to Wilfrid Blunt about the empire, though his chief interest of the moment was the condition and welfare of the poor in England. According to Blunt, he upheld an 'optimistic Liberal Imperialism where the British Empire was to be maintained in part by concession, in part by force, and the constant invention of new scientific forces to deal with the growing difficulties of Imperial rule'. Moreover: 'We get no advantage from it and it is a lot of bother. The only thing one can say for it is it is justified if it is undertaken in an altruistic spirit for the good of the subject races.' Blunt formed the impression that it was 'the vanity of Empire that affects him more than the supposed profit or the necessities of trade, which he repudiates'.[13] At the very least, this was probably true at this time.

III

Churchill left the Colonial Office in April 1908, when Asquith appointed him president of the Board of Trade. Then he was home secretary from February 1910, and first lord of the Admiralty from September 1911. He made remarkable contributions to the work of all these major departments. When war broke out in 1914 he was still just under forty. Some of the most interesting problems about his early political career raise the following questions, much debated by his contemporaries: how far was he affected by military modes of thought? Why – and how deeply – did he become a social reformer? Why did the Liberal Party recoil from clasping him to its bosom? And to what extent is it true that phrase-making mattered to him more almost than anything else?

'The whole spirit of his politics', wrote an acute observer in 1908, 'is military. It is impossible to think of him except in terms of actual warfare. The smell of powder is about his path.'[14] Halévy agreed: Churchill became an ultra-liberal, but 'he remained a soldier at heart'.[15] On the other hand, Lord Eustace Percy felt that although 'his imagination was most easily moved by the idea of a display of power', it was untrue to speak of Churchill as a natural militarist.[16]

Churchill had entered Sandhurst in 1893. By 1895 he decided that 'the more I see of soldiering the more I like it, but the more I feel convinced that it is not my *métier*'. He appears to have valued military experience mainly as giving him a chance to strengthen his hand for the political game by providing him with the money and fame to enter politics with aplomb. Several times before 1900 he declared his ambition to become prime minister. All his life he regarded military service as an essential ingredient of a political career. In November 1896 he felt that two years in Egypt, with a campaign thrown in, would qualify him 'to be allowed to beat my sword into a paper cutter and my sabretache into an election address'. From India in August 1897 he wrote:

It might not have been worth my while, who am really no soldier, to risk so many fair chances on a war which can only help me directly in a profession I mean to discard. But I have considered everything and I feel that the fact of having seen service with British troops while still a young man must give me more weight politically.[17]

In July 1898 he wrote to Lord Salisbury:

I am vy anxious to go to Egypt and to proceed to Khartoum with the Expedition. It is not my intention, under any circumstances to stay in the army long. I want to go, first, because the recapture of Khartoum will be a historic event: second, because I can, I anticipate, write a book about it which from a monetary, as well as from other points of view, will be useful to me.[18]

He left the army in 1899 and took up journalism. Later, as a politician – he entered parliament in 1901 – Churchill loved military metaphor, but it did not stop at that. The recollection of army methods occasionally influenced policy and procedure. An example may be taken from his Home Office days. In connection with his attempts to ameliorate the punishment of juvenile delinquents, he proposed to introduce a kind of disciplinary probation, in which some form of 'penal drill', or physical training, 'at once highly salutary and extremely disagreeable', would figure prominently; he believed there was no better cure for civil rowdyism than military drill.[19] His conduct of the Tonypandy episode was in fact restrained, but during the railway strike of 1911 he was observed to be in an excited state of mind, having, C.F.G. Masterman thought, 'rather a whiff-of-grapeshot attitude towards these matters'. He gave the impression of calling in troops prematurely and giving them wide discretionary powers; he appeared intensely to relish mapping the country, directing emergency operations, and issuing rather wild bulletins which exasperated the trade unions. When Lloyd George negotiated a settlement of the strike, Churchill seemed almost disappointed.[20] As First Lord of the Admiralty he spent a great deal of time afloat in the official yacht *Enchantress*, making voyages of inspection and study. John Morley shook his head over 'the splendid *condottiere* at the Admiralty'. Churchill was undeniably fascinated by war and the disposition of great fleets and armies. He never missed an opportunity to visit big army manœuvres, German in 1906 and 1909, French in 1907, English in 1908 and 1910. He retained an active interest in the Yeomanry, and in 1909 hankered after 'some practice in the handling of large forces'. But during the German manœuvres of 1909 he wrote to his wife, 'Much as war attracts me & fascinates my mind with its tremendous situations – I feel more deeply every year – & can measure the feeling here in the midst of arms – what vile & wicked folly & barbarism it all is.' A letter written at midnight on 28 July 1914 also brings out his conflicting thoughts: 'Everything tends towards catastrophe & collapse. I am interested, geared up & happy. Is it not horrible to be built like that? The preparations have a hideous fascination for me. I pray to God to forgive me for such fearful moods of levity. Yet I wd do my best for peace, & nothing wd induce me wrongfully to strike the blow.'[21] We may, therefore, reasonably suppose that while Churchill seemed capable of fusing, or confusing, political and military ideals, he was no warmonger. Whether or not the 'whiff of grapeshot' hung about him is another question.

Was he an authentic social reformer? His achievements were immense, including the establishment of labour exchanges, unemployment insurance, and trade boards to fix minimum rates of pay in sweated industries.

His radicalism, however, was possibly more the result of pugnacity than conviction. Lady Asquith thought that his reform utterances rang false, that 'he was – quite unconsciously – wearing fancy dress, that he was not himself'. His social reforming impulse certainly proved to be a passing phase and not an inherent passion. Why did he take it up? It may be observed that Churchill could not have been courting popularity by responding to pressures from below, since working-class demand for a 'welfare state' was almost non-existent in Edwardian England. But there was a proven administrative necessity for reform, and Churchill, under the influence of Bismarckian example, and the ideas of Lloyd George, the Webbs, and possibly W.S. Blunt, responded with constructive measures to remedy what he called 'the patent inadequacy of existing social machinery'. A clue to Churchill's motive is that his reform achievements were rooted and grounded in paternalism, and in the ulterior motive which goes with it. Social reform to him was not an end in itself; not to recognise this could make it seem false. All Churchill's speeches upon social reform were full of concern for the stability of society, of anxiety about state resources of 'inestimable advantage running thriftlessly to waste'.[22] As early as 1898 Churchill declared: 'To keep our Empire we must have a free people, an educated and well fed people. That is why we are in favour of social reform.' In 1901, after reading Seebohm Rowntree's report on urban poverty, he could 'see little glory in an Empire which can rule the waves and is unable to flush its sewers', and he urged parliament to take note of the fact that the degraded condition of the poor was 'a serious hindrance to recruiting' for the army and navy.[23] In 1908 he wrote to Asquith of his consciousness that Germany was organised not only for war but for peace, while Britain was 'organized for nothing except party politics and even in that we are not as well organized as the United States of America'. Social reforms would benefit the state and fortify the party.[24] In 1909 he said that without big social changes he could see nothing ahead but 'savage strife between class and class, and [England's] increasing disorganization with the increasing waste of human strength and human virtue'. The scion of Blenheim, with in some ways an almost eighteenth-century attitude to social problems, was appalled by the fact that 'the whole of our educational system . . . stops short at the age of 14', just when boys and girls 'ought to receive training and discipline to make them good craftsmen and careful housekeepers'. He believed that up to the age of eighteen every boy and girl, 'as in the old days of apprenticeship', should be learning a trade as well as earning a living.[25]

There was, he argued, only one foundation for the stability of society and empire: 'a healthy family life for all'. If children were under-fed, the family bread-winner unemployed and uninsured, and homes broken up, it was 'the stamina, the virtue, the safety and honour of the British race that are being squandered'. According to his analysis, so narrow was the margin upon which even the industrious and respectable working-class family relied, that when sickness or unemployment came knocking at the door, the family might become 'scattered on the high-roads, in the casual wards, in the public houses and prisons of the country. No one can measure the suffering to individuals which this process causes. No one can measure the futile, unnecessary loss which the State incurs.' The removal of preventable misery would, he declared, increase the stability of society, and remove the 'gnawing anxiety of suspense' about its future. For the seeds of imperial ruin and national decay were, he thought, at home, in

the unnatural gap between rich and poor, the divorce of the people from the land, the want of proper discipline and training in our youth, the exploitation of boy labour, the physical degeneration which seems to follow so swiftly on civilized poverty, the awful jumble of an obsolete Poor Law, the horrid havoc of the liquor traffic, the constant insecurity in the means of subsistence and employment which breaks the heart of many a sober, hard-working man, the absence of any established minimum standard of life and comfort among the workers, and, at the other end, the swift increase of vulgar, joyless luxury – here are the enemies of Britain. Beware lest they shatter the foundations of her power.[26]

It seems clear, then, that although Churchill's innate sense of compassion was fully aroused, he became a social reformer primarily from concern about the power of the state to maintain Britain's world position and effectiveness. For precisely the same reason he later took up Irish grievances, to bring an end to 'hatreds which disturb the foundations of the State', and also seamen's grievances, to check the spread of Syndicalism in the navy.[27]

How completely did social problems absorb his interest between 1908 and 1911? He deplored the controversy over the House of Lords as 'mere politics', distracting attention from 'boy prisoners, truck, the feeble-minded . . .'[28] As late as May 1911 he declared that there was no proposal in the field of politics about which he cared more than the great insurance scheme.[29] Yet at the Board of Trade he wrote memoranda on many topics falling outside the concern of his department: on the army estimates and on British military needs in June 1908; on South African unification in January 1909; on the Suez Canal in October 1909; on the financial difficulties of German naval expansion in November 1909; and on the total abolition of the House of Lords in February 1910.[30]

Nevertheless, whatever his motives and whatever his concurrent interests, there is little doubt that Churchill should have credit at least equal with Lloyd George for the social welfare measures of the Liberal government in this period. He may legitimately be regarded as one of the main founding fathers of the welfare state. One of the reasons why this has not been fully recognised is that Churchill did not want to upstage Lloyd George. He never claimed to have been more than a lieutenant playing a minor part, but, as Halévy recognised, he was an advanced social reformer in his own right. Despite the fact that his speeches some-times merely echoed what Lloyd George had already said, he also added a good deal, and with regard to railway nationalisation and afforesta-tion schemes, Lloyd George possibly picked up something from him. Furthermore, Churchill devised unemployment insurance before Lloyd George really turned his own mind to insurance legislation. Churchill insisted on holding back his unemployment scheme until Lloyd George was ready with health insurance, so that the two could be presented together. This had the effect of minimising Churchill's contribution. Again, Churchill had a much more highly developed ability to diagnose the state of English society and the problems confronting it. And he sug-gested solutions and plans of modernisation which were more compre-hensive than anything thought of by Lloyd George.

The comprehensiveness of his social vision and programme of reform is not adequately brought out in the official biography. It was, after all, Churchill who said, in 1908, that the aged had been rescued from the Poor Law by old age pensions, but

we have yet to rescue the children; we have yet to distinguish effectively between the *bona fide* unemployed workman and the mere loafer and vagrant; we have yet to transfer the sick, the inebriate, the feeble-minded, and the totally demor-alized to authorities specially concerned in their management and care . . . We ought to be able to set up a complete ladder, an unbroken bridge or causeway, as it were, along which the whole body of the people may move with a certain assured measure of security and safety against hazards and misfortunes . . . a large, coherent plan.[31]

In January 1909, he envisaged a 'comprehensive, interdependent scheme of social organisation', to be realised through 'a massive series of leg-islative proposals and administrative acts'.[32] If he had to sum up the immediate future of democratic politics in a single comprehensive word, he would say 'insurance' – insurance from dangers abroad and from dangers at home.[33] In the highly revealing peroration to his speech on the famous 1909 budget, he declared:

We are not going to measure the strength of Great Powers only in their material forces. We think that the security and the predominance of our country depends upon the maintenance of the vigour and health of its population, just as its true glory will always be found in the happiness of its cottage homes. We believe that if Great Britain is to remain great and famous in the world we cannot allow the present social and industrial disorders, with their profound physical and moral reaction, to continue unabated and unchecked. We propose to you a financial system; we also unfold a policy of social reorganization which will demand sacrifice from all classes, but which will give security to all classes. By its means we shall be able notably to control some of the most wasteful processes at work in our social life; and without it . . . our country will remain exposed to some fatal dangers against which fleets and armies are of no avail.

Churchill even supported Lloyd George's proposals for a land tax with an attack on the 'unreformed and vicious system' of unearned increment on land.[34] He repeatedly aired not only his view that 'the immediate future of British railways . . . depends upon amalgamation', but his envy of 'the splendid possession of the state railways by the German government'.[35] He circulated a paper on mental health to the Cabinet in 1909.[36]

Why, notwithstanding such intelligent good works, did he not commend himself more completely to the Liberal Party establishment? His official biographer does not give us many suggestions, or many of the opinions entertained about Churchill by his colleagues, but we know that the majority of Liberal leaders were lukewarm about these social reforms. They were, perhaps, not unmindful of Rosebery's warning that if some members of the Liberal Party committed it to permanent hostility to property in all its forms, the party would be squeezed out between socialism and conservatism. At any rate, they believed that Churchill and Lloyd George were running too fast and too far ahead of the main body of sober Liberals, and were thus responsible for the government's losing votes in elections. Asquith sometimes felt inclined summarily to cashier them both. There was considerable opposition within the Cabinet to unemployment insurance. Lewis Harcourt in 1910 believed some of Churchill's speeches to have done the party much harm, 'even with the advanced men of the *lower* middle class'.[37] Furthermore, Churchill's conduct in the railway strike focused attention on several of his faults. We might also add that at Cabinet meetings he could be a nuisance: at least one of his colleagues found him 'as long-winded as he was persistent'.[38] Asquith's critical judgment in 1915 was pertinent:

It is a pity that Winston hasn't a better sense of proportion, and also a larger endowment of the instinct of loyalty . . . I am really fond of him, but I regard his future with many misgivings . . . He will never get to the top in English politics, with all his wonderful gifts; to speak with the tongue of men and angels, and to spend laborious days and nights in administration, is no good if a man does not inspire trust.[39]

Here we have the explanation of the precariousness of Churchill's position. He was thought to be deficient in discrimination and loyalty, and he was not trusted. His biographer-son gives an illuminating account of how an attack on Lord Milner in 1906 did his reputation and popularity immense damage. Attention might also be drawn to the way in which his less than complete loyalty to Lord Elgin, his departmental chief at the Colonial Office, upset the inner ring of the political elite. He had an unhappy gift for putting people's backs up by an apparently gratuitous offensiveness of manner. He also seemed to lack both consistency and stability, as well as sensitivity to the feelings of others. He loved the limelight too much, and would not suppress a streak of levity and playfulness. He was unduly obstinate and aggressive in argument. He was not generally credited with acting from either conviction or principle.[40]

The essential journalism of some of his phrase-making also added to his unpopularity. Did his facility in this direction amount to an obsession? How did it influence his policies? Some of his friends in 1908 feared that his tendency to see first the rhetorical potentialities of any policy was beginning to get out of hand. In any case, since Churchill was proud to have spent half his life earning a living by dealing in words, his craftsmanship in the manipulation of language calls for analysis. One of the disappointments of the official biography is its reluctance to examine Churchill's use of English, or even sufficiently to provide the kind of evidence from which deductions could be made. His love of verbal play for its own sake is barely indicated. Some of this word-juggling was pretty weak; one example must suffice here. It did not, perhaps, specially illuminate Lloyd George's Port of London Authority Bill to say that without it, the docks, 'which have already been called obsolescent, will have to be allowed to obsolesce into obsoleteness'. Some of his favourite words and phrases do not emerge often enough to permit the reader to get the flavour of his language – grace, courage, generous, dark, millions, horrible, vicious, solid, sombre, sullen, squalid, abyss, minimum standard. Why cut out from a letter to Asquith about social reform the splendidly characteristic sentence: 'how much better to fall in such noble efforts than to perish by slow paralysis or windy agitation'.[41] It would be worth stressing the similarity of the language he used successively about the South African problem, the House of Lords problem, the Irish problem, and finally the Hitler problem. We can learn something about Churchill simply from the difficulty of ascribing context accurately to many passages of his speeches. Consider, for instance, the following utterance:

We base our hopes for the future on our faith in the wisdom and genius of the British people, and on the power which that people have always shown to rise to the height of great consequences and to defend against invasion and insult the primary rights and freedoms of their race.

This was not 1940, but 1909; the invasion was not by Hitler, but by the House of Lords, who had rejected Lloyd George's budget.[42] As he moved from one government department to another, Churchill took with him, not only his private secretary Eddie Marsh but, as it were, his phrase-book, from which well-tried word patterns were revised to meet new situations. This process probably explains the ease and readiness with which the Second World War rhetoric flowed. Its most famous word patterns had been polished and perfected through thirty-five years of refurbishing. Consider, for example, the pre-1914 genesis of 'Never in the field of human conflict was so much owed by so many to so few' (20 August 1940):

Never before were there so many people in England, and never before have they had so much to eat.   (1899, during Oldham by-election)[43]

I do not think it is very encouraging that we should have spent so much money upon the settlement of so few.
(April 1906, on land settlement in South Africa)[44]

Never before in Colonial experience has a Council been granted where the number of settlers is so few.
(November 1907, on the Legislative Council for Kenya)[45]

. . . nowhere else in the world could so enormous a mass of water be held up by so little masonry.   (1908, on a dam at Ripon Falls across the Victoria Nile)[46]

Never before has so little been asked and never before have so many people asked for it.   (1910, on Irish demands for Home Rule)[47]

One thing at least is clear. There were *two* outstanding periods in Winston Churchill's political career: we must take account of the importance and creativity of his work and ideas not only between 1940 and 1945, but also between 1905 and 1911. They are crucial to understanding him. Moreover, they suggest strongly that Churchill's commitment to empire in the total political scheme of things might not be as central as is often assumed.

Notes

1 CO 879/91, Confidential Print, African (S) 804, 'A note upon the Transvaal Constitution as established by Letters Patent', by Winston Spencer Churchill (WSC), 2 January 1906.
2 CO 520/39, no. 6993, minute by WSC, 17 May 1906.
3 CO 446/52, no. 5712, minute by WSC, 24 February 1906, partly quoted in M. Perham, *Lugard*, vol. II, *The years of authority, 1898–1945* (1960), pp. 247–61, at pp. 248–9.

4 CO 417/434, no. 38258, minutes 23 October 1906, and telegram, secretary of state to Lord Selborne, 31 October, and despatch, 10 November 1906. WSC's minute is quoted at length from RH, *Elgin and Churchill at the Colonial Office* (1968) (p. 492), by Martin Gilbert in *Churchill's political philosophy* (Oxford, 1981), pp. 40–2, without acknowledgement.

5 Lucy Masterman, *C.F.G. Masterman, a biography* (1934), p. 97: 'he is just an extraordinarily gifted boy, with genius and astonishing energy'; A.G. Gardiner, *Prophets, priests and kings* (1908), 'Winston Churchill', pp. 104–11: 'He has the curiosity and animation of a child in fairyland' (p. 106). See also Violet Bonham Carter, *Winston Churchill as I knew him* (1965), p. 20.

6 CO 417/434, no. 16276, minute by WSC, 17 May 1906.

7 Randolph Churchill, *Winston S. Churchill*, vol. II, *1901–1914* (1967), p. 153.

8 CO 48/592, no. 23907, 29 July 1907. Jan Hofmeyr was leader of the Afrikaner Bond.

9 CO 54/699, minute, 12 February 1906: 'The cadets must continue to solve the riddle of life for themselves.'

10 L.S. Amery, *My political life*, vol. I, *1896–1914* (1953), p. 196.

11 Sir Charles Dilke Papers, British Library Add. Mss 43877, WSC to Dilke, 24 January 1906.

12 WSC, *Liberalism and the social problem: speeches, 1906–1909* (1909), pp. 75–82, 11 October 1906 (speech in Glasgow on 'Liberalism and socialism').

13 W.S. Blunt, *My diaries: part 2, 1900–1914* (1920), pp. 287–95, 2 October–25 November 1909.

14 Gardiner, *Prophets, priests and kings*, p. 106.

15 E. Halévy, *A history of the English people in the 19th century*, vol. VI, *The rule of democracy, 1905–1914* (tr. E. Watkin, 2nd edn, 1952), p. 583.

16 Lord Eustace Percy of Newcastle, *Some memories* (1958), p. 189.

17 Randolph Churchill, *Winston S. Churchill*, vol. I, *Youth, 1874–1900* (1966), p. 349, and previous quotations from pp. 259, 300, 352, 361.

18 Ibid., vol. I, pp. 392–3.

19 Cabinet memorandum, CAB 37/103, no. 103, 'The abatement of imprisonment', 25 October 1910.

20 Masterman, *C.F.G. Masterman*, pp. 205–8. Masterman was under-secretary at the Home Office, 1909–12.

21 R. Churchill, *Winston S. Churchill*, vol. II, pp. 225, 710.

22 W.S. Churchill, 'The untrodden field in politics', *The Nation*, 7 March 1908, pp. 812–13.

23 R. Churchill, *Winston S. Churchill*, vol. I, p. 422, and vol. II, p. 31.

24 Churchill to Asquith, 29 December 1908, quoted in R. Jenkins, *Asquith* (1964), p. 193.

25 R. Churchill, *Winston S. Churchill*, vol. II, pp. 325, 277; W.S. Churchill, *The people's rights: selected from his Lancashire and other recent speeches* (1910), p. 111.

26 *PD, Commons*, vol. 26, c. 510 (25 May 1911), National Insurance Bill, 2nd reading; Churchill, *The people's rights*, pp. 29, 113.

27 Halévy, *A history of the English people*, vol. VI, p. 598; R. Churchill, *Winston S. Churchill*, vol. II, p. 465.

28 Masterman, *C.F.G. Masterman*, p. 176.

29 *PD, Commons*, vol. 26, c. 508 (February 1910).

30 Cabinet memoranda, CAB 37/93 no. 93; 94, no. 98; 97, no. 6; CAB 37/101, no. 143 and no. 147; CAB 37/102, no. 3, 14 February 1910.

31 Churchill, *The people's rights*, p. 117. Richard Toye, *Lloyd George and Churchill: rivals for greatness* (2007), ch. 2, pp. 38–71, is the most recent account of their work for the welfare state.

32 W.S. Churchill, *Liberalism and the social problem* (1909), pp. 237–8 (30 January 1909, 'The approaching conflict').

33 Ibid., p. 309 (23 May 1909, speech in Manchester on the budget resolutions).

34 *PD, Commons*, vol. 4, c. 854 (3 May 1909), Ways and means: Budget proposals.

35 *PD, Commons*, vol. 3, c. 838 (5 April 1909), Railway amalgamation; CAB 37/101, no. 147, 3 November 1909.

36 CAB 37/108, no. 189, 'The feeble-minded', by Dr Tredgold, covering note by WSC (May 1909).

37 Jenkins, *Asquith*, p. 205, footnote; see also British Library, Ripon Papers, Add. Mss 43542/48, Lord Bryce to Lord Ripon, 20 October 1908.

38 R.B. Haldane, *An autobiography* (1929), p. 217.

39 Jenkins, *Asquith*, pp. 339–40.

40 R. Churchill, *Winston S. Churchill*, vol. II, pp. 179–88; RH, *Elgin and Churchill at the Colonial Office*, pp. 499–500. David Reynolds, *In command of history: Churchill fighting and writing the Second World War* (2004), p. 504, has a good phrase about his 'iron whim'.

41 *PD, Commons*, vol. 196, c. 626 (12 November 1908); R. Churchill, *Winston S. Churchill*, vol. II, pp. 307–8.

42 Churchill, *The people's rights*, p. 48.

43 Quoted in W.S. Churchill, *My early life: a roving commission* (1930), p. 238.

44 *PD, Commons*, vol. 155, c. 845 (5 April 1906), civil services and revenue departments estimates, 1906–7.

45 Quoted in G. Bennett, *Kenya, a political history: the colonial period* (1963), p. 22.

46 W.S. Churchill, *My African journey* (1908), p. 31. All that was required, he thought, would be two or three short dams between islands, and the cost would be 'inconceivably small'. In fact, the Owen Falls dam which realised his vision was not completed until 1954. It took six years to build, cost £22 million, was 2,725 feet long and 85 feet high.

47 Quoted in Amery, *My political life*, vol. I, p. 404.

11   Churchill and the colonial empire

[This is a revised version of 'Churchill and the British empire', in
Churchill (ed. Robert Blake and Wm. Roger Louis, Oxford, 1993); the
change of title indicates better the limits of coverage, India being the
subject of a separate chapter in that volume, by Sarvepalli Gopal. As
published, the article was subject to editorial cuts, and the notes were
truncated. The original, intended, text is here restored.]

Not altogether enthusiastically, Churchill returned to the Colonial
Office on 13 February 1921 as secretary of state in Lloyd George's
coalition government. He remained there for twenty months until the
formation of Bonar Law's Conservative ministry towards the end of
October 1922. This chapter focuses upon Churchill's policies towards
the dependent colonies during this period,[1] so it excludes a consideration
of the Imperial Conference of 1921 (which he masterminded), and of the
conclusion of the Irish Treaty (to which he contributed considerably).
But the analysis is set within the broader context of Churchill's attitude
towards the colonial empire during his ministerial career as a whole.

Despite his fertile engagement with the colonies as parliamentary
under-secretary of state, 1905 to 1908, the question arises: was Churchill
thereafter even interested in the colonial empire? Was it not the case that
'His interest in the empire never absorbed him entirely at the Colonial
Office, and it may indeed have been very nearly exhausted by it'?[2] He
never set foot again in India after leaving it in 1897, or in South Africa
after 1900. Although he made many trips across the Atlantic and several
to North Africa and the Middle East, he never visited Nigeria and the
Gold Coast, let alone Australia and New Zealand or Malaya and Hong
Kong. His last sight of a British African colony was in 1907–8. He meant
to revisit Kenya and Uganda as secretary of state but never made it.
Leo Amery's opinion was that England was his fundamental concern
and the ultimate object of policy, enhanced by the prestige and power
of an empire beneficently ruled; Commonwealth patriotism never seriously influenced his thinking, his eloquence, or his actions. Attlee came
to a strikingly similar conclusion: Churchill was 'rather insular about

Britain. He talked a good deal about the Commonwealth . . . But Britain
– England – really was his limit so far as feeling went. This may be why
his judgment on Commonwealth affairs was often bad – notably on
India.' It may also be the reason why, India excepted, on no aspect of
Churchill studies has so little been written by so few as 'Churchill and
the empire'.[3]

I

The coruscating minutes in red ink, the elegantly polished memoranda,
and the long reflective letters to colleagues which characterised the earlier
period (1905–8) are simply not there for the years 1921–2. It may not
be strictly true that 'he who drafts the document wins the day',[4] but it is
certainly the case that ministers who write the best papers most readily
ensure the attention of historians: something Churchill understood
perfectly well. So what was he trying to tell us, both archivally and auto-
biographically, *ex silentio*? On investigation, it rapidly becomes clear, in
fact, that the astonishing Churchillian written output on colonial issues
for the earlier period was the product of a very particular combination of
circumstances. The Liberal government from 1905 was faced with the
aftermath of African partition as well as of South African war. It had one
major constructive job to do: to settle the future of southern Africa. And
at the same time it was earnestly trying to introduce a new tone into colonial administration. Put crudely, this involved cutting down proconsular
pretensions and reasserting trusteeship. Churchill himself was seeking to
make his name. A post which enabled him to combine helping forward
a South African settlement with exposing abuses of power and bureaucratic incompetence was ideal for his purpose.[5] Also, he was long enough
in office, almost two and a half years, to have some real impact.

In 1921 everything was different. By this date he had developed a
habit of concentrating on one problem at a time; this led to a backlog of
files, and then insufficient time for reflective comment. (L.S. Amery in
fact believed that, Iraq and Ireland apart, Churchill neglected the work
of the Colonial Office.)[6] There was no government mission to purify
colonial rule in 1921, and without this political imperative Churchill
found it hard to reactivate an interest in colonies. Moreover, Churchill
was now an experienced Cabinet minister, no longer needing to impress
his seniors. Nor did the Colonial Office occupy a central position in post-
war government policy as it had done briefly in 1905–6. When Curzon
as foreign secretary complained that Churchill was constantly interfering
in foreign policy (and how would Churchill have liked it if Curzon had
made unauthorised interventions in colonial policy?), Churchill shoved

a note across the Cabinet table, insisting on his right to an opinion, because 'there is no comparison between those vital matters which affect the whole future of the world, and the mere departmental topics with which the Colonial Office is concerned'.[7]

Some allowance has to be made for self-defensiveness as well as perhaps for self-deprecation, but of the sincerity of Churchill's anxiety about the vulnerability of Britain's post-war position in the world there can be no doubt. 'The whole accumulated greatness of Britain is under challenge,' he wrote in 1922. Every separate foreign or nationalist embarrassment, created by the 'rascals and rapscallions of mankind', he saw as a threat to its crumbling global position. A humiliation by the Turks at Chanak would above all else be a disastrous blow to imperial prestige. Straitened economic circumstances meant that 'the British Empire cannot become the policeman of the world'. Yet there was trouble everywhere, and so 'we may well be within measurable distance of universal collapse and anarchy throughout Europe and Asia'. All over the world, countries were 'relapsing in hideous succession into bankruptcy, barbarism or anarchy', not least within the ambit of the Pax Britannica. Ireland was suffering an 'enormous retrogression of civilisation and Christianity'. Egypt and India were in revolt, on the edge of a blind and heedless plunge back into 'primordial chaos'.[8] His predecessor Lord Milner had complained that 'the whole world was rocking', and in this situation colonial business was pushed aside.[9] It was the same for Churchill. Russia and Turkey, America and Japan – these were the issues that he felt should preoccupy him. Nor were his domestic British causes forgotten either. He was a notably disputatious member of the Cabinet. Nevertheless, during Churchill's time as secretary of state, important decisions were taken for the future of Palestine and Iraq, Kenya and Southern Rhodesia, and it is these problems that should mainly be considered here.

II

We may start by stating the legacy of his earlier years as an undersecretary. There was a negative impact, as has been seen. Was there anything more positive? Perhaps the most significant point is the substantial contribution the colonial experience had made to his perceptions of domestic and international policy: the potential value of state intervention to protect the welfare of the poor at home, and international intervention to protect the democratic rights of small states abroad. More specifically, the main conclusions he had come to were that the empire should be a 'family not a syndicate', and that justice should be done to all individuals within it, not least its own servants. An especially incandescent example had been his defence of the Batawana chief Sekgoma in Bechuanaland.[10] In addition he had acquired an incisively opinionated world-view. South Africa was 'a country of conflicting dualities and vicious contradictions, where everything is twisted, disturbed and abnormal'. Natal had by its treatment of the Zulu people shown itself to be the tyrannical 'hooligan of the British Empire'. Sir Frederick Lugard's Northern Nigeria – 'a wild and poor country just thawing into civilisation' – was a nuisance and Churchill could see no reason why 'these savage tribes should not be allowed to eat each other up without restraint'. Somaliland was 'just a wilderness of stone and scrub', and there was little point in trying to hold the interior. Kenya's 'first few ruffians' among the settlers should not be allowed 'to steal it from us, upon some shabby pretence of being a responsibly governed Colony'. The Kikuyu were 'light-hearted, tractable, if brutish children . . . capable of being instructed and raised from their present degradation'. (Mau Mau later took him greatly by surprise.) Uganda was an African pearl, highly suitable for a 'practical experiment in state socialism'. Its Bagandan elite he regarded as vital, powerful, and popular; nevertheless he could not resist the quip that the British officer class was, 'in all that constitutes fitness to direct, as superior to the Baganda as Mr Wells's Martians would have been to us'.[11] By contrast, he was anxious that the political capacities of European peoples in their own lands should be properly recognised. The plea that Malta was a 'battleship' he thought inadequate reason for denying it self-government. He recognised the restraints imposed by the Turkish minority presence in Cyprus, but was still unconvinced that enough was being done for Greek Cypriot aspirations – views which later came back to haunt him when the cry was for Enosis. Further afield, the remoter regions of the Churchillian world-picture were full of vivid if desk-bound impressions. The New Hebrides were 'an antipodean archipelago'; the Tristan da Cuhnans were 'a kind of poor version of the Bounty mutineers'; while the Seychelles was the place where the sale of postage-stamps ensured that 'Christianity was sustained by variations in the watermark'. His views were not immutable; some of his opinions were subject to subsequent modification, as we shall see. It simply is not true that Churchill's world-view was stuck in the attitudes of the 1890s' subaltern, nor even in those of the Edwardian junior minister.

Perhaps the two early interests which induced the closest involvement both developed directly out of his being in those days MP for Manchester North-West, a constituency with a community of notable Jewish businessmen and Lancashire cotton manufacturers. As well as embracing Zionism, he became an enthusiast for developing the empire's 'great estates', taking a close interest in the work of the British Cotton

Growing Association. At one of its meetings in Manchester in 1907 he said he looked forward to the emergence of 'a second India' in British West Africa, based on railways and cotton, with 'the two Nigerias, the Gold Coast and Sierra Leone woven together as one vast dependency of the Crown'. 'Cotton', he was fond of saying, 'is the thread which unites the material interests of British industrial democracy' with the development of the tropical possessions of the empire.[12] When Milner was about to be appointed secretary of state for the colonies in January 1919, Churchill told Lloyd George he ought to be given £50 million a year to develop Africa. (The amount of the first Colonial Development and Welfare allocation in 1929 was £1 million a year, while even after 1945 it was only £12 million annually.) As secretary of state himself, Churchill was quick to reassure the Manchester cotton entrepreneurs that he remained keen to promote their interests. He hoped to do this by diverting government expenditure from its unproductive new responsibilities in the Middle East: 'In Africa the population is docile and the country fertile. In the Middle East the country is arid and the population is ferocious. A little money goes a long way in Africa, and a lot of money goes very little way in Arabia.'[13] Already in May 1921 he was protesting to the prime minister that it was 'a most improvident policy to starve and neglect the whole development of our tropical colonies'. The comparatively small sums he needed to 'foster an active productivity' in the 'very valuable estates' of East and Central Africa were being denied him by the Treasury. They had slashed more than £600,000 from his estimates of £1.5 million for Tanganyika alone, so that it was 'rapidly relaxing' from the level of development it had attained under German rule, and its great railway was falling into serious disrepair. Since colonial development would also create a demand for British manufactures and open up supplies of raw materials for British industry, he warned Lloyd George that he would unrepentantly continue to press for a switch of expenditure to Africa away from their sterile obligations in the Middle East.[14] This was a major part of the theme of his first public survey of colonial problems, made during the Supply debate in July 1921, when he reiterated the comparison between 'tractable and promising' African colonies and Middle Eastern regions 'unduly stocked with peppery, pugnacious, proud politicians and theologians, who happen to be at the same time extremely well armed and extremely hard up'.[15] The trouble was, however, that Churchill was never able to persuade his colleagues to make this diversion of expenditure, and, being himself an incurably parsimonious minister, he was not prepared to campaign for *additional* financial resources.

Ironically, therefore, the Middle East proved to be an easier place than Africa for the fulfilment of expectations held of him. Churchill had some success in laying down a position which held the line for Zionists through to the White Paper of 1939 – which he never accepted, but could not dislodge, as government policy in wartime. Three characteristically Churchillian concerns underpinned his attraction to Zionism: his interests in strategy and geopolitics, in the development of 'great estates', and in visionary schemes of social engineering. As early as 1908 he had declared: 'The establishment of a strong, free Jewish state astride the bridge between Europe and Africa, flanking the land roads to the East, would not only be an immense advantage to the British Empire, but a notable step towards the harmonious disposition of the world among its peoples.'[16]

As prophecy this proved to be tragically naive. As geopolitics it is a good example of what one general called his imprecise 'cigar-butt strategy', making a sweeping gesture over a map.[17] But it is not essentially different from Amery's conception of Palestine as the keystone of the geopolitical arch which would enable the 'Southern British world', running from Cape Town through Cairo, Baghdad, and Calcutta to Sydney and Wellington, to go quietly about its business. The mobilisation of Jewish support for the Allied war effort through the Balfour Declaration of 1917 was something Churchill regarded as a 'definite, palpable' political and strategic advantage to Britain. But he also believed that here was the chance to remove an 'inefficient and out-of-date' Turkish control which had 'long misruled one of the most fertile countries in the world'. Merely maintaining an economic status quo was, of course, anathema to any good Victorian, and Churchill wanted to let the Jews come in and develop this 'great estate':

Left to themselves, the Arabs of Palestine would not in a thousand years have taken effective steps towards the irrigation and electrification of Palestine. They would have been quite content to dwell – a handful of philosophic people – in the wasted sun-scorched plains, letting the waters of the Jordan continue to flow unbridled and unharnessed into the Dead Sea.[18]

(The *rallentando* effect in this final cadence must have been worth hearing.) Finally, Zionism appealed to him because 'such a plan contains a soul'. He once told a hostess that her distinctly floppy-looking pudding required a theme. If even puddings needed a theme in the Churchillian scheme of things, how much the more did politics. So he liked strong, romantic, even audacious schemes in government: the reconciliation of Briton and Boer in a South African Union, the Salvation Army settlement proposal which through 'super-economic influence' might transform Southern Rhodesia, the 'big slice of Bismarckianism' thrust over 'the whole underside of our industrial system', the strategic push through the 'soft underbelly of Europe', the quixotic wartime offer of an Anglo-French political union, and so forth. His support for these, and for Zionism, is all of a piece. For Zionism, as he declaimed in 1905, 'enlists in its support energies, enthusiasms and a driving power which no scheme of individual colonisation can ever demand'. And so in 1921 he would not go back either officially or personally on a British pledge, which he regarded as a commitment to 'a great experiment which deserves a fair chance', even if this meant maintaining a considerable garrison, encouraging an armed Jewish gendarmerie, and holding in suspense for the time being the representative institutions which would curtail Jewish immigration.[19]

Churchill, however, had no desire to sully his hands with the perplexing realities of administering Palestine, and he was content to rely – and rely heavily – on John Shuckburgh (assistant under-secretary of state) for the working out of the government's Palestine policy which was eventually enshrined in the White Paper of June 1922. (Churchill was reluctant to rush into a public declaration.) Its purpose was to gloss or modify the Balfour Declaration by a careful balancing of the allegedly incompatible earlier promises. Starting from Churchill's premise that 'we have a double duty to discharge', the White Paper argued that the Balfour Declaration did *not* mean 'that Palestine as a whole should be converted into a Jewish National Home, but that such a Home should be founded *in* Palestine'. There was to be a Jewish 'centre' in Palestine, 'internationally guaranteed and formally recognised to rest upon ancient historic connection'. (The Jews must know they were there as of right and not on sufferance.) On the other hand, the future development of the existing Jewish community must not lead to the imposition of a Jewish nationality on the inhabitants of Palestine as a whole; and Jewish immigration should not be so great as to go beyond the economic capacity of the country to absorb it. There must be no subordination of the Arab population, or its language or its culture. Churchill thus rejected both an Arab national state and a Jewish national state; instead there ought to be a shared bi-national state. This was the first clear attempt to articulate properly the essential duality of British policy, promoting collaboration within a common territory. But neither Jews nor Arabs were really interested in such an outcome. The British delusion was that Arabs and Jews were ultimately reconcilable.[20]

In Churchill's view they would be reconciled through economic development – in the shape of hydroelectric schemes, hill terracing, irrigation, and agricultural improvements. This would divert Zionist attention from politics, and demonstrate to Arabs the practical advantages of the

Jewish influx. A new Palestine would be created by the Jews performing an archetypal European settler function, bringing the 'good gifts' of
prosperity, and a 'higher economic and social life to all'. Accordingly the
Arabs should see them 'as their friends and helpers, not expellers and
expropriators', and could not be allowed to prevent continuing Jewish
immigration. It was not perhaps entirely tactful to accuse the Arabs of
being 'guilty of a breach of hospitality'. He also appealed to them not to
deny history, for 'all history shows the relationship of these two races' to
be closely intertwined. Hence his rather exasperated cry: 'Why can't you
live together in amity and develop the country peacefully?'[21]

At the War Office in 1920, Churchill had already attacked the waste of
money in the newly acquired Mandate of Iraq, or Mesopotamia as it was
then known. Of the lands of the Marsh Arabs, he wrote: 'A score of mud
villages, sandwiched in between a swampy river and a blistering desert,
inhabited by a few hundred half-naked families, usually starving, are now
occupied . . . by Anglo-Indian garrisons on a scale which in India would
maintain order in wealthy provinces of millions of people.'[22] As secretary
of state for the colonies, his role in this turbulent land was to set up a
system of 'informal control', gradually reducing British military responsibilities without a 'policy of scuttle'. (He could not, however, do much
about prospecting for oil because of complications with the Americans.)
His intention was that Iraq should become 'an independent Native State
friendly to Great Britain, favourable to her commercial interests, and
casting hardly any burden upon the Exchequer' – a native state, that is,
analogous to princely states in India (which, incidentally, he thought
would be a good model for India as a whole). The costs of the enormous
post-war garrison would be run down, and a treaty relationship would
be substituted for the remainder of the mandatory period. Not to cut
costs in this way would be 'politically indefensible and from an imperial
viewpoint would misapply our limited and over-strained resources'. The
Cabinet approved the terms of the proposed treaty in 1922 as satisfactory.[23] All this was the classic mid-Victorian policy of 'informal empire'.
The difference was that instead of gunboats in the background there
would be aircraft overhead; only the reliance on nascent but 'proven
aerial power' would make it possible for Iraq to be held with such a small
military force as he now envisaged. Churchill, as ever, was quick to take
up the latest technological tools for the task in hand. This use of aircraft,
he claimed, 'may ultimately lead to a form of control over semi-civilised
countries which will be found very effective and infinitely cheaper'. He
argued that air power could be used as an instrument of imperial control
in India and Afghanistan as well;[24] and in years to come he would also
urge its value in intimidating the Mau Mau rebels.[25]

Out of the frustrations of the Middle East – which occupied too much of his time (he was the first but not the last secretary of state for whom this was true) – came a few authentic Churchillian flashes. In Iraq, he said, the British were paying huge sums for the privilege of living on 'an ungrateful volcano'. It was 'a poor, starving, backward, bankrupt country', a 'wild land filled with a proud and impecunious chief and extremely peppery well-armed politicians'. King Faisal (the government's chosen imperial collaborator) was getting into 'a perpetual ferment' and becoming tiresome – 'has he not got some wives to keep him quiet?'[26] When the re-employment of 'Philby of Arabia' in Transjordan (after dismissal from Iraq) was urged upon him by officials he riposted: 'I cannot take a Philby in a poke', but would like to see him first. When Shuckburgh decided, somewhat prematurely, that King Abdullah in Transjordan was 'a complete failure', Churchill was not to be seduced: 'I do not mean to throw him over easily. He has an impossible task.'[27] When the Opposition complained that a major concession in Palestine was being made to Rutenberg, who was a Jew, Churchill replied that of course he was a Jew, but they could hardly inscribe over the portals of the new Zion 'No Israelite need apply'. The House of Commons rocked with laughter, apparently.[28]

As far as Kenya is concerned, we find Churchill pursuing the same kind of balancing act between conflicting interests as he was attempting in Palestine. In the early 1920s, the Kenya debate was dominated by a crisis over the Indian problem. Indian colonising pretensions tended to grow as their existing overseas communities felt more and more excluded politically; there was vague talk of turning East Africa into the 'America of the Hindu'.[29] Unsurprisingly Churchill had some hard words for the Indian delegation in August 1921. They must accept as 'an agreed fact' the reservation of the Kenya highlands for white settlement, since the Europeans had gone there on the basis of the Elgin Pledge of 1908. It was 'no good expecting that could be set aside as if it were nothing', for this would be a breach of British good faith. He was not prepared to tell the white settlers they were going to be put unfairly into a minority position under an Indian majority government; such a system would actually 'make the path of the Indians far harder and would cause every kind of disaster', since Europeans simply would not stand for being subordinated in this way. Of course he would apply Rhodes's maxim of 'equal rights for [all] civilised men' – *except* in the highlands. Nevertheless he thought it a valuable principle, because 'it would be absurd to give equal electoral rights to the naked savages of Kikuyu and Kavirondo', even though they were human beings: 'there has to be a line'. He dismissed with an equally patronising sneer the Indian claim to have developed

Kenya: they had helped, but 'you would not have invented the railway let alone constructed it'. In conclusion, he said his aim was to find 'an interdependent general settlement', or at least 'a general proposition', which would reassure the settlers, protect the 'aboriginal native' (who had the first claim), and give Indians the benefits of applying 'equal rights'.[30] However grudgingly, he was committed to doing something to improve the lot of the Kenyan Indians, and, although it is noticeable that he took a more favourable view of the possibilities of European rule in Africa than he had done fifteen years before, he had a much less indulgent attitude towards settler shortcomings than Milner or Amery.

Instructions to construct a package deal along these lines were discussed in the Colonial Office with the governor, Sir Edward Northey, and presented to him in a memorandum dated 26 August 1921. This memorandum set out nicely balanced concessions to each side, but it did not represent a Cabinet decision on policy: rather, the matter would not go to the Cabinet until the governor had held full local consultations and reached an agreement. The memorandum shifted significantly beyond both previous policy and local advice, in the direction of greater partnership with Indians, by ruling against commercial segregation in towns, and by declaring in favour of a common electoral roll in elections to the Legislative Council. Officials were careful to note that by supporting a common roll embracing all races Churchill was insisting on an essential change on behalf of the Indians.[31] At the same time, Kenya must not become predominantly Indian, since fear of this was general among the settlers. The contrary pressures on Churchill were complex indeed. At the end of November, Northey reported that even his compromise proposals had completely failed. He had not been able to persuade the Europeans to entertain in any shape or form the idea of a common roll franchise with Indians. This was the rock on which the talks foundered, the settlers arguing that it would 'cut away the very foundation on which we feel our future is fixed'. They also began to dig their heels in over residential segregation as a supposedly pledged principle. In his telegram reporting all this, the governor stressed 'the very serious position which I am satisfied will occur if the demands of Indians are accepted *in toto*. Europeans have organisation complete for resistance as last resource.'[32] This was neither the first nor the last of such warnings about settler revolt. The Colonial Office was not unduly alarmed by them, although they certainly indicated the desirability of not taking a decision in a hurry and not refusing to make some concession.[33] Meanwhile the settlers announced their intention of sending a deputation under Lord Delamere to the secretary of state. Since his own proposals had already been leaked, Churchill was convinced he had no option but to see them, despite E.S. Montagu's protest (as secretary of state for India) against the further delay it would involve.[34]

At his meetings with Churchill in February 1922, Delamere indicated willingness to be flexible over some Indian demands, provided urban residential segregation was 'definitely laid down', and provided some sort of immigration control board was set up, on which Europeans would have an 'effective' voice. Churchill reported to Montagu: 'I feel bound to tell you that my mind is working very much on the same lines.' Montagu was furious: 'I cannot possibly agree . . . I cannot consent to any permanent disability on Indians *qua* Indians.' For Montagu this was the last straw in his fraught relations with Churchill on this and other questions. In October 1921 he had been angered and bewildered by Churchill's description, in a personal letter, of the Indians in East Africa as 'mainly of a very low class of coolies and the idea that they should be put on an equality with the Europeans is revolting to every white man throughout British Africa'. This sentence Montagu thought 'might have been written by a European settler of a most fanatical type'; in any case nobody had suggested giving political rights to a low class of coolies.[35] Then in January 1922 came the bombshell of Churchill's unexpected (but not off-the-cuff) remarks at the annual East African Dinner. There should, he said, be no invidious legislative distinctions or colour bar to advancement, and a broad imperial view should be taken of the position of Indians in Kenya and Uganda. Nevertheless – and here came the balancing announcements – European settlers could be relieved of their anxiety: the pledged exclusive reservation of the white highlands had been 'definitely settled'. A federal amalgamation of East African colonies was also to be studied. Moreover, there was a grandiloquent peroration: 'We do not contemplate any settlement or system which will prevent . . . Kenya . . . from becoming a characteristically and distinctively British colony, looking forward in the full fruition of time to responsible self-government.'[36] This statement – though welcomed by Delamere as a 'charter' courageously laying 'the foundations of a future self-governing colony, in the face of very great opposition' – did not mean much in practice. (It was heavily qualified.) But in combination with the other remarks it put Montagu into a cool rage of amazement. He took 'the strongest exception' to Churchill's 'unjustifiable and indefensible' way of proceeding, which had gravely breached Cabinet conventions and anticipated a Cabinet decision on the highlands. Churchill had also made a further pledge to the Europeans, which brushed aside all the suggestions Montagu had made. Why was Churchill apparently dissociating himself from 'our policy as a government'? Churchill defended himself before a Cabinet committee by warning against any attempt to force a withdrawal of his remarks:

The demands of Indians as regards their treatment in East Africa were unreasonable, and if they were conceded they would throw the whole of British East Africa into confusion. We had no force there to coerce the white population, who felt strongly on this question, and any repudiation of the statement he had made might lead to them ejecting the Indians from East Africa . . . [Indians] claimed that they must be treated as ordinary voters. This was quite impossible in Africa.[37]

At the full Cabinet on 13 March Montagu formally charged Churchill with having acted without Cabinet authority. Churchill simply rejected this out of hand: he had initiated no new unapproved policy, created no precedent, and had not even exceeded his departmental discretion. Montagu, he alleged, had agreed with the proposals now being made, although he did not like them.[38] No other minister is recorded as having expressed any view, but it is impossible to suppose that Churchill would have found much support. The truth is that he could not on occasion resist doling out some sensational journalistic copy, regardless of the consequences.

In the wake of this nasty ministerial quarrel, it was decided that the two under-secretaries of state should be left to thrash out an agreed inter-departmental formula: Edward Wood (later Lord Halifax) for the Colonial Office and Lord Winterton for the India Office. The Wood–Winterton scheme was announced in September 1922 and provisionally accepted by the two secretaries of state for reference to the government of Kenya and the government of India. (On the merits Churchill did not specifically endorse it.) Since the proposals stuck to a common electoral roll and envisaged neither urban segregation nor immigration restriction or control, they caused a storm of protest in Nairobi, and the threat of settler resistance heated up. Churchill shocked the settlers by recalling Northey, and, according to Sir Ralph Furse's memoirs, Churchill let it be known he would send a cruiser to Mombasa and blockade them.[39] However, it fell to his successor, the Duke of Devonshire, actually to defuse the crisis. As is well known, he did this by abandoning the common roll, sugaring the pill for Indians by rediscovery of the principle that African interests must be paramount if they conflicted with those of immigrants, whether Indian or European. Churchill's attempt to balance the interests of all three was thus summarily and dramatically dropped. He had tried to give the Indians something of substance and make a declaration on behalf of the settlers, while preserving the status quo for Africans, whereas Devonshire denied the Indians the substance and made a declaration on behalf of Africans, merely preserving the status quo for the settlers.

Concurrently Churchill was also juggling with conflicting claims upon the future of Southern Rhodesia, where Smuts and the dream of a 'Greater South Africa' pulled in one direction, and Sir Charles Coghlan and the desire for settler autonomy in another.[40] Within ten days of taking office in February 1921, Churchill asked Lord Buxton (the recently retired high commissioner) to head a committee to make an urgent investigation of constitutional prospects after the end of British South Africa Company rule. Buxton reported in mid-May 1921, suggesting a referendum on the possibility of responsible government (internal self-government). Churchill accepted this proposal, despite Smuts's protest that it would prejudice Rhodesia's future possible entry into the Union, under the procedure provided for in the Act of Union. Churchill did not think it need do so, but Smuts kept up the pressure, and on 21 September 1921 Churchill decided to let Smuts declare the terms on which Southern Rhodesia would be admitted as a province of the Union. It was, he said, his 'personal wish' to proceed in this way. The referendum would now offer a choice between the two alternative solutions for Rhodesia's future. The Cabinet agreed Churchill should continue to hold discussions with all the parties, putting 'the bias a little in favour of joining the Union'. Stronger pressure would be counterproductive. In the event, 59.43 per cent of the white Rhodesians voted against the Union.[41]

Both sides disapproved of Churchill's stance and tactics, which suggests a certain even-handedness. Coghlan complained that Churchill was 'out to get us into the Union if he could', while Smuts blamed Churchill for the adverse result from the Union point of view. Undoubtedly Churchill preferred the Union solution as a way of strengthening geopolitically the British position in southern Africa. (As early as 1906 he had recognised the potential of Southern Rhodesia as 'the weight which swings the balance in South Africa decisively on the side of the British Crown'.) With all the empire's other problems, he would gladly have despatched the Rhodesians into the care of the local imperial collaborator, who happened also to be a statesman of international standing. Financial constraints made it in any case impossible to match the generous inducements Smuts had offered. Churchill did not think a Union government would ill-treat the Africans, and pointed to the recent Native Affairs Act (1920) – certainly quite liberal by South African standards – as evidence. At the same time, he was throughout extremely careful to avoid dictating a solution to the settlers. It is surely not without significance that he refused to give Smuts the unequivocal pro-Union lead for which the latter had urgently appealed as necessary to ensure the outcome. Churchill's advisers were in genuine doubt as to how to respond to this. Churchill himself did nothing. And this was in sharp contrast to his unorthodox rush barely a year earlier to break official precedent by congratulating Smuts on winning the South African election of February 1921.[42]

III

Before we come to a conclusion, a brief look at Churchill's subsequent encounters with the empire is necessary. His pessimism about an impending 'wreck of our great estates' persisted for the rest of his career, and he worried about India.[43] As is notorious, he opposed the Government of India Act, 1935 ('a monstrous monument of sham built by the pygmies'[44]), and he had no intention of helping a constitutional solution forward in India in the 1940s. On the other hand, the Viceroy, Lord Wavell, and Secretary of State Amery felt that Britain owed a great deal to Churchill for his firm line against emerging forms of international trusteeship and accountability, which might allow 'America to push us off the map'. Churchill himself thought it was 'pretty good cheek' for the Americans 'now coming to school-marm us into proper behaviour' in the empire. And he was not going to 'preside over the liquidation of the British Empire' in Hong Kong or anywhere else at their behest.[45]

It was not only Americans he was wary of in the higher direction of imperial affairs. Colonials such as Australia's prime minister John Curtin, who wanted all Australian and New Zealand forces to be concentrated in the Pacific, received scant consideration. With his mind on the total strategic picture, and the empire as the buttress of British power, Churchill took the simple view that Dominion troops should be available for general deployment as seemed best as judged from the 'effective centre of gravity' in London.[46] Clearly, however, he was becoming increasingly out of touch with feelings and developments in Commonwealth countries. This was true even in respect of South Africa, with which he was comparatively familiar. A notable illustration of this was his accusation in 1941 that the high commissioner, Lord Harlech, was 'unconscious' of some of the 'basic realities' of South Africa. Harlech had diagnosed the British South African community as too introverted, refusing to take an interest in public life, and he pointed to Natal as the worst offender. The situation there was 'lamentable', he thought, because it played into the hands of the Afrikaners, who were thus outstripping the British intellectually and beginning to monopolise political leadership. This was an important attempt to sound a warning about the future fundamental weakness of the Union within the Commonwealth; Churchill could not see this, and dismissed Harlech's judgments as 'supercilious and superficial' (though he relented to the extent of excising these words from the

circulated version of his memorandum). Instead, he offered the following decidedly fanciful analysis: 'Natal is one of the very few spots in the
British Empire where the people are really devoted to the Old Country.
They have the New Zealand touch.' The maintenance of a distinctive
British standpoint and loyalist community – 'the Ulster of South Africa',
which the 'predominant Dutch find it most necessary to woo' – was of
positive value in reducing the risk of civil war. Moreover, 'There ought
to be room for many different kinds of people and many different kinds
of culture in the British Commonwealth and Empire. Totalitarianism
has great attractions to some minds; but he would be a poor artist who
tried to paint a picture by mixing up all the colours in the paint-box.'
Churchill added that if South Africa had declared itself neutral in 1939,
'there was always Natal, which would instantly have seceded from the
Union and placed the fine port of Durban at our disposal'. There was no
real evidence for this assertion.[47]

In the last phase, as prime minister in the 1950s, South Africa
remained one of the few parts of the empire he kept an eye on.[48] He was
against the transfer of the High Commission Territories to be administered by South Africa 'in accordance with very old-fashioned ideas'.
He was determined to maintain British interests in the Simon's Town
naval base as an effective link in the imperial line of communications to
Australasia. Negotiations over its future had begun under the Labour
government but ran into stalemate. Determined that South Africa's strategic ports – 'more important to the British Commonwealth of Nations
than Gibraltar or Malta' – should not 'go down the drain like Southern
Ireland', Churchill held out for the best possible terms, despite the
need for economies in the defence estimates. In this respect he maintained continuity of policy with the tough bargaining stance of Attlee
and Shinwell, and expressly rejected the advice of Secretary of State
Lord Ismay and the attempt of the Commonwealth Relations Office not
only to reopen negotiations but to do so on a more conciliatory footing.
Following Churchill's lead, the Defence Committee accordingly agreed
in March 1952 not to take any fresh initiative. By the summer of 1954,
however, the South African government was again pressing, and pressing hard, for the transfer of Simon's Town. Why? asked Churchill. Was
it because Dr Malan as prime minister was working towards the final
severance of South Africa from Britain? If so, the surrender of Simon's
Town would be taken as a symbol of British decline and fall. In his last
extended minute on South Africa, written nearly fifty years after the first,
he returned again to his Natal fantasy. If South Africa declared itself a
republic and quit the Commonwealth – which might not happen, though
anti-British sentiment and the division between Britain and white South

Africans on the colour question was growing – Natal might 'remain faithful to the Crown', in which case Britain would need to be in a strategic position 'to defend her rights to an independent choice, by force of arms if necessary'.[49] In the Cabinet, although admitting that the significance of Simon's Town was becoming largely symbolic, Churchill was 'reluctant to contemplate any transaction which would be presented as yet another surrender of the political rights and responsibilities of the United Kingdom'. Nor did he want to do anything which might discourage the 'loyalist elements in South Africa'.[50] So the hard bargaining continued. It was strongly kept up, too, by Eden, who had no love for South Africa. As a result in 1955 Britain obtained agreements on Simon's Town which were astonishingly favourable. Whilst not actually congratulating him, Churchill assured Eden he did not see what else he could have done: 'we live in days when neither South Africa nor Naval defence stand on their foundations of a few years ago'.[51]

One reason for Churchill's vigilance over Simon's Town was his realisation that the Suez Canal was no longer of much value as a Commonwealth link, nor the Egyptian base of such strategic importance. Negotiations over the future of the Canal Zone were far more difficult than those with South Africa, and Churchill was more consistently attentive to the Egyptian files than to any others from overseas. His approach was fundamentally pragmatic. We must not be misled by his anxiety about the domestic political reaction and his private growling about evacuation.[52] Officially, Churchill recognised that there was much to be said for a fresh start on a new basis of 'vigorous and effective' troop redeployment throughout the Middle East.

The same pragmatic if rather reluctant good sense was displayed in Africa. He 'noted' (rather than personally approved) the declaration made on behalf of his government that continuity in the goals of colonial policy would be maintained (November 1951). He grumbled that they were forced to make constitutional concessions to Nkrumah's Gold Coast as the 'consequences of what was done before we became responsible'. But there was no obstruction – and no atavistic reassertions of imperiousness. During the anti-Mau Mau operations, Michael Blundell found him keen to promote a conciliatory settlement.[53] There must be nothing like mass executions by courts, Churchill warned the Cabinet, because British public opinion would criticise anything resembling that. And there was also a nice Churchillian intervention on behalf of cattle seized from the Kikuyu: 'Is it true that they are dying for want of attention? They must be fed, watered and milked; who is doing this? Remember they belong to the innocent as well as to the guilty. I hope that this point is being well-looked after by the Government on the spot.'[54]

Finally, it is by no means unfitting that Churchill's last recorded utterance in the Cabinet on colonial problems showed him in his statesmanlike mode. Concern had been expressed about the tensions caused throughout the Commonwealth by Indian communities, and by Indian government encouragement of opposition to colonial rule in multi-racial societies. Churchill, however, advised against any drastic action which might offend India, because they needed India's moderating influence and help with major international problems in Asia. Nor, he suggested, should it be assumed that Indian immigrant communities would prove an embarrassment: they might in some cases be 'a balancing factor'. Thus he steered the Cabinet to the conclusion that they should watch the problems carefully but avoid any precipitate action. Precisely the same policy was adopted with respect to West Indian immigration into Britain.[55]

IV

There have been some extraordinary academic judgments upon Churchill's attitude to empire, as crude as they are emotive: for example, it is alleged that he was 'a profound and reactionary imperialist' and a 'malignant racist'.[56] The conclusion to a brief chapter like this is not the place to start a semantic analysis, but perhaps it may be asserted: *racism* is the institutionalised form of racial prejudice, manifesting itself in social and economic domination, while *imperialism* is the structured form of pride in empire, manifesting itself in territorial and international domination. If these definitions – or perhaps any others – are valid, then Churchill was neither a racist nor an imperialist. That he believed in British superiority over non-Europeans and thought the empire was a good thing is not denied. But he loathed racial exploitation, and he never had an imperial programme. He expressly rejected 'imperial federation' and Joseph Chamberlain's creed that the future lay with great empires rather than small states; and in practice he was mainly interested in the colonial empire only when he had to be by virtue of office. Adverse judgment of his attitudes has focused too much on what Churchill *said*, mostly when relaxing in private, rather than on what he *did*.[57] Of course he had his personal preferences – pro-Zionist in Palestine, pro-settler in Kenya, pro-Union in Southern Rhodesia, and so forth – but in no case were his private prejudices allowed to distort his ministerial actions or official decisions whilst at the Colonial Office, decisions which were invariably geared towards compromise, reconciliation, and even-handed justice, however paternalistic the presentation might be.

The Churchill who emerges from this investigation is a pragmatist and a conciliator, a man who believed the empire should be useful to Britain, but also bring benefits and harmony to the populations it ruled. He may never have referred to the 'dual mandate', but in many ways it reflected his ideas. He saw nothing reprehensible in using the empire to advance British national interests and power, because 'the mutually advantageous exchange of goods and services between communities is the foundation alike of the prosperity and peace of the world'; but if Britain was never to have any advantage from the colonies except the satisfaction of behaving in a purely philanthropic way, then 'a good many people would argue that we had better spend our money on improving the health and social services of our workers at home'.[58] If parts of the empire were not useful, or cost too much to maintain, then there was no point in holding on to them, at least formally. This pragmatic outlook was a consistent thread in his policy from Northern Nigeria in 1906 and Somaliland in 1907, through to Egypt in 1954, by way of Iraq in 1922. Even so, the duties of a trustee, when deliberately entered into, as in Palestine, must be upheld; while as far as India was concerned, he found it hard to believe that the Raj was as yet expendable (in terms of his own far from incoherent criteria) without danger to both sides.

This quintessential pragmatist always asked what was feasible, even if some of his answers were adventurous. Churchill was opposed to sending gunboats to Nanking in 1927, because 'punishing China is like flogging a jellyfish'.[59] No latter-day Palmerston he. (After 1945 the neo-Palmerstonians were all on the Labour side.) Indeed, he yielded nothing to Cobden and Bright, or to J.A. Hobson and E.D. Morel for that matter, in his hatred of imperial exploitation. In 1899 he published an account of the reconquest of the Sudan, in which he compared Kitchener's campaign of vilification of the Mahdi to 'the habit of the boa constrictor to besmear the body of his victim with a foul slime before he devours it'. Bold stuff. It bothered him that the inevitable gap between conquest and dominion in the Sudan might become filled with 'the greedy trader, the inopportune missionary, the ambitious soldier and the lying speculator'.[60] As an under-secretary, he denounced Milner's Chinese labour scheme in the Rand mines as 'a horrible experiment', and he accused the government of using Cyprus as 'a milch-cow' (though he was probably mistaken about this): 'There is scarcely any spectacle more detestable than the oppression of a small community by a Great Power for the purpose of pecuniary profit.' That was a courageous thing for a junior minister to write in an official memorandum in 1907, and it remains one of the fiercer critiques of British policy still on the Cyprus files, which is saying quite a lot.[61] Churchill paid dearly within the Establishment for such opinions. If similar protests cannot be quoted from a later period it is not because he became less radical, but because administration was largely purged of earlier abuses – a process in which Churchill himself had played no small part. In the context of his reputation as a stereotypical 'diehard' on India, it is worth recalling the sensitivity and insight into the fundamental flaw of British rule which he showed, however belatedly, in his reflection of 1953: 'If we had made friends with them and taken them into our lives instead of restricting our intercourse to the political field things might have been very different.'[62] His efforts as secretary of state to reconcile Jews and Arabs in Palestine, and Europeans and Indians in Kenya, may not have met with much success, but he surely deserves credit for trying: nothing could have been further from the easy option of 'divide and rule'. If in India the last word for him remained with Lord Morley rather than Lord Macaulay,[63] in other respects his vision was entirely in the liberal cultural tradition of Macaulay's 'imperishable empire' and of Sir Charles Dilke's 'Greater Britain'. This is nicely illustrated by his minute on promoting the worldwide use of the C.K. Ogden–I.A. Richards system of 'Basic' English. This, he wrote, 'would be a gain to us far more durable and fruitful than the annexation of great provinces'; it would also help to promote his policy of closer union with the United States, by making it even more worthwhile for the latter to 'belong to the English-speaking club'. Unfortunately for 'Basic', the support of Churchill proved to be the kiss of death.[64]

Notes

1 The best account of Churchill as secretary of state for the colonies is Henry Pelling, *Winston Churchill* (1974), pp. 261–78. Sir Martin Gilbert's official biography, *Winston S. Churchill*, vol. IV, *1916–1922* (1975) omits all discussion of Africa, including, incredibly, Kenya. Gilbert's *Companion* to volume IV, *Part 3: Documents, April 1921 to November 1922*, is, patchily, more helpful, especially on the Middle East; but even here Southern Rhodesia does not appear in the index, despite the presence of one (marginal) document about it on p. 1877.

2 RH, *Elgin and Churchill at the Colonial Office, 1905–1908* (1968), p. 505, reflecting to some extent the opinion of Wilfrid S. Blunt, *My diaries, part II, 1900–1914* (1920), pp. 287–95; quoted on p. 308 above.

3 L.S. Amery, *My political life*, vol. I, *1896–1914* (1953), p. 196; Clement Attlee, 'Churchill on balance', in P. Stansky, ed., *Churchill: a profile* (New York, 1973), p. 198. There is however an important unpublished essay by Piers Brendon arguing for a more central place for empire in Churchill's outlook: 'Churchill and empire' (see above, Introduction, p. 39).

4 J. Lynn and A. Jay, *The complete 'Yes, minister': the diaries of a cabinet minister, by the Rt Hon. James Hacker, MP* (revised omnibus edn, 1984), p. 161.

5 Churchill's targets were identified early as a soldier and war correspondent:

see *The River War: an historical account of the reconquest of the Soudan* (2 vols., 1899), and *London to Ladysmith* (1900); see also F. Woods, ed., *Young Winston's wars: original despatches, 1892–1900* (1972).

6 J. Barnes and D. Nicholson, eds., *The Leo Amery diaries*, vol. I, *1896–1929* (1980), p. 392; see also R. Furse, *Aucuparius: recollections of a recruiting officer* (Oxford, 1962), p. 85.

7 Gilbert, *Companion*, vol. IV, pt 3, p. 1543.

8 Gilbert, *Churchill*, vol. IV, pp. 859, 913–15, and *Companion*, vol. IV, pt 3, pp. 1999–2004, 2043, 2080, 2094; see also Keith Jeffery, *The British army and the crisis of empire, 1918–1922* (Manchester, 1984), p. 149.

9 Sydney Buxton Papers, Milner to Buxton, 10 May 1919.

10 RH, *Elgin and Churchill at the Colonial Office*, p. 492.

11 The East African quotations are from Churchill, *My African journey* (1908); the others are from RH, *Elgin and Churchill at the Colonial Office*.

12 British Cotton Growing Association pamphlet no. 20, *Speeches by the Rt Hon. Winston S. Churchill, MP, on the Northern Nigerian railway* (Manchester, 1907).

13 British Cotton Growing Association pamphlet no. 74, *Speeches at the banquet given to . . . Secretary of State for the Colonies, 7 June 1921*.

14 Quotation from *The Times*: Gilbert, *Companion*, vol. IV, pt 3, pp. 1474–5.

15 *PD, Commons*, vol. 144, cc. 1620–9 (14 July 1921). In this survey, Churchill also had a good deal to say about disappointing progress in East Africa, for nowhere was 'more magnificent, spacious and wonderful'. As to its racial problems, it was 'very difficult for him to say' where right and justice might lie: Africans, Indians, and settlers all had a claim on the respect of government, but the natives were their greatest trust, 'because they are the most helpless'.

16 I. Friedmann, *The question of Palestine, 1914–1918: British–Jewish–Arab relations* (1973) pp. 7, 17–18; for Churchill and Palestine generally, see M.J. Cohen, *Churchill and the Jews* (1985), though I feel Cohen may be too sceptical about the sincerity of Churchill's Zionism (at least until the murder of Lord Moyne in 1944), and the reality of his strategical interest in it.

17 B. Fergusson, ed., *The business of war: the war narrative of Major-General Sir John Kennedy* (1957), p. 180 (21 November 1941).

18 *PD, Commons*, vol. 156, c. 335 (4 July 1922), debate on Supply.

19 CAB 23/25, no. 45, Cabinet minutes, 31 May 1921; CAB 23/26, no. 70(21)6 (f. 311), Cabinet minutes, 18 August 1921; CO 733/18, no. 5285, minute by Churchill, 5 April 1922: all repr. in Gilbert, *Companion*, vol. IV, pt 3, pp. 1484, 1606, 1853.

20 *White Paper on Palestine* (1922), Cmd 1700.

21 *PD, Commons*, vol. 156, c. 334 (4 July 1922), Supply debate; remarks to Arab delegation, 22 August 1921, repr. in Gilbert, *Companion*, vol. IV, pt 3, pp. 1610–18.

22 Jeffery, *The British army and the crisis of empire*, p. 149.

23 CAB 24/123, CP 3328, Cabinet memo by WSC, 4 August 1921, 'Policy and finance in Mesopotamia, 1922–1923'; Gilbert, *Companion*, vol. IV, pt 3, pp. 1577–80.

24 Gilbert, *Companion*, vol. IV, pt 3, pp. 1648, 1701, 1801, 1869.

25 PREM 11/472, Defence Committee minutes, D 4(53)4, 6 March 1953.

26 Gilbert, *Companion*, vol. IV, pt 3, pp. 1511, 1577, 1675, 1974.

27 CO 733/6, nos. 50764 and 52088, minutes 8, 25 and 26 October 1921.

28 *PD, Commons*, vol. 156, cc. 334–5 (4 July 1922); Gilbert, *Companion*, vol. IV, pt 3, p. 1926.

29 There are several accounts of this important period of decision-making for Kenya, including W.K. Hancock, *Survey of British Commonwealth affairs*, vol. I, *Problems of nationality, 1918–1936* (Oxford, 1937), pp. 209–27; M.R. Dilley, *British policy in Kenya colony* (New York, 1937; London, 1966), pp. 156–61; R. Gregory, *India and East Africa: a history of race relations within the British empire, 1900–1930* (Oxford, 1971), pp. 198–213; G. Bennett, 'Settlers and politics to 1945', in V.T. Harlow and E.M. Chilver, eds., *History of East Africa*, vol. II (Oxford, 1965), pp. 294–9; H. Tinker, *Separate and unequal: India and the Indians in the British Commonwealth, 1920–1950* (1976), pp. 43–59.

30 CO 533/270, no. 40187, 11 August 1921: record of proceedings of the Indian delegation on 9 August 1921.

31 CO 533/270, no. 41679, secretary of state to governor, 16 August 1921; CO 533/264, no. 52967, secret instructions to governor (i.e. not agreed by the Cabinet).

32 CO 533/265, no. 59593, telegram to secretary of state, 29 November 1921, and no. 3128, despatch to the governor, 14 December 1921.

33 CO 537/782, minute by Sir G. Fiddes, 20 August 1921, ticked and initialled by WSC, 22 August 1921.

34 CO 533/265, no. 59593, letters from WSC to E.S. Montagu, 7 and 19 December 1921, and Montagu to WSC, 10 December 1921.

35 Gilbert, *Companion*, vol. IV, pt 3, p. 1649, Montagu to WSC, 12 October 1921; CO 533/288, no. 19600, letters from WSC to Montagu, 4 February 1922, and Montagu to WSC, 28 January and 10 February 1922.

36 CO 533/287, no. 7297, speech, 27 January 1922.

37 Gilbert, *Companion*, vol. IV, pt 3, pp. 1743–7, Montagu to WSC, 31 January 1922, CAB 23/29, ff. 223–4, Cabinet minutes, 13 February 1922. Churchill had a genuine point about coercing the settlers, since the only local force available was non-white, and it was unthinkable to use black troops against white settlers. Officials believed this would be fatal to European prestige and provoke an immediate revolution in South Africa.

38 CAB 23/29, f. 258, Cabinet minutes, 17(22)1, 13 March 1922; Gilbert, *Companion*, vol. IV, pt 3, p. 1805. Churchill's claim merely to be repeating precedent over the highlands reservation was disingenuous: the Elgin Pledge was not a legal restriction, but a matter of 'administrative convenience', and this 'non-racial' formula was now disappearing. The problem for Churchill was, of course, that the settlers had come to regard a stricter safeguard as the test of the government's good faith, and would not agree to anything without it.

39 Furse, *Aucuparius*, p. 85.

40 For the background, see J.P.R. Wallis, *The story of Sir Charles Coghlan and*

the liberation of Southern Rhodesia (1950), pp. 183–94; C. Palley, *The constitutional history and law of Southern Rhodesia, 1838–1965* (1966), ch. 10; L.H. Gann, *A history of Southern Rhodesia; early days to 1934* (1965), pp. 244–7, which perhaps makes Churchill seem to be too sympathetic to the settlers. See also RH, *The failure of South African expansion, 1908–1948* (1972), pp. 59–71.

41 CAB 23/27, f. 95, Cabinet minutes, 78(21)5, 20 October 1921; for correspondence with Smuts and high commissioner, see CO 537/1182–1184 (1921).

42 CO 537/1203, no. 6957, telegram to Smuts, 11 February 1921; and CO 537/1184, no. 50699, Smuts to WSC, 5 September 1921; Gilbert, *Companion*, vol. IV, pt 3, p. 1877, WSC to Lord Hugh Cecil, 26 April 1922.

43 Essential reading for Churchill's Indian policy is his *India: speeches and an introduction* (1931). Also valuable are N. Mansergh *et al.*, eds., *India, the transfer of power, 1942–7*, vols., III and IV (1971 and 1973), September 1942 to August 1944; and R.J. Moore, *Churchill, Cripps and India, 1939–1945* (Oxford, 1979).

44 Inaccurately transcribed as 'shame' by Gilbert, *Churchill*, vol. V, *1922–1939* (1976), p. 595, thus destroying the point of Churchill's criticism, which was not that the federal proposals were unworthy, but that they were unworkable. R.R. James, *Churchill: a study in failure, 1900–1939* (1970), p. 212, makes the same mistake. The correct wording was proved by N. Mansergh in *The Commonwealth experience* (1st edn, 1969), p. 267, note.

45 Mansergh *et al.*, eds., *Transfer of power*, vol. III, p. 809, Wavell to Amery, 15 April 1943; W.S. Churchill, *The Second World War*, vol. V (1952), p. 824, minute to home secretary, 7 January 1943. See also W.R. Louis, *Imperialism at bay, 1941–1945: the United States and the decolonisation of the British empire* (Oxford, 1977), pp. 200, 433–4.

46 J.D.B. Miller, *Sir Winston Churchill and the Commonwealth of Nations*, John M. Macrossan Lecture, 1966 (Queensland, 1967); T.R. Reese, *Australia, New Zealand and the United States: a survey of international relations, 1941–1968* (Oxford, 1969), pp. 20–3. Churchill was not perhaps totally insensitive to Australian feelings: in September 1941 he minuted: 'We have got to treat these people, who are politically embarrassed, but are sending a splendid army into the field, with the utmost consideration' (PREM 4/50/5). Churchill's wartime policy is now thoroughly discussed in Andrew Stewart, *Empire lost: Britain, the Dominions and the Second World War* (2008).

47 PREM 4/44/1, note by WSC, WP(G) (41)109, 7 October 1941, commenting on Lord Harlech's report to the prime minister about his visit to Natal, 20 October 1941. The only Natalian who voiced secessionist notions was G. Heaton Nicholls in the neutrality debate, 4 September 1939, and nobody had taken him seriously.

48 RH, *Britain's declining empire: the road to decolonisation, 1918–1968* (2006), ch. 3, esp. pp. 215–20 on southern Africa. See also D. Goldsworthy, '"Keeping change within bounds": aspects of colonial policy during the Churchill and Eden governments, 1951–1957', *JICH*, vol. 18 (1990), pp. 81–108.

49 CAB 131/12, Defence Committee minutes, D 1(52)1, 12 March 1952; PREM 11/1765, minutes 30 August and 6 September 1954.

50 CAB 128/27/2, Cabinet minutes, CC 57(54)4, 27 August 1954, and CC 58(54)2, 1 September 1954.

51 PREM 11/1765, WSC to Eden, 4 July 1955.

52 Doubts vividly recorded in Lord Moran, *Winston Churchill: the struggle for survival, 1940–1965: the diaries* (1966), pp. 478, 482, 580–2.

53 M. Blundell, *So rough a wind: the Kenya memoirs* (1964) pp. 183–4; CAB 128/26/1, Cabinet minutes CC 33(53)1, 25 May 1953.

54 PREM 11/472, minute M 552/52, 26 November 1952. For Gibraltar apes, see *The Second World War*, vol. VI (1954), p. 607, minute 1 September 1944.

55 CAB 128/28, Cabinet minutes CC 15(55)1, 17 February 1955.

56 C. Thorne, *Allies of a kind: the United States, Britain and the war against Japan, 1941–1945* (1978), pp. 669, 725, 750.

57 I agree with Paul Addison that too much can be made of Churchill's derogatory remarks in private (many of them recorded by Moran in *Winston Churchill: the struggle for survival*), e.g. the silly descriptions of a bygone age about camel-dung-eating Arabs, dirty Baboos, little yellow men. See Addison, 'The political beliefs of Winston Churchill', *Transactions of the Royal Historical Society*, 5th series, vol. 30 (1980), pp. 23–47. For a recent reassessment of Churchill's position on Africa, as more liberal, better informed, more enlightened than most of his contemporaries, see Roland Quinault, 'Churchill and black Africa', *History Today*, vol. 55/6 (2005), pp. 31–6.

58 Churchill, *The Second World War*, vol. V, p. 824, minute to home secretary, 7 January 1943.

59 W.R. Louis, *British strategy in the Far East, 1919–1939* (Oxford, 1971), p. 133.

60 Churchill, *The River War* (revised edn, 1902), p. 10.

61 Memo by WSC, 'The condition of Cyprus', 19 October 1907, confidential print, Med. no. 65.

62 Moran, *The struggle for survival*, pp. 449–50.

63 Winston S. Churchill, *Great contemporaries* (1937), p. 99: Morley's thought, fears, and outlook 'made a strong impression on me'.

64 Churchill, *The Second World War*, vol. V, p. 571, minute, 11 July 1943; see also PREM 8/180 (1946).

12   Smuts in context: Britain and South Africa

[This chapter is expanded from a paper first published (under the title 'South Africa, Cambridge, and Commonwealth History') in *The Round Table: the Commonwealth Journal of International Affairs*, vol. 90, no. 360 (2001), which in turn was based upon a modified version of the Smuts Distinguished Lecture, University of Cambridge, November 2000, delivered under the auspices of the Managers of the Smuts Memorial Fund, to commemorate the fiftieth anniversary of the death of Jan Christiaan Smuts – not an occasion for denigration.]

He was a man who raised the name of South Africa, with all its special . . . problems, to the highest rank of respect . . . among the freedom-loving nations of the world.

A noble and outstanding figure in his faithful and courageous support of his own countrymen when they seemed to be opposed by overwhelming forces . . . one of the most enlightened, courageous and noble-minded men . . . of the twentieth century.[1]

No, these words are not a eulogy to Nelson Mandela. They were in fact spoken in the House of Commons by Churchill and Attlee respectively after the death on 11 September 1950 of Field Marshal Jan Christiaan Smuts, the only other South African leader of world stature besides Nelson Mandela. The general eagerness today to honour Mandela has its parallel in the adulation once accorded to Smuts. For the last two and a quarter years of his life, he was chancellor of Cambridge University, between Baldwin and Tedder. That Cambridge should, in an uncontested election, choose a prime minister of unregenerate South Africa to be its chancellor may strike many now as odd, and the tributes quoted above as singularly inappropriate. Fifty years after his death, Smuts's reputation is in eclipse, and he is widely perceived as 'a racist and an imperialist'. We in Cambridge may all unite, however, in a grateful commemoration of the sequel to the university's action over the chancellorship: the establishment of the Smuts Memorial Fund for Commonwealth Studies in 1952. The princely sum of £150,000 was raised rapidly in times of austerity by public subscription to commemorate Smuts's part, as Attlee put it, 'in

342

the development of the conception of the Commonwealth and his devotion to the University of which he was Chancellor'.[2] Today (2007) the fund has an annual income of about £300,000. It not only provides for the professorship of the history of the Commonwealth, but has financed a broad range of Commonwealth studies, through six Smuts Readers, many visiting and post-doctoral fellowships and studentships, and most recently a Smuts Librarian. In addition the Managers arrange lectures, and regularly make substantial grants to faculty libraries, for graduate study, research, and travel, and towards the costs of publication. After more than half a century of enjoying this munificence, we should remind ourselves of how it all came about, and so perhaps arrive at a better understanding of the significance of Smuts himself.

I

Jan Smuts arrived in Christ's College, Cambridge as an undergraduate law student in 1891. There, he later claimed, he found 'hospitality, friendship, comradeship . . . an atmosphere of culture and a spiritual home'. This recollection was a little too rosy, I suspect. At least for his first year, he was short of money, lonely, 'utterly desolate' – and very cold. He lodged at 13 Victoria Street, probably for all three years. On the edge of the residential district known as 'The Kite', close to college, it is an artisan's dwelling, basic even by local standards. (There is no commemorative plaque.) Smuts kept himself to himself. He did not join the Union. Eventually he became friendly with two or three of the dons, and was drawn into a small group of South African students who accompanied him to the new St Columba's Presbyterian Church in Downing Street. One Boat Race day they persuaded him to go with them on a cheap railway excursion to London. Somehow he gave them the slip between Liverpool Street and Putney, escaping to spend an enjoyable day – in the library of the Middle Temple. Unsurprisingly, Smuts took firsts in both parts of the Law Tripos. Extraordinarily, he sat both examinations in the same year, 1894. He was awarded the George Long Prize for Roman Law and was remembered as a student of exceptional brilliance. Christ's offered him a fellowship. He turned it down.[3]

On his return to South Africa, and after becoming at the age of twenty-eight state attorney in the Transvaal government, Smuts played a resourceful part as a Boer general in the South African Anglo-Boer War – 'faithful and courageous' indeed, in support of his own countrymen when 'opposed by overwhelming forces'. His opening salvo was to dictate for anonymous publication a vitriolic denunciation of British policy, *A century of wrong* in the English translation, in which British rule and intervention in South Africa was repeatedly described as a perfidious record of duplicity, fraud, and violence.[4] This is not altogether wide of the mark. Victorian policy *was* aggressive and subject to maddening vacillations. As a young Boer commando-leader, Smuts carried in his knapsack not only the proverbial field marshal's baton, but also a Greek New Testament and a volume of Kant. This would have been unusual on the opposite side. It was, after all, *Ruff's guide to the turf* which consoled General Buller, and Jerome K. Jerome's *Three men in a boat (To say nothing of the dog)* which was found in the knapsack of a British soldier killed at Spion Kop.

After the war, the British regime under Lord Milner tried to consolidate military victory with a scheme to introduce more English settlers. The target was 7,800 but only 568 arrived, at a cost of £2.5 million – the subject of a premonitory Churchillian quip: never has 'so much money been spent upon the settlement of so few'. When an anti-jingoistic Liberal government came into office in Britain in December 1905, with Churchill a junior minister at the Colonial Office, Smuts seized the chance to campaign for the restoration of self-government to the Transvaal. His meeting with the Liberal prime minister, Sir Henry Campbell-Bannerman, proved to be the defining moment of Smuts's political life. Unfortunately, like all 'defining moments', perhaps, it was based on self-delusion. What Smuts could not know was that the decision had already been taken in principle, and that in any case ministers had been warned to be on their guard against a man described by the Colonial Office South African expert as 'a Boer and a lawyer', who would argue with 'all the cunning of his race and calling'. Plainly, no one in Whitehall in 1906 could discern the Commonwealth angel imprisoned in the Afrikaner block of marble. Smuts was totally convinced he had persuaded Campbell-Bannerman to be magnanimous. Campbell-Bannerman, like the good politician he was, let him believe it. Moreover, whether the policy was genuinely magnanimous is an issue on which I am agnostic.[5] Be that as it may, Smuts hung a portrait of Campbell-Bannerman behind his desk, and again and again recalled the 'magnanimity' of the Liberal post-war settlement. During his inaugural address as chancellor at Cambridge, he dwelt upon this 'highlight of statesmanship': Campbell-Bannerman had performed, he said, 'an immortal service to the British Empire, aye, to the cause of man everywhere'. 'My very presence here today', he added, 'bears witness to that great deed of political wisdom.'[6]

This was not how the Conservative Opposition saw it in 1906. The former prime minister, A.J. Balfour, denounced the Liberals' constitution for the Transvaal as 'the most reckless experiment ever tried in the development of a great colonial policy'. Remarkably, however, only three years later, Balfour endorsed its logical corollary, the South Africa Act of Union, as 'one of the great landmarks of imperial policy . . . which is going to produce admirable fruits'.[7] The judgment of history may be that the Liberal government in these years was at first neither so reckless, nor in 1909–10 so successful, as Balfour thought. But there was certainly a shift of opinion in favour of the Boers. Rapid progress towards South African unification was expedited because it suited both the British and the Boer leadership. The British government wanted to promote Anglo-Boer friendship and establish a large, effective, and grateful Union in order geopolitically to strengthen a weak link in the imperial chain. The Boers wanted it in order to assert themselves against the mining magnates, rid South Africa of British interference, consolidate white supremacy, and create a firm base for Afrikaner national expansion. Botha and Smuts, once in power in the Transvaal, quickly commended themselves, their administration winning almost golden opinions in London for frankness, friendliness, reasonableness, and helpfulness.[8] The new self-governing regime seemed to compare more than favourably with troublesome communities in the 'British world' elsewhere, especially 'White Australia' and the Kenya settlers. There was even testimony to improvement in the treatment of Africans. The Boers had recovered well from the aftermath of war, astutely led by Botha and Smuts, while the British failed to grasp how far they were losing ground. In consequence they indulged in some wishful thinking.[9] So there was a 'window of opportunity' for the unification movement, a short-lived period of perhaps unreal and transient goodwill.

There was a willingness in London to let the South African politicians settle their own constitution. Largely at Smuts's insistence, this was to be unitary and not federal in structure, and it followed the Westminster model, not the old Boer oligarchical republican constitutions. This guaranteed its credibility in Britain. The Union constitution – despite some myths to the contrary – was in no sense 'imposed' from London. The British government, and the Conservative Opposition, calmly accepted most of what Smuts wanted. The result froze the African franchise and political advancement, and neutralised the threat to an Afrikaner regime from urban and predominantly English-speaking voters. It also entrenched the Transvaal in an advantageous position by making Pretoria the seat of the executive. Smuts had every reason to be pleased with his efforts. He may well have concluded that he could continue to manipulate the British to secure his own ends.[10]

Now, throw in some calculations about South African national interest as a precarious 'small nation' (in inverted commas), and it is easy enough to explain why Smuts became reconciled to the Empire-Commonwealth. But how did Cambridge fix upon him as its chancellor? No records are available about such decisions. My guess is that the prime movers were the Master of his old college, Christ's, Canon Charles Raven, providentially in place as vice-chancellor, and the Master of St John's, E.A. Benians. Benians was the central figure in Cambridge imperial and Commonwealth history for the whole of the first half of the twentieth century. Unlike the Oxford historians of empire, inspired and financed by men who identified with the imperial triumphalism of the South African War, Cambridge historians like Benians and Professor Eric Walker regarded the war – which coincided exactly with Benians's formative undergraduate years – as an intolerable blot on Britain's record. Writing only a few years afterwards in the *Cambridge modern history*, Benians pulled no punches, denouncing a 'devastating, embittering' war which, he implied, the Afrikaners ('formidable, stubborn and skilful opponents' though they were) should never have had to fight, a war in which Britain inflicted 'the severest injury' on a 'distracted country'.[11] To the Cambridge dons who thought like this, making Smuts their chancellor was an act of expiation, even more than it was an assertion of the university's aspirations to an international status.

Of Smuts's fame and distinction there could in any case be no doubt: OM, CH, KC, FRS, LLB, Honorary LLD, an Honorary Fellow of Christ's since 1915, a field marshal in the British army, a creator of the Royal Air Force, a member of Lloyd George's War Cabinet, twice prime minister of South Africa, a founder of the League of Nations, a principal architect of the inter-war British Commonwealth. Lawyer and scientist, soldier, and mythic philosopher-king, Smuts had a wholly exceptional range of talents and experiences. In 1917, the journalist C.P. Scott said, 'Smuts was perhaps the most popular man in the country.'[12] He made a tremendous impression on all who met him. The Master of Magdalene, A.C. Benson, wrote in 1917 that he looked like a radiant Scandinavian royal prince, 'the embodiment of grace and sympathy and freedom . . . a beautiful spirit, I felt'. Benson did not automatically admire the famous. Compare his opinion of Churchill: 'he looked like a real cad', 'like some sort of *maggot*'.[13]

To some extent there are genuine parallels between Smuts and Mandela: both were well born but essentially country-boys at heart, with an affinity for the natural world, a Christian upbringing, and an English-language education, who both became lawyers and acclaimed guerrilla leaders, both inspirational personalities, generously preaching reconciliation.[14] But there is of course another side, or limitation, to Smuts. For all his admirable internationalism, scholarly learning, paternalist sympathies, and constant talk of justice, fair play, human fellowship, and interdependence, of the world as a holistic 'great society of companionship',[15] he did nothing to promote the political advancement of Africans. Inertia was perhaps largely to blame: sins of omission rather than commission. But whether it was from inaction or indifference, caution or obtuseness, few among condescending posterity have much good to say of the Smuts who failed to grapple with this problem. 'Colour queers my poor pitch everywhere,' he complained in 1946. Some are no doubt tempted to mutter, 'serve him right'. Smuts drafted the opening sentence of the preamble to the United Nations Charter, proclaiming the UN's faith in basic human rights, the importance of safeguarding the 'essential worth and integrity of the human personality'. The words were soon to be flung in his face as evidence of hypocrisy.[16] 'Human rights' to him meant dignity rather than equality. Smuts was, however, a prisoner of the ideologies of his generation – ideologies often virtually indistinguishable from those of the Edwardian Liberal Party – and before we get too judgmental, let us remind ourselves of the spacious perspectives of Mandela: 'I cared more that he had helped the foundation of the League of Nations, promoting freedom throughout the world, than the fact that he had repressed freedom at home.'[17] Let us also note that in speaking of non-Europeans, Smuts never descended to the crude contempt of a Field Marshal Montgomery or the cruel jokes of a Churchill.

More than most of us, perhaps, Smuts had his blind spots and contradictions. He was a South African patriot who seemed to care more about Europe than Africa. His own people became increasingly puzzled by him and sceptical, giving him a derogatory nickname, 'Slim Jannie', implying that he was two-faced and unscrupulous.[18] Afrikaner nationalists see him as a clever son of the veldt who sold his birthright for a mess of British imperial potage, a prodigal son who not only never really came home, but was so compromised at the end of his life as to accept the chancellorship of a British university. He had been unsuccessful in promoting South Africa's international interests after 1945. And so the South African white electorate rejected him in 1948. Too Anglophile for the Afrikaners, too much the wily old Afrikaner opportunist for the British South Africans, and the victim of a psephological quirk in the electoral provisions of the Union constitution – which as its founding father he was too punctilious, or too proud, to remove – Smuts lost to Dr Malan's National Party, who entered into power on a minority of the votes.[19]

Plate 12.1 Smuts with Hertzog (Smuts on the right). When General J.B.M. Hertzog's National Party defeated Smuts in the election of 1924, Whitehall was more alarmed than it would be in 1948. But in 1933 Smuts and Hertzog were reunited in an uneasy coalition led by Hertzog, known as 'the Fusion government', 1934–40.

II

The fall of Smuts surprised the British governing elite and the African National Congress leaders alike, but by neither was it regarded as a disaster. Who and what they were dealing with came into sharper focus. Indeed, on hearing that Smuts had died, the British high commissioner in South Africa, Sir Evelyn Baring (son of the great Lord Cromer), is recorded as sleeping more soundly in his bed. It is an unexpected reaction, and it needs a little explanation.[20]

The Union of South Africa was an inherently expansionist state from the beginning. The South Africa Act of 1909 provisionally envisaged a transfer from Britain to the Union of responsibility for the three High Commission Territories (Basutoland, Bechuanaland, and Swaziland), geopolitically enmeshed in the South African geographical region. The British government began to repent of this 'Greater South Africa' plan as early as 1913, disillusioned by the harsh and decidedly unmagnanimous Natives Land Act introduced by General Botha's government in that year. Nevertheless, every South African prime minister from Botha in 1911 to Verwoerd in 1961 pressed for the transfer of the High Commission Territories. As trustee, the British government was increasingly determined not to hand them over without African consent. This ever-hardening resistance was the principal cause of the steady deterioration of Anglo-South African relations in the inter-war years. To counter this deterioration, British policy-makers clung to Smuts as some sort of collaborative agent. There were two snags to this. One was that Smuts was of dubious value in such a role, simply because he was unrepresentative of the Afrikaner community, indeed insensitive to some of its most cherished aspirations, such as republicanism. The other was that Smuts had his own agenda and was the most committed and persistent expansionist of them all.[21] He had defined Boer war aims in 1899 with the slogan: 'from Zambesi to Simon's Bay: Africa for the Africander'. Later, his territorial ambitions extended not only to Rhodesia and the High Commission Territories, but to South-West Africa, and to at least part of Mozambique, and possibly even to Kenya as well. What High Commissioner Baring feared was that Attlee's post-war government, grateful for an £80 million gold loan which Smuts had arranged, would do a deal with Smuts, transferring Swaziland to him, sacrificing it as a compromise, the better perhaps to protect the other two Territories from a similar fate. It was, however, inconceivable that any such deal would be done with a South African government not headed by Smuts. And so the removal of Smuts from the scene enabled Baring to 'sleep more soundly in his bed'. Thus, paradoxically, in the moment of its triumph

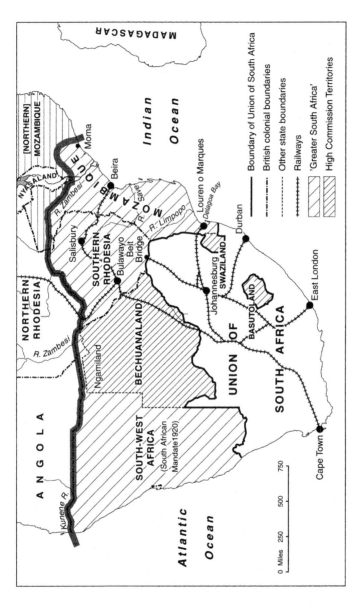

Map 12.1 Plans for a 'Greater South Africa'. The heavy northern line represents the limit of Smuts's abortive 'immediate' aim from 1916–19, with a plan to remove Portugal from southern Mozambique (with possible compensation
in south-east Tanganyika), either at Moma, or at the exit of the Zambesi (or alternatively at the exit of the Save, with
Southern Rhodesia taking the area between the two rivers and the port of Beira). *Source*: S.E. Katzenellenbogen, *South
Africa and southern Mozambique* (1982), p. 123, 'Smuts's expansionist aims'.

in winning the election of 1948, the National Party ensured the defeat of the foundation-dream of a 'Greater South Africa'.

Apart from pursuing the contentious issue of northward expansion, long after the British planners had given it up as an aim for South Africa, Smuts was for the last forty years of his life not merely *persona grata* to both sides of British politics, but widely admired as a statesman of the first rank. 'He's certainly impressive and very good company,' wrote Sir Alexander Cadogan in his diary, and 'one of the few men whom I think the PM [Churchill] really respects and to whom he will listen'.[22] Probably his closest friends were an English Quaker family, the Gilletts, with whom he corresponded regularly.

Smuts's views on race – relations between black and white South Africans – were hardly systematic, and they were not geared to immediate practical solutions to 'the native problem'. Of black South Africans, notoriously he said, 'I don't believe in politics for them.' On the other hand, he did not regard racial differences as innate and immutable, accepting that characteristics could change and acculturation develop, although probably slowly. He latched on to British doctrines of trusteeship as a convenient and principled middle way between racial equality and white superiority. He quoted Lugard's *Dual mandate* with approval, and he agreed that trusteeship carried the obligation to rule justly, even while it might function as a paternalistic vehicle for discrimination. Although he upheld the right to local residential segregation, he rejected all ideas of enforcing it by state legislation. Indeed, by 1942 he had concluded that 'the policy of keeping Europeans and Africans completely apart' would not work. The economic and social facts refuted the theory that whites and blacks could live in separate territorial compartments. 'The whole trend both in this country and throughout Africa has been in the opposite direction.' He constantly insisted that close contact was the reality, that South Africa was a unitary and dynamic economy, within which black and white had little option but to work together, because each needed the other. Mr Justice Fagan's Report of the Native Laws Commission (1948) embodied his social philosophy. It declared that territorial separation of the races was a self-deceiving dream.[23]

In many ways, Smuts's attitude was little different from those of the intellectual and official elites in 1930s and 1940s Britain. If his abhorrence of miscegenation seemed to take him closer to the more extreme doctrines of Stellenbosch and Bloemfontein, these were just as prevalent in Oxford and Kensington, as the reaction to Seretse Khama's marriage painfully showed.[24] It should therefore be possible to argue that Smuts had an essential Britishness of outlook, which was the source of his breadth of vision. It may be possible to understand his attitude to race, and, as it developed, to apartheid, by standing back, taking a longer perspective than that of his own lifetime, and examining the dynamics of British policy towards the apartheid state, particularly after 1948. By looking at the South African problem in this way, through British eyes, we may be able to conjecture how Smuts himself would have reacted to the racial policies of the Afrikaner regime after his death.

I suppose that most ordinary British people have a notion that the main concern of their governments with respect to South Africa has been one of economic interest – the protection of gold supply, trade, and investment – and that this objective compromised a proper stand against apartheid, even to the extent of actually supporting South Africa at the United Nations. Afrikaners are now further maintaining that it was the British government, not their National Party, which was in some fundamental way actually to blame for the invention of apartheid. There are misconceptions here. I want to comment on three of them, and in so doing, place Smuts more accurately in context, as South Africa lurched off in directions he would not have taken.

First, as to the nature of British interests in South Africa. Although it is true that there were long-standing economic linkages which were mutually beneficial, of less obvious but probably greater weight with Cabinet ministers were the strategic imperatives for trying to maintain as good relations as possible. The Cape route to India and Australia had to be kept open; South Africa was a major source of uranium; and it might be a useful anti-communist ally in the cold war. Even more central to Whitehall's concerns, it was essential not fatally to upset South Africa over the High Commission Territories, so vulnerable to all sorts of pressure, quite apart from the threat of incorporation. Preservation of over-flying rights to maintain air access was a serious consideration. The top priority of British South African policy was now the containment of South African expansion. Like Smuts, Whitehall planners viewed the world geopolitically. In fact, stopping the territorial spread of the apartheid regime was probably the most useful and realistic thing British governments could do to combat it, and they succeeded. Against all the odds, Lesotho, Botswana, Swaziland, and Namibia emerged into independence, and South Africa's boundaries today remain precisely those of 1910.[25]

Secondly, did British governments 'support' apartheid by an indulgent attitude at the United Nations over anti-South African resolutions? If this were ever true, the charge largely ceased to be valid from April 1960, when for the first time, instead of abstaining, the British delegation voted in favour of a General Assembly resolution condemning South Africa. This was in the aftermath of the horrifying shootings at Sharpeville, but it was also in accordance with the warning unequivocally issued by Prime Minister Macmillan in February during his famous 'wind of change' speech. There were, he declared, aspects of South African policy 'which make it impossible to support you without being false to our own deep convictions about the political destinies of free men, to which in our territories we are striving to give effect'.[26] (It is often forgotten that this was the climax and principal message of Macmillan's speech, and not the 'wind of change', added as an afterthought; the whole sub-text was that South Africa was becoming a liability to the West in the cold war.) Before April 1960, however, Britain had only *appeared* to support South Africa. Such alignment as there was with South Africa at the UN was made, not out of love for Malan and his successor Strijdom, but for compelling reasons of Britain's own as a colonial power. If UN intervention in the affairs of South and South-West Africa were successfully established, there would be a dangerous precedent for 'interference' in British colonies. (See above, p. 258.)

Of the reality of British ministerial detestation of apartheid and its exponents there can be no doubt, and it was uniform across the political spectrum. Labour colonial secretaries denounced apartheid as 'totally repugnant' and a 'wicked racial policy'.[27] Eden hated Strijdom: 'obstinate, rude and purblind', an offensive bully.[28] For Macmillan, white supremacy was 'clearly wrong', and he was personally committed to saying so publicly. Even Baroness Thatcher had to say, 'I held no brief for apartheid.'[29] Sir John Maud, high commissioner from 1959 to 1962, filled his despatches with scathing observations. 'To a Western European', he wrote, Verwoerd's government 'seems to owe more to the 17th century than to the 20th century – though there is an ominous Hitlerian smell about it.' Afrikaners had somehow 'missed the spirit of the century', allowing themselves to become 'a police state run by Transvaal thugs'. Dr Verwoerd (prime minister, 1958–66) he regarded as an arrogant, ruthless and authoritarian intellectual, a formidable, enigmatic, doctrinaire fanatic of 'impregnable insularity', 'frighteningly self-righteous'. The minister for external affairs, Eric Louw, Maud dismissed as an embittered, spiteful, pedantic, vain, dreary, self-righteous neurotic, as unprepossessing as he was unpopular, 'disturbingly reminiscent of Dr Goebbels'.[30]

In Sir John Maud's analysis, the British government would simply have to sit it out with this objectionable regime, just as they were sitting it out with that other conspicuous tyranny, Soviet Russia. He was convinced that apartheid would collapse in the end, because it was 'inconceivable that in this multi-racial state the criterion of advancement will forever remain the colour of your skin'. Verwoerdism must collapse, 'for the simple reason that it is not only evil but cannot be made to fit the facts: it is a policy for putting back in their shells eggs which were broken long ago (when South Africa first began to become industrialised)'. These acute insights were matched by almost prophetic predictions: 'In the end the policy will have to be modified in the interests of economic good sense.' And again: 'Christianity is a much more serious long-term threat than Communism to white supremacy.'[31]

So let us be quite clear about it: no British government 'supported' apartheid. Indeed, to have done so would have made nonsense of decolonisation and destroyed British international credibility, especially with those Afro-Asian nations whose friendship was needed in the East–West struggle. At the same time, it was necessary to keep on terms as good as possible with the South African government, *despite* apartheid. A reasonable working relationship remained necessary even after South Africa was driven out of the Commonwealth, which took its stand on human rights and non-racialism, in 1961. South Africa still had to be treated as half-ally and half-untouchable at the same time. British governments equivocated on the complex issue of sanctions, trying to distinguish in arms sales between weapons which might be used for internal repression and those required for external defence, and thus continued to pay a price in domestic and international criticism, which they believed to be unavoidable in order to preserve essential higher interests. As a Labour minister told his Cabinet colleagues in 1951, those who would ostracise South Africa and have nothing to do with it, 'completely fail to understand the realities of the situation'.[32] Nevertheless, there is no doubt where even Conservative ministerial sympathies lay. Secretly, the Macmillan government provided crucial facilities for Nelson Mandela, Oliver Tambo, and the ANC, meeting in and moving through Bechuanaland *circa* 1960.[33] British governments walked an agonising tightrope between co-operation with South Africa on matters of mutual concern, and provocation by policies such as promoting independence for the High Commission Territories. I have no experience of tightrope walking myself, but I understand the art is to keep the eye firmly fixed on a distant point. Sir John Maud showed Whitehall how to do this. Always remember, he advised, that one day there would almost certainly be a black government in Pretoria, so 'keep faith' with the black majority, keep a foot in the door, and meanwhile do not antagonise the National Party government to no good purpose. The return of the new South Africa to the Commonwealth in 1994 surely vindicates the essential soundness of this British strategy.[34]

Thirdly, does the British government – or Smuts for that matter – in fact have any responsibility for the invention of apartheid – as is now being vigorously asserted among Afrikaners anxious to make common cause with the blacks as brothers in their shared experience of British oppression? Not to beat about the bush, this is rather obviously a self-serving attempt to deflect the blame from where it properly belongs. No one is denying that the British treated South Africa badly in the nineteenth century, but everything changed in 1906, as Smuts recognised. Nor can we deny that apartheid had some of its roots in Edwardian policies of segregation. Separate black urban locations were, after all, well established in South Africa before 1910. But such arrangements were common throughout the British and French empires. At the turn of the century the world's most notorious racial villain was not South Africa but 'White Australia'. Separate ethnic 'quarters' in any case seem almost to be a historic and universal principle of urban life. Segregation may have been the framework within which apartheid developed. However, there is a fundamental difference between segregation and apartheid.[35] Smuts condemned apartheid as 'a crazy concept, born of prejudice and fear'. (This suggests that Chief Luthuli was wrong in his crushing judgment that 'it did not seem to us of much importance' whether Smuts or Malan won the election of 1948.[36]) What happened from 1948 was that a seismic shift took place, from pragmatic, occasional, and limited measures of discrimination and separation, to an ideological, unified, and systematic denial of black rights in all spheres of life: something dogmatic, rigorous, and totalising. Ad hoc arrangements were superseded by an unmerciful programme, regulating not just physical space, but human movement and social relationships too. The difference is neatly exemplified in the extension of specific legislation against inter-racial prostitution in the 1927 Immorality Act, to an ideologically driven criminalisation of racial mixture in the Prohibition of Mixed Marriages Act of 1949, the highly symbolic first act of the apartheid regime.[37] At best, apartheid was evidence of a preposterous vanity about the Self compounded by a fathomless ignorance about 'the Other'. But it was more sinister than this. Apartheid was given a religious sanction as a doctrine worked out by the Dutch Reformed Church, ideologically underpinned by twenty years of clerical thought – I refuse to call it theology, since its biblical arguments were almost entirely spurious – and then injected into the Afrikaner political elite in the 1940s. Theocratic appeals to divine sanction of course always conveniently place laws beyond modern principles of rational criticism. God had instituted boundary lines between races, it seems, and that was all there was to be said.[38] As prime minister, Dr Malan lectured the African National Congress to the effect that racial differences were 'permanent and not man-made . . . Afrikanerdom is but a creation of God. Our history is the highest work of the Architect of the Centuries.'[39] The minister for Bantu Administration, De Wet Nel, said in May 1959, introducing the so-called 'Promotion of Bantu Self-Government Bill' – the cornerstone of the notorious 'grand apartheid' of bantustans or African homelands – apartheid is 'not a mere abstraction which hangs in the air. It is a divine task which has to be implemented and fulfilled systematically.'[40] Whatever criticisms can be made of Smuts,[41] this was emphatically not his language or world-view, let alone that of any British government. However fumblingly, Smuts tried to find ways in which South Africans of different race and colour could live together. The National Party forced them to live apart. The difference could not be more stark.[42] What the Afrikaner regime taught in its schools they called 'Christian-National thought'. This has been memorably described by one historian as an eclectic amalgam of neo-Calvinism, neo-Nazism, and pseudo-scientific eugenics, with a dash of hopeless romanticism.[43] Only this peculiar Afrikaner concoction, and not any kind of British input, can adequately explain why segregation-ist policies held in common around the British empire as the twentieth century began, were gradually repudiated everywhere else, but in South Africa were reinvented as something much worse in the 1950s.

III

It was Nelson Mandela who in 2001 spoke of relations between Britain and South Africa in terms of 'a special relationship and its mutual benefits, which history has bound us in'.[44] It was something Smuts might have said, a generous yet realistic appreciation of the closeness of the ties between the two countries. South Africa had by far the largest concentration of British-descended population of any country in Africa, and there were economic and geopolitical reasons for each to remain in friendly relationship despite their differences, latterly sharpened by the explosive issues of race. So it was always an *uneasy* special relationship. Smuts himself embodied historically many of the points of conflict and continuing tension, as well as finding a path to their partial resolution, a resolution never free of ambivalence. The ambivalence was mutual. It was much harder to resolve once the Afrikaner community committed itself to the theocratic doctrine of apartheid, 'the creed of despair', the evasion of reality.[45] It led to the departure of South Africa from the Commonwealth in 1961. This 'parting of the ways' underlined the unease but could not entirely destroy the inherently 'special' nature of their historic relationship.

This was of course an outcome, some ten years after his death, that would have shattered Smuts. Of all the contexts in which we may place him, the Commonwealth was one to which he attached particular value, for it was where he found a platform and a fulfilment which South Africa was less and less able to provide. For Smuts, the Commonwealth represented the continuing basis of an essential Anglo-Afrikaner reconciliation at home, and the beautiful prospect of peace abroad, 'the beginning of great things for the World'. Was he mistaken so consistently to make Anglo-Afrikaner co-operation his first priority? Within the context of multi-racial South Africa, almost certainly. But 1961 shows that the relationship between the two white groups could never be taken for granted. History does not find it easy to exonerate Smuts for his perverse passivity in the face of the more fundamental issue of the black South African communities. Those who rush to judgment, however, would do well to ponder the measured assessment of Professor Mansergh:

Yet however large race relations may loom in the mind of a succeeding generation they should not be allowed to obscure foresight or achievements in other fields, at least as immediate in their importance and as challenging in their nature, in earlier times. Union itself, a memorable part in two world wars, an unrivalled perception of the principles that determined the transformation of Empire into Commonwealth – these were things in their own day of counterbalancing weight. In the perspective of history, after all, it was not colour but war, peace and their consequences that dominated the years of Smuts' political maturity from 1897 down to 1945 and what the times immediately demanded, Smuts supremely gave.[46]

In other words, even 'great men' have to be understood in context, as a product of their times, and also as constrained by their practice of politics as the art of the possible.

Notes

1 *PD, Commons*, tributes and memorial to Field Marshal Smuts, vol. 478, cc. 1097–1102 (13 September 1950); vol. 488, cc. 1224–6 (7 June 1951); vol. 502, cc. 2440–3 (20 June 1952).
2 *Cambridge University Reporter*, vol. 82 (1951–2), p. 719, Report of the Council of the Senate (4 February 1952), and pp. 1358–60 (28 May 1952).
3 W.K. Hancock, *Smuts*, vol. I, *The sanguine years, 1870–1919* (Cambridge, 1962), ch. 3, pp. 33–46.
4 Iain R. Smith, 'Jan Smuts and the South African War', *South African Historical Journal*, vol. 41 (1999), pp. 172–95.
5 RH, 'Smuts and the decision of the Liberal government to grant responsible government to the Transvaal, January and February 1906', *Historical Journal*, vol. 8 (1965), pp. 380–98. This case-study of an oral tradition was reinforced by Bentley B. Gilbert, 'The grant of responsible government to the Transvaal: more notes on a myth', *Historical Journal*, vol. 10 (1967), pp. 457–9.
6 *Cambridge University Reporter*, vol. 78 (1948), pp. 1300–3 (13 June 1950).

For the first time, microphones were allowed in the Cambridge Senate House, and Smuts's address was recorded for world broadcast. See also Hancock, *Smuts*, vol. II, *The fields of force, 1919–1950* (Cambridge, 1968), pp. 507–8.

7 *PD Commons*, vol. 162, cc. 798–804 (31 July 1906); *PD, Lords*, vol. 9, cc. 1000–8 (16 August 1909).

8 G.P. Gooch, *Under six reigns* (1958), pp. 119–20. Gooch compared Botha's reputation to that of General Eisenhower.

9 But not J.A. Hobson. He saw Union as the 'dominion of Afrikanerdom': 'A nice propriety of loyal speech in some of the Boer leaders may indeed be adduced in support of this romantic view of history', while 'our national sentimentalism befogs our vision', since it delights us 'to imagine reconciliation' (*The crisis of Liberalism: new issues of democracy*, 1909, p. 235).

10 Phyllis Lewsen, *The South African constitution: euphoria and rejection* (Witwatersrand, 1986); L.M. Thompson, 'The compromise of Union', in M. Wilson and L.M. Thompson, eds., *The Oxford history of South Africa*, vol. II, *1870–1966* (Oxford, 1971), pp. 358–64.

11 E.A. Benians, 'The European colonies', in A.W. Ward *et al.*, eds., *Cambridge modern history*, vol. XII, *The latest age* (Cambridge, 1910), pp. 643–8, 671.

12 T. Wilson, ed., *The political diaries of C.P. Scott, 1911–1928* (1970), p. 306.

13 A.C. Benson, *The happy warrior: a sight of General Smuts at Cambridge* (Cambridge, 1917, reproduced from *The Church Family Newspaper*, 7 June 1917); Benson Diary, Magdalene College Archives, F/ACB/165, ff. 30r–31r (16 May 1917), and, for Churchill, F/ACB/113, f. 8r (1910) and 154, f. 40v (1915).

14 Penny Grimbeek, 'Jan Smuts and Nelson Mandela', *Christ's College Magazine*, no. 224 (1999), pp. 35–8.

15 Christ's College Library, post-medieval manuscripts and papers, no. 126, J.C. Smuts, typescript, notes for an address in College Chapel, 21 October 1934. 'Holism', a term Smuts invented in 1926, 'simply means that we are not alone, not mere individual atoms by ourselves in this world'.

16 W.K. Hancock, *Smuts and the shift of world power* (SOAS pamphlet, London, 1964), p. 12; P. Marshall, 'Smuts and the preamble to the UN Charter', *The Round Table*, no. 358 (2001), pp. 55–65; S. Dubow, 'Smuts, the United Nations, and the rhetoric of race and rights', *Journal of Contemporary History*, vol. 43 (2008), pp. 45–73.

17 Nelson Mandela, *Long walk to freedom: the autobiography* (1994), pp. 57–8.

18 Sarah Gertrude Millin, his biographer, several times asked him, 'General, I don't understand you. What is the secret of your being?' 'My secret, Mrs Millin, is that I am a very unco-ordinated personality': quoted in H. Duncan Hall, *Commonwealth: a history of the British Commonwealth of Nations* (1971), pp. 394–5. See also more generally, Nicholas Mansergh, *The Commonwealth experience* (1st edn, 1969), pp. 370–8, 'General J.C. Smuts: he was defeated'.

19 Hancock, *Smuts*, vol. II, pp. 505–6. Constituencies were supposed to be equal in size by the total number of voters ('one vote one value'); but the South Africa Act allowed a reduction of up to 15 per cent in the number

of voters in rural seats and a 15 per cent increase in the size of urban constituencies, a system which Smuts had pressed for against the advice of the British government. Under this 'rural weighting', 85 rural votes could become 'equal' to 115 urban votes. On a strict 'one vote one value' system, Smuts would have won the straight fight against Malan's National Party in 1948.

20 C. Douglas-Home, *Evelyn Baring: the last proconsul* (1978), p.171. In the Colonial Office, Sir A. Dawe sounded a warning in 1943: 'There is always the danger that we may be deluded by the ephemeral magnetism of General Smuts's personality into taking a step which would have grave consequences to our long-term interests in Africa': S.R. Ashton and S.E. Stockwell, eds., *Imperial policy and colonial practice, 1925–1945* (BDEEP, 1996), pt I, p. 350 (17 July 1943).

21 J.C. Smuts, *Plans for a better world: speeches* (1942), pp. 243–54, 'Greater South Africa'. The South African edition was overtly entitled *Greater South Africa: plans for a better world* (Johannesburg, 1940). See also J. van der Poel, ed., *Selections from the Smuts Papers*, especially vol. V, *September 1919–November 1934* (Cambridge, 1973); and P.R. Warhurst, 'Smuts and Africa: a study in sub-imperialism', *South African Historical Journal*, vol. 16 (1984), pp. 82–100.

22 D. Dilks, ed., *The diaries of Sir Alexander Cadogan, 1938–1945* (1971), p. 467 (3 August 1942). Cadogan was permanent under-secretary of state for foreign affairs for the whole of the Second World War.

23 For Smuts's views on race, see Hancock, *Smuts*, vol. II, pp. 473–91, and especially his presidential address to the South African Institute of Race Relations in 1942: *Selections from the Smuts Papers*, vol. VI, *December 1934–August 1945*, pp. 331–43. N. Garson, 'Smuts and the idea of race', *South African Historical Journal*, vol. 57 (2007), pp. 153–78, and Dubow, 'Smuts, the United Nations, and the rhetoric of race and rights', are both fair-minded discussions.

24 Smuts declared: 'If there is one thing on which all South Africans are agreed it is this, that racial blood mixture is an evil . . . a universally admitted evil' (*House of Assembly Debates*, vol. 68, Cape Town, 1949, p. 6175, 19 May 1949, the Prohibition of Mixed Marriages Bill).

25 RH, ed., *The Labour government and the end of empire, 1945–1951* (BDEEP, 1992), pt IV, pp. 284–90, document no. 429. 'Relations with the Union of South Africa', Cabinet memorandum by P.C. Gordon Walker, 25 September 1950.

26 RH and W.R. Louis, eds., *The Conservative government and the end of empire, 1957–1964* (BDEEP, 2000), pt I, pp. 167–74, document no. 32, address by Mr Macmillan to both houses of the South African Parliament, Cape Town, 3 February 1960.

27 RH, ed., *The Labour government and the end of empire*, pt I, Introduction, p. lxiv.

28 Prime Minister's Office, PREM 11/1367, minutes by Eden, July–August 1956.

29 Margaret Thatcher, *The Downing Street years* (1993), p. 513.

30 RH and Louis, eds., *The Conservative government and the end of empire*, pt II, p. 407, editorial note to document no. 450.

31 Ibid., pt II, pp. 455–62, document no. 462, valedictory despatch by Sir J. Maud, 14 May 1963.

32 RH, *The Labour government and the end of empire*, pt IV, p. 315, document no. 433, Cabinet memorandum by P.C. Gordon Walker, 16 April 1951.

33 Mandela, *Long walk to freedom*, pp. 364–5; T. Tlou, N. Parsons, and W. Henderson, *Seretse Khama, 1921–1980* (Braamfontein, 1995), pp. 200–2.

34 RH and Louis, eds., *The Conservative government and the end of empire*, pt II, pp. 455–68, including document no. 463, briefing despatch, Lord Home to Sir H. Stephenson, 28 June 1963.

35 S. Dubow, *Racial segregation and the origins of apartheid in South Africa, 1919–1936* (Oxford, 1989).

36 Albert Luthuli, *Let my people go* (1962), p. 197.

37 A. du Toit, 'Political control and personal morality', in R. Schrire, ed., *South Africa: public policy perspectives* (Cape Town, 1983), pp. 54–83. See also *South Africa House of Assembly Debates* (Cape Town, 1949), vol. 68 (24 and 25 May 1949), cc. 6344–6511, and vol. 69 (24 June 1959), cc. 9065–71.

38 Susan S. Ritner, 'The Dutch Reformed Church and apartheid', *Journal of Contemporary History*, vol. 2 (1967), pp. 17–36.

39 Gwendolen M. Carter, *The politics of inequality: South Africa since 1948* (1958), p. 370.

40 T. Dunbar Moodie, *The rise of Afrikanerdom: power, apartheid, and the Afrikaner civil religion* (Berkeley, CA, 1975), p. 265.

41 E.g. by Shula Marks, 'White masculinity: Smuts, race and the South African War', Raleigh Lecture on History, 2000, *Proceedings of the British Academy*, vol. 111 (2001), pp. 199–223; but see criticisms of this by Garson, 'Smuts and the idea of race', esp. p. 166 and n. 25.

42 Smuts warned against 'the deification of race' – 'Race in the Nazi ideology becomes something divine: your race is your God' (1942 address to the South African Institute of Race Relations).

43 S. Dubow, 'Afrikaner nationalism, apartheid and the conceptualization of "race"', *Journal of African History*, vol. 33 (1992), pp. 209–37.

44 RH and P. Henshaw, *The lion and the springbok: Britain and South Africa since the Boer War* (2003), pp. xi, 350.

45 C.W. de Kiewiet, *The anatomy of South African misery* (Oxford, 1956).

46 Mansergh, *The Commonwealth experience*, p. 377. For a conclusion less favourable to Smuts, I would recommend Saul Dubow's article on his biographer: 'W.K. Hancock and the question of race', in W.R. Louis, ed., *Ultimate adventures with Britannia: personalities, politics, and culture in Britain* (2009), ch. 18, pp. 247–61.

Part V
Sexuality

13   Empire and sexual opportunity

[The article thus entitled first appeared in the *Journal of Imperial and Commonwealth History* in January 1986 (vol. 14, no. 2). It was not well received by feminists and others who found it did not conform to their own concerns about gender, racial and patriarchical domination, or emerging 'queer theory'. A debate was conducted with Mark T. Berger in the pages of the *Journal* in 1988: 'Imperialism and sexual exploitation: a response to Ronald Hyam's *Empire and sexuality*', and my 'Reply' (vol. 17, no. 1). Two years later I published *Empire and sexuality: the British experience* (Manchester University Press). This was also criticised for being 'under-theorised', which was disappointing, as I had attempted to develop a 'surplus energy' theory of imperialism (however inadequate), and had written a good deal about the interpretation of sexuality, the theory of sublimation, and my own concept of the 'parergal' character of sexual activity. In the 1990s there were two review articles about my work: (1) by Margaret Strobel, 'Sex and work in the British empire' (*Radical History Review*, vol. 54 (1992), pp. 177–86), and (2) by Richard A. Voeltz, 'The British empire, sexuality, feminism, and Ronald Hyam' (*European Review of History/Revue Européenne d'Histoire*, vol. 3, no. 1 (1996), pp. 41–5). Voeltz amusingly demonstrated the ambivalence of a body of work which could be regarded both as a radically subversive critique of empire, and as phallocentric imperialist apologetics; he concluded, however, that evaluating my view of the subject 'remains a daunting proposition'.

Much of the material here was refined in *Empire and sexuality*, but, for the historiographical record, the original text is retained. However, at fifty-six pages it was too long to reprint in full, so I have omitted the sections on 'The British home-base', and the twentieth-century 'Reaction'. In its reduced form it considers first 'The sexual imperative', especially as we can observe it overseas, and then provides a synoptic view of the principal settings within which the 'Arcana Imperii' had their clandestine manifestations in the nineteenth century. The 1986 version was densely footnoted, in order to establish the academic credibility of the subject. These notes have been much simplified, renumbered, and brought up to date where necessary.]

When in 1960 I first began research on the British empire, to write about its sexual aspects seemed so chimerical a project that I then put aside such evidence as I came across. The whole position has, however, since been entirely transformed by the successful reconstruction of the history of sex in British society, and by the progressive removal of reticence from political biography. We historians of empire were slow to make any parallel contribution. Although most imperial historians accept that Du Bois was right to point to the colour question as a major problem for the twentieth century, we have been much more reluctant to take up the challenge of his observation that he could forgive the West almost everything, including the slave trade, but not the way the white man took sexual advantage of black women [. . .] We are thus still in danger of pursuing a picture of European expansion which is both bowdlerised and incomplete: and, in comparison with metropolitan domestic history, out of date.[1]

I

The expansion of Europe was not only a matter of 'Christianity and commerce', it was also a matter of copulation and concubinage. Sexual opportunities were seized with imperious confidence. Gustave Flaubert spoke for all those who regarded visits to oriental lands, especially at government expense, as providing additional sexual education even for the experienced womaniser. In 1850 he wrote from Cairo: 'Here . . . one admits one's sodomy . . . We have considered it our duty to indulge in this form of ejaculation.' Such behaviour was not always popular. The deep-seated hostility of the Afghan people towards the British may well have been due to their resentment of the undisciplined lust with which British soldiers fell upon the women of Kabul in 1841. Roberts was determined to have no repetition in 1879, and the return of the troops to Peshawar as a result created an exceptional demand for sex, disrupting the routine services of Indian army prostitutes for several months.[2] The Ndebele rebels in 1896 and the Zulu in 1906 also had grievances about the British treatment of their women. The Nandi and the Masai resented the demand for women generated by the building of the Uganda Railway. Crossing the colour line was sometimes done in contempt, with cynicism and racial discrimination. The Southern Rhodesia Immorality Act (1903) protected white women but not black. Similarly the Europeans in 1926 in Papua New Guinea also imposed the death penalty for the attempted rape of a white woman by a black man, and life imprisonment for indecent assault; but black women received no such protection.[3] The Pax Britannica was also a 'pox Britannica':[4] Britain spread venereal diseases around the globe along with its race-courses and botanical gardens, steam engines and law-books. Britain did not merely sell cotton clothes to all the world, but also exported nude photographs. George Cannon, William Dugdale, and Henry Hayler were world leaders among the entrepreneurs of so-called pornography.[5] There was a flourishing free trade in prostitution.

Paradoxically, alongside this often insensitive activity, the British had another export too, and a very influential counterbalancing one: their official prudery. Practice and theory diverged. Britain had 'an ultra squeamishness and hyper-prudery peculiar to itself': narrow, blinkered, defective, and intolerant attitudes towards sex which it all too success-fully imposed on the rest of the world. One of the worst results of the expansion of Europe was the introduction of its guilty inhibitions about sex into societies previously much better sexually adjusted than any in the West. Many Third World leaders have short-sightedly traded in the traditional open attitudes of their societies in pursuit of a sterile con-formity to a supposedly more civilised, but in fact fundamentally infe-rior, model of behaviour.

Imperial history, then, cannot neglect sexual activity, because it is there. But more than that: no area of history can entirely ignore sex, because sex matters to most people and has a direct bearing on their relationships. Innumerable autobiographies testify to this. Here, two quotations from members of the colonial services will have to suffice. Lugard wrote: 'The real key to the study of a life lies in a knowledge of the emotions and passions . . . Of these the sexual instinct is recognised as the most potent for good or ill, and it has certainly been so in my life.' Victor Purcell (Malayan official turned historian) did not regard himself as particularly promiscuous, but 'I have never been able to distinguish the sexual urge and the urge to live.'[6]

Sexual needs can be imperative. Margery Perham observed in 1932 Francophone African migrant labourers in Kano queueing up to be circumcised in order to visit the Muslim prostitutes of the town.[7] Many men have pursued the illusion of sexual satisfaction (most wanted when it is least obtainable, least needed when it is most available) to the point of obsession. Some men took risks with their careers at which the histo-rian can only marvel. For ten years Milner maintained a secret mistress called Cécile in a 'seedy backstreet in Brixton' (1891–1901). Even on a working holiday in England at the end of the crucial year 1898 he van-ished on a six-day bicycling trip with her on the South Downs. Rosebery may also have had something to hide: we simply do not know for sure, but the maintenance of a villa in Naples looks suspiciously like a typical ploy of late Victorian upper-class homosexuals. Eldon Gorst in Egypt was reprimanded by Cromer in 1898 for being too conciliatory with the opposite sex (and not conciliatory enough with his colleagues). But there were many others whose private life became disastrously public. Sir Henry Pottinger was dismissed within a year as governor of Cape Colony in 1847. (Theal records: 'No other Governor of the colony ever lived in such open licentiousness as he. His amours would have been inexcusable in a young man; in one approaching his 60th year they were scandalous.'[8]) Valentine Baker, brother of Samuel the explorer, wrecked his army career by assaulting a lady in a railway carriage in 1875, and had to transfer to the Turkish army. Parnell was reduced to humiliating sub-terfuges, disguises, and scrambles on fire-escapes in order to maintain contact with Kitty O'Shea before the storm broke. It was an ardent affair which manifestly interfered with the proper performance of his duties as a party leader. Lovers of boys took particularly horrendous chances. General Sir Eyre Coote (a former MP) made regular Saturday excur-sions in 1815 into Christ's Hospital School, London, and was eventually caught with his trousers down in a flogging-and-groping session with six boys aged fourteen and fifteen. The Anglo-Boer War hero Sir Hector Macdonald was discovered in 1903 in a railway compartment with the blinds down, on the line between Colombo and Kandy, conducting (in all probability) a masturbation session with four Sinhalese boys. Trivial enough in itself, this led to another seven or eight immediate allega-tions, and the threatened exposure of an alleged habitual and systematic pattern of serious sexual contacts (perhaps producing up to seventy witnesses), with both local boys and the sons of the European commu-nity, aged twelve and upwards. Roberts already knew that Macdonald in South Africa was 'given to quaint practices . . . love-making to quite young girls – but this must be something much worse'. Indeed it was. There was even the possibility that Macdonald had used the services of a homosexual procurer convicted of murder in 1902. Macdonald shot himself, to the enormous relief of the authorities. Although no offence under Ceylon law had occurred, it could conceivably have built up into the most prodigious scandal in imperial history if Macdonald had come to trial in Britain. It is probably for this reason that the case-file was apparently destroyed immediately after his death.[9] Lewis Harcourt (ex-colonial secretary) in 1922 exposed his erection (or 'stalagmite' as he called it) to a house-guest, thirteen-year-old Etonian Edward James, who complained to his mother. For 'Loulou' also, suicide was the sequel.[10]

We can thus demonstrate the scandalous collapse of a number of imperial careers. More generally, it is helpful for the historian to know who or what sustains leaders in a crisis, or officials in their routines; to know to whom they turn to make the strain endurable, to whom they write in their loneliness, to know what inner image is the linchpin of their lives. Asquith was certainly not the only prime minister, or even

First World War leader, to be kept (more or less, in his case) on an even keel by exchanging letters with a lady-love. Others also had their 'pole-stars', their Venetia Stanleys, and Asquith was not even alone in endangering security by indiscreet disclosures. Contemporaneously, Field Marshal Sir John French, despite what one would have thought more than adequate experience in these matters, was ridiculously swept off his feet by Winifred Bennett, writing to her almost daily in 1915 and signing himself 'Peter Pan' to her 'Wendy'. His battle-cry before Neuve Chapelle was 'Winifred'. Admiral Beatty's appointment as commander-in-chief practically coincided with the inauguration of his affair with Eugénie Godfrey-Faussett, his 'fairy queen'; it was essential compensation for a wife with mental health problems. Lloyd George had his mistress-secretary, Frances Stevenson, whose unwanted pregnancy obtruded itself at the height of the war leadership crisis. Contemplating an earlier war, Milner found crucial relaxation in Cape Town (in the fateful autumn of 1899) with Lady Edward Cecil, his 'godsend'. When at last she was free, he married her in 1921. Earlier still, Nelson (whose flagrantly happy adultery long embarrassed naval hagiographers) truly observed that if there were more Emma Hamiltons there would be more Nelsons. However, not all life, even in the empire, takes place on the battlefield, and routine may be just as hard to get through, especially overseas. Palmerston livened up those long years behind desks at the War Office with sexual relaxations: he successfully fitted intercourse into the interstices of the working day. The words 'fine day' in his diary in fact recorded a successful proposition; sometimes there were five such entries a week, some of them on the same day, though he also failed quite often with his overtures. For twenty-eight years Palmerston maintained a mistress before they were free to marry. Even Gladstone had extra-marital emotional support in Mrs Thistlethwaite, a high-class ex-courtesan. Though he was a faithful husband (and thus almost unique among nineteenth-century prime ministers), his nocturnal perambulations seeking out (beautiful) prostitutes for 'rescue' carried its own special risks of misinterpretation and catastrophe. (His success rate was less than one per cent.) More seriously, perhaps, Gladstone was himself deeply perplexed by his own mixed motives, and for several years flagellated himself as a punishment, an act which must surely only have reinforced the cycle of excitement and doubt.

Turning overseas, and looking for the moment no further than India: Clive probably did not fornicate his way across the subcontinent, at least not after he was married, and, in view of the temptations in his path, was probably 'astonished at his own moderation'. However, a revealing letter survives from John Dalton, his bachelor-days chum, which not only refers to their both having been 'clapped' more than once, but looks forward to a joint exploration of the brothels of Covent Garden, and expresses relief that in spite of rumours about marriage 'you fuck as usual'.[11] Wellesley notoriously lived a life of sexual tempestuousness; his brother Wellington (certainly no abstainer himself: 'publish and be damned!') was so shocked as to wish him castrated. Metcalfe (acting governor-general 1835–6) had three Eurasian sons between 1809 and 1817, though his failure to marry a white woman also had something to do with his delight in the 'pure love which exists between man and man'. Northbrook as viceroy, 1872–6, was unpopular for reasons directly related to his private misfortunes: the double bereavement of both wife and son made him taciturn. He found dubious consolation with 'a notorious white woman' called Mrs Searle at Ranikhet in 1875, while at the same time becoming over-lyrical about children. Boys were certainly John Nicholson's principal solace; one of his few surviving long letters reveals him much concerned about the supply of humming-tops and Jew's harps with which to amuse the boys of Waziristan. But in general women were the order of the day, sometimes in bulk. Sir David Ochterlony (the Resident of Delhi, 1803–25) took thirteen Indian mistresses. Colonel James Skinner (founder of the crack regiment 'Skinner's Horse') was said to have had a harem of fourteen wives, though the family hotly denied there were ever more than seven; eighty children claimed him as their father. Both Wolseley and Burton as young soldiers in the Indian army had mistresses.

Of course not everyone behaved in this way. Kinsey identified perhaps about 2 per cent of men as fundamentally apathetic about sex. Such people are unresponsive to erotic stimulus, attach little importance to sex, and find little hardship in abstinence. A tentative list of 'high achievers' belonging to this category of 'a-sexuals' might include Benjamin Jowett and A.C. Benson (dons), General Gordon, Kitchener and Montgomery (soldiers), Sir Matthew Nathan and Sir Edward Twining (governors), and Winston Churchill and Harold Macmillan (politicians). Let Dean Inge and A.C. Benson be their spokesmen. Inge wrote in his diary: 'in a decent, well-ordered life, sex does *not* play a very important part'. In his diary Benson wrote: 'for me the real sexual problem does not exist . . . I don't want to claim or to be claimed . . . and thus a whole range of problems means nothing to me.'[12] Macmillan's sustained innocence and detachment (refusing all overtures at Eton and Oxford) left him ill-equipped to deal either with the romantic friendship between his wife and Robert Boothby, or with the Profumo Affair, which haunted the twilight of his premiership. ('I had no idea of [this] strange underworld . . . all this kind of thing was not only distasteful but unthinkable.'[13]) It must not be supposed that 'a-sexuals', those who by and large opt out, pose no problems for others by their abstinence. They often lose touch with reality. Benson represented more than one generation of school-masters unable to come to terms with adolescent sexuality ('the dread possibility', 'the dark shadow on the life of a schoolmaster, his most anxious and saddest preoccupation'). Such men gratuitously attempted to stamp out teenage masturbation. General Gordon was quite happy provided he could give the occasional bath to a dirty urchin and talk to him of God. But Gordon was probably unsuited to high responsibilities by the very fact of his not really caring about anything in life except his 'Gravesend laddies', or 'kings', as he revealingly called them. Kitchener, whose private life focused on merely sentimental relationships with young officers, and who became involved in the Purity Movement, caused havoc in the First World War by his reluctance to introduce VD prophylaxis for the army in Europe.

Above all there is the classic case of Montgomery, a man incontestably fitted for high command if not for anything else. Sex was something he largely repudiated, even during his ten years of marriage, and despite (or more likely because of) his deep-rooted tenderness towards boys. Montgomery was sometimes said to be able to derive an almost unfair advantage by his ability to concentrate on his career, especially after his wife's early death in 1937; but clearly there were repressed drives and tensions which fundamentally affected for the worse his behaviour and judgment. What, after all, is one to make of a man who wrote letters to schoolboys signed 'Fondest love, Montgomery of Alamein'? Behind a relentless generosity to his prepubertal protégés, Montgomery was unforgiving equally of the Farrar genetic inheritance from his mother, and of his son's divorce. Nor could he, for similar reasons of revulsion, get on with Auchinleck. He issued wholly unrealistic orders to his men about restricting access to wives. His crack-down upon the flesh-pots of Egypt in 1931–3 and against VD in the war got him into serious trouble. Of all public figures he was the most absurdly virulent and irrational in 1965 in attacking the Wolfenden proposals for reforming the laws con-cerning homosexuality, even suggesting in the House of Lords an age of consent fixed at eighty.[14]

Others were more obviously and consciously driven by their sense of frustration. For some, marriage meant all too literally living out the proverbial lifetime of repentance: among them Lord Wellington, Viceroy Ellenborough, Herbert Morrison, Rider Haggard, and governors Sir Donald Cameron and Sir Gordon Guggisberg. In fact Guggisberg had two unsuccessful marriages ('he failed at any time to build a domestic life or background . . . and this needs to be understood in approaching his governorship', of the Gold Coast, 1917–27). Then of course there were others who bore the burden of jilting or bereavement. Lugard's whole career was shaped by an early rejection in love, while Dalhousie, losing a wife half-way through his viceroyalty when he was forty-one, was as poignant a widower as any ('almost too hard to bear . . . my whole future is shivered by it'). Such men were tough and they kept going: but the strain not infrequently made them harder to work with.[15]

I have argued so far that imperial history should take account of sex not only because it is a fact of empire, but also because the sex-drive, even in its weakest manifestations, has repercussions on how men relate to other people and how they go about their work. A third reason for study may be added. There is already a tendency to attribute great explanatory power to an ill-defined concept of 'sublimation'. It is said to be an animating force behind empire-building. Ensor suggested in 1936 (and all credit to him for raising the issue at that time) that the late Victorian elite and professional business classes 'spent, there can be little doubt, far less of their time and thought on sex interests than either their continental contemporaries or their twentieth-century successors; and to this saving their extraordinary surplus of energy in other spheres must reasonably be in part ascribed'. Some forty years on, Lawrence Stone has a similar conclusion for a broader period: 'The sublimation of sex among young male adults may well account for the extraordinary military aggressiveness, the thrift, the passion for hard work, and the entrepreneurial and intellectual enterprise of modern Western man.' Gann and Duignan, in an aside, hint at empire-building as possibly 'a sublimation or alternative to sex'.[16] There are innumerable biographers and historians too who talk loosely about their subjects' 'sublimating themselves in hard work' (this is explicitly done by Magnus on Kitchener, Sinclair on Sir George Grey, Wraith on Guggisberg, Montgomery on Montgomery, Yarwood on Revd Samuel Marsden, Higgins on Rider Haggard). Other writers are looking for connections between private vision and public policy: Keynes could be a test-case here.

It is clearly high time to scrutinise rigorously these explanatory tendencies and speculations, and pay more attention to the various experts. Freud thought that apparently non-sexual activities could be an expression of the sexual instinct. He considered that the price of Western civilisation was sexual restraint. These may well be important insights, but his concept of sublimation has never been properly investigated. Kinsey's opinion needs to be pondered. 'Sublimation', he argues, is not a scientific concept. We cannot switch or divert sexual energy as if it were an electrical current; it is not enough to say that busy and successful people are 'sublimated' merely because they are energetic in non-sexual pursuits. As for those 2 per cent of apathetic 'a-sexuals' Kinsey has identified: such sexual inactivity is, he considers, no more sublimation of the sex-drive than blindness and deafness are sublimations of the perceptive capacities. Kinsey could not find in his sample (5,300 men) *any* clear-cut case of sublimation, and concluded 'sublimation is so subtle, or so rare, as to constitute an academic possibility rather than a demonstrated actuality'.[17] However, sublimation remains a technical term in psychoanalysis. Perhaps therefore we should accept that sublimation seems to have some explanatory value when applied to 'artistic creation and intellectual inquiry' among highly gifted individuals (as Freud intended its use to be restricted, or as he mostly used it himself), but the term has far less point when applied to ordinary people or to political and economic activities. It certainly seems useful to distinguish between sublimation and a-sexuality. As far as expansionist enterprise is concerned, even if a simple 'surplus energy' theory remains a possibility, the formation of empires cannot be explained specifically by the sex-drive. If 'sublimation' is suspect with regard to ordinary individuals, it is certainly inapplicable to the activities of whole societies. It would be nonsense to suggest that more than a minority of men initially went overseas in order to find sexual satisfaction. (The minority, however, could make a dynamic contribution – and one could cite Barth, Eyre, Stanley, Speke, and Thesiger as examples of explorers who enjoyed the intimate comradeship of boys which their remote travels brought.) Exploration aside, a 'surplus sexual energy' theory will not explain the fundamental motives behind expansionist enterprises, but it may show *how they were sustained*. It is relevant not so much to the question of why empires were set up, but to how they were run.

II

Since recent research has indicated that the amount and range of sexual opportunity available in Britain, at least before the Purity Campaign of the 1880s,[18] was greater than has hitherto been supposed, it probably follows that many young Victorian Britons going overseas expected to indulge in casual sex as a routine ingredient of life. Moreover, empire unquestionably gave them an enlarged field of opportunity. Greater space and privacy were often available. Inhibitions relaxed. European standards might be held irrelevant. Abstinence was represented as unhealthy in a hot climate. Boredom could constitute an irresistible imperative. The Indian army conveniently arranged for prostitutes. Local girls would offer themselves; or boys, especially in Ceylon. The white man's status put him in a strong position to get his way. As Bucknill reported to the government in 1906: 'of course the lascivious-minded man of European race can always, in any part of the world, find means of gratifying his wishes'.[19] The expatriate was in fact *more* likely to resort to prostitution overseas simply because the non-European prostitute was a much more attractive proposition than her British counterpart. Asian prostitutes were amusingly playful hostesses. By contrast, British whores were nasty, dirty, and coarse, drawn from deprived backgrounds. In India and Japan prostitution was an honourable estate, and not furtively conducted. Asian prostitutes were likely to be higher up the social scale, educated, and with a proper training for their art. Captain Edward Sellon, writing of India in the years 1834 to 1844, praised the cleanliness, the sumptuous dress, the temperance, the ability to sing and entertain that he had encountered in Indian high-caste courtesans:

I now commenced a regular course of fucking with native women. They understand in perfection all the arts and wiles of love, are capable of gratifying any tastes, and in face and figure they are unsurpassed by any women in the world . . . It is impossible to describe the enjoyment I experienced in the arms of these syrens. I have had English, French, German and Polish women of all grades of society since, but never, never did they bear a comparison with those salacious, succulent houris of the far [*sic*] East.[20]

An army officer told Havelock Ellis that he had known perhaps sixty prostitutes, of whom the Japanese were easily the best (clean, charming, beautiful, and taking an intelligent interest); next came Kashmiris and Chinese. ('G.R.' seems to have known what he was talking about in constructing his ladder of erotic delight: he had also experienced French, German, Italian, Spanish American, American, Bengali, Punjabi, 'Kaffir', Sinhalese, Tamil, Burmese, Malay, Greek, and Polish prostitutes; white women in the East he described as 'insupportable'.)

It is thus hardly surprising that the differential between VD rates in the services at home and abroad reflected a more intensive resort to prostitutes overseas, even at a relatively late date. The quinquennial figures for 1921–6 show that the incidence of VD in the army at home was 40 per thousand. In Egypt it was 103 per thousand, Malta 105, India 110, Ceylon 184, South China 169, and North China 333 per thousand. For the navy (1928 figures) the incidence was 82 per thousand at home; for Africa, the Mediterranean, and West Indian stations it was 156, for India and Ceylon 204, and for the China station 304. The places of highest risk to the sailor were Shanghai, Yokohama, and Singapore, where the combination of numerous multi-racial brothels and lack of alternative entertainment in port proved to be lethal.[21] Of course not all VD among sailors was spread by female harlots: it was also acquired *inter se*, so to speak. Churchill's description of the navy as founded upon 'Nelson, rum, buggery and the lash' was not just a good phrase. And evidence from the quarterdeck in the 1790s suggests that only *indiscriminate* mutual masturbation was frowned upon among cadets.

Running the empire would probably have been intolerable without resort to sexual relaxation. The historian has to remember the *misery* of empire: the heat and the dust, the incessant rain and monotonous food, the inertia and the loneliness, the lack of amusement and intellectual stimulus. There were no cars, no radios, sometimes not even enough white neighbours to make up a proper game of tennis or bridge. Sir Robert Hart in the Chinese Customs administration, separated from his wife for years on end, acutely felt this isolation: ('I am utterly *alone* and have not a single *friend* or *confidant* – man, woman or child . . . there are *spasms of loneliness* which hit hard'). Before his marriage he had a Chinese mistress, who bore him three children. Speaking for European administrators in Malaya, Richard Winstedt (schools inspector and director of education, 1916) reflected that it was hardly any surprise that the white exile in the out-stations took to himself 'one of the complaisant, amusing, good-tempered and good-mannered daughters of the East'. Those who did not do so tended to have mental troubles. In thirty-two years in Malaya he personally knew fourteen Europeans who shot themselves: all had been of sound mind when they went out. As far as Africa was concerned, Joyce Cary wrote as a district officer in Nigeria in 1917 that he could perfectly well appreciate why his French counterparts took local mistresses, and could equally understand 'the queer cases out here of fellows drinking themselves to death, or getting homicidal mania, or breaking down nervously into neurotic wrecks in the back-bush by themselves'. When Cary wrote this he had already had four months without conversing with another white person, but, being newly married (though unaccompanied by his wife) and a keen reader, he reckoned he knew how to guard against nerves, drink, and idleness.[22] Language barriers and other cultural impediments to relationships sometimes led Europeans into sexual intimacy with non-Europeans almost as an act of baffled despair.

It could well be thought that empire exercised a corrupting influence. It certainly unfroze restraint, and produced some imaginative feedback. It can hardly be an accident that all the classics of British erotic literature were written by men who were widely travelled inside and especially outside Europe. The author of 'Fanny Hill', *Memoirs of a Woman of Pleasure* (1748–9), John Cleland, had been a consul at Smyrna and spent thirteen years in the legal department of the East India Company at Bombay, becoming well versed in oriental ways and thought. The anonymous but identified author of the *Romance of Lust* (4 vols., 1873–6) knew India and Japan well and died in India in 1879. 'Walter' of *My Secret Life* had been to every country in Europe, together with visits to Russia,

America (where he certainly had sex with Amerindian women), Egypt, and possibly Lebanon. Among the writers of the major unpublished erotica, Captain Searight had saturation experience as an Indian army officer, and Sir Edmund Backhouse was a professor in Peking (Beijing). H.S. Ashbee, erotic bibliographer extraordinary, had travelled to India, China, Japan, Egypt, Tunis, and America.

There thus seems every reason to take seriously the allegations of the anonymous contributor to the *Pall Mall Gazette* in 1887 who argued that empire was inconsistent with morality. He suggested that about 500,000 people 'maintained' British relations with the empire: servicemen, officials, travellers, clerks. They were usually unaccompanied by women, and the great majority (basically as a consequence of deferred marriage) fell to the 'level of the immoral heathen', forming 'immoral relations with natives', coming to regard English morality as a local English institution, to be left behind 'along with Crosse and Blackwell's pickles or Keen's mustard, the corresponding substitutes abroad being better adapted to local conditions'. He complained that these servants of empire could cap the Sermon on the Mount with quotations from the 'Kama Shastra' (*sic*), and were beginning to think 'like Burton and his appalling footnotes'. Alternatively, some, out of duty, controlled themselves on posting, and then spent furloughs of uninterrupted debauchery in London, where they were not under observation. 'The empire was a Moloch, created by men not of a moral class' (he instanced Wellesley, Wellington, Nelson, Palmerston, and, surprisingly, Dalhousie); 'Purity' was to them an invention of Arnold of Rugby (actually it was not), and a sickly plant. At every turn he saw 'the necessity, the universality, and the eternity of sexual vice assumed as the basis of action and legislation'. The result was the creation of a heathen, ribald, sensual class of Britons absolutely unbound by convention. The editor could offer little by way of disagreement on this subject of 'deep and painful interest', merely observing that incontinence, like bloodshed, was perhaps now tending to diminish in the empire; and anyway strictly speaking the evils were due to trade rather than empire (a false distinction, as we now know), because only a quarter of the half-million were 'state employed'.[23]

Let us now look at sexual opportunity in some different types of imperial situation, both formal and informal, in an attempt to see how sexual interaction underpinned the operative structures of British expansion.

Plantations and trading posts

Whatever the theoretical objections to the work of Gilberto Freyre, there has been ample support for his dictum that 'there is no slavery without sexual depravity'. On all plantations, whether worked by slaves or by indentured labourers (but especially the former), there was obvious sexual exploitation.[24] Women were likely to be victims of the system. According to Jordan, the sexual leit-motiv of race relations on plantations was emphasised and sustained by a simple fact of everyday life: the slaves were in fact semi-nude, a circumstance which strengthened the sexual undertones in daily contact. It was common practice in the American South for boys of up to fourteen or fifteen years to wait at dinner clad only in a shirt which did not always cover what were optimistically called their 'private parts'. In the eighteenth-century West Indies it was almost customary for white men of every social rank (but especially of the lower classes) to sleep with black women. Coloured mistresses were kept openly, and the practice was integral to West Indian life. Informal liaisons were common even for married proprietors and their teenage sons. It was not considered reprehensible for a young white to begin his sex-life by seducing a slave woman. Samuel Taylor, the richest early Victorian planter in Jamaica, had several estates – with a family on each. According to Green, 'sexual licence was among the most distinctive characteristics of British Caribbean society'. According to Cooper, in the Arab plantations of Zanzibar, 'sexual subordination was often an important dimension of slavery', while miscegenation was 'normal and accepted'. The Dutch VOC in South Africa had a company slave lodge at Cape Town which was the leading brothel of the area and highly visible: 'slavery, poverty and prostitution were largely synonymous'. Some other writers, notably Genovese, while not questioning the exploitation that went on, warn against viewing plantations as harems. He argues that the blacks could and did resist, and some women practised steady concubinage with whites, valuing it as conferring status and advantages on their off-spring (though this did not extend to manumission in South Africa). In 1860 perhaps only 20 per cent or less of the Afro-American population had white blood, though it became much higher thereafter.[25]

Still, a clear libidinous pattern is inherent in slavery everywhere. Many of its objectionable features have been shown to resurface in indentured labour from India and the Pacific islands in the nineteenth century – a 'new system of slavery' for men, and of prostitution for women.[26] The women accompanying Indian labourers were often of low character; perhaps a quarter of them were already involved in prostitution. On the tea and sugar plantations of Assam and Ceylon, Mauritius and Fiji, Guiana and Trinidad, many planters exercised a *droit de seigneur*, though there were also some long-term relationships. A serious strike occurred on a Guiana plantation in 1904 because the manager and his overseers were having 'immoral relations' with the women. At the same time on another estate belonging to the same company there was much resentment over the manager's allowing one of his overseers to live openly with the Creole wife of an estate coolie. The government were embarrassed at the publicity but took no decisive action. From Fiji in 1913 it was reported that the morality of an estate compared unfavourably with that of an Indian village. Indian leaders were convinced that the indentured system condemned their women to prostitution, and this was a major reason why they objected to it. Some Melanesian contract labourers told their anthropologist that they had been passive partners to white plantation overseers. In 1914 Tamils went on strike in Malaya, demanding, among other things, an end to the molesting of female labourers. In Ceylon, many nineteenth-century writers referred to young girls being offered to planters by villagers, but in the 1870s it was noted that unions with Tamil or Sinhalese women were not as frequent as formerly. Edward Carpenter recorded (in 1892) that in Ceylon he met a tea-planter from Assam who was walking out hand-in-hand with boys and youths in Kandy. Planters, Carpenter observed, found their isolated lives very dreary, and it was not correct for them to associate too closely with their own employees (domestic servants were a different matter, however); but 'Ajax' wrote to him from Assam that he got very fond of his coolies and was 'quite attached to some'.

Frontier trading posts also articulated regular patterns of sexual interaction, whether under the Royal African Company in the eighteenth century, or the East India Company in India and on the China coast to the 1830s, where recruits were contractually prevented from marrying during their first five-year term. The taking of local mistresses (the *bibi*, or 'sleeping dictionary') was thus common. The classic case in many ways, however, was in the Canadian fur trade. The Hudson's Bay Company would have preferred celibacy in its employees, but this proved impossible, not least because the Amerindians could not understand it. By the early nineteenth century practically all the officers and many of the lower-ranked employees of the company had contracted non-Christian marriages *à la façon du pays*. Almost all Amerindian societies were accustomed to cement friendship-bonds with strangers by the loan of women. In 1821 George Simpson officially recommended such connections, especially in new areas: 'Connubial alliances are the best security we can have of the goodwill of the Natives. I have therefore recommended the gentlemen to form connections with the principal families immediately on their arrival, which is no difficult matter . . .'

Simpson was a very successful officer with the Hudson's Bay Company, becoming a wealthy governor-in-chief of Rupert's Land in 1839 and gaining a knighthood. 'The little emperor of the plains', as he was

known, exercised a strong influence on European social life there for
four decades until 1860. Even before he arrived in North America he
had fathered at least two bastards in Scotland, so he was not the man to
ignore the easy opportunities of the fur trade. He had five children by
four women in the 1820s; thereafter he tried to keep his new British wife
with him, but this was not a happy or successful experiment. The introduction of a white wife increased the tendency of fur traders to despise
local women. Simpson disparagingly referred to his 'bits of brown' (or
copper), his 'commodities' or 'articles', upon whom he would 'settle his
bollocks' or in whom he would 'deposit a little of my spawn'. (It also
has to be said that he was a possessive and tyrannical husband.) Once
in authority he was always nervous about the unrestrained lust of the
younger men in the business. Even the arrival of two washerwomen at
York Factory worried him, and he ordered that the 'young bucks' should
be kept away from them ('otherwise we shall have more fucking than
washing').

The company itself was also careful to avoid a cause of dispute with the
Amerindians, by insisting that men made provision for their offspring. If
employees grew tired of their Indian mates, it was usual to arrange some
alternative 'country marriage' for them. Certainly Simpson's friend
McTavish, McKenzie the governor of Red River, and McGillivray in the
north-west all behaved within the conventions of this system. It is always
difficult to measure the presence of affection, but the *system* itself seems
rather harsh. Simpson was keen to drive moralising missionaries off his
patch. The Revd John West did not last long as chaplain of Red River,
while the first missionary in Saskatchewan, the Revd James Evans, was
recalled by the Wesleyans in the mid-1840s after Simpson alleged sexual
misconduct against him. Evans may well not have been guilty, but scandalous allegations always wrecked a missionary's career.[27]

Convict settlements and mining compounds

The immorality of convict settlements was notorious. The Revd Samuel
Marsden described early Australia as 'a dreadful society for whoredoms
and all kinds of crimes'. Only about 10 per cent of the first convicts
in Australia were women, and their services were much in demand.
Prostitution was as old as the colony and not confined to any particular
area. Even in the 1820s for a woman to become a concubine instead
of a prostitute was considered an improvement in morals. Prostitution
offered female convicts one of their few chances of saving enough money
to buy a passage back to Britain. But perhaps the most striking feature
of the convict system was the opportunity it provided for sex between

men and boys. Sodomy was believed by several well-informed observers (Revd W.B. Ullathorne, H.P. Fry, John Frost) to be 'the prevailing crime' at mid-century in Van Diemen's Land and Norfolk Island. 'Deeply rooted and extensively practised . . . so easy to arrange and so difficult to detect', this offence (in theory warranting the death penalty at home) was treated as less serious than pipe-smoking. While merciless floggings were imposed for petty misdemeanours, the local authorities turned a blind eye to sodomy, which was sometimes vicious in character. Where legal action could not be avoided, offenders were often merely charged with 'disorderly conduct'. Under Russell's 'probation' system of 1840 the problem became more obvious by the concentration of young offenders. John Frost believed that it was 'almost impossible for a good-looking youth to be sent to any of these places without falling victim to this hellish system, for if other means fail, he will be forced'. Thousands, he warned, were annually sent 'to a fate worse than death'. The reformatory at Point Puer was particularly notorious.[28] Governor Eardley-Wilmot was sacked by Colonial Secretary Gladstone in 1846 largely because of his inability to solve or hush up this problem, though charges of a scandalous personal life were also directed against him. In South Africa, inter-racial sex between males occurred in the Robben Island prison.

Mining compounds in southern Africa later in the century also show how 'closed' situations led to homosexual solutions, causing alarm to the imperial authorities. From the earliest days of the migrant labour system, boys were recruited to fag or do 'women's work' in the compounds. They acted, in their hundreds, as cooks, cleaners, and bed-warmers. Some were so small that they were obviously incapable of mining work, and their surrogate female roles (sometimes institutionalised by payment of *lobola*, 'bridewealth') quickly shaded off into a high incidence of sodomy. Technically it was *hlo bongo* (intracrural intercourse) which was more commonly practised under this system of *nkotshane* (Shangaan; literally, 'dirty young wives', thus 'boy-wives', pejorative). In South Africa women were not allowed into compounds. In Rhodesia, the *chibaro* labour system did permit the presence of women. This did little to reduce the incidence of *nkotshane*, and only added further problems, such as the use of young girls born to the compound camp-followers. The services of the women were also disputed, and VD began to affect productivity. The government and mining companies therefore decided to introduce a system of regulated prostitution. Another point to notice is that *chibaro* paid such low wages that some labourers were obliged to sleep with each other in a shared blanket.

Chinese labour on the Witwatersrand was the subject of a bitter 'anti-slavery' campaign in Britain, and among the objections to it were fears that it was leading to an explosion of sodomy among the gold tips. A thorough investigation was conducted for the government in 1906 by J.A.S. Bucknill (commissioner of patents in the Transvaal). Since the subject was the 'unmentionable' his report was never published, but many of the witnesses showed a remarkable knowledge of Chinese and African sexual practices. The Revd F. Alexander and a busybody called Mr Leopold Luyt had made charges about the fearful scale of the problem, and alleged that the Chinese were teaching sodomy to the blacks. These charges, Bucknill concluded, were all grossly exaggerated. Chinese sexual conduct was not flagrant or a public scandal, and not like the 'bare-faced harlotry of Johannesburg'; mostly the Chinese did what they did in secret in disused mine-shafts. Syphilis of the rectum seemed practically unknown among them. Perhaps 6 or 7 per cent of the Chinese labourers were 'buggerboys' (*t'utzu*), most of them actors or barbers ('acting and immorality go hand-in-hand . . . all actors are very lewd fellows'). Bucknill concluded: 'I have been unable to satisfy myself that there is any great or alarming prevalence of this vice on the Rand.' The medical officer of health for the Rand even thought there was less sodomy among the Chinese than there was in London for a corresponding number of males. On the other hand, one particularly well-informed witness was convinced that some of the Chinese were carrying on with 'very little Kaffir piccanins on the veld'. Everyone agreed, however, that the Chinese were not teaching sodomy to the Africans, since it was already common among the Shangaan and other east-coasters, as well as among those from Zambesia and Lake Malawi, though the Zulu, Swazi, Sotho, and Xhosa were not involved. Some five or six Chinese theatres were closed down in the compounds and a few dozen catamites were repatriated. The government could not be said to have over-reacted. It emerged incidentally that Portuguese soldiers and police were enthusiastic participants in the *nkotshane* system.[29]

Mission stations

As pioneers on the moving frontier of European expansion in the early nineteenth century, missionaries quite often ran into trouble, especially in the south Pacific.[30] Some of the early London Missionary Society missionaries in Tahiti slept with Tahitian women. Some defected from the mission for Tahitian or Tongan women, among them B. Broomhall, T. Lewis, and G. Vason, the latter taking several wives. Sex was pressed upon the missionaries. Mostly they resisted, but their children often did not, finding the pervasive sensuality of the South Seas most enjoyable.

Missionaries soon aimed to send their offspring back to Britain for their education, in order to reduce their 'premature' exposure to sex. There were sexual problems to trouble the founder of the CMS New Zealand mission (1814), Samuel Marsden. At the Bay of Islands, in the 1820s, the Revd Thomas Kendall was found to have been living for some years openly with a Maori girl, Tungaroa. Kendall confessed his fornication but denied its seriousness: 'where is there a female of my own nation who can charge me with a lascivious look?' – an imperial double standard indeed. Then there was the awful fate of the Revd Mr Yate, a missionary in New Zealand from 1828. Yate was a brilliant evangelical publicist for the mission but was dismissed and sent home in disgrace in 1837. His downfall came as a result of a return trip to New Zealand when he had had unguarded liaisons with two sailors, Edwin Denison and Dick Deck (*sic*). It then emerged that he had been sexually active with many of his young male converts, perhaps fifty to a hundred of them. Piripi Tohi testified to mutual masturbation, Samuel Kohe to intracrural intercourse, Pehi to fellation for a pound of tobacco. Since there was no evidence of anal penetration, there was no legal case against him, and he argued (as any good Buddhist monk would have done) that only adultery with a woman was a sin. His colleagues knew God did not agree, and, to avoid divine retribution, burnt all his property and shot his horse.

Bishop Selwyn's Melanesian Mission operated in the New Hebrides, the Santa Cruz Group, and the Solomons; its base was in Auckland, which it was hoped would become an antipodean Lindisfarne. Although the mission was held in high regard by the Victorians, partly because it was sanctified by the martyrdom of Bishop Patteson's murder in 1871, its *modus operandi* was fraught with sexual temptation. An essential part of the technique was to tour the islands recruiting and gathering Melanesian boys for education and training away from home. Some missionaries enjoyed this task too much. In 1874 Charles H. Brooke was dismissed after over-exploiting his solitary visits to Mboli in the Solomons. In the late nineteenth century adolescent sex was 'rampant' at St Barnabas, Norfolk Island. Thirteen Melanesian teachers were suspended for their sexual behaviour in 1899 alone. And in the 1890s three white missionaries were sacked: A.E. Forrest, Arthur Brittain, and C.G.D. Browne. Forrest was the most painful case. He had given excellent service, but had sex with so many boys that the bishop thought the whole mission at Santa Cruz was ruined. Forrest's defence was that the islanders did not think his conduct wrong. 'If so', argued Bishop Wilson, 'his work during the nine years he has been there has been worth nothing.' Moreover, Forrest would not disappear into penitent obscurity, but remained at Santa Cruz as an independent trader, liberally practising 'gross indecency' up to the point of imprisonment in 1901. He then created a further sensation by escaping; he resumed his activities until he committed suicide in 1908, being remembered among the locals as the white man hounded to death by vindictive Christians. There was another round of problems in the late 1920s. E.N. Wilton, assistant bishop of northern Melanesia, was compelled to resign in 1929 after only one year in office because of allegations of sexual misconduct. This was followed in 1931 by the dramatic resignation of the bishop himself, F.M. Molyneux, because of whispered homosexual accusations.

Meanwhile in Papua New Guinea, the Anglican mission suffered resignations over women in the late 1890s and early 1900s. Missionaries complained about digger morals, but the diggers retorted that the mission stations were the worst. The bishop of north Queensland, 1913–47, J.O. Feetham, waxed indiscreetly eloquent in public about delightful Papuan youths, who seemed to him to combine the character of St John with the physique of Apollo.

In Africa the missionary had fewer temptations to face than in the Pacific islands. Nevertheless there was a young transgressor missionary-bishop of the Orange Free State, Edward Twells, who fled back to Britain in 1870 and never again held any benefice before his death thirty years later. And there were a number of eccentrics who aroused a good deal of suspicion and occasionally disgust. Skertchly reported in 1874 that the house of the Wesleyan Mission in Dahomey under the Revd Peter Bernasko had for twenty years been the most notorious brothel on the coast, especially after Bernasko had sole charge of it from 1863. Bernasko traded in palm oil, got very drunk, neglected his mission, fathered a dozen children, and prostituted his older daughters. Shortly after arriving in Kenya in 1902 to join the King's African Rifles, Meinertzhagen discovered three Italian White Fathers with the Kikuyu at Tusu, doing a 'roaring trade in enticing boys and girls to the mission', there to live a most immoral life: 'they are certainly not "white", but doubtless will soon be fathers'. With them was an Englishman called Smith who had slept with at least seven girls, saying they could not be true Christians until they had slept with a Christian.[31] (Meinertzhagen got him deported.) Mission stations certainly produced a crop of plausible excuses for unchastity [. . .].

Of course the behaviour of almost all Victorian missionaries was entirely orthodox, and inter-racial marriage for themselves was unthinkable (at least after about 1810). As a group they were firmly on the side of chastity, and for that very reason seldom received much support from expatriate whites.

Settler communities and the Colonial Service

In the colonies sexual conventions were often relaxed. Canada was a good place for an emigrant paterfamilias, remarked Sir Francis Bond Head: within a year he would 'find all his sons will be *free* and all his daughters *confined*'.[32] Servants were exploited, just as they were at home. In South Africa, Africans believed that black maids in European houses would be seduced by their employers, and this led in fact to a refusal in the 1890s to enter their service. This is why from 1897 there was an increase in the employment of Zulu house-boys and male nursemaids. Despite the occasional 'black peril' scare, these blacks rarely abused their often intimate responsibilities. But the police superintendent of Durban in 1903 alleged that not more than 10 per cent of black girls who came to towns looking for work 'escaped ruin' at the hands of white seducers.[33]

In every colony, wherever the unmarried white man found himself isolated, liaisons with local women were common in the nineteenth century. Among some white traders and hunters there was 'a partial equation of frontier life . . . with sexual freedom and indulgence . . . a no-man's land in terms of moral conduct'. In the early nineteenth century there was sexual interaction with the indigenous peoples of New Zealand, Australia, and South Africa, and some miscegenation, even in Cape Colony. (It was commoner still in India before the 1780s.) Later in the century there was widespread miscegenation in Central Africa. Not all district commissioners in Africa kept concubines, but some undoubtedly did, especially in the lonelier districts [. . .]. A few committed the ultimate sin and 'went native', like J.E. Stephenson, who, as administrator in Northern Rhodesia under the British South Africa Company, was sent to burn down a village in arrears with its taxes and was effectively put off his stroke by the two girls deputed to the task. He resigned, settled in the bush, married three African wives, had several children, and acquired a great reputation as a magician. Although he maintained the white man's dignity, he was never again received in European society.[34]

The presence of colonial society always imposed the need for discretion, as gossip was rife. But however stifling colonial society became, there was often a convenient safety-valve nearby, usually provided by the Portuguese. From the Rhodesias help was at hand at Beira and Lourenço Marques; from Hong Kong it was in Macao, where the early European traders kept their weekend mistresses; from India there was Goa, to say nothing of Rangoon or Port Said, or a Himalayan hill station, where even white women could refuse to conform to Victorian stereotypes. Prostitution in Africa was mainly disorganised and not brothel-based, but Europeans tended to make it more institutionalised. Port Said, Singapore, and Macao were inter-continental sex capitals and initiation centres for whites new to empire. Before 1914 a young man's first experience of the East might well be in a brothel in one of these cities. By the 1930s every street in Macao is said to have had one. Burma had the reputation of being a marvellous place for 'rest and recuperation'. The girls were cheap and sensuous. If the army had any doubts about their cleanliness, then an officer could burn their huts and restock with Japanese. Even into the twentieth century (and despite some official attempt to curtail the practice), W.N. Willis (an investigator who had lived there) believed that 90 per cent of the British in Burma took temporary mistresses. A special school was founded in Rangoon to educate children with European fathers. There was nothing comparable in British Africa. (Francophone Africa was different.) It was essentially all a matter of 'social distance'.

As a high-minded but nervous imperial ruling class emerged, and where fairly close-knit white communities were established, with white wives as regular participants and moral guardians, the practice of concubinage waned. This happened in India from the 1860s, in the wake of the steamships and the Suez Canal. The *memsahibs* also brought big changes to Ceylon, South Africa, and New Zealand by 1900, though not as yet to Burma or tropical Africa. Black mistresses disappeared in Central Africa, however, as the Zambian copper-belt was opened up. The longer a place remained not subject to the scrutiny of the *memsahib* the longer would persist the traditional solution to the problem of sexual deprivation. Sarawak was probably the last bastion of concubinage: even into the 1950s something of the old ways seems to have persisted. Things were also fairly free-and-easy in Malaya, until the 1930s, at any rate.[35] In the proto-Malay civil service, C.F. Bozzolo was the founding father of the administration: an impeccable and popular governor of Upper Perak, he had a harem said to be of dimensions befitting a patriarch. His successor, Hubert Berkeley, kept up the tradition. Indeed he embellished it, because he press-ganged into his harem some girls from the local orphanage, which he raided. Even in 1908 Berkeley could offer a recruit a 'sleeping dictionary' of quality, a Malay schoolmistress. In 1911 only 20 per cent of European men in Malaya were married. Planters (apart from a few proprietary ones) required their company's permission to marry, and many never did. Every village in the Federated Malay States, if it was big enough to have a post office, had its brothel. Most of them were Japanese. In very small towns without a rest house, the brothel doubled as a European hotel. These brothels were in regular use by Europeans. Sir Malcolm Watson, who was well placed to know (being a malariologist in constant touch with planters and officials) estimated that 90 per cent of Europeans in out-stations had Asian mistresses.

Opinions as usual vary about the extent of homosexual activity indulged in by Europeans: in Malaya it has been put as high as two-thirds, and this option certainly presented itself more overtly than it did in Africa. There was a major scandal in the 1930s when the diary of a professional Chinese catamite fell into the hands of the police, resulting in an official inquiry, and the disgrace of 'several prominent persons'. The press was forbidden to report the case. There were some speedy deportations, and the two men left behind both committed suicide. Purcell heard about this; he also knew of a civil servant who lived incestuously with his sister on a remote station, of a baronet who ditched his family to elope to Siam with a Chinese girl, and of certain Johore planters who indulged in wife-swapping. He himself had a temporary mistress in Canton.[36] The young journalist R.H. Bruce Lockhart in the early 1920s had no difficulty at all in living with a well-born Malay girl for several months while working on a rubber plantation. It was still a recognised custom. These plantation concubines were often Muslims divorced for barrenness, who subsequently purged themselves by undertaking a pilgrimage to Mecca.

III

Thus far we have noted some examples of the more or less spontaneous irregularities which occurred in the evolution of sexual opportunity in the overseas empire. But there were also more specific and institutionalised forms of sexual interaction: the 'regimental brothels' of the formal empire, and the prostitution networks of informal empire.

The Indian army and the 'lal bazar'

In the early nineteenth century marriage in the army below the rank of major was the exception. A subaltern could not marry, and a man might well be into his thirties before he became a captain. Marriage allowances were not in any case paid until the age of thirty, and quotas were in force. Not unusually only 12 per cent of a regiment was allowed to marry, and only 6 to 10 per cent of privates could have their wives in barracks. Officers overseas often maintained mistresses, while the other ranks created havoc in the taverns and brothels of any town available to them. A French nunnery was opened in the Montreal brothel-district in the 1840s in an attempt to quieten down the British garrison. The general position in the Indian army had been for a long time much as John Masters described it for the 1930s:

It is useless to pretend that our life was a normal one. Ours was a one-sexed society, with the women hanging on to the edges . . . In India there was always an unnatural tension . . . and every man who pursued the physical aim of sexual relief was in danger of developing a cynical hardness and a lack of sympathy . . . Of those who tried sublimation, some chased polo balls and some chased partridge, some buried themselves in their work, and all became unmitigated nuisances . . . And some took up the most unlikely hobbies, and some went to diseased harlots . . . and some married in haste, only to worry over who was now seducing their wives in the hill stations where they had seduced so many other people's wives. And a few homosexuals followed their secret star with comparative comfort in that large and easy-going country . . .[37]

In earlier times, a private or NCO could (according to Colour-Sgt Calladine of the 19th Foot, stationed in Ceylon) apply for written leave from the officer of his company to sleep out of barracks. When Calladine's regiment left Colombo after twenty-five years, in 1820, a great crowd of Sinhalese women saw them off, some of them with three or four children by the regiment.[38] But by the end of the 1850s, the taking of mistresses in India and Ceylon was in decline, and VD was becoming a serious problem. Especially worrying was the health of the army in the 'Mutiny' districts, where efficiency was essential. The first army 'lock' hospitals were established at Lucknow and Mian Mir (near Lahore). The problem was this. The British army represented 'the scum of the earth enlisted for drink'. However harsh Wellington's verdict, even in 1914 Flexner described it as an army 'recruited from the adventurous and derelict',[39] while Sir George White (commander-in-chief in India, 1888) remarked that 'our soldiers came from a class upon which the prudential motives operating against immoral conduct have little effect'. As Ballhatchet points out, the army had on hand many young, unmarried men, fitter and better fed than their age-mates outside. Leisure was really a choice between lying idly on a barrack bunk, perhaps for eighteen hours a day (for going out in the sun or masturbating were both believed to drive you mad), drinking oneself silly in the canteen, or going to a prostitute (and risking VD). There was also a dilemma for the authorities. To increase the marriage quotas would be expensive, because it would mean paying more allowances and building extra married quarters. To allow men out into the unregulated and often dirty brothels ('sand rags') of the cities and villages would increase VD and troubles with the locals, especially if Tommy were drunk. To exclude prostitutes from cantonments might turn them into replicas of Sodom and Gomorrah. The general army view was that continence was impossible, and the dominant consideration in India was the preservation of the soldier's health, for he was an enormously costly import.

Thus between the mid-1850s and 1888 a system was in operation under which regulated prostitution was available in seventy-five cantonments where the British Indian army was stationed (including one in Ceylon).[40] The aim was to keep the women free from disease. Under it, Indian prostitutes were admitted to the cantonments, to the *lal bazar* (the red-light brothel area of the regimental lines), after medical examination and registration. They remained subject to periodical checks, and by 1865 'lock' hospitals (not so punitive in their regime as in Britain) were available in all cantonments to treat prostitutes suffering from VD. They were grouped in their own houses, caravanserai style, with a superintendent, paid from cantonment funds, but they were free to move, and their conditions were not significantly different from the tens of thousands of other Indian residents serving the army's every need. In Lucknow the brothel was a substantial building with fifty-five rooms. There was no theoretical proportion of prostitutes to the number of soldiers: it was left entirely to the operation of supply and demand. But it seems that the number of prostitutes in a large cantonment (at least in three of the principal ones, Ambala, Mirat, and Lucknow) varied from 60 to 110 at any one time, according to the seasonal total of soldiers stationed there. The maximum average complement of British troops at one of these cantonments would be about 3,750; in other words, on average about one prostitute to forty-four men. The women were supposed to be 'reserved' for white use. Obstacles were placed on their receiving Indian clients, but many military police appear to have done no more than make sure the prostitutes were not seen to consort with Indians (in effect this meant that Indians could use them while the whites were on morning parade). Indian clients were kept out of the more strictly regimental lines, but the cantonment was a big place, and there were other, cheaper (4- to 6-anna) prostitutes in the general bazar and at a greater distance from the regimental lines. When the regiment travelled, the whole supporting bazar marched too, the prostitutes along with the cooks, the ginger-pop makers, the barbers, and *dhobis*. The organisation did not seem particularly shocking to its defenders. The British had not brought prostitution to India; they had only incorporated and regulated part of an old and honourably established business. Few of the girls appeared to be younger than fifteen. The regimental prostitute earned comparatively good money (one rupee per session, often enough) and was not generally ill-treated. With a recognised status, she could enlist the help of the military police in enforcing payment, and she could complain to the authorities. Admittedly she stood at some risk from drunken clients after pay-day or at Christmas, but the soldiers were not normally unkind. The officers recognised the importance of trying to ensure a sufficient number of women, who were moderately young and attractive, for otherwise the men would seek out unregulated women.

Evidence can occasionally be supplemented from unofficial sources. Frank Richards, a private in the Indian army between 1902 and 1909, records a vivid vignette of the brothel or 'rag' at Agra. There were thirty or forty Indian girls aged twelve to thirty for the garrison of 1,500 white men. The brothel was open from 12 noon to 11 p.m. It was 'generally accepted' that a healthy young man in India could not keep away from women, though Richards knew a number who did and he admired them. It was impossible, he said, to walk out of barracks without being offered 'jiggy-jig'. Much emphasis was laid on washing afterwards, in order to avoid VD: hot water was provided in a small lavatory in the street. At Agra, the 'rag' was right opposite the Protestant church, and it was possible to stand in the road and hear both the preacher and the cries of the soliciting girls. Small boys of six to nine years ran errands and acted as punka-wallahs: 'wicked little devils' they were, and 'very knowledgeable about sex'. Truly the soldiers of the king-emperor at Agra were in a different world from the barracks at Colchester. Richards also mentions that at Curzon's *durbar* a half-caste prostitute aged fifty announced her retirement after thirty-six years and kept open free house for five hours. Enormous numbers paid their farewell respects.[41]

Inevitably the whole system became caught up in the wake of the anti-Contagious Diseases Acts campaign in Britain. By 1888 criticism was strong enough for the Indian cantonment arrangements to be officially suspended. Many of their main features in practice went on unchanged, however, as two formidable American lady 'Purity' investigators (Mrs E.W. Andrew and Dr K. Bushnell) discovered in 1892/3 and in 1899/1900. 'Lock' hospitals continued under the sanitised name of 'voluntary venereal hospitals'. The critics had not fully understood the position anyway. The government's special committee on the working of the system (comprising Denzil Ibbetson of the Indian Civil Service, Surgeon-Colonel Cleghorn and Maulvi Samiullah Khan) emphatically rejected the picture suggested by its opponents:

of trembling groups of miserable women . . . their scanty earnings limited by authority, and accompanied by constant brutality . . . released from their confinement only in order to be subjected to the unspeakable indignity of personal examination . . . condemned to drag on a hopeless life of abject poverty and degradation, of shame, and self-abhorrence, of futile yearning for escape, till fading charms cause their rejection as articles no longer serviceable . . . For such a picture . . . we find no shadow of foundation.[42]

The regulated system had not, on the other hand, produced any dramatic reduction of VD, but suspension at once made matters lamentably

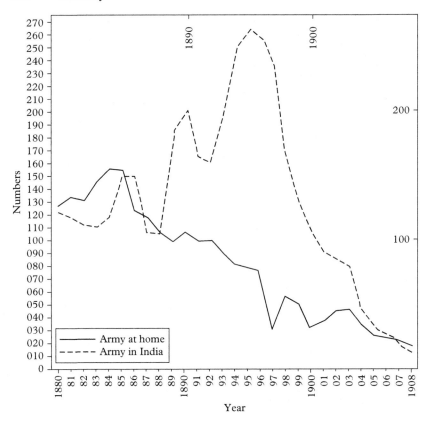

Figure 13.1 Venereal disease in the British army at home and in India; admissions per thousand for syphilis, 1880–1908. *Source*: Flexner, *Prostitution in Europe*, pp. 374–5.

worse. Between 1889 and 1892 nearly half the British soldiers in Bengal were treated for VD; officially the rate was 522.3 per thousand. (See Figure 13.1.) Maybe 'VD' was loosely defined, and some of the 'syphilis' cases might have been no more than festering abrasions caused by 'impure coition' (that is, fellatio) in a hot climate. Even so, the British soldier was certainly more vulnerable to VD than his Indian counterpart, who was more likely to be married. Perhaps this was in part also because he had more money to squander, or was more careless when drunk, or less canny in spotting female symptoms, or perhaps he simply maintained his uncircumcised equipment badly. At all events, in 1895 Secretary of State Lord George Hamilton wanted to bring back the old regulated precautions. Viceroy Elgin, with his habitual good sense and foresight, warned that this might eventually only produce another swing of the Purity pendulum, with the backlash overturning all that they had gained. He therefore suggested simply restarting a voluntary VD examination, taking powers to expel diseased prostitutes from cantonments, and, while they were in hospital, stopping the pay of men who caught VD. Such a penalisation, he hoped, might restrain the troops and at the same time remove the reproach that the authorities punished only the Indian women. The War Office refused to adopt this, largely from anxiety lest it encouraged men to conceal their infections. The new rules actually adopted in 1897 were as follows: no special registration of prostitutes (apart from that required for all inhabitants of cantonments); girls not to be allowed to live in the regimental bazar, only in the main bazar (*sadr bazar*), where most of them already were by now; VD to be compulsorily treated like any other contagious disease. (Improved recreational facilities were also recommended.) Some gratifying decline in VD seemed to result.[43] But 'regimental brothels' persisted into the twentieth century. Essentially the army outwitted the civilian objectors and Purity-mongers. The situation only really changed as recreation became diversified.

'White slavery' and international prostitution

The 'white slave traffic' was but a sub-branch of a more general phenomenon, as the League of Nations recognised in 1921 by renaming it the 'traffic in women and children'. In this international prostitution Britain was essentially a customer rather than a supplier. Unlike the French, British empire-builders never took their own prostitutes with them. Indeed, any British prostitute found in India or elsewhere was sent back home. Their presence was thought to be bad for prestige. International prostitution was fed by the French, the Italians, and Central European Jews (especially from Poland), together with some Russians. Above all, there were the Chinese and Japanese. Indians and Filipinos were not significantly involved in this movement.

Japanese brothels were renowned the world over for their excellent management, technical proficiency, cleanliness, and quietness. Even as late as 1930 Japan maintained 11,154 licensed brothels in 541 different quarters (*yoshiwara*, after the Tokyo prototype), including those in the Japanese empire. In Japan itself there were 50,056 prostitutes. The Japanese maintained a vast network of prostitution extending from Kyūshū, north to Siberia and east to Cape Town, with Singapore, Mauritius, and Australia as major termini. Queensland and the eastern gold-fields of Western Australia were operated on quite a scale: well over 200 Japanese prostitutes were working in Australia in 1896, about half of them in Queensland. The principal Japanese trafficker, Muraoka Iheiji Jiden, claimed to have superintended the smuggling of 3,222 women from Japan to Singapore, and often thence to Mauritius and Australia (some pardonable exaggeration probably has to be allowed for).[44]

Chinese prostitution was highly developed. Shanghai had more than 40,000 prostitutes (including clandestines) around 1900. Overseas, the Chinese had prostitutes wherever there were Chinese men at work. During the early 1930s there were 6,000 Chinese 'known' prostitutes in Malaya, 4,000 in Hong Kong, 1,000 in Macao, and 1,000 in Thailand. There were 2,600 registered brothels in Hong Kong. The Chinese did a not inconsiderable trade in little girls to the United States. There was also a definite and long-standing trade in small boys to Indonesia. *Ti-chou* troupes of young Chinese boy-actors contained some exquisitely expert anal technicians, and their tours among overseas Chinese communities caused considerable excitement and trouble, especially in Thailand, Malaya, and Sumatra. When in the 1930s the British authorities decided to ban Chinese theatricals in Malaya there was such an outcry from the *Ti-chou* community that the British were forced into a compromise whereby boy-actors would still be allowed to perform, but were to be recruited locally and not imported.[45]

The principal problem for British administrators, however, was posed by orthodox Chinese brothels in Malaya. William Pickering (Protector of Chinese) calculated that in 1893 there were 235 brothels in Singapore, housing 2,400 licensed prostitutes, catering for a population of 55,000 Chinese men; of these prostitutes all but 300 were also available to Europeans. Since there were ten Chinese men to every one Chinese woman in Malaya, and since Chinese men so famously knew how to take care of sexual needs without women anyway, Pickering concluded it would be pointless, even undesirable, to check free (that is, uncoerced) prostitution, though he realised that this advice was as 'unEnglish, unChristian and abnormal as the situation itself'. In Malaya in 1894 there were 587 registered brothels containing 4,514 Chinese, 450 Japanese, 81 Malay, and 50 other known prostitutes of various origin. (With keepers and servants the total inmates came to 6,596.) In addition there was Singapore, which alone had 246 brothels in 1894 with 1,871 registered prostitutes; and Penang had 103 houses with 981 inmates. By 1899 the figures had increased still further. Singapore had 311 brothels (236 Chinese, 48 Japanese, 10 European, 9 Tamil, and 8 Malay houses) in the recognised red-light district: with 861 Chinese, 294 Japanese, 37 European, 13 Tamil, and 28 Malay known prostitutes. Also, there were about half a dozen male brothels in Singapore with about a dozen inmates; half of these houses were reserved for the Chinese. In Penang by 1899 there were 736 Chinese registered prostitutes, 71 Japanese, and 86 Indians. British government policy in Malaya as in India was directed towards the abolition of compulsory registration and inspection.[46]

In the geography of 'white slavery' the main route was from Europe to Latin America, especially to Brazil, Argentina, and Uruguay. Buenos Aires was something of an international Mecca or Golconda magnet. But there was also a major supply-line running to North Africa, Egypt, and Constantinople (and taking in Greeks on the way). This line, especially after the opening of the Suez Canal in 1869, led on to Bombay, Colombo, Singapore, Saigon, Hong Kong, and Shanghai. From Shanghai there was a further forward extension by rail to Harbin in Manchuria, or by sea to Manila in the Philippines. The Russians had their own export-line (for unemployable Siberian peasants), to Manchuria and north China, focusing upon the frontier town of Harbin (the centre for railway construction in the region). Harbin in 1932 had a population of 100,000 Russians and contained nine licensed brothels. Most of the 2,000 white prostitutes in Shanghai around 1900 were Russians. There were also Russian women in Peking and Tientsin. The Italians had a direct line to the gold-fields of Western Australia. As the Witwatersrand mines developed, Johannesburg was brought on to the international vice circuit, partly from New York and partly via the Suez Canal. New York was always a major city in the network, with a westward supply-line via San Francisco to Hong Kong and Shanghai, and further branches to Singapore or to the Philippines. The southern route from New York linked up Texas, New Orleans, Cuba, Panama, and ultimately Cape Town and Johannesburg. (See Map 13.1.)

Perhaps one of the most surprising features of the European section of the international prostitution network was the extent to which Jews were involved in it. Arthur Moro, an officer in the London Jewish Association for the Protection of Girls and Women, lamented in 1903: 'We have positive evidence that to almost all parts of North and South Africa, to India, China, Japan, Philippine Islands, North and South America and also to many of the countries in Europe, Yiddish-speaking Jews are maintaining a regular flow of Jewesses, trafficked solely for the purpose of prostitution.' The roots of this phenomenon, spreading to five continents, were in destitution, discrimination, persecution, massive migrations, and urbanisation in Central Europe with a weakening of traditional controls in towns. To put it in perspective, however, there were more French prostitutes in Paris than there were Jewish harlots in all the world, and the French were also heavily represented in a global diaspora embracing Buenos Aires, the Rand, and Manchuria.

The organisers of this transnational traffic were officially regarded

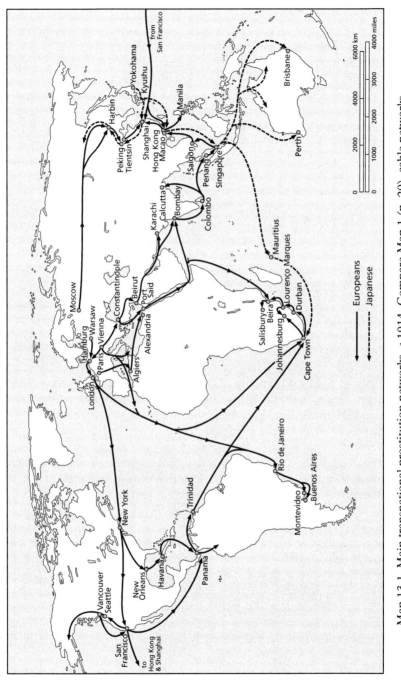

Map 13.1 Main transnational prostitution networks, c.1914. Compare Map 1 (p. 20), cable networks.

with extreme disgust, but they were by any standard remarkably resourceful entrepreneurs. Husband and wife teams were typical, the one a pimp (or *souteneur*, or 'boy' as they called themselves), the other a brothel-madam. They lived peripatetic lives, and passed on their know-how to their sons and daughters. Whole families from the Polish underworld were involved – for example the Stanger sisters, one procuring in Europe, one running a brothel in Port Arthur, another operating in Tientsin. Sadie Solomon was one of the best-travelled figures in the New York underworld, having run brothels in Johannesburg, Brazil, Buenos Aires, Panama, Texas, and Vancouver by 1914, when she was said to be worth $50,000. Nathan Spieler gave up pretzel-baking to run brothels in Shanghai, Constantinople, Bombay, and Singapore, and he was known in the Philippines too. The big-time players had nicknames which resounded in several continents: 'Sadie the Afrikaner' and 'Jenny the Factory' are self-explanatory soubriquets. In Argentina, after two sons of a rabbi had apparently had difficulty in obtaining a Jewish burial for their father because they were well-known pimps, a chartered burial society was set up with its own cemetery for those excluded from the Ashkenazi cemetery on grounds of uncleanness. By the 1920s this had evolved into the Zwi Magdal Society, a pimps' fraternity controlling a thousand brothels and three thousand girls. By such enterprise did prostitution thrive.[47]

The outstanding characteristics of these sexual entrepreneurs were their mobility, their readiness to diversify, and their ruthless professionalism. Movement was essential to the whole business. Customers needed new faces, and so the maintenance of a chain of brothels along a well-established passing-on route was essential. There was no formal direction, just a worldwide camaraderie of pimps and women constantly on the move. The League of Nations investigating team in the 1920s bumped into the same pimps in Buenos Aires, Cairo, Paris, Warsaw, and Antwerp. Pimps were well informed about each other's movements. Many made regular recruiting trips to Europe, sometimes as many as five times a year, probably bringing back no more than one girl at a time (to avoid attracting suspicion). In 1913 the Polish authorities even claimed that traffickers convened annually for a sort of trade fair in Warsaw. The enterprising George Cuirassier swooped into South Africa to meet the extra demand created by the South African War, having already operated in France, Manchuria, Argentina, Mexico, and the United States. Such men always knew where the big events were, whether it was races in a Mexican border town attracting 100,000 Americans a day, or a gymnastic gala in Geneva. Then there was their willingness to take on sidelines. They sold 'pornography' to potential customers and cocaine to weary women. They posed for sexual pictures, or perhaps entered into partnership with a sex photographer. Some were involved in smuggling. They were patient in outwitting the authorities. Making detours was a regular device to reduce the risk of immigration scrutiny – money could always be made en route. They obtained false marriage certificates, went through pseudo-marriage ceremonies, even actual marriage ceremonies. They regularly ordered reinforcements by telegraph. Their professionalism was particularly geared to obtaining 'green' girls (the raw newcomers), and to training them in anal and oral practices. This constituted the vital breakthrough into the 'big time', because a prostitute expert in these 'refinements' could receive forty men a day, compared with six to eight men serviced by straightforward intercourse. Moreover, the tariff was higher, and so a prostitute who had extended her range in this way was reckoned to be worth more than half a dozen ordinary prostitutes.

The League of Nations inquiry held between 1924 and 1927 visited 28 countries and 112 cities and conducted 6,500 interviews. It confirmed that Latin America was the major destination for white prostitutes. The proportion of foreign women in Brazilian brothels was 80 per cent; in Montevideo it was 42 per cent and in Argentina 75 per cent. Buenos Aires had 4,500 foreign prostitutes; there were 585 known brothels. Perhaps a quarter of its prostitutes were French – certainly the largest single group. A clear majority of *all* European prostitutes exported ended up in Argentina. Turning to North Africa, in Alexandria there were 670 brothels in 1923, with 1,356 known prostitutes: one-third were French, and more than 40 per cent foreign. Algeria had 580 European prostitutes, and Tunisia 115. In both countries the winter tourist season imposed an increased demand. Some houses were operated in conjunction with Marseilles and Paris, the telegraph again being a vital adjunct to business. The parallel inquiry into the situation in the East, covering the whole area from Beirut to Tokyo, was conducted in 1930–2. It came up with the following figures. In Calcutta there were 25 French prostitutes, 10 Russian, one Italian, one Greek, and one Australian. There were 20 whites in Hong Kong (half of them French), 20 in Bombay (mostly Jews), 15 in Shanghai (including 5 Americans and 3 Australians), 10 or more in the Philippines (plus 122 Japanese), and 23 in Colombo. Colombo provided the League with its best proof of boy-prostitution (involving Tamil teenagers working in the docks), but nowhere could they uncover much evidence of any substantial *traffic* in boys.

Thus the international diffusion of European prostitutes was remarkably wide at its heyday in the late nineteenth and early twentieth centuries. There was an elaborate informal organisation, efficiently run on the best entrepreneurial lines. The nodal distributive points were Buenos Aires,

New York, Alexandria, Constantinople, Hong Kong, and Shanghai. The whole international network relied heavily on technological advance: on condoms, cables, and canals (Suez and Panama). Southern Africa would not have been brought so quickly into the network but for the Suez Canal, and the railway link from Lourenço Marques to Johannesburg (1895). This soon brought 750 Jewish prostitutes to the region. About a third of the girls were French (the red-light district of Johannesburg was called Frenchfontein), and a fifth of them were Germans. There were at least 133 brothels in Johannesburg by 1896, and probably a similar number in Cape Town. Most of the inhabitants were white. Johannesburg's connection to the international network also owed something to the exodus from New York brothels during the police clean-up campaign of 1892–5. By 1909 Smuts was launching his own purge, and broke the hold of the immigrant vice merchants. Prostitution in South Africa reverted once more to its indigenous base.[48] Reversal of the trend towards turning the whole world into the white man's brothel had begun.[49]

IV

Empire provided ample opportunities for sexual indulgence throughout the nineteenth century, though this was more obvious in frontier situations and the fighting services than in settled expatriate communities. Indeed, the willingness of Victorian Britons to endure the deprivations involved in working overseas probably depended quite crucially on the easy availability of a range of sexual consolations. Sexual consciousness was heightened among soldiers and traders alike. Sexual relationships soldered together the invisible bonds of empire. In the erotic field, as in administration and commerce, some degree of 'collaboration' from the indigenous communities was essential to the maintenance of imperial systems. The empire-builder was exposed to more relaxed attitudes and alternative life-styles; even some evangelical missionaries took advantage of these exotic opportunities. After the orchestrated reduction of sexual opportunity in Britain itself from the 1880s, the formal and informal empire continued to provide some compensation, until Purity tightened its grip overseas.

The evidence uncovered in this chapter is fragmented and often tantalising. It is necessarily impressionistic and superficial. The effect is rather like peering only into the relatively clear surface layer of the waters of a particularly deep and opaque pool, since most sexual activity is simply not observable, still less recorded. The sources used here were in the main generated because something went wrong. Private behaviour became officially or publicly scandalous, and therefore the subject of investigation and record. The surviving evidence is thus biased towards the sensational and the discreditable. The larger (and presumably irrecoverable) truth is probably gentler and more ordinary than the rather lurid and perfervid picture presented above. Sexual preoccupation may well be even more pervasive than we can document, but its expression is likely to have been generally less exploitative than the record suggests. Though sex cannot of itself enable men to transcend racial barriers, it generates some admiration and affection across them, which is healthy, and which cannot always be dismissed as merely self-interested and prudential. However, if we are to regard such inter-racial sexual liaisons as damaging, then we should also be prepared to accept that at least equally damaging has been the willingness of the Third World to adopt the peculiar Purity laws and conventions of Britain in the 1880s as if they represented ultimate truths about human civilisation. They do not.

Notes

1 Happily, no longer the case. Following upon Kenneth Ballhatchet's pioneering *Race, sex and class under the Raj: imperial attitudes and policies and their critics, 1793–1905* (1980) there has been much significant work, more especially: Richard Aldrich, *Colonialism and homosexuality* (2003); Philippa Levine, *Prostitution, race and politics: policing venereal disease in the British empire* (New York, 2003); and John Iliffe, *The African AIDS epidemic: a history* (Athens, OH, 2006). From the explosion of writing about gender in the empire, three essays stand out: Rosalind O'Hanlon, 'Gender in the British empire', in *OHBE*, vol. IV, *The twentieth century* (ed. W.R. Louis and J.M. Brown, 1999), ch. 16, pp. 379–97; Philippa Levine, 'Sexuality, gender and empire', in Levine, ed., *Gender and empire* (*OHBE*, Companion Series, 2004), pp. 134–55; and Helen Callaway, 'Purity and exotica in legitimating the empire: cultural construction of gender, sexuality and race', in Terence Ranger and Olufemi Vaughan, eds., *Legitimacy and the state in twentieth-century Africa: essays in honour of A.H.M. Kirk-Greene* (1993, 2001), pp. 31–88. There are also important studies of other empires, notably: Owen White, *Children of the empire: miscegenation and colonial society in French West Africa, 1895–1960* (Oxford, 1999); and (on the Dutch) Ann L. Stoler, *Race and the education of desire: Foucault's 'History of Sexuality' and the colonial order of things* (Durham, NC, 1995), and Hanneke Ming, 'Barracks-concubinage in the Indies, 1887–1920', *Indonesia*, vol. 35 (1983), pp. 65–93.
2 F. Steegmuller, ed., *The letters of Gustave Flaubert, 1830–1857* (1980), pp. 11, 121; F M Lord Roberts of Kandahar, *Forty-one years in India* (1898 edn), p. 397.
3 S. Marks, *Reluctant rebellion: the 1906–08 disturbances in Natal* (Oxford, 1970), p. 47; A. Inglis, *The White Women's Protection Ordinance: sexual anxiety and politics in Papua* (Sussex, 1975).
4 L. Doyal and I. Pennell, '"Pox Britannica": health, medicine and under-

development', *Race and Class*, vol.18 (1970), pp. 155–72; I. McCalman, 'Unrespectable radicalism: infidels and pornography in early 19th-century London', *Past and Present*, no. 104 (1984), pp. 74–110. More recently: L.Z. Sigel, 'Filth in the wrong people's hands: postcards and pornography in Britain and the Atlantic world, 1880–1914', *Journal of Social History*, vol. 33 (2000), pp. 859–86.

5 'Pisanus Fraxi' [H.S. Ashbee], *Index librorum prohibitorum* (1877), p. xvii.

6 M. Perham, *Lugard*, vol. I, *The years of adventure, 1858–1898* (1956), pp. 59–73; V. Purcell, *Memoirs of a Malayan official* (1965), p. 251.

7 M. Perham, *West African passage: a journey through Nigeria, Chad, and the Cameroons, 1931–1932* (ed. A.H.M. Kirk-Greene, 1983), pp. 75–6.

8 G.M. Theal, *History of South Africa since 1795*, vol. III, *Cape Colony, 1840–1860* (1908), pp. 50–2.

9 For Macdonald: The National Archives, CO 537/410, no. 6835, and CO 537/411, no. 41391; National Army Museum, Roberts Papers, 7101/23/46, ff. 113, 114, and 7101/23/122, ff. 108–9 (1903); Aldrich, *Colonialism and homosexuality*, pp. 187–90.

10 Edward James, *Swans reflecting elephants: my early years* (ed. G. Melly, 1982), pp. 26–8.

11 M. Bence-Jones, *Clive of India* (1974), p. 27.

12 Magdalene College Archives, F/WRI/37 (Inge Diary, 31 January 1940); F/ACB/179, f. 44 (Benson Diary, 21 March 1925); A.C. Benson *The schoolmaster: a commentary* (1908), pp. 148–9.

13 Harold Macmillan, *Memoirs*, vol. VI, *At the end of the day, 1961–1963* (1973), pp. 437–44.

14 T.E.B. Howarth, ed., *Monty at close quarters: recollections of the man* (1985), contributions by Lucien Trueb and Richard Luckett.

15 R.E. Wraith, *Guggisberg* (1967), pp. 247–9; J.D. Baird, ed., *Private letters of the Marquess of Dalhousie* (1910, 1972), pp. 257–8.

16 R.C.K. Ensor, *England, 1870–1914* (Oxford, 1936), p. 170; L. Stone, *The family, sex and marriage in England, 1500–1800* (1977), pp. 54, 490–1, 579–80, 657; L.H. Gann and P. Duignan, *The rulers of British Africa, 1870–1914* (Stanford, CA, 1978), p. 240.

17 A.C. Kinsey *et al.*, eds., *Sexual behavior in the human male* (Philadelphia, 1948), pp. 205–13.

18 E.J. Bristow, *Vice and vigilance: purity movements in Britain since 1700* (Dublin, 1977).

19 CO 537/540, no. 38767, comment by J.A.S. Bucknill (7 December 1906) on his Report on 'unnatural vice and other immorality' among Chinese labourers in the Witwatersrand mines, September 1906.

20 Quoted in Ashbee, *Index librorum prohibitorum*, pp. 379–81, from Sellon, *Ups and downs of life* (1867), p. 42.

21 League of Nations Reports, *Traffic in women and children* (1929), p. 80.

22 J.K. Fairbank, K.F. Bruner, and E. Matheson, eds., *The I.G. in Peking: letters of Robert Hart, 1868–1951* (Cambridge, MA, 1975), vol. II, p. 1078 (8 August 1896); R. Winstedt, *Start from alif: count from one, an autobiographical mémoire* (Kuala Lumpur, 1969), pp. 17–18, 102–4; for Joyce Cary, M.

Crowder, *Revolt in Bussa: a study of British 'Native Administration' in Nigerian Borgu, 1902–1935* (1973), p. 168.

23 *Pall Mall Gazette*, vol. 45 (19 May 1887), pp. 2–3, 'Is empire consistent with morality? No!', by a Public Servant.

24 G. Freyre, *The masters and the slaves: a study in the development of Brazilian civilisation* (New York, 1946), p. 323.

25 W.D. Jordan, *White over black: American attitudes towards the Negro, 1750–1872* (Chapel Hill, NC, 1968), pp. 136–7, 161–2; W.A. Green, *British slave emancipation in the sugar colonies: the great experiment, 1830–1865* (1976), pp. 20–2; F. Cooper, *Plantation slavery on the east coast of Africa* (New Haven, CT, 1977), pp. 17, 35, 195–9; E.D. Genovese, *Roll, Jordan, roll!: the world the slaves made* (1975), pp. 413–31.

26 H. Tinker, *A new system of slavery: the export of Indian indentured labour overseas, 1830–1920* (1974); K. Saunders, ed., *Indian indentured labour in the British empire, 1834–1920* (1984).

27 J.S. Galbraith, *The little emperor: Governor Simpson of the Hudson's Bay Company* (Toronto, 1976); Jennifer S.H. Brown, *Strangers in blood: fur trade company families in Indian country* (Vancouver, 1980).

28 *Accounts and Papers*, vol. 7, reprint, *Crime and punishment: juvenile offenders, I, Session 1847* (Irish UP Series, British Parliamentary Papers, Shannon, 1970); R. Hughes, *The fatal shore: a history of the transportation of convicts to Australia, 1787–1868* (1987).

29 CO 537/542, no. 9752, 'Confidential inquiry into alleged prevalence of unnatural vice among the natives in the mines of Witwatersrand', 1907; C. van Onselen, *Studies in the social and economic history of the Witwatersrand, 1886–1914*, vol. II, *New Nineveh*, pp. 179–87, and *'Chibaro': African mine labour in Southern Rhodesia, 1900–1933* (esp. pp. 174–182, 'Sex in the service of industry and the state'); T. Dunbar Moody, 'Migrancy and male sexuality in the South African gold mines', *Journal of Southern African Studies*, vol. 14 (1988), pp. 228–56.

30 N. Gunson, *Messengers of grace: evangelical missionaries in the South Seas, 1797–1860* (Melbourne, 1978); D. Hilliard, *God's gentlemen: a history of the Melanesian Mission, 1849–1942* (Brisbane, Queensland, 1978); D. Wetherell, *Reluctant mission: the Anglican Church in Papua New Guinea, 1891–1942* (Brisbane, Queensland, 1977); J. Binney, 'Whatever happened to poor Mr Yate?', *New Zealand Journal of History*, vol. 9 (1975), pp. 111–25.

31 R. Meinertzhagen, *Kenya diary, 1902–1906* (Edinburgh, 1957), pp. 13, 34.

32 John Murray Papers, Sir Francis Bond Head to John Murray II (20 August 1838) – I owe this reference to Ged Martin.

33 Van Onselen, *Studies in the social and economic history of the Witwatersrand*, vol. II, 'Witches of suburbia: domestic service on the Witwatersrand, 1890–1914'; N. Etherington, 'Natal's black rape scares of the 1870s', *Journal of Southern African Studies*, vol. 15 (1988), pp. 36–53.

34 K.S Rukavina, *Jungle pathfinder: the biography of 'Chirupula' Stephenson* (1951).

35 J. de Vere Allen, 'The Malayan Civil Service, 1874–1941', *Comparative Studies in Society and History*, vol. 12 (1970), pp. 149–78; J.G. Butcher, *The*

British in Malaya, 1880–1940: the social history of a European community in South-East Asia (Kuala Lumpur, 1979), esp. ch. 8, 'European men and Asian women'; R.H. Bruce Lockhart, *Return to Malaya* (1936). More recently, and most vividly, C.A. Bayly and T.N. Harper, *Forgotten armies: the fall of British Asia, 1941–1945* (2004), pp. 37–69 ('A Malayan pastorale' and 'Malaise').

36 Purcell, *Memoirs of a Malayan official*, pp. 249–51. Information about Malayan scandals is hard to come by, but it is known that quite a number of European 'deviant cases' were rounded up by the police in Kelantan after 1945, including several civil servants. Mervyn (Mubin) Sheppard, the last in the long line of outstanding British scholar-administrators, who made important contributions to independent Malaya, had joined the Malay Civil Service in 1928; his superiors more or less forced him into (a disastrous) marriage in 1940, after a relationship with a Malay youth. Again, in the 1950s, a relationship with a young Malay protégé became scandalous, and this precipitated Sheppard into embracing Islam (from which we may infer that he had been circumcised in infancy). My thanks to Dr T.N. Harper and Dr S.P. Martland for discussing with me sexuality in Malaya.

37 John Masters, *Bugles and a tiger* (1956), pp. 153–4.

38 M.L. Ferrar, ed., *The diary of Colour-Sgt George Calladine, 19th Foot, 1793–1837* (1922), pp. 72–7.

39 A. Flexner, *Prostitution in Europe* (1914), p. 371. For 'lock hospitals', see D.M. Peers, 'Soldiers, surgeons and the campaign to combat sexually transmitted diseases in colonial India, 1805–1860', *Medical History*, vol. 42 (1998), pp. 137–60.

40 *Accounts and Papers*, vol. 64, *Report of the committee . . . into the Indian cantonments . . . with regard to prostitution and the treatment of veneral diseases* (C. 7148, 1893); more generally, Ballhatchet, *Race, sex and class*, and Levine, *Prostitution, race and politics*, together with D.M. Peers, 'Privates off parade: regimenting sexuality in the 19th-century Indian army', *International History Review*, vol. 20 (1998), pp. 823–54.

41 Frank Richards, *Old-soldier sahib* (1936), pp. 303–4.

42 *Report of the committee . . . Indian cantonments*, p. 273.

43 India Office Records, Elgin Viceroy Papers, F 84/15, Elgin to Secretary of State Lord George Hamilton (10 May 1897).

44 League of Nations Reports on *Traffic in women and children*, 1923–1937, esp. on *The Far East* (C.849.M.393.1932.IV, pp. 103–4); D.C.S. Sissons, '"Karayuki-san": Japanese prostitutes in Australia, 1887–1916', *Historical Studies (Australia and New Zealand)*, vol. 17 (1977), nos. 68 and 69 (in two parts).

45 League of Nations Report, *Traffic in women and children: Conference of central authorities in Eastern countries at Bandoeng, February 1937*, minutes of meetings (C.476.M.318.1937.IV).

46 The National Archives, CO 273/121, no. 13612, annual report by W.A. Pickering, on Chinese Protectorate, Singapore and Penang (12 April 1883); CO 273/197, no. 18487, report by G.T. Hare (12 September 1894); CO 273/258, no. 30403, report by A.H. Capper; R.N. Jackson, *Pickering: Protector of Chinese* (Kuala Lumpur, 1965), pp. 92–9.

47 E.J. Bristow, *Prostitution and prejudice: the Jewish fight against white slavery, 1870–1939* (Dublin, 1982).

48 Van Onselen, *Studies in the social and economic history of the Witwatersrand*, vol. I, *New Babylon*, pp. 102–62 ('Prostitutes and proletarians').

49 For the twentieth century, see Nils Ringdal, *Love for sale: a global history of prostitution* (1997, tr. from Norwegian by R. Daly, 2004), and two essays on the efforts of the League of Nations to combat international prostitution: B. Metzger, 'Towards an international human rights regime during the inter-war years: the League of Nations' combat of traffic in women and children', in K. Grant, P. Levine, and F. Trentmann, eds., *Beyond sovereignty: Britain, empire and transnationalism, 1860–1950* (Basingstoke, 2007), pp. 154–79; and D.M. Pomfret, '"Child slavery" in British and French Far-Eastern colonies, 1880–1945', *Past and Present*, no. 201 (2008), pp. 175–213.

14 Penis envy and 'penile othering' in the colonies and America

[The first half of this chapter is a revised version of a commissioned contribution to *Sex* (*The Erotic Review*, ed. Stephen Bayley, 2001), entitled 'Does size matter?: African and Afro-American super-sexuality'; the second half has been written for this volume.

The chapter registers an extraordinary reversal. Male circumcision, from being regarded as a barbarous mark of 'the Other', was adopted for a full half-century as an emblem of the imperial elite. Although circumcision provides unusually clear evidence of a cultural connection to empire, it is ignored by cultural and post-colonial historians. Its significance, however, has been picked up by traditionalist historians such as Piers Brendon (*The decline and fall of the British empire, 1781–1997* (2007), p. 206) and Anthony Kirk-Greene (*Britain's imperial administrators, 1858–1966* (2000), pp. 11–12).]

Perceptions of the penis signify as one of the ways in which European men saw people 'other' than themselves. Their assessments of the male body were part of their attitudes towards race, which perpetually hinged upon a sense of difference. And the sorts of 'other' penis they saw differed in two main ways, or so it seemed: in their size and in whether or not they were circumcised. In 1810, when Byron wanted to draw out the main differences between the 'Turks and ourselves', he seized upon the fact that 'we have a foreskin and they have none' – adding that 'we talk much and they little . . . we prefer a girl and a bottle, they a pipe and a pathic'.[1] It was a commonplace that Africans had larger generative organs – the macrophallic obsession or fantasy. A perceived white inadequacy in comparison was mainly dealt with by declaring a large penis to be a sign that blacks were closer to beast life than man, and it was linked to a supposed hypersexuality, condemned as uncivilised. The threat of forcible circumcision at times induced little short of panic among Europeans captured by Muslims, sometimes as prisoners of war, especially in India, sometimes as victims of piracy and shipwreck in the Mediterranean. This was an 'othering' because it was only at the end of the nineteenth century that British males began fashionably to be circumcised as a routine. Before that it was a contemptible sign of the

Other, practised only by Jews, Muslims, and some African, Melanesian, and Amerindian peoples. It was despised as mutilation.

I

John Ogilby's splendid compilation of travellers' tales, *Africa* (1670), recorded that Negro men sported 'large Propagators'. From at least the fifteenth century, it was widely put about in Europe that Africans were exceptionally well-equipped sexually. Coupled with this belief in the larger black penis was an apprehension that African sexual prowess and staying-power were also greater than those of white men. By the eighteenth century these propositions were probably well diffused in educated circles, and it was assumed that the 'noble savage' had an impressive 'propagator'.[2]

Probably the first systematic attempt to integrate the penis into racial classification was in 1799 when Charles White of Manchester, a respected scientist, published *An account of the regular gradation in Man*, which said the black member was 'invariably' longer and more solid than the white man's. Others followed him during the nineteenth century. James Hunt, in *On the Negro's place in nature* (1863), cited an 'eminent' French anthropologist, Dr Pruner Bey: 'the penis is always of an unusually large size', with 'very large' seminal vesicles. Bey added for good measure: sexual gratification, together with drunkenness, gambling, and ornamentation of the body, 'are the most powerful levers in the life of the Negro'.[3] Observable bodily difference was important in establishing categories of race, and travellers and anthropologists embraced the theory of the big propagator 'as a heuristic device alongside others for racial classification'.[4]

However, the notion of a black 'super penis' only began to assume widespread and obsessional significance in the 1860s, as a result of the deterioration of race relations throughout the Anglo-Saxon world. These processes were especially notable in the increasing segregation, negrophobia, and sexual paranoia of the American South following the end of slavery, and they persisted well into the twentieth century. The Afro-American novelist James Baldwin once remarked that white Southerners were obsessed with the black man's organ, and whenever a black man was lynched – and several thousand were from the 1880s to the 1930s – the first thing done 'was to cut his penis off'. As one commentator has said, 'To really kill a black man, you first had to kill his penis.'

Many commentators dismiss these propositions about size as myths, as no more than part of the racist paraphernalia and thus automatically discredited. They argue that there is no essential difference between penis size in blacks and whites, and that blacks were stigmatised as 'sexually depraved' as part of the battery of justification for European influence in Africa and domination in the New World. They suggest that the image of the black super-stud was invented in order to deter white women from seeking inter-racial liaisons. Had not Shakespeare himself identified the danger when he wrote that 'it is an old saying that black men are pearls in beauteous ladies' eyes'? (*Two Gentlemen of Verona*, V, ii, 10–13, published around 1589–93). These sexual worries were, in the opinion of many historians of race, 'the ultimate basis of racial antagonism' (J.S. Walvin), since all racism derives from fear of competition. Assumptions about an aggressive black sexuality were certainly deeply ingrained in Britain and throughout the American and colonial world.[5]

One of the first historians to challenge the 'myth' – if that is what it was – was the Brazilian writer Gilberto Freyre in his celebrated book translated as *The masters and the slaves: a study of the development of Brazilian civilisation* (1946). Freyre argued that Negro sexuality was in fact characterised by a greater moderation than European sexuality, and was in constant need of sharp stimulation, hence the need for such aids as 'aphrodisiac dances'. He pointed out that appearances could be deceptive, with many a giant-framed Negro having the 'penis of a small boy'; moreover, he declared, the sexual organs of 'primitive people' were comparatively underdeveloped.[6]

On the other hand, the alternative picture has never lacked its advocates, even in recent times. Professor J. Philippe Rushton, professor of psychology at the University of Western Ontario in Canada, as the twentieth century drew to its close, attempted to demonstrate statistically in *Race, evolution and behaviour* that blacks have larger genitals and smaller brains than whites or Asians, and that there was an inverse correlation between penis size and brain power. He summed up his thesis thus: 'It's a trade-off. More brain or more penis. You can't have both.'[7]

Whatever the facts, of course, the important thing is what people think is the case.[8] Thus the notion of the black 'super penis' remains a 'classic instance of the influence of sexual insecurity upon perception'. As W.D. Jordan writes of the American South:

Whatever the objective facts, the belief blended flawlessly with the white man's image of the Negro. If a perceptible anatomical difference did in fact exist, it fortuitously coincided with the already firmly established idea of the Negro's special sexuality; it could only have served as a striking confirmation of that idea, as salt in the wounds of the white man's envy.[9]

It has been further suggested that Amerindians were the subject of less prejudice because their 'propagators' were supposed to be a little smaller than those of the whites, and their sex-drives lower, while they were 'more likely' to evolve trans-sexual roles. A German writer, W.L. van Eschege, in 1818 committed himself to the view that the Brazilian Indians had 'an extraordinary small size of penis, consonant with their feminine nature'. A specific contrast with blacks was made by K. von Martius in 1843.[10] Intermarriage with American Indians was never illegal. Nor was it in New Zealand with the Maori. Were historians therefore in a position to posit an emerging general theory that penis length determines whether sexual fears are present or not? Is this the crucial reason why white men got on well with the Maori? Not really. Professor Sinclair acknowledged that the absence of a feeling of sexual rivalry or jealousy towards Maori males was important in comparatively good race relations in New Zealand. He was unable to suggest an explanation. 'But there is no real or imagined difference in sexual organs or practices to cause jealousy.' Although the negative point is not unimportant, there are more significant reasons for inter-racial respect, in New Zealand and elsewhere. In the Maori case these included martial spirit and lighter skin colour.[11]

Of course there has never been any shortage of exaggeration in white estimates of their own phallic prowess. Vic Gatrell has analysed 'phallic narcissism' in eighteenth-century bawdy songs circulating in London. A ditty by Charles Morris compared the penis with 'the tree of life':

> This tree will in most countries produce,
> But till 18 years growth 'tis not much fit for use,
> Then nine or ten inches, for it seldom grows higher,
> And that's as much as the heart can desire.[12]

In France the Marquis de Sade described his principals in *The 120 days of Sodom* (written in about 1784) as endowed with 'engines' or 'devices' of anything from eight to thirteen inches in length, and between 'seven and fifteen-sixteenths around' and 'eight and a quarter inches circumferentially'.[13] All Europeans of course, and mostly preposterous.

So what are the 'objective facts'? Men vary in their sexual drive and capacity, in the intensity of their need for sexual satisfaction, and even in the dynamic power of their ejaculatory force, just as they vary in every other attribute and characteristic. And, whether white or black, manifestly they vary – dramatically – in penis size. The scientific measurement of the phallus is known as phalloplethysmography, literally an assessment of volume.[14] Linear estimation is made upon the erect upper surface of the penis, from the urethral opening to the junction with the stomach. From a variety of such studies, the issue of size can be resolved.

Adult erections normally range from 4.5 inches to 9 inches (11.5 to 23 centimetres). That is to say, some men have erections which are twice as long as others. Almost all, however, are between 5 inches and

7 inches, though 8 inches is not uncommon; 6 inches (15 centimetres), plus or minus, may be regarded as standard, a respectable average. There is an inherent improbability about anything genuinely and verifiably in excess of 9.5 inches, although there has never been any shortage of claimants. In 1890 a French doctor, A. Charpy, documented an erection of 14.5 inches, and this is frequently cited as the record length in man. Unfortunately, virtually all the subjects available for scientific measurement appear to have been Caucasian. Even the great Kinsey himself was dissatisfied with his 'black' sample (mostly of the lower social level) and encountered problems in gaining the confidence of Afro-American groups. Although the data were routinely collected, his *Sexual behavior in the human male* (1948) is therefore silent on the whole issue. Privately, Kinsey said he dared not publish his findings because they confirmed the racial stereotype that blacks did indeed have larger penises, higher frequencies of sexual activity, and rose to orgasm more slowly than quick-firing whites; he feared that American neo-Nazis would say 'we told you so'. Perhaps not entirely incidentally he found that black women were more likely than white women to have clitorises which stood out more than one inch. The longest penises reported were, however, white.[15]

The Kinsey data subsequently published suggest the following conclusions, comparing a sample of white college students, 4,694 in number, with black college students, 177 in number. The black sample is small, but indicative. On estimated measurements of the length of erect penis – the most important point of comparison – it appears that 37% of whites had erections of less than six inches, but only 26% of blacks; there was almost no difference in the proportion of those between six and seven inches (56% as against 54%); but of those over seven inches, whites accounted for 6.8% as against 20% blacks, the latter including 3% at nine inches (0.4% of whites). (See Table 14.1.) Erect circumferences at the widest point showed 70% of whites measured up to five inches, 65% of blacks, with blacks having 5% more measurements in excess of five inches round. Measured flaccid length must be considered as seriously unreliable, but revealed a similar pattern: little difference in the majority middle range of about three to four inches; with more whites than blacks shorter than this, more blacks than whites longer. As far as other possible indicators of sexual avidity and technique were concerned, Kinsey found, for example, that 42% of white boys first masturbated at the age of ten or earlier, while 68% of blacks began this early. The length of time in sustained erection in coitus to orgasm indicated that only 12% of whites managed fifteen minutes or more, while 22% of black men fell into this category. Premature ejaculation – defined as sustaining coitus for less

Table 14.1. *The Kinsey data: estimated length of erect penis, white men and black men (per cent)*

Length to nearest quarter inch	White		Black
	College student	Non-college student	College student
2.0–3.75	0.6	1.2	0
4.0–4.75	6.5	9.6	3.1
5.00	12.4	13.4	9.9
5.25	1.4	0.8	1.2
5.50	13.1	11.6	10.6
5.75	2.9	2.2	1.2
6.00	28.7	28.9	19.3
6.25	2.5	1.8	2.5
6.50	13.3	12.2	16.8
6.75	1.2	0.6	0.6
7.00	10.7	9.8	14.9
7.25	0.6	1.0	0
7.50	2.4	2.9	6.2
7.75	0.2	0.2	0
8.00	2.4	2.9	9.3
8.25	0.1	0	0
8.50	0.6	0.6	1.2
8.75	0.1	0	0
9.00	0.3	0.2	3.1
9.25	0	0	0
9.50	–	0	0
9.75	0	0	0
10.00	0.1	0	0

Source: Derived from Gebhard and Johnson, *The Kinsey data*, table 69, p. 116. The size of the sample was 4,694 white college students (plus 766 non-college), and 177 black college students. The standard question was: 'How long is your penis when it is hard, measuring on the top side from your belly out to the tip?'

than two minutes – was characteristic of 17.6% of white men, but only 9.7% of black men.[16]

So Kinsey was probably right, and there is a marginal correlation between blackness and penis size, a black penis on average being a little larger that the white man's. But exactly the same variations in size can be observed in black as well as white. There are documented cases of Africans with smaller-than-average appendages, most famously the warrior-leader Shaka, ruler of Zululand between about 1818 and 1828. Shaka was taunted by other boys when he was eleven: 'Look at his cock: it is just like a little earthworm' ('Ake ni-bone umtondo wake: ufane nomsundu nje'). Whether puberty brought any relative improvement is not known, but Shaka took his revenge later by impaling his boyhood tormentors.[17]

Anyone who has seen ethnographic photographs or television pictures of the Masai of Kenya, or the Nuer and Nubians of the Sudan, will probably agree that their men do appear mainly to be well endowed. But a goodly flaccid length should not be assumed to extend proportionately into its erect state. The appearance, or actuality, of impressive penises in Africans may derive not so much from genetic determination as from lifestyle. Going routinely nude in hot climates would certainly seem to help, while regular sexual usage would seem to be an essential concomitant – a factor which may explain recent claims that (supposedly promiscuous) homosexuals have significantly longer propagators than (supposedly apathetic) heterosexuals. Some African peoples may also have resorted to artificial devices for lengthening the penis. And circumcision, though not practised by all Africans, may provide a 'value added' increment by exposing the glans to a subtle degree of continuous stimulation.

As far as sexual desire, capacity, and performance are concerned, any special African reputation would seem to rest on even shakier foundations than that of significantly superior penis size. There is nothing instinctive about the capacity to provide sophisticated sexual performance. It has to be learned, and it takes time and patience. Although it is perfectly possible that Africans cultivated their sexuality more than many Europeans, and were less inhibited about it, there is little evidence that they evolved an art of sexuality in any way comparable to that of the Indians or the Chinese, or even the Japanese; still less can such an evolution have happened among Afro-Americans in the unpropitious circumstances of a slave plantation. Indeed, if by 'sexual capacity' we mean maintenance of continuous erection over the space of many hours or a whole night, the world champions would undoubtedly be the Taoist masters of sex. Although the *Kama Sutra* may reflect a culture that was adept at strategies of arousal and the variation of positions for sexual intercourse, only the Tao philosophers of sex concentrated on techniques for improving erectile function (or curing dysfunction and combating old-age deterioration), for developing sexual energy, multiplying and controlling male orgasm, and practising semen retention, or any of the other arts which alone can maximise male sexual performance as such.[18]

III

Forcible circumcision has come to be associated especially with European captives in the state of Mysore in the 1780s. Mysore was ruled by two remarkable Muslims, Haidar Ali and, from 1782 his son Tipu Sultan.

The state of Mysore was a powerful kingdom which posed a significant threat to British military power in India, and it was not until 1792 that it was defeated. Tipu was known as 'the Tiger of Mysore' and tiger symbolism was pervasive: the sultan's troops wore tiger-striped uniforms. The British saw him as a bogeyman, and attributed to him a Muslim religious fanaticism 'for which there is no factual basis'.[19]

It is in the context of this cautious judgment that we need to evaluate the captivity narratives, with Linda Colley as our guide.[20] Many such stories were published, for example William Thomson's *Memoirs of the late war in Asia* (1788), and *Narrative of the sufferings of James Bristow, 1792–1794*. The former was from the perspective of the officer class, the latter that of the private soldier, but both detailed cases of forcible circumcision. Of the others, the memoir of an officer called Cromwell Massey seems to be the most interesting. He was imprisoned in Seringapatam from 1780 to 1784. At some point in 1781 he received reports that fifteen 'healthy looking young men', British private soldiers, had refused to join Mysore's armies. Having refused, they were taken one by one to be body-shaved, stretched naked on their backs over a large bowl, arms and legs held down by guards, and forcibly relieved of their foreskins. However, there is also evidence that some British captives voluntarily surrendered themselves to incorporation in Tipu's military machine, and perhaps were then circumcised more considerately with drugging. Massey also learned that at Bangalore, fifty-one boys and young men had been circumcised, including five midshipmen. At one point Massey scribbled in his manuscript, 'terribly alarmed this morning for our foreskins'.

There were reports in the British press that Tipu recruited some of the youngest captives, drummer-boys and cabin-boys, once circumcised, to act as *ramzainis* or dancing-boys in his court, and this may have involved cross-dressing. In 1784 some 1,700 British-born male captives remained alive in Mysore, and almost a quarter were either forced or chose to go over to their captors. According to Colley, this made defeat worse, because circumcision 'seemed a particularly indelible assault on their identity, an irreversible "othering" . . . the British bodies involved in this Mysore captivity panic could be viewed in terms of national humiliation: not just emblems of defeat and lapses in solidarity in India, but of emasculation as well'. These were 'physical mutilations that could be interpreted as affronts to British masculinity', as an 'ultimate and definitive emblem of national castration and unmanning'. Colley then quotes the words of one ensign: 'I lost with the foreskin of my yard all those benefits of a Christian and Englishman which were and ever shall be my greatest glory.' Although she recognises that this is 'at once comic, tortured and eloquent', she still seems to take it too seriously, for it is surely no more than a humorous bit of bravado. Colley, with her sub-Freudian 'symbolic castration thesis', apparently sees circumcision as part of a campaign of feminisation. From an anthropological perspective, this is nonsense. The universal meaning of circumcision is making properly male, conferring a 'badge of manhood'.[21] It achieves gender differentiation, an entry into masculine personality and a sexual role, by a conquest of 'feminine elements', marking a change 'from a state of infantile filthiness to a state of clean maturity', or, as the Merina describe it, *mahasoa* ('making sweet and clean').[22] It is most unlikely that Mysoreans saw it generally in any other way. To them circumcision was in part a heightening of masculinity, and it may even have been seen as conferring a favour. What we do not hear about from captives is subsequent gratitude for the increment of sexiness which the operation probably conferred. Fears about it beforehand were surely no more than apprehension about the pain and risk involved in *forcible* circumcision. But there is an inference that the benefits were soon realised, for there were those who agreed to this 'indelible' incorporation. So far from these 'mutilations' being interpreted as 'affronts to British masculinity', they may be evidence of Tipu's willingness to show respect to amenable British soldiers, in line with his drilling Mysorean troops in accordance with British army regulations.

The circumcision scares in Mysore and Bangalore certainly seem unusual in the context of other Muslim captivity scenarios. The North African corsairs, 'Barbary pirates', are thought to have captured some 20,000 Britons, including women and children, during the seventeenth and eighteenth centuries. Many became galley-rowers or other menials, subject to sexual abuse and often dying of disease. But their apprehensions were associated with sodomy rather than circumcision. Up to 1750, Colley tells us, there are five times more references to men and boys in Barbary and Ottoman captivity being buggered than to rape of females. (This is interesting, because it suggests Muslims did not bother to circumcise those they despised.) But once again, and fancifully, Colley reads into this a humiliation metaphor, this time of penetration, 'a particularly acute expression of the fear and insecurity' felt politically in the face of 'Muslim aggression': a fear of national 'penetration from without'. This declined, she says, when Muslims 'were no longer in a position seriously to threaten European males', after the shift in the relative balance of geopolitical power.

IV

There is of course a strange, even astonishing, footnote to all this – though perhaps one should call it a foreskin note. Within a little more than a hundred years from the idea that circumcision was an alien form of 'othering', it became a fashionable practice in Britain, America, and the white colonies. Traditionally, circumcision would be an unwelcome reminder to Christians of their Jewish origins, and religious art (the infant Jesus as well as the adolescent David) was unable to be honest about this.[23] But a most remarkable reversal occurred, symbolised by the shift from Victorian missionary opposition to it as a heathen abomination, to the colonial bishop of the 1920s who enthusiastically incorporated circumcision into Christian ritual (see p. 192 above).[24]

How then did experience of empire influence changing perceptions of the ideal British male body – beyond the obvious need of imperial wars and administration for fit young men? No longer associated with pagan barbarism or contemptible Jewishness, circumcision became especially popular from the 1890s with parents of the upper middle classes, just that sector of society upon which the empire relied for its management.[25] By the mid-1930s perhaps two-thirds of this class were circumcised, though in Britain overall, it was about one-third of males; while in the United States it was approaching two-thirds, and set to rise by the 1970s to 90 per cent. There seems little dispute that in some way this was connected to cults and theories of manliness. But in what particular concept or intention? Was it circumcised masculinity as representing physical fitness, or masculinity as non-masturbating 'clean' living? I have argued elsewhere that the procedure was 'primarily an imperial phenomenon', since the fundamental objective can be seen in the way in which British military and Indian medical authorities strongly favoured infant circumcision. They believed it would eliminate a tiresome cause of trouble for the future servants and soldiers of empire operating in hot climates. I have accordingly been criticised for being 'clearly mistaken' in refusing to subscribe to the orthodoxy that circumcision must 'inescapably' be held to be essentially an anti-masturbation device, at a time when 'self-abuse' was abhorred as an unmanly evil and an actual disease. It has recently been reasserted that circumcision was widely believed to dampen autoerotic urges, and therefore that a moral objective was central to it.[26]

Three observations may be offered in response. First, if combating 'self-abuse' was the primary driving force, I doubt if there can ever have been such a striking example of the law of unintended consequences. Circumcision could have precisely, even dramatically, the opposite effect, focusing more attention on the penis, not less. At my suburban lower-middle class grammar school in the late 1940s, where – typically for our social class– approximately 20 per cent of the boys had been circumcised as infants in the mid-1930s, all the most sexually precocious and physically confident boys, the most dedicated masturbators, were those in this group.[27] Secondly, this seems to confirm the anthropological proposition (mentioned above) that circumcision is essentially 'making more properly male', maybe even enhancing sexual function. If so, there is an instructive parallel to be drawn between the British adoption of circumcision from the 1890s and the Victorian and Edwardian fashion for moustaches. The history of the British moustache shows it unequivocally to be an imperial response to Indian contempt for 'unmanly' clean-shaven men. In India moustaches were cultivated as a symbol of virility. British soldiers got the message and started to copy the Indian fashion from about 1800. Its popularity was confirmed from the 1850s, with increasing official approval: in 1854 moustaches were made compulsory for European troops of the East India Company's Bombay Army. Civilians now began to copy the military with equal enthusiasm. The moustache became the mark of a British gentleman, a privilege, a badge of manhood which the servant classes were discouraged from aping; it was the necessary attribute of officers during the First World War, from Kitchener downwards. So, if the moustache 'became the emblem of empire, roughly coterminous with the Raj, but largely derived from it', might not the same be true of cicumcision?[28] This had long been a procedure used by Indian army doctors, and it was increasingly seen, perhaps, as appropriate in an empire of 70 million Muslim subjects. But it was its 'manliness' which was most significant. Cultivating a moustache and removing the foreskin were thus both Indian-inspired and complementary redefinitions of masculinity for British men.

In addition, there is a third consideration. Doctors, and particularly army doctors (who saw more young men than ordinary GPs), were concerned about foreskins as 'a harbour for filth'. They were horrified by phimosis, the consequent smegmatic accumulation, and its potential for assisting the development of venereal disease and cancer (both penile and cervical). It was this equation with uncleanliness, not unchastity, which really alarmed them.[29] The healthiness of Jewish communities provided perhaps a supportive medical model at home.[30] The masturbation hypothesis certainly wove in and out of the 1890s debate (including the supposition that Jews were less given to onanism), but it was certainly not unchallenged or accepted by all doctors at the time.[31] It is the imperial hypothesis which supplies for most people today the more convincing explanation.[32]

The way in which military-imperial contexts were highly significant is most easily demonstrated with the phenomenally successful circumcision campaign in the USA, where the percentages kept leaping forward:

10% in 1900, 15% by 1910, 25% by 1920, 40% by 1930, 65% by 1940, 77% by 1950, 83% by 1960, 90% by 1970. It was war that provided the engine: the conquest of the Philippines in 1898, the two world wars, and then Korea and Vietnam. Balanitis – infected penile swelling – was a serious risk in tropical climes, and there was almost fanatical pressure on American service personnel to submit to what was officially only a 'voluntary–advisable' recommendation for circumcision. A further incentive was provided by reports that the Japanese nailed bamboo splinters through the foreskins of prisoners of war. For every returning circumcised GI-soldier there was one more voice in favour of having their new-born sons circumcised.[33]

With pressures like these, an anti-masturbation hypothesis is redundant. The evidence is sustained over the generations. In 1895 a comparison was made in Netherlands India (Java) between 15,000 indigenous circumcised Muslim soldiers and the 18,000 uncircumcised European soldiers with whom they lived side by side; this revealed 16% Javanese with VD but 41% Europeans (those with syphilis were 0.8% and 4.1% respectively).[34] And today in Africa it is no surprise that Muslim circumcising communities in West Africa have lower rates of infection with HIV-Aids. It is accepted that foreskin-absorption is significant in the spread of the disease, and therefore that circumcision offers some protection.[35]

But there is an intriguing additional possibility. Already in the American conquest of the Philippines a connection had been made between uncircumcised and uncivilised.[36] This would seem directly connected to the absence of circumcision among Afro-Americans. So did white Americans take to it as a means of differentiating themselves from the uncircumcised blacks? A new adaptation of 'othering'? The new symbol of virility? '*You* may have large propagators, but *we* look readier for business'? Circumcision was never attractive to Afro-Americans. The Filipino, however, adopted a compromise version, a mild form of circumcision which provided all the presumed benefits, without the sometimes disfiguring effects of radical American circumcision.

It was of course the ineptitude of Westernised circumcision procedures which in the end turned the tide against it, with neither the Americans nor the British able to emulate the skill of the Jewish *mohel*. In the UK the reaction set in from the late 1940s with the conjuncture of the end of recruitment to the Indian Civil Service, the introduction of a cost-conscious National Health Service, and a medical re-evaluation. Too often, circumcision had been left in the hands of general practitioners, sometimes with wretched results.[37] But there was a growing recognition that, done properly, it was a delicate, time-consuming operation, requiring considerable finesse, which was mostly lacking.[38] In the United States the reaction was delayed until the 1980s, developing then amid a welter of cries about 'mutilation', 'castration', 'oppression', and a denial of 'male rights' – in other words, a regressive backlash invoking language strikingly similar to that used in the 1780s in the British captivity panics in India.

Notes

1 L. Crompton, *Byron and Greek love: homophobia in nineteenth-century England* (Berkeley, CA, 1986), p. 143. Surprisingly, perhaps, there is no reference to circumcision in a discussion of the 'male iconography of primitiveness' in Philippa Levine's fascinating article, 'States of undress: nakedness and the colonial imagination', *Victorian Studies*, vol. 50 (2008), pp. 189–219.

2 The best scholarly account is David M. Friedman, *A mind of its own: a cultural history of the penis* (2001, 2002, 2003), ch. 3, 'The measuring stick', pp. 80–114.

3 Charles White, *An account of the regular gradation in Man and in Different Animals and Vegetables, and from the Former to the Latter* (1799), p. 611; James Hunt, *On the Negro's place in nature* (1863).

4 See Rudi C. Bleys, *The geography of perversion: male-to-male sexual behaviour outside the West and the ethnographic imagination, 1750–1918* (1996), p. 133.

5 James S. Walvin, *Black and white: the Negro and English society, 1555–1945* (1973), pp. 208–9.

6 Gilberto Freyre, *The masters and the slaves: a study of the development of Brazilian civilisation* (New York, 1946: a translation by S. Putnam of *Cas grande e senzala*, 1933), pp. 323, 428. This remarkable book, which went through forty editions to 2000, had a 'daring and open approach to sex': see Peter Burke and Maria Lúcia G. Pallares-Burke, *Gilberto Freyre: social theory in the tropics* (Witney, Oxon, 2008), pp. 57–9.

7 J. Philippe Rushton and Anthony E. Borgaert, 'Race differences in sexual behaviour', *Journal of Research in Personality*, vol. 21 (1987), pp. 529–51.

8 Fritz Fanon, *Black skin, white masks* (New York, 1967), p. 170.

9 W.D. Jordan, *White over black: American attitudes towards the Negro, 1550–1812* (Chapel Hill, NC, 1968), esp. ch. 4, 'Fruits of passion: the dynamics of interracial sex', pp. 136–76. See also E.D. Genovese, *Roll, Jordan, Roll!: the world the slaves made* (1975), pp. 428, 462; and C.H. Stember, *Sexual racism: the emotional barrier to an integrated society* (New York, 1976), pp. 57–61.

10 Bleys, *The geography of perversion*, pp. 123, 133.

11 Keith Sinclair, 'Why are race relations in New Zealand better than in South Africa, South Australia or South Dakota?' *New Zealand Journal of History*, vol. 5 (1971), pp. 121–7.

12 V.A.C. Gatrell, *City of laughter: sex and satire in eighteenth-century London* (2006), pp. 295–303, on 'phallic obsession'.

13 D.A.F. Marquis de Sade, *Les 120 journées de Sodome* (written *c.*1784, tr. P. Casavini, Paris, 1962).

14 I use the term phalloplethysmography loosely. I believe the term penile

plethysmography was first used by the Canadian psychologist Kurt Freud for a volumetric measuring technique involving the 'weight' as well as length of the penis. It is too good a term to waste on such a restrictive form of measurement. See Bleys, *The geography of perversion*, p. 143, n. 152.

15 Alfred C. Kinsey, Wardell B. Pomeroy, and Clyde E. Martin, *Sexual behavior in the human male* (Philadelphia, 1948); J. Gathorne-Hardy, *Alfred C. Kinsey: sex the measure of all things: a biography* (1998), pp. 221, 261.

16 Paul H. Gebhard and Alan B. Johnson, *The Kinsey data: marginal tabulations of the 1938–1963 interviews conducted by the Institute for Sex Research* (Philadelphia, 1979): pp. 116–20 (tables 69–73 on penis size), p. 179 (table 130, 'First pre-pubertal masturbation'), and p. 373 (table 324, 'Time between intromission and ejaculation in coitus in first marriage').

17 Ali Mazrui, 'The resurrection of the warrior tradition in African political culture, from Shaka the Zulu to Amin the Kakwa', *Journal of Modern African Studies*, vol. 13 (1975), pp. 67–84, repr. in *Soldiers and kinsmen in Uganda: the making of a military ethnocracy* (Beverly Hills, CA, 1975), pp. 195–212.

18 Jolan Chang, *The Tao of love and sex: the ancient Chinese way to ecstasy* (New York, 1977); Stephen T. Chang, *The Tao of sexology: the book of infinite wisdom* (San Francisco, 1986).

19 C.A. Bayly, ed., *The Raj: India and the British, 1600–1947* (National Portrait Gallery Catalogue, 1990), pp. 155–6. Allen Edwardes, *The rape of India: a biography of Robert Clive and a sexual history of the conquest of Hindustan* (New York, 1966) seems to preserve folklore about Tipu's treatment of captives, but, although a clever reconstruction, it is not a reliable work of scholarship.

20 Linda Colley, *Captives: Britain, empire and the world, 1600–1850* (2002, 2003), pp. 43–65, 128–31 on Barbary corsairs, and ch. 9, pp. 269–307, esp. pp. 288–9 and 304–5 on Tipu's captives in Mysore; and 'Going native, telling tales: captivity, collaborations and empire', *Past and Present*, no. 168 (2000), pp. 170–93.

21 A Presbyterian missionary described the Xhosa 'cult of manhood' inspired by circumcision (1858): quoted by Richard Price, *Making empire: colonial encounters and the creation of imperial rule in nineteenth-century Africa* (Cambridge, 2008), p. 63.

22 Maurice Bloch, *From blessing to violence: history and ideology in the circumcision ritual of the Merina of Madagascar* (Cambridge, 1986). See also V.W. Turner, *Essays in the ritual of social relations* (ed. M. Gluckman, 1962), p. 173; K.E. and J. Paige, *The politics of reproductive ritual* (California, 1981), pp. 9–18, 122–5, 148–54, 263–7; C. Harrington, 'Sexual differentiation in socialisation, and some male genital mutilations', *American Anthropologist*, vol. 70 (1968), pp. 951–8.

23 D. Steinberg, *The sexuality of Christ in Renaissance art* (1984), appendix. Paintings of 'The Circumcision' of Jesus depict only the preparatory moment. Donatello's 'David' is more subtle than Michelangelo's; he has no loose foreskin, and partial retraction – a cunning compromise: see Fred Hartt, *Donatello: prophet of modernism* (1974), pp. 209–23. For the Jewish-perception perspective, see S.L. Gilman, *Freud, race and gender* (Princeton, NJ, 1993), pp. 49–72, and 222, n. 14.

24 H. Junod, *The life of a South African tribe*, vol. I, *Social life* (2nd edn 1926; repr. 1962), p. 524.

25 For a more detailed analysis of the dozen years before 1903 as the crucial period of debate on the issue, see RH, *Empire and sexuality*, pp. 75–7. See also E.M. Gordon, 'The history of circumcision', *British Journal of Urology International*, vol. 83, no. 1 (1999), pp. 1–12; and D.L. Gollaher, *Circumcision: a history of the world's most controversial surgery* (New York, 2000).

26 R. Darby, 'The masturbation taboo and the rise of routine circumcision: a review of the historiography', *Journal of Social History*, vol. 36 (2003), pp. 737–57, and his book review, 'A post-modern theory of wanking: *Solitary sex: a cultural history of masturbation*, by Thomas Laqueur (New York, 2003)', *Journal of Social History*, vol. 38 (2004), pp. 205–10. Laqueur's book is almost entirely about the eighteenth century.

27 For 1930s and 1940s statistics (there are no reliable earlier ones), see D. Gairdner, 'The fate of the foreskin: a study of circumcision', *British Medical Journal* (1949, vol. 2), pp. 1433–7 (critical of the procedure); D. MacCarthy, J.W.B. Douglas, and C. Mogford, 'Circumcision in a natural sample of four-year-old children' [the national survey of those born on 4 March 1946], *British Medical Journal* (1952, 4 October 1952); T.E. Osmond, 'Is routine circumcision advisable?', *Journal of Royal Army Medical Corps*, vol. 99 (1953), p. 254 (a study of National Servicemen).

28 Piers Brendon's brilliant insight, occurring thematically in *The decline and fall of the British empire, 1781–1997* (2007), pp. 123–4, and *passim*; from the 1890s, 'the rise of the moustache complemented the fall of the foreskin' (p. 206).

29 J. Hutchinson, *Archives of surgery*, vol. 2 (1891), pp. 15, 267–9, and vol. 4 (1893), no. clxi; *British Medical Journal* (1903, vol. 2), Dr R.E. Foott (a former army surgeon), 22 August 1903. In 1899, Captain F.W. Porter reported that in his last tour of duty in India he had performed a hundred circumcisions, and, back at the Station Hospital, Colchester, had operated twenty-five times in six months, always operating 'whenever there is a sore on the prepuce': *British Medical Journal* (1899, vol. 2), 8 July 1899.

30 A. Davin, 'Imperialism and motherhood', *History Workshop Journal*, vol. 5 (1978), pp. 14–18; J.M. Winter, *The Great War and the British people* (1986), pp. 15–16. Particularly among the Welsh, there does seem to have been a new admiration for Jewishness in the early twentieth century – 'one of the most striking ways in which the British male of this date expressed a feeling of kinship with the Jews was the popularity of circumcision': A.N. Wilson, *After the Victorians* (2005), pp. 100–1. Correlation with social class is, however, preferred by Brian Harrison, *Seeking a role: the United Kingdom, 1951–1970* (New Oxford History of England, 2009), pp. 256–7.

31 'A consultant of a children's hospital', *British Medical Journal* (1901, 5 October), pp. 1023–4: to circumcise to prevent later masturbation 'is pure quackery', and it is 'absurd to suppose it can thus be eradicated'.

32 The novelist Anthony Powell, *Journals, 1982–1986* (1994), p. 6: born in 1904, Powell had long been puzzled as to why he had been circumcised,

but found the 'first real answer' after reading John Spurling, *The British Empire, Part One: a play* (1982) – Spurling was a former district officer in the Cameroons, and followed RH in arguing that it 'started in the 1890s', the heyday of empire.

33 Bud Berkeley, *Foreskin: a closer look* (Boston, 1993), esp. pp. 75–86. G.J. Barker-Benfield, *The horrors of the half-known life: male attitudes towards women and sexuality in 19th-century America* (New York, 1976) discusses the way in which male identity was eroding in late nineteenth-century America, and the strategies for assertion and for control of women's sexuality. Circumcision, male and female, would fit into this scenario. See also L. Coveney, M. Jackson, S. Jeffreys *et al.*, *The sexuality papers: male sexuality and the social control of women* (1984), ch. 1, and p. 50.

34 Report by Dr Breitenstein, 1895, quoted in I. Bloch, *The sexual life of our time* (tr. M. Eden Paul, 1908), p. 376.

35 John Iliffe, *The African AIDS epidemic: a history* (2006), pp. 29, 32, 42–55, 62, 140.

36 S.C. Miller, *'Benevolent assimilation': the American conquest of the Philippines, 1899–1903* (New Haven, CT, 1982), p. 75.

37 Lord Hailsham of St Marylebone, *A sparrow's flight: memoirs* (1990), p. 17 (in fact the opening page). Born in 1907: 'my mother had me circumcised', and it had to be redone when he was nearly ready for private school; without anaesthetic, 'I was just laid across the doctor's knees . . . I can still remember the pain, the blood, and my sense of total betrayal by the adult world'. As a result, his younger brother was lucky enough to be circumcised by a Jewish *mohel*. (The royal family employed a *mohel* in 1948.)

38 'It needs a nice technique, fine instruments, fine suturing material, and perfect haemostasis': J.P. Blandy, 'Circumcision', *British Journal of Hospital Medicine* (February 1968), pp. 551–3 – an influential restatement of the post-imperial orthodoxy, discouraging infant circumcision.

15   Concubinage and the Colonial Service: Silberrad and the Crewe Circular, 1909

[Reprinted from the *Journal of Imperial and Commonwealth History*, vol.14 (1986). Some material has been added.

When first published, this article was seen as controversial. Margaret Strobel felt it 'trivializes the incident in Kenya', partly because it did not examine the 'collusion of male interests, African and European, that characterized much of colonialism' ('Sex and work in the British empire', *Radical History Review*, vol. 54 (1992), pp. 177–86). This seems to me a valid (feminist) criticism. For a (non-feminist) critique, see Ged Martin, *Past futures: the impossibility of history* (Toronto, 2004), pp. 181–4. Martin questions my claim to a neutrality of historical judgment about sexual behaviour. Is there not, he suggests, a 'hidden judgmentalism', which provides 'a tacit endorsement of one side of the Silberrad case to the exclusion of any other?' Martin thinks more sympathy is shown to the European officer than to African women as 'victims'; that Silberrad is made to seem unlucky in being found out, and especially unfortunate when his behaviour was made public by a 'moralising busybody' called Routledge, who, as Martin puts it, 'engaged the ultimate weapon of English moral outrage, writing to *The Times*'. My portrayal of Silberrad's denouncer, he adds, is 'particularly partisan'. The only answer to this criticism is that I probably see this case too closely through the eyes of the Colonial Office; politicians and officials alike were more cross and concerned about what Routledge had done than what Silberrad had done. It was certainly not unusual for them to take a sympathetic approach towards youthful transgressors, at least before the reaction of 1909.

Discovery of the text of the Crewe Circular filled a historical gap, and it is reproduced in facsimile here for the first time.]

In an earlier chapter, I tried to show how sexual attitudes and activities influenced the lives of the imperial elite, and I argued that sexual dynamics operated in such a way as crucially to underpin the British empire and Victorian expansion.[1] Without the easy range of sexual opportunities which imperial systems provided, the long-term administration and exploitation of tropical territories, in nineteenth-century conditions, might well have been impossible. This, however, was far from being an uncontested proposition in late Victorian Britain itself, when it was increasingly urged that, if the British empire was to survive, the imperial race must exercise sexual restraint, and government must intervene to enforce it. Through a fanatical Purity Campaign, sexual opportunity was from the mid-1880s gradually reduced, first at home, and then overseas. This present chapter deals with the most important specific decision in this process as it affected the 'men on the spot', the Colonial Service officers. Some historians of empire were aware that a sexual directive was issued by the British authorities in 1909, but the text of this significant document was not reproduced until 1986, and its origins deserve clarification. The change of official attitude towards the sexual arrangements hitherto made by many unmarried district officers and others may be regarded as one of the few tangible elements differentiating the so-called 'new imperialism' from what had gone before. It also marked a striking divergence from French policy in West Africa.

At the beginning of the twentieth century, although concubinage with local women was no longer the fashion in India and the white Dominions, it was still widely practised in certain parts of the empire by members of the British Colonial Services, as well as by white traders, railway engineers, and unmarried settlers. It was common in Burma, Malaya, and Sarawak, in Kenya and Uganda, in Nyasaland, Northern and Southern Rhodesia, in the Gold Coast and other parts of West Africa. In the lonelier districts it was probably the norm for bachelors. There were occasional reports of 'veritable harems of native women' being maintained by high-ranking officials, from the Ghansi district of western Bechuanaland to Upper Perak in Malaya. Missionaries made protests about it from Mashonaland to Papua. The attitudes of authority varied. The Brookes in Sarawak actively encouraged concubinage, and discouraged white wives. Sir Hugh Clifford was sympathetic to it in Malaya. By contrast, Sir Harry Johnston professed to be repelled by the way it was regularly practised in Uganda by many of the best and most hard-working officials. He was not the only administrator who condemned concubinage as demoralising and undesirable. Certainly, too, that was the view taken in Burma in the 1890s by the lieutenant-governor: 'What cannot be done in England ought to be equally impossible in Burma.'[2] The Colonial Office rule, however, was that a man's private life did not concern the government so long as it did not cause a public scandal, and a blind eye was officially turned to concubinage. Provided there was no interference with married women, many officials believed it did no harm to relations with African societies. With that proviso, it was held that 'the acquisition of a native wife, twenty wives, no wife, a motor-cycle or an ice-machine would provoke in a native the same amount of respect, or contempt, or astonishment, or indifference'. Indeed, it was said of a governor who received the messengers of a paramount chief, while in his shirt-sleeves and pulling a motor-bicycle to pieces, that 'he might have filled Government House ten times over with concubines and not excited in the native mind a tithe of the contempt for the British administration that was caused by this very innocent, though very thoughtless, action'.[3]

Moreover, concubinage was deliberately practised by French empire-builders as the easiest and pleasantest means of gallicising West Africa. 'A temporary union with a well-chosen native woman' was recommended semi-officially by L.G. Binger (director of African affairs, Colonial Ministry) in 1902. It was defended as a necessary part of the French 'colonial moral code', as being as desirable for the health and hygiene, discipline and prestige of the French official as it was for his imperial authority and linguistic competence.

Although most common before 1914, French inter-racial unions continued well into the 1930s, and even beyond, and some officials resented it when European families began to come out from the 1920s. By this time there were perhaps 3,000–4,000 *métis* (mixed race) children, and an orphanage was provided for those abandoned by their fathers. An administrator in Niger, André Thiellement, later wrote openly about the prospects for concubinage which he had experienced, and L. Le Barbier in *La Côte d'Ivoire* (1916) argued that a union with an African woman was a manifestation of a superiority which could enhance the prestige and position of the Europeans. This is in stark contrast to the British approach.[4]

Indeed, the Colonial Office in 1909 decided upon a completely opposite policy, condemning concubinage as an 'injurious and dangerous evil'. Lord Crewe as secretary of state for the colonies (1908–10) issued a confidential circular to this effect, dated 11 January 1909, and known to history as 'the Crewe Circular'.[5] Now Lord Crewe was very much an Establishment character, level-headed, courteous, and unemphatic, with an improbably precise handwriting. He was a Gladstonian Liberal, good at administration, but an indifferent public speaker. He was passionate about horse-racing and proud of his selective breeding of short-horn cattle. He was unembarrassed by the sexual scandals which led to the promulgation of what was referred to at the time as 'the morals despatch', the 'immoral relations memo', or 'the concubine circular'. It warned new recruits to the Colonial Service of the 'disgrace and official ruin which will certainly follow' should they enter into 'arrangements of concubinage with girls or women belonging to the native populations'

(Annex 'A'). The warning to those already in post was less explicit (Annex 'B'). The text is reproduced in the appendix (Plate 15.1).

Why then did the British imperial authorities turn so unexpectedly and so decisively against concubinage in 1909? Broadly speaking, the answer lies in the convergence of two reformist programmes operating at different levels of British society. The more general of these was the Purity Campaign launched in the mid-1880s, establishing a comprehensive code for the enthronement of sexual restraint, and attacking promiscuity and prostitution. This campaign was certainly in part concerned to maintain an 'imperial race', and the more specific programme of 'colonial service reform', directed at the empire elite, was a natural offshoot. Kenneth Ballhatchet has shown how it came to be believed that 'the social distance between the official elite and the people had to be preserved' in India. Terence Ranger has explained the desperate official need, with the coming of formal rule, to turn European activity in Africa away from the 'tatty, squalid, rough and inefficient' towards a more respectable, ordered, and convincing rulership. A proper imperial ruling class, it was thought, had to be brought into being: benevolent, but more aloof and conformist than its *ad hoc* heterogeneous prototype, with its often colourful and even outrageous characters. Under the new recruiting procedures adopted by the Colonial Office after 1900, graduates were preferred, and more than a third of British governors were to be the sons of Anglican clergymen.[6] Nevertheless, although sexual respectability appealed to many in its hierarchy, the Colonial Office had not *planned* a vigorous assault upon concubinage, if only because this would in many areas have led to the dismissal of a great many officers. Crewe was forced to act faster and more forcibly than intended, mainly as the result of the unwelcome publicity given to the activities of a particular individual in Kenya. The 'Silberrad case' was the catalyst.

Perhaps the standards of white officers, civil and military, were nowhere as dubious as they were in the newly formed British East Africa Protectorate (Kenya). Arriving at Nairobi in 1902 to join the King's African Rifles, Richard Meinertzhagen discovered that his brother officers were mostly

regimental rejects and heavily in debt; one drinks like a fish, one prefers boys to women and is not ashamed. On arrival here I was amazed and shocked to find that they all brought their native women into mess; the talk centres round sex and money and is always connected with some type of pornography . . . Nearly every man in Nairobi is a railway official. Every one of them keeps a native girl, usually a Masai, and there is a regular trade in these girls with the local Masai villages. If a man tires of his girl he goes to the village (*minyatta*) and gets a new one, or in several cases as many as three girls. And my brother officers are no exception.

Meinertzhagen also referred later to a civil administrative officer who committed suicide after forcing his King's African Rifles bugler-boy to commit 'an act of indecency'; and to another (W. Mayes) who had installed half a dozen Nandi concubines in his house after deserting his wife in Mauritius. In northern Nyanza province there was a district commissioner who (it was alleged) 'combined tax collection with rape'.[7]

Hubert Silberrad was an assistant district commissioner at Nyeri, near Fort Hall in central Kenya. Not much is known about his background. He was educated at Wren's School, and studied engineering at technical college. After working with the Imperial British East Africa Company he took up his post at Nyeri in May 1903. He acquired from his colleague C.W.I. Haywood two local girls, when Haywood left to be promoted to district commissioner at Kisumu in April 1905. The girls were called Nyambura and Wameisa. Haywood had paid forty goats' bridewealth for each of them. Both girls had apparently lived happily with Haywood, but Wameisa, who was still no more than twelve, was reluctant to be passed on to Silberrad, while Nyambura came to live with him in return for a monthly wage. A third girl, aged twelve or thirteen, whose name was Nyakayena, was passed to Silberrad by her husband, Mugalla, an *askari* (African policeman). Mugalla subsequently disputed her custody with Silberrad. In February 1908 they scuffled together at Silberrad's kitchen door, and Silberrad locked up the *askari* in the guardroom for a night, on grounds of insubordination. At this point Silberrad was descended upon by two outraged neighbours, Mr and Mrs W.S. Routledge. They took Nyakayena and Nyambura away from Silberrad, and Routledge reported the matter to the governor, riding four days in the rains to Nairobi in order to do so. Routledge was a settler who had lived in Nyeri for six years, enjoying the sport and claiming to study African life and interests; he was an Oxford graduate, but at best a self-styled anthropologist. More obviously he was an interfering busybody, who appeared to be jealous of Silberrad's authority. It was also unfortunate for Silberrad that the *askari*, Mugalla, was an uncircumcised Masai, and, as a result, peculiarly touchy about his sex-life.

The governor, Sir James Hayes Sadler, took the unusual step of ordering a private investigation by Judge Barth. This was held between 25 and 29 March 1908, and the judge reported on 13 April. The allegations seemed to be substantially true, but in Haywood's case uncomplicated and not particularly shocking. The judge was inclined to believe Wameisa's evidence that she went reluctantly to Silberrad but had consented to do so; Silberrad may have thought she came to him willingly enough, but it was dangerous for an officer to assume there was no difficulty just because there was no disobedience. He considered that

Silberrad was unjustified in taking the *askari*'s girl in circumstances that amounted to poaching. There was, however, no evidence that Silberrad had purchased or corrupted any of the girls. The most serious aspect of the case was his action over the *askari*, for the dispute between them had very obviously brought administration into disrepute. The matter then went before the Executive Council, which (rejecting Wameisa's plea of unwillingness) recommended by two to one that Silberrad should lose one year's seniority and not be put in charge of a district for two years. Haywood was severely admonished by the governor, after which he returned to duty. (He apparently remained in post until 1914.) Hayes Sadler, who had served in the Indian army until 1899, knew about demi-official circulars condemning open concubinage in Burma, and in May 1908 caused a similar admonition to be circulated in Kenya. This stated that 'morals apart', such proceedings tended to lower the British name, were incompatible with an officer's position and prestige, and were 'in every way detrimental to the interests of good government'. Such lax behaviour must be ended, and any further cases would be 'severely dealt with and may entail serious consequences'. He hoped this threat would check a practice 'which there is now reason to believe is more general than was supposed'. His personal recommendation in the Silberrad case was that he should be degraded to the bottom of the list of assistant district commissioners. (Silberrad was actually head of the list of twenty-eight for promotion.)[8]

The case went to the Legal and General department of the Colonial Office and not to the East African desk. The first principal minute was written by T.C. Macnaghten on 26 June 1908. He believed that the governor's suggested punishment was too severe and would ruin Silberrad's career. Even the Executive Council's recommendation seemed harsh. It would be more appropriate to censure him and merely pass him over twice for promotion. Macnaghten understood that there were many officers in Kenya who had lived more loosely than Silberrad and Haywood, and it was hard that they should have been made scapegoats. The treatment of the *askari* was certainly awkward and discreditable. The governor, he felt, was right to warn administrative personnel of the possibility of dismissal in future cases. Macnaghten was well aware that important issues of future policy were now forced upon the Colonial Office. The existing state of affairs 'could not be tolerated indefinitely'. In the old days it 'was not unnatural that a loose morality should be common', and perhaps only a small percentage of unmarried white officials had abstained entirely from concubinage. But now things were changing rapidly. Africans were 'emerging from savagery, and a better class of white official is being introduced'. It was time for a general ruling to be laid down. But he hoped that specific cases 'may be leniently dealt with – at any rate for a good many years to come'.

Macnaghten's minute anticipated quite accurately the reaction of senior officials. To Sir Francis Hopwood (permanent under-secretary) and H.B. Cox (legal assistant under-secretary) it was a 'nasty and delicate' business. The general question unhappily and acutely arising was 'whether the fact that an officer keeps a black mistress is in itself a scandal requiring the attention of the government'. Barefaced promiscuity, such as maintaining several women simultaneously in different places, could not be tolerated, and the governor's steps to raise the standards of morals among white officers in Kenya must be supported. But they should proceed carefully, since no previous indications of official disapproval had been given. To discourage concubinage in future, a general circular should be issued, but officers ought not to be threatened: rather, an appeal should be made to their sense of propriety and good conduct. These conclusions were arrived at rather reluctantly, and the officials' distaste for Routledge's actions was reinforced by his demand (made direct to the secretary of state) that Silberrad's punishment should be a deterrent to others. If, Routledge said, he was not satisfied with the government's decision, he would, 'as representing the public', see that the whole matter was revealed to Parliament and the press. The Office was thoroughly indignant at this threat, especially since it was now known that Routledge had himself almost certainly followed local custom and had intercourse with African girls before his marriage. It was also obvious that Routledge had a grudge against Silberrad, who had taken official action against him on liquor charges involving his Masai workers and porters. Routledge's importunate demands were counterproductive. The fact that he was 'disposed to be nasty' in public was probably one of the considerations which led Crewe not to adopt the governor's tough punishment proposals, but to accept instead the Executive Council's more moderate recommendation that Silberrad should lose one year's seniority (from April 1908), and not be put in charge of a district for two years. Meanwhile, Silberrad was to take five months' leave (three months on full pay and two months on three-quarters). In conveying these decisions to Silberrad on 30 July 1908 the secretary of state emphasised his condemnation of the aggravating offence of Silberrad's being involved in an altercation with a black subordinate over a girl, for this was a clear example of how concubinage could bring the government service into disrepute. Crewe told the governor that his conduct of the affair was generally approved, but he rejected Routledge's claim to be treated as 'representing the public'. Unfortunately the governor (while not disagreeing in principle) had promised to keep Routledge informed of the outcome of the Silberrad case. This gave Routledge the chance to stir up further trouble later.[9]

The Colonial Office asked the India Office for a copy of the Burmese circular to which Hayes Sadler had drawn attention, and did not begin any drafting of its own until this had been received at the end of November. (The Indian bureaucracy took five months to disgorge the information.) In the meantime, Silberrad took his leave, and had the good sense or good fortune to get married in England. He then returned to Kenya as assistant district commissioner at Kiambu, only some fifty miles from Nyeri, his previous posting. This was a mistake, and the move was to be strongly criticised.[10]

The egregious Routledge (to say nothing of Mrs Routledge) felt that Silberrad was getting off the hook altogether too lightly. And so he employed his ultimate weapon by writing to *The Times*, portentously signing himself W. Scoresby Routledge, MA (Christ Church, Oxon.), Erichsen Prizeman, University College Hospital (Lond.). His letter was published on 3 December 1908. In it, Routledge denounced the government for not acting severely enough to check the 'abuses' in Kenya or stop the 'demoralisation' of African women by British officials. He 'named' Hubert Silberrad in full, and revealed the details of his case. He protested that Silberrad's punishment was 'utterly insufficient'. And since the Colonial Office was proposing only to 'discourage' concubinage, the issue was 'Whether the representatives of the Crown are to be allowed to withdraw ignorant girls, committed to their charge, from the well-defined lines of tribal life, and to lead them into courses of which the inevitable tendency is to end on the streets of Nairobi.' Was not this calculated 'adversely to affect the power and influence' of British administration?

Officials reacted angrily. Routledge had (as they feared) hurled his publicity bombshell, and had done so knowing not only that these sexual transactions were 'exceedingly common' in Kenya, but also that Silberrad was trying to make a fresh start through marriage. The letter made use of accurate quotations from Judge Barth's report, but how had Routledge been able to see it? The letter was 'dangerously clever', full of 'venomous personal malice' and 'monstrous cruelty'; it could *not* have been written purely in the public interest. The reference to 'the streets of Nairobi' Macnaghten regarded as 'a wilful attempt on the part of a man who must know better to hoodwink the uninformed members of the British Public into supposing that Mr Silberrad's offence is as bad as that of a man who commits a similar offence with a young girl in England, and that he has been the cause of a similar social and moral downfall'. He regarded Sir Harry Johnston's opinion as extremely pertinent: that almost every girl in East-Central Africa ceased to be a virgin well before puberty.

Two days after *The Times* letter, Crewe recorded his opinion, opening with a gloomy reflection that perhaps they were about to witness the British public in what Lord Macaulay had called one of its 'periodical fits of morality':

> We are all agreed that conduct of this kind is not merely morally reprehensible (which is not directly our affair), but disadvantageous to the public service . . . The whole subject is very properly one for admonition, and where necessary for censure, with a view to its becoming the standard of opinion in the Service that these connections are degrading. But we cannot hope to eradicate the trouble entirely.

Crewe could see no essential difference from any other 'offence against morals of its class'. It therefore did not seem to him a case for a vindictive punishment or for ruining Silberrad's career. He distrusted Routledge's motives. It was 'very "strong" indeed' to give Silberrad's name to the press, when he could have withheld it, and this procedure 'would make me personally decline Mr Routledge's acquaintance'.[11]

The interest of Members of Parliament was immediately aroused by Routledge's thundering exposure. Colonel Seely (as parliamentary under-secretary) had to make a Commons Statement on 7 December, based on Crewe's minute and drafted by Hopwood. This defended the punishment as sufficiently severe, involving considerable pecuniary loss. Seely also announced that the government was going to warn all members of the Colonial Service that such actions were 'damaging and unworthy' and could lead to the 'gravest consequences' as a penalty. Although this statement got the House generally into a fair humour, some MPs remained agitated, and immediately afterwards a deputation confronted Seely in his room. This consisted of Sir Clement Hill (formerly superintendent of African Protectorates at the Foreign Office), Mr H. Pike Pease, Sir G. Scott Robertson (a former Indian administrator), and Josiah Wedgwood (then much interested in African affairs). Some members of the deputation maintained that there was evidence of a general laxity in the administration of the East Africa Protectorate. Sir Clement Hill denied this, and no immediate action was contemplated about it, but Seely agreed to show the deputation advance copies of the proposed circular. Seely felt he had survived the parliamentary ordeal pretty well, but prompt action was necessary: 'feeling was very strong in all parts of the House, and the Prime Minister informed me that he was much concerned; the danger of the situation is that in this matter what one may call the high – official – disciplinary – Tory mind makes common cause with the humanitarian – pro-native – Liberal mind . . .' Seely was thus now convinced (despite the misgivings of Hopwood, Cox, and Antrobus) that a warning on the lines of the Burmese circular should be automatically presented to all personnel in the colonies most affected, and that this was essential in fairness to officers. He agreed with Macnaghten that it would otherwise be unjust to deal severely with future cases. He also thought that such action would not be represented as vindictive self-righteousness or 'unctuous rectitude', because such confidential instructions had from time to time been given in the older dependencies in the past, and been extraordinarily effective; as a result, concubinage by officials was now almost at an end in India, South Africa, and New Zealand. His advisers were in full agreement that officers in Africa obviously needed instruction: like Haywood, they seemed to regard government resentment of their conduct as an unwarranted interference merely on moral grounds. As Macnaghten observed, Haywood 'does not seem to have the slightest idea that such practices are more detestable from the point of view of the Service than they are from the point of view of morals: that interference with native women has even led to risings in the past and might do so again', though admittedly the Silberrad case had not evoked African protest.[12]

For more than a week, the energies of the Colonial Office were much absorbed by this issue. Seely and Crewe each wrote several minutes which were as long as any written by either of them about anything. Crewe made his decision on 12 December. The difficulty as he saw it was in 'launching by surprise against the whole Colonial Service, young and old, married or unmarried, a thunderbolt forged for reasons of which they will have heard nothing, to the effect that if they engage in relations with native women they run the risk of being dismissed'. He proposed to get out of this difficulty by issuing two different circulars, with a covering letter instructing governors on their use. A drastic circular would warn new recruits of severe treatment, but a more general circular would be issued to all officers already in the service. This would impress on them the danger and scandal to the public service, but it would not contain threats of dismissal. The principle of the drastic circular might, however, if necessary be applied at any time to any officer. Macnaghten now set to work to draft the circulars. In front of him was the text of Lieutenant-Governor Sir Frederick Fryer's demi-official Burmese Minute (1903), which consolidated the substance of earlier confidential circulars issued in Burma. None of its phrasing was in fact copied.[13]

Ministers continued to face criticism throughout December. On 11 December Mrs Routledge had an interview with Colonel Seely. She complained that the severity of Silberrad's punishment had not been increased, and repeated the objection to Haywood's being let off with a reprimand. Seely replied that it would be especially inequitable to increase Silberrad's penalty after all the adverse publicity, and without new facts being adduced. And he reminded Mrs Routledge that Haywood had been exonerated of all serious charges, and had in fact been doubly reprimanded, by the governor and by the secretary of state. Next day, the Office was agitated over an article in the *Spectator* entitled 'A canker in imperial administration', which also took the line that Silberrad's punishment was inadequate and Seely's Commons Statement unsatisfactory. The empire would be ruined if officials exercised their powers to gratify their animal passions (the argument ran); the accepted standard in East Africa was lower than in the empire as a whole, and had reached a point of peril. The administrative personnel was unsatisfactory, and the blame really lay with the government for paying such low salaries. The article concluded with a suggestion that someone like Sir George Goldie should head a commission of inquiry. Officials thought that the article made some reasonable points, even if it was unfair in the particular case of Silberrad. After all (they reflected), he had only acted in accordance with the common local custom of officials and he had not used force; the object of the punishment decided upon was to be severe without marring his future efficiency or breaking his spirit. It was true (they agreed) that the administration was sub-standard: it had been created in a hurry, and some unsatisfactory people were taken over from the Imperial British East Africa Company, Silberrad among them. Many of them had now been got rid of, but, as Antrobus observed, it was impracticable to make a clean sweep of every unsatisfactory official. The Treasury was indeed paying less than the Colonial Office had repeatedly urged; and small salaries (about £250 a year for an assistant district commissioner) were a genuine hardship, discouraging marriage. An inquiry into concubinage was clearly impracticable, however. It was bound to be unsavoury, and what evidence would be admissible? Would it extract confessions, or demand denunciations from colleagues? Hopwood said they should stick to the policy of issuing a circular, and not be unduly rattled by newspaper criticism. Crewe summed up their reaction to the *Spectator* article:

There are several unsatisfactory features in the administration of British East Africa . . . But I do not propose that the Congregation of the Holy Office should institute a special enquiry into the British East Africa morals. We must try to elevate the general standard by sending good men there in all ranks. This is particularly necessary from the presence of a population of settlers, whose standard in all cases cannot be high.[14]

The Times carried several letters commenting on the Silberrad case, together with an editorial on 26 December. This emphasised that Seely's Statement had by no means entirely disposed of public anxiety, 'which will demand some definite assurance that such offences will in future be rigorously put down'. There was some exchange as to whether or not an African girl was 'ready for marriage' at twelve. Some correspondents asserted that 'the honour of Britain' was at stake, but a former administrative officer, writing anonymously, thought Silberrad's punishment was too severe. T.F. Victor Buxton (heir to the baronetcy) contributed the most forceful of the letters (9 January 1909), strongly urging much greater governmental stringency in dealing with such problems. Public servants, he wrote, could not divest themselves of the prestige attaching to their office; 'if therefore we are to rise to our responsibilities as an Imperial race – if we are not to bring grievous discredit upon the Christianity we profess – it is essential that those who represent us abroad should be clean-living men, whose conduct may command the respect of the peoples they govern'. This went right to the heart of the issues of the Silberrad case as perceived by the British 'Establishment'. The Colonial Office sent Buxton a copy of the draft circular, which he thought admirable. In the interests of dampening down simmering agitation, Seely also sent copies to other *Times* correspondents.

Macnaghten had submitted his drafts on 16 December. They expressly dealt with concubinage and not with occasional 'illicit acts'. Antrobus saw no good reason for distinguishing between new and serving officers, and issuing two different warnings, but Crewe insisted that this was necessary. It was decided to issue the circular overseas, and not at home, in case it fell into the hands of the parents of recruits and horrified them. Much attention was paid to eliminating any impression that the government regarded the morality of its servants as generally questionable. On the whole Macnaghten's drafts were approved, the principal amendments being to the annexes, where Hopwood made a number of changes. At a late stage of drafting, Crewe decided to remove the requirement on governors to *report* cases (following the Burma precedent), merely asking them instead to 'make it the subject of official action'. Considerable thought was given to the question of exactly which colonies and protectorates should receive the Circular. It would obviously be a bad blunder to send it to the West Indies, Mauritius, and the Seychelles, where black and white regularly lived together and inter-married, and it was not in fact sent to them. Antrobus held that it was irrelevant to Ceylon and Hong Kong, but he was overruled. (On receiving it, however, the governor of Ceylon protested his certainty that no civil servant there now lived in concubinage with local women, and the Colonial Office had

to agree that he need not issue the Circular in Ceylon.) The Circular
was never intended for places not thought to be affected, or for those
areas not under the direct responsibility of the Crown. It was thus not
sent to Malta, Gibraltar, Sarawak, the Federated Malay States, South
Africa (including the High Commission Territories), North-Western
and North-Eastern Rhodesia (which were under the British South Africa
Company).[15]

Crewe finalised the wording on 3 January, and the Circular was published on 11 January 1909. It had no heading, but a file for possible
replies was opened with the title 'Immoral relations with native women'.
Each recipient colony was sent enough copies of Annex 'B' to distribute
to all its serving white officers, and several years' supply of the sterner
Annex 'A', which was to be handed to newcomers, and to such old-
timers as seemed seriously in need of special exhortation. When supplies
ran out, the Colonial Office would arrange for reprinting. With the single
exception of Sir Henry McCallum's protest from Ceylon, no replies or
comments appear to have been received.[16]

The Silberrad case was again raised in the House of Commons on
27 July 1909, during the Colonial Office part of the Supply debate.
The main speakers were H.J. Wilson (who had attacked the Indian
Contagious Diseases Acts in 1888 and planned to outlaw all fornication),
and Josiah Wedgwood, who called for 'less leniency' and 'more reproba-
tion' from the Colonial Office over concubinage. Alfred Lyttelton (as
a former colonial secretary) uttered caustic remarks about deplorable,
reprehensible, miserable weakness on the part of the government: it was
monstrous, he said, to pride ourselves about keeping natives from drink
if we did not stop this sort of thing, and Joe Chamberlain would never
have allowed it. Seely's defence was the familiar one that they could not
dismiss Silberrad, because he had been given no previous warning of
this possibility; but he had been effectively punished, and it was anyway
only an 'isolated' offence. The Circular was a positive and 'very stern'
warning; the phrase 'grave consequences' in his Statement would be read
as meaning 'end of career'.[17]

Many critics felt Silberrad had been re-employed too near to the scene
of his offence, and he was transferred to Nyasaland in July 1909 as a '2nd
grade Resident'. There he remained until 1923, his career irretrievably
stuck.

When a similar problem in North-Eastern Rhodesia looked like
attracting attention in May 1910, Crewe authorised discussions with
the British South Africa Company to persuade them to take the same
serious view of concubinage as had now been adopted by the Colonial
Office. This led to the dismissal of R.A. Osborne. Seely was convinced

that concubinage arose out of loneliness, and the solution was to spend more money on salaries and travelling allowances, so as to make it easier for married men to join the service. Crewe agreed there was much to be said for increasing the number of married officers, but the 'real difficulty is that isolated posts at which temptation may be strongest to the officers are just those at which life is most difficult for a white woman'. The Rhodesian discussion again threw up doubts as to whether or not the hard line on concubinage was actually required by any African demand for it. There was general agreement in the CO that it probably was not. The decisive factor was metropolitan puritanical insistence, backed by bureaucratic preoccupation with preserving racial prestige and social distance. As Crewe's successor Lewis Harcourt put it: 'we must recognise the exigencies and prejudices of Parliamentary Government'.[18] It is worth emphasising that the pressure was political. Missionary comment was decidedly muted. A short and ambivalent editorial note in the *Church Missionary Review* conceded that Routledge had served 'the honour of the ruling race in Africa' by his unsavoury revelations, but concentrated on urging people to remember the better side to the 'white intrusion', such as the work of the medical missions.[19]

How effective was the 'immoral relations' Circular? It can hardly be said to have been welcomed. Some 'respectable' married men were furious at being presented with it. Lugard seems to have run into trouble when he tried to reinforce the message in Nigeria in 1914. Thereafter few governors ever wanted to impose it actively. Guggisberg of the Gold Coast, for example, wrote in 1927: 'In my view, while I expect Heads of Department to set an example to, and to advise their juniors, it is not advisable to pry too closely into the lives of officers so long as they do their work efficiently and do not cause a scandal.'[20] Crewe's unequivocal directive could not possibly be ignored, and in African colonies by the mid-1920s the consequences of doing so were generally understood. Even so, there is some evidence that in Kenya, Nigeria, and the Sudan discreet liaisons still took place. As late as 1927 in Wajir, with the King's African Rifles, Brian Montgomery was offered a Somali *bibi*, or 'sleeping dictionary'. In Kenya, Cashmore recalls that 'a majority of single white officers probably did, on a casual basis, sleep with African women'; on several occasions he found himself co-judge with one of them, 'an ex-chief's daughter', in local needlework competitions.[21] In the Sudan, which boasted of an exceptionally high moral code from the establishment of the Political Service in 1899, it is possible that down to 1924 (but not after that?), one medical officer at least was still advising newcomers that there was no objection to 'temporary marriage' with Sudanese women, provided it was in an out-district.[22] In Nigeria, an officer who served there between 1939 and 1959 assumed in his unpublished memoir that a 'fair proportion' of his colleagues 'sought solace' regularly or occasionally with black women; and even in the late 1940s an assistant district officer had to be sent back to Britain for flaunting an affair with an African woman too publicly.[23] Bechuanaland had a reputation as something of a haven for inter-racial liaisons, although British officials there were strongly opposed to any legislation which was 'too South African'.[24]

Some dismissals for 'immorality' occurred even in Papua in the five years before 1914.[25] Malayan officers showed a marked decline in resort to concubinage in the decade after 1909: according to J.G. Butcher by 1928 it was certainly practised by less than 10 per cent of them, and may have been down to 2 per cent. Several officers married their Malayan mistresses. In the opinion of the secretary for Chinese affairs (1922) the Circular had deterred officers in Malaya not only from concubinage, but also from resort to 'known' brothels. European residential segregation and the increasing presence of white wives in the colonies were important factors in changing sexual patterns, and it is therefore difficult to make precise statements about the continuing significance of Crewe's Circular in bringing about the demise of concubinage. To deny its impact would be wrong, but it was not issued in a vacuum and its application was not universal. The issue of the Circular did not reactivate the earlier (rather half-hearted) discouragement of concubinage in Burma. No dismissals were being made there. The weight of public, and therefore of official, concern was clearly concentrated on Africa. It never applied to Sarawak, where concubinage continued to flourish until the end of Brooke rule in 1946, and possibly even beyond.[26]

It was from Sarawak that Denis Garson wrote in 1948, eulogising its 'delightful relationship of races': 'It is impressive the way the Administrative staff mix with the people, though I suspect that its origins would not earn the commendation of moralists or of the author of the famous confidential despatch on morals.' The point was, he felt, that 'the good here must not be lost – the ease of race relations'. He greatly feared that the new generation of 'memsahibs' would only impose their small-minded standards in Sarawak as they had done to the detriment of India and Malaya and elsewhere.[27] Some members of the Colonial Office hierarchy were thus certainly aware that the stiff and aloof social relations of the twentieth-century empire, partly promoted by the Crewe Circular, were not something to be proud of.

To some older members of the Colonial Service, the formal end of concubinage was a matter of regret, but not very deeply so. Margery Perham, for her part, doubted whether most British men in the 1930s actually wanted that kind of 'un-English' intimacy with Africans.[28]

The temptations were greater in the Pacific islands, where many of the women conformed more closely to European standards of beauty. But even there, the culture gap meant that sustained relationships were almost impossible for educated Europeans. Sir Ronald Garvey in the Solomon Islands at the end of the 1920s was, for a whole year, attracted to a chief's daughter called Tanualoa, aged eighteen: 'Sadly I must record that the affair got little beyond a few coy glances . . . neither of us had either the spur or the ready opportunity to pursue that chemical attraction.'[29] George Bristow, who was a district administrator in the New Hebrides and the Solomons between 1950 and 1973, recalls:

I left the Pacific convinced that I had never come across a European in my 24 years there who could be said truly to have 'gone native'. It is, I am convinced, a social and mental impossibility. It is more conceivable for a native to become Europeanised, civilised, educated – whatever the word is . . . But it is impossible to take the step down. Not merely because it is difficult for the white man to surrender his standards – quite a few poor whites made a pretty fair fist of that – but mainly because the native will not accept you. Your native-reared children, yes. But not you.[30]

Bristow had been told as much by a Gilbertese girl, Teresa, with whom he had 'an association'. She maintained that her people would never accept him, even if they liked and respected him, because they believed he would never be able 'to become Gilbertese, both materially and psychologically'.[31]

Notes

1 RH, 'Empire and sexual opportunity', *JICH*, vol. 14 (1986): see chapter 13 above. For the East African background, see H.A.C. Cairns, *Prelude to imperialism: British reactions to Central African society, 1840–90* (1965), pp. 53–7; R. Meinertzhagen, *Kenya diary, 1902–06* (Edinburgh, 1957), pp. 9–13; L.H. Gann and P. Duignan, *The rulers of British Africa, 1870–1914* (London, 1978), pp. 226, 240–3.

2 R. Oliver, *Sir Harry Johnston and the scramble for Africa* (1957), p. 316; C.J. Edwards, *The Revd John White of Mashonaland* (1935), p. 51. K. Ballhatchet, *Race, sex and class under the Raj: imperial attitudes and policies and their critics, 1793–1905* (1980), pp. 145–55, gives a full discussion of concubinage in Burma, 1888–1903. In the Gold Coast, the colonial secretary at Accra issued in March 1907 a circular letter on his own authority (and unknown to the Colonial Office), threatening those who kept concubines with being reported to the secretary of state (see Gann and Duignan, *Rulers of British Africa*, pp. 386–7, n. 55).

3 The National Archives, CO 417/484, no. 38728 (South Africa: High Commission), minute by C.B. Sandby, 12 January 1911. Crown copyright

documents quoted and reproduced by permission of the Controller of HM Stationery Office.

4 J.D. Hargreaves, ed., *France and West Africa: an anthology of historical documents* (1969), pp. 206–9, 'Colonisation through the bed': Dr Barot, *Guide pratique de l'Européen dans l'Afrique Occidentale* (1902), Introduction and pp. 328–31. See also Margery Perham, *West African passage: a journey through Nigeria, Chad and the Cameroons, 1931–32* (ed. A.H.M. Kirk-Greene, 1983), pp. 133–4, 140, 179. There is now an excellent study by Owen White, *Children of the empire: miscegenation and colonial society in French West Africa, 1895–1960* (Oxford, 1999), esp. pp. 7–30. He quotes an apocryphal story by L. Vignon (1929) that when the British tried to clamp down in Burma in the 1890s (see above, p. 418), at a sportsday in Rangoon a race was held between two horses, 'Governor's Circular' and 'Physical Necessity' – the latter won (p. 16).

5 CO 854/168 (Circulars: Secret and Confidential, 1907–15), 11 January 1909. There is no convenient sequence of files on the genesis of the Circular and the Silberrad case which prompted it: materials are scattered in some half-dozen volumes of Kenyan correspondence, viz. CO 533/44, 46, 48, 49, 51, 52, 56 (East Africa Protectorate, 1908). The brief discussion in T.H.R. Cashmore, 'Studies in district administration in the East African Protectorate, 1895–1918' (PhD thesis, University of Cambridge, 1966), pp. 39–41, is inaccurate as well as incomplete. The same applies to C. Allen, ed., *Tales from the Dark Continent: images of British colonial Africa in the twentieth century* (1980 edn), pp. 19–20.

6 Ballhatchet, *Race, sex and class*, p. 164; T.O. Ranger, 'The invention of tradition in colonial Africa', in E. Hobsbawm and T.O. Ranger, eds., *The invention of tradition* (1983), p. 215; I.F. Nicolson and C.A. Hughes, 'A provenance of proconsuls: British colonial governors, 1900–60', *JICH*, vol. 4 (1975), p. 200.

7 Meinertzhagen, *Kenya diary*, pp. 9–13, 148, 176.

8 CO 533/44, no. 21793 and 46, no. 33653.

9 CO 533/44, no. 21793 and 56, no. 25633.

10 CO 533/48, no. 45971 and 49, no. 30560.

11 CO 533/52, no. 44293 and 51, no. 44448.

12 *PD, Commons*, vol. 198, cc. 68–73; minute by Seely, 8 December 1908, CO 533/52, no. 45005 (the key file on the Circular).

13 CO 533/52, no. 45005. The Burmese circulars remained demi-official, because it was felt specific formal rules would become public knowledge and only draw unwelcome attention to the situation. The India Office reported that the circulars had 'unfortunately' led some officers to marry their mistresses, and the only really effective way of extinguishing concubinage seemed to be through 'the more general presence of English ladies and the social pressures exerted by them' (CO 533/49, no. 43627).

14 Minute, 21 December 1908, CO 533/52, nos. 45714 and 45715.

15 CO 533/52, no. 45005; CO 854/168; CO 54/723, no. 6285 (Ceylon). The recipient colonies and protectorates were: Fiji, Western Pacific, East Africa Protectorate, Nyasaland Protectorate, Somali Protectorate, Uganda

Protectorate, Gambia, Gold Coast, Northern Nigeria, Southern Nigeria, Sierra Leone, [Ceylon], Hong Kong, Straits Settlements, Weihaiwei.

16 CO 862/15, nos. 190–1 (Replies to Circular Despatches). As to Ceylon, R.E. Stubbs remained sceptical: if the report from McCallum was true, 'things are better than they were a few years ago. You will remember the case of the Engineer who was considered "socially impossible" because he used to play cricket with his half-caste bastards – the objection being not that they were bastards or half-castes, or, altogether, that he played cricket with them, but that he did so on ground adjoining the Lawn Tennis Club's courts.' (Minute, 23 December 1909, CO 54/723, no. 6285).

17 *PD, Commons*, vol. 8, cc 1031–8, 1048, 1067–9, 1077–80, 1119–28.

18 Harcourt's minute, 16 January 1911, CO 417/482, no. 13936; 483, no. 19358; 484, no. 38758; see also Gann and Duignan, *Rulers of British Africa*, p. 241.

19 *Church Missionary Review*, vol. 60 (January 1909), p.61, 'Editorial notes: the honour of the ruling race in Africa'.

20 CO 96/670, no. 4049, Gold Coast, 1927. See also H. Kuklick, *The imperial bureaucrat: the colonial administrative service in the Gold Coast, 1920–1939* (Stanford, CA, 1979), pp. 122–30.

21 T.H.R. Cashmore, quoted by Piers Brendon, *Decline and fall of the British empire, 1781–1997* (2007), p. 559; see also p. 528, quoting a district officer in Nigeria who recalled in 1966: 'you could sleep with black women if you did it very discreetly, but you couldn't drink with black men' – a revealing confession.

22 R.O. Collins and F.M. Deng, eds., *The British in the Sudan, 1898–1956: the sweetness and the sorrow* (1984); K.D.D. Henderson, *Set under authority: being a portrait of the life of the British district officer in the Sudan, 1898–1955* (Castle Cary, 1987), pp. 27–8. There was an allegation, which may be malicious, that Sir Harold MacMichael (who served in the Sudan from 1905 to 1933 and rose to be acting governor-general), because of an attraction to the daughter of a chief, diverted a railway line so as to pass unnecessarily through his territory: see T. Segev, *One Palestine complete* (2000), p. 416. Apart from the fact that no source is given, the reason for doubting this story is that as a new recruit in 1905 MacMichael privately described the women of Khartoum as 'the most repulsive objects of hideosity I *ever* saw . . . their faces are like gargoyles and they smell appallingly of unguents' (Brendon, *Decline and fall*, p. 363). As to the 'homosexual' side of things, Alan Hollinghurst's novel *The swimming-pool library* (1988) suggests the possibility of an intense erotic appreciation of Sudanese males by some Sudan civil servants, but it was admiration at a distance; perhaps the character of Lord Nantwich was based on Wilfrid Thesiger, who joined the Sudan Political Service in 1935 (I owe this suggestion to Piers Brendon).

23 Helen Callaway, 'Purity and exotica in legitimating the empire: the cultural construction of gender, sexuality and race', in T. Ranger and O. Vaughan, eds., *Legitimacy and the state in twentieth-century Africa: essays in honour of A.H.M. Kirk-Greene* (1993, 2001), pp. 45–7.

24 P.T. Mgadla, 'Of mistresses and concubines: miscegenation and European

"shame" in the Bechuanaland Protectorate, 1911–1950', *South African Historical Journal*, vol. 51 (2004), pp. 47–66.

25 A. Inglis, *The White Women's Protection Ordinance: sexual anxiety and politics in Papua* (Brighton, 1975), pp. 15–16.

26 J.G. Butcher, *The British in Malaya, 1880–1941: the social history of a European community in colonial South-East Asia* (Kuala Lumpur, 1979), pp. 206–12. See also R. Winstedt, *Start from alif: count from one, an autobiographical mémoire* (Kuala Lumpur, 1969), pp. 17–18; V. Purcell, *The memoirs of a Malayan official* (1965), pp. 297–8; A. Mackirdy and W.N. Willis, *The white slave market* (1912), pp. 249; C. Allen, ed., *Tales from the South China seas: images of the British in South-East Asia in the twentieth century* (1984 edn), pp. 151–2.

27 Magdalene College Archives, Group F: A.D. Garson Diaries (1947–57), vol. I, pp. 77–8 (22 January 1948), quoted by permission of the Master and Fellows of Magdalene College, Cambridge. Garson was head of training, appointments, transfers, and promotions, 1948–62.

28 Perham, *West African passage*, p. 140 (24 February 1932).

29 Ronald Garvey, *Gentleman pauper* (Bognor Regis, 1984), p. 41. Garvey served in the Western Pacific High Commission and the New Hebrides, and as governor of Fiji, 1952–58.

30 In 1991–2 I corresponded with Will Stober, a former British administrative officer in the New Hebrides Anglo-French Condominium (Vanuatu since independence, 1980). He was involved in a project to collect bio-data of former members of the colonial administration in the New Hebrides. Although there was no formal attempt to record sexual experiences, Stober generously shared with me such meagre written and anecdotal evidence as came to light. This included a copy of an unpublished letter to him from George Bristow (dated 12 March 1985), from which this quotation is taken. Stober died in 1997.

31 The literary and semi-autobiographical evidence points in the same direction, i.e. ambivalence, with reservations finally outweighing the temptations of concubinage: see especially Michael W. Young, 'Gone native in isles of illusion: in search of Asterisk in Epi', in James G. Carrier, ed., *History and tradition in Melanesian anthropology* (Berkeley, CA, 1992), ch. 7, pp. 193–223. This is a study of two works by Robert Fletcher, *Isles of illusion: letters from the South Seas*, ed. Bohun Lynch (1923, repr. 1986, ed. Gavin Young), and a novel *Gone native: a tale of the South Seas* (1924), both written under the alias Asterisk. Fletcher was a coconut-plantation manager in the New Hebrides, who had a son by an Aoban woman, but he concluded that the 'game was not worth the candle' and returned to be a schoolmaster in England.

Appendix

Downing Street,

11th January 1909.

Sir,

I desire to inform you that my attention has recently been called to one or two instances of misconduct on the part of officials in the Crown Colonies and Protectorates which have resulted in scandal and grave discredit to the public service.

2. In the cases in question it has been established that Government Officers have entered into an arrangement of concubinage with girls or women belonging to the native population of the district in which they were stationed, and, as it would appear that the point of view from which such practices are regarded by His Majesty's Government may not hitherto have been fully appreciated by all members of the Colonial and Protectorate Services, I think it desirable that it should be explicitly stated, and that it should be made clear to all members of those Services, that quite apart from all questions of morality, I regard such conduct as both injurious and dangerous to the public service.

3. I am satisfied that much has been done in various parts of the Empire to diminish the evils to which I refer; but I am compelled to recognise that they still exist in some parts of it. It is my earnest wish that the improvements which have been brought about in the past by the pressure of public opinion and the personal influence of senior officers should also have full effect in those territories under the administration of the Colonial Office in which such practices may still continue; and I have very carefully considered whether any additional measures can be adopted with a view to diminishing still further the risk of misconduct of this kind.

The Officer Administering

Plate 15.1 The Crewe Circular on concubinage, January 1909
(*Source*: CO 854/168).

4. *In order to bring the view of His Majesty's Government with regard to such practices under the notice of the Colonial and Protectorate Services as a whole, I have caused two Circulars to be prepared (of which copies are enclosed), and I desire that the one marked "A" may be communicated to all British officers who in future enter the service of any of the Colonies or Protectorates in which such practices have existed or may still exist at the time when they enter upon their duties, and that the one marked "B" should be similarly communicated to all British officers at present in the service of those Colonies and Protectorates.*

5. *It will be open to you in your discretion to communicate in the sense of the Circular marked "A" with any officers already in the service in whose cases you may think an additional warning desirable; and it will also be understood that summary punishment for offences of this character may at any time be applied to individual officers, irrespective of whether that Circular has or has not been issued to them, should the facts show such action to be necessary.*

6. *I am confident that the Governors and leading officials will spare no effort to diminish these abuses where they may be found still to exist, and that for this purpose they will be able to rely upon the assistance of the senior officers of the districts in which instances of such misconduct may possibly occur.* *You will, no doubt, explain to these officers that it will in future be their duty, whenever an instance of conduct to which I have referred comes to their notice, to make it the subject of official action.*

I have the honour to be,

Sir,

Your most obedient, humble Servant,

CREWE.

Plate 15.2

Enclosure " A " in Circular of 11th January 1909.

CONFIDENTIAL.

Downing Street,
January 1909.

It has been brought to my notice that officers in the service of some of the Crown Colonies and Protectorates have in some instances entered into arrangements of concubinage with girls or women belonging to the native populations.

2. The moral objections to such conduct are so generally recognised that it is unnecessary to dwell upon them. There is, however, another aspect of this question on which I must lay stress, namely, the grave injury to good administration which must inevitably result from such ill conduct between Government officials and native women.

Gravely improper conduct of this nature has at times been the cause of serious trouble among native populations, and must be strenuously condemned on that account ; but an objection even more serious from the standpoint of the Government lies in the fact that it is not possible for any member of the administration to countenance such practices without lowering himself in the eyes of the natives, and diminishing his authority to an extent which will seriously impair his capacity for useful work in the Service in which it is his duty to strive to set an honourable example to all with whom he comes in contact.

3. I am anxious to make it clear that this circular is not intended to cast any reflection upon those who are about to be admitted into the ranks of an honourable profession. Its object is simply to advise those who enter the service of a danger in their path, and to warn them of the disgrace and official ruin which will certainly follow from any dereliction of duty in this respect.

CREWE.

Plate 15.3

Enclosure " B " in Circular of 11th January 1909.

Downing Street,
January 1909.

It has been brought to my notice that officers in the service of some of the Crown Colonies and Protectorates have in some instances entered into arrangements of concubinage with girls and women belonging to the native populations of the territories in which they were performing their duties.

2. These illicit connections have at times been a cause of trouble with native populations; and another objection equally serious from the standpoint of the Government lies in the fact that it is not possible for any member of the administration to countenance such practices without lowering himself in the eyes of the natives and diminishing his authority over them.

3. I will not for a moment believe that such practices receive anything but the gravest condemnation from the members of the Service. Their admirable work and excellent conduct are fully appreciated by His Majesty's Government, and I feel sure that this Circular will be accepted by the Service as an appeal for loyal co-operation in vigorously reprobating and officially condemning all such cases of concubinage between Civil Servants and native women whenever and wherever they are detected.

CREWE.

Plate 15.4

16 Greek love in British India: Captain Searight's manuscript

[Not previously published. Although a brief account of Searight's sexual adventures and writings was offered in *Empire and sexuality: the British experience* (1990, 1991, 1998), this chapter attempts a far more detailed analysis, contextualisation, and assessment. Drafted in 2005.]

Little has been written about same-sex behaviour by British men in India. Everybody knew it went on, but it is rare for tangible evidence to have survived. Many scholars have lamented this frustrating absence from the archives. One of the leading historians of colonial sexualities, A.L. Stoler, writes apologetically about her account, focused mainly on the Dutch empire: 'My silence on this issue and the prominent place I give to heterosexuality reflects my long-term and failed efforts to identify any sources that do more than assume or obliquely allude to this "evil".'[1] Another authority, Professor Tapan Raychaudhuri, in his study of 'Love in a colonial climate' confirms that sources are conspicuously silent on British 'homosexuality' in Bengal.[2] Nevertheless, it is widely recognised that the British army in India was given to same-sex activities, in the context of what has been described as the 'prevailing homosocial structure of desire in British India'.[3] There are snippets of evidence from the 1830s and 1840s, such as Sir Richard Burton's notorious investigation of the boy-brothels of Karachi in 1845,[4] but the rest is silence, broken only by the terrible tragedy of Major-General Sir Hector Macdonald in Ceylon, committing suicide in 1903 after allegations of sex with a considerable number of Sinhalese boys.[5] It has always been understood that a major justification for 'regimental brothels' in India was the fear that without access to female prostitutes, there would be, as one viceroy put it, 'ever more deplorable evils . . . an increase in unnatural crimes'.[6] But when same-sex scandals did occur they were mostly treated officially by hushing them up. Newspapers seldom got hold of the stories. Courts martial were held in camera. Court cases were often struck from the record, reflecting an official reluctance to admit that this white 'imperfection' existed. Prosecuting offences mattered less than denying their existence.[7]

440

Memoirs are equally destitute. Some writers give hints as to what others may have done, seldom themselves: 'a few homosexuals followed their secret star with comparative comfort in that large and easygoing country'.[8] What might be missing is perhaps suggested by one of Havelock Ellis's case-studies from the late nineteenth century, an Indian army officer referred to as 'G.R.', who supplied brief details of sexual relationships with other officers, one of whom himself admitted to several similar experiences in the army.[9] Even when they are written, few sexual memoirs or confessional diaries escape destruction as a result of the later qualms of the author himself or of his family and executors. Hence the survival of a lengthy erotic manuscript, of indisputable authenticity, written by a serving Indian army officer, Captain Kenneth Searight, is of great significance.[10] It is a highly original anthology, part autobiographical, part semi-autobiographical, part literary fantasy. The evidence has to be carefully sifted, but embedded in it is a chronicle of imperial experience, all the more important because of its unique revelation of a prolonged and intensive set of sexual relationships with Indian boys. It is not a draft, but a final version, as carefully penned as any gospel in a monastic scriptorium.[11]

I

Its author was born Arthur Kenneth Searight, in Kensington, London, on 15 November 1883, and he belonged to an army family. At Charterhouse, his boarding school, aged fourteen, he fell in love with a class-mate and enjoyed regular mutual masturbation with him. He left school in 1900 to go to the Royal Military College at Sandhurst. He joined the Queen's Own Royal West Kent Regiment as a second lieutenant on 2 March 1904. In October 1907 he became a lieutenant. After a brief tour of duty in Russia, he began a tentative exploration of London's sexual underground, but by the time he was posted to India in 1909, aged twenty-six, he still had had sexual experiences with only three or four other partners. His initiation into the quite different scale of sexual opportunity provided by service of the empire began typically enough in Port Said. In India he was initially stationed at Lebong, near Darjeeling; from 1911 he was transferred to Peshawar, near the North-West Frontier. From there he explored a wide area of the Punjab and Rajastan, aided from 1914 by his post as a railway transport officer, visiting Karachi, Lahore, Cherat, Simla, Bombay, and, once again, Port Said. By the time the First World War broke out he was a captain, and in common with the rest of his regiment had a quiet time in India – spending most of 1917 in Bangalore – until posted to Mesopotamia (Iraq) in 1918 as a 'general staff officer' in the North Persian Force. He was described then in *The Army List* as on 'special appointments (class FF)', with the grade of 'interpreter, first class', and speaking Arabic, Baluchi, Persian, and Pushtu. By the beginning of 1920 he was in the War Office on 'special employment', then joined the Egyptian Expeditionary Force until August 1921. After leaving the army in 1925, having completed twenty-one years' service, he is believed to have retired to Rome, but he ended his days in Folkestone. He died on 28 February 1957, aged 73, from broncho-pneumonia and alcoholic hepatic cirrhosis. His death was registered by a spinster-sister from London.

Searight called himself a 'pederast', which he understood in its original Greek sense as an adult male who had sexual relations with adolescent boys. Sometimes known as 'Greek love', the appropriate technical term for this is hebephilia (*hebe* = puberty, *ephebos* = youth). It is to be sharply distinguished from paedophilia, which prefers prepubertal partners; and whereas a paedophile may be attracted to little girls as well as boys, sexual relations with a young girl would be unthinkable to a 'Greek' boy-lover like Searight. Most of his partners were Indian boys aged between thirteen and fifteen. In the climate of today's revulsion – but without in any way attempting to condone his activities – it is necessary to repeat: Searight was not a paedophile in its modern sense of a dangerous child-molester preying upon the very young.[12] It should also be remarked that his preference for adolescent boys is by no means as unusual historically as it may seem today, from our newly acquired perspective of symmetric civil partnerships between two male adults. Despite the tendentious attempts of this now ascendant 'gay' culture to claim a historical legitimacy and pedigree, it is abundantly clear that the vast majority of men in supposedly 'homosexual' cultures in the past – whether in ancient Greece and Rome, medieval Christian or later Buddhist monasteries, Renaissance Italy (especially Florence), the Ottoman courts, pre-communist China or pre-Meiji Japan, Nelson's navy, or even late Victorian and Edwardian England[13] – were involved in asymmetric relationships, usually with boys and not other mature men.[14] Western art attests to the boy-centredness of its homoerotic past, and is indeed full of images of beautiful boys and androgynous youths, from angels to card-sharps.[15]

Searight's intellectual horizons and psychological inspiration were typical for an Edwardian 'homosexual', public school and classically educated.[16] His inner world was entirely formed within the Hellenist paradigm of inter-generational man–boy relationships (*erastes* and *eromenos*). He was familiar with the relevant writings of Plato, Petronius, and Ovid. He can quote Greek love-poetry, and makes frequent allusion to the iconic mythological figures of Greek love, especially Ganymede, its quintessential emblem. Equally important, however, is to recognise that Searight's exceptional confidence in his sexual orientation was profoundly enhanced by exposure to contemporary cultures which, decoupling sex from guilt, did not share British sexual *mores* arising out of a narrowly parochial interpretation of Judaeo-Christian teaching, particularly its assumption that anal intercourse was unnatural. Italy was important to him in this regard, since every boy there seemed to be open to seduction. It was well known to the British in India that Muslim sexuality was ambivalent, even hypocritical – Qur'anic prohibitions co-existing with harems of young boys kept by nawabs. It was also understood that indigenous homoerotic camaraderie was widespread in Punjab, Sind, and Rajputana – precisely those areas where, as luck would have it, Searight spent so much of his army service. All British soldiers knew that even the fiercest Pathan warrior liked same-sex activity.[17] And every Pathan boy, as Searight wrote in his autobiographical poem, was eager 'to let on hire/His charms to indiscriminate desire,/To wholesale Buggery and perverse letches [*sic*]'. To get a boy in Peshawar, he wrote, 'was easier than to pick the flowers by the wayside'.

'Same-sex love in India', it has recently been asserted, 'is as old as the hills and sacred rivers.'[18] The continuities of Indian homoeroticism are now being closely studied. It seems clear that ancient literary texts, whether pre- or post-Muslim, Hindu or Buddhist, are certainly not innocent of it, while Persian and Urdu poetry is full of lyrical praise of 'flower-faced' pubescent boys. An example would be Dargah Quli Khan's *Portrait of a city*, with its rhapsodic evocations of Delhi's boy-dancers, singers, and wrestlers in the 1780s.[19] But what about modern literature? Under the pseudonym 'Ugra', Pandey Bechan Sharma published *Chaklet*, 'Chocolate', in 1927 in Calcutta, a collection of eight stories about the love of adolescent boys. Beautiful young boys are known as 'chocolate', but also, indicatively, as 'pocket-book' and 'money-order'. *Chaklet* claims to draw on real-life experiences, and acknowledges that *laundebaazi* ('boy chasing'), the sexual love of boys (including sodomy), was, like chocolate, ubiquitous, 'a widespread practice', especially in UP (the United Provinces). Ugra quoted Urdu literature, but also highlighted the opportunities for men and boys to meet in 'modern' sites such as schools, colleges, clubs, hostels, cinemas, parks, fairs, swimming-places, and jails. The book was hugely popular, and reprinted as late as 1953 (third edition), but by then it was also the subject of a homophobic backlash. This was part of a nationalist critique, worried about the image of India as 'effeminate'. The reference to jails seems to be confirmed by the United Provinces Jails Inquiry Report of 1929, which found male-to-male sex 'frequent' and easy to conceal from guards.[20] As to what went on in schools, at the CMS school in Srinigar, Kashmir, the headmaster introduced boxing as an 'alternative to sodomy', and had staff beaten for 'immorality'.[21] Many Indian intellectuals thought schools and colleges promoted 'homosexuality'. Mayo College at Ajmir for the sons of Indian notables, and schools attached to the theosophy movement, had a reputation in this regard. A Rajput nobleman, Amar Singh, an officer in the Indian army, and in charge of the Imperial Cadet Corps College, sedulously tried to keep his establishment pure, but the prevalence of 'homosexuality' (which he loosely called 'sodomy') is a recurring subliminal theme in the diary he kept from 1898 to 1915. He records in detail a major case which led to the expulsion of a pupil.[22] His observations can be corroborated from an unlikely source: Gandhi wrote an article in *Young India* (26 July 1929) referring to a recent Bihar Government Education Department inquiry, which found 'unnatural vice' not only among boys but between teachers and boys. Gandhi believed the practice was widely increasing.[23]

One of the puzzling things about Searight's account is that he gives no hint of any collaborators in his sexual enterprise, and there is no suggestion of any kind of network of the like-minded. We need not doubt that there were other expatriates with a similar interest in Indian boys at the same time, even if we cannot identify many of them. Possibly the best known to history would be the 'Revd' (later 'Bishop') Charles Leadbeater (1854–1934), renegade clergyman and theosophist friend and colleague of Annie Besant. He travelled in India and Ceylon from 1884 onwards. In 1888 he picked up Jinarajasdasa, a Sinhalese boy who became his constant companion. In 1906 Leadbeater was charged with teaching boys to masturbate, under the guise of occult training. He took baths with them and slept naked with them. He made no secret of his theory that assisting boys with their sexual development was a spiritual necessity. He was forced to resign from the Theosophical Society. But on becoming president of the society in 1909, Besant immediately reinstated him, and together they identified an exceptionally attractive Brahman boy, Jiddu Krishnamurti, as a reincarnation of the World Teacher. They set about training him in the Hindu College, which Besant had set up in Benares in 1897. There were scandalous reports and charges implying something more serious than Leadbeater's habitual addiction to mutual masturbation with young boys. Krishnamurti's father took a custody case to court in 1913, where the truth of the sexual allegations was not established. Leadbeater fled to Australia.[24]

Lewis Thompson (1909–49) was an aspiring poet who, with Rimbaudian ideas and independent means, left for India in 1932 and never returned to the UK, travelling through Ceylon and India, making friends with the locals and adopting Indian dress. By 1943 he was installed as librarian and writer-in-residence at the Rajghat School in Benares, which had a theosophical orientation. The published extracts from his journal document an intensely committed, almost overwhelming adoration of young Indian boys, celebrating his inexhaustible delight in their 'mystic radiance', their eyes 'soft, mysterious, subtle as perhaps only Hindu eyes can be'. For Thompson, these relationships – whether sexual or not does not emerge from what has been published – were a 'subtle field of the most delicate spiritual knowledge and perfection'. His posthumously published reflections (or 'wisdom sayings') only touch on the 'famous charm of children'; he has a few cryptic pages on sexuality, which he argues must not be suppressed, but allowed to flourish as the 'spontaneous, undifferentiated expression of affection and delight'.[25]

Men like Leadbeater and Thompson testify to the attraction which Indian boys might hold for European men.[26] Searight, however, would seem to be unique in his comprehensive vision of inter-generational relationships, and in the quantity of material which he wrote down about them.

II

Captain Searight's manuscript is labelled and entitled *Paidikion* – that is, the book of boyhood, a hymn to boyishness, and subtitled 'an anthology of the book of Hyakinthos and Narkissus'. He filled 566 pages of a lined notebook, bound in very dark green, a small fat format, similar to a hymn-book, 4¾ inches by 6¼ inches. There are three items in it of particular interest to the imperial historian: an autobiographical poem in rhyming couplets, 'The furnace', 2,706 lines in length (137 pages); a hundred-page novella, 'Simla: the tale of a secret society'; and crucially, a six-page coded listing of Searight's sexual encounters, 129 in number, and headed 'Paidiology'. The autobiography covers the years from 1897 to 1915, while the 'Paidiology' extends the evidence through to 1917, when he was thirty-four. The remainder of the manuscript is taken up with seven stories, ranging in length from nine to seventy-one pages. Eight photographs of nude boys are interspersed, the majority of them from the famous Italian studios of von Gloeden, Galdi, and von Pluschow. In addition there are six in-fill fragments, each occupying a page. These include fourteen lines of untranslated verse, 'Pathan love songs to his boy'; a list of the words for 'boy' in twenty-four languages; and an extraordinary table of the 'measurements of the young male body'. This last is a complicated but ingeniously constructed tabulation of eighteen basic measurements, from age nine to nineteen inclusive, made at two-year intervals – such things as the distance between neck-nipple-navel-penis-knee-foot, the length of arms, and the size of hands and ankles (front and side readings in some cases), together with the length and circumference of the penis, both flaccid and erect. It may seem highly eccentric to measure systematically, even the distance between nipples or the width of the hand, until one recalls that Indian police relied on meticulous measurements of this sort before the introduction of finger-printing.[27] There is no indication of whether these are measurements made on one boy only, or whether the figures are averages (more likely), and if so, what was the size of the sample.

The 'Paidiology' list at the back of the volume consists almost entirely of the 125 boys from the Indian period, 1909 to 1917, and it is certainly incomplete, with allocated spaces at the end not filled in. The tables record for each boy his forename, age, and 'race', together with the place of meeting, and the year-date, and 'references', that is, the sexual acts performed (see Plate 16.4). The final column (presumably) records the total number of orgasms experienced with each partner. The coded 'references' are represented by thirty-three different symbols, a neat system of pictograms, where a dotted circle represents the anus, an upright stroke the phallus, and so on, with active and passive signs (dashes either above or below the pictogram). Included in the list are eleven British young men, most probably all soldiers; those partners over the the age of nineteen were exclusively British, with names like Cyril, Fred, Jack, Douglas, and Herbert. The average number of orgasms Searight calculated page by page at 12.3 per partner, higher in his earlier years, lower in the later. The highest number of orgasms with individuals were achieved with Pathans aged thirteen and fourteen, during the years 1912 to 1915: 73 in one case, 82 and 93 in others; the record was 96, inspired by Serbiland, a fourteen year old, who was originally engaged to help him with lessons in 'higher Pushtu'. (Serbiland seems to have been a pederastic variant of the 'sleeping dictionary'.) Besides these, there were six other boys in the age-group twelve to fifteen with whom he had more than thirty orgasms. In other words, he had many young Indian friends on a regular basis. About half the total number of 125, with whom he had three orgasms or fewer, may be regarded as casual contacts. Invariably the boys – Mahmud, Abdul, Umar, Mazuffar, and the rest – came to his cantonment tent or bungalow, or, when he was travelling, to his hotel room. Searight's 'Paidiology' tabulation would have excited the admiration of Kinsey, and it is probably the first attempt of its kind at a coded sexual recording.

The autobiographical poem, 'The furnace', 'an autobiography in which is set forth the secret diversions of a paiderast', is in three 'acts': 'Smoke' (lines 1–606), covering his schooldays and attendance at a 'crammer's' (similar to a small tutorial college), with only the 'mere suggestion of hidden fires'; 'The spark' (lines 607–1504), dealing with his post-adolescent frustrations, and early years in the army, until India provided ignition; and finally 'The flame' (lines 1505–2706), when the furnace of his desire was well and truly raging, from 1912 to 1915. His schoolboy friendship with Stanley Winch (his real name) is touchingly recollected. Fevered auto-masturbation dominates the next section, followed by his first attempt at active anal intercourse, with a nineteen-year-old Piccadilly rent-boy. Port Said, however, provided the first real 'breath of freedom'; he then, 'thus encouraged, at once began/To explore the amorous realms of Hindustan'. To begin with, his contacts in Bengal were with Gurkha boys in their mid-teens, Kaul, Lachman, Bahadur, and Lobzang the Tibetan, 'slim brown enchanters', the first to 'help me satisfy this burning thirst', though not proceeding beyond what he called 'intercrural' intercourse. A defining moment occurred in Calcutta in 1911 when he was approached in Chowringhee Road – a highly respectable location – by fourteen-year-old seductive Narayan, who, once they had found a room, penetrated him, and thus 'taught me how the passive love is won'. He was then posted to Peshawar, near the North-West Frontier, where things developed exponentially. Passionate Pathans are contrasted with the 'mild Hindus' of Bengal: 'I groaned; the boy's untamed ferocity/So different to the young Bengali's love/Filled me with anguish.' The established pattern now and henceforward was for sessions of both active and passive anal sex:

> Scarce passed a night but I in rapturous joy
> Indulged in mutual sodomy, the boy
> Fierce eyed, entrancing, . . .
> And when his luscious bottom-hole would brim
> Full of my impoured essences, we'd change
> The role of firing-point . . .
> Then half-an-hour . . . and back again I'd come
> To plunge my weapon in his drenching bum.

It was in Cherat that he met Serbiland, with a face of almost English whiteness, 'so beautiful in profile', with 'splendid eyes', sparkling brilliantly, shy and timid at first – but Searight cultivates him, because 'if I had let him go, some wild Pathan' would have taken advantage of him. He was thrilled by the 'exquisite beauty' of his phallus, 'smoother than satin', 'curved like an Oriental scimetre' (*sic*). An initial attempt to enter Serbiland anally 'miserably failed', the boy commenting '*Warkote*', meaning he was too small behind. However, he proved immediately adept in the active role, and then it was a point of honour to give as much pleasure as he had taken. Searight was full of admiration:

> In fact I was enamoured of this boy
> More than I cared to own. I would employ
> The subtlest means to entice him & to win
> His real affection; while if I did sin
> In tempting him to spend his precious seed
> I did not spare myself nor grudge the mead
> Of my intenser passion, nor did he
> See any sin in my immodesty.

'The Paidiology' confirms active and passive anal intercourse with Serbiland, and fellation, in a total of ninety-six orgasms. In returning eventually to barracks at Peshawar, 'I left my darling tearfully.'

After this episode, it is perhaps rather surprising that the central climax of the poem deals not with Indian boys but with the period of his six-month long leave in 1912. Travelling via Port Said, Sicily, and Naples, he arrived back in England, where he picked up a horseguard in Hyde Park and had other adventures in London pubs.[28] Taormina in 'ardent Sicily' had enchanted him, and he found it a 'natural home'. On his return journey, in congenial Naples once again, where 'paiderastic love in flame unchecked/ Is what these Neapolitans expect', he met an exceptionally attractive grey-blue-eyed boy, Cecillo ('Francesco' in the 'Paidiology'), aged fifteen.[29] The account of their friendship is one of the most lyrical and erotic sections of the entire manuscript. Cecillo proved to be 'a wanton little scamp', who delighted in mock-gladiatorial fights and 'luscious tonguing':

> Those misty eyes of his, more opalescent
> Than sapphire blue: each pencilled crescent
> Of wide set brow; each eyelash curled aloft,
> His wondrous colouring, a skin so soft
> That down on the smooth surface of a peach
> Were rougher in comparison; a chin
> Square and just dimpled; while again on each
> Delicious cheek the velvet of his skin
> Was broken by a dimple as he smiled.
> . . .
> Ah sweet Cecillo, you could e'er entice
> My soul itself to very paradise . . .
> Indeed no spurious sense of shame divided
> His whole subjection, nor our love one-sided:
> For if I revelled in his nether most
> The oral orifice would play the host
> With equal fervour till at either end
> Cecillo would encourage me to spend
> With naïve impartiality.

Although not mentioned in the autobiography, it was immediately after this, on the P&O liner from Port Said to Bombay, that Searight met

E.M. Forster. The main part of the poem was already complete, and Forster read it. (I shall say more about Searight's influence on Forster below.) In the final section of the autobiography, pride of place is again given to a European lad, this time a German prostitute aged sixteen, called Mischell, whom he met on another trip to Port Said. Searight highlighted this as 'an episode of paramount importance' for its satisfying intimacy. The autobiography ends in 1915, with 'fifty adolescents' gratefully recalled, and final obeisance made to his compulsive devotion to 'strange and solitary rites/Before the mirror'.

Considering that the author was no more than an amateur poet, and that this was his first and as far as we know his only attempt, it is surprisingly well done. The constant imperative to sustain the rhyme imparts a playful lightness of touch. Paradoxically, this account of his secret sexual life ends just as Searight entered – as we deduce from the 'Paidiology' – a more promiscuous phase. This was marked by a faster turnover of partners, fewer steady friendships, and increasing sexual commitment, or depravity, according to one's view, as he began routinely to incorporate analingus into the programme, and became increasingly keen on urolagnia. In 1917 the listing of partners suddenly stops, and a projected second volume was abandoned. Like Pepys and Rimbaud, Searight stopped writing while still quite young. Perhaps, like them, he was conscious that he couldn't go on producing to the level of colourfulness achieved in his youthful intimate outpourings. Or perhaps discretion took over, or he decided to concentrate on his military career in intelligence, or to develop his linguistic interests, which became his new obsession.

In India, at first, Searight was excited by contrasting skin colour, the sight of 'my rod of ivory between the mons/Of buttocks fashioned out of bronze', but there came a time when he began to long for English whiteness. An important feature to notice is that Indian boys occupy lines 1185 to 1652 of the autobiographical poem, together with lines 2456 to 2467, and 2653–4: that is, only 480 out of 2,706 lines, 18 per cent – 30 per cent of the record of his Indian experience. The autobiography is thus highly selective, biased in favour of describing the European encounters, and very far from reflecting the actual predominance of Indian partners. There may of course be an artistic reason for this, but it could also be considered as 'racist', or proof of exploitativeness, taking advantage of Indian boys although they were not really what he wanted. However, there is in fact no doubting the affection he felt for many of these boys. What they can seldom have provided was a meeting of minds, something that was important for a man of his intelligence. One thinks of E.M. Forster's despairing cry after a sexual relationship with an

Indian he came to consider 'such a goose': 'what relation beyond carnal-ity could one establish with such a people?'[30]

'Simla' is the longest and best of the fiction. Essentially it is a love-story about a friendship between a twenty-two-year-old British army officer, 'Ken', and an Anglo-Armenian schoolboy, 'Eric'.[31] Ken first met Eric when the latter was ten. He saw him again a year later, but the main action takes place in and near Simla two more years on, and over a period of six days. It is an extremely plausible account of how a thirteen-year-old boy might be courted, with the first meetings all at successive after-school tea-times. Following visits to a film-show and a fancy-dress party, by the fifth day there is developing a mutual sexual awareness, and the first tentative grope takes place. Eric agrees to come back the next day, bringing two slightly older chums from Christ Church School with him. The prospect puts Ken into an overnight fever of impatience: 'It's ages since I've seen a real white boy properly.'

Almost one-third of the novella is devoted to these lovingly described pre-sexual preliminaries. There is every reason to suppose that they describe an actual relationship. We know from the 'Paidiology' that Searight was in Simla and nearby Kasauli and Mashobra in 1915 and had sex with four *Indian* boys there, Natu, Hita Ram, Said Amir, and Ghulam Rasul. But Eric is a character vividly brought to life, so that he is probably based on a real boy, much as the fourteen-year-old Polish boy Wladyslaw Moes provided the inspiration for Thomas Mann's Tadzio in *Death in Venice* (1911). The main narrative of 'Simla', however, consists of a series of five orgies of ever-deepening intensity and abandon, a semi-autobiographical fantasy, possibly transposed from sessions with the Indian boys. A coda returns the novella to the original spirit of a tender love-affair, when Eric sleeps naked with Ken, a quietly elegiac end to a wildly eventful day, during which the narrator and three English school-boys had broken all manner of taboos. The climactic scene involved coprophilia. (This may seem far-fetched, but it might be worth remem-bering that for Indians there is nothing inherently private or repulsive about defecation, and therefore it would not have been difficult for Searight to fantasise about sexualising it.)

We should probably therefore conclude that 'Simla' is in part a displacement fantasy, and understanding this is central to understand-ing Searight. It confirms what we have already suspected from 'The furnace', that he had sex with Indian boys 'because they were there', but would have preferred to be disporting with European partners. Indeed, he confesses that a young artillery bandsman even as old as twenty was 'better than all Eastern catamites'.

This makes it all the more puzzling that the adult Searight appears not to have had sex with young British teenagers, since he manifestly wanted to do so. It was of course illegal, but that was hardly a deterrent for a man of his determination. A man 'taking an interest' in a boy even in England itself would not have necessarily attracted unfavourable attention at this date – or indeed for several decades more – and particularly not in community settings such as boarding schools, scout troops, mission settlements[32] – and army camps. Searight's self-denying ordinance is all the more surprising in the light of another unpublished autobiographical confession, which in one sense is even more shocking than his, since it indicates that English schoolboys in India might be seduced not only by soldiers (or ex-soldiers) but by Indians themselves.

This revealing memoir by Guy Wheeler provides insight into the boy-sexual atmosphere of Bombay – through which Searight passed several times and where he had sex with Indian boys.[33] Wheeler writes from the perspective of a young British boy growing up there in an army family in the early 1930s, and attending the Cathedral High School as a chorister. Aware of the sexual antics of naked *chokra* boys on the beach, and of Indian lingam-worship, and having often seen Indians 'tossing themselves off under the mango trees', when the scoutmaster warned Guy's troop of the perils of 'beastliness', with its risk of causing the fall of the empire, 'we thought it was rubbish'. Guy had two sexual encounters with English adults. One was at a swimming-place with a British 'Tommy'. The other, which developed into a regular relationship, was with an ex-army physical training instructor, now a shop assistant, nicknamed 'Trader Horn' (after the popular book and film of that name). 'Tommy' told the young boy that soldiers 'fucked each other wherever he had been, from Aldershot to the North-West Frontier', and he himself preferred doing it 'with another bloke'. Both men got Guy to masturbate them. This detailed account does not allow us to say that 'Tommy' and 'Trader Horn' picked up Indian boys, but if they were prepared to take the surely larger risk with English youngsters, it hardly seems probable they would have passed up the chances with Indian juveniles. Their silence about this may simply mean only that they were not prepared to admit it to a son of the Raj. What Guy Wheeler's memoir does provide, however, is evidence in reverse, so to speak, and astonishingly, evidence of Indians seducing European boys. Two instances are given. On the first occasion it was a session with a native cook in a friend's house, and on the second it was with an Indian hospital orderly, supervising Guy's bath after a tonsilectomy. Like the European seducers, both Indian men asked the boy to masturbate them. There are many telling details in the account. Two must suffice here. After climaxing, the orderly exclaimed, 'Ganesh has got lucky today!' And Guy was surprised that Indian sperm was white not brown. By the time he was sent off to St Paul's School in London at the age of thirteen, his outlook was thoroughly sexualised. As he comments, for a boy growing up in Bombay, 'pricks were as plentiful as lollipops – if you knew where to look'.

III

What sort of man does Searight's manuscript reveal him to be? Obviously he was clever and imaginative, enjoyed recording and classifying, and he possessed unusual literary and linguistic skills. Apart from his relatively ordinary experience of mutual masturbation at school, he was a late starter as a devotee of anal intercourse. There is nowhere any suggestion that he was inhibited by religious interdictions. Ken Searight was not a religious person. He was, however, highly sexed, deeply narcissistic, a compulsive masturbator. He never had any emotional involvement with women, whom he thoroughly despised. Instead, he indulged in an almost pagan worship of the naked bodies of boys 'in the full flush of puberty', which he found incomparably lovely and entrancing, something 'splendid, vivid, clean as the lillies of the field'. He was captivated by the paradoxical contrast of smooth skin, slender boyish frame, and 'rose-bud anus', with the precocious manly penis and luxuriant pubic hair. (He readily admitted to being a pubic hair fetishist.) Unsurprisingly for one who enjoyed so many Muslim partners, he was an admirer of circumcision, although it had not yet become popular in time for his generation of the British middle classes. As to his more-or-less political views, Searight laments the contemporary evaluation of homosexuals, who were scorned with 'contemptuous hatred', and the way in which boy-love has been 'boycotted, maligned, abused, and cursed'. He makes one caustic reference to 'English legislation', and a favourable one to the Napoleonic Code, which 'thank God, admits that love has other mode'. Throughout the manuscript there are very few references to modern literature, whether technical or creative: just two nods towards Oscar Wilde and one to Tite Street (where Wilde had been the most famous resident), and another to 'a problem in modern ethics' (which was the title of a book by A.J. Symonds). Otherwise there is almost nothing of contemporary resonance. The First World War is nowhere mentioned, and there is only a single passing whiff of anti-German prejudice. Searight certainly liked to drink, and enjoyed 'a night's carouse'. He was definitely a public school snob. He did not care for the 'inherent coarseness' of London street-boys, with their 'regrettable Cockney twang', unworthy of their breathtakingly smooth skins. In his stories the narrators are invariably toffs. His favourite adjective is 'ripping', just as in innumerable Victorian and Edwardian school stories.

The way the manuscript is written up in itself tells us a lot about its author. It is done with meticulous, almost obsessive care. The handwriting is not untypical of scholarly hands of the period, small, compact, and written with a very fine steel nib like a mapping-pen; it is not italic, but slightly sloping backwards, at its best hardly more than a print-script, but fluid and with some ligatures. As the pages, and presumably the years, progress, the writing becomes smaller, more cursive, and less attractive. There are neat decorative embellishments, mostly stylised drawings of genital parts. Numerals are finely rendered, the pagination being in red ink. The spelling is somewhat erratic, but the text is almost free of corrections and entirely without erasures.

It is not part of my purpose here to determine Searight's place in the history of erotic literature, so I shall confine myself to a couple of observations. A central issue in evaluating works which attract the derogatory label 'pornography' is to assess how far the author departs from 'reality'. It is a constant refrain of opponents of the genre that its practitioners are ignorant of physiology and descend into ludicrous exaggeration. On the other hand, commentators have to be careful not to dismiss as fanciful that which is simply beyond their own personal comprehension or experience.[34] Searight was no sexual boaster, recording his own phallus as of modestly typical size (five inches at the age of fourteen increasing to six inches as an adult), and those of his characters and partners as within the normal range. He is in fact extremely knowledgeable, describing such things as male multiple orgasm, juvenile anal dilatation, and anal or prostatic orgasm independent of penile stimulation, all of which are now known to be 'real' and not just figments of a heated pornographic imagination. We can also claim for him a high degree of originality. There was very little European attempt after the Graeco-Roman era to develop a same-sex literature until the end of the nineteenth century, and almost none of that dwelt solely upon inter-generational liaisons. It is in any case most unlikely that Searight would have had access to such clandestine publications as existed. Moreover, several of the practices he describes had never been given literary form before, at least not from the perspective he adopts, nor had the psychological motivations and emotional implications been addressed in the same way. The prevailing tone of late Victorian and Edwardian erotica was that of a jolly romp. For Searight, by contrast, sexuality and erotic writing were both a good deal more than a bit of fun.

Be that as it may, Searight is a more significant figure than a mere pornographer, however serious, or even an exemplar of sexual opportunism within the empire, however revealing. He has two other claims to fame. One is as the inventor of an artificial language, and the other is as a some-time friend of E.M. Forster, upon whom he may have exercised a creative influence.

In retirement, Searight concentrated on constructing a new universal language, which he called Sona.[35] He published his scheme in 1935 through the good offices of C.K. Ogden, the Cambridge polymath genius, inventor of Basic English, and the editor of a series called Psyche Miniatures. Ogden wrote an introduction to Searight's book in the series. Although he thought Sona a worthwhile scheme, he not unnaturally thought 'Basic' was the better option. Searight for his part agreed with Ogden that a good international neutral language would be useful, especially if a nation could adopt it as a second language. Rather like Ogden too, he regarded national and dead languages as unsuitable models. Instead, and it is the most interesting feature of Sona, he believed that too many constructed languages were European-based, ignoring what Chinese, Japanese, and Arabic had to teach. Indeed, the result on the page looks very much like transliterated Japanese. Sona has 360 radicals and 15 particles. Thus he was able to claim that 'by the nature of Sona's method of simple agglutination its power of forming words is almost unlimited'. The word 'Sona' itself was formed from SO (help, auxiliary) + NA (negative, neutral); while – to pick the obvious example – 'boy' was KORA (from KO small + RA male). In a final section of his book, Searight translated the 850 words of Basic into Sona.

As far as I am able to judge, Searight's project was both logical and learned. And it is far from forgotten. There is now a website devoted to the promotion of Sona. Devotees aim to organise a Sona community together, to help people learn and practise it, to promote its use and advancement by interactive discussion, and to write new works in Sona – 'fiction, essays, reference material and poetry' – breathing life into the grammar and vocabulary. The website does not disguise the fact that its hero was a 'pederast'.[36]

The other aspect of Searight which extends his significance was his contact with and possible influence upon E.M. Forster. They met on Searight's return voyage between Port Said and India after his long leave in 1912. At the time Forster was living in London, but he was accompanied by his friend Goldsworthy Lowes Dickinson, a notable history don at King's College, Cambridge, who specialised in the history of political thought. Dickinson recorded the encounter: 'We discovered one interesting figure – a young officer called Searight, of a romantic Byronic temperament: Homosexual and perpetually in love with some boy or other, with a passion for literature.' Dickinson added that Searight was 'writing an autobiography of which he showed us parts, in a style which also seemed to belong to Byron – not good, I suppose, but curiously moving'. Forster and Dickinson later joined Searight for a few days at Peshawar.[37] There, they met at least one of Searight's boys, possibly Mahmud, the fourteen-year-old inspirer of ninety-three orgasms; at any rate, five years later Forster reported to Dickinson his own growing friendship in Alexandria with Mohammed el-Adl, a teenage tram-conductor, as being 'like Searight's affair . . . this will convey to you age, race, rank, though not precisely relationship'.[38] Their conversations with Searight would undoubtedly have discussed the difficulty for Englishmen to get into real contact with Indians. As Dickinson put it in his diary – immediately after the references to Searight – 'the barrier, on both sides, of incomprehension is almost impassable. I feel this incomprehension very strongly myself . . . It is really distressing to feel the gulf – everyone salaaming to the white man, cringing and begging, not allowed to do a thing for oneself; and never knowing what is or is not proper for a sahib.'[39]

The fact that Forster five years later could assume Dickinson would remember Searight suggests a considerable impact on them both. Forster's biographer acknowledges that 'India made a profound impression on him' in 1912–13, but argues that it was only the visit to Egypt in 1917–19 which made him sexually 'more active'. Whether or not our uninhibited Indian army officer might have pushed him earlier in this direction, Forster was certainly shaken up by their encounter, and began writing more definitely about homosexual themes. *Maurice* was begun shortly afterwards, and perhaps was directly prompted by Searight's autobiography. Though *Maurice* does not concern intergenerational sex, and was not released for publication until 1971, it is a major statement about homosexuality in the early twentieth century. In the 'terminal note' to *Maurice* (dated September 1960), Forster says the novel was 'the direct result of a visit to Edward Carpenter'. This may seem to deflate Searight's influence, but there would have been little point in adding the name of unknown Searight to that of such an iconic figure, author of *The intermediate sex* (1908), even if Searight had some part in the novel's genesis.[40] There has indeed been continuing speculation that the eponymous hero may have been modelled on him.[41] (Youthful Maurice certainly could not have been based upon patriarchal Carpenter.) Although elements of Maurice's character are probably drawn from Searight, *Maurice* is in no sense 'his' story. However, Maurice represents 'suburbia', and Forster repeatedly stresses that he is 'a suburban gentleman' (as distinct from the other main characters who are 'county', 'academic', and 'servant/tradesman'). Maurice is from a comfortable home, his father is dead, and he is attractive, 'powerful and handsome'; he is 'destitute of religious sense', and 'rather a snob'. At school he was average-mediocre, and now, to begin with, inexperienced, chastely romantic, given to 'public schoolishness', and to quoting Plato – and then he rebels. This is indeed consistent with how we might describe the younger Searight. Forster also suggests Maurice is not very bright mentally, is 'constitutionally lazy' and of 'a slow nature' – which sounds rather less like Searight, indeed not like him at all.

There is, however, a more plausible case to be made for Searight as the model for one of Forster's other characters. Richard Aldrich was the first to realise that 'The other boat' was a story 'vaguely inspired' by Captain Searight.[42] The important point here – not in fact noticed by Aldrich – is that Forster almost certainly wrote this story in 1913 immediately after returning from India, and moreover, revised it in 1957–8, that is, just after Searight's death. The action takes place on a P&O liner between Suez and Bombay, and concerns an Indian army officer, Captain Lionel March, who had been successful in getting his captaincy early: 'He was what any rising young officer ought to be – clean-cut, athletic, good looking without being conspicuous.' He conducted himself with 'dash and decision', his 'demeanour assured, his temper equable'. But: 'He was the conventional type, who once the conventions are broken, breaks them into little pieces.' The story tells how he had to share a cabin with a seductive Indian half-caste, Cocoanut, 'a personable adolescent', whom he had once met in childhood. Eventually they sleep together and 'did what they both wanted to do'; Lionel asks if it hurt.

The characterisation sounds like Searight, even if the specific episode does not seem to fit; and if indeed Lionel is based on him, one particular feature of the delineation is especially significant – the ambivalence of Lionel's racial attitude. He refers to Cocoanut with other Europeans as 'a dagoe', 'a wog', but also speaks to him directly about his 'fuzzywuzzy family'. Furthermore, 'In England he would never have touched him, no not with tongs.'

It is perfectly possible that Searight may have told Forster a great deal about his background. Is Forster recalling such details when he tells the reader that Lionel was the eldest son, with four brothers and sisters, of an army major (now dead) who had shamed the family by 'going native' in Burma? Or when he suggests that until this sexual adventure he had been expecting to get married? But whether or not these details are true for Searight, it is still highly possible that he has been immortalised in one of Forster's finest pieces of writing, wherein the author sharply and convincingly describes an East–West sexual encounter. It is one of Forster's most erotic and strongest statements of support for personal sexual emancipation, and his most powerful indictment of the imperial nexus;[43] this is Forster 'at the height of his powers', writing with 'a tragic grandeur unsurpassed even in *A passage to India*'.[44] Of course, Forster gives the tale a grim finale. Lionel commits suicide after murdering the boy, and there is a terrific scandal. The paradox of love between an English officer and an Indian boy is unresolvable in any literary way except in tragedy.[45]

IV

In real life it could not have been more different. Searight manipulated the imperial situation, spectacularly securing his own personal gratification, and as far as one can tell doing no harm to anyone. It is, however, tantalisingly difficult to say what his attitude actually was towards the empire, or indeed India's place in it. The idea that 'homosexuals' might have been an unassimilable counter-force to the imperial project, might have had a subversive empathy with 'otherness', is not easy to prove in general. And there is no evidence here that Searight forged a counter-allegiance or became a critic of the Raj in the way that Forster did, or that he was either deliberately or unwittingly 'subverting imperialism', or the cult of hyper-masculinity said to have been necessary to maintain it.[46] Although Searight does seem to have acquired a respect for Asian cultures, which is reflected in his artificial language, he appears simply to have been a good army officer who just happened to like sex with boys.

When first posted to India, he went most reluctantly, and even returned again regretfully after six months' leave, despite knowing the pleasures that awaited him. India itself he described as 'the amorous realms of Hindustan', 'this lascivious Eastern region'. To some extent he subscribed to the stereotypes:[47] the 'soft, effeminate Bengali', 'that much-despised race', and, typically, he preferred the martial races, the fierce but homoerotically inclined Pathan, this 'fascinating Breed . . . of young savages', who performed their sexual roles in highly energetic fashion. He gives little away about how he actually met these boys. One was the son of his *chowkidar* (caretaker/night watchman); most of them probably offered themselves on the street – after all, for an Indian young-ster, considerable fascination might attach to a friendly European.[48] He is equally reticent about inducements he may have offered. It is likely that he sometimes provided 'a night's carouse' (mentioned once, for Hindu boys), but he records no cash payments.[49]

Searight's manuscript gives the merest glimpse of Calcutta's 'teeming long bazaars', and of the North-West Frontier camping-grounds, 'where my tent/Stood silent in the moonlight & where paced/The sentry on his rounds'. The hill-station of Simla is more affectionately etched. From his hotel there:

The windows of my room looked out over the mist obscured Himalayas. Nothing intervened, between them and myself but the grey mist and the ocean of heavy rain clouds through an occasional rift in which one caught a rare vision of black, towering hills covered with sombre pine woods . . . I would stand gazing through the clouds of driving rain – rain that for six months scarcely stops, the fresh scent of it in my nostrils – revelling in the sense of solitude, in the wild beauty of the misty hills.

Simla, however, was for him a place of 'vast proprieties', all unaware that 'in her highly proper brass-hatted domains stalked the dreaded spectre of Sodomy', unaware of the debaucheries among the English schoolboys of her 'most moral, Bishop-shepherded School', Christ Church. In the novella 'Simla' we almost enter into the social life of the Raj. There are amateur theatricals ('Where the rainbow ends' and 'The Pied Piper'), and there are newfangled amenities like a 'cinematograph' and a scout troop. There are regimental guest-nights, sports days, and fancy-dress balls.

Of his duties as a soldier there is almost complete silence; just one mention of learning an indigenous language – which in fact opened up a sexual opportunity; another of guard-duty at Peshawar Fort – which appears not to have interfered with his programme of evening sexual entertainment. Physical descriptions of individual boys apart – such as the one with 'mystic eyes, big as a young gazelle's' – little can be discerned of what he thought of Indians *en masse*. Although he admired buttocks of handsome bronze, he preferred the 'pale and amber coloured Indian complexion' to darker skins. Politically, a single reference to 'that endless contest/Twixt English pride and native insolence' seems fairly objective; many Indians he believed were 'Anglophobes'. The nearest he comes in the entire manuscript to a subversive comment is perhaps in the story 'Kid' about a London rent-boy, but even there it is so casually slipped in that it would be easy to miss. The men who ran the boy-brothel are called 'Thesiger' and 'Isaacs': which we can interpret as a snide dig at J.N. Thesiger, who as Lord Chelmsford was viceroy of India, 1916–21 (well known for the Montagu–Chelmsford reforms), and at R.D. Isaacs, who as Lord Reading, followed Chelmsford as viceroy, 1921–6.[50]

To sum up: Captain Searight's manuscript provides a unique insight into the mind-set of a boy-lover unashamedly practising the intergenerational sexuality of Greek love in an imperial setting. Some of it is explicit and authentic documentary record. If the stories which make up the rest of it do not relive actual experiences, they nevertheless embody fragmentarily some real episodes and are true representations of the mental world of a hypersexual personality, a statement of pederastic fantasies and imaginings of a particularly comprehensive kind, probably never equalled.

That the overall context is the Indian Raj in the heyday of British rule adds enormously to the interest and significance of the manuscript, providing a fascinating glimpse into a forbidden sexual world otherwise hidden from us, all the more genuine for Searight's obvious and fundamental preference for white partners. Nevertheless, as a fastidiously class-conscious, career-minded, and studiously intelligent army officer, he did not pursue the possibility of sex with young English boys. Indian boys thus seem to have been essentially substitutes and surrogates. *Laundebaazi* mainly provided him with physical excitement rather than emotional consummation – and this in spite of the fact that he was undoubtedly fond of some Indian youngsters. The way in which India – indeed, the empire as a whole – functioned as a safety-valve for the satisfaction of prohibited sexual desires is thus graphically illustrated. It is an ironic paradox that the service of the empire made it possible to circumvent some of its basic values.[51]

One other characteristic of Searight's imaginative writings stands out, and it is not unconnected. Unlike Forster, he wrote no stories about an inter-racial sexual relationship. What does this unexpected gap mean? Perhaps sheer satiety has something to do with it. In 1912, even though it was eaten into by the period of his overseas long leave, he had 144 orgasmic sessions with Indian boys. In a more typical year, 1915, he had almost 200 such sessions. These figures suggest an astonishing expenditure of energy in acting out an obsessive commitment, pursued, one would have thought, to a point of extinction. It was a life-style reflecting, if nothing else, the huge amounts of spare time available during army service in India, not excluding wartime.

For some eight or nine years, and perhaps even longer if we can add in his later time in Iraq and Egypt, Searight indulged continuously in activities of a highly suspect nature, and as far as we know, 'got away with it'. This is indeed remarkable. For as one historian has reminded us, an officer who merely spoke to his men about sexual transgression was cashiered in 1916.[52] Clearly Searight could rely on the complicity and loyalty of his partners, both Indian and European, and no complaints were lodged. His inter-generational relationships were entirely outside the institutional frameworks, and they were almost by definition therefore non-coercive, since he had no official responsibility for or control over Indian boys. To some that will seem an irrelevance, and no excuse. But it is perhaps worth asking whether any teenagers would present themselves, as some of Searight's young friends did, for

96, 73, 58, 54, 36, or even 18 orgasmic sessions, unless they enjoyed themselves. Moreover, Searight must have been extremely careful not to draw attention to himself. Richard Aldrich puts the essential point well: 'Nothing suggests that Searight encountered difficulties in his military life because of his sexual nature and prolific activities. For a man of discretion, even with a great appetite, often for young boys, ample sexual opportunities presented themselves in India and other places in Europe and overseas.'[53]

Paul Scott's 'Raj Quartet' encapsulates an orthodoxy when Count Bronowsky reflects the fears of all in authority in British India when he advances his theory that Captain Ronald Merrick's search for fulfilment through young Indian boys threatened the entire edifice of racial separation on which the empire depended.[54] The case of Captain Searight suggests that we may have to think again. Neither Ken and his kind, nor the rulers of empire, seem to have had too much to worry about on account of inter-racial 'homosexuality' discreetly practised.[55]

Notes

1 A.L. Stoler, *Race and the education of desire: Foucault's 'History of sexuality' and the colonial order of things* (Durham, NC, 1995), pp. 180–1.
2 T. Raychaudhuri, 'Love in a colonial climate: marriage, sex and romance in nineteenth-century Bengal', *Modern Asian Studies*, vol. 34 (2000), pp. 349–78, esp. p. 365. E.M. Collingham, *Imperial bodies: the physical experience of the Raj, c.1800–1914* (Cambridge, 2001) has little on sex and nothing on homosexuality.
3 Nancy L. Paxton, *Writing under the Raj: gender, race and rape in the British colonial imagination* (New Brunswick, NJ, 1999), p. 294.
4 R. Aldrich, 'Burton, Sir Richard (Francis)', in R. Aldrich and G. Wotherspoon, eds., *Who's who in gay and lesbian history*, vol. I, *From antiquity to World War II* (New York and London, 2001), p. 74; F.M. Brodie, *The devil drives: a life of Sir Richard Burton* (1967, 1971), pp. 76–7. Lawrence James, *Raj: the making and unmaking of British India* (1997, 1998), pp. 213–14 discusses the case of Lt-Col. Edward Smythe of the 5th Madras Cavalry, and allegations of sodomy with his men, c.1830. See also S. Sneade Brown, *Home letters from India, 1828–1841* (1878), p. 76 (8 November 1831).
5 R. Aldrich, 'Macdonald, Sir Hector Archibald', in Aldrich and Wotherspoon, eds., *Who's who in gay and lesbian history*, vol. I, pp. 284–5; RH, *Empire and sexuality: the British experience* (Manchester, 1990, 1991, 1998), pp. 32–5.
6 India Office Records, Mss Eur F/84/15, Elgin Viceroyalty Papers, Lord Elgin to Secretary of State Lord George Hamilton, 10 May 1897. For the general background, see K. Ballhatchet, *Race, sex and class under the Raj: imperial attitudes and policies and their critics, 1793–1905* (1980).
7 D.M. Peers, 'Privates off parade: regimenting sexualities in the nineteenth-century Indian empire', *International History Review*, vol. 20 (1998), pp.

823–54; P. Stanley, *The White Mutiny: British military culture in India* (New York, 1998).

8 John Masters, *Bugles and a tiger* (1956), pp. 153–4. Much of the novel-writing is rather limited too, suggesting that most homosexual experience for British men took place in princely courts: see J.R. Ackerley, *Hindoo holiday* (1932) at 'Chhokrapur', E.M. Forster at Chattapur, or Paul Scott's 'Count Bronowski' at 'Mirat' in the 'Raj Quartet' – see R.J. Moore, *Paul Scott's Raj* (1990), pp. 143–4.

9 Havelock Ellis, *Studies in the psychology of sex*, vol. III, *Analysis of the sexual impulse* (Philadelphia, 1903, 1922), appendix B, history no. XIII, pp. 306–15.

10 I was invited to examine the original manuscript in the early 1970s, when it was in the hands of a London antiquarian bookseller, before it was sold to a private collector; authorship had been established and a full bibliographical analysis made by Toby Hammond for the short-lived *International Journal of Greek Love* (Oliver Layton Press, New York, 1966), vol.1, no. 2, pp. 28–37 ('Paidikion'). The details of Searight's life and movements as they emerge in the manuscript can be validated by internal corroboration between the 'Autobiography' and the 'Paidiology' listings, and externally cross-checked against *The Charterhouse register, 1872–1900* (ed. R.B. Stedman, Godalming, 1904), p. 475; *The Army List, The Half-Yearly Army List,* and *The Indian Army List, passim,* and C.T. Atkinson, *The Queen's Own Royal West Kent Regiment, 1914–1919* (1924). A copy of his death certificate, dated 4 March 1957, is available from the General Register Office, sub-district of Folkestone, Kent.

11 Searight first entered mainstream historiography in my book *Britain's imperial century, 1815–1914: a study of empire and expansion* (1st edn, 1976), where there is a short paragraph and a quotation (pp. 136–7). Next, I wrote a more extended account in *Empire and sexuality* (pp. 128–31). Since then, Lawrence James referred to Searight (unfortunately calling him 'Seabright') in *Raj: the making and unmaking of British India*, p. 508. He also appears in Niall Ferguson's popular work *Empire: how Britain made the modern world* (2003), p. 264. Meanwhile Richard Aldrich published a sub-section on 'Captain Searight and his friends' in *Colonialism and homosexuality* (2003), and there are multiple references to Searight in this book (pp. 279–81, 299, 310, 324–5). Searight's 'epic verse autobiography' is mentioned in Graham Robb, *Strangers: homosexual love in the 19th century* (2003), p. 172, implying that it was written by a 'sex maniac with a passion for accounting'.

12 Ardent admiration and openly accepted love for teenage boys was unquestionably a core value in ancient Greece – amounting to the prominent 'centre-piece of its public identity' – but the nature and extent of its sexual expression was complicated, and remains difficult to recover historically: see James Davidson, *The Greeks and Greek love: a radical reappraisal of homosexuality in ancient Greece* (2007), from which this quotation is taken (p. 365), and D.M. Halperin, *One hundred years of homosexuality, and other essays on Greek love* (New York, 1990). But it is clear that the ancient Greeks were not 'paedophiles' in the modern sense: to quote a leading criminologist, 'hebephilia is not the same as child molestation' (D.J. West, *Male prostitution* (1992), p. 328).

13 It is a curious coincidence that in the half-dozen years before the outbreak of war in 1914, when Searight was working on his autobiographical poem, a number of more famous authors were also engaged in writing literary explorations of homosexual desire, stories, poems, and seminal justifications of Greek love, which have become canonical in the genre. Most famous of all was Thomas Mann's *Death in Venice* (*Der Tod in Venedig*), written in 1911. In France, André Gide was slowly preparing the text of *Corydon*, which first appeared in an unsigned private edition in 1911. It is a scholarly argument, in four dialogues, a defence of Greek love. Whilst living in Venice in 1909 and 1910, Frederick Rolfe (Baron Corvo) was writing *The desire and pursuit of the whole*, a full-length novel about the sixteen-year-old androgynous Zildo, together with some more explicit and revelatory letters later published as *The Venice Letters*. In Britain, an underground, full-bloodied homoerotic classic, a school-story with a difference, *Memoirs of a voluptuary*, was published anonymously, probably about 1908. (The dating to some extent is determined by two characters called 'Elgar' and 'Benson', a dig at 'Land of hope and glory', so not earlier than 1902.) Also in 1908, one of the 'Uranians', the Revd E.E. Bradford, brought out *Sonnets, songs and ballads*, the first of a series of volumes of slushy poetry in praise of boyhood. And of course, E.M. Forster began writing *Maurice* in 1913.

14 Louis Crompton, *Homosexuality and civilisation* (Cambridge, MA, 2003) tried to make this linkage between past and present sexual modes of 'homosexuality', but the whole thrust of most of the evidence in his book serves only to disprove such tendentiousness. For understanding similar sexual modes in the Arab and Asian worlds, the key works include: Tsuneo Watunabe and Jun'ichi Iwata, *The love of the samuri: a thousand years of Japanese homosexuality* (tr. D.R. Roberts, 1989); Bret Hinsch, *Passions of the cut sleeve: the male homosexual tradition in China* (Berkeley, CA, 1990); Walter G. Andrews and Mehmet Kalpakli, *The age of the beloveds: love and the beloved in early modern Ottoman and European culture and society* (Durham, NC, 2005). See also Adrian Carton, 'Desire and same-sex intimacies in Asia', and Vincenzo Patanè, 'Homosexuality in the Middle East and North Africa', in R. Aldrich, ed., *Gay life and culture: a world history* (2006), pp. 271–331.

15 Dominique Fernandez, *A hidden love: art and homosexuality* (Munich, Berlin, London, and New York, 2002, from the original French, 2001) is the master-work; see esp. pp. 157–81 on 'The Far East'.

16 R. Jenkyns, *The Victorians and ancient Greece* (Blackwell, Oxford, 1980); A. Hickson, *The poisoned bowl: sex, repression and the public school system* (1995); J.R. de Honey, *Tom Brown's universe: the development of the Victorian public school* (1977).

17 F. Yeats-Brown, *Bengal Lancer* (1930), p. 13 for observations on the Edwardian Punjab; Philippa Levine, *Prostitution, race and politics: policing venereal disease in the British empire* (New York, 2003), p. 294, and p. 353, n. 205. See also, for a more anthropological angle, L. Dupree, *Afghanistan* (Princeton, NJ, 1993), p. 198. David Omissi, *The sepoy and the Raj: the Indian army, 1860–1940* (1994), records the case of a Pathan soldier stationed in the

UK at Milford-on-Sea who had 'a beautiful white boy' as his mess-mate (pp. 65–6).

18 Santanu Das, review of Brinda Bose and Subhabrata Bhattacharyya, eds., *The phobic and the erotic: the politics of sexualities in contemporary India*, in the *Times Literary Supplement* (15 June 2007), no. 5437, p. 33, where the point is made that Western labels are misleading, because 'thousands of Indian men' have sex with other males without any notion of Western sexual identity as 'homosexual' or 'gay'.

19 Ruth Vanita and Saleem Kidwai, eds., *Same-sex love in India: readings from literature and history* (New York, 2000), esp. pp. 27, 46–8, 119–21, 175–83; R.M. George, I. Chatterjee, G. Gopinath, 'Tracing "same-sex" love from antiquity to the present in South Asia', *Gender and History*, vol. 14 (2002), pp. 6–30.

20 Ruth Vanita, ed., *Queering India: same-sex love and eroticism in Indian culture and society* (New York, 2002), pp. 129–34; Charu Gupta, 'Impossible love and sexual pleasure in late-colonial north India', *Modern Asian Studies*, vol. 36 (2002), pp. 195–221, esp. pp. 197–202.

21 This was C.E. Tyndale-Biscoe (1863–1949): see J.A. Mangan, *The games ethic and imperialism: aspects of the diffusion of an ideal* (1986), pp. 180–1.

22 S.H. and L.I. Rudolph, eds., *Reversing the gaze: Amar Singh's diary: a colonial subject's narrative of imperial India* (Boulder, CO, 2002), esp. pp. 239–54, 278–9, 336–7.

23 Vanita and Kidwai, eds., *Same-sex love in India*, pp. 255–6. See also Suparna Bhaskaran, 'The politics of penetration', in Vanita, ed., *Queering India*, p. 17: an advice column in a Bengali weekly, *Sanjibani* (1893), suggested Indian schoolboys indulging in 'unnatural and immoral habits' could be cured by visits to prostitutes.

24 G. Tillett, *The elder brother: a biography of Charles Webster Leadbeater, 1854–1934* (1982); A.H. Nethercot, *The last four lives of Annie Besant* (1963), chs. 7 and 8; G. Wotherspoon, 'Leadbeater, C.W.' in *Who's who in gay and lesbian history*, vol. I, p. 254; Anne Taylor, 'Besant, Annie', in the *ODNB*, vol. V, pp. 504–7. Aged sixty-eight, Leadbeater was embroiled in a major scandal in Sydney, publicised all over Australia; once again the charges were dismissed, his young friends denying any impropriety: in the immortal words of Mandy Rice-Davies, 'they would say that, wouldn't they?'

25 J. Geraci, ed., *Dares to speak: historical and contemporary perspectives on boy-love* (Swaffham, Norfolk, 1997), pp. 148–63, 'The journals of Lewis Thompson'; Richard Lannoy, ed., *Lewis Thompson, mirror to the light: reflections on consciousness and experience* (1984), esp. pp. 51–2, 99, 152–3.

26 Richard Aldrich in his major study *Colonialism and homosexuality* casts the net wider than British India; see the review by Ross G. Forman in *Victorian Studies*, vol. 47 (2005), pp. 293–5 for an assessment of its importance. Other names could be added to the Indian list, such as A.F. Scholfield, an almost exact contemporary of Searight's (1884–1969), who was Keeper of the Records of the Government of India, 1913–19, and subsequently Librarian of Trinity College, Cambridge, and University Librarian, 1923–49. Scholfield is believed to have had a large collection of photographs of Indian boys, and

as a Fellow of King's College was remembered 'for his immense kindness to generations of boy-choristers': see *King's College Annual Report* (1970), and Noel Annan, *Our age: portrait of a generation* (1990), p. 102; *Who was who*, vol. VI (1961–70), p. 1009.

27 B.S. Cohn, *An anthropologist among the historians and other essays* (Delhi, 1990), esp. 'The census, social structure and objectification in South Asia', pp. 224–54.

28 For the sexual underground of Edwardian London, Searight's manuscript provides several indications; for recently published studies, see Matt Cook, *London and the culture of homosexuality, 1885–1914* (Cambridge, 2003); M. Houlbrook, 'Soldier-heroes and rent-boys: homosexualities, masculinities and Britishness in the Brigade of Guards, *c.*1900–1960', *Journal of British Studies*, vol. 47 (2003), pp. 351–88.

29 One of Searight's most polished short stories is 'Nel bagno, a Neapolitan tale', possibly based on a sexual experience in a bath-house which he either had himself or heard about from someone else. It is a well-focused piece, written with gusto, but it is not for the faint-hearted. For the significance of Italy and Sicily to British homosexuals, see Richard Aldrich, *The seduction of the Mediterranean: writing, art and homosexual fantasy* (1993); Mark Holloway, *Norman Douglas: a biography* (1976); among the novels, Roger Peyrefitte, *The exile of Capri* (1959, tr. 1961).

30 'Kanaya', 1922, first published in E. Heine, ed., *The hill of Devi, and other Indian writings by E.M. Forster* (1982 edn); see also E.M. Forster, *Indian journals and essays* (1983), pp. 194–208.

31 The choice of the name Eric may be a satirical swipe at the romantically agonised but chaste atmosphere of Dean F.W. Farrar's well-known school story, *Eric, or Little by little* (1858). In the book – which is dedicated to the bishop of Calcutta – Eric's parents were serving in India.

32 Matt Houlbrook, *Queer London: perils and pleasures in the sexual metropolis, 1918–1957* (Chicago, IL, 2005), pp. 182–6, 232–6. For an interesting examination of the 'cultural shift' in New York City from the 1920s, with an unprecedented new concern for boys, instead of the 'limited recognition of sexual dangers posed to boys', see Stephen Robertson, '"Boys, of course, cannot be raped": age, homosexuality and the redefinition of sexual violence in New York City, 1880–1955', *Gender and History*, vol. 18 (2006), pp. 357–79.

33 Guy Edmund Wheeler, writing as 'Edmund Fahey', 'The pathography of a cuckoo', part 1, 'An imperial bastard': memoirs, [n.d.], deposited at the Royal Commonwealth Society Library (Cambridge University Library) in 1993; typescript, 111 pp. I am grateful to Vyvyen Brendon for drawing my attention to this source; she later referred to Wheeler in her book *Children of the Raj* (2005), pp. 166–9, 176, 275, though she does not discuss his seduction. An epigraph to the typescript quotes my article on 'Empire and sexual opportunity' (*JICH*, 1986: see above, ch. 13) about empire as a 'matter of copulation and concubinage', p. 35; it is good to know that people are now more willing to reveal their sexual experiences for posterity.

34 Ignorance should have been dispelled by the epoch-making publication of

Alfred Kinsey's *Sexual behavior in the human male* (New York, 1949) – for example, pp. 175–80 on juvenile multiple orgasm. For an example of censorious misunderstanding of human sexual potentialities, see Steven Marcus, *The other Victorians: a study of sexuality and pornography in nineteenth-century England* (1964, reissued in 2008 as a 'classic'). The most scholarly guide to the literature is P.J. Kearney, *The Private Case: an annotated bibliography of the Private Case erotica in the British (Museum) Library* (1981). It seems probable that Searight's 'Paidikion' manuscript is the best and most significant evocation of Greek love since *L'Alcibiade fanciullo a scola* (1652): for which see P.-J. Salazar, 'Rocco, Antonio', in *Who's who in gay and lesbian history*, vol. I, pp. 373–5.

35 Kenneth Searight, *Sona: an auxiliary neutral language* (Kegan Paul, Trench, & Trubner, London, 1935), 119 pp.

36 See http://sonauiki.org/Main/SonaUiki. My thanks to Andrew Ward for locating this website.

37 D. Proctor, ed., *The autobiography of Lowes Dickinson* (1977), pp. 178–9; see also P.M. Furbank, *E.M. Forster: a life*, vol. I, *1879–1914* (1978), pp. 224, 231–3.

38 Aldrich, *Colonialism and homosexuality*, p. 311, quoting from the Forster Papers in King's College Library, Forster to Dickinson, June–August 1917.

39 *Autobiography of Lowes Dickinson*, p. 179.

40 E.M. Forster, *Maurice: a novel* ('finished 1914', later revised, and posthumously published), 1971 edn, 'terminal note', pp. 235–41, and introduction by P.M. Furbank, pp. v–vi; see also O. Stallybrass, introduction to the Abinger Edition of *A passage to India* (1978), p. xi.

41 See http://sonauiki.org/Main/KennethSearight.

42 Aldrich, *Colonialism and homosexuality*, pp. 324–5. For 'The other boat', see E.M. Forster, *The life to come and other stories* (Abinger edn, vol. VIII, ed. O. Stallybrass, 1972), pp. 65–82. It was intended as the opening for an Indian novel, which did not go well. The title mirrors a metaphor for the empire as 'the view from the boat'.

43 Aldrich, *Colonialism and homosexuality*, p. 325.

44 Stallybrass, introduction to *The life to come and other stories*, p. xvii.

45 An interesting contrast with the idyllic pastoral ending of the cross-class affair in *Maurice*.

46 Grant Parsons, 'Another India: imagining escape from the masculine self', in P. Darby, ed., *At the edge of international relations: post-colonialism, gender, and dependency* (New York, 1997), p. 172: sceptical of the argument in Christopher Lane, *The ruling passion: British colonial allegory and the narrative of homosexual desire* (Durham, NC, 1995), pp. 2–4.

47 M. Sinha, *Colonial masculinity* (1995), and 'Giving masculinity a history: some contributions from the history of India', *Gender and History*, vol. 11 (1999), pp. 445–60.

48 Levine, *Prostitution, race and politics*, pp. 292–4: the inspector-general of police in Colombo reported (1917) 'on any night there may be seen in public places a number of boys from 14 to 18 years of age . . . waiting to be spoken to'. For street-solicitation in newly independent Pakistan, see Michael

Davidson, *The world, the flesh and myself* (1962), pp. 244–5, and *Some boys* (unexpurgated New York edn, 1971), pp. 33–49.

49 Except one payment to a London rent-boy: a sovereign. (This was generous by the contemporary standards of a regular patron like Roger Casement, who seems not to have paid more than ten shillings, and sometimes less: P. Singleton-Gates and M. Girodias, eds., *The Black Diaries: an account of Roger Casement's life and times* (Paris, 1959), entry for 24 June 1910.) In 'Simla', Ken rewards the boys with beer and Chianti.

50 F.J.N. Thesiger (1868–1933) served in the Indian army (1914–16), while R.D. Isaacs was made Lord Chief Justice in 1913 and vilified on appointment, by Kipling among others, after his suspicious share-dealing in the Marconi scandal of 1912. Reference to these two figures may or may not suggest a date after 1917 for completion of the manuscript.

51 Aldrich, *Colonialism and homosexuality*, p. 325.

52 Lawrence James, *Raj*, p. 508, quoting War Office records, WO 92/3, no. 6d.

53 Aldrich, *Colonialism and homosexuality*, p. 281.

54 Moore, *Paul Scott's Raj*, pp. 143–4.

55 On the issue of 'exploitation', I suggested in the Introduction (p. 46), that readers would make up their own mind. However, I would draw attention to a review by Andrew Williams of Antony Copley's book, *A spiritual Bloomsbury: Hinduism and homosexuality in the writings of Edward Carpenter, E.M. Forster and Christopher Isherwood* (Lanham, Boulder, and New York, 2006), in *Round Table*, vol. 97, no. 399 (2008), pp. 891–2. Williams concluded from this study that accusations of 'exploitative behaviour' are 'crass and uninformed'; that such men can be regarded as having rejected class-bound attitudes, thus becoming pioneers of a cultural interaction which led to the development of a more cosmopolitan and open-minded Britain, which the Commonwealth now celebrates.

Appendix

Plate 16.1 The opening of Searight's autobiographical poem. The picture is an original water-colour, pasted in – possibly of Searight himself as a boy?

332   THE FURNACE   82

The passage lubricates with his spittle
He thrust his rampant member in a little,
Slowly, caressingly as though he tried
1600 To thus prolong the pleasure; my inside
Yearned with insatiable desire the while
To feel his semen mingle with my bile...
I raised my buttocks & my fingers seized
The hesitating ravisher and squeezed
His swelling testicles & thus persuaded
The young Pathan immediately invaded
My palpitating orifice & lunged.
Straight to the hilt where in and out he plunged
With ever quickening velocity!
1610 I groaned: the boy's untamed ferocity,
So different to the young Bengali's love,
Filled me with anguish till each savage shove
Seemed splitting me in twain; and then at last
In exquite sensations anguish passed.
To mad enjoyment as the boy had sunk
And filled my entrails with his burning spunk.

Plate 16.2 Sex with Serbiland (from the autobiographical poem).

THE THIRTY THREE JOYS OF PAIDERASTY   3

AND THEIR SYMBOLS

Breast ° • , Penis b , Anus O . Mouth 7 , Pubic hair S , Stomach C , Semen ꝺ , Faeces 0
Urine w , Thighs ∧ , Autoerotic sign I , Active sign ‾ , Passive sign __ , Flagellation ∼

#	Symbol	Onanism	#	Symbol	
1	ı	Auto-masturbation	17	ē	Active sodomy
2	·H	Mutual masturbation	18	☺	Passive sodomy
3	ⱶ	Masturbation	19	∧	Intercrural coitus
4	◦ʲ◦	Breast masturbation	20	bd	Intergenital friction
5	∧	Thigh masturbation	21	°ʲ°	Pectoral coitus
6	⊕	Anal masturbation	22	∩	Armpit coitus
7	⅀	Fellattio	23	bc	Interventral friction
8	<7	Mutual fellattio	24	SS	Pubic friction
9	↓	Auto-fellattio	25	⸈	Pubic fellattio
10	⊙	Anilinctus	26	⊥	Auto-flagellation
11	⊚	Mutual anilinctus	27	=	Mutual flagellation
12	•ʲ•	Breast sucking	28	∼	Flagellation
13	①	Anal onanism	29	ſ	Feeling
14	♂	Spermolagnia	30	3̄	Superemination
15	♀	Coprolagnia	31	ō	Superfaecation
16	⩊	Urolagnia	32	w̄	Micturation

33 I ⚥ I Spatolagnia , Mucelagnia

Plate 16.3 Paidiology code.

PAIDIOLOGY						535
No	Age	Place	Date	Name	Race	Reference
101	17	Chaklala	1916	Azam Khan	Path.	Λ.ō.ọ.ⱡ.bd	
102	13	Chaklala	1917	Dilbar	Path.	Λ.ō.ọ.H.ⱡ.♛	33
103	9	Bangalore	1917	Hanuman	Madras	ſ	⸗
104	16	Bangalore	1917	Ghulam Haidar	Mosl.	Λ.ō.ọ.H.ⱡ.⊙.	11
105	15	Bangalore	1917	Majid.	Mosl.	bd	2
106	16	Bangalore	1917		Mosl.	bd.Λ	1
107	16	Bangalore	1917	Sirdar Khan	Mosl.	bd	3
108	16	Bangalore	1917	Abdul Razak	Mosl.	ō.ⱡ	15
109	15	Bangalore	1917	Amir	Mosl.	ō.ⱡ.bd.Λ	2
110	8	Bangalore	1917	Ramsawmy	Tamil	Λ.bd	2
111	14	Bangalore	1917	Abdur Rahim	Mosl.	ſ.f.	c
112	14	Bangalore	1917	Said Wahab	Mosl.	ō.¡	1
113	17	Bangalore	1917	Shah Sham	Mosl.	ō.bd.Λ	1
114	23	Bangalore	1917	P..	Eng.	ⱡ.⊙.Λ	1
115	16	Bangalore	1917	Vishnanaikhu	Brahmin	Λ.♛.mv.bd.ō.	12
116	16	Bangalore	1917	Ranga Nathrao	Brahmin	Λ.ⱡ.⊙.ō.ọ.w	3
117	10	Bangalore	1917	Satya	Hindu	Λ	1
118	16	Bangalore	1917	Ramrá	Hindu	Λ.bd.f	7
119	15	Bangalore	1917	Krishna	Hindu	ō	1
120	16	Bangalore	1917	Piru	Moslem	bd	1
	303 (15.2)		1528 (15.2)		(12.3) 1480 (4.3)	99

Plate 16.4 Part of the Paidiology listing for 1917.

Part VI

Imperial historians

17 Imperial and Commonwealth history at Cambridge, 1881–1981: founding fathers and pioneer research students

[First published in the *Journal of Imperial and Commonwealth History*, vol. 29 (2001), an essay for which Professor Sir Christopher Bayly, Professor John Lonsdale, and Dr Doug Munro provided valuable insights. Now revised and updated.

Professor Tony Hopkins first suggested this subject for investigation, after hearing me outline an oral history of it as part of my valedictory talk to the Cambridge Commonwealth Seminar in October 1999. At about the same time, the appearance of the admirable essay by Professor Sir Andrew Roberts in the *Oxford history of the British empire*, vol. V, *Historiography* ('The British Empire in tropical Africa: a review of the literature to the 1960s', 1999) provided further stimulus, not least because of its emphasis on Oxford and London, with comparatively little on Cambridge's contribution.]

Almost exactly a century separates the publication of two of Cambridge's most celebrated contributions to imperial history: Seeley's *Expansion of England* (1883) and Gallagher's Ford Lectures, *Decline, revival and fall of the British empire* (1982), published two years after his premature death. The early 1980s marked the end of an era in other ways too, as imperial and Commonwealth history itself everywhere became fragmented, unfashionable, and increasingly embattled. The old conceptual unities as they had been worked out in the previous half-century now collapsed, particularly under the pressure of the inexorable advance of area studies.[1] Although framed by this chronology, the purpose of this investigation into a potentially rich historiographical landscape is not to memorialise or assess the writings of the famous professorial names – Robinson and Gallagher, Mansergh and Stokes – but to contextualise them and focus upon lesser known but nevertheless significant ancestors, and to trace developing patterns of teaching and research down to 1981. In any case, the earlier occupants of the Vere Harmsworth chair of imperial and naval history (established in 1919), interesting characters though they were, had little real impact on the work of the Cambridge History Faculty, not least because it lacked a proper examination paper

473

in the subject until 1945. J.Holland Rose (1919–33) was mainly interested in William Pitt and Napoleon, but made some study of sea-power in British history.[2] Admiral Sir Herbert Richmond (1933–5) was exclusively a naval historian, and had to retire after only two years in office.[3] Eric Walker was a South African specialist whose tenure (1936–51) was badly affected by the war and a severe nervous breakdown from which he never fully recovered.[4]

I

Extra-European history in Cambridge was slow to get off the ground. In 1866 the University rejected the offer from a benefactor to endow a lectureship in the history and institutions of the United States.[5] Moreover, the study of imperial and American history began, not in the History Faculty, but in the Faculty of Economics and Politics. When the Historical Tripos was inaugurated in 1873, the emphasis was heavily on English constitutional and economic history, together with a great deal of 'political philosophy'. In fact the Regius professor of modern history, J.R. Seeley (1869–95), would have preferred to call it the Politics Tripos, wanting to 'turn away from the past to the present': 'Our university is, and must be, a great seminary of politicians.' Nobody thought it possible or desirable to cover recent history or to extend the geographical range even to Scotland and Wales.[6] Seeley lectured on a varying set of topics, including 'political science' and 'international history and English foreign policy', chiefly in the eighteenth century, 'the age of Frederick the Great', the wars of the Spanish Succession and Louis XIV, and Napoleon. Only in one academical year, 1881–2, did he turn to the empire, giving a course of sixteen lectures with the title 'Greater Britain'. The published version, *The Expansion of England*, was a famous and influential book, but hardly representative of Seeley's main interests or of student studies in Cambridge. Nevertheless, it was an inspired and intelligent foray, and, as the first professional historian to tackle the subject, he was historiographically a pioneer.[7]

From the perspective of the Cambridge curriculum, a more influential figure was Professor Alfred Marshall, the founding father of the Economics Tripos in 1903, and a passionate believer in the importance both of extra-European history and of recent history as 'absolutely essential to the economist'. He could see no hope of the Historical Tripos catering for them, and so he established in Part I Economics two compulsory papers on 'recent economic and general history'. One dealt mainly with Britain (not just England) in the nineteenth century, and the other chiefly with the British empire and the United States. In Part

II he provided for a special subject dealing with the 'recent and general history' or the existing political and administrative organisation of a foreign country, or India, or 'some other dependency or colony of the United Kingdom'.[8]

Marshall was a professorial Fellow of St John's College, where one of his protégés was E.A. Benians, the first Johnian entrance Scholar in history (1898). Benians, who had been educated by his parents, gained a double first (1901, 1902), won the Adam Smith prize for economic history, and wrote a substantial fellowship dissertation on 'The progress of settlement in Canada'.[9] Marshall recruited him in 1906 to lecture on the 'recent economic and general history' of the British empire and the United States.[10] Benians continued to give these lectures until 1931, when the Economics Tripos was reformed, and, to his dismay, the compulsory Part I paper was given a narrower focus and transferred into Part II as one option among many. Meanwhile Benians had become a Fellow of St John's (1906), a college lecturer in history (1910), and senior tutor (1926). In 1926 under the new system of university lectureships, he became a lecturer in the History Faculty, where he taught early modern Europe until he resigned in 1934, after election as Master of St John's (1933), a post which he held until his death in 1952. He was vice-chancellor between 1939 and 1941, in which year he was chosen to be chairman of the Advisory Historical Committee to the War Cabinet.

Although mostly a forgotten figure today, Benians played the central role in the development of imperial and American history in Cambridge for almost the whole of the first half of the twentieth century. He intermitted his fellowship in 1911–12 in order to travel the world. He either supervised or examined almost every doctoral candidate in imperial subjects. The mastership of St John's more or less put an end to his published output as well as his lecturing, but he remained dedicated to promoting the study of empire and American history. After their demotion in the Economics Tripos he worked tirelessly to secure a permanent home for them in the Historical Tripos, and was very largely instrumental in the setting up of the American history paper in 1943 and the 'Expansion of Europe' in 1945 (see below). He also masterminded the editing of six of the eight volumes of the *Cambridge history of the British empire*, the principal Cambridge achievement before 1960 in the study of the empire, published between 1929 and 1959. Inevitably there are stodgy chapters, but it also contains some of the finest writing ever achieved within its field: such chapters as those by C.W. de Kiewiet on 'Social and economic developments in Native tribal life' (vol. VIII), J.H. Clapham on 'The Industrial Revolution and the colonies' (vol. II), C.R. Fay on 'The movement towards free trade, 1820–1853' – in which the term 'informal empire' was invented (vol. II, p. 399) – and A.F. Madden on 'Changing attitudes and widening responsibilities, 1895–1914' (vol. III).[11] Benians commissioned several promising young historians, giving them the opportunity to cut their teeth on a major assignment, even if, owing to delays in publication, this was not always apparent. Among them were three future 'knights' of the historical profession, Hancock, Hinsley,[12] and Habakkuk,[13] together with R.E. Robinson, CBE, writing, respectively, on the first years of the Australian Commonwealth (vol. VII), foreign policy (vol. III), free trade and commercial expansion (vol. II), and 'imperial problems in British politics, 1880–1895' (vol. III). (Robinson was somewhat embarrassed by his chapter, as it affronted his later self-image as a thinker rather than a researcher, but in fact by trawling the multi-volumed Victorian political biographies it did well a job that had to be done.) The trouble with the *CHBE* was that its sheer size and scale, and rigorous professionalism, to say nothing of the densely packed typography, have all helped to ensure that it has remained outside the capacity of students and scholars alike fully to absorb. The repeated use of 'our empire' and similar possessives grates upon modern susceptibilities. The confident editorial assertion (vol. II, p. viii) that 'no great empire was ever built with so little show or use of force' does not convince today's more sceptical readership. Nevertheless, the *CHBE* remains a valuable resource, in all its entombing magnificence.[14]

Apart from some early contributions to historical geography, and two little books on the United States (1943 and 1946), Benians's principal writings were for the Cambridge Histories. He contributed a remarkably comprehensive blockbuster of a chapter on 'The European colonies' for the final volume of the *Cambridge modern history* (vol. XII, *The latest age* (1910), pp. 602–71), together with 'Canada, 1763–1847' for volume X (1907). In the *Cambridge history of the British empire* he wrote 'The beginnings of the new empire, 1783–1793' and 'Colonial self-government, 1852–1870' in volume II, and 'The Western Pacific, 1788–1885' in the Australian volume, together with two chapters in volume III, one of them on Victorian commercial policy, a subject he also tackled in the *Cambridge history of British foreign policy*, volume II (ed. A.W. Ward and G.P. Gooch (1923)). The best of these chapters are models of their kind: informative and stylish, and written with real verve.

Like others of his contemporaries, Benians's outlook on the empire and the emerging Commonwealth was conditioned by the fact that his undergraduate days coincided precisely with what we must now learn to call the Anglo-Boer South African War. It is natural for later generations to feel uncomfortable with the admiration of Benians, Eric Walker, and others, not only for the Commonwealth, but also for the Afrikaners, but it has to be remembered that they genuinely felt the Afrikaners had performed formidably well in a devastating war which they should never have had to fight. To Benians, after 'making a shipwreck' of the 'first empire' by the loss of the American colonies, and after the 'tragic scenes' and 'ill-starred events' of the South African War,[15] the way the British had achieved the emergence of the Commonwealth – 'a union of states and nations in a free and peaceful co-operation' – was indeed little short of miraculous, especially considering its heterogeneity of membership and racial and geographical diversity. The Commonwealth, however imperfect and whatever its aggressive origins, was nothing to be ashamed of, but 'a moral conception, a great partnership', whose justification was 'to teach the way of freedom, to teach nations to live together in society'.[16]

It is no doubt a matter for regret that such a gifted historian as Benians also happened to be so admired as a good administrator and committee chairman, and so valued a counsellor, noted for his 'judicious foresight', tact, insight, kindness, and fairness. If the mastership of St John's had not taken precedence over a chair, and monopolised so much of his time, he might have produced books which would have secured his historical reputation.[17] As it is, apart from those sadly neglected 'Cambridge' chapters, Benians is memorialised only in small – but undeniably elegant – ways: briefly in the St John's Benians Fellowship for visiting Commonwealth scholars,[18] permanently in the handsome slate oval tablet in the central place of honour in St John's College Chapel, and in the dedication to Frank Thistlethwaite's seminal book, *The great experiment* (1955).[19] Thistlethwaite was probably Benians's most highly regarded pupil, and he steered him into American history. Thistlethwaite recalled Benians as 'my great mentor . . . He was a great man; his tall, quiet presence masked the immense strength of character which had carried College and University through the War and into an altered post-war world.'

Hardly any British academic of his generation worked harder than Benians to reduce the general ignorance about imperial and American history. He did not of course labour alone. There were other stalwarts of the History Faculty who shared some of his concerns and interests and supported his aims in the 1920s and 1930s. Foremost among them, perhaps, was Harold Temperley, the Peterhouse don who became its Master (1938), and the first professor of modern history (1931). Essentially a foreign policy historian, Temperley had, however, written on 'The new colonial policy, 1840–1870' for the *Cambridge modern history* (vol. XI, 1909) and, most illuminatingly, on 'The Peace of Paris' (Britain's 'colonial moment' if ever there was one) for the *Cambridge*

Plate 17.1 E.A. Benians in 1933.

history of the British empire (vol. I, 1929), while his masterpiece, *The foreign policy of Canning, 1822–1827* (1925), aroused his continuing interest in the Americas.[20] He was the first president of the new Commonwealth Institute (1934), and he supervised some of the earlier imperial research students. Then there was Sir James Butler, Regius professor from 1947 to 1954, who had a lifelong interest in the constitutional aspects of empire history, lecturing upon them fairly regularly from the late 1920s; he was the author of three chapters on imperial questions (1838–80) for the *Cambridge history of the British empire* (vols. II and III).[21] Finally, there was George Kitson Clark, Fellow of Trinity, a bluff, burly, and pompous character who played a major role in the Faculty for several decades and superintended the teaching of modern English constitutional history. He was a particularly useful and active ally in planning the introduction of the papers in American and Expansion history in the mid-1940s. He was also Gallagher's mentor, and later still, Anil Seal's and John Lonsdale's.[22]

II

As every student of it believes, 'The Expansion of Europe' paper – the forerunner of today's 'Empires and world history' – is the jewel in the crown of the Cambridge Historical Tripos. It is also, since the later 1960s, the essential pivot around which all the other extra-European papers spin. It dates, however, only from 1945. It was then thirty-five years since a paper in 'English colonial history' had first been called for in a Senate House discussion. When the Tripos was being reviewed in 1909, Benians complained that a corner in an English constitutional history paper and an occasional 'special period' was 'not an adequate treatment of colonial history'. Moreover, looking merely at a colony's institutions 'isolated from the study of their history seemed to him to be barren'. What would be far more interesting and instructive was the 'story of the growth of nations in new countries'. He received some support from fellow Johnian T.R. Glover, as the ancient historians also had grievances, but even Temperley thought it impossible to accommodate a new paper. Archdeacon Cunningham disapproved of the very idea of these 'modern subjects' in which lazy men could 'browse around'.[23]

The position was radically changed by the Second World War, which made it possible to argue persuasively that ex-servicemen, returning in large numbers, would be looking for wider opportunities to study those non-European countries with which so many of them had come into contact. Academically, the publication of Hancock's masterly *Survey of British Commonwealth affairs, 1918–1939* (2 vols., 1937–42) demonstrated the exciting possibilities of the broader sweep.[24] The general ethos of the Tripos inevitably imposed a somewhat Eurocentric core upon the 'Expansion' paper; nevertheless the imaginativeness of the concept remains striking more than half a century later:

The subject shall include exploration; the relevant missionary, humanitarian and political movements; the development of overseas trade and investment; the reaction of extra-European countries to European influence, including the effects on peasant economy of the opening of international markets and the industrialisation of colonial territories; the foundation of colonial empires, with the general features of the imperial policy of the principal European countries; the problems of native self-government; international relations in the colonial sphere, with the relevant military and naval history.

Or, put more succinctly, it dealt with 'the political, economic and cultural contacts of the principal countries of Europe – including Russia – with the remainder of the world in the period since 1400'.[25] The new paper was made available to start with on an experimental basis, and in both parts of the Tripos, though it was soon confined to Part II for almost twenty years. Examination papers were at first divided regionally, but this was abandoned, leaving only a division into two sections at 1783, with candidates being required to answer at least one question (out of four) from each period. The experiment was an immediate success. According to John Fage, one of its very first takers, it was a bold and pioneering paper, leading the way in British universities. He added, 'scratch many a British historian of Africa or Asia of my generation, and it is likely that you will find a former student of "The Expansion of Europe" at Cambridge'.[26] Perhaps that is pitching it a little high; some of the most devoted practitioners of extra-European history in later years did not in fact study it as Cambridge undergraduates, among them Jack Gallagher, Eric Stokes, Anil Seal, John Iliffe, John Lonsdale, and T.N. Harper.

We have all tended to accept at face value the myth that Robinson and Gallagher 'really created the subject'.[27] Although they certainly exploited its potential to the full, they had no part whatsoever in devising or launching it, or in compiling the first book-lists which defined its scope and character. They were perhaps not always particularly generous in publicly acknowledging their debts to their Cambridge predecessors, such as E.A. Benians or J.W. Davidson. And we must not forget that the new paper represented a major *Faculty* commitment, one which it was determined actively to promote. The Faculty obtained lectureships in Colonial Studies, Latin American and Far Eastern history. E.E. Rich provided the initial outline Expansion lecture course, and continued to do so for many years, to ever declining audiences. Before the war he had lectured on English economic history, and his interest in the empire developed through research on the Hudson's Bay Company and the North American fur trade. Professor E.A. Walker lectured on 'the British empire', and, more surprisingly, on 'Africa'. 'Percy' Spear, as bursar of Selwyn (1945–63), was available to cover Indian history. As an Indianist, Spear's output was highly respected, and he was significant in the historiography as a 'transitional' practitioner between older and newer approaches (not that he would ever discuss issues like Clive's sex life).[28] J.H. Parry, already a university lecturer, Fellow and Tutor of Clare College, provided real backbone to the lectures on the fifteenth and sixteenth centuries, as can be seen in their published version, *Europe and the wider world* (1949; 3rd edn 1966). Parry in fact gave the very first lecture for the Expansion paper, in October 1945. He moved on to a distinguished career elsewhere.[29]

Probably the key figure in inaugurating the paper was James W. Davidson.[30] A New Zealander, Jim Davidson came to St John's College as a graduate student, preparing a doctoral dissertation on 'European penetration of the South Pacific, 1779–1842'. His supervisor was Professor Walker and he was Holland Rose Student, 1940–1. During the war he worked in naval intelligence for the Admiralty (based at the Scott Polar Institute in Cambridge), writing the historical sections of its geographical handbooks on the Pacific. He also worked for Margery Perham's Nuffield project on colonial government, starting a book on the government of Northern Rhodesia. After the war, he was lecturing from the Lent Term 1945, and from January 1947 he became the first holder of the lectureship in colonial studies,[31] for which the only other serious candidate was Victor Kiernan of Trinity (a gifted young Marxist).[32] Davidson proceeded to lecture on 'Europe and the Pacific', 'the government of dependencies', and on the West Indies.

What made Davidson's work so innovative was his attempt to get beyond the conventional study of colonisation and international relations, and make a contribution to the history of European expansion rather than British imperial history, by using social anthropology and by concentrating on analysing the changes in the life of 'native peoples'. The preface to his thesis (PhD 1942) advanced a manifesto which speaks the authentic discourse of what was to become the Expansion paper: 'The Imperial Historian forgets at his peril that the cattle-ranching of Uruguay and Australia, the fruit-growing of Honduras and Samoa, the experiments in governing non-European peoples in Java, Mexico and Uganda, and the investment of capital in India and China all form parts of one great [if disorderly] movement.' Davidson went on to write one of the classic works of extra-European history, the pioneer account of colonial nationalism in the Pacific, *Samoa mo Samoa: the emergence of the independent state of Samoa* (Melbourne, 1967). Since Western Samoa was the first ex-colonial independent state (1 January 1962) in the region, a book on 'Samoa for the Samoans' bears much the same relationship to the Pacific as early works on Ghanaian nationalism do to African history. Davidson first went to Samoa while on leave from Cambridge between April and July 1947, being invited by the prime minister of New Zealand (Peter Fraser) to make a report on the New Zealand mandated territory. There was an unashamed romanticism in the way Samoa and its peoples captivated him, and eventually he rented a house there, became constitutional adviser, and a member of the Legislative Assembly. Meanwhile, he was attracted to the opportunities the new Australian National University

(ANU) at Canberra would provide to complete a general history of the Pacific. Although Davidson loved and enjoyed Cambridge, especially St John's (which he made his residuary legatee), and would be 'very sorry' to leave it, he was ambitious, and a research chair in Canberra seemed a good career move, from which he might return to Britain in ten years or so.[33] However, the increasingly irresistible call to be a 'scholar-in-action' in the Pacific, together with a disappointing lack of publications in the 1950s, prevented this. In fact, he came to regard his work as a constitutional adviser to a number of emergent Pacific states as more important than writing history.

Although it is well known that Davidson was the 'father of Pacific history', its first professor anywhere in the world, creator of a lively department at ANU, and founder of the *Journal of Pacific History*, his role as the progenitor of 'the Expansion of Europe' is not properly recognised – truly a case of a prophet being without honour in his own land. He staked his claim in his inaugural lecture in Canberra (November 1954):

the substitution of the broadly defined framework of European expansion for the limited one of imperial history represents a major advance. I think, too, that it is an advance which historians are becoming willing to make. Ten years ago, I was able to suggest to the Faculty of History in the University of Cambridge that 'The Expansion of Europe' (defined in terms similar to those which I have used here) should be included as a subject in the Historical Tripos. The suggestion fell on fertile ground. The war years themselves had shown how little the old-style imperial historians could contribute to an understanding of the changing European position in Asia and Africa. And younger members of the university who were serving outside Europe were asking, in their letters and in their brief re-appearances on leave, questions to which historical research had provided no answers. My proposal had come, as I suspected, at the very moment when men were prepared to take action. It was accepted; and a year later we began teaching the subject to undergraduates. Elsewhere, as inquiries showed, scholars had begun thinking along similar lines. If we – or, more particularly, I, as the instigator of the proposal – could claim any originality, it was merely in having formulated a detailed definition a little earlier than others.[34]

Although Davidson was not averse to self-promotion, there is no reason to doubt this account. The expansion of Europe was, then, an idea whose time had come, and Davidson was the Cambridge historian who saw it first. As he declared, 'imperial history must give way to the history of European expansion', since imperial history, if it insisted on orienting all its material around the imperial factor, ignoring the 'non-imperial setting' and 'informal empire', becomes, indeed, 'the negation of true historical explanation' (p. 7). Conceptually he acknowledged a debt to Hancock[35] and Fay; but his old supervisor Walker was not unsympathetic to the idea either.[36]

While at Cambridge, Davidson was forced by the archaic absurdities of the supervision system to teach Tudor history, and it cannot be claimed that he did it well. Nor, it seems, was he a good lecturer; indeed P.E.H. Hair considers that his only redeeming feature was that 'he followed E.E. Rich, who was nearly as bad, in another way'. It was not that he was ill-prepared; rather that he seemed ill at ease and not able to relate well to the audience. He was more enthusiastic in Expansion supervisions, 'throwing himself into an armchair and curling up with his sandals very visible'. Whenever possible, he steered undergraduates into the literature on race relations, such as the works of W.E.B. Du Bois and Gilberto Freyre. His contemptuous rejection of all forms of racial prejudice was already an obvious characteristic even before he went to Samoa.[37] He was quick to encourage talent among his pupils, such as Robinson, Hair, and George Shepperson.[38] Shepperson regarded him as 'a very kindly and stimulating teacher', and hoped it would be remembered that 'he was also one of the post-war pioneers of African studies in Britain'. Davidson, in fact, with his unique double role as historical innovator and political *liberator populus*, continues to grow in reputation, and this despite his early death at the age of fifty-seven.[39]

Davidson had two notable research students in Cambridge. One was Angus Ross, a fellow New Zealander (from Otago) who came to King's College to write a thesis on New Zealand's aspirations in the Pacific.[40] The other was Jack Gallagher, who embarked on a study of British colonial policy and West Africa, 1830–86.[41] This he abandoned on election as a Fellow at Trinity in 1948, in accordance with the old Cambridge protocol which held a doctorate to be a second best to a college fellowship. After Davidson left in 1950 Gallagher was appointed to the vacant colonial studies lectureship. His first lecture course was on 'Europe and West Africa' (1948–9). From Michaelmas 1950 Gallagher was also lecturing on 'the British empire'. When E.E. Rich (now elevated to the Vere Harmsworth chair) began to devote most of his time to a special subject ('Responsible government in Canada, 1837–54'), from October 1953 Gallagher took over the basic outline course in 'Expansion to 1850'. R.E. Robinson – who had helped Davidson see his book on Northern Rhodesia through the press – first appeared on the podium in Lent 1953 with 'British imperialism, 1870–1914', and, as a lecturer from 1954, then continued the Expansion course after 1850. One or other, or sometimes both, of them gave a major part of the outline courses for almost the next thirty years. While Robinson tended to lecture mainly (but excitingly and with great originality and perception) on Victorian British expansion, Gallagher's all-embracing global range was magnificent.

One of the most interesting of the other lecturers was Victor Purcell, who held the first lectureship in Far Eastern history.[42] He was generally underestimated by undergraduates; a bulky, elderly, and dreary-looking don, he was a poor lecturer with a jerky style and he could never attract decent audiences. Purcell was, however, a very considerable figure. As an undergraduate at Trinity (after service in the First World War) his interests were largely literary, and he abandoned the Historical Tripos in order to join the Malayan Civil Service. Malaya occupied him for the years 1921 to 1946. He specialised on its Chinese community, and ended as the principal adviser on Chinese affairs for the British administration. After the Second World War he was United Nations consultant on South-East Asian affairs (1946–8), before returning to Cambridge in 1949. Purcell was one of the few Cambridge history dons ever to become embroiled in major public controversy, as a bitter opponent of General Sir Gerald Templer as high commissioner in Malaya, 1952–4, believing him to be 'terroristic' and an impediment to a political solution to the Malayan Emergency. He made a good case for this view. Purcell thought that European powers had provided indispensable services by bringing colonial countries into the scientific and technological age, but that they were not sympathetic enough to colonial nationalism and too slow to recognise changing circumstances. Purcell was a man of the broadest interests, and prodigiously industrious: he was not just a historian and civil servant (in the classic 'scholar-official' tradition), but 'a controversialist, a raconteur, a traveller, a delightful autobiographer, and a poet'.[43]

By the mid-1960s new blood was beginning to emerge, together with some startling new directions, which led to an increase in the number of extra-European options. The teaching team for the next generation was assembled. Eric Stokes joined it in October 1963.[44] Geoffrey Scammell contributed to maritime expansion from an early modernist perspective from 1966.[45] Anil Seal began lecturing in Lent 1963 ('The growth of Indian nationalism, 1857–1947'), followed by me in Easter 1964 (unimaginatively advertised under 'Topics in expansion since 1700', but actually exploring racial attitudes, or 'racism' as it would now be called). After Gallagher's departure to the Beit chair in Oxford in 1963, his lecture course to 1850 was essentially covered by Seal, while I attempted to reinforce the century from 1760 to 1860, at which point Robinson continued to take over. After Robinson's departure in 1971 my portion was extended to 1914. Seal and I then continued to provide the principal outline courses for the rest of the twentieth century.

It had been agreed in March 1963 to move Expansion from Part II to Part I in order to develop extra-European studies further; this was done in 1966–7. As a result of the conjunction of internal pressures for a fundamental reform of the Tripos, and external pressures arising out of the report (1961) by Sir William Hayter (Warden of New College, 1958–76) recommending a big extension of 'area studies' in British universities, a new schedule of papers for Part II was agreed in May 1964 for introduction in 1966. There were options in South Asian, Latin American, and African history, together with the 'Commonwealth'. South Asia – India for the most part – was in the hands of Stokes and Seal, Spear retiring at about this time. They were soon joined by Gordon Johnson who held his appointment jointly with the Oriental Studies Faculty. Johnson added entrepreneurial skills to his academic laurels (double first, Trinity 1963, 1964), making *Modern Asian Studies* into the leading British journal in its field and playing a major role in launching the *New Cambridge history of India*, as well as the Cambridge South Asian series of publications.[46] In the early 1970s, Stokes brought to Cambridge and St Catharine's C.A. Bayly, Gallagher's star research student in Oxford; Bayly began lecturing in 1975.[47] Meanwhile, D.A. Brading (a Pembroke double first, 1959, 1960), who had done his doctoral research in London under R.A. Humphreys, was appointed to the Latin American lectureship formerly held by John Street and Christopher Platt; Brading began lecturing in 1974. Mexico was his particular interest.[48]

From 1965 I assisted Robinson with a pilot course on African history. In the following year we were greatly helped by the advent of John Lonsdale and Sydney Kanya-Forstner (a Fellow of Gonville and Caius College, 1965–72), but it was still all rather makeshift until the real Africanist experts were ready to take over: Lonsdale himself, together with, briefly, the formidable Ivor ('Asante') Wilks, and then from 1971 John Iliffe. The 'two Johns' were, like Seal and Hyam slightly earlier, a pair of age-mates with double firsts. (Iliffe in fact had a starred first, 1961).

The new Commonwealth paper fitted awkwardly into this scheme, but had (understandably) been insisted on by Professor Mansergh – the first Smuts professor, who arrived in 1953 – whose field it was. Although conceptually it grew out of the toe-hold in English constitutional history, it was also perceived as an Oxford cuckoo in the nest. The Oxford model was thought to be too document-orientated, 'whiggish', and celebratory. Few of us in Cambridge believed the 'Commonwealth' was abstractable from larger unities or in itself a satisfactory organising concept for study. A symptomatic problem was its tendentious and teleological opening date, fixed precisely at 1839, thus implying Lord Durham's report was its approved foundation charter. The unsoundness of this approach was soon to be exposed by Ged Martin in *The Durham Report and British policy: a critical essay* (Cambridge, 1972). (Martin was probably the only student of Expansion who chose to make the white colonies his field.) However, as the recent development of 'British world' studies has proved, there clearly was a theoretical case for keeping the history of Canada, Australia, New Zealand, and 'white supremacist' South Africa going in Cambridge through the Commonwealth paper. In any case it would have been dangerous to initiate radical changes, since this would involve public debate which might result in the loss of this 'slot' for extra-European history. The paper was given a lift when Jack Gallagher lectured for it in the 1970s. Over the years valuable contributions were periodically made by research Fellows such as Ged Martin, B.R. Tomlinson, and T.N. Harper (all of them at Magdalene College), and by distinguished Smuts visiting Fellows like Angus Ross, G.C. Bolton, J.D.B. Miller, Rodney Davenport, P.S. Gupta, and R.V. Kubicek. That the paper survives at all today is largely due to Anthony Low, who, shortly before he retired as Smuts professor, injected into it new themes vulgarly known as 'the fours Ss' – science, sport, sex, and society – thus making it more attractive if not actually fashionable. In 2002 the paper was redeveloped as 'The British Empire and Commonwealth from 1780 to the present day'.

The Expansion paper had always been overloaded, and, as the possibilities of reading a sound literature on the twentieth century developed, there was frustration too. With some misgivings about fracturing the unity of the subject, a new paper called 'The Third World' from about 1918 (popularly referred to as 'The West and the rest') was split off from it. First examined in 1978, it took several years to settle down. Its content was not easy to define and make coherent, while too many weaker students supposed it to be a trendy soft option, which it certainly was not.

One other opportunity existed for extra-European history in the Tripos, and that was the final-year special subject.[49] Among the earliest on offer were American and Canadian ones. Temperley in the later 1920s devised a special subject on 'Secession and the preservation of the United States, 1820–65'. In the mid-1930s J.R.M. Butler mounted one on 'The evolution of self-government in British North America, 1837–54', which was re-run by Rich twenty years later. Meanwhile Professor Walker had opened up a more unusual opportunity with 'The unification of South Africa, 1895–1910', which ran from 1938 to 1941. Since 1950 it has been the convention that there should always be at least one extra-European special subject and usually there are two; they normally run for five years. From 1951, Victor Purcell put on no fewer than three successive special subjects: Sino-British relations, 1834–42, the Boxer Rebellion, and the British in Malaya, 1867–1909. The 1960s

opened with Mansergh's lucid and authoritative 'Anglo-Irish settlement, 1922–25'; and in the mid-1960s Spear introduced the first Indian
special, centering on the years 1818 to 1835. Stokes followed this with
a rather technical approach to the 'Great Indian Mutiny and Rebellion'.
More accessible was Gordon Johnson's special subject on the collapse
of the Mahratta empire in India, 'British expansion in an Asian political system, 1802–20', which ran for many years from the mid-1970s.
Concurrently, G.V. Scammell offered 'The establishment of Portuguese
Power in Asia, 1550–55'. The first Africanist special was Iliffe's on
Buganda (1978).

One other special subject, at first sight somewhat tangential, must
be mentioned. This was 'British interests and politics and the Peace of
Paris, 1759–63', given between 1957 and 1962 by the remarkable Betty
Behrens, whose principal interest was the *ancien régime* in Europe.[50] This
was in fact a very cleverly designed post-Namierite 'imperial and naval'
topic. It certainly taught me most of what I know about the eighteenth-
century empire, and it also inspired a most important piece of research
on India by a pupil of Miss Behrens at Newnham College, Pamela
Nightingale (see below, p. 491).

III

The 'doctor of philosophy' research degree was introduced at Cambridge
in the early 1920s. The *Cambridge Historical Journal* was launched in
1923. But in the period before the Second World War Cambridge had
nothing to compare with Professor A.P. Newton's imperial history
research group in London, and its associated series of 'Imperial Studies'
published by Longman (nineteen volumes, 1927–42).[51] Cambridge
research students ploughed very lonely furrows until in 1958 Nicholas
Mansergh founded the Seminar in Commonwealth and European
Expansion, the forerunner of today's World History Seminar.[52] With
his Oxford and London background, he was well aware of the extent to
which Cambridge had fallen behind in providing a forum for research
students and visiting scholars. This was of wider historic importance as
the very first open research seminar in the History Faculty, as opposed
to private after-dinner gatherings like those organised by Kitson Clark
for his own pupils. It anticipated Elton's famous Tudor Seminar by
two years (no doubt to the chagrin of that inveterate enemy of extra-
European history). Robinson and Gallagher pitched in fairly often,
but it was essentially Mansergh's show, and it met in his rooms in St
John's. In the early years nearly all the papers were given by research
students.

The pre-war generation of research students included some well-known names, including Victor Kiernan, J.W. Davidson, and the Canadian G.S. Graham, who spent two years in Trinity, working under Holland Rose on British policy in Canada, 1774–94 (PhD 1929);[53] T.G.P. Spear, working on the English social life of the nabobs in eighteenth-century India, under Dr W.A.J. Archbold (PhD 1931); Victor Purcell, studying Western education in modern China (PhD 1935); W.O. Aydelotte on Bismarck's dispute with Britain over South-West Africa, supervised by Temperley (PhD 1935);[54] also with Temperley (and later Walker) was Sybil E. Crowe of Girton, who found it difficult to define a topic within late nineteenth-century colonial issues, but eventually settled very successfully for the Berlin West African Conference (PhD 1939).[55] One of the earliest pieces of research was on the occupation of the Falkland Islands after 1770 (by W.G. Down, PhD 1927, supervised by Holland Rose). Another intriguing thesis was presented by R.A. Humphreys (double first, 1928, 1929)[56] on 'Lord Shelburne and British imperialism', rather oddly supervised by Professor Sir Ernest Barker (PhD 1932, apparently unknown to Harlow, the examiners being Benians and Professor Newton). After taking a double first (1934, 1935) J.H. Parry embarked on a study of Spanish colonial government (PhD 1940), starting off in Harvard under R.B. Merriman and returning under Walker, who cannot have been much help (there is no acknowledgement in the thesis of a supervisor). Parry enterprisingly used the Seville Archive of the Indies, and the Mexican National Archives. Michael Greenberg (another double first, 1935, 1936) exploited the Jardine, Matheson Papers in the University Library to elucidate the opening of China in the early nineteenth century, supervised by Professor Sir John Clapham (PhD 1949, but never deposited).[57] One notable Cambridge product of this period was C. Northcote Parkinson,[58] but his Tripos results (1931–2) were poor and he went off to London to be supervised by Newton on trade in the eastern seas. H.S. Ferns, a Canadian, also began research before the war, after taking a distinction in Part II in 1938, but was interrupted by the war; his supervisors on British enterprise in Argentina in the nineteenth century were C.R. Fay and the professors of economic history, Clapham and Postan (PhD 1951).[59]

Then came the war. A considerable number of undergraduates took Part I before war service, returning afterwards to take Part II. They included Gallagher (1939, 1946), Robinson (1941, 1946), Shepperson (English 1942, History 1947),[60] K. Ballhatchet (1942, 1947),[61] J.D. Fage (1941, 1946), and R.A. Oliver (English 1942, History 1946). Scammell had his Part I preparation interrupted. Not all of these managed double firsts under these trying circumstances, but those who did were Gallagher, Shepperson, and Ballhatchet. Not all stayed to do their research in Cambridge, but all of them were deeply influenced by their wartime experiences. For example, George Shepperson had Nyasalanders under his command in Burma. Geoffrey Scammell, after serving with the Royal Navy in Palestine, Goa, Malaya, and the eastern seas, returned to Cambridge and became a medieval research student working on Crusader castles under Dr R.C. Smail, but the 'call of the East' gradually took over, converting him into an early extra-Europeanist. As Fage has observed, whether or not ex-servicemen precipitated nation-alist protest in Africa, they certainly boosted the academic study of Africa and the empire.[62]

John Fage may indeed stand as an archetype for this war-split genera-tion.[63] He was a Scholar of Magdalene College. His interests decisively switched from medieval European history after he had spent two years training as a Royal Air Force pilot in Southern Rhodesia, where he was thrilled by the Victoria Falls, and fascinated by Bulawayo ('a dusty, glaring mid-West American sort of place'). He saw much of southern Africa, East Africa, and Madagascar. After the war he knew precisely what he wanted to do, which was to find out why Southern Rhodesia got control of its black population with internal self-government in 1923. Thus he became one of the first students of the Expansion of Europe paper introduced in October 1945. Obtaining a Bartle Frere Exhibition – but pipped by Gallagher to the Holland Rose studentship – he started research under Benians, and then transferred to Walker. Both his super-visors liked his intelligence, keenness, industry, and pleasantness as a man. Walker also admired his sense of humour and skill at map-making – which was to bear important fruit as *An atlas of African history* (1957, 1978) – to say nothing of his ability to 'handle a fairly complicated subject firmly'. Benians singled out his 'breadth of view, power of planning and arrangement, and sound critical judgement'. On the strength of such references, Magdalene elected him to a bye-fellowship, and, exception-ally, extended his tenure.[64] One of his tutors, F.McD.C. Turner (brother of the principal of Makerere), considered Fage to be 'one of the best, if not the best pupil I have ever had' (in twenty years): he was 'capable of quite exceptionally acute analysis, and combines great thoroughness with balance and lucidity'. On completing his thesis (examined by Rich and Hancock), Fage decided not to try to pursue an academic career in Cambridge,[65] because a teaching fellowship would yield at most £400 a year and, being now married, he did not consider this would be enough. Instead, he took a lectureship at Achimota in the Gold Coast, which paid more than twice as much. (The University College of Rhodesia and Nyasaland did not open until 1955, otherwise he would have sought to go there.) To begin with at Achimota he lectured out of his Cambridge notes on Expansion, but quickly turned himself into a pioneer Africanist. He was the effective founder of its department of history.

Meanwhile, Fage's future collaborator, Roland Oliver of King's, who started out as a church historian, was working under the professor of ecclesiastical history, Norman Sykes, on missionary activity in East Africa. Presumably not encountering much opposition, in 1948 he secured a lectureship at the School of Oriental and African Studies in London on 'the tribal history of East Africa'. His well-rounded thesis was examined by Benians and Jack Simmons (of Oxford and Leicester).[66]

Robinson was long remembered in the annals of the Degree Committee. Supervised by Walker, he set a record for the number of changes of title, wobbling between 'native policy', 'governance', 'trusteeship', and 'political and administrative development' for a range of shifting geographical locations and dates. Eventually he settled on 'The Trust in British Central Africa, 1889–1948' (PhD 1950). He created further sensations by citing documents well within the government's 'fifty-year rule of access' (more or less: in 1948 records were open only to 1902), or any other. As a result, his examiners (Benians, and Miss Perham, replacing Sir Reginald Coupland, who had fallen ill) had to be given security clearance in order to read it, were not allowed to check references, and the thesis, when deposited, was put under embargo and could not be read by anybody, including the members of the Degree Committee who had formally passed it. This all came about because Robinson as a research officer in the African Studies Branch of the Colonial Office had secretly read these documents; the thesis was duly completed with the connivance of his powerful patron, Andrew Cohen, who was head of the African department at the time. The substance of the thesis Robinson eventually published in the *Festschrift* for Mansergh.[67]

Three more research students after the war began research on India with Dr. T.G.P. Spear. Eric Stokes (double first, 1947, 1948) studied Utilitarian influences in the making of British Indian policy, 1820–40 (PhD 1952). Hugh Tinker started on 'local self-government in India, 1870–1939' but transferred to London.[68] Maurice Cowling abandoned 'British social policy in India, 1860–1910', and turned to British domestic politics instead. Two students worked on the Far East under Victor Purcell. James Ch'eng investigated the Taiping Rebellion, using Chinese sources (PhD 1950).[69] Nicholas Tarling tackled British policy towards the Dutch and indigenous princes in Malaya in the half-century before 1871 (PhD 1956).[70] A handful of Cambridge graduates without firsts went off to do research elsewhere, often producing work of exceptional quality. These included W.D. McIntyre (Peterhouse),[71] Roger Anstey[72] and J.E. Flint of St John's,[73] W.D. Tordoff of Magdalene,[74] (J.)R. Gray of Downing,[75] and T.H. Beaglehole of King's.[76] Another point to notice is that some graduate students who did not do research at all, or not within the imperial field, later made a name for themselves in it, for example W.H. Morris-Jones,[77] John Omer-Cooper,[78] Anthony Kirk-Greene,[79] H.R.C. Wright,[80] Frank Welsh,[81] Piers Brendon[82] (and somewhat later, David Cannadine[83]). One of the star performers in the Historical Tripos in the late 1950s, J.M.D. Elvin of King's, learned classical Chinese as a graduate student, and later became professor of Chinese history at the School of Pacific and Asian Studies, ANU Canberra.[84]

Three notable dissertations were written in the 1960s, from very different perspectives, by Pamela Nightingale (née Bottoms), Anthony Reid, and Ged Martin. Nightingale's path-breaking work on British commercial expansion in India in the late eighteenth century was written before the publication of Professor P.J. Marshall's main studies and was supervised by Spear (PhD 1964). Reid, a New Zealander at King's, was the first Cambridge student to specialise on Indonesia, studying the contest for North Sumatra, 1858–88, and he was Purcell's last protégé (PhD 1965).[85] My undergraduate pupil Ged Martin's investigation of British policy in the years before Canadian Confederation showed how the study of mid-Victorian colonial politics could be reinvigorated; he was supervised by the American constitutional expert Professor J.R. Pole (PhD 1972).[86]

By the end of the 1950s, however, most research students were gravitating to the Mansergh–Robinson–Gallagher research axis, where the pattern of investigation was beginning to assume some coherence. Before the mid-1950s, it was highly unusual to become a Cambridge research student in history unless one was a high-flyer intending to pursue an academic career in Cambridge. The *Cambridge Historical Journal* was the principal vehicle for publication, and it was a tightly enclosed world as far as examiners were concerned too. With the advent of free state education from primary to PhD level under the 1944 Education Act, and with the increase in the 1960s of the number of new universities, many more young men and women decided to embark on research degrees, leading to a considerable expansion in their numbers. Before the war there had been fewer than 300 research students in history at any one time; by 1960 this had risen to 1,200, and by 1970 numbers had doubled to 2,400; while the number of university teachers of history almost doubled in the 1960s (from 800 to 1,500).[87] The lifting of restrictions on access to government archives, first to a fifty-year rule and then to a thirty-year rule of access, also enhanced the opportunities for genuinely original research for the post-1960 generations. These two factors enabled research supervisors to construct interlocking patterns of investigation among their pupils in a way never previously possible.

Robinson assigned to one of his earliest students the crucial task of studying Palmerston's African policy: Robert Gavin's thesis on this (PhD 1959) underpinned much of the earlier part of *Africa and the Victorians*.[88] He set D.G. Hoskin to work on the interactions between the Egyptian and Irish crises, but this proved to be too large a topic; the resulting dissertation (PhD 1964) on the 'genesis and significance of the 1886 Home Rule split' in the Liberal Party is still cited (though Hoskin himself died young). Robinson steered Bernard Porter and me into investigating the opposite sides of the imperial policy coin: Porter on left-wing critics (PhD 1967),[89] and myself on Liberals in government (African policy, 1905–9: PhD 1963). From Harvard, T.R. Metcalf worked under Robinson on trusteeship in India and the impact of the Mutiny (PhD Harvard 1959).[90] The next wave of researchers was decidedly Africanist: J.M. Lonsdale on the conquest of the Nyanza Province of Kenya (PhD 1964); John Iliffe on German administration in Tanganyika (PhD 1965);[91] A.S. Kanya-Forstner (whom Robinson supervised jointly with Gallagher) on the French conquest of western Africa (PhD 1965).[92] Robinson's first African pupils included G.M.P. Bakhiet on the Sudan (PhD 1965), O. Omisini working on tropical development in West Africa, 1880–1906 (PhD 1968), and B.E. Kipkorir on educational policy in Kenya (PhD 1970) – none of these were published as books. (Kipkorir became Kenyan ambassador to the United States.)

Not all Robinson's 1960s undergraduate pupils at St John's remained with him. For example, M.J. Twaddle[93] and A.J. Stockwell[94] went to London, while A.N. Porter was supervised by Hinsley (who had a special interest in the causes of war) on the background to the South African War (PhD 1971).[95] Most of those with South African interests tended to gravitate towards Mansergh. Apart from myself, D.J. Denoon also had both Robinson's and Mansergh's guidance, while working on reconstruction in the Transvaal after the war.[96] C.F. Goodfellow published his thesis on *Great Britain and South African Confederation, 1870–1881* in 1966; his tragic death shortly afterwards deprived the second volume of the *Oxford history of South Africa* of two chapters, considerably weakening its political backbone.[97] Mansergh also looked after N.G. Garson from Witwatersrand who was investigating Swaziland and regional geopolitics in the partition era.[98] Mansergh's other main research areas were Ireland and Canada. His students on Irish problems included David Steele (Gladstone's 1870 Land Act: PhD 1963), and David Fitzpatrick (Irish politics, 1913–21: PhD 1975).[99] P.G. Wigley[100] and N. Hillmer[101] took successive chronological portions of Anglo-Canadian relations between the wars (PhDs, 1971, 1975).

Gallagher's first graduate student was (probably) Oliver MacDonagh, working on Irish emigration,[102] but his most celebrated research student was Anil Seal, who also became Fellow of Trinity. Half-Indian, half-Hungarian, Seal swiftly produced an elegant and powerfully argued account of the origins of Indian nationalism which transformed our understanding of Indian politics (PhD 1962).[103] Later in his career Seal proved to be a brilliantly successful fundraiser, thus adding an immeasurably important further contribution to Commonwealth studies. There was considerable inter-penetration between Gallagher's pupils and Seal's, and the combined group did indeed build up together an identifiable school of Cambridge Indianists, who rescued Indian history from its earlier simplicities. The 'school' tended to see Indian politics in terms of elites, factions and local self-interest groups, and the mainsprings of political action in power struggles. This could only be controversial and the results were not always easy to read.[104] Nevertheless many important monographs emerged, and the guiding hand of Seal was apparent in many of them. The group included many now senior people, such as Gordon Johnson (Seal's first research student), Judith Brown,[105] B.R. Tomlinson,[106] Rajnarayan Chandavarkar,[107] David Washbrook,[108] Francis Robinson,[109] and Ayesha Jalal,[110] together with C.J. Baker, Richard Gordon, Christine Dobbin, David Page, Rajat K. Ray, Claude Markovits, Ian Copland, and Basudev Chatterji. Many of these contributed to the two volumes of collected essays which appeared in 1973 and 1981, to which the reader is referred for further details,[111] although we may highlight here the bursting upon the scene in the mid-1970s of the 'Washbaker' phenomenon. Both Washbrook and Baker published in 1976 their theses on Indian politics, on Madras (1870 to 1920) and South India (1920 to 1937) respectively, having the previous year collaborated on a study of political institutions and political change in south India (between 1880 and 1940). Baker, before leaving the field for a business career, published perhaps the best of all the books of the 'Cambridge school', *An Indian rural economy, 1880–1955: the Tamilnad countryside* (Oxford, 1984). Associated with these Indianists was Keith Jeffery, who amplified the defence aspects of Gallagher's theme, 'the crisis of empire, 1919–22', with a study of Sir Henry Wilson (PhD 1978) before taking up more definitely Irish history in its imperial setting.[112]

The Indianists gathered around Eric Stokes produced a solid and integrated corpus of studies of mainly nineteenth-century Indian agrarian history: of rural society, revenue collection, and demographic change.

They included Neil R.F. Charlesworth (PhD 1974: western India), Mrs Ratnalekha Ray (PhD 1974: Bengal), Clive Dewey (PhD 1973: agrarian indebtedness generally), Chittabrata Palit (PhD 1975: Bengal), Peter J. Musgrave (PhD 1976: United Provinces), Simon J. Commander (PhD 1980: northern India). In addition, Ernest C.T. Chew studied Sir Alfred Lyall (PhD 1970), and Susan Bayly (S.B. Kaufmann) wrote upon popular Christianity in south India (PhD 1980). Susan Bayly spoke for the entire group in recording her debt to Stokes as 'a sparkling, inspiring and generous PhD supervisor'.[113]

The story of the development of Africanist research under Lonsdale and Iliffe belongs mainly to the post-1981 period, but one of the earliest and brightest of Lonsdale's pupils was R.D. Waller (double first, Peterhouse, 1968, 1969), the pioneer in Cambridge of African oral history (PhD 1978). When Waller asked the permission of the Degree Committee to add specimen oral texts as appendices to his thesis, exclusive of the word-limit, Professor Elton led the attack: how could examiners verify the evidence, and how were they to know the texts had not been concocted by the candidate? Professor Walter Ullmann saved the day for the future of Cambridge African history. 'What's the problem?', he expostulated with Germanic high drama, '*all* my sources are forgeries!' (he was professor of medieval ecclesiastical history).[114]

IV

It seems reasonable to conclude that a great deal of valuable and innovative research was undertaken by doctoral candidates in Cambridge in the period before 1981, and especially since 1945. This covered a broad spectrum, from imperial policy-making to informal enterprise in Latin America and China. Cambridge intellectual initiatives have also helped to improve the historiography of all parts of the empire, from South Africa to Samoa, from Ireland to India, from Canada to Kenya, from New Zealand to Namibia, from Malaya to Sudan. Finally, it may be noted that the seven volumes of the *Cambridge history of Africa* began to come off the presses in 1975, and the twelve volumes of the *Cambridge history of China* in 1978. Nor would they be the last in the extra-European field.

The shifts of interest over the past seventy years since the establishment of the Vere Harmsworth chair emerge clearly. The eighteenth century attracted most of the earliest attention, and gave some justification for the chair's orientation towards naval history. The immediate post-war generation moved into the nineteenth century, and those with overseas war service or national service behind them often had an interest awakened in Afro-Asian history. John Lonsdale and myself were the last of the conscripts: Lonsdale served with the King's African Rifles in Kenya, with intellectual results plain to see; I served with the Royal Air Force in deepest Herefordshire and never saw an aeroplane – the influence of this experience is not so readily apparent. Serious work in twentieth-century archives only became possible from 1958 (when the fifty-year rule was established), but was enthusiastically embraced. And then area studies boomed, though they have recently retreated a little, at least as far as undergraduate interests are concerned, since British and Western European history have staged a comeback we had not expected.

Many of our immediate ancestors were intensely ambitious to reach beyond their historical investigations. They became involved in affairs of state, and they were keen to train the next generation of leaders, whether administrative or academic. Indeed, training some of the former was unavoidable, for so long as the Colonial Service Courses remained in Cambridge.[115] The events of empire were often experienced by them as 'near realities, not as distant phenomena or issues in high politics', whether it was Mansergh as a boy of eight in County Tipperary hearing the shots which killed two policemen at Soloheadbeg on 29 January 1919, the episode which heralded the opening of the Irish War of Independence;[116] or Purcell struggling to protect the interests of the *mui tsai*, the Chinese prostitutes in Malaya;[117] or Robinson and Fage learning to fly in Rhodesia, or Hinsley at Bletchley Park arranging to sink the *Bismarck*. Several of them served in Whitehall departments: Mansergh again (Dominions Office), Davidson, and Robinson. Davidson represented the apotheosis of 'participant history' (as he himself called it), for in his case it even came to displace the primacy of the academic role.[118]

'Imperial history', Sir Christopher Bayly has reminded us, 'has always been intensely political.'[119] Historians have seldom been able to disjoin themselves completely from contemporary issues or the perceived place of empire in the scheme of things, let alone fashionable theories and methodologies. Not unnaturally, the politics of Cambridge imperial historians has ranged over the entire gamut, from true-blue right-wingers and freemasons (like Rich) to 'green-pillarbox' Irish nationalists, and from persistent Marxists (Kiernan) to lapsed communist fellow-travellers; just as religious standpoints have embraced regular church-goers – not all to be insensitively lumped together as 'High Anglicans', as Robinson was apt to do – like Holland Rose, Mansergh, and Stokes, as well as quiet agnostics and lapsed Catholics (not quite the same thing either). It is broadly true to say that in Cambridge imperial historiography, as in so much else, the Second World War was a great divide. While the empire seemed to be a going concern, historians found it important to study how it was run; in the era of decolonisation they strove to understand the growth of nationalism and the dynamics of imperial collapse; just as today, bombarded with exogenous influences, we have won through (if that is the right expression) to post-colonial theory, globalisation, sex and gender issues, the cultural imperative, and the linguistic turn. Before the Second World War, Cambridge imperial historians tended to admire – though not, in the Oxonian way, to celebrate – the empire. Since the war, attitudes have been quintessentially ambivalent, and in my judgment almost uniformly so. Indeed, it is impossible to see how it could reasonably be otherwise, since scholarship reveals elements both good and bad in Britain's imperial performance. We are also likely to be agreed that, with all its complex variety and opportunities to enter into other, non-European worlds, we have had bequeathed to us – if rather haphazardly – as Gallagher once put it, 'such a wonderful subject'.[120]

Notes

1 D.K. Fieldhouse, 'Can Humpty-Dumpty be put together again? Imperial history in the 1980s', *JICH*, vol. 12 (1984), pp. 9–23.

2 J. Holland Rose: see *Dictionary of national biography, 1941–50* (1959), pp. 736–7. See further below, chapter18.

3 G.M. Trevelyan, 'Admiral Sir Herbert Richmond', *Autobiography and other essays* (1949), pp. 222–34, reprinted from *Proceedings of the British Academy*, vol. 32 (1946), pp. 325–37.

4 Ken Smith, *The changing past: trends in South African historical writing* (Athens, OH, 1989), pp. 121–31; C. Saunders, *The making of the South African past: major historians on race and class* (Cape Town and Johannesburg, 1988), pp. 112–15.

5 Ged Martin, 'The Cambridge lectureship of 1866: a false start in American studies', *American Studies*, vol. 7 (1973), pp. 17–29.

6 G.S.R. Kitson Clark, 'A hundred years of the teaching of history at Cambridge, 1873–1973', *Historical Journal*, vol. 16 (1973), pp. 535–53; J.O. McLachlan, 'The origin and early development of the Cambridge Historical Tripos', *Cambridge Historical Journal*, vol. 9 (1947), pp. 78–105.

7 Sir John Seeley (1834–95): see *ODNB*, vol. XLIX, pp. 670–3, by R.T. Shannon; Peter Burroughs, 'John Robert Seeley and British imperial history', *JICH*, vol.1 (1973), pp. 191–211; Deborah Wormell, *Sir John Seeley and the uses of history* (Cambridge, 1980); and comments by C.A. Bayly and Wm. Roger Louis in Robin W. Winks, ed., *OHBE*, vol. V, *Historiography* (Oxford, 1999), pp. 8–10, 57.

8 *Cambridge University (CU) Reporter*, vol. 33 (1902–3), pp. 528–38, report on the proposed regulations for a Tripos in Economics (10 May 1903); p. 773, discussion (14 May 1903); pp. 1133–4, 'supplementary regulations'.

9 Benians Box, Biographical Collection, St John's College Library, Cambridge.

10 *CU Reporter*, vol. 37 (1906–7), p. 70.

11 C.R. Fay, DSc (1884–1961), Fellow of Christ's College (1908–22), Reader in Economic History, 1930; formerly professor of economic history at Toronto, 1921–30. Madden's chapter had to be written with barely six month's notice after Vincent Harlow's sudden death, and when the typescript was complete it was stolen: Madden had left it in a briefcase in his car in Oxford. Some days later it was discovered in two halves, the pages scattered alternately over each side of a high-walled lane between Queen's College and New College, where they had been thrown by the disgruntled thief, who presumably had been hoping for atomic secrets at least (Letter from A.F. Madden to the author, 8 April 2000).

12 F.H. Hinsley, Kt (1985), OBE, FBA (1918–98), Master of St John's College (1979–89) and vice-chancellor (1981–83); *ODNB*, vol. XXVII, pp. 292–4, by Richard Langhorne, and *Proceedings of the British Academy* vol.120.

13 H.J. Habakkuk, Kt (1976), FBA (1915–2002), born John Guest but invented 'Hrothgar' as first name and adopted his mother's surname. An undergraduate at St John's, he had a distinction in Part II (1936); Fellow, Pembroke College, Cambridge, 1938–50; Chichele professor of economic history, Oxford (1950–67), principal of Jesus College, Oxford (1967–84), and vice-chancellor (1973–7). See *Proceedings of the British Academy for 2003*, vol. 124, *Biographical memoirs of Fellows, vol. III* (2004) by F.M.L. Thompson.

14 For an important contemporary evaluation of vol. II, see J.W. Davidson, 'The history of empire', *Economic History Review*, vol. 16 (1946), pp. 68–73, particularly critical of W.F. Reddaway's contribution. However, it is pleasing to see that in so thoroughly modern, even post-modern, a book as *Gentlemanly capitalism and British imperialism: the new debate on empire* (1999), the editor, R.E. Dumett, praises *CHBE* vol. II as a 'classic volume' (p. 7, n. 13). There is also praise for Habakkuk's acutely perceptive chapter, in P.J. Cain and A.G. Hopkins, *British imperialism, 1688–2000* (2nd edn, 2002), pp. 214–15. For an astringent overall assessment of *CHBE*, see Wm. Roger Louis in *OHBE*, vol. V, *Historiography*, pp. 11–12, 25.

15 These quotations are all taken from his chapter in the *Cambridge modern history*, vol. XII, pp. 643–8, 671. In the light of them we can see that making Smuts the university's chancellor (1948) – in which Benians presumably played a leading part – would have seemed an act of expiation: see RH, 'Smuts, Cambridge, and Commonwealth History', *The Round Table: The Commonwealth Journal of International Affairs*, no. 360 (2001), pp. 401–14 (chapter 12, p. 346 above).

16 Speeches by E.A. Benians, notes, probably for a talk to LSE on 'Universities and the empire', *c.*1940: Mss W 5, St John's College Library. A very similar formulation appears in the preface to *CHBE*, vol. II, p. viii.

17 G.M. Trevelyan in 1933 dissuaded Benians from applying for the Vere Harmsworth chair, on the grounds that he would and should become

Master of St John's (letter to Benians, 2 January 1934, quoted by Peter Linehan in the forthcoming quincentenary history of St John's College, 2011). For obituaries, see J.S. B[oys] S[mith], 'Ernest Alfred Benians', *The Eagle* [the magazine of St John's College], no. 240 (1953), pp. 4–9, and *Cambridge Independent Press*, 15 February 1952. Benians does not appear in the *ODNB*, but Dr Linehan is writing an entry for the online supplement.

18 So named from 1986, reflecting his having inspired the Dominions Fellowship set up in 1946–7 (Overseas Fellows file, St John's College Archives, consulted by permission of the Master, Fellows, and Scholars), but from 1993 subsumed in the 'Overseas Visiting Scholars' scheme (*The Eagle*, 2003, pp. 30–1).

19 Frank Thistlethwaite, CBE (1915–2003), Fellow of St John's College, 1945–61, and university lecturer in the Economics Faculty, with W.R. Brock becoming the History Faculty lecturer in American history instead: see Thistlethwaite's memoir, *Cambridge years, 1945–1961* (privately printed, Cambridge, 1999), pp. 34–40, 78, 131). His seminal work, *The great experiment*, was Cambridge's first textbook on American history, selling 40,000 copies, translated into fourteen languages. Thistlethwaite became the inaugurating vice-chancellor of the University of East Anglia. He made a most important contribution to Expansion studies through his work on Atlantic migrations: 'Birds of passage: some aspects of the history of migration', *Reports of the 11th International Congress of Historical Sciences*, vol. 6 (1960), pp. 32–60, etc.

20 H.W.V. Temperley, OBE, LittD, FBA (1879–1939): *DNB, 1931–40* (1949), pp. 849–50. *The foreign policy of Canning*, which I read at the age of sixteen, triggered my own interest in Britain's overseas policy. There is a biography by John D. Fair, *Harold Temperley: a scholar and romantic in the public realm* (Newark, DE, 1992).

21 J.R.M. Butler, Kt, OBE (1889–1975): *DNB, 1971–80* (1986), pp. 113–14.

22 G.S.R. Kitson Clark, LittD (1900–75); ibid., p. 470.

23 *CU Reporter*, vol. 39 (1908–9), 4 May 1909, pp. 964–74; see also 'Notes on the development of the Historical Tripos, 1875–1932', Tripos Reform Papers, box I (1875–1955), no. 1, History Faculty Archives, University Library, Cambridge.

24 R.E. Robinson believed this was the work which 'inspired Kitson Clark' to campaign for the new paper: 'Oxford in imperial historiography', in F. Madden and D.K. Fieldhouse, eds., *Oxford and the idea of Commonwealth: essays presented to Sir Edgar Williams* (1982), p. 42.

25 *CU Reporter*, vol. 75 (1944–5), pp. 729–30, 15 May 1945, report of the History Faculty Board on the addition of a paper on the Expansion of Europe (24 April 1945); see also pp. 882–3 for the first prescribed reading list.

26 J.D. Fage, 'British African studies since the Second World War: a personal account', *African Affairs*, vol. 88 (1989), pp. 397–413, and *To Africa and back: memoirs* (Birmingham, 2002), pp. 66–7. The paper also attracted Roland Oliver, hoping to study the expansion of Christianity in colonial lands, but in retrospect he did not think it then a well-designed course, 'nor

was it taught by any of the more exciting teachers in the university': *In the realms of gold: pioneering in African history* (1997), p. 45.

27 Anil Seal in the preface to J.A. Gallagher, *Decline, revival and fall of the British empire: the Ford Lectures and other essays* (Cambridge, 1982), p. xvi.

28 T.G.P. Spear, OBE (died 1982), originally from St Catharine's, took a doctorate in Indian history before spending twenty years in India, becoming head of the history departments at St Stephen's College, Delhi, and Delhi University. During the war he was in the Government Information Service at Delhi and briefly government whip in the legislative assembly. In recognition of many years' contribution to Faculty lecturing in Cambridge, in 1963 he was appointed to a single-tenure five-year lectureship which took him to retirement in 1968. See *Selwyn College Calendar* (1983–4), p. 23, 'Obituaries: Dr T.G.P. Spear'; and C.A. Bayly, 'The Orient: British historical writing about Asia since 1890', in Peter Burke, ed., *History and historians in the 20th century* (2002), pp. 104–5. The Spear Papers are in the Centre of South Asian Studies, Cambridge. His best-known book is *India, a modern history* (Ann Arbor, 1961, new edn 1972).

29 J.H. Parry, CMG, MBE (1914–82), Fellow of Clare, 1938–49; Royal Navy, 1940–5, first professor of modern history, University College of the West Indies, 1949–56, principal of University College, Ibadan, 1956–60, and of Swansea 1960–5, vice-chancellor of University of Wales, 1963–5, Gardiner professor of oceanic history and affairs, Harvard, 1965–82; author of *The Spanish theory of empire in the sixteenth century* (Cambridge, 1940) and *The age of reconnaissance* (1963); recreations, 'sailing, fishing, mountain walking, ornithology'.

30 J.W. Davidson (1915–73), Fellow of St John's College, 1944–51, professor of Pacific history, Australian National University, 1949–73. Dr Doug Munro is writing a full-scale biography of Davidson, and has been of the greatest possible assistance, not least with supplying copies of letters in the Davidson Papers in the National Library of Australia at Canberra, and allowing me to see various papers in draft, particularly Doug Munro, 'J.W. Davidson: the making of a participant historian', in B.V. Lal and P. Hempenstall, eds., *Pacific lives, Pacific places: bursting boundaries in Pacific history* (Canberra, 2001), pp. 98–116, and 'Becoming an expatriate: J.W. Davidson and the brain drain', *Journal of New Zealand Studies*, new series, vol. 2–3 (2003–4), pp. 19–43.

31 Davidson's referees were Benians, Kitson Clark, the historical geographer H.C. Darby, the anthropologist Dr Raymond Firth, and Margery Perham (application dated 24 July 1946, Lectures and Lecturers records, Box 1, no. 3, 1946, History Faculty Archives).

32 E.V.G. Kiernan, double starred first (1933, 1934), author of *British diplomacy in China, 1880–85* (Cambridge, 1939) and two volumes of Urdu poetry; eight years in India, then returned to Cambridge for two years, before going to Edinburgh (becoming professor of history) – a Marxist, author of *The lords of human kind: European attitudes to the outside world* (1969) and *European empires from conquest to collapse: 1815–1960* (1982).

33 JWD to his mother, 6 July 1948 (Box 65, Davidson Papers, Xerox copy supplied by Doug Munro). On the death of his sister, St John's College received A$445,000 (£156,000) from the Davidson estate (*The Eagle*, 2002, p. 178).

34 J.W. Davidson, *The study of Pacific history: an inaugural lecture* (Canberra, 1955). A more than usually inspiring example of the genre, it was reprinted with revisions (and omitting the paragraph about the Expansion of Europe in Cambridge) as 'Problems of Pacific history' in the inaugural number of the *Journal of Pacific History*, vol. 1 (1966), pp. 5–21. For further examples of Davidson's synoptic flair, see 'New Zealand, 1820–1870: an essay in re-interpretation', *Historical Studies, Australia and New Zealand*, vol. 1 (1953), pp. 349–59, and 'Scholarship and the government of colonies', ibid., vol. 7 (1957), pp. 406–20 (a study of Raffles, Sir George Grey, and Arthur Hamilton Gordon), together with 'China, Japan and the Pacific, 1900–31', in *New Cambridge modern history*, vol. XII, *1898–1945* (2nd edn, 1968, ed. C.L. Mowat), pp. 329–72 (co-author); see also n. 14 above.

35 Hancock was the examiner for his MA thesis on the Scandinavians in New Zealand.

36 Walker thought highly of Davidson, arguing strongly for him to get the Oxford Beit chair instead of V.T. Harlow (who did not impress Walker: conversation with EAW, 1962), in May 1948 (JWD to his mother, 23 May 1948, MS 5105, box 65, Davidson Papers, Xerox copy courtesy of Dr Munro). Walker further hoped that Davidson would succeed him in the Vere Harmsworth chair (to which E.E. Rich was elected).

37 G. Shepperson, P.E.H. Hair, and Doug Munro, 'J.W. Davidson at Cambridge: some student evaluations', *History in Africa: a Journal of Method*, vol. 27 (New Brunswick, NJ, 2000), pp. 215–27. I am most grateful to Professor Shepperson and Dr Munro for allowing me to see this article in draft. The Biographical Collection in St John's College Library has a useful box of Davidsoniana, mostly built up from photocopies supplied by Dr Munro.

38 P.E.H. Hair (died 2001) was Ramsey Muir professor of modern history at Liverpool, 1979–90, arriving at African history via research on the British and then Nigerian coal industries; he specialised on using Portuguese sources and studying early African languages – see *Africa encountered: European contacts and evidence, 1450–1700* (Aldershot, 1997). For Shepperson, see n. 60 below.

39 The literature on Davidson is already considerable. Of the obituaries, the most critical is F. West, 'Obituary: James Wightman Davidson', *JICH*, vol. 2 (1973), pp. 114–17; see also H.E. Maude, 'James Wightman Davidson', *Journal of Pacific History*, vol. 8 (1973), pp. 5–9; D. Scarr, 'Obituary: James Wightman Davidson', *Historical Studies*, vol. 16 (1974), pp. 157–61, repr. in *Journal of Pacific History*, vol. 28, no. 2 (1993), special issue in honour of J.W. Davidson on the twentieth anniversary of his death, important for the bibliography compiled by H. Forster, pp. 278–81.

40 Angus Ross, PhD 1949, published version, *New Zealand aspirations in the Pacific in the nineteenth century* (Oxford, 1964).

41 Degree Committee Minute Book, vol. 3, f. 58, History Faculty Archives.
42 This was not an easy post to fill, and the first attempt failed in July 1948 after the withdrawal of Kiernan, leaving only Spear and G.M. Friters as candidates; Purcell was appointed after interview (very unusual in those days) in April 1949; after his retirement in 1963 he was not replaced (Box on Appointments, 1929–73, Minute Book of the Appointments Committee, pp. 90, 96, History Faculty Archives).
43 V.W.W. Purcell, CMG, LittD (1896–1965); see his *Memoirs of a Malayan official* (1965), ch. 5, 'Cambridge'; S. van der Sprenkel, 'Memoir', in J. Ch'eng and N. Tarling, eds., *Studies in the social history of China and South-East Asia: essays in memory of Victor Purcell* (Cambridge, 1970), pp. 3–20; for sympathetic sidelights see T.N. Harper, *The end of empire and the making of Malaya* (Cambridge, 1999), pp. 58, 83, 276, 311. See also p. 365 above.
44 Stokes ran a popular course for Expansion on 'theories of imperialism', which Robinson asked him to give, in order, he said, 'to provide intellectual respectability' to the subject. The *CU Reporter* is the source for all details about lecture courses.
45 G.V. Scammell (1925–2006), undergraduate at Emmanuel College; served with the Royal Navy in the eastern seas, 1942–6; lecturer at Durham; Fellow of Pembroke College, 1965; author of *The world encompassed: the first European maritime empires, c.800–1650* (1981); *The first imperial age: European overseas expansion, c.1400–1715* (1989); *Ships, oceans and empire: studies in European maritime and colonial history, 1400–1750* (1995); and a striking synoptic survey, 'After Da Gama: Europe and Asia since 1498', *Modern Asian Studies*, vol. 34 (2000), pp. 513–43. A keen sailor.
46 G. Johnson (b. 1943), Fellow of Trinity College (1966–74), lecturer in the history of South Asia (1974), president of Wolfson College, Cambridge, since 1994, director of the South Asian Studies Centre (to 2001), editor of *Modern Asian Studies* (1971–2008); his thesis was published as *Provincial politics and Indian nationalism: Bombay and the Indian National Congress, 1880–1915* (Cambridge, 1973).
47 C.A. Bayly, LittD, FBA, Kt (2007), Vere Harmsworth professor since 1992. His landmark work, *Rulers, townsmen and bazaars: North Indian society in the age of British expansion, 1770–1870*, was published in 1983.
48 D.A. Brading, LittD, FBA, professor of Mexican history (1999). John Street had a double first in Spanish (1942, 1946) and completed a PhD on 'British influences in the independence of the River Plate provinces, 1806–16'; his opportunity came with the departure of J.H. Parry in 1949. Street was succeeded by D.C.M. Platt, an Oxford man who held the lectureship from 1969 to 1972, before taking up the chair of Latin American history in Oxford; he died in 1989, aged fifty-five.
49 *CU Reporter, passim.*
50 C.B.A. Behrens (1904–89), Fellow of Newnham College and then of Clare Hall, university lecturer in history from 1938, author of two masterpieces in unrelated fields: *Merchant shipping and the demands of war* (HMSO, 1955) and *Society, government and the Enlightenment: the experiences of eighteenth-century France and Prussia* (1985). Sir Keith Hancock told me, *c.*1964,

that he regarded her as the best and most brilliant historian in post-war Cambridge, and I was happy to concur. She discomfited Regius Professor Sir Herbert Butterfield to his face and destroyed Regius Professor Sir Geoffrey Elton's *The practice of history* in a review in the *Historical Journal*, vol. 12 (1969), pp. 190–3; and she criticised Hancock for some 'scissors and paste' writing (Louis, 'Sir Keith Hancock and the British empire: the Pax Britannica and the Pax Americana', *English Historical Review*, vol. 120 (2005), p. 950, n. 60, or p.1014 in his collected essays). See also Noel Annan, *The dons: mentors, eccentrics and geniuses* (1999), pp. 245–55; Jonathan Steinberg, *'Based on fact but told like a novel': the historical legacy of C.B.A. Behrens* (a memorial lecture, Newnham College, Cambridge, 1989); Jonathan Haslam, *The vices of integrity: E.H. Carr, 1892–1982* (London and New York, 1999), pp. 228–95, *passim*, for her disastrous marriage in 1966 to E.H. Carr; and *ODNB*, vol. IV, pp. 850–1.

51 This section on research students is based mainly on the History Faculty Degree Committee Minute Books, vols. 1–4 (1922–50), and the dissertations index, Manuscripts Room, Cambridge University Library, together with personal knowledge. I have usually noted 'double firsts' obtained as an undergraduate, since these are distinctly less common in the academic community than doctorates.

52 Oliver, *In the realms of gold*, p. 49: 'I do not think that any research student in any of the universities in which I have subsequently taught was ever subjected to quite the tests of self-reliance cultivated in post-war Cambridge.'

53 G.S. Graham (1903–88), professor of history, Queen's University, Canada (1936–46), Rhodes professor of imperial history, London (1949–70); his best-known book is probably *Empire of the North Atlantic* (Toronto, 1950, 1959); for assessments, see *OHBE*, vol. V, pp. 332–4, and *ODNB*, vol. XXIII, pp. 186–7 by John Flint. His seminar at the Institute of Historical Research 'became an engine for the decolonisation of imperial history, influencing the profession in every country of the Commonwealth' – he had more than two hundred graduate students in university posts, including Kenneth Dike and Jacob Ajayi.

54 Published as *Bismarck and British colonial policy: the problem of South-West Africa, 1883–1885* (Philadelphia, 1937). Aydelotte subsequently moved into British parliamentary history and quantification.

55 Published as *The Berlin West African Conference, 1884–1885* (1942): 'still the standard work' (A.D. Roberts, *OHBE*, vol. V, p. 470), which 'convincingly demolished many nostrums' (J.E. Flint, ibid., p. 455).

56 R.A. Humphreys, OBE, DLitt (1907–99), professor of Latin American history, London (1948–74), president of the Royal Historical Society (1964–8).

57 Published as *British trade and the opening of China, 1800–1842* (Cambridge, 1951).

58 C. Northcote Parkinson, famous for *Parkinson's Law: the pursuit of progress* (1958); published his thesis as *Trade in the eastern seas* (Cambridge, 1937); professor of history at Singapore (1950–8); author of *British intervention in Malaya, 1867–1870* (Singapore, 1960); recreations 'painting, travel, sailing, badminton'.

59 H.S. Ferns (1913–92), professor of political science, Birmingham (1961–81), thesis published as *Britain and Argentina in the nineteenth century* (Oxford, 1960); recreations, 'journalism, idling, pottering about'.

60 G.A. Shepperson, CBE (b. 1922), King's African Rifles (1942–6); emeritus professor of Commonwealth and American history, Edinburgh; author (with T. Price), *Independent African: John Chilembwe and the origins, setting and significance of the Nyasaland Rising of 1915* (Edinburgh, 1958, 5th edn 1987, reissued 2001). See also p. 5 above.

61 K. Ballhatchet, Reader in Indian history at Oxford, then professor at SOAS; author of *Social policy and social change in western India, 1817–1830* (1957), and *Race, sex and class under the Raj: imperial attitudes and policies and their critics, 1793–1905* (1980).

62 J.D. Fage, 'British African studies since the Second World War', *African Affairs*, vol. 88 (1989), p. 397.

63 J.D. Fage (1921–2002): lecturer at SOAS, London (1959–63), professor of African history, Birmingham (1963–84); with R. Oliver, co-founder and co-editor of *Journal of African History* (1960) and of *Cambridge history of Africa* (7 vols., 1975–86), and co-author of the *Penguin short history of Africa* (1962: seven edns, tr. into German, Italian, Spanish, Catalan, Portuguese, Dutch, Finnish, Afrikaans, and Japanese, with sales of several hundred thousand); recreation 'doing things to houses and gardens'. See J.D. Fage, 'Reflections on the genesis of Anglophone African history after World War Two', *History in Africa*, vol. 20 (1993), pp. 15–26; D.R., 'John Donnelly Fage', *Journal of African History*, vol. 27 (1986), pp. 193–201 (*Festschrift*); R. Oliver, 'John Fage: a personal recollection', ibid., vol. 44 (2003), pp. 1–2: the idea of establishing a journal was 'very fundamental to John's thinking'. Fage's autobiography *To Africa and back* (Birmingham, 2002) explains how he was 'mentally and morally quite exhausted' by the war and 'could not recapture the confident form' of his intellectual achievements before it (pp. 67–8). His principal book was *A history of Africa* (1978, 4th edn 2002: Hutchinson's 'History of human society' series).

64 Tutorial Files, Magdalene College Archives, H/FRS/JDF (references from Benians, Walker, and Turner, 1946–8). Magdalene bye-fellowships were normally for one year only, but in all other respects the same as research fellowships, normally of three years' duration; at this time the college elected to one research fellowship once every three years. Fage was a Bye-Fellow, 1947–9.

65 In 1948 Gallagher and Fage gave a joint course of eight lectures on Africa, and this pilot scheme became a formal proposal for the Lent Term of 1949, with Gallagher down to give the first four lectures on 'European political and economic penetration of West Africa', and Fage the next four on 'European settlement and native problems in Central and East Africa', *CU Reporter*, vol. 79 (1948–9), p.1072; Fage's were never given. I'm not sure this quite justifies the claim by A.D. Roberts that these were the first lectures on tropical Africa in Cambridge (*OHBE*, vol.V, p. 477), since Walker had anticipated them.

66 Roland Oliver (b.1923 at Srinagar, Kashmir), published his thesis as *The missionary factor in East Africa* (London, 1952); he spent the war years at

Bletchley Park, and after Cambridge, his entire career at the School of Oriental and African Studies in London, being professor of the history of Africa, 1963–86. He supervised forty-two theses, of which twenty-six were published. See M.C., 'Roland Oliver', *Journal of African History*, vol. 29 (1988), pp. 1–4, special issue in honour of Roland Oliver, and Oliver, *In the realms of gold.*

67 'The moral disarmament of African empire, 1919–1947', in N. Hillmer and P. Wigley, eds., *The first British Commonwealth: essays in honour of Nicholas Mansergh* (London, 1980), pp. 86–104, repr. from *JICH*, vol. 8.

68 H.R. Tinker (1921–2000), Scholar of Sidney Sussex College, captain in the Indian army (1941–5) serving in Burma, professor of history at Rangoon, Cornell, London; director of the Institute of Race Relations (1970–2), professor of politics, Lancaster (1977–82); thesis published as *The foundations of local self-government in India, Pakistan and Burma* (1954). He three times stood at general elections as a Liberal candidate. Tinker's son, David, was killed in the Falklands War, 1982; three years later Tinker completed *A message from the Falklands: the life and gallant death of David, Lieutenant RN*, which became one of the most powerful anti-war classics of the century. See *Sidney Sussex College Annual* (2000), pp. 115–16; *ODNB* by P. Lyon, vol. LIV, pp. 819–21; *Who's Who*: recreation – 'pottering'.

69 J.C. Ch'eng began his research under Victor Kiernan; his thesis was published as *Chinese sources for the Taiping Rebellion* (Hong Kong, 1963).

70 [P.]N. Tarling, LittD; thesis first published in *Journal of the Malayan Branch of the Royal Asiatic Society*, vol. 30, no. 3 (1957), repr. as *British policy in the Malay Peninsula and Archipelago, 1824–1871* (Kuala Lumpur, 1969); emeritus professor of history, University of Auckland; editor of the *Cambridge history of Southeast Asia* (2 vols., 1992).

71 W. David McIntyre, OBE: emeritus professor of history at the University of Canterbury, Christchurch, New Zealand; his London thesis was published as *The imperial frontier in the tropics, 1865–1875* (1967), a superb study.

72 R.T. Anstey, who wrote a thesis on the Congo and was the author of *The Atlantic slave trade and its British abolition, 1760–1810* (1975), died young, the first professor of modern history at the University of Kent at Canterbury.

73 J.E. Flint, professor emeritus of history at Dalhousie University, Nova Scotia; his thesis was published as *Sir George Goldie and the making of Nigeria* (1956).

74 W.D. Tordoff, supervised by G.S. Graham; thesis published as *Ashanti under the Prempehs, 1888–1935* (Oxford, 1965); author of *Government and politics in Africa* (1984, 1993); professor of politics at Dar es Salaam, Zambia and Manchester.

75 [J.] Richard Gray, professor of African history, University of London, 1972–89, in succession to Roland Oliver, his former supervisor; author of *History of the southern Sudan, 1839–1889* (Oxford, 1961).

76 Tim Beaglehole was the son of J.C. Beaglehole, whose *Life* he wrote (Wellington, 2006); his research supervisor was Kenneth Ballhatchet in London, and his thesis was published as *Thomas Munro and the development of administrative policy in Madras, 1792–1818: the origins of 'the Munro system'* (Cambridge, 1966).

77 W.H. Morris-Jones (1918–99), a graduate of LSE working at Christ's College on political thought, supervised by Professor Sir Ernest Barker; lieutenant-colonel in the Indian army (1941–6), professor of political theory, Durham (1955), professor of Commonwealth history and director, Institute of Commonwealth Studies, London, 1966–83. He specialised in Indian politics.

78 John Omer-Cooper was born in Grahamstown and educated at the Rhodes University and Corpus Christi College, Cambridge, where he took Part II of the Historical Tripos (1955). He became an assistant lecturer at the University of Ibadan, pro-vice-chancellor of the University of Zambia, and professor of history at the University of Otago, 1974–96. He was the author of *The Zulu aftermath* (1966). See his *Tales from the life of a peripatetic historian: extracts from a valedictory lecture* (1996).

79 A.H.M. Kirk-Greene, CMG, studied at Clare College, Cambridge, Modern Languages Tripos, Part I, 1948. He wrote many books on the history of the Colonial Service.

80 H.R.C. Wright, double first (1938, with distinction, 1939); author of *East Indian economic problems in the age of Cornwallis and Raffles* (1961).

81 Frank Welsh, author of *A borrowed place: the history of Hong Kong* (New York, 1993, 1997), *A history of South Africa* (1998), and *Great southern land: a new history of Australia* (2004), all written after a business career.

82 Piers Brendon, author of *The decline and fall of the British empire, 1781–1997* (2007), Magdalene College 1960–3, and later Fellow of Churchill College, where he was Keeper of the Churchill Archives Centre.

83 David Cannadine, Kt (2009), LittD, FBA, director of the Institute of Historical Research, University of London, author of *Ornamentalism: how the British saw their empire* (2001); a Clare College student (double first, 1971, 1972, starred in Part I, later a Fellow of Christ's), supervised in Part II Commonwealth History by Ged Martin.

84 J.M.D. Elvin, starred first, 1959 in Part II. Elvin's research was undertaken within the Oriental Faculty; his books include *The retreat of the elephants: an environmental history of China* (Yale, 2004). Jonathan Spence (Clare College) was an exact contemporary, who went off to do research at Yale, and became an equally famous sinologist.

85 Nightingale's thesis was published as *Trade and empire in western India* (Cambridge, 1970). A.J.S. Reid became professor of South-East Asian history, Research School of Pacific Studies, ANU Canberra. That other pioneer Indonesian specialist, Benedict Anderson, read Classics (double first, 1956, 1957) at King's.

86 G.W. Martin, president of the Cambridge Union, research Fellow of Magdalene College (1970–2), director of the Centre of Canadian Studies, University of Edinburgh and professor of Canadian studies (to 2001); author of *Britain and the origins of Canadian Confederation, 1837–1867* (Basingstoke, 1995).

87 Sir David Cannadine, *Making history, now and then: discoveries, controversies and explorations* (2008), p. 24.

88 Gavin's important thesis remained unpublished, to the detriment of almost every biography of Palmerston; something of his approach may, however,

be seen in his review article, 'Palmerston and Africa', *Journal of the Historical Society of Nigeria*, vol. 6 (Ibadan, 1971), pp. 93–9, criticising Jasper Ridley, *Lord Palmerston*. Gavin taught for many years at Zaria before returning to Ulster. With R.A. Betley he edited documents on the Berlin West Africa Conference in 1973, and he published *Aden under British rule, 1839–1967* (1975).

89 B.J. Porter, Fellow of Corpus Christi College, 1966–8; professor of modern history, University of Newcastle (1992); thesis published as *Critics of empire* (1968, 2nd edn 2008); author of *The lion's share: a short history of British imperialism, 1850–1970* (1975; 4th edn 2004).

90 Published as *The aftermath of revolt: India, 1857–1870* (Princeton, NJ, 1965): Metcalf had to abandon the first sixty pages of his thesis, as it was pre-empted by Stokes, *The English Utilitarians and India* (Oxford, 1959); he is now professor of the history of India and the British empire at the University of California, Berkeley.

91 J.M. Lonsdale, Fellow of Trinity College, and J. Iliffe, LittD, FBA, Fellow of St John's College, both professors of African history.

92 Published as *The conquest of the Western Sudan: a study in French military imperialism* (Cambridge, 1969). Kanya-Forster was a Hungarian graduate of Toronto.

93 Twaddle wanted to explore oral history. For Robinson's doubts about this, see M. Twaddle, 'Historians and African history', in D. Rimmer and A. Kirk-Greene, eds., *The British intellectual engagement with Africa in the twentieth century* (2000), p. 151. Twaddle completed his biography of the Uganda warlord Semei Kakungulu, and became a leading historian of Uganda, at the Institute of Commonwealth Studies in London.

94 A.J. Stockwell, professor of imperial and Commonwealth history, Royal Holloway College, University of London, leading historian of Malaya; he began his career as a civil servant.

95 Andrew Porter, Rhodes professor of imperial history, King's College, University of London (1993–2008); thesis published as *The origins of the South African War* (Manchester, 1980).

96 Donald Denoon, professor of Pacific history, Australian National University, and formerly professor of history, University of Papua New Guinea; thesis published as *A grand illusion: the failure of imperial policy in the Transvaal Colony 1900–1905* (1973).

97 Goodfellow became head of the history department at Roma, the Lesotho Campus of the University of Botswana, Lesotho, and Swaziland, and committed suicide by throwing himself off a cliff overlooking the university in 1966; see Saunders, *The making of the South African past*, pp. 150, and 213, n. 24.

98 'The Swaziland question and a road to the sea, 1887–1895', *Argief-jaarboek vir Suid-Afrikaanse Geskiedenis* (Archives Yearbook for South African History), vol. 2 no. 2 (Cape Town, 1957), pp. 261–434 (MA thesis), written at Sidney Sussex College, 1955.

99 E.D. Steele's career was spent at Leeds; thesis published as *Irish land and British politics: tenant right and nationality, 1865–70* (Cambridge, 1974); in

1991 he published a study of Palmerston's last ten years. D.P.B. Fitzpatrick: associate professor of modern history and Fellow of Trinity College, Dublin.

100 Published as *Canada and the transition to Commonwealth, 1917–1926* (Cambridge, 1977); lecturer in Commonwealth and Canadian history, Edinburgh, before his early death.

101 Published as *The in-between time: Canadian external policy in the 1930s* (Toronto, 1975): professor of history, Carleton University.

102 O.O.G.M. MacDonagh, 'Irish overseas emigration and the state during the great famine' (PhD 1952). MacDonagh become a Fellow of St Catharine's College, then became more interested in the state than the empire, and went on to a distinguished career.

103 Published as *The emergence of Indian nationalism: competition and collaboration in the later nineteenth century* (Cambridge, 1969); despite its undoubted influence, a factual account of some of the educational developments was anticipated by B.T. McCully, *English education and the origins of Indian nationalism*, in *Columbia University Studies in History* (New York, 1940).

104 T. Raychaudhuri, 'Indian nationalism as animal politics', *Historical Journal*, vol. 22 (1979). pp. 747–63; *OHBE*, vol. V, pp. 218, 231–2.

105 J.M. Brown, Fellow of Girton College (1968–71), Beit professor of the history of the British Commonwealth, Oxford and Fellow of Balliol College (1990): leading authority on Gandhi.

106 B.R. Tomlinson, research Fellow of Magdalene College (1978–80), professor of economic history, University of Strathclyde: his especially important pair of articles on 'India and the British empire', 1880–1935 and 1935–1947, appeared in the *Indian Economic and Social History Review*, vols. 12 and 13 (1975, 1976).

107 R. Chandavarkar (1954–2006), Fellow of Trinity College, and university Reader in Indian history.

108 D. Washbrook, Reader in modern South Asian history and Fellow of St Antony's College, Oxford.

109 Francis Robinson, professor of history of South Asia, Royal Holloway College, London.

110 Professor Jalal established her reputation with *The sole spokesman: Jinnah, the Muslim League and the demand for Pakistan* (Cambridge, 1985).

111 J. Gallagher, G. Johnson, and A. Seal, eds., *Locality, province and nation: essays on Indian politics, 1870–1940* (Cambridge, 1973); C. Baker, G. Johnson, and A. Seal, eds., *Power, profit and politics in 20th century India: essays in imperialism, nationalism and change* (Cambridge, 1981).

112 Keith Jeffery, LittD, MRIA, professor of history, University of Ulster at Jordanstown; thesis published as *The British army and the crisis of empire, 1918–1922* (Manchester, 1984).

113 S. Bayly, *Saints, goddesses and kings: Muslims and Christians in south Indian society, 1700–1900* (Cambridge, 1989), p.xii.

114 Personal information from JML, 17 March 2000.

115 The university at this time, through the Colonial Studies Committee, provided lectures for the Overseas Services Courses, which trained probationers

for the Colonial Service. Lecturers in extra-European history were expected to contribute. For example, Walker, Rich, and Gallagher were all involved in 1954, and for many years J.H. Plumb (Professor Sir John Plumb) lectured on African exploration, using his collection of eighteenth-century travellers' books – in 1952 he published, with C. Howard, *West African explorers*; see also J.D. Fage, *To Africa and back*, p. 67.

116 N. Mansergh, *The unresolved question: the Anglo-Irish Settlement and its undoing, 1912–72* (1991), p. 3.

117 Purcell, *Memoirs of a Malayan official*, pp. 163–4.

118 In 1957 Davidson wrote: 'The qualities are not very different that make for real success in scholarship and in the government of colonies', and he implied that Sir Arthur Gordon, governor of Fiji, New Zealand, and Ceylon, should have been able to fulfil his ambition of becoming Regius professor of modern history at Cambridge: 'Scholarship and the government of colonies', *Historical Studies, Australia and New Zealand*, vol. 5 (1953), p. 420.

119 *OHBE*, vol. V, p. 74.

120 Quoted by D.K. Fieldhouse in his inaugural address to the Cambridge Commonwealth Seminar, 1982, though not printed in the formal inaugural lecture, 'Can Humpty-Dumpty Be Put Together Again?' (see note 1 above).

18 The Oxford and Cambridge imperial history professoriate, 1919–1981: Robinson and Gallagher and their predecessors

[Newly written for this volume, this chapter incorporates material on Professor Mansergh which first appeared in the *Oxford dictionary of national biography*, vol. XXXVI (2004), and on professors Robinson and Gallagher in a review of the second edition of *Africa and the Victorians* (1981), in the *Journal of Imperial and Commonwealth History*, vol. 11 (1983), and in 'South Africa, Cambridge, and Commonwealth history', *Round Table: the Commonwealth Journal of International Affairs*, vol. 90, no. 360 (2001).

The aim here is to contribute towards a better understanding of these historians, and what they may or may not have achieved, rather than to assess their work critically or answer their critics.]

The elite group of Oxford and Cambridge professors of imperial history forms a natural unit for historiographical study.[1] Oxford was the pioneer in the field, both with infrastructure (libraries and scholarships) as well as appointments.[2] In 1905 the mining magnate Alfred Beit, shortly before he died, founded the Oxford professorship and a lectureship in colonial history. It was another generation before Cambridge had its first (partly) imperial chair. Thereafter there was considerable inter-penetration between the two universities. Of the Oxford professors, Gallagher, Robinson, and Judith Brown came from Cambridge, while Oxford supplied Walker, Mansergh, Fieldhouse, Low, and Bayly to Cambridge. Only Gallagher held chairs in both universities. Although one could not claim that all the leading British historians of empire in the twentieth century were professors at either Oxford or Cambridge, many of them were. Even Keith Hancock was at one time Chichele professor of economic history at Oxford (1944–9).

I

When the Oxford professorship of colonial history was established, many thought the history of the empire 'a "fancy" subject', a mere side-track of British history (which in Oxford finished in 1837). Nevertheless, the

509

first professor, Hugh Egerton, aimed to establish its relevance to modern politics, as well as 'to kindle a beacon, which shall attract young men, the trustees of the next generation'. He successfully established what his successor Coupland described as a 'fit and profitable field for scientific study'. Egerton's interest in the subject had been fired by his experience as an assistant private secretary to his cousin-by-marriage, Edward Stanhope, secretary of state for the colonies, 1886. This led Egerton to write *A short history of British colonial policy* (1897, 9th edn revised, 1932). He admired Seeley's *Expansion of England*, but sought to provide a more detailed account. This was followed by a short biography of Sir Stamford Raffles (1900) and an edition of the speeches of Sir William Molesworth (1903). In conformity with the historical teaching methods of the day, Egerton gave Oxford colonial history a strongly constitutional and documentary base. His collection of documents, *Canadian constitutional development: selected speeches and despatches* (with W.L. Grant, 1907), long remained on undergraduate reading-lists, for, as he observed in his introduction, it would be difficult to find another hundred-year period anywhere richer in constitutional experience, from military rule to self-governing Dominion (p. vii).[3]

Reginald Coupland held the chair from 1920 to 1950, with the title Beit professor of colonial history. Coupland's original research subject was the ancient Greek city-state, but Lionel Curtis was impressed by his lively mind, and persuaded him to take the Beit lectureship in 1913 in succession to himself. Even so, it was still a surprise when Coupland was elected as the professor. In his inaugural lecture, he passionately urged the relevance of the subject, arguing that the First World War had damagingly shown up how ignorant they were about the United States of America, and the economic interdependence of the rest of the world, especially Africa. He made an eloquent plea for the rising generation to find time to study 'the terrible story' of what Europeans had done in Africa. 'The outer peoples', overseas students, should be welcomed into the Oxford educational system. The conduct of government affairs would benefit from 'the scientific study of politics'. Coupland identified for study what he called the two paramount political problems of the time: nationality (or national self-determination), and the transcendent problem of colour (for 'the world is one'). The Commonwealth could help to solve both issues, especially 'the long march to the brotherhood of man', by its redeeming doctrine of trusteeship. But he made a prophetic warning (though we would read it now in terms more of Islamist fundamentalism than of race): if the 'untutored multitudes' were persuaded that the East could not profit from contact with the West, and regarded all British action as 'Satan's doing', the result would be a dreadful conflict, 'more terribly primitive in its impulses, more inexorable, more destructive than any of its predecessors, the authentic Armageddon, staining all in blood, and ruining the last hope of civilization'.[4]

Coupland became a prominent adviser to government, serving on royal commissions for India and Palestine, and on the staff of the Cripps mission in 1942. He has been described as 'a proconsul manqué'. As well as several books on India, he also wrote on the abolition of the slave trade, on Wilberforce, Raffles, Kirk, and Livingstone. But above all his reputation rests on two large-scale books about East Africa: *East Africa and its invaders* (1938), which went down to 1856, and *The exploitation of East Africa, 1856–1890: the slave trade and the scramble* (1939). These represented 'the first attempt by a serious and academic historian to reconstruct part of the history of tropical Africa', and Coupland deserves great respect for 'entering a neglected field' (John Fage). His long tenure of the chair helped to make him a central figure in putting colonial history on the map in the inter-war period. He believed that nationalist aspirations could be fulfilled within the constitutional structure of the empire. He planned a multi-volume history of nationalism in the British empire, but he never completed this.[5]

If Coupland was a beliverer in the moral rectitude of contemporary British rule, his successor Vincent Harlow – with the revised title of Beit professor of the history of the British empire – pushed even further in a religious-moralising direction. A vicar's son, he was a churchwarden and lay reader. Like Coupland, Harlow believed the future of the world might hang upon the success of the Commonwealth in the 'difficult art of inter-racial co-operation'. Harlow was driven not by the search for a meta-narrative or a master-concept, of which he was suspicious, but by the need to develop in the Commonwealth some 'intrinsic merit', a dynamic inspiration. This could be 'the Christian precept to regard the interests of a neighbour as of equal importance with one's own . . . the inescapable fact remains that the hard crust of [national self-interest] will never be dissolved by anything short of a spiritual evolution towards that absolute standard'. They had to have the courage and humility 'to impregnate politics with religion'. The Commonwealth must be based on respect for the 'moral value of individual liberty'. The Indian demand for equality was 'morally irresistible'. This credo was spelled out to a London audience in 1939. When he delivered his Oxford inaugural in 1950 there was much less in this vein, and more on the problems of writing history, but he did revealingly describe the Expansion of Europe in terms of 'Christendom invading the planet', and the Commonwealth as 'the vindication in corporate action of the absolute value of the spirit of man'. His other main message to Oxford was the methodological need for the historian to avoid specialist compartmentalisation, and 'see and present men and their thinking *whole*', in other words, to 'correlate the political, religious, economic, and social aspects of human thought and behaviour' in an 'intimate relationship . . . components of one . . . organic unity'. He pointed to the danger that 'insularity distorts', and so colony and metropole should be regarded as 'integral to one another'.[6]

This was valuable teaching as far as it went, but Harlow's vision remained Anglocentric, pervaded with a sense of moral purpose. His lectures are remembered as 'infused with a staunchly Christian interpretation'. His seminars for research students are said to have been 'more than a little serious and morally earnest', which could seem 'schoolmasterly and suffocating'. Harlow followed Coupland in attaching great importance to lecturing the probationers of the Colonial Service course. Sometimes he embarrassed them by bursting into tears when talking in a final lecture about their noble mission of trusteeship.[7]

Like many of his generation, Harlow's early historical interests were focused on the seventeenth- and eighteenth-century West Indies. He was Egerton's last pupil, and under his guidance wrote a big book on the history of Barbados.[8] His master-work, though, was the two-volume *The founding of the second British empire, 1763–1793*, which had a truly global scope. His research uncovered huge amounts of material not previously known to historians, and, by his incorporation of China and Latin America into the story, he was a pioneer practitioner of the history of 'informal empire'. He was imaginative enough to elucidate several general themes, though most of these were quietly dropped or modified in the second volume, after astute criticisms suggested by Richard Pares.[9] Nevertheless, Harlow's great work remains one of the finest achievements of the Oxford imperial historians, [10] and perhaps of a wider group as well. (I return to this below, p. 527.)

II

Cambridge is unusual, and may be presumed fortunate, in having two established chairs within the field of imperial and Commonwealth history. On the other hand, neither chair in its initial shape gave the Faculty of History what it wanted, which was a straightforward professorship of 'British imperial history'. Nor, originally, did either have any discernible relationship with a Tripos paper, so most of the incumbents had to find shelter in the tiny and neglected niche in modern English constitutional history, where a provision had existed since 1909 that examination questions *might* be set on the constitutional evolution of the colonies. This purely permissive regulation is indicative of its inherent tokenism, and it was in the main ignored by students whose narrow English-centredness was stretched to the limit by the less easily escaped Irish Question.

The first chair was the Vere Harmsworth professorship of naval history, established in 1919 by Lord Rothermere (formerly H.S. Harmsworth), who later modestly described himself in *Who's Who* as 'interested in newspapers'. In fact he was a Fleet Street magnate whose principal properties were the *Daily Mail*, the *Daily Mirror*, and the *Sunday Pictorial*.[11] Besides the naval chair – a war memorial for a beloved son killed in the First World War, while serving with the Royal Naval Division in France – he also endowed a chair of American history at Oxford, and the King Edward VII chair of English literature at Cambridge. He reserved to himself the right to nominate the first naval professor. J. Holland Rose was at the time not ostensibly a naval historian, still less an imperial one, but it was not at all a bad appointment. Like Seeley before him and Dom David Knowles in a later generation, Holland Rose had taken the Classical Tripos. He became a Fellow of Christ's College in 1914, and developed skills as a historical biographer and populariser. He wrote a two-volume life of William Pitt, and a life of Napoleon which went through eleven editions. He contributed chapters on sea-power to the *Cambridge history of the British empire* and other small items on naval history, but nothing of the same calibre as his Napoleon biography, which held the field in Britain until his death. He founded a studentship (1932) in his name to encourage the study of imperial history, which remains useful. His best-known pupil, who inherited many of his interests, was Gerald Graham, later Rhodes professor in London. A colleague described Rose thus: 'A man of middle height and full figure, somewhat important in manner and speech, of independent spirit and great determination, a Congregationalist in religion, most kind-hearted and friendly, fond of society and of children, and systematic in his habits of work and exercise. Music, walking, cycling, and his garden were his principal recreations.'[12] He visited the United States and South Africa in 1921 and 1933 on lecture tours. In 1932 he protested against the Faculty's decision to allow lectures to be given on so recent a subject as the Russian Revolution.[13] He was the model for the Cambridge don M.L.H. Gay in C.P.Snow's *Strangers and brothers*.

Mindful of the fact that Oxford had the Beit chair since 1905, Cambridge badly wanted a professor of imperial history, but no funds or endowments appeared to be forthcoming. In October 1932 and approaching retirement, Holland Rose himself proposed that his successor should be elided into the Vere Harmsworth professor of *imperial and naval* history. Harold Temperley and G.M. Trevelyan (as chairman of the Faculty Board) warmly supported this change of title as the best available way forward.[14] Rothermere agreed. The intention was that the chair would in future be open to one who professed solely (or chiefly) the history of the British empire *or* naval history: in other words that the chair might remain afloat, or be firmly planted on dry land, or become daringly amphibious. The Faculty was not only seeking to do more for imperial history. It was also concerned about the problem of incorporating naval history into the Tripos, and argued that it was in fact impossible except under the limited 'empire' rubric of constitutional history since 1688. Additionally, it seemed likely to be 'very difficult in practice to get on all occasions a really competent naval history professor'. All these points were made effectively by Trevelyan in the Senate House discussion. A couple of die-hard opponents made carping noises about the downgrading of naval history, but were easily silenced by the reminder that Lord Rothermere had agreed.[15]

Ironically, the first professor elected under the new dispensation was one 'solely professing naval history', Admiral Sir Herbert Richmond. We are unlikely ever again to have a professor who left school at the age of thirteen and went to sea as a midshipman in the Royal Navy. Between 1909 and 1911 Richmond was commander of the *Dreadnought*. Between 1926 and 1931 he was commandant of the Imperial Defence College. From 1920 onwards he wrote comprehensively on British sea-power and strategy in the mid-eighteenth century, most notably a three-volume work on *The navy in the war of 1739–1748* (1920). He was Vere Harmsworth professor for only two years (1934–6) before he had to retire, but he then moved from a professorial fellowship at Jesus College to become Master of Downing College for the remaining ten years of his life. His Ford Lectures (1943) were published in the year of his death, 1946, as *Statesmen and sea-power*. It was a very good book. Richmond was a close friend of Trevelyan, who admired him greatly. Since his navy days he had been a skilled model-maker, particularly of furniture. And he kept bees, 'but they were prone to sting him, and he not infrequently bore their marks and objurgated their unreasonable hostility'.[16]

Next came Eric Walker, from 1936 to 1951, a London-born Oxford man (Merton College). In 1911 he had become the second King George V professor of history at Cape Town at the age of twenty-five – slightly younger even than Hancock in his first chair at Adelaide.[17] Walker held the oldest independent chair of history in sub-Saharan Africa, and he observed ruefully 'history is . . . red-hot here'.[18] On his arrival in Cambridge, E.A. Benians (the leading Cambridge imperial historian) secured his election as a professorial Fellow at the rather less red-hot St John's College. Walker remained there until the 1960s, when he finally retired to South Africa to be cared for by his daughter. His tenure was disrupted not only by the war, but by a severe nervous breakdown, between 1944 and 1946, from which he never fully recovered. In his younger days, with his abundant fair hair and tall athletic build, he was said to have been a 'veritable Adonis'. In advanced age he was a rugged old oak of a figure, increasingly known for his impatience.

There were two dominant passions in Walker's life: rowing and South Africa. He was fanatical about the former, and very much the outspoken 'white liberal' on the latter.[19] Walker was an early producer of scholarly work on its controversial history, writing the lives of prominent men such as W.P. Schreiner and Judge J.H. de Villiers. In 1938 he published *The Great Trek*, timed for its centenary celebrations, and filling a gap which Coupland had identified as one of the 'unwritten epics of nationality'.[20] Walker helped to edit one of the most successful volumes of the *Cambridge history of the British empire*, on *South Africa*; he did attempt to bring Africans into the picture, notably by commissioning C.W. de Kiewiet's brilliant chapter on 'Social and economic developments in native tribal life'. In his own *History of South Africa* – for decades the undisputed principal textbook – he described his theme as 'the adjustment of the mutual relations' between 'Western civilisation, tribal Africa, and to a less degree, theocratic Asia'.[21] However, he clearly found the application of the tripartite theme difficult. In the words of his obituarist: although he displayed 'a mastery of detail woven into a closely connected narrative . . . where a younger generation were apt to look for more critical probings, socio-economic insights and Africanist perspectives, Walker kept to his own approach, his own style and his own interpretation'.[22] It was, perhaps, a polite way of saying that the enlarged and revised 1957 edition of the book,[23] and its author, were soon left behind by modern historical methods and the march of time itself.

It was a similar story with his general textbook, *The British empire: its structure and spirit* (1943, revised edn 1953). It failed to live up to the expectations aroused by his declaration that 'a group of states and dependencies which contains one-fourth of the human race in all its varieties from Bushmen of the Stone Age to professors of anthropology, presents an unrivalled field for the study of problems that are of world-wide importance today'. Nor was there any evidence of his promise to bring a new perspective: 'having lived so long on one of the outer marches, I cannot see the Empire quite as it appears to you at the centre'.[24] The book was an unashamedly Anglo-Saxonist Whiggish narrative. Sound enough for the nineteenth century, the twentieth century became a series of disconnected country narratives of political events, often only loosely related to imperial issues. In its final version (1953 edition), two-fifths of the book covered the period after 1914. It reads as though Walker had used nothing except newspaper reports. Hancock's 'moving frontiers' were not in evidence. Instead, there was a prophetic call to action. Since the disappearance of the empire would be 'a disaster for mankind', Walker hoped it would continue, changed indeed into a federation, but still recognisably 'the Empire'. The 'discordant cacophony' of the 'amorphous Commonwealth' could be voluntarily federated into a real government, a beneficent 'centre of stability', to which eventually the USA and the European democracies might rally in the interests of world peace and freedom. The British had, after all, long been 'great political amalgamators', as well as champions of personal liberty. Walker concluded *The British empire* with a reverential quotation from Smuts about freedom as the 'most ineradicable craving of human nature' (pp. 333–7). The idea of the empire as a standard-bearer for liberty, and its history as the unfolding story of Freedom, was excusably sharpened (at least in the short run) by the experience of the Second World War, and even Hancock was not immune to it. But Walker's continuing commitment to the Edwardian chimera of 'imperial federation' seems eccentric. The ecclesiastical style adds to the impression: it was a bit late by 1953 to speak of the empire as sustained by 'faith, hope and charity', or of the USA as its 'colossal flying buttress' (p. 244).

Walker encouraged his research students to drop in for tea on Sunday afternoons. His star pupil, the New Zealander 'Jim' Davidson, did this regularly, finding Walker and his wife 'both delightfully unpretentious people', whose greatest pleasure seemed to be bicycle rides on Saturday afternoons. In May 1939 Walker could not conceal from Davidson his vitriolic contempt for Neville Chamberlain's 'shambling and most disreputable government'.[25] Walker did everything he could to advance Davidson's prospects, and was disappointed when he was not elected as his successor in the chair, or indeed to the Beit professorship in Oxford.

The Cambridge succession fell to the first internal Faculty candidate to occupy the chair. Not altogether satisfactorily. 'Teddy' Rich was qualified by long service as a history lecturer, and by extensive research and editing of Hudson's Bay Company records (with assistants); he also wrote a three-volume history of the company (1961), and two smaller books on the fur trade.[26] He was, however, a dry-as-dust historian, widely regarded as fuddy-duddy. Some of his research on eighteenth-century Canada will retain its value for specialists, but his reputation has suffered the final eclipse of not rating even a single mention in the *Historiography* volume of the *OHBE*. In his inaugural lecture, Rich rather foolishly proclaimed his hope that he would be the last 'imperial and naval' professor, and that the chair would revert to being solely for naval historians, after what he called a 'brief but stimulating episode' under his two predecessors.[27]

III

Rich said this because the second Cambridge chair, the Smuts professorship, was now on the horizon, though fortunately his advice was ignored, thus enabling Jack Gallagher to be his successor in the Vere Harmsworth chair. The Smuts chair in the 'history of the British Commonwealth' was part of a national memorial to Jan Smuts (see above, pp. 342–3).[28]

Nicholas Mansergh was the first Smuts professor, arriving in 1953, and at once elected as a Fellow of St John's College.[29] He read history in pre-war Oxford under R.B. McCallum at Pembroke, and began research under W.G.S. Adams, the Gladstone professor of government, who shared his particular interest in Ireland. This led to a pair of 'political science' books, the *Irish Free State: its government and politics* (1934) and *The government of Northern Ireland* (1936). These were followed by a study of *Ireland in the age of reform and revolution* (1940), later revised and expanded attractively as *The Irish Question, 1840–1921: a commentary* (1965). During the war Mansergh became the Irish expert and director of the empire division of the Ministry of Information (leading to the award of the OBE), and then an assistant secretary at the Dominions Office (1946–7). Despite his natural gifts as a civil servant, he returned to academic life in 1947 as a research professor at the Royal Institute of International Affairs, where he wrote sequels to Hancock's *Survey of British Commonwealth affairs*, on external policy from 1931, and on post-war change to 1952. Surprisingly, he was not much called upon by Whitehall for advice: both the Colonial Office and the Commonwealth Relations Office turned instinctively to Oxford, and to Sir Reginald Coupland, Dame Margery Perham, and Sir Kenneth Wheare as its preferred constitutional experts. However, Mansergh did have an impact on Commonwealth development through a lecture delivered at Chatham House in December 1947, a remarkable statement which influenced the Irish and Indian governments and was much quoted by their politicians. In it, Mansergh predicted a more valuable future for an association based on shared values rather than reliance on 'out-of-date imperial terminology'.[30]

A member of the Anglo-Irish gentry, the Manserghs of Grenane, Tipperary, he was born into a family involved with the empire and the army. He was the son of a railway engineer – one of his father's survey photographs illustrates *The Commonwealth experience* (plate 7: the Beira–Salisbury line, *c.*1897). Mansergh was a striking figure, six feet three inches tall. August but always smiling and approachable, his patrician manner was kindly and dignified but never pompous. He was slow and deliberate of utterance, curiously adding an 'a' or 'ah' sound after dental consonants (during the Suez Crisis, 'I shall never vote Conservative again-ah' – actually a rare example of indiscretion). He was a life-long communicant member of the Church of Ireland, and a fine tennis player.[31]

Despite the war years and the mastership of St John's, Mansergh's output was large: five books on Irish history, six books on Commonwealth history, with three volumes of supporting 'documents and speeches', several revised editions, two major lecture-booklets, more than thirty-six articles (giving rise to two posthumous collections of essays), and, as editor-in-chief, the twelve magnificent and acclaimed volumes of documents, *Transfer of power in India, 1942–7* (1970–82), appearing at the rate of one a year. Although as with all his documentary collections, the introductions are rather thin, this series will remain a valuable research tool for a long time to come. In many ways, though, he would probably have regarded the centrepiece of his oeuvre as *The Commonwealth experience* (1969, new edn 1982), a history covering the years 1839 to 'the present'. Widely recognised as the finest book on the subject, it exemplifies that 'detachment with sympathetic insight' which he always aimed at. More than one of its chapters were model examples of the art of stylish historical synthesis. But a waning interest in the Commonwealth may push it to the margins of what is read in future.

In retirement Mansergh completed *The unresolved question: the Anglo-Irish settlement and its undoing, 1912–1972* (published posthumously, 1991), an unrivalled and humane study of Anglo-Irish relations in the wider Commonwealth context, which he understood better than anyone. If in his writing about Commonwealth history, Mansergh retained what was often described as an Olympian detachment, where Ireland was concerned this was much harder. For him, the events of Irish history were experienced as 'near realities, not as distant phenomena or as issues in high politics' (p. 3; see above, p. 495). If he contributed uniquely to the understanding of what an apparently nebulous Commonwealth actually was, he was also one of the most accomplished and fair-minded practitioners of the history of his beloved Ireland. His Irish perspectives enriched his Commonwealth studies, and his perception of the Commonwealth deepened his analysis of Ireland.[32] He was a precise and thoughtful scholar.[33] His weakness perhaps was a relative lack of interest in economic history and in the tropical dependencies. For these reasons some might judge him not to be quite in the same league as Hancock.[34] On the other hand, his commitment to an independent India is impressive, while his short monograph on *South Africa: the price of magnanimity, 1906–1961* suggests that he felt more deeply about the tragic plight of the black communities than Hancock had done.

As a Cambridge professor, Mansergh was notably – and success-fully – concerned to raise the profile of the study of both Irish and Commonwealth history. The rubric for the Smuts chair encouraged travel, and Mansergh took full advantage of this, travelling widely, and frequently to Canada and New Delhi, but also to Canberra, Duke, and Cape Town. He established Cambridge's first proper research seminar for graduate students, an immense advance, now transmuted into the World History Seminar. He cared about his pupils and knew exactly how to help and encourage them.

Mansergh's successor was Eric Stokes (from 1970 to 1981), who had graduated from Christ's College and taught in Singapore, Bristol, and Salisbury, Rhodesia as well as in Cambridge. His was a controversial appointment, which surprised many people who thought that R.E. Robinson should have been preferred. Could the little man bend the bow of Ulysses?

There was certainly a shift in aim. For Eric Stokes the point of Commonwealth history was that it could provide an entry into 'Third World' studies. He was one of those 'war-bred' historians for whom Commonwealth experience came 'early and unasked', in army service alongside soldiers drawn from all over the empire: 'We passed through a crucible that for some of us set the pattern of our lives.' Musing further on scholarly motivation, he believed that much of the drive into overseas history 'is a paradoxical attempt to register the authenticity of a totally separate world of existence, and at the same time to appropriate that experience into this narrow domestic circle; to enjoy, as it were, a dual emotional citizenship, like men, as Maine said, bound to make their watches keep true time in two longitudes at once.'[35]

Stokes was a curious and unconventional character, though impish rather than radical. He was much given to playing the Cockney 'cheeky-chappy', a role that his appearance did not entirely belie, with his fringed haircut and eye-magnifying spectacles; and his conversation was pep-pered with interrogative 'hurmmph's. There were those – and they were not only foreigners – who found him disconcerting and perhaps not easy to take with perfect seriousness. (If Peter Sellers had ever had to play a middle-aged professor, Stokes would have been the perfect model.) Nevertheless, he was a man of fertile intellect, a practising Christian, with many devoted pupils, while his premature death from cancer was a tragedy.

Eric Stokes was one of that gifted generation of historians who some-how managed to straddle both African and Indian history, Gallagher and Low being other examples. After his illuminating and much-read book, *The English Utilitarians and India* (1959), he became professor of history at the University College of Rhodesia and Nyasaland, explaining to a friend that he wanted 'to make some contribution to the awful African problem'.[36] There, he stimulated pioneering work on Central African history, published as *The Zambesian past* (1966), by various hands, including his own on Malawi and the Lozi of Barotseland. Back in Cambridge, Robinson urged him to lecture on 'theories of imperialism', which he did, although he decided mainly to promote Indian social and economic history, specialising himself in the neglected field of Indian agrarian history. Wrestling now with tenure and taxes, ryots and zemind-ars, rent-rate and land-settlement reports, he seemed set to become the Vinogradoff of Indian history. Because he died at the age of fifty-six, however, it is unclear what he might have achieved. But Professor Sir Christopher Bayly is no doubt right that an accessible big book was prob-ably beyond him: 'a love of paradox, scepticism, and a fundamental honesty about the limits of historical explanation would always have pre-vented him from bundling up his ideas on this subject in an appropriately dramatic form'.[37]

IV

For many, the names of Robinson and Gallagher are practically synony-mous with Oxbridge imperial and 'expansion of Europe' history in the second half of the twentieth century, and certainly they were the domi-nant presence from the 1950s to the 1980s. Their famous article 'The imperialism of free trade' (*Economic History Review*, 1953), redefined the shape of a subject in a way which it is seldom given to any scholars to do, and it is arguably the single most influential British journal article in any area of history since 1945 (though with just twenty-five footnotes, it would not be accepted for publication today). *Africa and the Victorians* (1961) is one of the half-dozen most admired books in the field, an exceptional achievement and satisfyingly controversial. It is history on the grand scale, though much shortened for publication: a strong theo-retical backbone, events brilliantly described, pen-portraits nicely drawn (on the 'intricacy' of Gladstone's nature: 'He could chop logic with the most sparkling of the High Churchmen, yet frame budgets with the grim-mest of the utilitarians').[38] Although it contains a good account of the origins of the South African War, not everyone accepts its central thesis on the partition of Africa, as driven by 'nationalist crises' in the south and in Egypt – since these were only part of a more widespread and fundamental destabilisation. But this hardly affects its status as a 'classic'. Legends about it abound: that it was hammered out in the bar of 'The Blue Boar', that it was rejected by both OUP and CUP, that Harold Macmillan 'never understood a word of it', that it would never have been finished but for Alice Denny (Mrs Robinson). The authors, too, are legendary. Much has been written about 'the Robinson and Gallagher thesis',[39] and about R.[40] and G.[41] themselves individually. I have myself three times written elsewhere about *Africa and the Victorians*,[42] so I will say no more about it here.

Both men were, of more or less working-class origins (R. was from Battersea, the son of a warehouse stock-keeper and salesman, G. was from Birkenhead, an Irish railwayman's son), and each attended his local grammar school. Both were formidable intellectuals who retained their anti-establishmentarianism and plebeian sympathies – they hated social injustice, and boasted that their motto was 'high thinking and low living'. Both fought mightily in the Second World War: R. was an RAF squadron leader in Bomber Command (awarded the DFC), while G. was a sergeant commanding a tank in the Royal Tank Regiment in the North African desert war ('like a latter-day T.E. Lawrence', who chose to enlist in the ranks).[43] Although both rejected their youthful religious affiliations (the one a Plymouth Brother, the other a Catholic, with a mother who hoped he was destined for the priesthood), each was a true-believing warrior-scholar. In another time and another place, either would have been as charismatic a jihadist as any Usman dan Fodio or al-Hājj 'Umar. But there were differences too. If Robinson was – to use their own conceptual terminology – a Resister (careful to perform the rituals of invulnerability, for example urinating against the aircraft wheels), then Gallagher was a Collaborator. Jack was never more content than when being a reconciler and a peacemaker. Where G. was charming and emollient, R. could be challenging and abrasive. While G. always nursed his pupils along genially, R. demanded unswerving loyalty before revealing his affectionateness. If R., once a very good-looking soccer Blue, cut a dashing figure, G. was decidedly sedentary: Buddha in a bow tie, perhaps, though some thought him more like the Cheshire Cat or Sir John Falstaff. G. gave no recreations in *Who's Who*, but R. proclaimed his life-long enthusiasm for 'room cricket'. Where G. was witty, R. was sardonic. G. was the more learned, a veritable polymath. Robinson's expertise was narrower, and he was the more committed theoriser, almost hypnotised by the search for 'a new unifying concept', the big hypothesis.[44] Both had verbal facility, but where G. was imaginative, R. was astringent. If G. had more eccentricities, R. had more vulnerabilities. While G. remained unmarried, R. became a family patriarch. However, Gallagher's joke that he was always on the look-out for a scented letter suggests much less amorous success than was actually the case.[45] Titans though they both became, they never ceased to be Young Turks at heart.[46] They always had irreverent nicknames for many of their colleagues, especially the professors: Hot Lips, Boyo, Daddy, Rhino, Electric Whiskers, Wet Legs in Cambridge,[47] while further afield there was Dormouse and the Great Stamboulski in Oxford, the Grand Eunuch of London, and the Playboy of the Western World.

Everyone liked and admired Jack Gallagher, but 'Robbie' was not without his detractors. He was perhaps less successful in smoothing away the hard edges of his background, and he was never one to put people at ease. Although he could be very amusing, he never quite managed to conceal his edgy seriousness about 'big issues'. His wartime experiences – two years being spent in pilot-training in Southern Rhodesia – had changed him profoundly. As with many of his contemporaries (Gallagher included), the naive socialist, the flirter with communism, and the pacifist idealist disappeared for good. He became somewhat contemptuous of dons who had led more sheltered lives. Battersea and Bomber Command were tough schools, and Barraclough (his Part I supervisor for the Historical Tripos) was an exceptionally rigorous task-master.[48] All left their mark. After the war, he was one of the first batch of Cambridge students taking 'The Expansion of Europe' paper, which he was taught by 'Jim' Davidson. But it was Eric Walker who superintended his research, approving his proposed topic as 'a good one'.[49]

Robinson secured a fellowship at St John's College with the draft of his doctoral dissertation on trusteeship in Central Africa, 1889–1939 (see above pp. 490–1).[50] Both referees, Professor Vincent Harlow and Ifor L. Evans,[51] commented how lucky he was in his material, based on privileged access to closed records in the Colonial Office. The documentation was 'quite unusually impressive', and his handling of it was 'balanced and fair-minded', showing insight into the interplay of diverse forces. He had filled an important gap. Harlow concluded that he had 'the makings of a really good historian'. Having been employed from 1947 to 1949 as a research officer in the newly established African Studies Branch at the Colonial Office,[52] under Andrew Cohen, Robinson decided not to become a permanent civil servant, believing – quite correctly – that he had neither the talent nor the charm required.[53] So he took up the research fellowship, which, in the conventions of the day, meant having to do a great deal of teaching. He became a university lecturer in 1954.

As a supervisor of undergraduates he could be stimulating but also a bit intimidating. Often sitting hunched up in his little dark room (once the bedroom of a grander seventeenth-century set), with only a few books, silences would be punctuated with much knocking out of a favourite pipe against the surround of a flickering gas-fire, before the delivery of unexpected one-liners ('it's all a load of balls, old boy' – this said with a rattling laugh; or 'Queer buggers, the Chinese' – more ruminatively). During the 1960s, research students absorbed a substantial amount of his energies. He also spent a good deal of time organising, chairing, and then editing the proceedings of a series of summer conferences known as the Cambridge Development Conferences, on Third World economic problems.[54] After *Africa and the Victorians* his mainstream historical publications stalled. He never attempted a large-scale general survey, though the opportunity must have come his way. It was becoming plain that he was essentially an essayist, a master of the creative and trenchant proposition.[55] In the 1970s he set out to write a biography of his hero, Sir Andrew Cohen, but we have only sketches for it.[56] There were several reasons for this. In part he felt that recent publications had pre-empted much of the story, but also that it would be difficult for him to recover significantly more of Cohen's scattered minutes and memoranda from the CO records. Unlike his earlier research project, no conveniently accessible 'confidential print' existed for the post-war period.

'A perfect circulation of elites', was Stokes's quip about the swapping of the Beit chair between R. and G. in 1971 and Gallagher's return to Cambridge. Alas, poor Eric! – he never understood just how mortified Robinson had been when Stokes was preferred over him for the Smuts chair in succession to Mansergh.[57] Privately, Robinson felt that Stokes, by applying for the Smuts professorship at all, had stabbed him in the back. Election to the Beit chair in Oxford gave him the intellectual recognition he needed for his morale, though he soon discovered that 'professors are figures of fun and everybody's dogs-bodies administratively speaking'.[58] In Oxford for the next sixteen years, he retained his concern for his 'old gang' in Cambridge, even spending his leave helping out in 1981 after Gallagher's death in 1980.

All who heard Gallagher's undergraduate lectures admired their global span. Where others might announce their courses as being about the British and other empires, Gallagher, tongue in cheek, announced that he was concerned with the 'Tokyo to Tipperary group of civilisations'. He tackled everything from 1500 onwards fearlessly but with careful preparation: the Spanish, the Portuguese, the Dutch, North American Indians, Jesuit missions, the profits of the Atlantic slave trade and its impact on Africa, eighteenth-century Quebec and Louisiana, Latin American independence, the British in West Africa, the French in North

R.1 to R.2.

Sorry to have delayed comment on drafts.Too much bloody teaching.

It is of course hard to comment without seeing the whole work,b
but one point occurred to me on the Comparison with Unionist policy;
Should it not be pointed out that one big difference was not simply
oneof basic principle and prejudice,but difference in situation.After all
the Unionists had got into being seeing things simplyxxx thro pro-brit,loyalist
eyes because when they were in office that was all they had to play with in
the way of south African cards.Of course they inclined that way in any case
because they were anglo-saxon believers and not brotherhood of man orientated
likethe Liberals.But the Liberals could afford to be liberal in a sense not
merely because of their unconscious presumptions but also because once again
they were playing from strength i.e. the occupation of the Transvaal which
ace had been acquired by a war thatthey had opposed.

It maybe that this pointis worth making explicit here .It has the
advantage of blurring thepresent impression that the difference between
Unionistand Liberal was entirely one of prinxi theoretical principle
and to that extent academic;whereas politics is never really quite like
that --or is it ? Obly propaganda is like that . You dont want to leave
the impression that the Liberals were angels and the Unionists devils.

Plate 18.1 Robinson's comments (first part), undated, but *c*.1965, on early drafts for my first book, *Elgin and Churchill at the Colonial Office.* This is typical of the kind of help he would give to research students. In line 11 the overtyped word is 'unconscious'.

Africa, country trade and the growth of British power in India, the East Indies and 'innovative' Raffles, the South Pacific islands and early settlement in Australia, the changing motives and methods of European expansion. As the 1960s opened, he developed a pioneering course on 'colonial nationalism', African, Indian, and Arab. He made the unfamiliar amusingly accessible: divisions in Islam were like those between Evangelicals and High Churchmen; Africa in the 1960s was similar to England under the Tudors (a dig at Geoffrey Elton). Nevertheless he warned that European models of nationalism (relying on 'economic stages' and class conflict) would only break down if applied to Africa and Asia. More revealing would be the political splits between young and old in elites coping with rapid change: 'Nationalism is pre-eminently the occupation of the young.'

By the early 1960s Gallagher's global approach was well advanced. He wanted 'a unified view of modern world history', with an emphasis on problems rather than regions. White migrations within the empire should be seen in the context of Chinese, Indian, and African movements. 'Looking in from the outside is the occupational vice which bedevils Western students of African or Asian history, even if the road to ethnocentricity is paved with the best of intentions.' The cartographers of old 'hid their ignorance of Africa by drawing elephants over blank patches; we modern historians cover ours with excuses about European attitudes'. Nor were traditional methods of Western political theory, least of all Marxism, of much help in understanding colonial nationalism. Partly this was because 'colonies do not have industrial revolutions. That is why they are colonies.' Much more to the point was to study the behaviour of local elites. The problem for imperial governments under pressure is why nationalists should 'accept cheques from crashing banks'. At the same time he disapproved of 'the shoddy arguments' which tried to hold Western regimes to Utopian standards: 'Colonialism is not the form of government hardest to endure, but the form of government safest to attack.'[59] As may be seen from these fizzing aphorisms, Gallagher had evolved a style that was (as John Darwin puts it), 'ironic and humorous, sometimes mocking and caustic, but never dull, repetitive or merely conventional'.[60]

For some, Jack was their 'great guru'. Those who knew him more as a colleague than as a mentor had many opportunities to observe, and be grateful for, his helpfulness and supportive kindness. He could be hard to get hold of, and he was notoriously contemptuous of institutional paperwork, though always punctilious about writing references for his pupils. On academic business he was patient, worthwhile to listen to, confident and fair-minded in his decisions, while on non-business he was convivial, a delightful companion and raconteur, intensely interested in everything and everybody, 'amused, irreverent, and sceptical'. He loved living in Trinity College, and Trinity made him its Vice-Master in the days of 'Rab' Butler. He was also dean in charge of discipline, boasting that he had not had a single case of sheep-shagging.

Gallagher's early work on eighteenth- and early nineteenth-century British relations with West Africa ought not to be forgotten, as we continue to ponder what he had to say on 'the crisis of empire, 1919–1922',[61] or the grass-roots intricacies of Bengal politics in the 1930s. By one of the most intriguing of role-reversals, of course, Gallagher's turn to India was confirmed by sitting at the feet of his own pupil, Anil Seal, there to have his drafts 'castigated and emended'.[62] The Ford Lectures (1974), however, gave him an opportunity to revert to doing what he did best, the broad survey, with plenty of literary allusions and stylistic fireworks. He tried out all six draft lectures at the Cambridge seminar; that was a memorable term for the seminar. He mastered the British political background, 'the home base', with relish. And he neatly avoided appropriating a directly Gibbonian title by flagging new interpretation about a revival associated with the wartime effort.[63]

The decline, revival and fall of the British empire eschews grand theory. One of its most memorable sentences reads, 'Here and there on the mountain of truth lie the frozen bodies of theorists, some still clutching their ice-picks, others gripping their hammers and sickles.' But if there is no fully articulated theory – and the main discussion does not go much beyond 1947 – there is an analytical framework based upon a 'triangle of forces', which he saw as bringing about imperial collapse.[64] This methodological tool can be called *Gallagher's nutcracker*. The essence of the analysis was that colonies crack, and independence emerges, when they are held between 'the two jaws of the nutcracker', international pressures and domestic constraints, and when essential leverage is applied by the third element, 'local-colonial politics', building enough pressure to persuade the British government to accept its demands. Gallagher was interested to see how crises interlocked, and 'one set of forces worked on the other in critical situations'. Although he was inclined to think that developments in the 'colonial political balance' were especially significant, in part because always present, he also recognised the salience of the response of the government in London to them, the willingness to 'open unto them', those who knocked. His *alter ego*, Robinson, refined this insight: imperial powers pack up and go when they run out of local collaborators ('Robinson's rule').[65] The influence of Gallagher's three inter-related elements clearly underpins all the chapters in the *Oxford history of the British empire*.

V

The premature death of Jack Gallagher (essentially from earlier neglected diabetes) and Eric Stokes in 1980–1 marked in some ways the end of an era, particularly in Cambridge, where a younger generation quickly came to the fore. Both Oxford and Cambridge had by the end of the 1970s become, if somewhat belatedly, leading centres for imperial, Commonwealth, Indian, and African history.[66] If a review is attempted of the performance of the eleven Oxbridge professors in the previous three-quarters of a century (Egerton, Coupland, Holland Rose, Richmond, Walker, Harlow, Rich, Mansergh, Stokes, Gallagher, and Robinson), it is perhaps surprising that more works of enduring significance did not emerge *during their tenures*. Coupland and Mansergh produced the biggest body of work as professors, and Mansergh's oeuvre is, taken as a whole, particularly impressive, though dominated by surveys and compilations rather than analytical research. Robinson and Gallagher wrote a number of enormously influential essays, and Cambridge clearly scored an outstanding hit with *Africa and the Victorians*, though this was a collaborative work produced before either of the authors obtained his chair. It is therefore hard to argue that at least before 1981, Harlow's *Founding of the second British empire* is not the best single piece of research-based narrative by the Oxbridge professors, a classic piece of scholarship.[67]

However, any genuine assessment of the achievements of these men ought to be set in a wider perspective. Who else outside this group, down to 1981, might occupy a place in the Valhalla of imperial historians? It is probably common ground that Keith Hancock has been the presiding genius or avatar of twentieth-century imperial history, rather than any of these Oxbridge historians. His *Survey of British Commonwealth affairs* decisively broke new ground, and remains a spectacular vision of how, ideally, the subject might develop.[68] Amongst other possible contenders, A.P. Newton, Harlow's predecessor as Rhodes professor of imperial history at London, from 1921 to 1938, is unlikely to win many votes.[69] Newton's academic career began as a lecturer in physics, but more mystifying than his switch to history was his penchant for mixing research on the spacious history of West Indies exploration with the narrowest technicalities of English constitutional history. Although Newton played a major role in the inter-war years in supervising research students in imperial history – and in getting their theses published – he wrote little of enduring significance himself.[70]

There are, however, three other historians from the inter-war years who made outstanding contributions to imperial history, albeit from slightly off-centre positions: William M. Macmillan (on South African and colonial dynamics), Richard Pares (on the eighteenth-century Atlantic empire), and Cornelius de Kiewiet (on nineteenth-century South Africa). In each case their reputations in this field suffered from truncated output. Pares was lost to early death, de Kiewiet to American university administration. Macmillan became distracted by unemployment, politics, and journalism. He was a Fabian socialist, playing 'a full and fearless part in public affairs'. His *Bantu, Boer and Briton: the making of a South African native problem* (1929, 1963) was an important landmark, part of a trilogy, in which the missionary Dr John Philip was the hero. As professor at the University of the Witwatersrand in the inter-war years, Macmillan was more influential on the development of South African historiography than his contemporary Eric Walker. His interests broadened, and in 1959 he published *The road to self-rule: a study in colonial evolution*. Notable for its lively and thoughtful discussion of big themes over a period of two centuries, it never quite established itself, being overshadowed by A.P. Thornton's more original, if metropolitan-based, *The imperial idea and its enemies*, published in the same year.[71]

Although Pares was professor of history at Edinburgh, from 1945 to 1954, he was a quintessentially Oxford academic. He made an impressive contribution to the history of the West Indies within the imperial economy. His *War and trade in the West Indies, 1739–1763* (1936) was a central text, a colossal study in 612 pages. Harlow went out of his way publicly to praise it as a 'notable synthesis', and rightly drew attention to its 'masterly reassessment of the negotiations leading up to the Treaty of Paris and the treaty itself'.[72] (It remains a standard analysis of this subject.) Pares was as fully a member of the 'historical establishment' as it is possible to be: the son of a historian of Russia (Bernard Pares), married to the daughter of the medievalist Sir Maurice Powicke, editor of the *English Historical Review* for the unusually long time of twenty years (1939–58), a Fellow of All Souls (1924–45 and 1954–8), and a Ford Lecturer. He was commissioned to write the *Oxford history of England* volume for 1760 to 1815, but he was defeated by ill-health. Crippled by 'progressive muscular atrophy' (a form of motor neurone disease) he become completely paralysed before dying at the age of fifty-six. But he did produce an admirable volume on *George III and the politicians* (1953), based on his Ford Lectures. Unquestionably he was among the most outstanding British historians of his time.[73] His empire studies are rewarding but quite technical in their approach: nothing, for instance, could be more misleading than the catchpenny title: *Yankees and Creoles*.[74] He also wrote a clutch of significant articles on imperial issues.[75]

De Kiewiet was a cosmopolitan figure. Born in Holland, brought up in South Africa, he attended the universities of Witwatersrand (where he was inspired by W.M. Macmillan), Paris, and Berlin, and was a PhD student under Newton in London. He was disillusioned by what he saw as 'the secondariness of imperial studies' in British universities in the 1920s : 'In not one of the British universities did scholarship in the greatest expansion of cultural influence since the Roman Empire acquire the dignity and the stature of the great traditional fields like medieval or constitutional history.' So in 1929 de Kiewiet emigrated to the USA. There he rose through teaching posts in the universities of Iowa and Cornell to become president of Rochester University in New York. It was from there that he observed after the Second World War a proper effort at last being made 'to realize the late-Victorian promise of an era of vigorous and creative imperial studies'. If this had happened sooner, he said, and the British had invested the study of their empire and Commonwealth with 'the stature, the intellectual excitement, the diversity and the imaginativeness which it deserved', fewer mistakes might have been made in the conduct of affairs, especially in Africa. For de Kiewiet history was the 'indispensable agent to wise and successful action' and decision-making.[76]

Although he wrote exclusively about South Africa, de Kiewiet saw this as definitely 'part of the history of the British empire', and he remained a strong advocate of imperial and Commonwealth studies as a way of understanding African problems. As a historian, de Kiewiet is under-recognised. Whilst Hancock was spinning his elegant literary excursions, and Sir Lewis Namier was shaping a new kind of eighteenth-century English history out of the voluminous Newcastle Papers, de Kiewiet was forging a new way of writing nineteenth-century colonial and African history out of the even more voluminous Colonial Office records. As a stylist he was the equal of Hancock, and while Namier wrote up only highly concentrated fragments, de Kiewiet published three major pioneering books and one small one, each a fully rounded study of its subject and together covering an extended period. *The anatomy of South African misery* was an early attempt to understand the pathology of apartheid. Lucid, elegant, and outspoken, it made him particularly well known and admired in the USA. His *History of South Africa, social and economic* (1941) remained for decades by far the best book on South African history. And until the advent of Wm. Roger Louis in the mid-1960s, establishing a new benchmark, no other scholar, Oxbridge professor or otherwise, achieved the same depth of archival penetration into government files.[77]

Notes

1 For the general background: W.R. Louis, 'Introduction' to *OHBE*, vol. V, *Historiography* (ed. R.W. Winks, 1999), pp. 1–42, and R.E. Robinson, 'Oxford in imperial historiography', in F. Madden and D.K. Fieldhouse, eds., *Oxford and the idea of Commonwealth: essays presented to Sir Edgar Williams* (Oxford, 1982), pp. 30–48.

2 For Oxford: F. Madden, 'The Commonwealth, Commonwealth history, and Oxford, 1905–1971', in Madden and Fieldhouse, eds., *Oxford and the idea of Commonwealth*; Richard Symonds, *Oxford and empire: the last lost cause?* (1986); Michael Bentley, *Modernizing England's past: English historiography in the age of modernism, 1870–1970* (Cambridge, 2005), 'Empire', pp. 70–81.

3 H.E. Egerton (1855–1927), *The claims of the study of colonial history upon the attention of the University of Oxford, an inaugural lecture, 1906* (Oxford, 1906); R. Coupland and N. Banerji, 'Egerton, Hugh', in *ODNB*, vol. XVII, pp. 995–6; J.G. Greenlee, '"A succession of Seeleys": the "Old School" re-examined', *JICH*, vol. 4 (1976), pp. 266–82. Egerton contributed a chapter to the *Cambridge history of the British empire* (hereafter *CHBE*), vol. I, on 'The literature and social life of the old empire', pp. 784–827.

4 Sir Reginald Coupland, KCMG, CIE, FBA (1884–1952). R. Coupland, *The study of the British Commonwealth: an inaugural lecture* (Oxford, 1921).

5 J.D. Fage, Introduction to Coupland's *The British anti-slavery movement* (2nd edn, 1964), pp. ix–xvii; W.R. Louis, foreword to *OHBE*, vol. V, p. ix, and Introduction, pp. 23–4; see also the entry on Coupland in *ODNB*, vol. XIII, pp. 660–1, by Alex May.

6 Vincent Harlow, CMG, Dlitt (1898–1961). V.T. Harlow, *The character of British imperialism: an inaugural lecture* (London, 1939), and *The historian and British colonial history: an inaugural lecture, 16 November 1950* (Oxford, 1951). Harlow had been Rhodes professor in London, 1938 to 1948. There is an illuminating discussion of Harlow in W.D. McIntyre, *The Britannic vision: historians and the making of the British Commonwealth of Nations, 1907–1948* (2009), pp. 53–6. See also Louis in *OHBE*, vol. V, pp. 35–7.

7 Symonds, *Oxford and empire*, p. 55; Madden, 'The Commonwealth, Commonwealth history, and Oxford', pp. 19–20.

8 V.T. Harlow, *A history of Barbados, 1625–1685* (Oxford, 1926), 347 pp., based on his BLitt dissertation.

9 R. Pares, 'The *"Founding of the second British empire"* vol. I', *English Historical Review*, vol. 68 (1953), pp. 282–5; RH, 'British imperial expansion in the late eighteenth century', *Historical Journal*, vol. 10 (1967), pp. 113–24.

10 Harlow also made three contributions to the *CHBE*: vol. II, 'The new imperialism, 1783–1815', pp. 129–87; and vol. VIII, *South Africa* (1936), 'The British occupation, 1795–1822', and 'Cape Colony, 1806–1822'.

11 Of Rothermere it was said 'a more perfect specimen of the plutocratic cad it would be hard to imagine' (Stephen Koss, *The rise and fall of the political press in Britain*, vol. II, *The twentieth century* (1984), p. 340, quoting Sir Robert Sanders. I owe this reference to Piers Brendon).

12 J. Holland Rose, LittD, FBA (1855–1942): entry by E.A. Benians in *DNB, 1940–1950* (1959), pp. 736–7; *ODNB* (2004), vol. XLVII, pp. 764–5, by T. Gotte.

13 University of Cambridge Archives (University Library), Faculty of History, Faculty Board Records, Minute Book, vol. 5 (1928–35), 24 May 1932.

14 Cambridge University Archives (University Library), History Faculty Board Minute Book, vol. 5, 18 October 1932.

15 *Cambridge University Reporter*, vol. 63 (1932–3), report of the Council of the Senate on the title of the Vere Harmsworth professorship, 17 January 1933, p. 665, discussion.

16 Sir Herbert Richmond, KCB, FBA (1871–1946). G.M. Trevelyan (quoting H. Thursfield), 'Admiral Sir Herbert Richmond', in *An autobiography and other essays* (1949), pp. 222–34, repr. from *Proceedings of the British Academy*,

vol. 32 (1946), pp. 325–37. See also entry in *ODNB*, vol. XLVI, pp. 875–6, by H.G. Thursfield and M. Brodie.

17 Eric A. Walker (1886–1976). C. Saunders, *The making of the South African past: major historians on race and class* (Cape Town and Johannesburg, 1988), pp. 112–15; Ken Smith, *The changing past: trends in South African historical writing* (Athens, OH, 1989), pp. 121–31 – this is a very substantial piece. The professor first appointed died while Walker was on the voyage out to South Africa to take up what he expected to be a lectureship (personal information from Professor Walker).

18 Quoted by H. Phillips, 'The South African College and the emergence of history as a university discipline in South Africa', *Historia: Joernaal van die Historiese Genootskap van Suid-Afrika*, vol. 49 (2004), p. 9.

19 See particularly his Cust Foundation Lecture, *The policy of apartheid in the Union of South Africa* (Nottingham, 1953), and 'The franchise in southern Africa', *Cambridge Historical Journal*, vol. 11 (1953), pp. 93–113. Walker took up rowing after a youthful sporting injury affected his agility.

20 Coupland, *The study of the British Commonwealth*, p. 11.

21 Preface to *A history of South Africa* (2nd edn, 1940). He wrote three chapters himself for the *CHBE*, vol. VIII, *South Africa, Rhodesia and the Protectorates* (1936), including the pivotal one on 'The struggle for supremacy, 1896–1902'.

22 N. Mansergh, 'Professor Eric Walker', *The Eagle* (The Magazine of St John's College Cambridge), vol. 67, no. 284 (Easter, 1976), p. 46.

23 The *History of southern Africa* (1957) is known to contain a fair number of errors (though not as many as Henry Pelling listed for A.J.P. Taylor's *English history, 1914–1945*), but an article by a South African historian detailing them was rejected by John Fage as editor of the *Journal of African History* out of respect for his former supervisor (personal information).

24 E.A. Walker, *The study of imperial history: an inaugural lecture* (Cambridge, 1937).

25 Letters of J.W. Davidson to his mother, National Library of Australia, Davidson Papers, MS 5105, box 64, transcripts referring to E.A. Walker, by the good offices of Dr Doug Munro. Davidson is discussed more fully in chapter 17 above.

26 E.E. Rich, LittD (1904–79): educated at Selwyn College; Fellow of St Catharine's College, 1930, Master, 1957; recreation, 'rowing'. He edited the *Cambridge Economic History of Europe*, vol. IV, *Economy of expanding Europe in the sixteenth and seventeenth centuries* (1967), contributing a chapter on 'Colonial settlement and its labour problems'.

27 E.E. Rich, *The crises of imperial history: an inaugural lecture* (Cambridge, 1952).

28 *Cambridge University Reporter*, vol. 82 (1951–2), p. 719, report of the Council of the Senate, 4 February 1952.

29 P.N.S. Mansergh, DLitt, FBA (1910–91). See D.W. Harkness, 'Philip Nicholas Seton Mansergh, 1910–1991', *Proceedings of the British Academy*, vol. 82 (1993), pp. 425–30; F.H. Hinsley, 'Professor Nicholas Mansergh', *The Eagle* (1991), pp. 35–9, repr. in the *Journal of Imperial and Commonwealth*

History, vol. 20 (1992), pp. 7–10; W.K. Hancock, 'Nicholas Mansergh: some recollections and reflections', in N. Hillmer and P. Wigley, eds., *The first British Commonwealth: essays in honour of Nicholas Mansergh* (1980), pp. 3–9. See also on Ireland, D.W. Harkness in *OHBE*, vol. V, *Historiography*, pp. 129–31, and on the Commonwealth, W.D. McIntyre, in ibid., pp. 560–3.

30 P.N.S. Mansergh, 'The implications of Eire's relationship with the British Commonwealth of Nations', *International Affairs*, vol. 24 (1948), pp. 1–18, repr. in *Nationalism and independence: selected Irish papers of Nicholas Mansergh* (ed. Diana Mansergh, Cork, 1997), pp. 92–116. The lecture was attended by ministers, officials, and diplomats, and a copy was forwarded to the Cabinet Committee on Commonwealth Relations by Sir Stafford Cripps and Mr Attlee (CAB 134).

31 RH, 'Mansergh, P. Nicholas S.', in *ODNB* (2004), vol. XXXVI, pp. 542–3.

32 J.J. Lee, Foreword to *Nationalism and independence: selected Irish papers*, pp. xiii–xvii.

33 Insisting, for example, that Churchill had spoken of the 'sham' not 'shame' of the Government of India Bill (1935), proving that Churchill's leading biographers were wrong: see p. 340 above, n. 44.

34 R.E. Robinson, 'Oxford in imperial historiography', in Madden and Fieldhouse, eds., *Oxford and the idea of Commonwealth*, pp. 40–1.

35 E.T. Stokes, FBA (1924–81). His inaugural lecture (1971) was printed as '"The voice of the hooligan": Kipling and the Commonwealth experience', in N. McKendrick, ed., *Historical perspectives: studies in English thought and society in honour of J.H. Plumb* (1974), pp. 285–301. Stokes was an exhibitioner at Christ's College, Cambridge, who served in the Royal Indian Mounted Artillery, 1944–6. He took a double first in the Historical Tripos (1947, 1948). Among other articles reflecting his commitment to the 'Third World' were two for *Past and Present*: 'Traditional resistance movements and Afro-Asian nationalism: the 1857 Mutiny-Rebellion in India', no. 48 (1970), pp. 100–18, and 'The first century of British colonial rule in India: social revolution or social stagnation?', no. 58 (1973), pp. 136–60.

36 Quoted by C.A. Bayly, in 'Stokes, Eric Thomas', in *ODNB*, vol. LII, pp. 858–9. See also Bayly's obituary notice in *Proceedings of the British Academy*, vol. 97 (1988), pp. 466–98, and his remarks in Peter Burke, ed., *History and historians in the 20th century* (Oxford, 2002), pp. 111, 114–15, on Asian historiography.

37 Bayly, *Proceedings of the British Academy*, p. 498. *The peasant armed: the Indian revolt of 1857* (Oxford, 1986) owes its readability to Bayly's skilful editing.

38 R.E. Robinson and J. Gallagher, *Africa and the Victorians: the official mind of imperialism* (1961), p. 89.

39 Wm. Roger Louis, ed., *Imperialism: the Robinson and Gallagher controversy* (New York, 1976); for Robinson's response, see *Africa and the Victorians* (2nd edn, 1981), pp. ix–xxiii, 473–99; also illuminating on the partnership is the memoir by Robinson and Anil Seal, 'Professor John Gallagher, 1919–1980', *JICH*, vol. 9 (1981), pp. 119–24. Two articles by D.C.M. Platt remain the most significant challenges to the original thesis: '"Imperialism of free trade": some reservations', *Economic History Review*, vol. 21 (1968),

pp. 296–306, and 'Further objections to an "Imperialism of free trade"', *Economic History Review*, vol. 25 (1973), pp. 77–91.

40 R.E. Robinson, DFC, CBE (1920–99): see George Shepperson, 'Ronald Robinson: scholar and good companion', in A.N. Porter and R. Holland, eds., *Theory and practice in the history of European expansion overseas: essays in honour of Ronald Robinson* (1988), pp. 1–8; A.N. Porter, 'Professor Ronald Robinson, 1920–1999', *JICH*, vol. 27, no. 3 (1999), pp. xi–xiii; Peter Linehan, 'Professor Ronald Robinson, 1920–1999', *The Eagle* (1999), pp. 110–15; 'Ronald Robinson', obituary in the *Guardian* (26 June 1999) by Peter Clarke.

41 J.A. Gallagher, FBA (1919–80): see Anil Seal, 'John Andrew Gallagher, 1919–1980', in Gallagher, *Decline, revival and fall of the British empire*, Preface, pp. vii–xxvii, together with reminiscences by Graham Chinner and Richard Cobb; Madden, 'The Commonwealth, Commonwealth history and Oxford', pp. 21–35; John Darwin, 'The decline and rise of the British empire: John Gallagher as a historian of imperialism', in W.R. Louis, ed., *Yet more adventures with Britannia: people, politics and culture in Britain* (Austin, TX, 2005), pp. 235–49, and *Proceedings of the British Academy*, vol. 150 (2007), pp. 57–75. Robinson is subsumed under 'Gallager, John Andrew' in *ODNB*, vol. XXI, pp. 312–15, by A.S. Thompson. Although Thompson gives an effective feel for their achievements, I cannot imagine many other historians saying, 'It would probably not be an understatement to say that Robinson and Gallagher were to Commonwealth-imperial history what the Beatles were to pop music.'

42 Review article, 'The partition of Africa', *Historical Journal*, vol. 7 (1964), pp. 154–69; review of 2nd edn, *JICH*, vol. 11 (1983), pp. 238–9; 'The partition of Africa: a critique of Robinson and Gallagher', in RH and G.W. Martin, *Reappraisals in British imperial history* (1975), pp. 139–66.

43 W.R. Louis, 'Introduction', *OHBE*, vol. V, *Historiography*, p. 32.

44 Robinson, 'Oxford in imperial historiography', p. 33. 'If the firm was given to "the higher generalisation", Jack was not usually to blame: for the "poor man's Bismarck", who liked to see himself applying *realpolitik* to history as to life, was sceptical of speculation' (Robinson and Seal, 'Professor John Gallagher', p. 122.)

45 For more detail than would be appropriate here, see Katharine Whitehorn, *Selective memory: an autobiography* (2007), pp. 42–50: Whitehorn was his girlfriend in the early 1950s and remained a lifelong friend.

46 Indeed, one of R.'s contemporaries found it hard to think of him as a don – almost a case, he thought, of 'poacher turned game-keeper': Logie Bruce Lockhart, 'Robbie as an undergraduate' (1999, St John's College Library, Biographical Collection, printed in *The Eagle* (2000), pp. 15–17).

47 Richard Cobb lists these 'mysterious' names in 'Jack Gallagher in Oxford' (see note 41), p. xxiii. Not all were imperial historians: the list includes George Kitson Clark, John Saltmarsh, Charles Wilson, and David Joslin (personal knowledge).

48 Geoffrey Barraclough was a charismatic History Fellow of St John's College, 1936–45, and professor of medieval history at Liverpool, 1945–56; he then

dramatically switched to 'contemporary history' as professor of international history at the University of London. Robinson used to tell the story of how he and his supervision partner were concerned at Barraclough's ascetic life-style, and, thinking it would be sufficiently cerebral, invited Barraclough to play chess; Barraclough crossly replied, 'My job is to stimulate your intellects, not titillate your emotions.'

49 St John's College Archives, file 'Robinson, R.E.', letter from E.A. Walker to F. Thistlethwaite, 15 October 1946, consulted by permission of the Master, Fellows, and Scholars of St John's College, and with the help of the archivist, Malcolm Underwood.

50 St John's College Archives, admission to Title A fellowships, referees' reports, D/93/81 (1949), quoted by permission of the Master, Fellows, and Scholars of St John's College; and D/93/82, summaries of dissertations. As Harlow put it, Robinson was 'in a position comparable with that of a gold-prospector, who has been directed to a rich outcrop, studded with nuggets; his mechanical labour cannot fail to be richly rewarded'. It is always good to know what the leading scholars of one generation thought of those who would be the next. Unfortunately, Trinity College has not preserved reports on Gallagher's fellowship dissertation, 'The British penetration of West Africa, between 1830 and 1865' – which Darwin describes as showing 'astonishing intellectual assurance', with an almost Dickensian cast of characters (*Yet more adventures with Britannia*).

51 Ifor Evans was one of Benians's favourite protégés in history and economics, who was a Fellow of the College, 1923–34 and university lecturer in the Economics Faculty. He wrote pioneering books on Africa, now utterly forgotten: *The British in tropical Africa: an historical outline* (396 pp., Cambridge, 1929) and *Native policy in southern Africa: an outline* (177 pp., Cambridge, 1934), the former a survey intended mainly for the Colonial Service probationers. Evans became principal of the University College of Wales, Aberystwyth.

52 J.M. Lee, *Colonial development and good government: a study of the ideas expressed by the British official classes in planning development, 1939–1964* (Oxford, 1967), p. 84. Robinson's main task seems to have been to provide a historical rationale for the change of policy from Indirect Rule to 'local self-government': see RH, ed., *The Labour government and the end of empire, 1945–1951* (BDEEP, 1992), pt I, pp. 148–57, document nos. 48, 49, 'Theories of Native Administration, 1927–1947', and 'Some recent trends in Native Administration Policy in the British African Territories'. See also R.E. Robinson, 'Why "Indirect Rule" has been replaced by "Local Government" in the nomenclature of British native administration', *Journal of African Administration*, vol. 2 (1950), pp. 12–15.

53 RER to his tutor, Frank Thistlethwaite, 9 July 1947: St John's College Archives, file 'Robinson, R.E.' However, in later years, Robinson was a member of the Bridges Committee on Training in Public Administration. In 1980 he was one of the UK team of observers at the February election in Southern Rhodesia which led to the independence of Zimbabwe.

54 D.K. Fieldhouse, 'Ronald Robinson and the Cambridge Development

Conferences, 1963–1970', *JICH*, vol. 16 (1988), pp. 173–99. Fieldhouse was gently sceptical about the effectiveness of these conferences on the ideology of development policy.

55 Outstanding among the essays, perhaps, are: 'European imperialism and indigenous reactions in British West Africa', in H. Wesseling, ed., *Expansion and reaction*, vol. I (Leiden, 1978), and 'Non-European foundations of European imperialism', in R. Owen and R. Sutcliffe, eds., *Studies in the theory of imperialism* (1972), ch. 5.

56 For example, the entry in *DNB, 1961–1970* (1981), pp. 227–9, revised in *ODNB*, vol. XII, pp. 418–19; and 'Sir Andrew Cohen (1909–1968)', in L.H. Gann and P. Duignan, eds., *African proconsuls: European governors in Africa* (New York and London, 1978), pp. 353–64.

57 Stokes evidently had powerful backers, not just the Master of his College (Professor E.E. Rich), and Professor 'Jack' Plumb (for many years an elector to the chair, who did not like Robinson), but also Professor Sir Cyril Philips, director of the School of Oriental and African Studies in London, and a leading Indianist.

58 RER to the author, letters 12 May 1970 and 27 August 1993.

59 J.A. Gallagher, review article on L.H. Gann and P. Duignan, *White settlers in tropical Africa* (Harmondsworth, 1962), *Historical Journal*, vol. 5 (1962), pp. 198–203. This was a hard-hitting analysis of a relatively slim contribution to the Penguin African Series.

60 Darwin, *Proceedings of the British Academy*, vol. 150, p. 74.

61 Gallagher, 'Fowell Buxton and the new African policy, 1838–1842', *Cambridge Historical Journal*, vol. 10 (1950), pp. 36–58; 'Economic relations in Africa', in J.O. Lindsay, ed., *New Cambridge modern history*, vol. VII, *1713–63* (1957), pp. 566–79; 'Nationalisms and the crisis of empire, 1919–22', in C. Baker, G. Johnson, and A. Seal, eds., *Power, profit and politics: essays in imperialism, nationalism and change in twentieth century India* (Cambridge, 1981, repr. from *Modern Asian Studies*, vol. 15 (1981), pp. 355–68).

62 Gallagher, 'Congress in decline: Bengal, 1930 to 1939', in J. Gallagher, G. Johnson, and A. Seal, eds., *Locality, province and nation: essays on Indian politics, 1870 to 1940* (Cambridge, 1973, repr. from *Modern Asian Studies*, vol. 7 (1973), pp. 269–325, at p. 269n.).

63 Gallagher, *The decline, revival and fall of the British empire: the Ford Lectures and other essays* (ed. Anil Seal, Cambridge, 1982).

64 Gallagher, *Decline, revival and fall*, pp. 73–4, 85, 94–9, 149–50. The Marxist Victor Kiernan complained in a review that there was too little emphasis on freedom-fighters, agitators, and mobs, and too much on 'bureaucratic wisdom' – 'this is a Kitson Clark approach to politics' (*Times Literary Supplement*, 16 January 1983, p. 16), an unkind jibe, since their old tutor had little of the world-historical view of either of his former pupils.

65 R.E. Robinson, 'The ex-centric idea of imperialism, with or without empire', in W.J. Mommsen and J. Osterhammel, eds., *Imperialism and after: continuities and discontinuities* (1986), pp. 267–89.

66 C. Bayly, 'Stokes, Eric', *ODNB*, p. 859. Professor Peter Hennessy recalls as a former Cambridge undergraduate 'that mixture of verve, erudition and wit

which marked (and still does) the Cambridge school of imperial historians' (*Times Educational Supplement*, 8 October 1993, p. 9).

67 'The most substantial piece of scholarship to appear from Oxford imperial historians in the [twentieth] century': F. Madden, 'The Commonwealth, Commonwealth history and Oxford, 1905–1971', in Madden and Fieldhouse, eds., *Oxford and the idea of Commonwealth*, p. 19. Putting *The founding of the second British empire* in the wider context, Roger Louis finds it to be 'one of the great works in the literature' (*OHBE*, vol. V, pp. 35–6); while David McIntyre in his latest book places it alongside Hancock's *Survey of British Commonwealth affairs*, as 'the most significant overall revision of the wide sweep of empire history' (*The Britannic vision*, p. 56).

68 According to the soundings of Roger Louis, Hancock was by common consent 'far and away the greatest historian of the Empire and Common-wealth': *OHBE*, vol. V, p. 30. However, he subsequently accepted that this claim 'needs a slight modification': the post-publication *OHBE* consensus 'proved to be a little more muted', but without altering the basic assess-ment ('Sir Keith Hancock and the British empire: the Pax Britannica and the Pax Americana', *English Historical Review*, vol. 120 (2005), p. 937, n.1).

69 For Newton's biographical details see *Who was who*, vol. IV, *1941–1950*, and for his contribution to supervising research students, A.D. Roberts, 'The British empire in tropical Africa', *OHBE*, vol. V, p. 475.

70 See the disparaging remarks of C.W. de Kiewiet: 'The incumbent of the most distinguished chair in Imperial Studies in all of Great Britain baffled his students by doing most of his research in Tudor constitutional history' (*The anatomy of South African misery*, 1956, p. 4). Perhaps Newton's best-known articles were 'The King's Chamber under the early Tudors', *English Historical Review*, vol. 32 (1917), and 'The establishment of the Great Farm of the English Customs', *Transactions of the Royal Historical Society*, 4th series, vol. 1 (1918).

71 Lucy Sutherland, 'William Miller Macmillan: an appreciation', in K. Kirkwood, ed., *African Affairs, No. 3* (St Antony's Papers, no. 21, Oxford, 1969), pp. 9–24; Hugh Macmillan and Shula Marks, eds., *Africa and empire: W.M. Macmillan, historian and social critic* (1989); and *OHBE*, vol. V, pp. 25, 518. Macmillan was awarded an Hon. DLitt by Oxford.

72 Harlow, *The historian and British colonial history*, p. 16.

73 Richard Pares, CBE, FBA (1902–58), *The historian's business, and other essays* (ed. R.A. and E. Humphreys, with an introduction by Lucy Sutherland, Oxford, 1961); entry in *ODNB*, vol. XLII, pp. 615–16, by Ian Christie; *Proceedings of the British Academy*, vol. 48 (1962), pp. 345–56, by A.L. Rowse; W.R. Louis, 'Introduction', *OHBE*, vol. V, *Historiography*, pp. 34–5.

74 Richard Pares, *Yankees and Creoles: the trade between North America and the West Indies before the American Revolution* (1956); *A West India fortune* (1950); *Colonial blockade and neutral rights, 1739–1763* (Oxford, 1938).

75 For example: 'American *versus* continental warfare, 1739–1763', *English Historical Review*, vol. 51 (1936), pp. 429–65; 'The economic factors in the history of the empire', *Economic History Review*, vol. 7 (1937), pp. 119–44,

which uses the phrase 'Free trade imperialism' (p. 132); 'The London sugar market, 1740–1769', *Economic History Review*, vol. 9 (1956), pp. 254–70.

76 Cornelius Willem de Kiewiet, *The anatomy of South African misery* (The Whidden Lectures, McMaster University; Oxford 1956), pp. 3–5. The lectures are an illuminating analysis of 'the delusion of apartheid', a 'creed of despair' and evasion of reality.

77 C.W. de Kiewiet, *A history of South Africa: social and economic* (Oxford, 1941, 1960). John Darwin rightly says this remains 'the most brilliant introduction to South African history' (*The empire project: the rise and fall of the British world-system* (Cambridge, 2009), p. 706, n. 1.) De Kiewiet's two Colonial Office studies were *British colonial policy and the South African republics, 1848–1872* (1929) and *The imperial factor in South Africa, 1872–1885* (Cambridge, 1937, 1965); he contributed two chapters on South African policy, 1854–72 to the *CHBE*, vol. VIII, *South Africa* (1936), pp. 391–448, while his celebrated essay, 'Social and economic developments in Native tribal life' formed ch. 30; and he edited (with F.H. Underhill) the *Dufferin–Carnarvon correspondence, 1874–1878* (Champlain Society Publication no. 33, Toronto, 1955). See W.H. Worger, 'Southern and Central Africa', in *OHBE*, vol. V, pp. 519–20.

Published writings of RH on imperial history

Excluding book reviews.

* Reprinted in this volume.
+ Reprinted in *The lion and the springbok*.

1964   'The partition of Africa', review article, *Historical Journal*, vol. 7 (1964), pp. 154–69; repr. in P.J.M. McEwan, ed., *Readings in African history*, vol. II, *Nineteenth-century Africa* (Oxford University Press, 1968, 1969)

1965   'Smuts and the decision of the Liberal government to grant Responsible Government to the Transvaal, January and February, 1906', *Historical Journal*, vol. 8 (1965), pp. 380–98

1967   'British imperial expansion in the late eighteenth century', review article, *Historical Journal*, vol. 10 (1967), pp. 113–24

1968   *Elgin and Churchill at the Colonial Office, 1905–1908: the watershed of the Empire-Commonwealth* (London, Macmillan, 1968)

1969   'Winston Churchill before 1914', review article, *Historical Journal*, vol. 12 (1969), pp. 164–73

1970   + 'African interests and the South Africa Act, 1908–1910', *Historical Journal*, vol. 13 (1970), pp. 85–105

1972   *The failure of South African expansion, 1908–1948* (London, Macmillan, 1972)

1973   (1) 'Are we any nearer an African history of South Africa?', review article, *Historical Journal*, vol. 16 (1973), pp. 616–26
(2) '[Churchill] at the Colonial Office, 1905–1908', in P. Stansky, ed., *Churchill: a profile* (New York, Macmillan, 1973), pp. 21–35; repr. from *Elgin and Churchill*, ch. 13

1974   (1) 'Expansion of Europe, imperial, African and Asian history since *c.*1800', in R.F. Bennett, ed., *First class answers in history* (London, Weidenfeld and Nicolson, 1974), pp. 135–65
+(2) 'The politics of partition in southern Africa, 1908–1961', *Joernaal vir die Eietydse Geskiedenis*, vol. 1 (Bloemfontein, 1974), pp. 3–12

1975   with Ged Martin, *Reappraisals in British imperial history* (London, Macmillan, 1975)

1976   *Britain's imperial century, 1815–1914: a study of empire and expansion* (London, Batsford, first edn, 1976)

1979   'The Colonial Office mind, 1900–1914', *Journal of Imperial and*

Commonwealth History, vol. 8 (1979), pp. 30–55; repr. in N. Hillmer and P. Wigley, eds., *The first British Commonwealth: essays in honour of Nicholas Mansergh* (London, Cass, 1980)

1980 'British imperial policy and South Africa, 1906–1910', in P.Warwick, ed., *The South African War* (London, Longman, 1980), pp. 362–85

1986 ★ (1) 'Empire and sexual opportunity', *Journal of Imperial and Commonwealth History*, vol. 14 (1986), pp. 34–90

+ (2) 'The political consequences of Seretse Khama: Britain, the Bangwato, and South Africa, 1948–1952', *Historical Journal*, vol. 29 (1986), pp. 921–47

★ (3) 'Concubinage and the Colonial Service: the Crewe Circular (1909)', *Journal of Imperial and Commonwealth History*, vol. 14 (1986), pp. 170–86

1987 + 'The geopolitical origins of the Central African Federation: Britain, Rhodesia, and South Africa, 1948–1953', *Historical Journal*, vol. 30 (1987), pp. 145–72

1988 ★ (1) 'Africa and the Labour government, 1945–1951', *Journal of Imperial and Commonwealth History*, vol. 16 (1988), pp. 148–72; repr. in A.N. Porter and R. Holland, eds., *Theory and practice in the history of European overseas expansion: essays in honour of Ronald Robinson* (London, Cass, 1988)

(2) 'Imperialism and sexual exploitation: a reply [to Mark Berger]', *Journal of Imperial and Commonwealth History*, vol. 17 (1988), pp. 90–8

(3) 'The pioneer missionaries', *Magdalene College Magazine*, no. 32 (1987–8), pp. 36–41

1990 *Empire and sexuality: the British experience* (Manchester University Press, 1990; repr. 1991, 1992, 1998; Japanese translation by Takehiko Honda (Tokyo, Kashiwa-shobo, 1998)

1992 editor, *The Labour government and the end of empire, 1945–1951*, vol. A 2, British Documents on the End of Empire Project (London, HMSO, 1992), in four parts

1993 ★ (1) 'Churchill and the British empire', in R. Blake and W.R. Louis, eds., *Churchill* (Oxford University Press, 1993), pp. 167–85

(2) *Britain's imperial century, 1815–1914* (new and revised 2nd edn, Basingstoke, Macmillan, 1993; repr. 2001)

1995 'Guy Clutton-Brock', in memoriam, a National Hero of Zimbabwe, *Magdalene College Magazine*, no. 39 (1994–5), pp. 2–7

1997 'After Victoria: an empire in flux?', *Humanities: the Magazine of the National Endowment for the Humanities* (Washington DC, July/August, 1997), pp. 25–9: anticipating the essay @ 1999(1)

1998 + 'The parting of the ways: Britain and South Africa's departure from the Commonwealth, 1951–1961', *Journal of Imperial and Commonwealth History*, vol. 26 (1998), pp. 157–75; repr. in P. Burroughs and A.J. Stockwell, eds., *Managing the business of empire: essays in honour of David Fieldhouse* (London, Cass, 1998)

1999 (1) 'The British empire in the Edwardian era', in J.M. Brown and W.R. Louis, eds., *OHBE*, vol. IV, *The twentieth century* (1999), pp. 47–63

* (2) 'Bureaucracy and "trusteeship" in the colonial empire', in *OHBE*, vol. IV, pp. 255–79

* (3) 'The primacy of geopolitics: the dynamics of British imperial policy, 1763–1963', *Journal of Imperial and Commonwealth History*, vol. 27 (1999), pp. 27–52; repr. in R.D. King and R.W. Kilson, eds., *The statecraft of British imperialism: essays in honour of Wm. Roger Louis* (London, Cass, 1999)

(4) 'Sir Richard Turnbull', in memoriam, *Magdalene College Magazine*, no. 43 (1998–9), pp. 2–5

2000   (1) '"Winds of change": the empire and Commonwealth', in W. Kaiser and G. Staerck, eds., *British foreign policy, 1955–1964: contracting options* (Basingstoke, Macmillan/Institute of Contemporary British History, 2000), pp. 190–208

(2) editor, with Wm. Roger Louis, *The Conservative government and the end of empire, 1957–1964*, vol. A 4, British Documents on the End of Empire Project (London, The Stationery Office, 2000), in two parts

2001   * (1) 'South Africa, Cambridge, and Commonwealth history', the Smuts Distinguished Lecture, University of Cambridge, November 2000, on the fiftieth anniversary of the death of Smuts, *Round Table: the Commonwealth Journal of International Affairs*, vol. 90, no. 360 (2001), pp. 401–14

* (2) 'The study of imperial and Commonwealth history at Cambridge, 1881–1981: founding fathers and pioneer research students', *Journal of Imperial and Commonwealth History*, vol. 29 (2001), pp. 75–103

* (3) 'Does size matter? African and Afro-American super-sexuality', in Stephen Bayley, ed., *Sex* (*The Erotic Review*, 2001), pp. 296–307

2002   *Britain's imperial century, 1815–1914* (extended 3rd edn, Basingstoke, Palgrave, 2002)

2003   with Peter Henshaw, *The lion and the springbok: Britain and South Africa since the Boer War* (Cambridge University Press, 2003)

2004   (1) 'Bruce, Victor Alexander, 9th Earl of Elgin', *ODNB*, vol. VIII, pp. 331–3

(2) 'Mansergh, (P.) Nicholas (S.)', in *ODNB*, vol. XXXVI, pp. 542–3

2006   *Britain's declining empire: the road to decolonisation, 1918–1968* (Cambridge University Press, 2006)

2007   (1) *Magdalene, anti-slavery, and the early human rights movement, from the 1780s to the 1830s*, Magdalene College Occasional Papers, no. 35 (2007)

(2) 'Peckard and the abolition of the slave trade', *Magdalene College Magazine*, no. 51 (2006–7), pp. 92–5

2010   *Understanding the British empire* (Cambridge University Press, 2010)

Index

CPSIA information can be obtained
at www.ICGtesting.com
Printed in the USA
LVOW01s1237130916
504337LV00015BB/275/P